Introduction to Distributed Algorithms

Introduction to Distributed Algorithms

Gerard Tel
Utrecht University

CAMBRIDGE
UNIVERSITY PRESS

PUBLISHED BY THE PRESS SYNDICATE OF THE UNIVERSITY OF CAMBRIDGE
The Pitt Building, Trumpington Street, Cambridge, United Kingdom

CAMBRIDGE UNIVERSITY PRESS
The Edinburgh Building, Cambridge, CB2 2RU, UK
40 West 20th Street, New York, NY 10011–4211, USA
10 Stamford Road, Oakleigh, VIC 3166, Australia
Ruiz de Alarcón 13, 28014 Madrid, Spain
Dock House, The Waterfront, Cape Town 8001, South Africa

http://www.cambridge.org

First published 1994
Second edition 2000
Reprinted 2001

Typeface Computer Modern 11/13pt   *System* LaTeX   [UPH]

A catalogue record for this book is available from the British Library

Library of Congress Cataloguing in Publication data
Tel, Gerard.
Introduction to distributed algorithms / Gerard Tel. – 2nd ed.
p.   cm.
Includes bibliographical references and index.
ISBN 0 521 79483 8
1. Electronic data processing–Distributed processing–Congresses.
2. Computer algorithms–Congresses.
QA76.9.D5 T44   2000
005.2'76–dc21   00-036292

ISBN 0 521 79483 8 paperback

Transferred to digital printing 2004

To Ineke,
Rik, Jan-Willem, and Rianne

Contents

x *Contents*

Preface

Distributed systems and distributed information processing have received considerable attention in the past few years, and almost every university offers at least one course on the design of distributed algorithms. There exist a large number of books about principles of distributed systems; see for example Tanenbaum [Tan96] or Sloman and Kramer [SK87], but these concentrate on architectural aspects rather than on algorithms. Since the first edition of this book, other texts on distributed algorithms have been published by Barbosa [Bar96], Lynch [Lyn96], and Attiya and Welch [AW98].

It has been remarked that algorithms are the backbone of every computer application; therefore a text devoted solely to distributed algorithms seems to be justified. The aim of this book is to present a large body of theory about distributed algorithms, which has been developed over the past twenty years or so. This book can be used as a textbook for a one- or two-semester course on distributed algorithms; the teacher of a one-semester course may select topics to his own liking.

The book will also provide useful background and reference information for professional engineers and researchers working with distributed systems.

Exercises. Each chapter (with the exception of Chapters 1 and 13) ends with a list of exercises and small projects. The projects usually require the reader to develop a small but non-trivial extension or application of the material treated in the chapter, and in most cases I do not have a "solution". If the reader succeeds in working out one of these small projects, I would be pleased to have a copy of the result.

A list of answers (sometimes partial) to most of the exercises is available for teachers; it can be obtained from the author or by anonymous ftp.

Corrections and suggestions. If the reader finds errors or omissions in this book, please inform the author (preferably by electronic mail). All constructive criticism, including suggestions for more exercises, is most welcome.

Acknowledgements. Draft versions of this book were proofread carefully by the following: Erwin Bakker, Hans Bodlaender, Stefan Dobrev, Petra van Haaften, Ted Herman, Jan van Leeuwen, Patrick Lentfert, Friedemann Mattern, Pascale van der Put, Peter Ružička, Martin Rudalics, Anneke Schoone, and Kaisa Sere. Their comments were very helpful in improving the quality of the manuscript. Also, some students of the fall courses on "Gedistribueerde Algoritmen" at Utrecht University provided me with helpful suggestions. The Department of Computer Science provided the technical support necessary for text processing and printing. Linguistic editing was performed by Susan Parkinson.

Gerard Tel, April 1994/February 2000.

1

Introduction: Distributed Systems

This chapter gives reasons for the study of distributed algorithms by briefly introducing the types of hardware and software systems for which distributed algorithms have been developed. By a distributed system we mean all computer applications where several computers or processors cooperate in some way. This definition includes wide-area computer communication networks, but also local-area networks, multiprocessor computers in which each processor has its own control unit, and systems of cooperating processes.

The different types of distributed system and the reasons why distributed systems are used are discussed in Section 1.1. Some examples of existing systems will be given. The main topic of this book, however, is not what these systems look like, or how they are used, but how they can be made to work. And even that topic will be further specialized towards the treatment of the *algorithms* used in the systems.

Of course, the entire structure and operation of a distributed system is not fully understood by a study of its algorithms alone. To understand such a system fully one must also study the complete architecture of its hardware and software, that is, the partition of the entire functionality into modules. Also, there are many important questions related to properties of the programming languages used to build the software of distributed systems. These subjects will be discussed in Section 1.2.

It is the case, however, that there are already in existence excellent books about distributed systems, which concentrate on the architectural and language aspects; see, e.g., Tanenbaum [Tan96], Sloman and Kramer [SK87], Bal [Bal90], Coulouris and Dollimore [CD88] or Goscinski [Gos91]. As already mentioned, the present text concentrates on algorithms for distributed systems. Section 1.3 explains why the design of distributed algorithms dif-

1

fers from the design of centralized algorithms, sketches the research field of distributed algorithms, and outlines the remainder of the book.

1.1 What is a Distributed System?

In this chapter we shall use the term "distributed system" to mean an interconnected collection of autonomous computers, processes, or processors. The computers, processes, or processors are referred to as the *nodes* of the distributed system. (In the subsequent chapters we shall use a more technical notion, see Definition 2.6.) To be qualified as "autonomous", the nodes must at least be equipped with their own private control; thus, a parallel computer of the single-instruction, multiple-data (SIMD) model does not qualify as a distributed system. To be qualified as "interconnected", the nodes must be able to exchange information.

As (software) processes can play the role of nodes of a system, the definition includes software systems built as a collection of communicating processes, even when running on a single hardware installation. In most cases, however, a distributed system will at least contain several processors, interconnected by communication hardware.

More restrictive definitions of distributed systems are also found in the literature. Tanenbaum [Tan96], for example, considers a system to be distributed only if the existence of autonomous nodes is *transparent* to users of the system. A system distributed in this sense behaves like a virtual, stand-alone computer system, but the implementation of this transparency requires the development of intricate distributed control algorithms.

1.1.1 Motivation

Distributed computer systems may be preferred over sequential systems, or their use may simply be unavoidable, for various reasons, some of which are discussed below. This list is not meant to be exhaustive. The choice of a distributed system may be motivated by more than one of the arguments listed below, and some of the advantages may come as a spin-off after the choice has been made for another reason. The characteristics of a distributed system may vary also, depending on the reason for its existence, but this will be discussed in more detail in Subsections 1.1.2 through 1.1.6.

(1) *Information exchange.* The need to exchange data between different computers arose in the sixties, when most major universities and companies started to have their own mainframe computer. Cooperation between people of different organizations was facilitated by

the exchange of data between the computers of these organizations, and this gave rise to the development of so-called *wide-area networks* (WANs). ARPANET, the predecessor of the current Internet, went on-air in December, 1969. A computer installation connected in a wide-area network (sometimes called a *long-haul network*) is typically equipped with everything a user needs, such as backup storage, disks, many application programs, and printers.

Later computers became smaller and cheaper, and soon each single organization had a multitude of computers, nowadays often a computer for each person (a personal computer or workstation). In this case also the (electronic) exchange of information between personnel of one organization already required that the autonomous computers were connected. It is even not uncommon for a single person or family to have multiple computers in the home, and connect these in a small personal home-network.

(2) *Resource sharing.* Although with cheaper computers it became feasible to equip each employee of an organization with a private computer, the same is not the case for the peripherals (such as printers, backup storage, and disk units). On this smaller scale each computer may rely on dedicated servers to supply it with compilers and other application programs. Also, it is not effective to replicate all application programs and related file resources in all computers; apart from the waste of disk space, this would create unnecessary maintenance problems. So the computers may rely on dedicated nodes for printer and disk service. A network connecting computers on an organization-wide scale is referred to as a *local-area network* (LAN).

The reasons for an organization to install a network of small computers rather than a mainframe are cost reduction and extensibility. First, smaller computers have a better price–performance ratio than large computers; a typical mainframe computer may perform 50 times faster than a typical personal computer, but cost 500 times more. Second, if the capacity of a system is no longer sufficient, a network can be made to fit the organization's needs by adding more machines (file servers, printers, and workstations). If the capacity of a stand-alone system is no longer sufficient, replacement is the only option.

(3) *Increased reliability through replication.* Distributed systems have the potential to be more reliable than stand-alone systems because they have a *partial-failure* property. By this it is meant that some nodes of the system may fail, while others are still operating correctly and can

take over the tasks of the failed components. The failure of a stand-alone computer affects the entire system and there is no possibility of continuing the operation in this case. For this reason distributed architectures are a traditional concern in the design of highly reliable computer systems.

A highly reliable system typically consists of a two, three, or four times replicated uniprocessor that runs an application program and is supplemented with a voting mechanism to filter the outputs of the machines. The correct operation of a distributed system in the presence of failures of components requires rather complicated algorithmical support.

(4) *Increased performance through parallelization.* The presence of multiple processors in a distributed system opens up the possibility of decreasing the turn-around time for a computation-intensive job by splitting the job over several processors.

Parallel computers are designed specifically with this objective in mind, but users of a local-area network may also profit from parallelism by shunting tasks to other workstations.

(5) *Simplification of design through specialization.* The design of a computer system can be very complicated, especially if considerable functionality is required. The design can often be simplified by splitting the system into modules, each of which implements part of the functionality and communicates with the other modules.

On the level of a single program modularity is obtained by defining abstract data types and procedures for different tasks. A larger system may be defined as a collection of cooperating processes. In both cases, the modules may all be executed on a single computer. But it is also possible to have a local-area network with different types of computers, one equipped with dedicated hardware for number crunching, another with graphical hardware, a third with disks, etc.

1.1.2 Computer Networks

By a computer network we mean a collection of computers, connected by communication mechanisms by means of which the computers can exchange information. This exchange takes place by sending and receiving messages. Computer networks fit our definition of distributed systems. Depending on the distance between the computers and their ownership, computer networks are called either *wide-area networks* or *local-area networks*.

A wide-area network usually connects computers owned by different organizations (industries, universities, etc.). The physical distance between the nodes is typically 10 kilometers or more. Each node of such a network is a complete computer installation, including all the peripherals and a considerable amount of application software. The main object of a wide-area network is the exchange of information between users at the various nodes.

A local-area network usually connects computers owned by a single organization. The physical distance between the nodes is typically 10 kilometers or less. A node of such a network is typically a workstation, a file server, or a printer server, i.e., a relatively small station dedicated to a specific function within the organization. The main objects of a local-area network are usually information exchange and resource sharing.

The boundary between the two types of network cannot always be sharply drawn, and usually the distinction is not very important from the algorithmical viewpoint because similar algorithmical problems occur in all computer networks. Relevant differences with respect to the development of algorithms include the following.

(1) *Reliability parameters.* In wide-area networks the probability that something will go wrong during the transmission of a message can never be ignored; distributed algorithms for wide-area networks are usually designed to cope with this possibility. Local-area networks are much more reliable, and algorithms for them can be designed under the assumption that communication is completely reliable. In this case, however, the unlikely event in which something does go wrong may go undetected and cause the system to operate erroneously.

(2) *Communication time.* The message transmission times in wide-area networks are orders of magnitude larger than those in local-area networks. In wide-area networks, the time needed for processing a message can almost always be ignored when compared to the time of transmitting the message.

(3) *Homogeneity.* Even though in local-area networks not all nodes are necessarily equal, it is usually possible to agree on common software and protocols to be used within a single organization. In wide-area networks a variety of protocols is in use, which poses problems of conversion between different protocols and of designing software that is compatible with different standards.

(4) *Mutual trust.* Within a single organization all users may be trusted, but in a wide-area network this is certainly not the case. A wide-area

network requires the development of secure algorithms, safe against offensive users at other nodes.

Subsection 1.1.3 is devoted to a brief discussion of wide-area networks; local-area networks are discussed in Subsection 1.1.4.

1.1.3 Wide-area Networks

Historical development. Much pioneering work in the development of wide-area computer networks was done in projects of the Advanced Research Projects Agency (ARPA) of the United States Department of Defense. The network *ARPANET* became operational in 1969, and connected four nodes at that time. This network has grown to several hundreds of nodes, and other networks have been set up using similar technology (MILNET, CYPRESS). The ARPANET contains special nodes (called interface message processors (IMPs)) whose only purpose is to process the message traffic.

When UNIX[1] systems became widely used, it was recognized that there was a need for information exchange between different UNIX machines, to which end the uucp program (UNIX-to-UNIX CoPy) was written. With this program files could be exchanged via telephone lines and a networks of UNIX users, called the *UUCP network*, emerged rapidly. Yet another major network, called BITNET, was developed in the eighties because the ARPANET was owned by the Department of Defense, and only some organizations could connect to it.

Nowadays all these networks are interconnected; there exist nodes that belong to both (called *gateways*), allowing information to be exchanged between nodes of different networks. The introduction of a uniform address space and common protocols has turned the networks into a single virtual network, commonly known as the *Internet*. It differs from a "monolithic" network by having many owners and the lack of a single authoritative body, but its organizational diversity is carefully hidden from the users. The electronic address of the author (`gerard@cs.uu.nl`) provides no information about the network his department is connected to.

Organization and algorithmical problems. Wide-area networks are always organized as *point-to-point* networks. This means that communication between a pair of nodes takes place by a mechanism particular to these two nodes. Such a mechanism may be a telephone line, a fiber optic or satellite connection, etc. The interconnection structure of a point-to-point network

---

[1] UNIX is a registered trademark of AT&T Bell Laboratories.

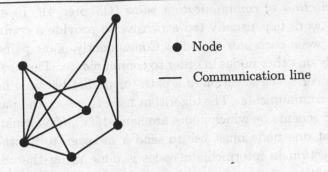

● Node

— Communication line

Figure 1.1 AN EXAMPLE OF A POINT-TO-POINT NETWORK.

can be conveniently depicted by drawing each node as a circle or box, and drawing a line between two nodes if there is a communication line between the two nodes; see Figure 1.1. In more technical language, the structure is represented by a *graph*, of which the edges represent the communication lines of the network. A summary of graph theory terminology is given in Appendix B.

The main purpose of wide-area networks is the exchange of information, for example in the form of electronic mail, bulletin boards, and remotely accessed files and databases. Most of these services are available through a single application, the web *browser*. The implementation of a suitable communication system for these purposes requires the solution of the following algorithmical problems, some of which are discussed in Part One of this book.

(1) *The reliability of point-to-point data exchange* (Chapter 3). Two nodes connected by a line exchange data through this line, but they must somehow cope with the possibility that the line is unreliable. Due to atmospheric noise, power dips, and other physical circumstances, a message sent through a line may be received with some parts garbled, or even lost. These transmission failures must be recognized and corrected.

This problem occurs not only for two nodes directly connected by a communication line, but also for nodes not directly connected, but communicating with the help of intermediate nodes. In this case the problem is even more complicated, because in addition messages may arrive in a different order from that in which they were sent, may arrive only after a very long period of time, or may be duplicated.

(2) *Selection of communication paths* (Chapter 4). In a point-to-point network it is usually too expensive to provide a communication line between each pair of nodes. Consequently, some pairs of nodes must rely on other nodes in order to communicate. The problem of *routing* concerns the selection of a path (or paths) between nodes that want to communicate. The algorithm used to select the path is related to the scheme by which nodes are named, i.e., the format of the address that one node must use to send a message to another node. Path selection in intermediate nodes is done using the address, and the selection can be done more efficiently if topological information is "coded" in the addresses.

(3) *Congestion control.* The throughput of a communication network may decrease dramatically if many messages are in transit simultaneously. Therefore the generation of messages by the various nodes must be controlled and made dependent on the available free capacity of the network. Some methods to avoid congestion are discussed in [Tan96, Section 5.3].

(4) *Deadlock prevention* (Chapter 5). Point-to-point networks are sometimes called *store-and-forward* networks, because a message that is sent via several intermediate nodes must be stored in each of these nodes, then forwarded to the next node. Because the memory space available for this purpose in the intermediate nodes is finite, the memory must be managed carefully in order to prevent deadlock situations. In such situations, there exists a set of messages, none of which can be forwarded because the memory of the next node on its route is fully occupied by other messages.

(5) *Security.* Networks connect computers having different owners, some of whom may attempt to abuse or even disrupt the installations of others. Since it is possible to log on a computer installation from anywhere in the world, reliable techniques for user authentication, cryptography, and scanning incoming information (e.g., for viruses) are required. Cryptographic methods (cf. [Tan96, Secion 7.1]) can be used to encrypt data for security against unauthorized reading and to implement electronic signatures for security against unauthorized writing.

1.1.4 *Local-area Networks*

A local-area network is used by an organization to connect a collection of computers it owns. Usually, the main purpose of this connection is to share

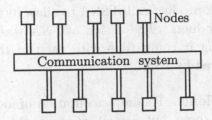

Figure 1.2 A BUS-CONNECTED NETWORK.

resources (files as well as hardware peripherals) and to facilitate the exchange of information between employees. Incidentally, networks are also used to speed up computations (by shunting tasks to other nodes) and to allow some nodes to be used as a stand-by for others in the event of their failure.

Examples and organization. In the first half of the nineteen-seventies, the Ethernet[2] local-area network was developed by the Xerox Corporation. While the names of wide-area networks, ARPANET, BITNET, etc., refer to specific networks, the names of local-area networks are usually product names. There was one ARPANET, one BITNET, and one UUCP net, and there is one Internet, but each company may set up its own private Ethernet, Token Ring, or SNA network.

Unlike wide-area networks, the Ethernet is organized using a *bus-like* structure, i.e., the communication between nodes takes place via a single mechanism to which all nodes are connected; see Figure 1.2. Bus-like organization has become very common for local-area networks, although there may be differences in what this mechanism looks like or how it is used.

The Ethernet design allows only one message to be transmitted at a time; other designs, such as the *token ring* (developed at the IBM Zürich Laboratory), allow for *spatial reuse*, which means that several messages can be transmitted via the communication mechanism at the same time. The bus organization requires little hardware and is therefore cheap, but it has the disadvantage that it is not a very *scalable* organization. This means that there is a fairly tight maximum to the number of nodes that can be connected by one bus. Large companies with many computers must connect them by several buses, and use *bridges* to connect the buses with each other, giving rise to a hierarchical overall network organization.

---

[2] Ethernet is a trademark of the Xerox Corporation.

Not all local-area networks use a bus organization. IBM has designed a point-to-point network product called SNA to allow its costumers to connect their various IBM products. The design of SNA was complicated by the requirement of making it compatible with each of the many networking products already offered by IBM.

Algorithmical problems. The implementation of local-area networks requires the solution of some, but not all, of the problems mentioned in the previous subsection on wide-area networks. Reliable data exchange is not so much of a problem because the buses are usually very reliable and fast. The routing problem does not occur in bus-like networks because each destination can be addressed directly via the bus. In ring-shaped networks all messages are usually sent in the same direction along the ring and removed by either the recipient or the sender, which also makes the routing problem practically void. There is no congestion in the bus because each message is received (taken from the bus) immediately after it is sent, but it is necessary to limit the congestion of messages waiting in the nodes to enter the bus. As messages are not stored in intermediate nodes, no store-and-forward deadlocks arise. Security mechanisms beyond the usual protection offered by an operating system are not necessary if all computers are owned by a single family or a single company that trusts its employees.

The use of local-area networks for the distributed execution of application programs (collections of processes, spread over the nodes of the network) requires the solution of the following distributed-control problems, some of which are discussed in Part Two.

(1) *Broadcasting and synchronization* (Chapter 6). If information must be made available to all processes, or all processes must wait until some global condition is satisfied, it is necessary to have a message-passing scheme that somehow "touches" all processes.

(2) *Election* (Chapter 7). Some tasks must be carried out by exactly one process of a set, for example, generating output or initializing a data structure. If, as is sometimes desirable or necessary, no process is assigned this task a priori, a distributed algorithm must be executed to select one of the processes to perform the task.

(3) *Termination detection* (Chapter 8). It is not always possible for the processes in a distributed system to observe directly that the distributed computation in which they are engaged has terminated. Termination detection is then necessary in order to make the computed results definitive.

(4) *Resource allocation.* A node may require access to some resource that is available elsewhere in the network, though it does not know in which node this resource is located. Maintaining a table that indicates the location of each resource is not always adequate, because the number of potential resources may be too large for this, or resources may migrate from one node to another. In such a case the requesting node may inquire at all or some other nodes about the availability of the resource, for example using broadcasting mechanisms. Algorithms for this problem can be based on the wave mechanisms described in Chapter 6; see, e.g., Baratz *et al.* [BGS87].

(5) *Mutual exclusion.* The problem of mutual exclusion arises if the processes must rely on a common resource that can be used only by one process at a time. Such a resource may be a printer device or a file that must be written. A distributed algorithm is then necessary to determine, if several processes request access simultaneously, which of them is allowed to use the resource first. Also it must be ensured that the next process begins to use the resource only after the previous process has finished using it.

(6) *Deadlock detection and resolution.* If processes must wait for each other (which is the case if they share resources, and also if their computation relies on data provided by other processes) a cyclic wait may occur, in which no further computation is possible. These deadlock situations must be detected and proper action must be undertaken to restart or continue the computation.

(7) *Distributed file maintenance.* When nodes place read and write requests for a remote file, these requests may be processed in an arbitrary order, and hence provision must be made to ensure that each node observes a consistent view of the file or files. Usually this is done by *time stamping* requests, as well as the information in files, and ordering incoming requests on the basis of their time stamps; see, e.g., [LL86].

1.1.5 Multiprocessor Computers

A multiprocessor computer is a computer installation that consists of several processors on a small scale, usually inside one large box. This type of computer system is distinguished from local-area networks by the following criteria. Its processors are homogeneous, i.e., they are identical as hardware. The geographical scale of the machine is very small, typically of the order of one meter or less. The processors are intended to be used together in one computation (either to increase the speed or to increase the reliability). If the main design objective of the multiprocessor computer is to improve the speed of computation, it is often called a parallel computer. If its main design objective is to increase the reliability, it is often called a replicated system.

Parallel computers are classified into single-instruction, multiple-data (or SIMD) machines and multiple-instruction, multiple-data (or MIMD) machines. The SIMD machines have one instruction interpreter, but the instruction is carried out by a large number of arithmetic units. Clearly, these units lack the autonomy required in our definition of distributed systems, and therefore SIMD computers will not be considered in this book. The MIMD machines consist of several independent processors and they are classified as distributed systems.

The processors are usually equipped with dedicated hardware for communication with other processors. The communication between the processors can take place either via a bus or via point-to-point connections. If a bus organization is chosen, the architecture is scalable only to a certain limit.

A very popular processor for the design of multiprocessor computers was the Transputer[3] chip developed by Inmos; see Figure 1.3. A Transputer chip contains a central processing unit (CPU), a dedicated floating point unit (FPU), a local memory, and four dedicated communication processors. The chips lend themselves very well to the construction of networks of degree four (i.e., each node is connected to four other nodes). Inmos also produces special chips dedicated to communication, called *routers*. Each router can simultaneously handle the traffic of 32 Transputer links. Each incoming message is inspected to see via which link it must be forwarded; it is then sent via that link. The popularity of these machines peaked in the first half of the nineties.

Another example of a parallel computer is the Connection Machine CM-5[4] system, developed by Thinking Machines Corporation [LAD+92] and continued by Connection Machines Services, Inc. Each node of the machine consists of a fast processor and a vector processing unit, thus offering internal parallelism in addition to the parallelism offered by having many nodes. As each node has a potential performance of 128 million operations per second, and one machine may contain 16,384 nodes, the entire machine may execute over 10^{12} operations per second. (A maximal machine of 16,384 processors occupies a room of 900m^2 and is probably very expensive.) The

---

[3] Transputer is a trademark of Inmos, now SGS-Thomson Microelectronics.
[4] Connection Machine is a registered trademark and CM-5 a trademark of Thinking Machines Corporation.

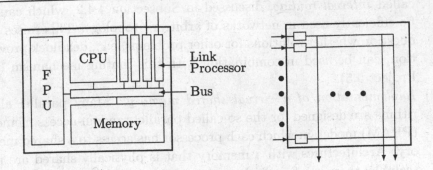

Figure 1.3 A TRANSPUTER AND A ROUTING CHIP.

nodes of the CM-5 are connected by three point-to-point communication networks. The *data network*, with a *fat tree* topology, is used to exchange data in a point-to-point manner between the processors. The *control network*, with a binary tree topology, performs dedicated operations such as global synchronization and combining inputs. The *diagnostic network* is invisible for the programmer and is used to propagate information about failed components. The computer can be programmed in both SIMD and (synchronous) MIMD mode.

In a parallel computer the computation is divided into subcomputations, each performed by one of the nodes. In a replicated system each node carries out the entire computation, after which the results are compared in order to detect and correct errors.

The construction of multiprocessor computers requires the solution of several algorithmical problems, some of which are similar to problems that arise in computer networks. Several of these problems are also discussed in this book.

(1) *Implementation of a message-passing system.* If the multiprocessor computer is organized as a point-to-point network a communication system must be designed. This poses problems similar to those that occur in the implementation of computer networks, such as transmission control, routing, and deadlock and congestion prevention. The solutions to these problems are often simpler than in the general case of computer networks. The routing problem, for example, is much simplified by regularity of the network's topology (i.e., a ring or grid) and the reliability of the nodes.

The Inmos C104 routing chips use a very simple routing algorithm called *interval routing*, discussed in Subsection 4.4.2, which cannot be efficiently used in networks of arbitrary topology. This raises the question whether solutions for other problems, e.g., deadlock prevention, can be used in combination with this routing mechanism (see Project 5.5).

(2) *Implementation of a virtual shared memory.* Many parallel algorithms are designed for the so-called parallel random-access memory (PRAM) model, in which each processor has access to a shared memory. Architectures with a memory that is physically shared are not scalable; there is a firm limit to the number of processors that can be served by a single memory chip.

Research is therefore directed towards architectures that have several memory nodes, connected to the processors by an interconnection network.

(3) *Load balancing.* The computational power of a parallel computer is exploited only if the workload of a computation is spread uniformly over the processors; concentration of the work at a single node degrades the performance to that of a single node. If all steps of the computation can be determined at compile time, it is possible to distribute them statically. A more difficult case arises when units of work are created dynamically during a computation; in this case, intricate techniques are required. The task queues of the processors must be compared regularly, after which tasks must migrate from one processor to another. For an overview of some techniques and algorithms for load balancing, see Goscinski [Gos91, Chapter 9] or Harget and Johnson [HJ90].

(4) *Robustness against undetectable failures* (Part Three). In a replicated system there must be a mechanism to overcome failures in one or more processors. Of course, computer networks must also continue their operation in spite of the failure of a node, but there it is usually assumed that such a failure can be detected by other nodes (see, e.g., the Netchange algorithm in Section 4.3). The assumptions under which replicated systems must remain correct are much more severe since a processor may produce an erroneous answer but otherwise cooperate in the protocols exactly like a correctly operating processor. Voting mechanisms must be implemented to filter the results of the processors, so that only correct answers are delivered as long as a majority of the processors operates correctly.

1.1.6 Cooperating Processes

The design of complicated software systems may often be simplified by organizing the software as a collection of (sequential) processes, each with a well-defined, simple task.

A classical example to illustrate this simplification is *Conway's record conversion*. The problem is to read 80-character records and write the same data in 125-character records. After each input record an additional blank must be inserted, and each pair of asterisks ("**") must be replaced by an exclamation mark ("!"). Each output record must be followed by an end-of-record (EOR) character. The conversion can be carried out by a single program, but writing this program is very intricate. All functions, i.e., replacement of "**" by "!", the insertion of blanks, and the insertion of EOR characters, must be handled in a single loop.

The program is better structured as two cooperating processes. The first process, say p_1, reads the input cards and converts the input to a stream of printable characters, not divided into records. The second process, say p_2, receives the stream of characters and inserts an EOR after every 125 characters. A design as a collection of processes is usually assumed for operating systems, telephone switching centers, and, as will be seen in Subsection 1.2.1, communication software in computer networks.

A design as a collection of cooperating processes causes the application to be *logically* distributed, but it is quite possible to execute the processes on the same computer, in which case it is not *physically* distributed. It is of course the case that achieving physical distribution is easier for systems that are logically distributed. The operating system of a computer installation must control the concurrent execution of the processes and provide the means for communication and synchronization between the processes.

Processes that execute on the same processor have access to the same physical memory, hence it is most natural to use this memory for communication. One process writes in a certain memory location, and another process reads from this location. This model of *concurrent processes* was used by Dijkstra [Dij68] and Owicki and Gries [OG76]. Problems that have been considered in this context include the following.

(1) *Atomicity of memory operations.* It is frequently assumed that reading and writing on a single word of memory are atomic, i.e., the read or write executed by one process is completed before another read or write operation begins. If structures larger than a single word are to be updated, the operations must be carefully synchronized to avoid the reading of a partially updated structure. This can be done, for

example, by implementing *mutual exclusion* [Dij68] on the structure: while one process has access to the structure, no other process can start reading or writing. The implementation of mutual exclusion using shared variables is intricate, because of the possibility that several processes may seek entry to the structure at the same time.

The wait conditions imposed by mutually exclusive access to shared data may reduce the performance of the processes, for example if a "fast" process must wait for data currently accessed by a "slow" process. In recent years attention has concentrated on implementations of atomic shared variables that are *wait-free*, meaning that a process can read or write the data without waiting for any other process. Reading and writing may now overlap, but by careful design of the read and write algorithms, atomicity can be ensured. For an overview of algorithms for wait-free atomic shared variables, see Kirousis and Kranakis [KK89], or Attiya and Welch [AW98].

(2) *The producer–consumer problem.* Two processes, one of which writes in a shared buffer and the other of which reads from this buffer, must be coordinated to prevent the first process from writing when the buffer is full and the second process from reading when the buffer is empty. The producer–consumer problem arises when the solution to Conway's conversion problem is worked out; p_1 produces the intermediate stream of characters, and p_2 consumes them.

(3) *Garbage collection.* An application that is programmed using dynamic data structures may produce inaccessible memory cells, referred to as *garbage*. Formerly, an application had to be interrupted when the memory system ran out of free space, in order to allow a special program called the *garbage collector* to identify and reclaim inaccessible memory. Dijkstra *et al.* [DLM+78] proposed an *on-the-fly* garbage collector, which could run as a separate process concurrently with the application.

Intricate cooperation between the application and the collector is required, because the application may modify the pointer structure in the memory while the collector is deciding which cells are inaccessible. The algorithm must be carefully analyzed to show that the modifications do not cause accessible cells to be erroneously reclaimed by the mutator. An algorithm for on-the-fly garbage collection with a simpler correctness proof was proposed by Ben-Ari [BA84].

The solutions to the problems listed here demonstrate that very difficult problems of process interaction can be solved for processes that communicate via shared memory. However, the solutions are often extremely. sophisticated and sometimes a very subtle interleaving of steps of different processes introduces erroneous results for solutions that seem correct at first (and second!) glance. Therefore, operating systems and programming languages offer primitives for a more structured organization of the interprocess communication.

(1) *Semaphores.* A semaphore [Dij68] is a non-negative (integer) variable whose value can be read and written in one atomic operation. A **V** operation increments its value, and a **P** operation decrements its value when it is positive (and suspends the process executing this operation as long as the value is zero).

Semaphores are an appropriate tool to implement mutual exclusion on a shared data structure: the semaphore is initialized to 1, and access to the structure is preceded by a **P** operation and followed by a **V** operation. Semaphores put a large responsibility for correct use onto each process; the integrity of shared data is violated if a process manipulates the data erroneously or does not execute the required **P** and **V** operations.

(2) *Monitors.* A monitor [Hoa74] consists of a data structure and a collection of procedures that can be executed on this data by calling processes in a mutually exclusive way. Because the data can be accessed solely via the procedures declared in the monitor, correct use of the data is ensured when the monitor is declared correctly. The monitor thus prevents unrestricted access to the data and synchronizes the access by different processes.

(3) *Pipes.* A pipe [Bou83] is a mechanism that moves a data stream from one process to another and synchronizes the two communicating processes; it is a pre-programmed solution to the producer–consumer problem.

The pipe is a basic communication mechanism in the UNIX operating system. If the program **p1** implements process p_1 of Conway's conversion problem and **p2** implements p_2, the UNIX command **p1 | p2** calls the two programs and connects them by a pipe. The output of **p1** is buffered and becomes the input of **p2**; **p1** is suspended when the buffer is full, and **p2** is suspended when the buffer is empty.

(4) *Message passing.* Some programming languages, such as occam and Ada, provide message passing as a mechanism for interprocess communication. Synchronization problems are relatively easy to solve using message passing; because a message cannot be received prior

to its sending, a temporal relation between events is induced by the exchange of a message.

Message passing can be implemented using monitors or pipes, and it is the natural means of communication for systems that run on distributed hardware (without shared memory). Indeed, the languages occam and Ada have been developed with physically distributed applications in mind.

1.2 Architecture and Languages

The software for implementing computer communication networks is very complicated. In this section it is explained how this software is usually structured in acyclically dependent modules called *layers* (Subsection 1.2.1). We discuss two network-architecture standards, namely, the ISO model of *Open Systems Interconnection*, a standard for wide-area networks, and the supplementary IEEE standard for local-area networks (Subsections 1.2.2 and 1.2.3). Also the languages used for programming distributed systems are briefly discussed (Subsection 1.2.4).

1.2.1 Architecture

The complexity of the tasks performed by the communication subsystem of a distributed system requires that this subsystem is designed in a highly structured way. To this end, networks are always organized as a collection of modules, each performing a very specific function and relying on services offered by other modules. In network organizations there is always a strict *hierarchy* between these modules, because each module exclusively uses the services offered by the previous module. The modules are called *layers* or *levels* in the context of network implementation; see Figure 1.4.

Each layer implements part of the functionality required for the implementation of the network and relies on the layer just below it. The services offered by layer i to layer $i + 1$ are precisely described in the layer i to layer $i + 1$ *interface* (briefly, the $i/(i + 1)$ interface). When designing a network, the first thing to do is to define the number of layers and the interfaces between subsequent layers.

The functionality of each layer must be implemented by a distributed algorithm, such that the algorithm for layer i solves a "problem" defined by the $i/(i + 1)$ interface, under the "assumptions" defined in the $(i - 1)/i$ interface. For example, the $(i - 1)/i$ interface may specify that messages are transported from node p to node q, but some messages may be lost,

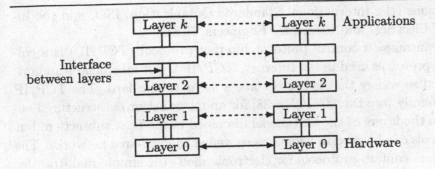

Figure 1.4 A LAYERED NETWORK ARCHITECTURE.

while the $i/(i+1)$ interface specifies that messages are transmitted from p to q reliably. The algorithmic problem for layer i is then to implement reliable message passing using unreliable message passing, which is usually done using acknowledgements and the retransmitting of lost messages (see Subsection 1.3.1 and Chapter 3). The solution of this problem defines the type of messages exchanged by the layer-i processes and the meaning of these messages, i.e., how the processes should react to these messages. The rules and conventions used in the "conversation" between the processes at layer i are referred to as the *layer-i protocol*.

The lowest layer of the hierarchy (layer 0 in Figure 1.4) is always the hardware layer. The 0/1 interface describes the procedures by which layer 1 can transmit raw information via the connecting wires, and a definition of the level itself specifies what types of wire are used, how many volts represents a one or a zero, etc. An important observation is that a change in the implementation of layer 0 (the replacement of wires by other wires or satellite connections) does not require the 0/1 interface to be changed. The same holds at higher layers: the layer interfaces serve to screen the implementation of a layer from other layers, and the implementation can be changed without affecting the other layers.

By the network *architecture* we mean the collection of layers and the accompanying definitions of all interfaces and protocols. As a network may contain nodes produced by various manufacturers, programmed with software written by different companies, it is important that products of different companies are compatible. The importance of compatibility has been recognized worldwide and therefore standard network architectures have been developed. In the next subsection two standards are discussed that have received an "official" status because they are adopted by influential organizations (the International Standards Organization, ISO, and the Institute of Electrical and Electronic Engineers, IEEE).

The Transmission control protocol/Internet protocol (TCP/IP) is a collection of protocols used in the Internet. TCP/IP is not an official standard, but is used so widely that is has become a *de facto* standard. The TCP/IP protocol family (see Davidson [Dav88] for an introduction) is structured according to the layers of the OSI model discussed in the next subsection, but the protocols can be used in wide-area as well as in local-area networks. The higher layers contain protocols for electronic mail (the simple mail-transfer protocol, SMTP), file transfer (the file-transfer protocol, FTP), and bidirectional communication for remote login (Telnet).

1.2.2 The OSI Reference Model

The International Standards Organization (ISO) has fixed a standard for computer networking products such as those used (mainly) in wide-area networks. Their standard for network architectures is called the *Open-Systems Interconnection* (OSI) reference model, and will be described briefly in this subsection. Because the standard is not entirely appropriate for use in local-area networks, additional IEEE standards for local-area networks are discussed in the next subsection.

The OSI reference model consists of seven layers, namely the *physical, data-link, network, transport, session, presentation,* and *application* layers. The reference model specifies the interfaces between the layers and provides, for each layer, one or more standard protocols (distributed algorithms to implement the layer).

The physical layer (1). The purpose of the physical layer is to transmit sequences of bits over a communication channel. As the name of the layer suggests, this goal is achieved by means of a physical connection between two nodes, such as a telephone line, fiber optic connection, or satellite connection. The design of the layer itself is purely a matter for electrical engineers, while the 1/2 interface specifies the procedures by which the next layer calls the services of the physical layer. The service of the physical layer is not reliable; the bitstream may be scrambled during its transmission.

The data-link layer (2). The purpose of the data-link layer is to mask the unreliability of the physical layer, that is, to provide a reliable link to the higher layers. The data-link layer only implements a reliable connection between nodes that are directly connected by a physical link, because it is built directly upon the physical layer. (Communication between non-adjacent nodes is implemented in the network layer.)

To achieve its goal, the layer divides the bitstream into pieces of fixed length, called *frames*. The receiver of a frame can check whether the frame was received correctly by verifying its *checksum*, which is some redundant information added to each frame. There is a feedback from the receiver to the sender to inform the sender about correctly or incorrectly received frames; this feedback takes place by means of *acknowledgement* messages. The sender will send a frame anew if it turns out that it is received incorrectly or completely lost.

The general principles explained in the previous paragraph can be refined to a variety of different data-link protocols. For example, an acknowledgement message may be sent for frames that are received (positive acknowledgements) or for frames that are missing from the collection of received frames (negative acknowledgements). The ultimate responsibility for the correct transmission of all frames may be at the sender's or the receiver's side. Acknowledgements may be sent for single frames or blocks of frames, the frames may have sequence numbers or not, etc.

The network layer (3). The purpose of the network layer is to provide a means of communication between all pairs of nodes, not just those connected by a physical channel. This layer must select the routes through the network used for communication between non-adjacent nodes and must control the traffic load of each node and channel.

The selection of routes is usually based on information about the network topology contained in *routing tables* stored in each node. The network layer contains algorithms to update the routing tables if the topology of the network changes (owing to a node or channel failure or recovery). Such a failure or recovery is detected by the data-link layer.

Although the data-link layer provides reliable service to the network layer, the service offered by the network layer is not reliable. Messages (called *packets* in this layer) sent from one node to the other may follow different paths, causing one message to overtake the other. Owing to node failures messages may be lost (a node may go down while holding a message), and owing to superfluous retransmissions messages may even be duplicated. The layer may guarantee a bounded packet lifetime; i.e., there exists a constant c such that each packet is either delivered at the destination node within c seconds, or lost.

The transport layer (4). The purpose of the transport layer is to mask the unreliability introduced by the network layer, i.e., to provide reliable *end-to-end* communication between any two nodes. The problem would be similar to the one solved by the data-link layer, but it is complicated by the possibility of the duplication and reordering of messages. This makes it impossible to use cyclic sequence numbers, unless a bound on the packet lifetime is guaranteed by the network layer.

The algorithms used for transmission control in the transport layer use similar techniques to the algorithms in the data-link layer: sequence numbers, feedback via acknowledgements, and retransmissions.

The session layer (5). The purpose of the session layer is to provide facilities for maintaining connections between processes at different nodes. A connection can be opened and closed and between opening and closing the connection can be used for data exchange, using a session address rather than repeating the address of the remote process with each message. The session layer uses the reliable end-to-end communication offered by the transport layer, but structures the exchanged messages into sessions.

A session can be used for file transfer or remote login. The session layer can provide the mechanisms for recovery if a node crashes during a session and for mutual exclusion if critical operations may not be performed at both ends simultaneously.

The presentation layer (6). The purpose of the presentation layer is to perform data conversion where the representation of information in one node differs from the representation in another node or is not suitable for transmission. Below this layer (i.e., at the 5/6 interface) data is in transmittable and standardized form, while above this layer (i.e., at the 6/7 interface) data is in user- or computer-specific form. The layer performs data *compression* and *decompression* to reduce the amount of data handed via the lower layers. The layer performs data *encryption* and *decryption* to ensure its confidentiality and integrity in the presence of malicious parties that aim to receive or corrupt the transmitted data.

The application layer (7). The purpose of the application layer is to fulfill concrete user requirements such as file transmission, electronic mail, bulletin boards, or virtual terminals. The wide variety of possible applications makes it impossible to standardize the complete functionality of this layer, but for some of the applications listed here standards have been proposed.

1.2.3 The OSI Model in Local-area Networks: IEEE Standards

The design of the OSI reference model is influenced to a large extent by the architectures of existing wide-area networks. The technology used in local-area networks poses different software requirements, and due to this some of the layers may be almost absent in local-area networks. If the network organization relies on a common bus shared by all nodes (see Subsection 1.1.4), the network layer is almost empty because each pair of nodes is connected directly via the bus. The design of the transport layer is very much simplified by the limited amount of non-determinism introduced by the bus, as compared to an intermediate point-to-point network. In contrast, the data-link layer is complicated by the fact that the same physical medium is accessed by a potentially large number of nodes.

In answer to these problems the IEEE has approved additional standards, covering only the lower levels of the OSI hierarchy, to be used in local-area networks (or, to be more precise, all networks that are bus-structured rather than point-to-point). Because no single standard could be general enough to encompass all networks already widely in use, the IEEE has approved three different, non-compatible standards, namely CSMA/CD, token bus, and token ring. The data-link layer is replaced by two sublayers, namely the *medium access control* and the *logical link control* sublayers.

The physical layer (1). The purpose of the physical layer in the IEEE standards is similar to that of the original ISO standard, namely to transmit sequences of bits. The actual standard definitions (the type of wiring, etc.) are, however, radically different, due to the fact that all communication takes place via a commonly accessed medium rather than point-to-point connections.

The medium access control sublayer (2a). The purpose of this sublayer is to resolve conflicts that arise between nodes that want to use the shared communication medium. A statical approach would once and for all schedule the time intervals during which each node is allowed to use the medium. This method wastes a lot of bandwidth, however, if only a few nodes have data to transmit, and all other nodes are silent; the medium remains idle during the times scheduled for the silent nodes.

In token buses and token rings access to the medium is on a round-robin basis: the nodes circulate a privilege, called the *token*, among them and the node holding this token is allowed to use the medium. If the node holding the token has no data to transmit, it passes the token to the next node. In a token ring the cyclic order in which nodes get their turn is determined by the physical connection topology (which is, indeed, a ring), while in a token bus the cyclic order is determined dynamically based on the order of the node addresses.

In the carrier sense multiple access with collision detection (CSMA/CD) standard, nodes observe when the medium is idle, and if so they are allowed to send. If two or more nodes start to send (approximately) simultaneously, there is a *collision*, which is detected and causes each node to interrupt its transmission and try again at a later time.

The logical link control sublayer (2b). The purpose of this layer is comparable to the purpose of the data-link layer in the OSI model, namely to control the exchange of data between nodes. The layer provides error control and flow control, using techniques similar to those used in the OSI protocols, namely sequence numbers and acknowledgements.

Seen from the viewpoint of the higher layers, the logical link control sublayer appears like the network layer of the OSI model. Indeed, communication between any pair of nodes takes place without using intermediate nodes, and can be handled directly by the logical link control sublayer. A separate network layer is therefore not implemented in local-area networks; instead, the transport layer is built directly on top of the logical link control sublayer.

1.2.4 Language Support

The implementation of one of the software layers of a communication network or a distributed application requires that the distributed algorithm used in that layer or application is coded in a programming language. The actual coding is of course highly influenced by the language and especially by the primitives it offers. Because in this book we concentrate on the algorithms and not on their coding as a program, our basic model of processes is based on process states and state transitions (see Subsection 2.1.2) and not on the execution of instructions taken from a prescribed set. Of course it is inevitable that where we present algorithms, some formal notation is required; the programming notation used in this book is presented in Appendix A.

In this subsection we describe some of the constructs one may observe in actual programming languages designed for distributed systems. We confine ourselves here to a brief description of these constructs; for more details and examples of actual languages that use the various constructs, see, e.g., Bal [Bal90]. A language for programming distributed applications must provide the means to express parallelism, process interaction, and non-determinism. Parallelism is of course required to program the various nodes of the system in such a way that the nodes will execute their part of the program concurrently. Communication between the nodes must also be supported by the programming language. Non-determinism is necessary because a node must sometimes be able to receive a message from different nodes, or be able to either send or receive a message.

Parallelism. The most appropriate degree of parallelism in a distributed application depends on the ratio between the cost of communication and the cost of computation. A larger degree of parallelism allows for faster execution, but also requires more communication, so if communication is expensive, the gain in computation speed may be lost in additional communication cost.

Parallelism is usually expressed by defining several *processes*, each being a sequential entity with its own state space. A language may either offer the possibility of statically defining a collection of processes or allow the dynamic creation and termination of processes. It is also possible to express parallelism by means of parallel statements or in a functional programming language. Parallelism is not always explicit in a language; the partitioning of code into parallel processes may be performed by a sophisticated compiler.

Communication. Communication between processes is inherent to distributed systems: if processes do not communicate, each process operates in isolation from other processes and should be studied in isolation, not as part of a distributed system. When processes cooperate in a computation, communication is necessary if one process needs an intermediate result produced by another process. Also, synchronization is necessary, because the former process must be suspended until the result is available. *Message passing* achieves both communication and synchronization; a *shared memory* achieves only communication: additional care must be taken to synchronize processes that communicate using shared memory.

In languages that provide message passing, "send" and "receive" operations are available. Communication takes place by the execution of the send operation in one process (therefore called the sender process) and the receive operation in another process (the receiver process). The arguments of the send operation are the receiver's address and additional data, forming the content of the message. This additional data becomes available to the receiver when the receive statement is executed, i.e., this implements the communication. The receive operation can be completed only after the send operation has been executed, which implements the synchronization. In some languages a receive operation is not available explicitly; instead, a procedure or operation is activated implicitly when a message is received.

A language may provide *synchronous* message passing, in which case the send operation is completed only after execution of the receive operation. In other words, the sender is blocked until the message has been received, and a two-way synchronization between sender and receiver results.

Messages can be sent point-to-point, i.e., from one sender to one receiver, or broadcast, in which case the same message is received by all receivers. The term multicast is also used to refer to messages that are sent to a collection of (not necessarily all) processes. A somewhat more structured communication primitive is the *remote procedure call* (RPC). To communicate with process b, process a calls a procedure present in process b by sending the parameters of the procedure in a message; a is suspended until the result of the procedure is returned in another message.

An alternative for message passing is the use of *shared memory* for communication; one process writes a value to a variable, and another process reads the value. Synchronization between the processes is harder to achieve, because reading a variable can be done before the variable has been written. Using synchronization primitives such as *semaphores* [Dij68] or *monitors* [Hoa78], it is possible to implement message passing in a shared-variable environment. Conversely, it is also possible to implement a (virtual) shared memory in a message-passing environment, but this is very inefficient.

Non-determinism. At many points in its execution a process may be able to continue in various different ways. A receive operation is often non-deterministic because it allows the receipt of messages from different senders. Additional ways to express non-determinism are based on *guarded commands*. A guarded command in its most general form is a list of statements, each preceded by a boolean expression (its guard). The process may continue its execution with any of the statements for which the corresponding guard evaluates to *true*. A guard may contain a receive operation, in which case it evaluates to true if there is a message available to be received.

1.3 Distributed Algorithms

The previous sections have given reasons for the use of distributed computer systems and explained the nature of these systems; the need to program these systems arises as a consequence. The programming of distributed systems must be based on the use of correct, flexible, and efficient algorithms.

In this section it is argued that the development of distributed algorithms is a craft quite different in nature from the craft used in the development of centralized algorithms. Distributed and centralized systems differ in a number of essential respects, treated in Subsection 1.3.1 and exemplified in Subsection 1.3.2. Distributed algorithms research has therefore developed as an independent field of scientific research; see Subsection 1.3.3. This book is intended to introduce the reader to this research field. The objectives of the book and a selection of results included in the book are stated in Subsection 1.4.

1.3.1 Distributed versus Centralized Algorithms

Distributed systems differ from centralized (uniprocessor) computer systems in three essential respects, which we now discuss.

(1) *Lack of knowledge of global state.* In a centralized algorithm control decisions can be made based upon an observation of the state of the system. Even though the entire state usually cannot be accessed in a single machine operation, a program may inspect the variables one by one, and make a decision after all relevant information has been considered. No data is modified between the inspection and the decision, and this guarantees the integrity of the decision.

Nodes in a distributed system have access only to their own state and not to the global state of the entire system. Consequently, it is not possible to make a control decision based upon the global state. It is the case that a node may receive information about the state of other nodes and base its control decisions upon this information. In contrast with centralized systems, the fact that the received information is old may render the information invalid, because the state of the other node may have changed between the sending of the state information and the decision based upon it.

The state of the communication subsystem (i.e., what messages are in transit in it at a certain moment) is never directly observed by the nodes. This information can only be deduced indirectly by comparing information about messages sent and received by the nodes.

(2) *Lack of a global time-frame.* The events constituting the execution of a centralized algorithm are totally ordered in a natural way by their temporal occurrence; for each pair of events, one occurs earlier or later than the other. The temporal relation induced on the events constituting the execution of a distributed algorithm is not total; for

some pairs of events there may be a reason for deciding that one occurs before the other, but for other pairs it is the case that neither of the events occurs before the other [Lam78].

Mutual exclusion can be achieved in a centralized system by requiring that if the access of process p to the resource starts later than the access of process q, then the access of process p must start after the access of process q has ended. Indeed, all such events (the starting and ending of the access of processes p and q) are totally ordered by the temporal relation; in a distributed system they are not, and the same strategy is not sufficient. Processes p and q may start accessing the resource, while the start of neither temporally precedes the start of the other.

(3) *Non-determinism.* A centralized program may describe the computation as it unrolls from a certain input unambiguously; given the program and the input, only a single computation is possible. In contrast, the execution of a distributed system is usually non-deterministic, due to possible differences in execution speed of the system components.

Consider the situation where a server process may receive requests from an unknown number of client processes. The server cannot suspend the processing of requests until all requests have been received, because it is not known how many messages will arrive. Consequently, each request must be processed immediately, and the order of processing is the order in which the requests arrive. The order in which the clients send their requests may be known, but as the transmission delays are not known, the requests may arrive in a different order.

The combination of lack of knowledge of the global state, lack of a global time-frame, and non-determinism makes the design of distributed algorithms an intricate craft, because the three aspects interfere in several ways.

The concepts of *time* and *state* are highly related; in centralized systems the notion of time may be defined by considering the *sequence* of states assumed by the system during its execution. Even though in a distributed system a global state can be defined, and an execution can be seen as a sequence of global states (cf. Definition 2.2), this view is of limited use since the execution can also be described by other sequences of global states (Theorem 2.21). Those alternative sequences usually consist of different global states; this gives the statement "the system assumed this or that state during its execution" a very dubious meaning.

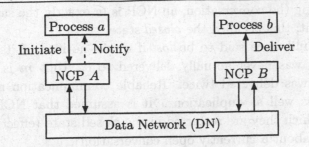

Figure 1.5 A SIMPLIFIED NETWORK ARCHITECTURE.

Lack of knowledge of the global state could be compensated for if it were possible to predict this global state from the algorithm that is being executed. Unfortunately, this is not possible due to the inherent non-determinism in the execution of distributed systems.

1.3.2 An Example: Single-message Communication

We shall illustrate the difficulties imposed by the lack of knowledge of the global state and the lack of a global time-frame by an example problem, discussed by Belsnes [Bel76], namely the reliable exchange of information via an unreliable medium. Consider two processes, a and b, connected by a data network, which transmits messages from one process to the other. A message may be received an arbitrarily long time after it is sent, but may also be lost altogether in the network. The reliability of the communication is increased by the use of network control procedures (NCPs), via which a and b access the network. Process a initiates the communication by giving an information unit m to NCP A. The interaction between the NCPs (via the data network, DN) must ensure that the information m is delivered at process b (by NCP B), after which a is notified of the delivery (by NCP A). The communication structure is depicted in Figure 1.5.

Even if only a single information unit is to be transported from a to b, the network's unreliability forces NCP A and NCP B to engage in a conversation consisting of several messages. They maintain state information about this conversation, but because the number of possible conversation partners for each process is large, it is required that state information is discarded after the message exchange is complete. The initialization of status information is called *opening* and its discarding is called *closing* the conversation. Observe that, after closing the conversation, an NCP is in exactly the same state as before opening it; this is called the *closed* state.

Information unit m is said to be *lost* if a was notified of its receipt by b, but the unit was never actually delivered to b. Unit m is said to be *duplicated* if it was delivered twice. Reliable communication mechanisms prevent losses as well as duplications. It is assumed that NCPs may fail (crash), after which they are restarted in the closed state (effectively losing all information about a currently open conversation).

No reliable communication is achievable. As a first observation, it can be shown that no matter how intricately the NCPs are designed, it is not possible to achieve completely reliable communication. This observation can be made independently of the design of the data network or the NCPs and only relies on the assumption that an NCP may lose information about an active conversation.

To see this, assume that after initialization of a communication by a, NCP A and NCP B start a conversation, during which NCP B is supposed to deliver m to b after the receipt of a message M from NCP A. Consider the case where NCP B crashes and is restarted in the closed state after NCP A has sent message M. In this situation, neither NCP A nor NCP B can tell whether m was already delivered when NCP B crashed; NCP A because it cannot observe the events in NCP B (lack of knowledge of the global state) and NCP B because it has crashed and was restarted in the closed state. Regardless of how the NCPs continue their conversation, an error may be introduced. If NCP A sends the message to NCP B again and NCP B delivers the message, a duplication may arise. If notification to a is given without delivery, a loss may arise.

We shall now evaluate several possible designs for the NCPs with respect to the possibility of losing or duplicating messages. We shall try to design the protocols in such a way that losses are avoided in any case.

A one-message conversation. In the simplest possible design, NCP A sends the data unaltered via the network, notifies a, and closes, in a single action upon initialization. NCP B always delivers a message it receives to b and closes after each delivery.

This protocol introduces a loss whenever the network refuses to deliver a message, but there is no possibility of introducing duplications.

A two-message conversation. A limited protection against loss of messages is offered by the addition of acknowledgements to the protocol. In a normal conversation, NCP A sends a data message $\langle \textbf{data}, m \rangle$ and waits for the receipt of an acknowledgement message $\langle \textbf{ack} \rangle$ from NCP B. When this message is received, NCP A closes the conversation. NCP B, upon receipt of the $\langle \textbf{data}, m \rangle$ message, delivers m to b, replies with an $\langle \textbf{ack} \rangle$ message, and closes. Summarizing, an error-free conversation consists of three events.

1. NCP A send $\langle \textbf{data}, m \rangle$
2. NCP B receive $\langle \textbf{data}, m \rangle$, deliver m, send $\langle \textbf{ack} \rangle$, close
3. NCP A receive $\langle \textbf{ack} \rangle$, notify, close

The possibility of loss of a data message forces NCP A to send $\langle \textbf{data}, m \rangle$ again if the acknowledgement is not received after some time. (Due to lack of knowledge of the global state, NCP A cannot observe whether $\langle \textbf{data}, m \rangle$ was lost, $\langle \textbf{ack} \rangle$ was lost, or NCP B crashed between receiving $\langle \textbf{data}, m \rangle$ and sending $\langle \textbf{ack} \rangle$.) To this end, NCP A awaits the receipt of an acknowledgement for a limited amount of time, and if no such a message is received, a timer runs out and a *timeout* occurs. It can be easily seen that this option of retransmission introduces the possibility of a duplicate, namely, if not the original data message, but its acknowledgement, was lost, as in the following scenario.

1. NCP A send $\langle \textbf{data}, m \rangle$
2. NCP B receive $\langle \textbf{data}, m \rangle$, deliver m, send $\langle \textbf{ack} \rangle$, close
3. DN $\langle \textbf{ack} \rangle$ is lost
4. NCP A timeout, send $\langle \textbf{data}, m \rangle$
5. NCP B receive $\langle \textbf{data}, m \rangle$, deliver m, send $\langle \textbf{ack} \rangle$, close
6. NCP A receive $\langle \textbf{ack} \rangle$, notify, close

But not only do acknowledgements introduce the possibility of duplicates, they also fail to safeguard against losses, as the following scenario shows. Process a offers two information units, m_1 and m_2, for transmission.

1. NCP A send $\langle \textbf{data}, m_1 \rangle$
2. NCP B receive $\langle \textbf{data}, m_1 \rangle$, deliver m_1, send $\langle \textbf{ack} \rangle$, close
3. NCP A timeout, send $\langle \textbf{data}, m_1 \rangle$
4. NCP B receive $\langle \textbf{data}, m_1 \rangle$, deliver m_1, send $\langle \textbf{ack} \rangle$, close
5. NCP A receive $\langle \textbf{ack} \rangle$, notify, close
6. NCP A send $\langle \textbf{data}, m_2 \rangle$
7. DN $\langle \textbf{data}, m_2 \rangle$ is lost
8. NCP A receive $\langle \textbf{ack} \rangle$ (step 2), notify, close

Message m_1 is duplicated as in the previous scenario, but the first acknowledgement was delivered slowly instead of lost, causing a loss of a later in-

formation unit. The slow delivery is not detected due to the lack of a global
time.

The problem of reliable interprocess communication can be solved more
easily if a weak notion of global time is assumed, namely, that there exists an
upper bound T on the transmission delay of any message sent through the
network. This is considered a *global* timing assumption, because it induces
a temporal relation between events in different nodes (namely, the sending
by NCP A and a receipt by NCP B). The receipt of messages from earlier
conversations can be prevented in this protocol by closing the conversation
in NCP A only $2T$ after sending the last message.

A three-message conversation. As the two-message protocol loses or duplicates an information unit when an acknowledgement is lost or delayed, one
may consider adding a third message to the conversation, informing NCP B
that NCP A has received the acknowledgement. A normal conversation then
consists of the following events.

1. NCP A send $\langle \mathbf{data}, m \rangle$
2. NCP B receive $\langle \mathbf{data}, m \rangle$, deliver m, send $\langle \mathbf{ack} \rangle$
3. NCP A receive $\langle \mathbf{ack} \rangle$, notify, send $\langle \mathbf{close} \rangle$, close
4. NCP B receive $\langle \mathbf{close} \rangle$, close

A loss of the $\langle \mathbf{data}, m \rangle$ message causes a timeout in NCP A, in which case
NCP A retransmits the message. A loss of the $\langle \mathbf{ack} \rangle$ message also causes a
retransmission of $\langle \mathbf{data}, m \rangle$, but this does not lead to a duplication because
NCP B has an open conversation and recognizes the message it has already
received.

Unfortunately, the protocol may still lose and duplicate information. Because NCP B must be able to close even when the $\langle \mathbf{close} \rangle$ message is
lost, NCP B must retransmit the $\langle \mathbf{ack} \rangle$ message if it receives no $\langle \mathbf{close} \rangle$
message. NCP A replies saying that it has no conversation (a $\langle \mathbf{nocon} \rangle$
message), after which NCP B closes. The retransmission of $\langle \mathbf{ack} \rangle$ may arrive, however, in the next conversation of NCP A and be interpreted as an
acknowledgement in that conversation, causing the next information unit to
be lost, as in the following scenario.

1. NCP A send $\langle$ **data**, $m_1 \rangle$
2. NCP B receive $\langle$ **data**, $m_1 \rangle$, deliver m_1, send $\langle$ **ack** $\rangle$
3. NCP A receive $\langle$ **ack** $\rangle$, notify, send $\langle$ **close** $\rangle$, close
4.   DN $\langle$ **close** $\rangle$ is lost
5. NCP A send $\langle$ **data**, $m_2 \rangle$
6.   DN $\langle$ **data**, $m_2 \rangle$ is lost
7. NCP B retransmit $\langle$ **ack** $\rangle$ (step 2)
8. NCP A receive $\langle$ **ack** $\rangle$, notify, send $\langle$ **close** $\rangle$, close
9. NCP B receive $\langle$ **close** $\rangle$, close

Again the problem has arisen because messages of one conversation have interfered with another conversation. This can be ruled out by selection of a pair of new conversation identification numbers for each new conversation, one by NCP A and one by NCP B. The numbers chosen are included in all messages of the conversation, and are used to verify that a received message indeed belongs to the current conversation. The normal conversation of the three-message protocol is as follows.

1. NCP A send $\langle$ **data**, $m, x \rangle$
2. NCP B receive $\langle$ **data**, $m, x \rangle$, deliver m, send $\langle$ **ack**, $x, y \rangle$
3. NCP A receive $\langle$ **ack**, $x, y \rangle$, notify, send $\langle$ **close**, $x, y \rangle$, close
4. NCP B receive $\langle$ **close**, $x, y \rangle$, close

This modification of the three-message protocol excludes the erroneous conversation given earlier, because the message received by NCP A in step 8 is not accepted as an acknowledgement for the data message sent in step 5. However, NCP B does not verify the validity of a $\langle$ **data**, $m, x \rangle$ before delivering m (in step 2), which easily leads to duplication of information. If the message sent in step 1 is delayed and retransmitted, a later-arriving $\langle$ **data**, $m, x \rangle$ message causes NCP B to deliver information m again.

Of course, NCP B should also verify the validity of messages it receives before delivering the data. We consider a modification of the three-message conversation in which NCP B delivers the data in step 4 rather than in step 2. Notification is now given by NCP A *before* delivery by NCP B, but because NCP B has already received the information this seems justified. It must be ensured, though, that NCP B will now deliver the data in any case; in particular, when the $\langle$ **close**, $x, y \rangle$ message is lost. NCP B repeats the $\langle$ **ack**, $x, y \rangle$ message, to which NCP A replies with a $\langle$ **nocon**, $x, y \rangle$ message, causing NCP B to deliver and close, as in the following scenario.

  1.   NCP A send $\langle \mathbf{data}, m, x \rangle$
  2.   NCP B receive $\langle \mathbf{data}, m, x \rangle$, send $\langle \mathbf{ack}, x, y \rangle$
  3.   NCP A receive $\langle \mathbf{ack}, x, y \rangle$, notify, send $\langle \mathbf{close}, x, y \rangle$, close
  4.   DN $\langle \mathbf{close}, x, y \rangle$ is lost
  5.   NCP B timeout, retransmit $\langle \mathbf{ack}, x, y \rangle$
  6.   NCP A receive $\langle \mathbf{ack}, x, y \rangle$, reply $\langle \mathbf{nocon}, x, y \rangle$
  7.   NCP B receive $\langle \mathbf{nocon}, x, y \rangle$, deliver m, close

It turns out that, in order to avoid loss of information, NCP B must deliver the data even if NCP A does not confirm having a connection with identifications x and y. This renders the validation mechanism useless for NCP B, leading to the possibility of duplication of information as in the following scenario.

  1.   NCP A send $\langle \mathbf{data}, m, x \rangle$
  2.   NCP A timeout, retransmit $\langle \mathbf{data}, m, x \rangle$
  3.   NCP B receive $\langle \mathbf{data}, m, x \rangle$ (sent in step 2), send $\langle \mathbf{ack}, x, y_1 \rangle$
  4.   NCP A receive $\langle \mathbf{ack}, x, y_1 \rangle$, notify, send $\langle \mathbf{close}, x, y_1 \rangle$, close
  5.   NCP B receive $\langle \mathbf{close}, x, y_1 \rangle$, deliver m, close
  6.   NCP B receive $\langle \mathbf{data}, m, x \rangle$ (sent in step 1), send $\langle \mathbf{ack}, x, y_2 \rangle$
  7.   NCP A receive $\langle \mathbf{ack}, x, y_2 \rangle$, reply $\langle \mathbf{nocon}, x, y_2 \rangle$
  8.   NCP B receive $\langle \mathbf{nocon}, x, y_2 \rangle$ in reply to $\langle \mathbf{ack}, x, y_2 \rangle$,
                      deliver m, close

A four-message conversation. The delivery of information from old conversations can be avoided by having the NCPs mutually agree upon their conversation identification numbers before any data is delivered, as in the following conversation.

  1.   NCP A send $\langle \mathbf{data}, m, x \rangle$
  2.   NCP B receive $\langle \mathbf{data}, m, x \rangle$, send $\langle \mathbf{open}, x, y \rangle$
  3.   NCP A receive $\langle \mathbf{open}, x, y \rangle$, send $\langle \mathbf{agree}, x, y \rangle$
  4.   NCP B receive $\langle \mathbf{agree}, x, y \rangle$, deliver m, send $\langle \mathbf{ack}, x, y \rangle$, close
  5.   NCP A receive $\langle \mathbf{ack}, x, y \rangle$, notify, close

The possibility of a crash of NCP B forces the error handling to be such that a duplicate may still occur, even when no NCP actually crashes. An error message $\langle \mathbf{nocon}, x, y \rangle$ is sent by NCP B when an $\langle \mathbf{agree}, x, y \rangle$ message is received and no conversation is open. Assume that NCP A does not receive an $\langle \mathbf{ack}, x, y \rangle$ message, even after several retransmissions of $\langle \mathbf{agree}, x, y \rangle$; only $\langle \mathbf{nocon}, x, y \rangle$ messages are received. Because it is possible that NCP B crashed before it received $\langle \mathbf{agree}, x, y \rangle$, NCP A is forced to start a new conversation (by sending $\langle \mathbf{data}, m, x \rangle$) to prevent loss of m! But it is also possible that NCP B has already delivered m, and the $\langle \text{ack}, x, y \rangle$ message was lost, in which case a duplicate is introduced.

It is possible to modify the protocol in such a way that NCP A notifies and closes upon receipt of the $\langle \text{nocon}, x, y \rangle$ message; this prevents duplicates, but may introduce a loss, which is considered even less desirable.

A five-message conversation and comparison. Belsnes [Bel76] gives a five-message protocol that does not lose information and that introduces duplicates only if an NCP actually crashes. Consequently, this is the best possible protocol, seen in the light of the observation that no reliable communication is possible, earlier in this subsection. Because of the excessive overhead (five messages are exchanged by the NCPs to transmit one information unit), it must be doubted whether the five-message protocol must really be preferred to the much simpler two-message protocol. Indeed, because even the five-message protocol may introduce duplicates (when an NCP crashes), the process level must deal with them somehow. So then the two-message protocol, which may introduce duplicates but can be made free of losses if conversation identifications are added as we did for the three-message protocol, may as well be used.

1.3.3 Research Field

There has been ongoing research in distributed algorithms during the last two decades, and considerable progress towards maturity of the field has been made especially during the nineteen-eighties. In previous sections we have pointed at some technical developments that have stimulated research in distributed algorithms, namely, the design of computer networks (both wide- and local-area) and multiprocessor computers. Originally the research was very much aimed towards application of the algorithms in wide-area networks, but nowadays the field has developed crisp mathematical models, allowing application of the results and methods to wider classes of distributed environments. However, the research maintains tight connections with the engineering developments in communication techniques, because the algorithmical results are often sensitive to changes in the network model. For example, the availability of cheap microprocessors has made it possible to construct systems with many identical processors, which has stimulated the study of "anonymous networks" (see Chapter 9).

There are several journals and annual conferences that specialize in results concerning distributed algorithms and distributed computation. Some other journals and conferences do not specialize solely in this subject but contain a lot of publications in the area nonetheless. The annual symposium on Principles of Distributed Computing (PoDC) has been organized every year since 1982 up to the time of writing in North America, and its proceedings are published by the Association for Computing Machinery, Inc. International Workshops on Distributed Algorithms (WDAG) were held in Ottawa (1985), Amsterdam (1987), Nice (1989), and since then annually with its proceedings being published by Springer-Verlag in the series *Lecture Notes on Computer Science*. In 1998 the name of this conference has changed to Distributed Computing (DISC). The annual symposia on theory of computing (SToC) and foundations of computer science (FoCS) cover all fundamental areas of computer science, and often carry papers on distributed computing. The proceedings of the SToC meetings are published by the Association for Computing Machinery, Inc., and those of the FoCS meetings by the IEEE. The *Journal of Parallel and Distributed Computing (JPDC)* and *Distributed Computing* publish distributed algorithms regularly, and so does *Information Processing Letters (IPL)*.

1.4 Outline of the Book

This book was written with the following three objectives in mind.

(1) To make the reader familiar with techniques that can be used to investigate the properties of a given distributed algorithm, to analyze and solve a problem that arises in the context of distributed systems, or to evaluate the merits of a particular network model.

(2) To provide insight into the inherent possibilities and impossibilities of several system models. The impact of the availability of a global time-frame is studied in Section 3.2 and in Chapters 12 and 15. The impact of the knowledge by processes of their identities is studied in Chapter 9. The impact of the requirement of process termination is studied in Chapter 8. The impact of process failures is studied in Part Three.

(3) To present a collection of recent state-of-the-art distributed algorithms, together with their verification and an analysis of their complexity.

Where a subject cannot be treated in full detail, references to the relevant scientific literature are given. The material collected in the book is divided into three parts: Protocols, Fundamental Algorithms, and Fault Tolerance.

Part One: Protocols. This part deals with the communication protocols used in the implementation of computer communication networks and also introduces the techniques used in later parts.

In Chapter 2 the model that will be used in most of the later chapters is introduced. The model is both general enough to be suitable for the development and verification of algorithms and tight enough for proving impossibility results. It is based on the notion of transition systems, for which proof rules for safety and liveness properties can be given easily. The notion of causality as a partial order on events of a computation is introduced and logical clocks are defined.

In Chapter 3 the problem of message transmission between two nodes is considered. First a family of protocols for the exchange of packets over a single link is presented, and a proof of its correctness, due to Schoone, is given. Also, a protocol due to Fletcher and Watson is treated, the correctness of which relies on the correct use of timers. The treatment of this protocol shows how the verification method can be applied to protocols based on the use of timers.

Chapter 4 considers the problem of routing in computer networks. It first presents some general theory about routing and an algorithm by Toueg for the computation of routing tables. Also treated are the Netchange algorithm of Tajibnapis and a correctness proof for this algorithm given by Lamport. This chapter ends with compact routing algorithms, including interval and prefix routing. These algorithms are called *compact* routing algorithms, because they require only a small amount of storage in each node of the network.

The discussion of protocols for computer networks ends with some strategies for avoiding store-and-forward deadlocks in packet-switched computer networks in Chapter 5. The strategies are based on defining cycle-free directed graphs on the buffers in the nodes of the network, and it is shown how such a graph can be constructed using only a modest amount of buffers in each node.

Part Two: Fundamental Algorithms. This part presents a number of algorithmical "building blocks", which are used as procedures in many distributed applications, and develops theory about the computational power of different network assumptions.

Chapter 6 defines the notion of a "wave algorithm", which is a generalized scheme to visit all nodes of a network. Wave algorithms are used to disseminate information through a network, to synchronize the nodes, or to compute a function that depends on information spread over all the nodes.

As it will turn out in later chapters, many distributed-control problems can be solved by very general algorithmic schemes in which a wave algorithm is used as a component. This chapter also defines the time complexity of distributed algorithms and examines the time and message complexity of a number of distributed depth-first search algorithms.

A fundamental problem in distributed systems is *election*: the selection of a single process that is to play a distinguished role in a subsequent computation. This problem is studied in Chapter 7. First the problem is studied for ring networks, where it is shown that the message complexity of the problem is $\Theta(N \log N)$ messages (on a ring of N processors). The problem is also studied for general networks and some constructions are shown by which election algorithms can be obtained from wave and traversal algorithms. This chapter also discusses the algorithm for spanning tree construction by Gallager *et al.*

A second fundamental problem is that of *termination detection*: the recognition (by the processes themselves) that a distributed computation has completed. This problem is studied in Chapter 8. A lower bound on the complexity of solving this problem is proved, and several algorithms are discussed in detail. The chapter includes some classical algorithms (e.g., the ones by Dijkstra, Feijen, and Van Gasteren and by Dijkstra and Scholten) and again a construction is given for obtaining algorithms for this problem from wave algorithms.

Chapter 9 studies the computational power of systems where processes are not distinguished by unique identities. It was shown by Angluin that in this case many computations cannot be carried out by a deterministic algorithm. The chapter introduces probabilistic algorithms, and we investigate what kind of problems can be solved by these algorithms.

Chapter 10 explains how the processes of a system can compute a global "picture", a snapshot, of the system's state. Such a snapshot is useful for determining properties of the computation, such as whether a deadlock has occurred, or how far the computation has progressed. Snapshots are also used to restart a computations after occurrence of an error.

Chapter 11 studies the effect of the availability of directional knowledge in the network, and also gives some algorithms to compute such knowledge.

In Chapter 12 the effect of the availability of a global time concept will be studied. Several degrees of synchronism will be defined and it will be shown that completely asynchronous systems can simulate fully synchronous ones by fairly trivial algorithms. It is thus seen that assumptions about synchronism do not influence the collection of functions that are computable by a distributed system. It will subsequently be shown, however, that there is an influence on the communication complexity of many problems: the better the synchronism of the network, the lower the complexity of algorithms for these problems.

Part Three: Fault Tolerance. In practical distributed systems the possibility of failure in a component cannot be ignored, and hence it is important to study how well an algorithm behaves if components fail. This subject will be treated in the last part of the book; a short introduction to the subject is given in Chapter 13.

The fault tolerance of asynchronous systems is studied in Chapter 14. A result by Fischer *et al.* is presented; this shows that deterministic asynchronous algorithms cannot cope with even a very modest type of failure, the crash of a single process. It will also be shown that weaker types of faults can be dealt with, and that some tasks are solvable in spite of a crash failure. Algorithms by Bracha and Toueg will be presented; these show that in contrast, randomized asynchronous systems are able to cope with a reasonably large number of failures. It is thus seen that, as is the case for reliable systems (see Chapter 9), randomized algorithms offer more possibilities than deterministic algorithms.

In Chapter 15 the fault tolerance of synchronous algorithms will be studied. Algorithms by Lamport *et al.* show that deterministic synchronous algorithms can tolerate non-trivial failures. It is thus seen that, unlike in the case of reliable systems (see Chapter 12), synchronous systems offer more possibilities than asynchronous systems. An even larger number of faults can be tolerated if processes are able to "sign" their communication to other processes. Consequently, implementing synchronism in an unreliable system is more complicated than in the reliable case, and the last section of Chapter 15 will be devoted to this problem.

Chapter 16 studies the properties of abstract mechanisms, referred to as *failure detectors*, by which processes can obtain an estimated view of crashed and correct processes. We show implementations of such mechanisms and how they can be used to implement specifications in faulty environments.

A different approach to reliability, namely via self-stabilizing algorithms, is followed in Chapter 17. An algorithm is stabilizing if, regardless of its initial configuration, it converges eventually to its intended behavior. Some theory about stabilizing algorithms will be developed, and a number of stabilizing algorithms will be presented. These algorithms include protocols for several graph algorithms such as the computation of depth-first search trees (as in Section 6.4) and the computation of routing tables (as in Chapter 4). Also, stabilizing algorithms for data transmission (as in Chapter 3) have been proposed, which may indicate that entire computer networks can be implemented using stabilizing algorithms.

Appendices. Appendix A explains the notation used in this book to represent distributed algorithms. Appendix B provides some background in graph theory and graph terminology. The book ends with a list of references and an index of terms.

Part One

Protocols

2

The Model

Several different models of distributed information processing are used frequently in the study of distributed algorithms. The choice of a particular model usually depends on what problem from the area of distributed computing is studied and what type of algorithm or impossibility proof is presented. In this book, although it covers a wide range of distributed algorithms and theory about them, an attempt is made to work in a single, general model, described in this chapter, as much as possible.

In order to admit impossibility results (the proof of the non-existence of an algorithm for some task) the model must be very precise. An impossibility result is a statement about *all* possible algorithms allowed in a system, hence the model must be precise enough to describe the relevant properties of all admitted algorithms. Yet a computational model is more than the detailed description of a particular computer system or programming language. There are many different computing systems, and we desire that the model is applicable to a *class* of related systems sharing the essential properties that make them "distributed". Finally, the model must be reasonably compact, because one may expect that all aspects of a model must be considered in proofs. Summarizing, the model must describe *precisely* and *concisely* the relevant aspects of a *class* of computing systems.

A distributed computation is usually considered as a collection of discrete events, each event being an atomic change in the configuration (the state of the entire system). In Section 2.1 this notion is captured in the definition of *transition systems*, leading to the notion of reachable configurations and a constructive definition of the set of executions induced by an algorithm. What makes a system "distributed" is that each transition is only influenced by, and only influences, *part of* the configuration, basically the (local) state of a single process. (Or the local states of a subset of interacting processes.)

43

Sections 2.2 and 2.3 consider consequences and properties of the model described in Section 2.1. Section 2.2 deals with the issue of how desired properties of a given distributed algorithm can be proved. In Section 2.3 a very important notion is discussed, namely the causality relation between the events of an execution. This relation gives rise to an equivalence relation defined on executions; a computation is an equivalence class under this relation. Clocks are defined, and a logical clock is presented as the first distributed algorithm to be discussed in this book. Finally, further assumptions and notation not incorporated in the basic model will be discussed in Section 2.4.

2.1 Transition Systems and Algorithms

A system whose state changes in discrete steps (transitions or events) can usually be conveniently described by the notion of a *transition system*. In the study of distributed algorithms this applies to the distributed system as a whole, as well as to the individual processes that cooperate in the algorithm. Therefore, transition systems are an important concept in the study of distributed algorithms, and are defined in Subsection 2.1.1.

In distributed systems transitions influence only part of the configuration (the system's global state). Each configuration itself is a tuple, and each transition refers to some of the components of this tuple only. The components of the configuration include the state of each individual process. For a precise description of the configurations different kinds of distributed system must be distinguished, depending on the mode of communication between processes.

Processes in a distributed system communicate either by accessing *shared variables* or by *message passing*. We shall take a more restrictive point of view and consider only distributed systems where processes communicate by exchanging messages. Distributed systems where communication is by means of shared variables will be considered in Chapter 17. The reader interested in communication by shared variables may consult the landmark paper by Dijkstra [Dij68] or that by Owicki and Gries [OG76]; a more recent treatment is Attiya and Welch [AW98].

Messages in distributed systems can be passed either *synchronously* or *asynchronously*. The main emphasis in this book is on algorithms for systems where messages are passed asynchronously. For many purposes synchronous message passing can be regarded as a special case of asynchronous message passing, as was demonstrated by Charron-Bost *et al.* [CBMT96]. Subsection 2.1.2 describes the model for asynchronous message passing precisely; in Subsection 2.1.3 the model is adapted to systems using synchronous message passing. Subsection 2.1.4 briefly discusses fairness.

2.1.1 Transition Systems

A transition system consists of the set of all possible states of the system, the transitions ("moves") the system can make in this set, and a subset of states in which the system is allowed to start. To avoid confusion between the states of a single process and the states of the entire algorithm (the "global states"), the latter will from now on be called *configurations*.

Definition 2.1 *A transition system is a triple $S = (\mathcal{C}, \rightarrow, \mathcal{I})$, where $\mathcal{C}$ is a set of configurations, $\rightarrow$ is a binary transition relation on $\mathcal{C}$, and $\mathcal{I}$ is a subset of $\mathcal{C}$ of initial configurations.*

A transition relation is a subset of $\mathcal{C} \times \mathcal{C}$. Instead of $(\gamma, \delta) \in \rightarrow$ the more convenient notation $\gamma \rightarrow \delta$ is used.

Definition 2.2 *Let $S = (\mathcal{C}, \rightarrow, \mathcal{I})$ be a transition system. An execution of S is a maximal sequence $E = (\gamma_0, \gamma_1, \gamma_2, \ldots)$, where $\gamma_0 \subset \mathcal{I}$, and for all $i \geq 0$, $\gamma_i \rightarrow \gamma_{i+1}$.*

A *terminal* configuration is a configuration γ for which there is no δ such that $\gamma \rightarrow \delta$. Note that a sequence $E = (\gamma_0, \gamma_1, \gamma_2, \ldots)$ with $\gamma_i \rightarrow \gamma_{i+1}$ for all i, is maximal if it is either infinite or ends in a terminal configuration.

Definition 2.3 *Configuration δ is reachable from γ, notation $\gamma \rightsquigarrow \delta$, if there exists a sequence $\gamma = \gamma_0, \gamma_1, \gamma_2, \ldots, \gamma_k = \delta$ with $\gamma_i \rightarrow \gamma_{i+1}$ for all $0 \leq i < k$. Configuration δ is reachable if it is reachable from an initial configuration.*

2.1.2 Systems with Asynchronous Message Passing

A distributed system consists of a collection of *processes* and a *communication subsystem*. Each process is a transition system in itself, with the annotation that it can interact with the communication subsystem. To avoid confusion between attributes of the distributed system as a whole and attributes of individual processes, we use the following convention. The terms "transition" and "configuration" are used for attributes of the entire system, and the (otherwise equivalent) terms "event" and "state" are used for attributes of processes. To interact with the communication system a process has not only ordinary events (referred to as *internal events*) but also *send events* and *receive events*, in which a message is produced or consumed. Let $\mathcal{M}$ be a set of possible *messages* and denote the collection of multisets with elements from $\mathcal{M}$ by $\mathbb{M}(\mathcal{M})$.

Definition 2.4 *The local algorithm of a process is a quintuple* $(Z, I, \vdash^i, \vdash^s, \vdash^r)$, *where* Z *is a set of* states, I *is a subset of* Z *of initial states,* $\vdash^i$ *is a relation on* $Z \times Z$, *and* $\vdash^s$ *and* $\vdash^r$ *are relations on* $Z \times \mathcal{M} \times Z$. *The binary relation* $\vdash$ *on* Z *is defined by*

$$c \vdash d \iff (c, d) \in \vdash^i \ \lor \ \exists m \in \mathcal{M} \left((c, m, d) \in \vdash^s \cup \vdash^r \right).$$

The relations $\vdash^i$, $\vdash^s$, and $\vdash^r$ correspond to state transitions related with internal, send, and receive events, respectively. In the sequel we shall denote processes by p, q, r, p_1, p_2, etc., and denote the set of processes of a system by $\mathbb{P}$. Definition 2.4 serves as a theoretical model for processes; of course, algorithms in this book are not described by an enumeration of their states and events, but by means of a convenient pseudocode (see Appendix A). The executions of a process are the executions of the transition system $(Z, \vdash, I)$.

We will however be interested in executions of the entire system, and in such an execution the executions of the processes are coordinated through the communication subsystem. To describe the coordination, we shall define a distributed system as a transition system where the configuration set, transition relation, and initial states are constructed from the corresponding components of the processes.

Definition 2.5 *A distributed algorithm for a collection* $\mathbb{P} = \{p_1, \ldots, p_N\}$ *of processes is a collection of local algorithms, one for each process in* $\mathbb{P}$.

The behavior of a distributed algorithm is described by a transition system as follows. A configuration consists of the state of each process and the collection of messages in transit; the transitions are the events of the processes, which do not only affect the state of the process, but can also affect (and be affected by) the collection of messages; the initial configurations are the configurations where each process is in an initial state and the message collection is empty.

Definition 2.6 *The transition system induced under asynchronous communication by a distributed algorithm for processes* $p_1, \ldots, p_N$ *(where the local algorithm for process* p_i *is* $(Z_{p_i}, I_{p_i}, \vdash^i_{p_i}, \vdash^s_{p_i}, \vdash^r_{p_i}))$, *is* $S = (\mathcal{C}, \rightarrow, \mathcal{I})$ *where*

(1) $\mathcal{C} = \{(c_{p_1}, \ldots, c_{p_N}, M) : (\forall p \in \mathbb{P} : c_p \in Z_p) \text{ and } M \in \mathbb{M}(\mathcal{M})\}$.

(2) $\rightarrow = (\cup_{p \in \mathbb{P}} \rightarrow_p)$, where the $\rightarrow_p$ are the transitions corresponding to the state changes of process p; $\rightarrow_{p_i}$ is the set of pairs

$$(c_{p_1}, \ldots, c_{p_i}, \ldots, c_{p_N}, M_1), \ (c_{p_1}, \ldots, c'_{p_i}, \ldots, c_{p_N}, M_2)$$

for which one of the following three conditions holds:

- $(c_{p_i}, c'_{p_i}) \in \vdash^i_{p_i}$ and $M_1 = M_2$;
- for some $m \in \mathcal{M}$, $(c_{p_i}, m, c'_{p_i}) \in \vdash^s_{p_i}$ and $M_2 = M_1 \cup \{m\}$;
- for some $m \in \mathcal{M}$, $(c_{p_i}, m, c'_{p_i}) \in \vdash^r_{p_i}$ and $M_1 = M_2 \cup \{m\}$.

(3) $\mathcal{I} = \{(c_{p_1}, \ldots, c_{p_N}, M) : (\forall p \in \mathbb{P} : c_p \in I_p) \wedge M = \varnothing\}$.

An execution of the distributed algorithm is an execution of this induced transition system. The events of an execution are made explicit with the following notations. The pairs $(c, d) \in \vdash^i_p$ are called the (possible) *internal events* of process p, and the triples in $\vdash^s_p$ and $\vdash^r_p$ are called the *send* and *receive* events of the process.

- An internal event e given by $e = (c, d)$ of p is called *applicable* in configuration $\gamma = (c_{p_1}, \ldots, c_p, \ldots, c_{p_N}, M)$ if $c_p = c$. In this case, $e(\gamma)$ is defined as the configuration $(c_{p_1}, \ldots, d, \ldots, c_{p_N}, M)$.
- A send event e given by $e = (c, m, d)$ of p is called *applicable* in configuration $\gamma = (c_{p_1}, \ldots, c_p, \ldots, c_{p_N}, M)$ if $c_p = c$. In this case, $e(\gamma)$ is defined as the configuration $(c_{p_1}, \ldots, d, \ldots, c_{p_N}, M \cup \{m\})$.
- A receive event e given by $e = (c, m, d)$ of p is called *applicable* in configuration $\gamma = (c_{p_1}, \ldots, c_p, \ldots, c_{p_N}, M)$ if $c_p = c$ and $m \in M$. In this case $e(\gamma)$ is defined as the configuration $(c_{p_1}, \ldots, d, \ldots, c_{p_N}, M \setminus \{m\})$.

It is assumed that for each message there is a unique process that can receive the message. This process is called the *destination* of the message.

2.1.3 Systems with Synchronous Message Passing

Message passing is said to be *synchronous* if a send event and the corresponding receive event are coordinated to form a single transition of the system. That is, a process is not allowed to send a message unless the destination of the message is ready to accept the message. Consequently, the transitions of the system are of two types: one corresponding to the internal state changes of a process, the other corresponding to the combined communication events of two processes.

Definition 2.7 *The transition system induced under synchronous communication by a distributed algorithm for processes* $p_1, \ldots, p_N$ *is* $S = (\mathcal{C}, \rightarrow, \mathcal{I})$ *where*

(1) $\mathcal{C} = \{(c_{p_1}, \ldots, c_{p_N}) : \forall p \in \mathbb{P} : c_p \in Z_p\}.$

(2) $\rightarrow = (\cup_{p \in \mathbb{P}} \rightarrow_p) \cup (\cup_{p,q \in \mathbb{P}: p \neq q} \rightarrow_{pq}),$ *where*

- $\rightarrow_{p_i}$ *is the set of pairs*

$$(c_{p_1}, \ldots, c_{p_i}, \ldots, c_{p_N}), \ (c_{p_1}, \ldots, c'_{p_i}, \ldots, c_{p_N})$$

for which $(c_{p_i}, c'_{p_i}) \in \vdash^i_{p_i};$

- $\rightarrow_{p_i p_j}$ *is the set of pairs*

$$(\ldots, c_{p_i}, \ldots, c_{p_j}, \ldots), \ (\ldots, c'_{p_i}, \ldots, c'_{p_j}, \ldots)$$

for which there is a message $m \in \mathcal{M}$ *such that*

$$(c_{p_i}, m, c'_{p_i}) \in \vdash^s_{p_i} \quad and \quad (c_{p_j}, m, c'_{p_j}) \in \vdash^r_{p_j}.$$

(3) $\mathcal{I} = \{(c_{p_1}, \ldots, c_{p_N}) : (\forall p \in \mathbb{P} : c_p \in I_p)\}.$

Some distributed systems allow hybrid forms of communication; the processes in them have communication primitives for passing messages in a synchronous as well as an asynchronous fashion. Given the two models defined above it is not difficult to design a formal model for this type of distributed system. The configurations of such a system include process states and a collection of in transit messages (namely, asynchronous messages). The transitions include all the types of transition presented in Definitions 2.6 and 2.7.

Synchronism and its impact on algorithms. It has already been remarked that for many purposes synchronous message passing can be regarded as a special case of asynchronous message passing. The collection of executions is restricted in the case of synchronous message passing to those executions where each send event is followed immediately by the corresponding receive event [CBMT96]. We therefore consider asynchronous message passing to be a more general model than synchronous message passing, and will develop algorithms mostly for this general case.

Some care must be taken, however, if an algorithm developed for asynchronous message passing is executed in a system with synchronous message passing. The reduced non-determinism of the communication subsystem must be balanced by increased non-determinism in the processes, otherwise a deadlock may result.

We illustrate this by an elementary example in which two processes are to send each other some information. In the asynchronous case, each process may first send a message and subsequently receive the message from the other process. The messages are temporarily buffered in the communication subsystem between their sending and their receipt. In the synchronous case, no such buffering is possible, and if both processes must send their own message before they can receive a message, no transition can take place. In the synchronous case, one of the processes must receive the message of the other process before it sends its own message. Needless to say, if both processes must receive a message before sending their own message, again no transition can take place.

An exchange of two messages can take place in a synchronous system only if one of the following two conditions is satisfied.

(1) It is determined in advance which of the two processes will send first, and which one will receive first. In many cases it is not possible to make this choice in advance, because it requires the two processes to execute different local algorithms.

(2) The processes have the non-deterministic choice either to send first and receive next, or to receive first and send next. In each execution one of the possible execution orders will be chosen for each process, i.e., the symmetry is broken by the communication subsystem.

When we present an algorithm for asynchronous message passing and state that the algorithm can also be used under synchronous message passing, the addition of this non-determinism, which is always possible, is assumed implicitly.

2.1.4 Fairness

In some cases it is necessary to restrict the behavior of the system to so-called *fair* executions. Fairness conditions rule out executions where events are always (or infinitely often) applicable, but never occur as a transition (because the execution continues with other applicable events).

Definition 2.8 *An execution is weakly fair if no event is applicable in infinitely many consecutive configurations without occurring in the execution. An execution is strongly fair if no event is applicable in infinitely many configurations without occurring in the execution.*

It is possible to incorporate fairness conditions in the formal model explicitly, as is done by Manna and Pnueli [MP88]. Most of the algorithms treated in this book do not rely on these conditions; therefore we chose not to incorporate them in the model, but state these conditions explicitly when they are used for a particular algorithm or problem. Also, it has been debated whether it is reasonable to include fairness assumptions in a model of distributed systems. It has been argued that fairness assumptions should not be made; rather, algorithms should be designed so as not to rely on these assumptions. A discussion of some intricate issues related to fairness assumptions is found in [Fra86].

2.2 Proving Properties of Transition Systems

Given a distributed algorithm for some problem, it is necessary to demonstrate that the algorithm is a correct solution to this problem. The problem specifies what properties the required algorithm must have; a solution must be shown to have these properties. The issue of verifying distributed algorithms has received considerable attention and there are numerous texts discussing formal verification methods; see [CM88, Fra86, Kel76, MP88]. In this section some simple, but frequently used methods to demonstrate the correctness of distributed algorithms are discussed. These methods rely only on the definition of transition systems.

Many of the required properties of distributed algorithms fall into one of two types: *safety requirements* and *liveness requirements*. A safety requirement imposes that a certain property must hold for each execution of the system in *every* configuration reached in that execution. A liveness requirement imposes that a certain property must hold for each execution of the system in *some* configuration reached in that execution. A formal treatment of what makes up a safety or liveness property was given by Alpern and Schneider [AS85]. They show that *every possible* specification (property of the set of executions) can be written as the conjunction of a safety and a liveness property.

These requirements may also occur in a weakened form, for example, that they must be satisfied with some fixed probability over the set of possible executions. Other requirements on algorithms may include that they rely only on the use of some given knowledge (see Subsection 2.4.4), that they are resilient to failures of some processes (see Part 3), that the processes are equal (see Chapter 9), etc.

The verification methods described in this section are based on the truth of *assertions* in the configurations reached in an execution. Such methods are called *assertional* verification methods. An assertion is a unary relation on the set of configurations, that is, a predicate that is true for a subset of the configurations and false for others.

2.2.1 Safety Properties

A safety property of an algorithm is a property of the form "Assertion P is true in each configuration of each execution of the algorithm". Informally this is formulated as "Assertion P is always true". The basic technique for showing that assertion P is always true is to demonstrate that P is an *invariant* according to the definitions that are to follow. The notation $P(\gamma)$, where γ is a configuration, is a boolean expression whose value is true if P holds in γ, and false otherwise.

The definitions are relative to a given transition system $S = (\mathcal{C}, \to, \mathcal{I})$. In the sequel, we write $\{P\} \to \{Q\}$ to denote that for each transition $\gamma \to \delta$ (of S), if $P(\gamma)$ then $Q(\delta)$. Thus $\{P\} \to \{Q\}$ means that if P holds before any transition, then Q holds after the transition.

Definition 2.9 *Assertion P is an invariant of S if*

(1) *for all $\gamma \in \mathcal{I}$, $P(\gamma)$, and*

(2) *$\{P\} \to \{P\}$.*

The definition says that an invariant holds in each initial configuration, and is preserved under each transition. It follows that it holds in each reachable configuration, as is formulated in the following theorem.

Theorem 2.10 *If P is an invariant of S, then P holds for each configuration of each execution of S.*

Proof. Let $E = (\gamma_0, \gamma_1, \gamma_2, \ldots)$ be an execution of S. It will be shown by induction that $P(\gamma_i)$ holds for each i. First, $P(\gamma_0)$ holds because $\gamma_0 \in \mathcal{I}$ and by the first clause of Definition 2.9. Second, assume $P(\gamma_i)$ holds and $\gamma_i \to \gamma_{i+1}$ is a transition that occurs in E. By the second clause of Definition 2.9 $P(\gamma_{i+1})$ holds, which completes the proof. $\square$

It is not the case that, conversely, an assertion that holds in each configuration of each execution is an invariant (see Exercise 2.2). Hence not each safety property can be proved by applying Theorem 2.10. It is the case, however, that each assertion that is always true is implied by an invariant; hence the assertion can be shown to be always true by applying the following theorem. (It must be noted, though, that it is often very difficult to find an appropriate invariant Q to which to apply the theorem.)

Theorem 2.11 *Let Q be an invariant of S and assume $Q \Rightarrow P$ (for each $\gamma \in \mathcal{C}$). Then P holds in each configuration of each execution of S.*

Proof. By Theorem 2.10, Q holds in each configuration, and as Q implies P, P holds in each configuration as well. □

It is sometimes useful to prove a weak invariant first, and subsequently use this to prove a stronger invariant. How an invariant can be made stronger is demonstrated by the following definition and theorem.

Definition 2.12 *Let S be a transition system and P, Q be assertions. P is called a Q-derivate if*

(1) *for all $\gamma \in \mathcal{I}$, $Q(\gamma) \Rightarrow P(\gamma)$; and*
(2) $\{Q \wedge P\} \rightarrow \{Q \Rightarrow P\}$.

Theorem 2.13 *If Q is an invariant and P is a Q-derivate, then $Q \wedge P$ is an invariant.*

Proof. According to Definition 2.9, it must be shown that

(1) *for all $\gamma \in \mathcal{I}$, $Q(\gamma) \wedge P(\gamma)$; and*
(2) $\{Q \wedge P\} \rightarrow \{Q \wedge P\}$. .

Because Q is an invariant, $Q(\gamma)$ holds for all $\gamma \in \mathcal{I}$, and because for all $\gamma \in \mathcal{I}$, $Q(\gamma) \Rightarrow P(\gamma)$, $P(\gamma)$ holds for all $\gamma \in \mathcal{I}$. Consequently, $Q(\gamma) \wedge P(\gamma)$ holds for all $\gamma \in \mathcal{I}$.

Assume $\gamma \rightarrow \delta$ and $Q(\gamma) \wedge P(\gamma)$. Because Q is an invariant, $Q(\delta)$ holds, and because $\{Q \wedge P\} \rightarrow \{Q \Rightarrow P\}$, $Q(\delta) \Rightarrow P(\delta)$, from which $P(\delta)$ is concluded. Consequently, $Q(\delta) \wedge P(\delta)$ holds. □

Examples of safety proofs relying on the material in this subsection are presented in Section 3.1.

2.2.2 Liveness Properties

A liveness property of an algorithm is a property of the form "Assertion P is true in some configuration of each execution of the algorithm". Informally this is formulated as "Assertion P is eventually true". The basic techniques used to show that P is eventually true are *norm functions* and *deadlock-freeness* or *proper termination*. A simpler technique may be used for algorithms that allow only executions with a fixed, finite length.

Let S be a transition system and P a predicate. Define **term** as the predicate that is true in all terminal configurations and false in all non-terminal configurations. We first consider situations where an execution reaches a terminal configuration. It is usually not desired that such a configuration is reached while the "goal" P has not been achieved; one speaks of *deadlock* in this case. On the other hand, termination is allowed if the goal has been reached; in this case one speaks of *proper termination*.

Definition 2.14 *System S terminates properly (or is deadlock-free) if the predicate* (**term** $\Rightarrow P$) *is always true in S.*

Norm functions rely on the mathematical concept of *well-founded sets*. This is a set with an order $<$, for which there are no infinite decreasing sequences.

Definition 2.15 *A partial order* $(W, <)$ *is well-founded if there is no infinite decreasing sequence*

$$w_1 > w_2 > w_3 \cdots .$$

Examples of well-founded sets that will be used in this book are the natural numbers with the usual order, and n-tuples of natural numbers with the lexicographic order (see Section 4.3). The property that a well-founded set has no infinite decreasing sequence can be used to show that an assertion P is eventually true. To this end it must be shown that there exists a function f from $\mathcal{C}$ to a well-founded set W, such that in each transition the value of f decreases or P becomes true.

Definition 2.16 *Let a transition system S and an assertion P be given. A function f from $\mathcal{C}$ to a well-founded set W is called a norm function (with respect to P) if for each transition $\gamma \to \delta$, $f(\gamma) > f(\delta)$ or $P(\delta)$.*

Theorem 2.17 *Let a transition system S and an assertion P be given. If S terminates properly and a norm function f (w.r.t. P) exists, then P is true in some configuration of each execution of S.*

Proof. Let $E = (\gamma_0, \gamma_1, \gamma_2, \ldots)$ be an execution of S. If E is finite, its last configuration is a terminated configuration, and as **term** $\Rightarrow P$ is always true in S, P holds in this configuration. If E is infinite, let E' be the longest prefix of E that contains no configurations in which P is true, and let s be the sequence $(f(\gamma_0), f(\gamma_1), \ldots)$ for all configurations γ_i that appear in E'. By the choice of E' and the property of f, s is a decreasing sequence, and hence, by the well-foundedness of W, s is finite. This implies also that E' is a finite prefix $(\gamma_0, \gamma_1, \ldots, \gamma_k)$ of E; by the choice of E', $P(\gamma_{k+1})$ holds. $\square$

If fairness properties are assumed, it can be concluded from weaker premises (than in Theorem 2.17) that P is eventually true; the value of the norm function need not decrease with *every* transition. A fairness assumption can

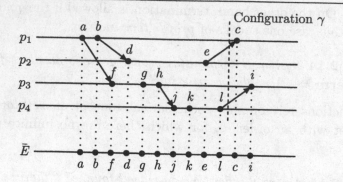

Figure 2.1 AN EXAMPLE OF A SPACE–TIME DIAGRAM.

be exploited to show that infinite executions contain transitions of a certain type infinitely often. It then suffices to show that f never increases, but decreases with each transition of this type.

In some cases we shall make use of the following result, which is a special case of Theorem 2.17.

Theorem 2.18 *If S terminates properly and there is a number K such that each execution contains at most K transitions, then P is true in some configuration of each execution.*

2.3 Causal Order of Events and Logical Clocks

The view on executions as sequences of transitions naturally induces a notion of time in executions. A transition a is then said to occur earlier than transition b if a occurs in the sequence before b. For an execution $E = (\gamma_0, \gamma_1, \ldots)$, define the associated sequence of events $\bar{E} = (e_0, e_1, \ldots)$, where e_i is the event by which the configuration changes from γ_i to γ_{i+1}. Observe that each execution defines a *unique* sequence of events in this way. An execution can be visualized in a *space–time diagram*, of which Figure 2.1 presents an example. In such a diagram, a horizontal line is drawn for each process, and each event is drawn as a dot on the line of the process where it takes place. If a message m is sent in event s and received in event r, an arrow is drawn from s to r; the events s and r are said to be *corresponding* events in this case.

As will be seen in Subsection 2.3.1, events of a distributed execution can sometimes be interchanged without affecting the later configurations of the execution. Therefore a notion of time as a total order on the events of an execution is not suitable for distributed executions, and instead the notion of causal dependence is introduced. The equivalence of executions under the reordering of events is studied in Subsection 2.3.2. We discuss in Subsection 2.3.3 how a clock for measuring causal dependence (rather than time) can be defined, and present Lamport's logical clock, an important example of such a clock.

2.3.1 Independence and Dependence of Events

It has been remarked already that the transitions of a distributed system influence, and are influenced by, only part of the configuration. This leads to the observation that two consecutive events, influencing disjoint parts of the configuration, are independent and can also occur in reversed order. For systems with asynchronous message passing this is expressed in the following theorem.

Theorem 2.19 *Let γ be a configuration of a distributed system (with asynchronous message passing) and let e_p and e_q be events of different processes p and q, both applicable in γ. Then e_p is applicable in $e_q(\gamma)$, e_q is applicable in $e_p(\gamma)$, and $e_p(e_q(\gamma)) = e_q(e_p(\gamma))$.*

Proof. To avoid a case analysis which are send, receive, or internal events, we represent each event by the uniform notation (c, x, y, d). Here c and d denote the process state before and after the event, x is the collection of messages received in the event, and y is the collection of messages sent in the event. Thus, an internal event (c, d) is denoted $(c, \varnothing, \varnothing, d)$; a send event (c, m, d) is denoted $(c, \varnothing, \{m\}, d)$; and a receive event (c, m, d) is denoted $(c, \{m\}, \varnothing, d)$. In this notation, event $e = (c, x, y, d)$ of process p is applicable in configuration $\gamma = (c_{p1}, \ldots, c_p, \ldots, c_{pN}, M)$ if $c_p = c$ and $x \subseteq M$. In this case

$$e(\gamma) = (c_{p1}, \ldots, d, \ldots, (M \setminus x) \cup y).$$

Now assume $e_p = (b_p, x_p, y_p, d_p)$ and $e_q = (b_q, x_q, y_q, d_q)$ are applicable in

$$\gamma = (\ldots, c_p, \ldots, c_q, \ldots, M),$$

that is, $c_p = b_p$, $c_q = b_q$, $x_p \subseteq M$, and $x_q \subseteq M$. An important observation is that x_p and x_q are disjoint; the message in x_p (if any) has destination p, while the message in x_q (if any) has destination q.

Write $\gamma_p = e_p(\gamma)$, and note that

$$\gamma_p = (\ldots, d_p, \ldots, c_q, \ldots, (M \setminus x_p) \cup y_p).$$

As $x_q \subseteq M$ and $x_q \cap x_p = \varnothing$, it follows that $x_q \subseteq (M \setminus x_p \cup y_p)$, and hence e_q is applicable in γ_p. Write $\gamma_{pq} = e_q(\gamma_p)$, and note that

$$\gamma_{pq} = (\ldots, d_p, \ldots, d_q, \ldots, ((M \setminus x_p \cup y_p) \setminus x_q) \cup y_q).$$

By a symmetric argument it can be shown that e_p is applicable in $\gamma_q = e_q(\gamma)$. Write $\gamma_{qp} = e_p(\gamma_q)$, and note that

$$\gamma_{qp} = (\ldots, d_p, \ldots, d_q, \ldots, ((M \setminus x_q \cup y_q) \setminus x_p \cup y_p)).$$

Because M is a multiset of messages, $x_p \subseteq M$, and $x_q \subseteq M$,

$$((M \setminus x_p \cup y_p) \setminus x_q \cup y_q) = ((M \setminus x_q \cup y_q) \setminus x_p \cup y_p),$$

and hence $\gamma_{pq} = \gamma_{qp}$. $\square$

Let e_p and e_q be two events that occur consecutively in an execution, i.e., the execution contains the subsequence

$$\ldots, \gamma, e_p(\gamma), e_q(e_p(\gamma)), \ldots$$

for some γ. The premise of Theorem 2.19 applies to these events except in the following two cases.

(1) $p = q$; or
(2) e_p is a send event, and e_q is the corresponding receive event.

Indeed, the theorem explicitly states that p and q must be different, and if e_q receives the message sent in e_p, the receive event is not applicable in the starting configuration of e_p, as also required. Thus, if one of these two statements is true, the events cannot occur in the reversed order; otherwise they can occur in reversed order and yet result in the same configuration. Note that from a global point of view *transitions* cannot be exchanged, because (in the notation of Theorem 2.19) the transition from γ_p to γ_{pq} is different from the transition from γ to γ_q. However, from the point of view of the process these *events* are indistinguishable.

The fact that a particular pair of events cannot be exchanged is expressed by saying that there is a *causal relation* between these two events. This relation can be extended to a partial order on the set of events of an execution, called the *causal order* of the execution.

Definition 2.20 *Let E be an execution. The relation $\prec$, called the causal order, on the events of the execution is the smallest relation that satisfies*

(1) *If e and f are different events of the same process and e occurs before f, then e ≺ f.*

(2) *If s is a send event and r the corresponding receive event, then s ≺ r.*

(3) *≺ is transitive.*

We write $a \preceq b$ to denote $(a \prec b \vee a = b)$. As $\preceq$ is a *partial* order, there may exist events a and b for which neither $a \preceq b$ nor $b \preceq a$ holds. Such events are said to be *concurrent*, notation $a \parallel b$. In Figure 2.1, $b \parallel f$, $d \parallel i$, etc.

Causal order was first defined by Lamport [Lam78] and plays an important role in the reasoning concerning distributed algorithms. The definition of $\prec$ implies the existence of a *causality chain* between causally related events. By this we mean that $a \prec b$ implies the existence of a sequence $a = e_0, e_1, \ldots, e_k = b$, such that each pair of consecutive events in the chain satisfies either (1) or (2) in Definition 2.20. The causality chain can even be chosen such that each pair satisfying (1) is a consecutive pair of events in the process where they occur, i.e., there is no other event between them. In Figure 2.1, a causality chain between event a and event l is the sequence a, f, g, h, j, k, l.

2.3.2 Equivalence of Executions: Computations

In this subsection it is shown that the events of an execution can be reordered in any order consistent with the causal order, without affecting the result of the execution. This reordering of the events gives rise to a different sequence of configurations, but this execution will be regarded as equivalent to the original execution.

Let $f = (f_0, f_1, f_2, \ldots)$ be a sequence of events. This sequence is the sequence of events related to an execution $F = (\delta_0, \delta_1, \delta_2, \ldots)$ if for each i, f_i is applicable in δ_i and $f_i(\delta_i) = \delta_{i+1}$. If this is the case, F is called the *implied execution* of the sequence f. We would like F to be uniquely determined by f, but this is not always the case; if for some process p no event in p is included in f, the state of p can be an arbitrary initial state. However, if f contains at least one event of p, then the first event in p, say (c, x, y, d), defines the initial state of p to be c. Therefore, if f contains at least one event in each process, δ_0 is uniquely defined, and this defines the entire execution uniquely.

Now let $E = (\gamma_0, \gamma_1, \gamma_2, \ldots)$ be an execution with an associated sequence of events $\bar{E} = (e_0, e_1, e_2, \ldots)$, and assume that f is a permutation of $\bar{E}$. This means that there exists a permutation σ of the natural numbers (or, of the set $\{0, \ldots, k-1\}$ if E is a finite execution with k events) such that

$f_i = e_{\sigma(i)}$. The permutation $(f_0, f_1, f_2, \ldots)$ of the events of E is *consistent* with the causal order if $f_i \preceq f_j$ implies $i \leq j$, i.e., if no event is preceded in the sequence by an event it causally precedes.

Theorem 2.21 *Let $f = (f_0, f_1, f_2, \ldots)$ be a permutation of the events of E that is consistent with the causal order of E. Then f defines a unique execution F starting in the initial configuration of E. F has as many events as E, and if E is finite, the last configuration of F is the same as the last configuration of E.*

Proof. The configurations of F are constructed one by one, and to construct δ_{i+1} it suffices to show that f_i is applicable in δ_i. Take $\delta_0 = \gamma_0$.

Assume that for all $j < i$, f_j is applicable in configuration δ_j, and $\delta_{j+1} = f_j(\delta_j)$. Let $\delta_i = (c_{p_1}, \ldots, c_{p_N}, M)$ and let $f_i = (c, x, y, d)$ be an event in process p; then event f_i is applicable in δ_i if $c_p = c$ and $x \subseteq M$.

To show that $c_p = c$ two cases are distinguished. In both cases we note that the causal order of E *totally* orders the events in process p; this implies that the events in process p occur in exactly the same order in f and $\bar{E}$.

Case 1: f_i is the first event in p of f; then c_p is the initial state of p. But then f_i is also the first event in p of $\bar{E}$, which implies that c is the initial state of p. Consequently, $c = c_p$.

Case 2: f_i is not the first event in p of f; let the last event in p of f before f_i be $f_{i'} = (c', x', y', d')$, then $c_p = d'$. But then $f_{i'}$ is also the last event in p before f_i in $\bar{E}$, which implies that $c = d'$. Consequently, $c = c_p$.

To show that $x \subseteq M$ we note that corresponding send and receive events occur in the same order in f and $\bar{E}$. If f_i is not a receive event, $x = \varnothing$ and $x \subseteq M$ holds trivially. If f_i is a receive event, let f_j be the corresponding send event. Because $f_j \prec f_i$, $j < i$ holds, i.e., the send event precedes f_i in f; consequently, $x \subseteq M$.

We have now shown that for each i, f_i is applicable in δ_i, and δ_{i+1} can be taken as $f_i(\delta_i)$. We must finally show that the last configurations of F and E coincide if E is finite. Let γ_k be the last configuration of E. If $\bar{E}$ contains no event in p, the state of p in γ_k equals its initial state. As f also contains no event in p, the state of p in δ_k also equals the initial state, hence the state of p in δ_k equals the its state in γ_k. Otherwise, the state of p in γ_k is the state after the last event in p of $\bar{E}$; this is also the last event in p of f, so this is also the state of p in δ_k.

The messages in transit in γ_k are exactly those messages for which the send event is not matched by a corresponding receive event in $\bar{E}$. But as

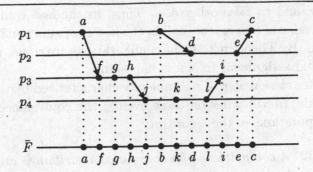

Figure 2.2 A SPACE–TIME DIAGRAM EQUIVALENT TO FIGURE 2.1.

$\bar{E}$ and f contain the same collection of events, the same messages are in transit in the last configuration of F. ◻

Executions $\bar{F}$ and E have the same collection of events, and the causal order of these events is the same for E and F. It is therefore also the case that $\bar{E}$ is an permutation of the events of F that is consistent with the causal order of F. If the condition of Theorem 2.21 applies, we say that E and F are *equivalent* executions, denoted as $E \sim F$.

Figure 2.2 shows the time diagram of an execution equivalent to the one depicted in Figure 2.1. Equivalent time diagrams can be obtained by "rubber band transformations" [Mat89c]. Assuming that the time axis of a process can be compressed and stretched as long as message arrows keep pointing "to the right", Figure 2.1 can be deformed to become Figure 2.2.

Although the depicted executions are equivalent and contain the same collection of events, they do not contain the same collection of configurations. Figure 2.1 contains a configuration (γ") in which the message sent in event e and the one sent in event l are in transit simultaneously. Figure 2.2 does *not* contain such a configuration, because the message sent in event l is received *before* event e takes place.

A global observer, who has access to the actual sequence of the events, may distinguish between two equivalent executions, i.e., may observe either one of the executions or the other. However, the processes cannot distinguish between two equivalent executions since it is not possible for them to decide which of two equivalent executions takes place. This is illustrated as follows. Assume that it must be decided whether the messages sent in events e and l were in transit simultaneously. There is a boolean variable *sim* in one of the processes, which must be set to true if the messages were in transit simultaneously, and to false otherwise. Thus, in the last configuration of Figure 2.1 the value of *sim* is true, and in the last configuration of Figure 2.2 its value is false. By Theorem 2.21, the configurations are equal, which shows that the required assignment to *sim* is impossible.

An equivalence class under $\sim$ is completely characterized by the collection of events and the causal order on these events; the equivalence classes are called the computations of the algorithm.

Definition 2.22 *A computation of a distributed algorithm is an equivalence class (under $\sim$) of executions of the algorithm.*

It makes no sense to speak about the configurations of a computation, because different executions of the computation may not have the same configurations. It does make sense to speak about the collection of events of a computation, because all executions of the computation consist of the same set of events. Also, the causal order on the events is defined for a computation. We will call the computation finite if its executions are finite. All executions of a computation start in the same configuration and, if the computation is finite, terminate in the same configuration (cf. Theorem 2.21); these configurations are called the initial and terminal configurations of the computation. We shall identify a computation with the partially ordered set of events belonging to it.

A result from the theory of partial orders implies that each order can occur for a pair of concurrent events of a computation.

Fact 2.23 *Let $(X, <)$ be a partial order and a, $b \in X$ satisfy $b \not< a$. There exists a linear extension $<_1$ of $<$ such that $a <_1 b$.*

Consequently, if a and b are concurrent events of a computation C, there exist executions E_a and E_b of this computation such that a takes place earlier than b in E_a, and b takes place earlier than a in E_b. The processes in the execution have no means of deciding which of the two events takes place first.

Synchronous message passing. A version of Theorem 2.19 can be formulated also for systems with synchronous message passing. In such systems two subsequent events are independent if they affect different processes, as formulated in the following theorem.

Theorem 2.24 *Let γ be a configuration of a distributed system with synchronous message passing and let e_1 be a transition of processes p and q,* *and e_2 be a transition of processes r and s, different from p and q, such that both e_1 and e_2 are applicable in γ. Then e_1 is applicable in $e_2(\gamma)$, e_2 is applicable in $e_1(\gamma)$, and $e_1(e_2(\gamma)) = e_2(e_1(\gamma))$.*

The proof of this theorem, which relies on the same arguments as the proof of Theorem 2.19, is left as Exercise 2.9. A notion of causality in synchronous systems can be defined similarly to Definition 2.20; the interested reader is referred to [CBMT96]. Theorem 2.21 also has its counterpart for synchronous systems.

Executions and Computations. We have defined executions first (as runs in a transition system) and subsequently introduced computations as equivalence classes of executions. This order reflects an operational view of what happens in a distributed system. Many other works take the more symbolic road of first introducing computations as partially ordered sets over events and subsequently introduce executions as linearizations of these posets. This is done, for example, in the work of Charron-Bost *et al.* [CBMT96] and in the standardized Message Sequence Charts formalism [RGG96]. The two approaches are equivalent.

2.3.3 Logical Clocks

In analogy to physical clocks, which measure real time, in distributed computations clocks can be defined that express causality. Throughout this section, Θ is a function from the set of events to an ordered set $(X, <)$.

Definition 2.25 *A clock is a function Θ from the events to an ordered set such that*

$$a \prec b \Rightarrow \Theta(a) < \Theta(b).$$

In the remainder of this section some examples of clocks are discussed.

(1) *Order in sequence.* In an execution E defined by the sequence of events $(e_0, e_1, e_2, \ldots)$, set $\Theta_g(e_i) = i$. Thus each event is labeled by its place in the sequence of events.

This function can be used by a global observer of the system, who has access to the order in which the events occur. It is, however, not possible to observe this order *within* the system, or, to put it differently, Θ_g cannot be computed by a distributed algorithm. This is a consequence of Theorem 2.19; assume that some distributed algorithm stores the value $\Theta_g(e_i) = i$ for the event e_i (which satisfies the premises of the theorem). In an equivalent execution, in which this event is exchanged with the next event, and consequently, has a different value of Θ_g, the same value i is stored in the process. To say it in different words, Θ_g is defined for executions, but not for computations.

(2) *Real-time clocks.* It is possible to *extend* the model that is the subject of this chapter by supplying each process with a hardware clock. In this way it is possible to record for each event the real time at which it occurs; the numbers obtained satisfy the definition of a clock.

Distributed systems with real-time clocks do not fit Definition 2.6 because the physical properties of clocks synchronize state changes at different processes. Time proceeds in all processes, and this induces transitions that change the state (namely, the clock reading) of all processes. It turns out that these "global transitions" change the properties of the model drastically; indeed, Theorem 2.19 no longer holds if real-time clocks are assumed. Distributed systems with real-time clocks are used in practice, however, and they will be treated in this book (see Section 3.2) and Chapters 12 and 15).

(3) *Lamport's logical clock.* Lamport [Lam78] has presented a clock function that assigns to event a the length k of the longest sequence $(e_1, \ldots, e_k)$ of events satisfying

$$e_1 \prec e_2 \prec \ldots \prec e_k = a.$$

Indeed, if $a \prec b$ this sequence can be extended to show that $\Theta_L(a) < \Theta_L(b)$. The value of Θ_L can be computed for each event by a distributed algorithm based on the following relations.

(a) If a is an internal or send event, and a' the previous event in the same process, then $\Theta_L(a) = \Theta_L(a') + 1$.

(b) If a is a receive event, a' the previous event in the same process, and b the send event corresponding to a, then $\Theta_L(a) = \max(\Theta_L(a'), \Theta_L(b)) + 1$.

In both cases, $\Theta_L(a')$ is supposed to be 0 if a is the first event in a process.

To compute the clock values by a distributed algorithm, the clock value of the last event of process p is stored in the variable θ_p (initialized to 0). In order to compute the clock value of a receive event, each message m contains the clock value θ_m of the event e in which it was sent. Lamport's logical clock is given as Algorithm 2.3. For event e in process p, $\Theta_L(e)$ is the value of θ_p immediately after the

var θ_p : integer   **init** 0 ;

(* An internal event *)
  $\theta_p := \theta_p + 1$;
  Change state

(* A send event *)
  $\theta_p := \theta_p + 1$;
  send $\langle$ **messg**, $\theta_p \rangle$; Change state

(* A receive event *)
  receive $\langle$ **messg**, $\theta \rangle$; $\theta_p := \max(\theta_p, \theta) + 1$;
  Change state

Algorithm 2.3 LAMPORT'S LOGICAL CLOCK.

occurrence of e, i.e., at the moment the state change in p takes place. It is left as an exercise to show that with this definition Θ_L is a clock.

It is not specified under what conditions a message must be sent or how the state of a process changes. The clock is a supplementary mechanism that can be added to any distributed algorithm to order its events.

(4) *Vector clocks.* For some purposes it is useful to have clocks that express not only causal order (as required by Definition 2.25) but also concurrency. Concurrency is expressed by a clock if concurrent events are labeled with incomparable clock values, that is, the implication in Definition 2.25 is replaced by an equivalence, giving

$$a \prec b \iff \Theta(a) < \Theta(b). \tag{2.1}$$

The existence of concurrent events implies that the domain of such a clock (the set X) is a non-totally-ordered set.

In Mattern's *vector clock* [Mat89b] $X = \mathbb{N}^N$, i.e., $\Theta_v(a)$ is a *vector* of length N. Vectors of length n are naturally ordered by the vector order, defined as follows:

$$(a_1, \ldots, a_n) \leq_v (b_1, \ldots, b_n) \iff \forall i \ (1 \leq i \leq n) : a_i \leq b_i. \tag{2.2}$$

(The vector order is different from the lexicographic order defined in Exercise 2.5; the latter order is total.) The clock is defined by $\Theta_v(a) = (a_1, \ldots, a_N)$, where a_i is the number of events e *in process p_i* for which $e \preceq a$. Like Lamport's clock, this function can be evaluated by a distributed algorithm.

Charron-Bost [CB89] has shown that it is impossible to use shorter vectors (with the vector order as in (2.2)). If the events of an arbitrary execution of N processes are mapped on vectors of length n such that (2.1) is satisfied, then $n \geq N$.

2.4 Additional Assumptions, Complexity

The definitions made so far in this chapter are sufficient to set the scene for the remaining chapters; the defined model serves as a framework for the presentation and verification of algorithms, as well as for impossibility proofs for solutions of distributed problems. In the various chapters additional assumptions and notation are used if appropriate. This section discusses some of this terminology, which is also common in the literature on distributed algorithms.

2.4.1 The Network Topology

So far, we have modeled the communication subsystem of a distributed system by the collection of messages currently in transit. Further, it has been assumed that each message can only be received by a single process called the destination of the message. In general it is not necessarily the case that each process can send messages to every other process. Instead, for each process a subset of the other processes is defined (called the *neighbors* of the process) to which it can send messages. If a process p can send messages to process q, a *channel* is said to exist from p to q. Unless stated otherwise it is assumed that channels are *bidirectional*, that is, the same channel allows q to send messages to p. A channel that accomodates only one-way traffic from p to q is called a *unidirectional* (or *directed*) channel from p to q.

The collection of processes and the communication subsystem is also referred to as a *network*. The structure of the communication subsystem is often represented as a *graph* $G = (V, E)$, in which the nodes are the processes, and an edge between two processes exists if and only if a channel between the two processes exists. A system with unidirectional channels can similarly be represented by a directed graph. The graph of a distributed system is also called its *network topology*.

Representation as a graph allows us to speak about the communication system in terms of graph theory; see Appendix B for an introduction to this terminology. Because the network topology is of major influence on the existence, appearance, and complexity of distributed algorithms for many problems, we include below a brief discussion of some commonly used topologies here; see Appendix B for more details. Throughout this book, unless stated otherwise, it is assumed that the topology is *connected*, that is, a path between any two nodes exists.

(1) *Rings.* The N-node *ring* is the graph on the nodes v_0 through v_{N-1} with edges $v_i v_{i+1}$ (indices are modulo N). Rings are frequently used for distributed control computations because of their simplicity. Also, some physical networks, such as Token Rings [Tan96, Section 4.3.3], arrange the nodes in a ring.

(2) *Trees.* A *tree* on N nodes is a connected graph with $N-1$ edges; it contains no cycles. Trees are used in distributed computations because they allow computation at a low communication cost, and furthermore, each connected graph contains a tree as a spanning subnetwork.

(3) *Stars.* A *star* on N nodes has one special node (the *center*) and $N-1$ edges, connecting each of the $N-1$ other nodes to the center. Stars are used in centralized computations, where one process acts as a controller and all other processes communicate with this special process only. Disadvantages of the star topology are the communication bottleneck that may arise in the center and the vulnerability of such a system to a failure of the center.

(4) *Cliques.* A *clique* is a network in which an edge exists between any two nodes. It is the graph that is "implicitly" assumed in situations where each process can directly communicate with all others, as in Chapters 13 through 16.

(5) *Hypercubes.* A *hypercube* is a graph $HC_N = (V, E)$ on $N = 2^n$ nodes. Here V is the set of bit strings of length n:

$$V = \{(b_0, \ldots, b_{n-1}) : b_i \in \{0, 1\}\},$$

and there is an edge between two nodes b and c if and only if the bit strings b and c differ in exactly one bit. The name of the hypercube refers to a graphical representation of the network as an n-dimensional unit cube, of which the corners are the nodes.

An example of each of these networks is given in Figure 2.4. The topology can be *static* or *dynamic*. A static topology means that the topology remains fixed during the distributed computation. A dynamic topology means that channels (sometimes even processes) can be added or removed from the system during the computation. These changes in the topology can also be modeled by transitions of the configuration, namely, if the process states reflect the set of neighbors of the process (see Chapter 4).

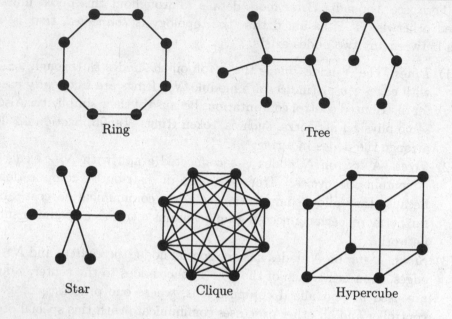

Figure 2.4 Examples of frequently used topologies.

2.4.2 Properties of the Channels

The model (as described in Subsection 2.1.2) can be refined by representing the contents of each channel separately in the configuration, that is, replacing the set M by a collection of sets M_{pq} for each (unidirectional) channel pq. As we have postulated that each message implicitly defines its destination, this modification does not alter the important properties of the model. Next some commonly made assumptions about the correspondence between send and receive events are discussed.

(1) *Reliability.* A channel is said to be *reliable* when every message that is sent in the channel is received exactly once (provided that the destination is able to receive the message). Unless stated otherwise, it is always assumed in this book that the channels are reliable. This assumption in fact adds a (weak) fairness condition; indeed, after a message has been sent, the receipt of this message (in a suitable state of the destination) is applicable from then on.

A channel that is not reliable may exhibit *communication failures*, which can be of several types, e.g., loss, garble, duplication, creation. These failures can be represented by transitions in the model of Definition 2.6, but these transitions do not correspond to state changes of a process.

The *loss* of a message occurs when the message is sent, but never received; it can be modeled by a transition that removes the message from M. The *garbling* of a message occurs when the message received is different from the message sent; it can be modeled by a transition that changes one message of M. The *duplication* of a message occurs when the message is received more often than it is sent; it is modeled by a transition that copies a message of M. The *creation* of a message occurs when a message is received that has never been sent; it is modeled by a transition that inserts a message in M.

(2) *The fifo property.* A channel is said to be *fifo* if it respects the order of the messages sent through it. That is, if p sends two messages m_1 and m_2 to process q and the sending of m_1 occurs earlier in p than the sending of m_2, then the receipt of m_1 occurs earlier in q than the receipt of m_2. Unless stated otherwise, fifo channels will *not* be assumed in this book.

Fifo channels can be represented in the model of Definition 2.6 by replacing the collection M by a set of *queues*, one for each channel. Sending is done by appending a message to the end of this queue, and a receive event deletes a message from the head. When fifo channels are assumed, a new type of communication failure arises, namely the reordering of messages in a channel; it can be modeled by a transition that exchanges two messages in the queue.

It sometimes happens that a distributed algorithm profits from the fifo property of the channels; see, e.g., the communication protocol in Section 3.1. Exploiting the order of receipt of messages decreases the amount of information that must be transported in each message. In many cases, however, an algorithm can be designed so as to function properly (and efficiently) even if messages can be reordered in the channel. In general, the implementation of the fifo property distributed systems may decrease the inherent parallelism of the computation, since it may require the buffering of messages (at the receiver's side of the channel) before the message can be processed. For this reason we chose not to assume the fifo property implicitly in this book.

A weaker assumption was proposed by Ahuja [Ahu90]; a *flush channel* is a channel that respects the order only of messages for which this is specified by the sender. Stronger assumptions can also be defined. Schiper *et al.* [SES89] defined *causally ordered message delivery* as follows. If p_1 and p_2 send messages m_1 and m_2 to process q in events e_1 and e_2, and it is the case that $e_1 \prec e_2$, then q receives m_1 before m_2. A hierarchy of delivery assumptions, consisting of full asynchronism, causally ordered delivery, fifo, and synchronous communication, was discussed by Charron-Bost *et al.* [CBMT96].

(3) *Channel capacity.* The *capacity* is the number of messages that can be in transit in the channel at the same time. The channel is *full* in each configuration in which it actually contains a number of messages equal to its capacity. A sending event is applicable only if the channel is not full.

Definition 2.6 models channels with unbounded capacity, i.e., channels that are never full. In this book it will always be assumed that the capacity of the channels is unbounded.

2.4.3 Real-time Assumptions

An essential property of the model presented is, of course, its distributiveness: the complete independence of events in different processes, as expressed in Theorem 2.19. This property is lost when a global time frame and the ability of processes to observe physical time (a physical clock device) are assumed. Indeed, when some real time elapses, this time elapses in all processes, and this will show up on the clock of each process.

Real-time clocks can be incorporated by equipping each process with a real-time clock variable; the elapse of real time is modeled by a transition that puts forward the clock of each process; see Section 3.2. Usually, a bound on the message transmission time (the time between sending and receiving the message) is assumed in conjunction with the availability of real-time clocks. This bound can also be included in the general model of transition systems.

Unless stated otherwise, real-time assumptions are not made in this book; that is, we consider *fully asynchronous* systems and algorithms. Timing assumptions will be used in Section 3.2, Chapter 12, and Chapter 15.

2.4.4 Process Knowledge

Initial process knowledge is the term used to refer to information about the distributed system that is represented in the initial states of the processes. If an algorithm is said to rely on such information it is assumed that the relevant information is correctly stored in the processes prior to the start of the execution of the system. Examples of such knowledge include the following information.

(1) *Topological information.* Information about the topology includes: the number of processes, the diameter of the network graph, and the topology of the graph. The network is said to have a *sense of direction* if a consistent edge-labeling with directions in the graph is known to the processes (see Appendix B).

(2) *Process identity.* In many algorithms it is required that the processes have unique names (identities), and that each process knows its own name initially. The processes are then supposed to contain a variable that is initialized to this name (i.e., differently for each process). Further assumptions can be made regarding the set from which the names are chosen, such as that the names are linearly ordered or that they are (positive) integers.

Unless stated otherwise, in this book it will always be assumed that processes do have access to their identity; in this case the system is referred to as a *named network*. Situations where this is not the case (*anonymous networks*) will be investigated in Chapter 9.

(3) *Neighbor identities.* If processes are distinguished by a unique name, it is possible to assume that each process knows initially the names of its neighbors. This assumption is referred to as *neighbor knowledge* and, unless stated otherwise, will not be made. Process names may be useful for purposes of message addressing; the name of the destination of a message is given when sending a message by *direct addressing*. A stronger assumption is that each process knows the entire collection of process names.

A weaker assumption is that the processes know of the existence but no of the names of their neighbors. Direct addressing can not be used in this case, and the processes use local names for their channels when addressing a message, which is called *indirect addressing* [SK87, p. 54]. Direct and indirect addressing are visualized in Figure 2.5. Direct addressing uses the process' identity as an address, while in indirect addressing the processes p, r, and s use different names (a, b, and c, respectively) to address messages with destination q.

2.4.5 The Complexity of Distributed Algorithms

The most important property of a distributed algorithm is its correctness: it must satisfy the requirements posed by the problem that the algorithm is

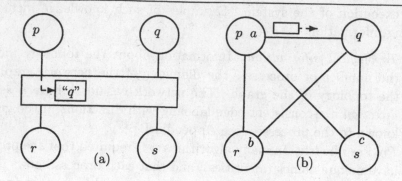

Figure 2.5 DIRECT (a) AND INDIRECT (b) ADDRESSING.

to solve. To compare different algorithms for the same problem it is useful to measure the consumption of resources by an algorithm. The lower this consumption, the "better" is the algorithm. The resource consumption of distributed algorithms can be measured in several ways.

(1) *Message complexity.* This is the total number of messages exchanged by the algorithm.

(2) *Bit complexity.* As the set M usually contains different messages, an amount of information must be transmitted in every message to identify it in M. For an algorithm that uses a small set M each message can be identified using only a small number of bits, while algorithms using many different messages require more bits in each message. As "long" messages are more expensive to transmit than "short" messages, one may also count the total number of bits contained in messages.

Most of the algorithms in this book use messages that contain $O(\log N)$ bits (where N is the number of processes), so their bit complexity exceeds their message complexity by a logarithmic factor. In most cases only the message complexity of algorithms will be analyzed, and the bit complexity will be computed only for algorithms using very long or very short messages.

(3) *Time complexity.* As our model of distributed algorithms does not contain a notion of time it is not obvious how the time complexity of distributed algorithms can be defined. Different definitions are found in the literature (see Section 6.4 for a comparison). The definition

used in this book is based on an idealized timing of the events of a computation according to the following assumptions.

(a) The time for processing an event is zero time units.

(b) The transmission time (i.e., the time between sending and receiving a message) is at most one time unit.

The time complexity of an algorithm is the time consumed by a computation, under these assumptions. Note that the assumptions are only made for the purpose of defining the time complexity of the algorithm. The correctness of an asynchronous algorithm must be proved independently of these assumptions.

(4) *Space complexity.* The space complexity of an algorithm equals the amount of memory needed in a process to execute it. The space in a process is the logarithm of the number of states of that process.

As the operation of distributed algorithms is non-deterministic, an algorithm may give rise to several computations for which these measures may not be equal. Therefore a distinction between worst-case and average-case complexity is made. The worst-case measure is the highest complexity of any computation of the algorithm. The average case, as implied, averages over all possible computations, but in order to do so a probability distribution over all computations must be defined.

Exercises to Chapter 2
Section 2.1

Exercise 2.1 *Define a model of distributed systems where messages can be passed both synchronously and asynchronously.*

Section 2.2

The following three exercises investigate the difference between an invariant and an always-true predicate, the disjunctivity and conjunctivity of invariants and derivates, and how invariants behave under parallel program composition.

Exercise 2.2 *Give a transition system S and an assertion P such that P is always true in S, but is not an invariant of S.*
(Hint: An example with three configurations is given in [GT90]. Can an example with two configurations be found?)

Exercise 2.3 *Assume P_1 and P_2 are invariants of a system S. Prove that $(P_1 \vee P_2)$ and $(P_1 \wedge P_2)$ are invariants.*
Assume P_1 and P_2 are Q-derivates of a system S. Prove that $(P_1 \vee P_2)$ and $(P_1 \wedge P_2)$ are Q-derivates of a system S.

Transition systems with the same set of configurations and initial configurations can be composed by combining their transition relations. Thus, the *parallel composition* of $S_1 = (\mathcal{C}, \rightarrow_1, \mathcal{I})$ and $S_2 = (\mathcal{C}, \rightarrow_2, \mathcal{I})$ is the system $S = (\mathcal{C}, \rightarrow, \mathcal{I})$, where $\rightarrow = (\rightarrow_1 \cup \rightarrow_2)$.

Exercise 2.4 *Let S be the parallel composition of S_1 and S_2.*
Prove that if P is an invariant of S_1 and S_2, then P is an invariant of S.
Prove that if P is a Q-derivate of S_1 and S_2, then P is a Q-derivate of S.
Give an example where P is always true in both S_1 and S_2, but not in S.

The next exercise concerns well-founded sets. A set can be well-founded, even when it has an element smaller than which there exist infinitely many elements in the set. The *lexicographic order* on vectors $a = (a_1, a_2, \ldots, a_n)$ and $b = (b_1, b_2, \ldots, b_n)$ is defined by the relation

$$a <_l b \iff a_1 < b_1 \ \vee \ (\ a_1 = b_1 \wedge (a_2, \ldots, a_n) <_l (b_2, \ldots, b_n)\ ).$$

Exercise 2.5 *Prove that $(\mathbb{N}^n, \leq_l)$ (where $n \geq 2$) has elements smaller than which there exist infinitely many elements.*
Prove that $(\mathbb{N}^n, \leq_l)$ is well-founded.

Section 2.3

Exercise 2.6 *Label the events of Figure 2.1 with the clock values assigned by Lamport's logical clock.*
Label the events with the clock values assigned by Mattern's vector clock.
Identify some pairs of concurrent events and check whether the labels assigned to these events are ordered.

Exercise 2.7 *Give a distributed algorithm (similar to Algorithm 2.3) that labels the events with the clock values assigned by Mattern's vector clock.*

Exercise 2.8 *Can one prove Theorem 2.21 by repeatedly applying Theorem 2.19 to events of E?*

Exercise 2.9 *Prove Theorem 2.24.*

Exercise 2.10 *Define the causal order for the transitions of a system with synchronous communication. Define clocks for such systems, and give a distributed algorithm for computing a clock.*

3

Communication Protocols

This chapter discusses two protocols that are used for the reliable exchange of data between two computing stations. In the ideal case, data would simply be exchanged by sending and receiving messages. Unfortunately, the possibility of communication errors cannot always be ignored; the messages must be transported via a physical medium, which may lose, duplicate, reorder, or garble messages transmitted through it. These errors must be detected and corrected by supplementary mechanisms, traditionally referred to as protocols, implemented in the computing stations.

The main function of these protocols is *data transmission*, i.e., the accepting of the information at one station and its delivery at the other station. Reliable data transmission includes the repeated sending of messages that are lost, rejecting or correcting messages that are garbled, and discarding duplicates of messages. To do so the protocol maintains state information, recording which data has already been sent, which data has been certified to be received, and so on. The necessity of using state information raises the issue of *connection management*, i.e., the initialization and discarding of state information. The initialization is called *opening* the connection and its discarding is called *closing* the connection. The difficulty of connection management is due to the possibility that a message remains in the communication channels when the connection is closed. Such a message could be received when no connection exists or during a later connection, and its receipt must not disturb the correct operation of the current connection.

The protocols discussed in this chapter are designed for different layers in a protocol hierarchy, such as the OSI reference model (Subsection 1.2.2). They are included in this book for different reasons; the first protocol is completely asynchronous, while the second protocol relies on the correct use of timers. In both cases the verification of the protocol concentrates on

74

the required *safety* property, that is, that the receiver will only deliver the correct data.

The first protocol (Section 3.1) is designed for the exchange of data between two stations that have a direct physical connection (such as a telephone line), and therefore belongs in the data-link layer of the OSI model. The second protocol (Section 3.2) is designed to be used by two stations that must communicate via an intermediate network (possibly containing other stations and connecting the end stations through different paths), and this protocol therefore belongs in the transport layer of the OSI model. This difference influences the required functionality of the protocols in the following two ways.

(1) *Errors considered.* For the two protocols different classes of transmission error will be considered. Messages cannot bypass each other in a physical connection and they cannot be duplicated; indeed, in Section 3.1 only the loss of messages is considered (for the garbling of messages, see below). In a network, messages can travel via different paths, and hence bypass each other; also, due to failures of intermediate stations messages may be duplicated as well as lost. Hence, in Section 3.2, the loss, duplication, and reordering of messages will be considered.

(2) *Connection management.* Further, connection management will not be considered for the first protocol, but will be for the second. A physical connection is usually supposed to operate continuously during a very long time, rather than being opened and closed repeatedly. This is not the case for connections with remote stations. Such a connection may be necessary temporarily for the exchange of some data, but it is usually too expensive to maintain a connection with every remote station indefinitely. Therefore the ability to open and close connections will be required for the second protocol.

The treatment of the first protocol shows that timer-based mechanisms are not essential to achieve the required safety properties of data transmission protocols. Section 3.1 serves as the first, large example of the proof of safety properties, relying on the proof tools described in Section 2.2. It is widely believed [Wat81] that the correct use of timers and a bound on the time for which a message can be in transit are necessary for a safe connection management. Thus in order to prove the safety of protocols for connection management the role of timers must be taken into account. Section 3.2 shows how the model of distributed systems (Definition 2.6) can be extended to processes using timers, and provides an example of this extension.

Garbling of messages. It is realistic to take into account the possibility that messages are garbled during transport. The contents of a message communicated via a physical connection can be damaged due to atmospheric noise, malfunctioning memory units, etc. It can however be assumed that the garbling of a message can be detected by the receiving process, for example by means of parity checks or more general checksum mechanisms (cf. [Tan96, Chapter 3]). The receipt of a garbled message is then treated as if no message were received, and thus the garbling of a message in fact causes the message to be lost. For this reason garbling is not treated explicitly; instead, the possibility of message loss is always considered.

3.1 The Balanced Sliding-window Protocol

In this section a symmetric protocol that allows information to be sent reliably in both directions is studied. The protocol is taken from [Sch91, Chapter 2]. As it is used for the exchange of information between stations that are directly connected through a line, the fifo property of channels may be assumed. This assumption is not used, however, until Subsection 3.1.3, where it is demonstrated that the sequence numbers used by the protocol can be bounded. The protocol is presented in Subsection 3.1.1, and proved correct in Subsection 3.1.2.

Two communication processes are denoted by p and q. The assumptions, requirements, and protocol are completely symmetric w.r.t. p and q. The input of p consists of the information it must send to q, and is modeled by an infinite array in_p of words. The output of p consists of the information it receives from q, and is also modeled by an infinite array of words, out_p. For the time being it is assumed that p has random read-access to in_p and random write-access to out_p. Initially the value of $out_p[i]$ is undefined and represented by *udef* for all i. The input and the output of process q are modeled respectively by arrays in_q and out_q. These arrays are all indexed by the natural numbers, i.e., they start with the word 0. It will be shown in Subsection 3.1.3 that the random access can be restricted to access to a "window" of finite length, shifting over the array. This is why the protocol is called a "sliding-window" protocol.

Process p contains a variable s_p, indicating the lowest numbered word that p still expects to receive from q. Thus, at any time, p has already written $out_p[0]$ through $out_p[s_p - 1]$. The value of s_p never decreases. Analogously q contains a variable s_q. The required properties of the protocol can now be stated. The safety property says that each process only outputs the correct data; the liveness property says that all data will eventually be delivered.

(1) *Safe delivery.* In every reachable configuration of the protocol

$$out_p[0..s_p - 1] = in_q[0..s_p - 1] \quad \text{and} \quad out_q[0..s_q - 1] = in_p[0..s_q - 1].$$

(2) *Eventual delivery.* For each integer $k \geq 0$, a configuration with $s_p \geq k$ and $s_q \geq k$ is eventually reached.

3.1.1 Presentation of the Protocol

Transmission protocols usually rely on the use of *acknowledgement* messages. An acknowledgement message is sent by the receiving process to inform the sender about data it has correctly received. If the sender of the data does not receive an acknowledgement it assumes that the data message (or the acknowledgement) was lost, and retransmits the same data. In the protocol of this section, however, no explicit acknowledgement messages are used. In this protocol both stations have messages to send to the other station; the messages of a station serve also as the acknowledgements for the other station's messages.

The messages exchanged by the processes are referred to as *packets*, and they are of the form $\langle \mathbf{pack}, w, i \rangle$, where w is a data word and i a natural number (called the *sequence number* of the packet). This packet, when sent by p (to q), transmits the word $w = in_p[i]$ to q, but also, as mentioned earlier, acknowledges the receipt of a number of packets from q. Process p can be a fixed number of l_p packets "ahead of" q if we postulate that the data packet $\langle \mathbf{pack}, w, i \rangle$ sent by p acknowledges the receipt of the words numbered $0..i - l_p$ from q. (The meaning of the packet is analogous when sent by q.) The constants l_p and l_q are non-negative and known to both p and q. The implied meaning of data packets as acknowledgements has two consequences for the transitions of the protocol:

(1) Process p can send the word $in_p[i]$ (as the packet $\langle \mathbf{pack}, in_p[i], i \rangle$) only after storing all the words $out_p[0]$ through $out_p[i - l_p]$, i.e., if $i < s_p + l_p$.

(2) When p receives $\langle \mathbf{pack}, w, i \rangle$, retransmission of words from $in_p[0]$ through $in_p[i - l_q]$ is no longer necessary.

Explanation of the pseudocode. After making these design choices it is not very difficult to give the code of the protocol; see Algorithm 3.1. A variable a_p is introduced for process p (and a_q for q) to indicate the lowest numbered word for which an acknowledgement has not yet been received by p (or q, respectively).

In Algorithm 3.1, action $\mathbf{S}_p$ is the sending of the ith word by p, action $\mathbf{R}_p$ the receipt of a word by p, and action $\mathbf{L}_p$ the loss of a packet with destination p. Process p can send any word of which the index falls within the bounds outlined above. When a message is received, a check is first made if an identical message has already been received (in case it is a retransmission). If not, the word contained in it is written to the output, and a_p and s_p are updated. There are also actions $\mathbf{S}_q$, $\mathbf{R}_q$, and $\mathbf{L}_q$, with p and q reversed.

Invariant of the protocol. The communication subsystem is represented by two queues, Q_p for the packets with destination p and Q_q for the packets with destination q. Observe that the renewed computation of s_p in $\mathbf{R}_p$ never gives a value smaller than the previous one, so s_p never decreases. To show that this algorithm satisfies the requirements given earlier, it will first be demonstrated that the assertion P is an invariant. (In this and other assertions i is a natural number.)

$$
\begin{aligned}
P \equiv \quad & \forall i < s_p : \ out_p[i] \neq udef & (0p)\\
\wedge \ & \forall i < s_q : \ out_q[i] \neq udef & (0q)\\
\wedge \ & \langle \mathbf{pack}, w, i \rangle \in Q_p \Rightarrow w = in_q[i] \wedge (i < s_q + l_q) & (1p)\\
\wedge \ & \langle \mathbf{pack}, w, i \rangle \in Q_q \Rightarrow w = in_p[i] \wedge (i < s_p + l_p) & (1q)\\
\wedge \ & out_p[i] \neq udef \Rightarrow out_p[i] = in_q[i] \wedge (a_p > i - l_q) & (2p)\\
\wedge \ & out_q[i] \neq udef \Rightarrow out_q[i] = in_p[i] \wedge (a_q > i - l_p) & (2q)\\
\wedge \ & a_p \leq s_q & (3p)\\
\wedge \ & a_q \leq s_p & (3q)
\end{aligned}
$$

Lemma 3.1 *P is an invariant of Algorithm 3.1.*

Proof. In each initial configuration Q_p and Q_q are empty, for all i, $out_p[i]$ and $out_q[i]$ are $udef$, and a_p, a_q, s_q, and s_p are 0; these imply that P is true. The transitions of the protocol will now be considered in turn to show that they preserve P. First note that the values of in_p and of in_q never change.

$\mathbf{S}_p$: To see that $\mathbf{S}_p$ preserves (0p), observe that $\mathbf{S}_p$ does not increase s_p and does not make any $out_p[i]$ equal to $udef$.

To see that $\mathbf{S}_p$ preserves (0q), observe that $\mathbf{S}_p$ does not increase s_q and does not make any $out_q[i]$ equal to $udef$.

To see that $\mathbf{S}_p$ preserves (1p), observe that $\mathbf{S}_p$ adds no packets to Q_p and does not decrease s_q.

To see that $\mathbf{S}_p$ preserves (1q), observe that $\mathbf{S}_p$ adds $\langle \mathbf{pack}, w, i \rangle$ to Q_q with $w = in_p[i]$ and $i < s_p + l_p$, and leaves the value of s_p unchanged.

var s_p, a_p : integer   **init** 0, 0 ;
       in_p : array of word   (* Data to be sent *) ;
       out_p : array of word   **init** *udef*, *udef*, ... ;

$\mathbf{S}_p$: $\{\, a_p \le i < s_p + l_p \,\}$
    begin send $\langle \mathbf{pack}, in_p[i], i \rangle$ to q **end**

$\mathbf{R}_p$: $\{\, \langle \mathbf{pack}, w, i \rangle \in Q_p \,\}$
    begin receive $\langle \mathbf{pack}, w, i \rangle$;
          if $out_p[i] = udef$ **then**
             begin $out_p[i] := w$;
                  $a_p := \max(a_p, i - l_q + 1)$;
                  $s_p := \min\{j \mid out_p[j] = udef\}$
             end
          (* **else** ignore, packet was retransmission *)
    end

$\mathbf{L}_p$: $\{\, \langle \mathbf{pack}, w, i \rangle \in Q_p \,\}$
    begin $Q_p := Q_p \setminus \{\langle \mathbf{pack}, w, i \rangle\}$ **end**

Algorithm 3.1 THE BALANCED SLIDING-WINDOW PROTOCOL (FOR p).

To see that $\mathbf{S}_p$ preserves (2p) and (2q), observe that $\mathbf{S}_p$ does not change the values of out_p, out_q, a_p, or a_q.

To see that $\mathbf{S}_p$ preserves (3p) and (3q), observe that $\mathbf{S}_p$ does not change the values of a_p, a_q, s_q, or s_p.

$\mathbf{R}_p$: To see that $\mathbf{R}_p$ preserves (0p), observe that $\mathbf{R}_p$ does not make any $out_p[i]$ equal to *udef*, and if it recomputes s_p it satisfies (0p) afterwards.

To see that $\mathbf{R}_p$ preserves (0q), observe that $\mathbf{R}_p$ does not change out_q or s_q.

To see that $\mathbf{R}_p$ preserves (1p), observe that $\mathbf{R}_p$ adds no packets to Q_p and does not decrease s_q.

To see that $\mathbf{R}_p$ preserves (1q), observe that $\mathbf{R}_p$ adds no packets to Q_q and does not decrease s_p.

To see that $\mathbf{R}_p$ preserves (2p), observe that $\mathbf{R}_p$ changes $out_p[i]$ to w on receipt of $\langle \mathbf{pack}, w, i \rangle$. As Q_p contained this packet before $\mathbf{R}_p$ is applied, (1p) implies that $w = in_q[i]$. The assignment $a_p := \max(a_p, i - l_q + 1)$ ensures that $a_p > i - l_q$ holds after the application.

To see that $\mathbf{R}_p$ preserves (2q), observe that $\mathbf{R}_p$ does not change the values of out_q or a_q.

To see that $\mathbf{R}_p$ preserves (3p), observe that when $\mathbf{R}_p$ assigns $a_p :=$

$\max{(a_p,\ i-l_q+1)}$ (on receipt of $\langle \mathbf{pack}, w, i \rangle$), (1p) implies $i < s_q + l_q$, hence $a_p \leq s_q$ holds after the assignment. $\mathbf{R}_p$ does not change s_q. To see that $\mathbf{R}_p$ preserves (3q), observe that s_p can only be increased in an application of $\mathbf{R}_p$.

$\mathbf{L}_p$: To see that $\mathbf{L}_p$ preserves (0p), (0q), (2p), (2q), (3p), and (3q) it suffices to observe that $\mathbf{L}_p$ does not change the state of any process. (1p) and (1q) are preserved because $\mathbf{L}_p$ only deletes packets (and does not insert or garble them).

The actions $\mathbf{S}_q$, $\mathbf{R}_q$, and $\mathbf{L}_q$ preserve P by symmetry.   □

3.1.2 Correctness Proof of the Protocol

It will now be demonstrated that Algorithm 3.1 ensures safe and eventual delivery. The safety is implied by the invariant, as shown in Theorem 3.2, but the demonstration of the liveness is somewhat harder.

Theorem 3.2 *Algorithm 3.1 satisfies the requirement of safe delivery.*

Proof. (0p) and (2p) imply $out_p[0..s_p - 1] = in_q[0..s_p - 1]$, and (0q) and (2q) imply $out_q[0..s_q - 1] = in_p[0..s_q - 1]$.   □

To prove the liveness of the protocol it is necessary to make some fairness assumptions and an assumption about l_p and l_q. Without these assumptions the liveness requirement is not satisfied by the protocol, as can be seen by the following arguments. The non-negative constants l_p and l_q are as yet unspecified; if they are both chosen to be 0 the protocol deadlocks in its initial configuration (each initial configuration is terminal). It is therefore assumed that $l_p + l_q > 0$.

A configuration of the protocol can be denoted $\gamma = (c_p, c_q, Q_p, Q_q)$, where c_p and c_q are states of p and q. Let γ be a configuration in which $\mathbf{S}_p$ is applicable (for some i). Let

$$\delta = \mathbf{S}_p(\gamma) = (c_p, c_q, Q_p, (Q_q \cup \{m\})),$$

and note that action $\mathbf{L}_q$ is applicable in δ. If $\mathbf{L}_q$ removes m, $\mathbf{L}_q(\delta) = \gamma$. The relation $\mathbf{L}_q(\mathbf{S}_p(\gamma)) = \gamma$ gives rise to an infinite computation in which neither s_p nor s_q is ever increased.

The protocol satisfies the eventual delivery requirement if the following two fairness assumptions are satisfied.

F1. If the sending of a packet is applicable for an infinitely long time, the packet is sent infinitely often.

F2. If the same packet is sent infinitely often, it is received infinitely often.

Assumption F1 ensures that a packet is retransmitted over and over again if an acknowledgement is never received; F2 excludes computations such as the one above where the retransmission is never received.

Neither of the two processes can be much ahead of the other: the difference between s_p and s_q remains bounded. This is why the protocol is called balanced, and implies that if the eventual delivery requirement is satisfied for s_p, then it is also satisfied for s_q, and vice versa. It also indicates that the protocol should not be used in situations where one process has many more words to send than the other.

Lemma 3.3 *P implies* $s_p - l_q \leq a_p \leq s_q \leq a_q + l_p \leq s_p + l_p$.

Proof. From (0p) and (2p) $s_p - l_q \leq a_p$ follows. (3p) reads $a_p \leq s_q$. From (0q) and (2q) $s_q \leq a_q + l_p$ follows. From (3q) $a_q + l_p \leq s_p + l_p$ follows. □

Theorem 3.4 *Algorithm 3.1 satisfies the requirement of eventual delivery.*

Proof. It will first be demonstrated that a deadlock of the protocol is not possible. The invariant implies that one of the two processes can send the packet containing the lowest numbered word that is still missing to the other.

Claim 3.5 *P implies that the sending of* $\langle \mathbf{pack}, in_p[s_q], s_q \rangle$ *by p or the sending of* $\langle \mathbf{pack}, in_q[s_p], s_p \rangle$ *by q is applicable.*

Proof. As $l_p + l_q > 0$, at least one of the inequalities of Lemma 3.3 is strict, i.e.,

$$s_q < s_p + l_p \quad \lor \quad s_p < s_q + l_q.$$

P also implies $a_p \leq s_q$ (3p) and $a_q \leq s_p$ (3q), hence it follows that

$$(a_p \leq s_q < s_p + l_p) \quad \lor \quad (a_q \leq s_p < s_q + l_q),$$

that is, $\mathbf{S}_p$ is applicable with $i = s_q$ or $\mathbf{S}_q$ is applicable with $i = s_p$. □

We can now show that in each computation s_p and s_q are increased infinitely often. According to Claim 3.5 the protocol has no terminal configurations, hence each computation is infinite. Assume that C is a computation in which s_p and s_q are increased only finitely often, and let σ_p and σ_q be the largest values that these variables take in C. By the claim, the sending of $\langle \mathbf{pack}, in_p[\sigma_q], \sigma_q \rangle$ by p or the sending of $\langle \mathbf{pack}, in_q[\sigma_p], \sigma_p \rangle$ by q is applicable forever after s_p, s_q, a_p, and a_q have reached their final values. Thus, by F1, one of these packets is sent infinitely often, and by F2, it is received

infinitely often. But, as the receipt of a packet with sequence number s_p by p causes s_p to be increased (and vice versa for q), this contradicts the assumption that neither s_p nor s_q is ever increased. Hence Theorem 3.4 is proved.
$\square$

We conclude this subsection with a brief discussion of the assumptions F1 and F2. F2 is the minimum quality requirement that must be satisfied by the channel connecting p and q in order to be able to exchange data. Obviously, if some word $in_p[i]$ never passes through the channel it is not possible to obtain eventual delivery of that word. Assumption F1 is usually implemented in a protocol by using a time-out condition: if a_p is not increased during a certain amount of time, $in_p[a_p]$ is transmitted again. As already remarked in the introduction of this chapter, safe delivery can be proved for this protocol without taking timing issues into consideration.

3.1.3 Discussion of the Protocol

Bounding the storage in the processes. Algorithm 3.1 does not lend itself to implementation in a computer network because an infinite amount of information is stored in each process (the arrays *in* and *out*) and because it uses unbounded sequence numbers. It will now be shown that it suffices to store only a bounded number of words at any moment. Let $L = l_p + l_q$.

Lemma 3.6 *P implies that sending* $\langle \mathbf{pack}, w, i \rangle$ *by p is only applicable for* $i < a_p + L$.

Proof. The guard of $\mathbf{S}_p$ requires $i < s_p + l_p$, hence $i < a_p + L$ is implied by Lemma 3.3.
$\square$

Lemma 3.7 *P implies that if* $out_p[i] \neq udef$ *then* $i < s_p + L$.

Proof. By (2p), $a_p > i - l_q$; hence $i < a_p + l_q$, and $i < s_p + L$ is implied by Lemma 3.3.
$\square$

The consequences of these two lemmas are depicted in Figure 3.2. Process p needs to store only the words $in_p[a_p..s_p + l_p - 1]$ because these are the words that p can send. They are referred to as the *sending window* of p (and represented as S in Figure 3.2). Whenever a_p increases, p discards the words that no longer fall in the sending window (they are represented as A in Figure 3.2). Whenever s_p increases, p reads the next words of the sending window from the source that produces the words. According to Lemma 3.6 the sending window of p contains at most L words.

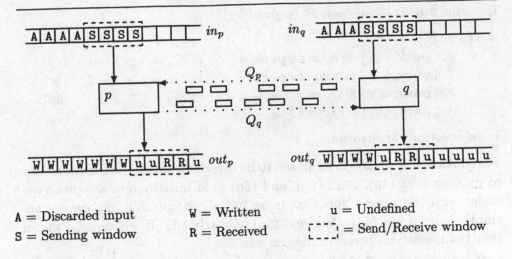

Figure 3.2 THE SLIDING WINDOWS OF THE PROTOCOL.

A similar argument bounds the space needed in p to store the arrays out_p. As $out_p[i]$ does not change any more for $i < s_p$, it may be assumed that p outputs these words irreversibly and no longer stores them (they are represented by W in Figure 3.2). As $out_p[i] = udef$ for all $i \geq s_p + L$, those values of $out_p[i]$ need not be stored in the process either. The subarray $out_p[s_p..s_p + L - 1]$ is referred to as the *receiving window* of p. The receiving window is represented in Figure 3.2 by u for *udef* words and R for words that have been received. Only the words that fall within this window are stored in the process. Lemmas 3.6 and 3.7 show that at most $2L$ words are stored at any moment in each process.

Bounding the sequence numbers. Finally it will be shown that sequence numbers can be bounded if the fifo property of the channels is exploited. Using the fifo assumption it can be shown that the sequence number of a packet that is received by p is always within a $2L$-range around s_p. Note that this is the first time the fifo assumption is used.

Lemma 3.8 *The assertion P', defined by*

$$P' \equiv P$$
$$\wedge \ \langle \textbf{pack}, w, i \rangle \ is \ behind \ \langle \textbf{pack}, w', i' \rangle \ in \ Q_p \Rightarrow i > i' - L \quad (4p)$$
$$\wedge \ \langle \textbf{pack}, w, i \rangle \ is \ behind \ \langle \textbf{pack}, w', i' \rangle \ in \ Q_q \Rightarrow i > i' - L \quad (4q)$$
$$\wedge \ \langle \textbf{pack}, w, i \rangle \in Q_p \Rightarrow i \geq a_p - l_p \quad (5p)$$
$$\wedge \ \langle \textbf{pack}, w, i \rangle \in Q_q \Rightarrow i \geq a_q - l_q \quad (5q)$$

is an invariant of Algorithm 3.1.

Proof. As P has already been shown to be invariant, we can restrict ourselves to proving that (4p), (4q), (5p), and (5q) hold initially and are preserved under each transition. Note that in an initial configuration the queues are empty, hence (4p), (4q), (5p), and (5q) hold trivially. It will now be shown that the transitions preserve these assertions.

$\mathbf{S}_p$: To see that $\mathbf{S}_p$ preserves (4p) and (5p), observe that $\mathbf{S}_p$ adds no packets to Q_p and does not change a_p.

To see that $\mathbf{S}_p$ preserves (5q), observe that if $\mathbf{S}_p$ adds a packet $\langle \textbf{pack}, w, i \rangle$ to Q_q, then $i \geq a_p$, which implies that $i \geq a_q - l_q$ by Lemma 3.3.

To see that $\mathbf{S}_p$ preserves (4q), observe that if $\langle \textbf{pack}, w', i' \rangle$ is in Q_q then by (1q) $i' < s_p + l_p$, hence if $\mathbf{S}_p$ adds a packet $\langle \textbf{pack}, w, i \rangle$ with $i \geq a_p$, then $i' < a_p + L \leq i + L$ follows by Lemma 3.3.

$\mathbf{R}_p$: To see that $\mathbf{R}_p$ preserves (4p) and (4q), observe that $\mathbf{R}_p$ adds no packets to Q_p or Q_q.

To see that $\mathbf{R}_p$ preserves (5p), observe that when a_p is increased (upon receipt of $\langle \textbf{pack}, w', i' \rangle$) to $i' - l_q + 1$, then for any remaining packets $\langle \textbf{pack}, w, i \rangle$ in Q_p we have by (4p) $i > i' - L$. Hence $i \geq a_p - l_p$ holds after the increase of a_p.

To see that $\mathbf{R}_p$ preserves (5q), observe that $\mathbf{R}_p$ does not change Q_q or a_q.

$\mathbf{L}_p$: Action $\mathbf{L}_p$ adds no packets to Q_p or Q_q, and does not change the values of a_p or a_q; hence it preserves (4p), (4q), (5p), and (5q).

It follows from the symmetry of the protocol that $\mathbf{S}_q$, $\mathbf{R}_q$, and $\mathbf{L}_q$ preserve P' as well. $\qquad \square$

Lemma 3.9 P' *implies that*

$$\langle \textbf{pack}, w, i \rangle \in Q_p \Rightarrow s_p - L \leq i < s_p + L$$

and

$$\langle \textbf{pack}, w, i \rangle \in Q_q \Rightarrow s_q - L \leq i < s_q + L.$$

Proof. Let $\langle \mathbf{pack}, w, i \rangle \in Q_p$. From (1p), $i < s_q + l_q$, and from Lemma 3.3 $i < s_p + L$. From (5p), $i \geq a_p - l_p$, and from Lemma 3.3 $i \geq s_p - L$. The statement about packets in Q_q is proved similarly. $\qquad\square$

According to the lemma it suffices to send the packets with sequence numbers modulo k, where $k \geq 2L$. Indeed, having s_p and $i \bmod k$ available allows p to compute i.

The choice of the parameters. The values of the constants l_p and l_q have an important influence on the efficiency of the protocol. Their effect on the throughput of the protocol is analyzed probabilistically in [Sch91, Chapter 2]. The optimal values depend on a number of system dependent parameters, such as

(1) the *communication time*, i.e., the time between two consecutive operations of a process,

(2) the *round-trip delay*, i.e., the average time it takes to pass a packet from p to q and the answer back from q to p,

(3) the *error probability*, the probability that a particular packet is lost.

The alternating-bit protocol. An interesting special case of the sliding-window protocol is obtained when $L = 1$, i.e., $l_p = 1$ and $l_q = 0$ (or vice versa). The variables a_p and a_q are initialized to $-l_p$ and $-l_q$ rather than 0. It can be shown that $a_p + l_q = s_p$ and $a_q + l_p = s_q$ hold always, hence only one of a_p and s_p (and of a_q and s_q) must be stored in the protocol. The well-known *alternating-bit protocol* [Lyn68] is obtained if the use of timers is further restricted to ensure that the stations send messages in turn.

3.2 A Timer-based Protocol

We shall now study the role of timers in the design and verification of communication protocols by analyzing a simplified form of Fletcher and Watson's Δt-protocol for end-to-end message communication. This protocol was proposed in [FW78], but the (somewhat simplified) treatment in this section is taken from [Tel91b, Section 3.2]. This protocol provides not only a mechanism for data transmission (as does the balanced sliding-window protocol of Section 3.1), but also opens and closes connections. It is resilient against loss, duplication, and reordering of messages.

The state information of (the data transmission part of) the protocol is kept in a data structure called the *connection record*. (It will be seen in Subsection 3.2.1 what information is kept in the connection record). The connection records can be created and deleted to open and close the connection. Thus a connection is said to be open (at one of the stations) if a connection record exists.

In order to concentrate on the relevant aspects of the protocol (namely, the connection management mechanism and the role of timers in this mechanism) a simplified version of the protocol is considered. Discussions of extensions of the protocol in order to make it more practical and efficient are found in [FW78] and [Tel91b, Section 3.2]. The following four simplifications are made in the protocol described here.

(1) *One direction.* The transmission of data is only considered in one direction, namely from p to q. Sometimes p will be referred to as the *sender*, and q as the *receiver*. It should be noted, however, that the protocol uses acknowledgement messages that are sent in the reverse direction, i.e., from q to p.

It will usually be the case that data must be transmitted in two directions. To handle this situation a second protocol, in which the roles of p and q are reversed, is executed in addition. It is then possible to introduce combined data/ack messages, containing both data (with the corresponding sequence number) and the information contained in an acknowledgement packet of the timer-based protocol.

(2) *Single-word receiving window.* The receiver does not store any data packets with a higher number than the one it expects. Only if the next packet to arrive is the expected one it is taken into account and immediately delivered. More intricate versions of the protocol would store early-arriving packets with a higher sequence number and deliver them after all packets with lower sequence numbers have arrived and have been delivered.

(3) *Simplified timing assumptions.* The protocol is expressed using a minimum number of timers. It is, for example, assumed that an acknowledgement can be sent by the receiving process at any time as long as the connection is open at the receiver's side. Alternatively it could be the case that an acknowledgement can only be sent within a smaller time interval, but this would make the protocol more complicated.

Also, the timer mechanisms used to trigger retransmission of data packets have been omitted from the description of the protocol, as in Section 3.1. Only the mechanism necessary to guarantee the safety of the protocol is included.

(4) *Single-word packets.* The sender may put only a single word in each

data packet. The protocol could be made more efficient if data packets were able to contain blocks of consecutive words.

The protocol is timer-based, that is, the processes have access to physical clock devices. With regard to the time and the timers in the system the following assumptions are made.

(5) *Global time.* A global measure of time extends over all processes of the system, that is, each event is said to take place at a certain time. Each event itself is assumed to have duration 0, and the time at which an event takes place is *not* observable by the processes.

(6) *Bounded packet lifetime.* The lifetime of a packet is bounded by a constant μ (the *maximum packet lifetime*). Thus, if a packet is sent at time σ and received at time τ, then

$$\sigma < \tau < \sigma + \mu.$$

If a packet is duplicated in a channel, each of the copies must be received within a time μ after the sending of the original packet (or become lost).

(7) *Timers.* The processes cannot observe the absolute time of their actions, but they have access to timers. A timer is a real-valued variable of a process, whose value continuously decreases in time (when not otherwise assigned explicitly). More precisely, if Xt is a timer, we denote its value at time t by $Xt^{(t)}$, and if Xt between t_1 and t_2 is not assigned a different value, then

$$Xt^{(t_1)} - Xt^{(t_2)} = t_2 - t_1.$$

Note that these timers run exactly in the sense that during time δ they decrease by exactly δ. In Subsection 3.2.3 we shall discuss the case where the timers suffer from a drift.

The input words for the sender are modeled, as in Section 3.1, by an infinite array in_p. Again, this array is never stored in p entirely; p can only access a part of it at any time. The part of in_p that can be accessed by p is extended (at the higher end) when p obtains a next word from the process that generates the words. This operation is referred to as the *acceptance* of a word by the sender.

In this section the modeling of words delivered by the receiver is different from the modeling in Section 3.1. Instead of writing an (infinite) array, the receiver hands words to the consuming process by an operation referred to as *delivering* the word. Ideally, each word of in_p should be delivered exactly once and the words should be delivered in the correct order.

The specification of the protocol, however, is weaker than this, and the reason is that the protocol is only allowed to treat each word of in_p during a bounded time interval. It cannot be guaranteed by any protocol that a word is received within a bounded time, because it is possible that all packets are lost during this time. Therefore the specification of the protocol allows for the possibility of a *reported loss*, where the sending protocol generates an error report indicating that the word may be lost. (If, for this reason, a higher-level protocol were to offer this word to p again a duplication could effectively occur; we will, however, not concern ourselves with this problem here.) The properties of the protocol that will be proved in Subsection 3.2.2 are:

(1) *No loss.* Each word of in_p is delivered by q or reported by p (as "possibly lost") within a bounded time after the acceptance of the word by p.

(2) *Ordering.* The words delivered by q occur in strictly increasing order in in_p.

3.2.1 Presentation of the Protocol

A connection is opened in the protocol when previously no connection exists and then (for the sender) a next word is accepted or (for the receiver) when a packet arrives that can be delivered. Thus in this protocol, to open a connection it is not necessary to exchange any control messages before data packets can be sent. This makes the protocol relatively efficient for applications where only a few words are transmitted in every connection (small bursts of communication). The predicate cs (or cr, respectively) is true when the sender (or the receiver, respectively) has an open connection. This is usually not an explicit boolean variable of the sender (or the receiver, respectively); instead an open connection is defined by the existence of a connection record. A process tests whether a connection is open by searching for the existence of a connection record in its list of open connections.

When the sender opens a new connection it starts numbering the accepted words from 0. The number of words already accepted in this connection is indicated by *High*, and the number of words for which an acknowledgement has already been received is indicated by *Low*. This would suggest (analogously to the protocol of Section 3.1) that the sender may transmit packets with sequence numbers ranging from *Low* to *High* − 1, but there is a twist to

Network constant:
μ : real ;   (* Maximum packet lifetime *)

Protocol constants:
U : real ;   (* Length of send interval *)
R : real ;   (* Receiver time-out value: $R \geq U + \mu$ *)
S : real ;   (* Sender time-out value: $S \geq R + 2\mu$ *)

Connection record of sender:
Low : integer ;   (* Acknowledged words of current connection *)
$High$: integer ;   (* Accepted words of current connection *)
St : timer ;   (* Connection timer *)

Connection record of receiver:
Exp : integer ;   (* Next expected sequence number *)
Rt : timer ;   (* Connection timer *)

Communication subsystem:
M_q : channel ;   (* Data packets for q *)
M_p : channel ;   (* Acknowledgement packets for p *)

Auxiliary variables:
B : integer **init** 0 ;   (* Words in previous connections *)
cr : boolean **init** false ;   (* Connection exists at receiver *)
cs : boolean **init** false ;   (* Connection exists at sender *)

Figure 3.3 VARIABLES OF THE TIMER-BASED PROTOCOL.

this. The sender may send a word only during a time interval, of length U, starting from the moment at which the sender accepts the word. To this end a timer $Ut[i]$ is associated with each word $in_p[i]$; it is set to U at the moment of acceptance, and must be positive for a word to be transmitted. Thus the sending window of p consists of those words of the range $Low...High - 1$ for which the associated timer is positive.

The protocol sends data packets consisting of a bit (the *start-of-sequence* bit; its meaning will be discussed below), a sequence number, and a word. For the purpose of analysis of the protocol each data packet carries a fourth field, called the *remaining packet lifetime*. It represents the maximum time that a packet can still spend in the channels before it must be received or become lost according to the bounded-lifetime assumption. The remaining packet lifetime is always μ when the packet is sent. The acknowledgement packets sent in the protocol consist only of the next sequence number expected by q; but again for the purpose of analysis each acknowledgement packet carries a remaining packet lifetime also.

A$_p$: (* Accept next word *)
    begin if not cs **then**
        begin (* Connection is opened first *)
            create $(St, High, Low)$; (* $cs := $ true *)
            $Low := High := 0$; $St := S$
        end ;
          $Ut[B + High] := U$; $High := High + 1$
    end

S$_p$: (* Send ith word from current connection *)
    $\{ \ cs \ \wedge \ Low \leq i < High \ \wedge \ Ut[B + i] > 0 \ \}$
    begin send $\langle \textbf{data}, (i = Low), i, in_p[B + i], \mu \rangle$;
        $St := S$
    end

R$_p$: (* Receive an acknowledgement *)
    $\{ \ cs \ \wedge \ \langle \textbf{ack}, i, \rho \rangle \in M_p \ \}$
    begin receive $\langle \textbf{ack}, i, \rho \rangle$; $Low := \max (Low, i)$ **end**

E$_p$: (* Generate error report for possibly lost word *)
    $\{ \ cs \ \wedge \ Ut[B + Low] \leq -2\mu - R \ \}$
    begin $error[B + Low] := true$; $Low := Low + 1$ **end**

C$_p$: (* Close the connection *)
    $\{ \ cs \ \wedge \ St < 0 \ \wedge \ Low = High \ \}$
    begin $B := B + High$; delete $(St, High, Low)$ **end**
    (* $cs := $ false *)

Algorithm 3.4 THE SENDER PROTOCOL.

The closing of the connections is controlled by timers, a timer St for the sender and a timer Rt for the receiver. The bounded send interval for each word and the bounded lifetime of packets imply that each word can be found in the channels only during a time interval of length $\mu + U$, starting at the moment of acceptance of the word. This allows the receiver to discard information about a certain word $\mu + U$ time units after the receipt of the word; after this time no duplicates can arrive, hence there is no risk of duplicate delivery. The timer Rt is set to R each time a word is delivered, the constant R being chosen so as to satisfy $R \geq U + \mu$. If a next word is delivered within R time units the timer Rt is refreshed, otherwise the connection is closed. The timer value of the sender is chosen such that an acknowledgement is never received while a connection is closed; to this end, a connection is maintained for a time interval of at least S after sending a packet, S being a constant chosen so as to satisfy $S \geq R + 2\mu$. The timer St

$\mathbf{R}_q$: (* Receive a data packet *)
$\{\ \langle \mathbf{data}, s, i, w, \rho \rangle \in M_q\ \}$
$\quad$ **begin** receive $\langle \mathbf{data}, s, i, w, \rho \rangle$;
$\qquad$ **if** cr **then**
$\qquad\quad$ **if** $i = Exp$ **then**
$\qquad\qquad$ **begin** $Rt := R$; $Exp := i + 1$; deliver w **end**
$\qquad\quad$ **else if** $s = true$ **then**
$\qquad\qquad$ **begin** create (Rt, Exp) ; (* $cr := true$ *)
$\qquad\qquad\qquad$ $Rt := R$; $Exp := i + 1$; deliver w
$\qquad\quad$ **end**
$\quad$ **end**

$\mathbf{S}_q$: (* Send an acknowledgement *)
$\{\ cr\ \}$
$\quad$ **begin** send $\langle \mathbf{ack}, Exp, \mu \rangle$ **end**

(* Close connection if Rt times out, see action **Time** *)

Algorithm 3.5 THE RECEIVER PROTOCOL.

---

is set to S each time a packet is sent, and a connection can be closed only if $St < 0$. If at that time there are still outstanding words (i.e., words for which no acknowledgement has been received) these words must be reported before the connection can be closed.

The start-of-sequence bit is used by the receiver when a packet is received in a closed connection, to decide whether a connection can be opened (and the word in the packet delivered). The sender sets the bit to true when all previous words have been acknowledged or reported (as possibly lost). When q receives a packet in an already open connection the contained word is delivered if and only if the sequence number of the packet equals the next expected sequence number (stored in Exp).

It remains to discuss the meaning of the variable B in the sender protocol. It is an auxiliary variable, introduced only for the purpose of the correctness proof of the protocol. The sender numbers the words in each connection starting from 0, but in order to distinguish between words in different connections all words are indexed consecutively with increasing numbers in the analysis of the protocol. Thus, where the sender indexes a word by i, the "absolute" number of the referred word is $B + i$, where B is the total number of packets accepted by p in earlier connections. The correspondence between "internal" and "absolute" word numbers is shown in Figure 3.7. In an implementation of the protocol B is not stored, and the sender "forgets" about all words of $in_p[0..B-1]$.

Loss: $\{\ m \in M\ \}$ (* M is either M_p or M_q *)
          begin remove m from M **end**

Dupl: $\{\ m \in M\ \}$ (* M is either M_p or M_q *)
          begin insert m in M **end**

Time: (* $\delta > 0$ *)
          begin forall i **do** $Ut[i] := Ut[i] - \delta$;
                $St := St - \delta$;
                $Rt := Rt - \delta$;
                if $Rt \leq 0$ **then** delete (Rt, Exp) ; (* $cr := false$ *)
                forall $\langle .., \rho \rangle \in M_p, M_q$ **do**
                        begin $\rho := \rho - \delta$;
                             if $\rho \leq 0$ **then** remove packet
                    end
    end

Algorithm 3.6 ADDITIONAL TRANSITIONS OF THE PROTOCOL.

The communication subsystem is represented by two multisets, M_p for the packets with destination p and M_q for the packets with destination q. The sender protocol is given as Algorithm 3.4 and the receiver protocol is given as Algorithm 3.5. There are additional transitions of the system, given as Algorithm 3.6, which do not correspond to steps in the processes' protocols. These transitions represent channel failures and the progress of time. In the transitions **Loss** and **Dupl** M stands for either M_p or M_q. The **Time** action decreases all timers in the system by an amount δ, which is what happens between the application of two discrete events with δ time units between them. When the receiver's timer reaches the value 0, its connection is closed.

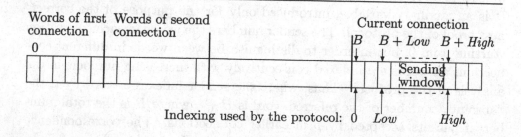

Figure 3.7 THE SEQUENCE NUMBERS OF THE WORDS.

3.2.2 Correctness Proof of the Protocol

The required properties of the protocol will be proved in a series of lemmas and theorems. The assertion P_0 defined below expresses that the sender's connection remains open as long as there are any packets in the system, and that the sequence numbers of those packets have the correct meaning in the current connection.

$$
\begin{aligned}
P_0 \equiv \quad & cs \Rightarrow St \leq S && (1) \\
\wedge \ & cr \Rightarrow 0 < Rt \leq R && (2) \\
\wedge \ & \forall i < B + High : \ Ut[i] \leq U && (3) \\
\wedge \ & \forall \langle .., \rho \rangle \in M_p, M_q : 0 < \rho \leq \mu && (4) \\
\wedge \ & \langle \mathbf{data}, s, i, w, \rho \rangle \in M_q \Rightarrow cs \wedge St \geq \rho + \mu + R && (5) \\
\wedge \ & cr \Rightarrow cs \wedge St \geq Rt + \mu && (6) \\
\wedge \ & \langle \mathbf{ack}, i, \rho \rangle \in M_p \Rightarrow cs \wedge St > \rho && (7) \\
\wedge \ & \langle \mathbf{data}, s, i, w, \rho \rangle \in M_q \Rightarrow (w = in_p[B + i] \wedge i < High) && (8)
\end{aligned}
$$

To interpret (3), the value of *High* is supposed to be zero in all configurations where no connection exists at the sender.

Lemma 3.10 P_0 *is an invariant of the timer based protocol.*

Proof. Initially no connections exist, there are no packets, and $B = 0$, which implies that P_0 is true.

$\mathbf{A}_p$: (1) is preserved because an assignment to St always results in $St = S$. (3) is preserved because before an increment of *High*, $Ut[B + High]$ is assigned the value U. (5), (6), and (7) are preserved because St can only increase. (8) is preserved because *High* can only increase.

$\mathbf{S}_p$: (1) is preserved because St is always set to S. (4) is preserved because each packet is sent with remaining packet lifetime equal to μ. (5) is preserved because a packet $\langle .., \mu \rangle$ is sent and St is set to S, and $S = R + 2\mu$. (6) and (7) are preserved because St can only increase in this action. (8) is preserved because the new packet satisfies $w = in_p[B + i]$ and $i < High$.

$\mathbf{R}_p$: Action $\mathbf{R}_p$ does not change any of the variables mentioned in P_0, and the removal of a packet preserves (4) and (7).

$\mathbf{E}_p$: Action $\mathbf{E}_p$ does not change any of the variables mentioned in P_0.

$\mathbf{C}_p$: Action $\mathbf{C}_p$ falsifies the conclusion of (5), (6), and (7), but (by (2), (5), (6), and (7)) is applicable only when their premises are false. $\mathbf{C}_p$ also changes the value of B, but as there are no packets in transit by (5) and (7), (8) is preserved.

R$_q$: (2) is preserved because Rt is always assigned as R (if at all). (6) is preserved because Rt is set to R only on receipt of a packet $\langle \textbf{data}, s, i, w, \rho \rangle$, and (4) and (5) imply $cs \land St \geq R + \mu$ when this happens.

S$_q$: (4) is preserved because each packet is sent with remaining packet lifetime equal to μ. (7) is preserved because a packet $\langle \textbf{ack}, i, \rho \rangle$ is sent with $\rho = \mu$ when cr is true, so by (2) and (6), $St > \mu$.

Loss: (4), (5), (7), and (8) are preserved because the removal of a packet can only falsify their premise.

Dupl: (4), (5), (7), and (8) are preserved because the insertion of a packet m is applicable only if m was in the channel already, which implies that the conclusion of the relevant clause was true even before the insertion.

Time: (1), (2), and (3) are preserved because St, Rt, and $Ut[i]$ can only decrease, and the receiver's connection closes when Rt reaches 0. (4) is preserved because ρ can only decrease, and a packet is removed when its ρ-field reaches 0. Observe that **Time** decreases all timers (including ρ-fields of packets) by *the same* amount, hence preserves all assertions of the form $Xt \geq Yt + C$, where Xt and Yt are timers, and C a constant. This shows that (5), (6), and (7) are preserved.

$\square$

The first requirement for the protocol is that each word is eventually delivered or reported as lost. Define the predicate $Ok(i)$ by

$$Ok(i) \iff error[i] = true \ \lor \ q \text{ has delivered } in_p[i].$$

It can now be shown that the protocol does not lose any words without reporting the fact. Define the assertion P_1 by

$$
\begin{aligned}
P_1 \equiv \ & P_0 \\
& \land \ \lnot cs \Rightarrow \forall i < B: \ Ok(i) & (9) \\
& \land \ cs \Rightarrow \forall i < B + Low: \ Ok(i) & (10) \\
& \land \ \langle \textbf{data}, true, I, w, \rho \rangle \in M_q \Rightarrow \forall i < B + I: \ Ok(i) & (11) \\
& \land \ cr \Rightarrow \forall i < B + Exp: \ Ok(i) & (12) \\
& \land \ \langle \textbf{ack}, I, \rho \rangle \in M_p \Rightarrow \forall i < B + I: \ Ok(i) & (13)
\end{aligned}
$$

Lemma 3.11 P_1 *is an invariant of the timer-based protocol.*

Proof. First observe that once $Ok(i)$ has become true for some i, it never becomes false thereafter. Initially there is no connection, there are no packets, and $B = 0$, which implies that P_1 holds.

$\mathbf{A}_p$: Action $\mathbf{A}_p$ may open a connection, but preserves (10) when doing so because the connection is opened with $Low = 0$ and $\forall i < B : Ok(i)$ holds by (9).

$\mathbf{S}_p$: Action $\mathbf{S}_p$ may send a packet $\langle \mathbf{data}, s, I, w, \rho \rangle$, but as s is true only when $I = Low$, this preserves (11) by (10).

$\mathbf{R}_p$: The value of Low may be increased if a packet $\langle \mathbf{ack}, I, \rho \rangle$ is received. Nevertheless, (10) is preserved because by (13) $\forall i < B + I : Ok(i)$ holds if this acknowledgement is received.

$\mathbf{E}_p$: The value of Low may be incremented when action $\mathbf{E}_p$ is applied, but the generation of an error report ensures that (10) is preserved.

$\mathbf{C}_p$: Action $\mathbf{C}_p$ falsifies cs, but is applicable only if $St < 0$ and $Low = High$. (10) implies that $\forall i < B + High : Ok(i)$ holds prior to the execution of $\mathbf{C}_p$, hence (9) is preserved. The premise of (10) is falsified in the action, and (5), (6), and (7) imply that the premises of (11), (12), and (13) are false; hence (10), (11), (12), and (13) are preserved.

$\mathbf{R}_q$: First consider the case that q receives $\langle \mathbf{data}, true, I, w, \rho \rangle$ while no connection exists (cr is false). Then $\forall i < B + I : Ok(i)$ by (11), and w is delivered in the action. As $w = in_p[B+I]$ by (8), the assignment $Exp := I + 1$ preserves (12).

Now consider the case that Exp is incremented as the result of the receipt of $\langle \mathbf{data}, s, Exp, w, \rho \rangle$ in an open connection. By (12), $\forall i < B + Exp : Ok(i)$ held before the receipt, and the word $w = in_p[B + Exp]$ is delivered in the action, hence the increment of Exp preserves (12).

$\mathbf{S}_q$: Sending $\langle \mathbf{ack}, Exp, \mu \rangle$ preserves (13) by (12).

Loss: An application of **Loss** can only falsify the premises of the clauses.

Dupl: The insertion of a packet m is applicable only if the premise of the relevant clause (and hence the conclusion) was true even before the insertion.

Time: No timers are mentioned explicitly in (9)–(13). The removal of a packet or closing by q may only falsify the premises of (11), (12), or (13).

$\square$

The first part of the protocol specification can now be proved after making an additional assumption. Without this assumption, the sender can be extremely lazy in reporting possibly lost words; it is specified in Algorithm 3.4 only that this reporting may *not* occur within $2\mu + R$ after the end of the word's sending interval, but not that it eventually must occur. So, let us now make the additional assumption that action $\mathbf{E}_p$ will actually be executed by p and within a reasonable time, namely *before* $Ut[B + Low] = -2\mu - R - \lambda$.

Theorem 3.12 (No Loss) *Each word of in_p is delivered by q or reported by p within $U + 2\mu + R + \lambda$ after the acceptance of the word by p.*

Proof. After acceptance of the word $in_p[I]$, $B + High > I$ holds and continues to hold. If the connection is closed within the specified period after the acceptance of the word $in_p[I]$, then $B > I$, and the result follows from (9). If the connection is not closed within this period of time and $B + Low \leq I$, the reporting of all words from the range $B + Low..I$ is enabled by a time $2\mu + R$ after the end of the sending interval of $in_p[I]$. This implies that this reporting has taken place $2\mu + R + \lambda$ after the end of the sending interval, i.e., $U + 2\mu + R + \lambda$ after the acceptance. This also implies $I < B + Low$, and hence the word was reported or delivered by (10).   □

To establish the second correctness requirement of the protocol it must be shown that each word that is accepted has a higher index (in in_p) than the previously accepted word. Denote the index of the most recently delivered word by pr (for convenience, write $pr = -1$ and $Ut[-1] = -\infty$ initially). Define the assertion P_2 by:

$$
\begin{aligned}
P_2 \equiv \quad & P_1 \\
& \wedge \langle \mathbf{data}, s, i, w, \rho \rangle \in M_q \Rightarrow Ut[B + i] > \rho - \mu && (14) \\
& \wedge\ i_1 \leq i_2 < B + High \Rightarrow Ut[i_1] \leq Ut[i_2] && (15) \\
& \wedge\ cr \Rightarrow Rt \geq Ut[pr] + \mu && (16) \\
& \wedge\ pr < B + High \wedge (Ut[pr] > -\mu \Rightarrow cr) && (17) \\
& \wedge\ cr \Rightarrow B + Exp = pr + 1 && (18)
\end{aligned}
$$

Lemma 3.13 P_2 *is an invariant of the timer-based protocol.*

Proof. Initially M_q is empty, $B + High$ is zero, $\neg cr$ holds, and $Ut[pr] < -\mu$, from which (14)–(18) follow.

$\mathbf{A}_p$: (15) is preserved because the newly accepted word gets timer value U, which by (3) at least equals the timer values of all earlier accepted words.

$\mathbf{S}_p$: (14) is preserved because $Ut[B + i] > 0$ and the packet is sent with $\rho = \mu$.

$\mathbf{C}_p$: (14), (16), and (18) are preserved because by (5) and (6) their premise is false when $\mathbf{C}_p$ is applicable. (15) is preserved because B is assigned the value $B + High$ and the timers do not change. (17) is preserved because B is assigned as $B + High$ and pr and cr do not change.

R_q: (16) is preserved because when Rt is set to R (upon accepting a word) $Ut[pr] \leq U$ by (3), and $R \geq 2\mu + U$. (17) is preserved because $pr < B + High$ follows from (8), and cr becomes true. (18) is preserved because Exp is set to $i + 1$ and pr to $B + i$, which implies that (18) becomes true.

Time: (14) is preserved because $Ut[B + i]$ and ρ are decreased by the same amount (and the removal of a packet only falsifies the premise). (15) is preserved because $Ut[i_1]$ and $Ut[i_2]$ are decreased by the same amount. (16) is preserved because cr does not become true in the action, and Rt and $Ut[pr]$ are decreased by the same amount. (17) is preserved, because its conclusion is only falsified if Rt becomes ≤ 0, which implies by (16) that $Ut[pr]$ becomes $\leq -\mu$. (18) is preserved because if cr is not falsified, B, Exp, and pr do not change.

The actions R_p, E_p, and S_q do not change any of the variables mentioned in (14)–(18). **Loss** and **Dupl** preserve (14)–(18) by the same arguments as used in earlier proofs. $\qquad\square$

Lemma 3.14 *It follows from P_2 that*

$$\langle \mathbf{data}, s, i_1, w, \rho \rangle \in M_q \Rightarrow (cr \vee B + i_1 > pr).$$

Proof. By (14), $\langle \mathbf{data}, s, i_1, w, \rho \rangle \in M_q$ implies $Ut[B + i_1] > \rho - \mu > -\mu$. If $B + i_1 \leq pr$ then, because $pr < B + High$ by (15), $Ut[pr] > -\mu$, so by (17) cr is true. $\qquad\square$

Theorem 3.15 (Ordering) *The words delivered by q occur in strictly increasing order in the array in_p.*

Proof. Assume q receives a packet $\langle \mathbf{data}, s, i_1, w, \rho \rangle$ and delivers w. If no connection existed before the receipt, $B + i_1 > pr$ (by Lemma 3.14), so the word w occurs after position pr in in_p. If a connection did exist, $i_1 = Exp$, hence $B + i_1 = B + Exp = pr + 1$ by (18), which implies that $w = in_p[pr + 1]$. $\qquad\square$

3.2.3 Discussion of the Protocol

Some extensions of the protocol have already been discussed in the introduction to this section. We conclude the section with a further discussion of the protocol and of the techniques introduced and used in this section.

The quality of the protocol. The *No Loss* and *Ordering* requirements are both safety properties, and they allow an extremely simple solution, namely a protocol that does not send or receive any packets, and reports every word as lost. It goes without saying that such a protocol, which does not achieve any form of data transport from sender to receiver, would not be considered a very "good" solution.

Good solutions of the problem not only satisfy the *No Loss* and *Ordering* requirements, but also report as few words as lost as possible. To achieve this goal the protocol of this section can be augmented with a mechanism by which each word is sent repeatedly (until the end of its sending interval) until it has been acknowledged. The sending interval must be long enough to repeat the transmission of a certain word several times, so that the probability that a word is lost becomes very small.

On the receiver's side a mechanism is provided for triggering the sending of an acknowledgement whenever a packet is delivered or received in an open connection.

Bounded sequence numbers. The sequence numbers used in the protocol can be bounded by proving for the protocol a result similar to Lemma 3.9 for the balanced sliding-window protocol [Tel91b, Section 3.2]. To this end it must be assumed that the acceptance rate of words (by p) is bounded in a way such that a word can only be accepted if the Lth previous word is at least $U + 2\mu + R$ time units old. The guard

$$\{(High < L) \vee (Ut[B + High - L] < -R - 2\mu)\}$$

must be added to action $\mathbf{A}_p$ to achieve this. Under this assumption it can be shown that sequence numbers in received data packets are within the $2L$-range around *Exp*, and the sequence number in acknowledgements is within the L-range around *High*. Consequently, sequence numbers may be transmitted modulo $2L$.

The shape of actions and invariants. With an assertional approach, reasoning about a communication protocol is reduced to a (large) exercise in formula manipulation. Formula manipulation is a "safe" technique because every step can be checked in great detail so the possibility of making an error in reasoning is small. It bears the risk that one loses an overview of the protocol and its relation to the formulas considered. The design issues of a protocol can be understood from both the pragmatic and the formal viewpoint. Fletcher and Watson [FW78] argue that control information must be "protected" in the sense that its meaning must not be changed by the

---

Time-ϵ: $\{\ \delta > 0\ \}$
    begin (* The timers in p decrease by δ' *)
        $\delta' := \ldots\ ;$ (* $\frac{\delta}{(1+\epsilon)} \leq \delta' \leq \delta \times (1+\epsilon)$ *)
        forall i **do** $Ut[i] := Ut[i] - \delta'\ ;$
        $St := St - \delta'\ ;$
    (* The timers in q decrease by δ'' *)
        $\delta'' := \ldots\ ;$ (* $\frac{\delta}{(1+\epsilon)} \leq \delta'' \leq \delta \times (1+\epsilon)$ *)
        $Rt := Rt - \delta''\ ;$
        if $Rt \leq 0$ **then** delete $(Rt, Exp)\ ;$
    (* The ρ-fields run exactly *)
        forall $\langle .., \rho \rangle \in M_p,\ M_q$ **do**
            begin $\rho := \rho - \delta\ ;$
                if $\rho \leq 0$ **then** remove packet
            end

    end

Algorithm 3.8 THE MODIFIED **Time** ACTION.

---

loss or duplication of packets; this is the pragmatic viewpoint. In the assertional approach towards verification the "meaning" of control information is reflected in the choice of particular assertions as invariants. The choice of these invariants and the design of transitions preserving them constitute the formal viewpoint. Indeed, as will be shown, Fletcher and Watson's observation can be restated in terms of the "shape" of formulas that can or cannot be chosen as invariants of a protocol resilient against the loss and duplication of packets.

All invariant clauses of P_2 regarding packets are of the form

$$\forall m \in M:\ A(m)$$

and it is indeed easy to see that such a clause is preserved by packet duplication or loss. In later chapters we shall see invariants with more general forms, e.g.,

$$\sum_{m \in M} f(m) = K$$

or

$$\text{condition} \Rightarrow \exists m \in M:\ A(m).$$

Assertions having these forms can be falsified by packet loss or duplication, and hence cannot serve in the correctness proof of algorithms that must tolerate these faults.

Similar observations apply to the shape of invariants in the **Time** action.

$$
\begin{aligned}
P_2' \equiv \quad & cs \Rightarrow St \leq S & (1') \\
\wedge \quad & cr \Rightarrow 0 < Rt \leq R & (2') \\
\wedge \quad & \forall i < B + High : \ Ut[i] \leq U & (3') \\
\wedge \quad & \forall \langle .., \rho \rangle \in M_p, M_q : 0 < \rho \leq \mu & (4') \\
\wedge \quad & \langle \mathbf{data}, s, i, w, \rho \rangle \in M_q \Rightarrow cs \wedge St \geq (1 + \epsilon)(\rho + \mu + (1 + \epsilon)R) & (5') \\
\wedge \quad & cr \Rightarrow cs \wedge St \geq (1 + \epsilon)((1 + \epsilon)Rt + \mu) & (6') \\
\wedge \quad & \langle \mathbf{ack}, i, \rho \rangle \in M_p \Rightarrow cs \wedge St > (1 + \epsilon) \times \rho & (7') \\
\wedge \quad & \langle \mathbf{data}, s, i, w, \rho \rangle \in M_q \Rightarrow (w = in_p[B + i] \wedge i < High) & (8') \\
\wedge \quad & \neg cs \Rightarrow \forall i < B : \ Ok(i) & (9') \\
\wedge \quad & cs \Rightarrow \forall i < B + Low : \ Ok(i) & (10') \\
\wedge \quad & \langle \mathbf{data}, true, I, w, \rho \rangle \in M_q \Rightarrow \forall i < B + I : \ Ok(i) & (11') \\
\wedge \quad & cr \Rightarrow \forall i < B + Exp : \ Ok(i) & (12') \\
\wedge \quad & \langle \mathbf{ack}, I, \rho \rangle \in M_p \Rightarrow \forall i < B + I : \ Ok(i) & (13') \\
\wedge \quad & \langle \mathbf{data}, s, i, w, \rho \rangle \in M_q \Rightarrow Ut[B + i] > (1 + \epsilon)(\rho - \mu) & (14') \\
\wedge \quad & i_1 \leq i_2 < B + High \Rightarrow Ut[i_1] \leq Ut[i_2] & (15') \\
\wedge \quad & cr \Rightarrow Rt \geq (1 + \epsilon)((1 + \epsilon)Ut[pr] + (1 + \epsilon)^2 \mu) & (16') \\
\wedge \quad & pr < B + High \wedge Ut[pr] > -(1 + \epsilon)\mu \Rightarrow cr & (17') \\
\wedge \quad & cr \Rightarrow B + Exp = pr + 1 & (18')
\end{aligned}
$$

Figure 3.9 THE INVARIANT OF THE PROTOCOL WITH TIMER DRIFT.

It has already been remarked that this action preserves all assertions of the form

$$Xt \geq Yt + C,$$

where Xt and Yt are timers and C is a constant.

Inaccurate timers. The **Time** action models idealized timers that decrease by exactly δ during δ time units, but in practice timers suffer from inaccuracies called *drift*. This drift is always assumed to be ϵ-*bounded* for a known constant ϵ, which means that during δ time units the timer decreases by an amount δ', satisfying $\delta/(1 + \epsilon) \leq \delta' \leq \delta \times (1 + \epsilon)$. (Typically ϵ is of the order of 10^{-5} or 10^{-6}.) This behavior of timers is modeled by the action **Time-ϵ** given in Algorithm 3.8.

It was observed that **Time** preserves assertions of the special form $Xt \geq Yt + C$ because the timers on both sides of the inequality are decreased by exactly the same amount, and $Xt \geq Yt + C$ implies $(Xt - \delta) \geq (Yt - \delta) + C$. A similar observation can be made for **Time-ϵ**. For real numbers Xt, Yt, δ, δ', δ'', r, and c satisfying $\delta > 0$ and $r > 1$,

$$
(Xt \geq r^2 \, Yt + c) \ \wedge \ \left(\frac{\delta}{r} \leq \delta' \leq \delta \times r \right) \ \wedge \ \left(\frac{\delta}{r} \leq \delta'' \leq \delta \times r \right)
$$

implies

$$(Xt - \delta') \geq r^2 (Yt - \delta'') + c.$$

Consequently, **Time-ϵ** preserves assertions of the form

$$Xt \geq (1 + \epsilon)^2 Yt + c.$$

The protocol can now be adapted to work with drifting timers by modifying the invariants accordingly. In order that the other actions should also preserve the modified invariants, the constants R and S of the protocol must satisfy

$$R \geq (1 + \epsilon)((1 + \epsilon)U + (1 + \epsilon)^2 \mu) \text{ and } S \geq (1 + \epsilon)(2\mu + (1 + \epsilon)R).$$

Barring the modified constants, the protocol remains the same. Its invariant is given in Figure 3.9.

Theorem 3.16 P_2' *is an invariant of the timer-based protocol with ϵ-bounded timer drift. The protocol satisfies the No Loss and Ordering requirements.*

Exercises to Chapter 3

Section 3.1

Exercise 3.1 *Show that the balanced sliding-window protocol does not satisfy the eventual delivery requirement if, of the fairness assumptions F1 and F2, only F2 holds.*

Exercise 3.2 *Prove that if $L = 1$ in the balanced sliding-window protocol and a_p and a_q are initialized to $-l_q$ and $-l_p$, then $a_p + l_q = s_p$ and $a_q + l_p = s_q$ always hold.*

Section 3.2

Exercise 3.3 *In the timer-based protocol the sender may report a word as possibly lost, when in fact the word was delivered correctly by the receiver.*

(1) *Describe an execution of the protocol where this phenomenon occurs.*
(2) *Is it possible to design a protocol in which the sender generates an error report within a bounded time, if and only if the word is not delivered by the receiver?*

Exercise 3.4 *Assume that, due to a failing clock device, the receiver may fail to close its connection in time. Describe a computation of the timer-based protocol in which a word is lost without being reported by the sender.*

Exercise 3.5 *Describe a computation of the timer-based protocol in which the receiver opens a connection upon receipt of a packet with a sequence number greater than zero.*

Exercise 3.6 *The* **Time-ε** *action does not model drift in the remaining packet lifetime of packets. Why not?*

Exercise 3.7 *Prove Theorem 3.16.*

Exercise 3.8 *A network engineer wants to use the timer-based protocol, but wants to allow possibly lost words to be reported earlier with the following modification of* E_p.

E_p: *(* Generate error report for possibly lost word *)*
        $\{\ Ut[B + Low] < 0\ \}$
        begin $error[B + Low] := true\ ;\ Low := Low + 1$ **end**

Does the protocol thus modified still satisfy the No Loss and Ordering requirements or must other changes be made as well?
Give an advantage and a disadvantage of this modification.

4

Routing Algorithms

A process (a node in a computer network) is in general not connected directly
to every other process by a channel. A node can send packets of information
directly only to a subset of the nodes called the *neighbors* of the node.
Routing is the term used to describe the decision procedure by which a
node selects one (or, sometimes, more) of its neighbors to forward a packet
on its way to an ultimate destination. The objective in designing a routing
algorithm is to generate (for each node) a decision-making procedure to
perform this function and guarantee delivery of each packet.

It will be clear that some information about the topology of the network
must be stored in each node as a working basis for the (local) decision
procedure; we shall refer to this information as the *routing tables*. With
the introduction of these tables the routing problem can be algorithmically
divided into two parts; the definition of the table structure is of course
related to the algorithmical design.

(1) *Table computation*. The routing tables must be computed when the
network is initialized and must be brought up to date if the topology
of the network changes.
(2) *Packet forwarding*. When a packet is to be sent through the network
it must be forwarded using the routing tables.

Criteria for "good" routing methods include the following.

(1) *Correctness*. The algorithm must deliver every packet offered to the
network to its ultimate destination.
(2) *Efficiency*. The algorithm must send packets through "good" paths,
e.g., paths that suffer only a small delay and ensure high throughput
of the entire network. An algorithm is called *optimal* if it uses the
"best" paths.

(3) *Complexity.* The algorithm for the computation of the tables must use as few messages, time, and storage as possible. Other aspects of complexity are how fast a routing decision can be made, how fast a packet can be made ready for transmission, etc., but these aspects will receive less attention in this chapter.

(4) *Robustness.* In the case of a topological change (the addition or removal of a channel or node) the algorithm updates the routing tables in order to perform the routing function in the modified network.

(5) *Adaptiveness.* The algorithm balances the load of channels and nodes by adapting the tables in order to avoid paths through channels or nodes that are very busy, preferring channels and nodes with a currently light load.

(6) *Fairness.* The algorithm must provide service to every user in the same degree.

These criteria are sometimes conflicting, and most algorithms perform well only w.r.t. a subset of them.

As usual, a network is represented as a graph, where the nodes of the graph are the nodes of the network, and there is an edge between two nodes if they are neighbors (i.e., they have a communication channel between them). The optimality of an algorithm depends on what is called a "best" path in the graph; there are several notions of what is "best", each with its own class of routing algorithms:

(1) *Minimum hop.* The cost of using a path is measured as the number of hops (traversed channels or steps from node to node) of the path. A minimum-hop routing algorithm uses a path with the smallest possible number of hops.

(2) *Shortest path.* Each channel is statically assigned a (non-negative) *weight*, and the cost of a path is measured as the sum of the weights of the channels in the path. A shortest-path algorithm uses a path with lowest possible cost.

(3) *Minimum delay.* Each channel is dynamically assigned a weight, depending on the traffic on the channel. A minimum-delay algorithm repeatedly revises the tables in such a way that paths with a (near) minimal total delay are always chosen. As the delays encountered on the channels depend on the actual traffic, the various packets transmitted through the network influence each other; the impact on the required routing algorithm will be discussed at the end of Section 4.1.

Other notions of the optimality of paths may be useful in special applications, but will not be discussed here.

Chapter overview. The following material is treated in this chapter. In Section 4.1 it will be shown that, at least for minimum-hop and shortest-path routing, it is possible to route all packets for the same destination d optimally via a spanning tree rooted towards d. As a consequence, the source of a packet can be ignored when routing decisions are made.

Section 4.2 describes an algorithm to compute routing tables for a static network with weighted channels. The algorithm distributively computes a shortest path between each pair of nodes and stores in each source node the first neighbor on the path for each destination. A disadvantage of this algorithm is that the entire computation must be repeated after a topological change in the network: the algorithm is not robust.

The Netchange algorithm discussed in Section 4.3 does not suffer from this disadvantage: it can adapt to failing or recovering channels by a *partial* recomputation of the routing tables. To keep the analysis simple it is presented as a minimum-hop routing algorithm, that is, the number of hops is taken as the cost of a path. It is possible to modify the Netchange algorithm to deal with weighted channels that can fail or recover.

The routing algorithms of Sections 4.2 and 4.3 use routing tables (in each node) that contain an entry for each possible destination. This may be too heavy a storage demand for large networks of small nodes. In Section 4.4 some routing strategies will be discussed that code topological information in the address of a node, in order to use shorter routing tables or fewer table lookups. These so-called "compact" routing algorithms usually do not use optimal paths. A tree-based scheme, interval routing, and prefix routing are discussed.

Section 4.5 discusses hierarchical routing methods. In these methods, the network is partitioned into (connected) clusters, and a distinction is made between routing within a cluster and routing to another cluster. This paradigm can be used to reduce the number of routing decisions that must be made during a path, or to reduce the amount of space needed to store the routing table in each node.

4.1 Destination-based Routing

The routing decision made when forwarding a packet is usually based only on the *destination* of the packet (and the contents of the routing tables), and is *independent* of the original sender (the source) of the packet. Routing can ignore the source and still use optimal paths, as implied by the results of this section. The results do not depend on the choice of a particular optimality criterion for paths, but the following assumptions must hold. (Recall that a path is *simple* if it contains each node at most once, and the path is a cycle if the first node equals the last node.)

(1) The cost of sending a packet via a path P is independent of the actual utilization of the path, in particular, the use of edges of P by other messages. This assumption allows us to regard the cost of using path P as a function of the path; thus denote the cost of P by $C(P) \in \mathbb{R}$.

(2) The cost of the concatenation of two paths equals the sum of the costs of the concatenated paths, i.e., for all $i = 0, \ldots, k$,

$$C(\langle u_0, u_1, \ldots, u_k \rangle) = C(\langle u_0, \ldots, u_i \rangle) + C(\langle u_i, \ldots, u_k \rangle).$$

Consequently, the cost of the empty path $\langle u_0 \rangle$ (this is a path from u_0 to u_0) satisfies $C(\langle u_0 \rangle) = 0$.

(3) The graph does not contain a cycle of negative cost.

(These criteria are satisfied by minimum-hop and shortest-path cost criteria.) A path from u to v is called *optimal* if there exists no path from u to v with lower cost. Observe that an optimal path is not always unique; there may exist different paths with the same (minimal) cost.

Lemma 4.1 *Let u, v be in V. If a path from u to v exists in G, then there exists a simple path that is optimal.*

Proof. As there are only a finite number of simple paths, there exists a simple path from u to v, say S_0, of lowest cost, i.e., for every *simple* path P' from u to v $C(S_0) \leq C(P')$. It remains to show that $C(S_0)$ is a lower bound for the cost of every (non-simple) path.

Write $V = \{v_1, \ldots, v_N\}$. By successively eliminating from P cycles that include v_1, v_2, etc., it will be shown that for each path P from u to v there exists a simple path P' with $C(P') \leq C(P)$. Let $P_0 = P$, and construct for $i = 1, \ldots, N$ the path P_i as follows. If v_i occurs at most once in P_{i-1} then $P_i = P_{i-1}$. Otherwise, write $P_{i-1} = \langle u_0, \ldots, u_k \rangle$, let u_{j_1} be the first and u_{j_2} be the last occurrence of v_i in P_{i-1}, and let

$$P_i = \langle u_0, \ldots, u_{j_1}(= u_{j_2}), u_{j_2+1}, \ldots, u_k \rangle.$$

By construction P_i is a path from u to v and contains all nodes of $\{v_1, \ldots, v_i\}$ at most once, hence P_N is a simple path from u to v. P_{i-1} consists of P_i and the cycle $Q = u_{j_1}, \ldots, u_{j_2}$, hence $C(P_{i-1}) = C(P_i) + C(Q)$. As there are no cycles of negative weight, this implies $C(P_i) \leq C(P_{i-1})$, and hence $C(P_N) \leq C(P)$.

By the choice of S_0, $C(S_0) \leq C(P_N)$, from which $C(S_0) \leq C(P)$ follows.

$\square$

If G contains cycles of negative weight an optimal path does not necessarily exist; each path can be beaten by another path that runs through the negative cycle once more. For the next theorem, assume that G is connected (for disconnected graphs the theorem can be applied to each connected component separately).

Theorem 4.2 *For each $d \in V$ there exists a tree $T_d = (V, E_d)$ such that $E_d \subseteq E$ and such that for each node $v \in V$, the path from v to d in T_d is an optimal path from v to d in G.*

Proof. Let $V = \{v_1, \ldots, v_N\}$. We shall inductively construct a series of trees $T_i = (V_i, E_i)$ (for $i = 0, \ldots, N$) with the following properties.

(1) Each T_i is a subtree of G, i.e., $V_i \subseteq V$, $E_i \subseteq E$, and T_i is a tree.
(2) Each T_i (for $i < N$) is a subtree of T_{i+1}.
(3) For all $i > 0$, $v_i \in V_i$ and $d \in V_i$.
(4) For all $w \in V_i$, the simple path from w to d in T_i is an optimal path from w to d in G.

These properties imply that T_N satisfies the requirements for T_d.

To construct the sequence of trees, set $V_0 = \{d\}$ and $E_0 = \varnothing$. The tree T_{i+1} is constructed as follows. Choose an optimal simple path $P = \langle u_0, \ldots, u_k \rangle$ from v_{i+1} to d, and let l be the smallest index such that $u_l \in T_i$ (such an l exists because $u_k = d \in T_i$; possibly $l = 0$). Now set

$$V_{i+1} = V_i \cup \{u_j : j < l\} \quad \text{and} \quad E_{i+1} = E_i \cup \{(u_j, u_{j+1}) : j < l\}.$$

(The construction is pictorially represented in Figure 4.1.) It is easy to verify that T_i is a subtree of T_{i+1} and that $v_{i+1} \in V_{i+1}$. To see that T_{i+1} is a tree, observe that by construction T_{i+1} is connected, and the number of nodes exceeds the number of edges by one. (T_0 has the latter property, and in each stage as many nodes as edges are added.)

It remains to show that for all $w \in V_{i+1}$, the (unique) path from w to d in T_{i+1} is an optimal path from w to d in G. For the nodes $w \in V_i \subset V_{i+1}$ this follows because T_i is a subtree of T_{i+1}; the path from w to d in T_{i+1} is the same as the path in T_i, which is optimal. Now let $w = u_j$, $j < l$ be a node in $V_{i+1} \setminus V_i$. Write Q for the path from u_l to d in T_i, then in T_{i+1} u_j is connected to d by the path $\langle u_j, \ldots, u_l \rangle$ concatenated with Q, and it remains

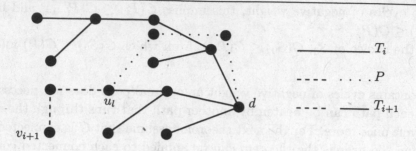

Figure 4.1 THE CONSTRUCTION OF T_{i+1}.

to show that this path is optimal in G. First, the suffix $P' = \langle u_l, \ldots, u_k \rangle$ of P is an optimal path from u_l to d, i.e., $C(P') = C(Q)$: the optimality of Q implies $C(P') \geq C(Q)$, and $C(Q) < C(P')$ implies (by the additivity of path costs) that the path $\langle u_0, \ldots, u_l \rangle$ concatenated with Q has lower cost than P, contradicting the optimality of P. Now assume that a path R from u_j to d has lower cost than the path $\langle u_j, \ldots, u_l \rangle$ concatenated with Q. Then, by the previous observation, R has a lower cost than the suffix $\langle u_j, \ldots, u_k \rangle$ of P, and this implies (again by the additivity of path costs) that the path $\langle u_0, \ldots, u_j \rangle$ concatenated with R has lower cost than P, contradicting the optimality of P. □

A spanning tree rooted towards d is called a *sink tree* for d, and a tree with the property given in Theorem 4.2 is called an *optimal sink tree*. The existence of optimal sink trees implies that it is no compromise to optimality if only routing algorithms are considered for which the forwarding mechanism is as in Algorithm 4.2. In that algorithm, *table_lookup*$_u$ is a local procedure with one argument, returning a neighbor of u (after consulting the routing tables). Indeed, as all packets for destination d can be routed optimally over a spanning tree rooted at d, forwarding is optimal if, for all $u \neq d$, *table_lookup*$_u(d)$ returns the father of u in the spanning tree T_d.

When the forwarding mechanism is of this form and no (further) topological changes occur, the correctness of routing tables can be certified using the following result. The routing tables are said to *contain a cycle* (for destination d) if there are nodes $u_1, \ldots, u_k$ such that for all i, $u_i \neq d$, for all $i < k$, *table_lookup*$_{u_i}(d) = u_{i+1}$, and *table_lookup*$_{u_k}(d) = u_1$. The tables are said to be *cycle-free* if they do not contain a cycle for any d.

(* A packet with destination d was received or generated at node u *)
if $d = u$
   then deliver the packet locally
   else send the packet to $table\_lookup_u(d)$

Algorithm 4.2 DESTINATION-BASED FORWARDING (FOR NODE u).

Lemma 4.3 *The forwarding mechanism delivers every packet at its destination if and only if the routing tables are cycle-free.*

Proof. If the tables contain a cycle for some destination d a packet for d is never delivered if its source is a node in the cycle.

Assume the tables are cycle-free and let a packet with destination d (and source u_0) be forwarded via $u_0, u_1, u_2, \ldots$. If the same node occurs twice in this sequence, say $u_i = u_j$, then the tables contain a cycle, namely $\langle u_i, \ldots, u_j \rangle$, contradicting the assumption that the tables are cycle-free. Thus, each node occurs at most once, which implies that this sequence is finite, ending, say, in node u_k $(k < N)$. According to the forwarding procedure the sequence can only end in d, i.e., $u_k = d$ and the packet has reached its destination in at most $N - 1$ hops. $\qquad\square$

In some routing algorithms it is the case that the tables are not cycle-free during their computation, but only when the table computation phase has finished. When such an algorithm is used, a packet may traverse a cycle during computation of the tables, but reaches its destination in at most $N - 1$ hops after completion of the table computation if topological changes cease. If topological changes do not cease, i.e., the network is subject to an infinite sequence of topological changes, packets do not necessarily reach their destination even if tables are cycle-free during updates; see Exercise 4.1.

Bifurcated routing for minimum delay. If routing via minimum-delay paths is required, and the delay of a channel depends on its utilization (thus assumption (1) at the beginning of this section is not valid), the cost of using a path cannot simply be assessed as a function of this path alone. In addition, the traffic on the channel must be taken into account. To avoid congestion (and the resulting higher delay) on a path, it is usually necessary to send packets having the same source–destination pair via different paths; the traffic for this pair "splits" at one or more intermediate nodes as depicted in Figure 4.3. Routing methods that use different paths towards the same destination are called *multiple-path* or *bifurcated* routing methods.

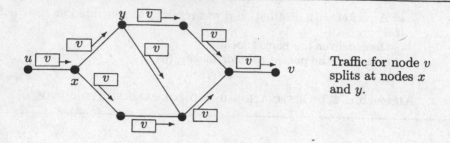

Traffic for node v
splits at nodes x
and y.

Figure 4.3 EXAMPLE OF BIFURCATED ROUTING.

Because bifurcated routing methods are usually very intricate, they will not
be treated in this chapter.

4.2 The All-pairs Shortest-path Problem

This section discusses an algorithm by Toueg [Tou80a] for computing simultaneously the routing tables for all nodes in a network. The algorithm
computes for each pair (u, v) of nodes the length of a shortest path from u to
v and stores the first channel of such a path in u. The problem of computing
a shortest path between any two nodes of a graph is known as the all-pairs
shortest-path problem. Toueg's distributed algorithm for this problem is
based on the centralized Floyd–Warshall algorithm [CLR90, Section 26.4].
We shall discuss the Floyd–Warshall algorithm in Subsection 4.2.1, and subsequently Toueg's algorithm in Subsection 4.2.2. A brief discussion of some
other algorithms for the all-pairs shortest-path problem follows in Subsection 4.2.3.

4.2.1 The Floyd–Warshall Algorithm

Let a weighted graph $G = (V, E)$ be given, where the weight of edge uv is
given by ω_{uv}. It is not necessary to assume that $\omega_{uv} = \omega_{vu}$, but it will be
assumed that the graph contains no cycles of total negative weight. The
weight of a path $\langle u_0, \ldots, u_k \rangle$ is defined as $\sum_{i=0}^{k-1} \omega_{u_i u_{i+1}}$. The *distance* from
u to v, denoted $d(u, v)$, is the lowest weight of any path from u to v (∞
if no such path exists). The all-pairs shortest-path problem is to compute
$d(u, v)$ for each u and v. (In Section 4.2.2 the algorithm will be augmented
to store the first edge of such a path as well.)

To compute all distances, the Floyd–Warshall algorithm uses the notion of

S-paths; these are paths in which all *intermediate* nodes belong to a subset S of V.

Definition 4.4 *Let S be a subset of V. A path $\langle u_0, \ldots, u_k \rangle$ is an S-path if for all i, $0 < i < k$, $u_i \in S$. The S-distance from u to v, denoted $d^S(u, v)$, is the lowest weight of any S-path from u to v (∞ if no such path exists).*

The algorithm starts by considering all $\varnothing$-paths, and incrementally computes S-paths for larger subsets S, until all V-paths have been considered. The following observations can be made.

Proposition 4.5 *For all u and S, $d^S(u, u) = 0$. Further, S-paths satisfy the following rules for $u \neq v$.*

(1) *There exists an $\varnothing$-path from u to v if and only if $uv \in E$.*

(2) *If $uv \in E$ then $d^\varnothing(u, v) = \omega_{uv}$, otherwise $d^\varnothing(u, v) = \infty$.*

(3) *If $S' = S \cup \{w\}$ then a simple S'-path from u to v is an S-path from u to v or an S-path from u to w concatenated with an S-path from w to v.*

(4) *If $S' = S \cup \{w\}$ then $d^{S'}(u, v) = \min\left(d^S(u, v), d^S(u, w) + d^S(w, v) \right)$.*

(5) *A path from u to v exists if and only if a V-path from u to v exists.*

(6) *$d(u, v) = d^V(u, v)$,*

Proof. For all u and S, $d^S(u, u) \leq 0$ because the empty path (consisting of zero edges) is an S-path from u to u of weight 0. No path has a smaller weight, because G contains no cycles of negative weight, so $d^S(u, u) = 0$.

For (1): an $\varnothing$-path has no intermediate nodes, so an $\varnothing$-path from u to v consists only of the channel uv.

For (2): this follows immediately from (1).

For (3): a simple S'-path from u to v contains node w either once, or zero times as an intermediate node. If it does not contain w as an intermediate node it is an S-path, otherwise it is the concatenation of two S-paths, one to w and one from w.

For (4): it can be shown by an application of Lemma 4.1 that (if an S'-path from u to v exists) there is a *simple S'* path of length $d^{S'}(u, v)$ from u to v, which implies $d^{S'}(u, v) = \min\left(d^S(u, v), d^S(u, w) + d^S(w, v) \right)$ by (3).

For (5): each V-path is a path, and vice versa.

For (6): each V-path is a path, and vice versa, hence an optimal V-path is also an optimal path.

$\square$

begin (* Initialize S to $\varnothing$ and D to $\varnothing$-distance *)
    $S := \varnothing$;
    forall u, v **do**
        if $u = v$ **then** $D[u, v] := 0$
        else if $uv \in E$ **then** $D[u, v] := \omega_{uv}$
                else $D[u, v] := \infty$;
    (* Expand S by pivoting *)
    while $S \neq V$ **do**
        (* Loop invariant: $\forall u, v : D[u, v] = d^S(u, v)$ *)
        begin pick w from $V \setminus S$;
            (* Execute a global w-pivot *)
            forall $u \in V$ **do**
                (* Execute a local w-pivot at u *)
                forall $v \in V$ **do**
                      $D[u, v] := \min\,(\,D[u, v], D[u, w] + D[w, v]\,)$;
        $S := S \cup \{w\}$
    end   (* $\forall u, v : D[u, v] = d(u, v)$ *)
end

Algorithm 4.4 The Floyd–Warshall algorithm.

Using Proposition 4.5 it is not difficult to design a "dynamic programming" algorithm to solve the all-pairs shortest-path problem; see Algorithm 4.4. The algorithm first considers $\varnothing$-paths, and incrementally computes S-paths for larger sets S (enlarging S by means of "pivot" rounds), until all paths have been considered.

Theorem 4.6 *Algorithm 4.4 computes the distance between each pair of nodes in $\Theta(N^3)$ steps.*

Proof. The algorithm starts with $D[u, v] = 0$ if $u = v$, $D[u, v] = \omega_{uv}$ if $uv \in E$ and $D[u, v] = \infty$ otherwise, and $S = \varnothing$. Hence by Proposition 4.5, parts (1) and (2), $\forall u, v : D[u, v] = d^S(u, v)$ holds. In a pivot round with pivot-node w the set S is expanded with w, and the assignment to $D[u, v]$ ensures (by parts (3) and (4) of the proposition) that the assertion $\forall u, v : D[u, v] = d^S(u, v)$ is preserved as a loop invariant. The program terminates when $S = V$, i.e., (by parts (5) and (6) of the proposition and the loop invariant) the S-distances equal the distances.

The main loop is executed N times, and contains N^2 operations (which can be executed in parallel or serially), which implies the time bound stated in the theorem. $\qquad\square$

```
var S_u    : set of nodes ;
    D_u    : array of weights ;
    Nb_u   : array of nodes ;

begin S_u := ∅ ;
      forall v ∈ V do
          if v = u
              then begin D_u[v] := 0 ; Nb_u[v] := udef end
              else if v ∈ Neigh_u
                  then begin D_u[v] := ω_uv ; Nb_u[v] := v end
                  else begin D_u[v] := ∞ ; Nb_u[v] := udef end ;
      while S_u ≠ V do
          begin pick w from V \ S_u ;
                (* All nodes must pick the same node w here *)
                if u = w
                    then "broadcast the table D_w"
                    else "receive the table D_w" ;
                forall v ∈ V do
                    if D_u[w] + D_w[v] < D_u[v] then
                        begin D_u[v] := D_u[w] + D_w[v] ;
                              Nb_u[v] := Nb_u[w]

                        end ;
                S_u := S_u ∪ {w}
          end
end
```

Algorithm 4.5 THE SIMPLE ALGORITHM (FOR NODE u).

4.2.2 Toueg's Shortest-path Algorithm

A distributed algorithm for computing routing tables was given by Toueg [Tou80a], based on the Floyd–Warshall algorithm described in the previous subsection. It must be verified that the Floyd–Warshall algorithm is suitable for this purpose, i.e., that its assumptions are realistic in distributed systems. The most important assumption of the algorithm is that the graph does not contain cycles of negative weight. This assumption is indeed realistic for distributed systems, where it is usually the case that each individual channel is assigned a positive cost. An even stronger assumption will be made; see A1 below.

In this subsection the following assumptions are made.

A1. Each cycle in the network has a positive weight.

A2. Each node in the network initially knows the identities of all nodes (the set V).

A3. Each node knows which of the nodes are its neighbors (stored in $Neigh_u$ for node u) and the weights of its outgoing channels.

The correctness of Toueg's algorithm (Algorithm 4.6) will be more easily understood if we first consider a preliminary version of it, the "simple algorithm" (Algorithm 4.5).

The simple algorithm. To arrive at a distributed algorithm the variables and operations of the Floyd–Warshall algorithm are partitioned over the nodes of the network. The variable $D[u, v]$ is a variable belonging to node u; by convention, this will be expressed by subscripting: write $D_u[v]$ from now on. An operation that assigns a value to $D_u[v]$ must be executed by node u, and when the value of a variable of node w is needed in this operation, this value must be sent to u. In the Floyd–Warshall algorithm all nodes must use information from the pivot node (w in the loop body), which sends this information to all nodes simultaneously by a "broadcast" operation. Finally, the algorithm will be augmented with an operation to maintain not only the *lengths* of shortest S-paths (as in the variable $D_u[v]$), but also the first channel of such a path (in the variable $Nb_u[v]$).

The assumption that a cycle in the network has positive weight can be used to show that no cycles occur in the routing tables after each pivot round.

Lemma 4.7 *Let S and w be given and suppose that*

(1) *for all u $D_u[w] = d^S(u, w)$ and*
(2) *if $d^S(u, w) < \infty$ and $u \neq w$, then $Nb_u[w]$ is the first channel of a shortest S-path to w.*

Then the directed graph $T_w = (V_w, E_w)$, where

$$(u \in V_w \iff D_u[w] < \infty) \quad and \quad (ux \in E_w \iff (u \neq w \wedge Nb_u[w] = x))$$

is a tree rooted towards w.

Proof. First observe that if $D_u[w] < \infty$ for $u \neq w$, then $Nb_u[w] \neq udef$ and $D_{Nb_u[w]}[w] < \infty$. So for each node $u \in V_w$, $u \neq w$ there is a node x for which $Nb_u[w] = x$, and this node satisfies $x \in V_w$.

For each node $u \neq w$ in V_w there is one edge in E_w, so the number of nodes of T_w exceeds the number of edges by one and it suffices to show that T_w contains no cycle. As $ux \in E_w$ implies that $d^S(u, w) = \omega_{ux} + d^S(x, w)$, the existence of a cycle $\langle u_0, u_1, \ldots, u_k \rangle$ in T_w implies that

$$d^S(u_0, w) = \omega_{u_0 u_1} + \omega_{u_1 u_2} + \cdots + \omega u_{k-1} u_0 + d^S(u_0, w),$$

i.e.,

$$0 = \omega_{u_0 u_1} + \omega_{u_1 u_2} + \cdots + \omega u_{k-1} u_0,$$

which contradicts the assumption that each cycle has positive weight.   □

The Floyd–Warshall algorithm can now be transformed in a straightforward way to obtain Algorithm 4.5. Each node initializes its own variables and executes N iterations of the main loop. The algorithm is not the ultimate solution, and it is not given completely because we have not specified how the broadcast of the table of the pivot node can be done (efficiently). For now it suffices to take for granted that because the operation "broadcast the table D_w" is executed by w and the operation "receive the table D_w" is executed by the other nodes, each node has access to the table D_w.

Some care must be given to the operation "pick w from $V \setminus S$", in order to guarantee that the nodes select the pivots in the same order. As it is assumed that all nodes know V in advance, we can simply assume that the nodes are selected in some prescribed order (e.g., the alphabetical order of the node names).

The correctness of the simple algorithm is expressed in the following theorem.

Theorem 4.8 *Algorithm 4.5 terminates in each node after N iterations of the main loop. When the algorithm terminates in node u, $D_u[v] = d(u, v)$, and if a path from u to v exists then $Nb_u[v]$ is the first channel of a shortest path from u to v, otherwise $Nb_u[v] = udef$.*

Proof. The termination and the correctness of $D_u[v]$ on termination follow from the correctness of the Floyd–Warshall algorithm (Theorem 4.6). The statement about the value of $Nb_u[v]$ follows because $Nb_u[v]$ is updated each time $D_u[v]$ is assigned.   □

The improved algorithm. In order to do the broadcast in Algorithm 4.5 efficiently, Toueg observes that a node u for which $D_u[w] = \infty$ at the start of the w-pivot round does not change its tables during the w-pivot round. If $D_u[w] = \infty$, $D_u[w] + D_w[v] < D_u[v]$ is false for every v. Consequently, only the nodes that belong to T_w (at the beginning of the w-pivot round) need to receive w's table, and the broadcast operation can be done efficiently by sending the table D_w only via the channels that belong to the tree T_w. That is, w sends D_w to its sons in T_w, and each node of T_w that receives the table (from its father in T_w) forwards it to its sons in T_w.

At the beginning of the w-pivot round a node u with $D_u[w] < \infty$ knows

```
var S_u    : set of nodes ;
    D_u    : array of weights ;
    Nb_u   : array of nodes ;

begin S_u := ∅ ;
      forall v ∈ V do
          if v = u
              then begin D_u[v] := 0 ; Nb_u[v] := udef end
              else if v ∈ Neigh_u
                      then begin D_u[v] := ω_uv ; Nb_u[v] := v end
                      else begin D_u[v] := ∞ ; Nb_u[v] := udef end ;
      while S_u ≠ V do
          begin pick w from V \ S_u ;
                (* Construct the tree T_w *)
                forall x ∈ Neigh_u do
                    if Nb_u[w] = x then send ⟨ys, w⟩ to x
                                   else send ⟨nys, w⟩ to x ;
                num_rec_u := 0 ; (* u must receive |Neigh_u| messages *)
                while num_rec_u < |Neigh_u| do
                    begin receive ⟨ys, w⟩ or ⟨nys, w⟩ message ;
                          num_rec_u := num_rec_u + 1
                    end ;
                if D_u[w] < ∞ then (* participate in pivot round *)
                    begin if u ≠ w
                              then receive ⟨dtab, w, D⟩ fromthis Nb_u[w] ;
                          forall x ∈ Neigh_u do
                              if ⟨ys, w⟩ was received from x
                                  then send ⟨dtab, w, D⟩ to x ;
                          forall v ∈ V do (* local w-pivot *)
                              if D_u[w] + D[v] < D_u[v] then
                                  begin D_u[v] := D_u[w] + D[v] ;
                                        Nb_u[v] := Nb_u[w]
                                  end
                    end ;
                S_u := S_u ∪ {w}
          end
end
```

Algorithm 4.6 TOUEG'S ALGORITHM (FOR NODE u).

who its father (in T_w) is, but not who its sons are. Therefore each node v must send a message to each of its neighbors u, telling u whether v is a son of u in T_w. The full algorithm is now given as Algorithm 4.6. A node can participate in the forwarding of w's table when it knows which of its neighbors are its sons in T_w. The algorithm uses three types of messages:

(1) A $\langle \mathbf{ys}, w \rangle$ message ($\mathbf{ys}$ stands for "your son") is sent by u to x at the beginning of the w-pivot round if x is the father of u in T_w.

(2) A $\langle \mathbf{nys}, w \rangle$ message ($\mathbf{nys}$ stands for "not your son") is sent by u to x at the beginning of the w-pivot round if x is not the father of u in T_w.

(3) A $\langle \mathbf{dtab}, w, D \rangle$ message is sent during the w-pivot round via each edge of T_w to transmit the value of D_w to each node that must use this value.

Assuming that a weight (of an edge or path) together with a node name can be represented by W bits, the complexity of the algorithm is expressed in the following theorem.

Theorem 4.9 *Algorithm 4.6 computes for each u and v the distance from u to v, and, if this distance is finite, the first channel of a path of this length. The algorithm exchanges $O(N)$ messages per channel, $O(N \cdot |E|)$ messages in total, $O(N^2 W)$ bits per channel, $O(N^3 W)$ bits in total, and requires $O(NW)$ bits of storage per node.*

Proof. Algorithm 4.6 is derived from Algorithm 4.5, which implies its correctness.

Each channel carries two $\langle \mathbf{ys}, w \rangle$ or $\langle \mathbf{nys}, w \rangle$ messages (one in each direction) and at most one $\langle \mathbf{dtab}, w, D \rangle$ message in the w-pivot round, which totals to at most $3N$ messages per channel. A $\langle \mathbf{ys}, w \rangle$ or $\langle \mathbf{nys}, w \rangle$ message contains $O(W)$ bits and a $\langle \mathbf{dtab}, w, D \rangle$ message contains $O(NW)$ bits, which gives the bound on the number of bits per channel. At most N^2 $\langle \mathbf{dtab}, w, D \rangle$ messages and $2N \cdot |E|$ $\langle \mathbf{ys}, w \rangle$ and $\langle \mathbf{nys}, w \rangle$ messages are exchanged, which totals to $O(N^2 \cdot NW + 2N \cdot |E| \cdot W) = O(N^3 W)$ bits altogether. The D_u and Nb_u tables maintained in node u require $O(NW)$ bits. $\square$

During the w-pivot round a node is allowed to receive and process only the messages of that round, i.e., those that carry the parameter w. If the channels satisfy the fifo property then the $\langle \mathbf{ys}, w \rangle$ and $\langle \mathbf{nys}, w \rangle$ messages arrive as the first messages after a node has started that round, one via each channel, and then the $\langle \mathbf{dtab}, w, D \rangle$ message is the next to arrive from $Nb_u[w]$ (if the node is in V_w). It is possible by careful programming to omit the parameter w from all messages if the channels are fifo. If the channels are not fifo it is possible that a message with parameter w' arrives while a node expects messages for round w, where w' is the pivot after w. In this case the parameter is used to distinguish the messages for each pivot round, and local buffering (either in the channel or in the node) must be used to defer processing of the w'-message.

Toueg gives a further optimization of the algorithm, relying on the following result. (Node u_2 is a *descendant* of u_1 if u_2 belongs to the subtree of u_1.)

Lemma 4.10 *Let $u_1 \neq w$, and let u_2 be a descendant of u_1 in T_w at the beginning of the w-pivot round. If u_2 changes its distance to v in the w-pivot round, then u_1 changes its distance to v in the w-pivot round.*

Proof. As u_2 is a descendant of u_1 in T_w,

$$d^S(u_2, w) = d^S(u_2, u_1) + d^S(u_1, w). \tag{1}$$

Because $u_1 \in S$,

$$d^S(u_2, v) \leq d^S(u_2, u_1) + d^S(u_1, v). \tag{2}$$

Node u_2 changes $D_{u_2}[v]$ in this round iff

$$d^S(u_2, w) + d^S(w, v) < d^S(u_2, v). \tag{3}$$

By applying (2), and then (1), and subtracting $d^S(u_2, u_1)$, we obtain

$$d^S(u_1, w) + d^S(w, v) < d^S(u_1, v), \tag{4}$$

implying that u_1 changes $D_{u_1}[v]$ in this round.   □

According to this lemma, Algorithm 4.6 can be modified as follows. After the receipt of the table D_w (message $\langle \mathbf{dtab}, w, D \rangle$) node u first executes the local w-pivot operation, and then forwards the table to its sons in T_w. When forwarding the table it suffices to send those entries $D[v]$ for which $D_u[v]$ has changed as a result of the local w-pivot operation. With this modification the routing tables are cycle-free not only between pivot rounds (as expressed in Lemma 4.7), but also during pivot rounds.

4.2.3 Discussion and More Algorithms

The presentation of Toueg's algorithm provides an example of how a distributed algorithm can be obtained in a straightforward manner from a sequential algorithm. To this end, the variables of the sequential algorithm are dispersed over the processes, and any assignment to variable x (in the sequential algorithm) is executed by the process holding x. Whenever the assigned expression contains references to variables held by other processes, communication between processes is required in order to pass the value of this variable and to synchronize the processes. Specific properties of the sequential algorithm can be exploited to minimize the required amount of communication.

Toueg's algorithm is reasonably simple to understand, has low complexity, and routes via optimal paths; its main disadvantage is its bad robustness. When the topology of the network changes the entire computation must be performed anew. In addition, the algorithm has two properties that make it less attractive from the viewpoint of distributed algorithms engineering.

First, as already mentioned, the uniform selection by all nodes of the next pivot node (w) requires that the set of participating nodes is precisely known in advance. As this knowledge is in general not available a priori, the execution of an additional distributed algorithm to compute this set (e.g., Finn's algorithm, Algorithm 6.9) must precede execution of Toueg's algorithm.

Second, Toueg's algorithm is based on repeated application of the *triangle inequality* $d(u, v) \leq d(u, w) + d(w, v)$. Evaluating the right-hand side (by u) requires information about $d(w, v)$, and this information is in general *remote*, i.e., available neither in u nor in any of its neighbors. Dependence on remote data necessitates the transport of information to remote nodes, which can be observed in Toueg's algorithm (the broadcasting part).

Alternatively, the following defining equation for $d(u, v)$ can be used in algorithms for shortest-path problems:

$$d(u, v) = \begin{cases} 0 & \text{if } u = v \\ \min_{w \in Neigh_u} \omega_{uw} + d(w, v) & \text{otherwise} \end{cases} \qquad (4.1)$$

Two properties of this equation make algorithms based upon it different from Toueg's algorithm.

(1) *Data locality.* In order to evaluate the right-hand side of Equation (4.1), node u only needs information available locally (namely, ω_{uw}) or at a neighbor (namely, $d(w, v)$). The transportation of data between remote nodes is avoided.

(2) *Destination independence.* Only distances *to* v (namely, $d(w, v)$ for neighbors w of u) are needed to compute the distance from u to v. Thus, the computation of all distances to a fixed destination v_0 can proceed independently of the computation of distances to other nodes, and also, can be studied in isolation.

In the remainder of this section two algorithms based on Equation (4.1) are discussed, namely, the Merlin–Segall and Chandy–Misra algorithms. Despite the advantage offered by data locality, the communication complexity of these algorithms is no improvement over Toueg's algorithm. This is due to the destination independence introduced by Equation (4.1); apparently, using results for other destinations (as is done in Toueg's algorithm) is a more profitable technique than introducing data locality.

If it does not lead to a reduced communication complexity, then what is the importance of data locality? Reliance on remote data requires the latter's repeated broadcast if data can change due to topological changes in the network (channel and node failures and repairs). Achieving these broadcasts (under the possibility of new topological changes during the broadcast) turns out to be a non-trivial problem with expensive solutions (see, e.g., [Gaf87]). Therefore, algorithms based upon Equation 4.1 can be more easily adapted to handle topological changes. This is exemplified in Section 4.3, where such an algorithm is discussed in depth.

The Merlin–Segall algorithm. The algorithm proposed by Merlin and Segall [MS79] computes the routing tables for each destination completely separately; the computations for different destinations do not influence each other. For a destination v, the algorithm starts with a tree T_v rooted towards v, and repeatedly updates this tree so as to become an optimal sink tree for destination v.

For destination v, each node u maintains an estimate for the distance to v ($D_u[v]$) and the neighbor to which packets for u are forwarded ($Nb_u[v]$), which is also the father of u in T_v. In an update round each node u sends its estimated distance, $D_u[v]$, to all neighbors *except* $Nb_u[v]$ (in a $\langle \mathbf{mydist}, v, D_u[v] \rangle$ message). If node u receives from neighbor w a message $\langle \mathbf{mydist}, v, d \rangle$ and if $d + \omega_{uw} < D_u[v]$, u will change $Nb_u[v]$ to w and $D_u[v]$ to $d + \omega_{uw}$. The update round is controlled by v and requires the exchange of two messages of W bits on each channel.

It is shown in [MS79] that after i update rounds all shortest paths of at most i hops have been correctly computed, so that after at most N rounds all shortest paths to v are computed. Shortest paths to each destination are computed by executing the algorithm independently for each destination.

Theorem 4.11 *The algorithm of Merlin and Segall computes shortest-path routing tables by exchanging $O(N^2)$ messages per channel, $O(N^2 \cdot W)$ bits per channel, $O(N^2 \cdot |E|)$ messages in total, and $O(N^2 \cdot |E|W)$ bits in total.*

The algorithm can also adapt to changes in the topology and the weight of channels. An important property of the algorithm is that during update rounds also the routing tables are cycle-free.

var $D_u[v_0]$: weight   **init** ∞ ;
      $Nb_u[v_0]$: node   **init** $udef$;

For node v_0 only:
    begin $D_{v_0}[v_0] := 0$;
           forall $w \in Neigh_{v_0}$ **do** send $\langle \mathbf{mydist}, v_0, 0 \rangle$ to w
    end

Processing a $\langle \mathbf{mydist}, v_0, d \rangle$ message from neighbor w by u:
    $\{ \langle \mathbf{mydist}, v_0, d \rangle \in M_{wu} \}$
    begin receive $\langle \mathbf{mydist}, v_0, d \rangle$ from w ;
         if $d + \omega_{uw} < D_u[v_0]$ **then**
            begin $D_u[v_0] := d + \omega_{uw}$; $Nb_u[v_0] := w$;
                forall $x \in Neigh_u$ **do** send $\langle \mathbf{mydist}, v_0, D_u[v_0] \rangle$ to x
            end
    end

Algorithm 4.7 THE CHANDY–MISRA ALGORITHM (FOR NODE u).

The Chandy–Misra algorithm. The algorithm proposed by Chandy and Misra [CM82] computes all shortest paths towards one destination using the paradigm of *diffusing computations*, that is, a distributed computation that is initiated by a single node, and joined by other nodes only after receiving a message.

To compute, for all nodes, the distance to node v_0 (and a preferred outgoing channel), each node u starts with $D_u[v_0] = \infty$ and waits for the receipt of messages. Node v_0 sends a $\langle \mathbf{mydist}, v_0, 0 \rangle$ message to all neighbors. Whenever node u receives a $\langle \mathbf{mydist}, v_0, d \rangle$ message from neighbor w, where $d + \omega_{uw} < D_u[v_0]$, u assigns $d + \omega_{uw}$ to $D_u[v_0]$ and sends a $\langle \mathbf{mydist}, v_0, D_u[v_0] \rangle$ message to all neighbors; see Algorithm 4.7.

It is not difficult to show that $D_u[v_0]$ is always an upper bound for $d(u, v_0)$, i.e., $d(u, v_0) \leq D_u[v_0]$ is implied by an invariant of the algorithm; see Exercise 4.3. To demonstrate that the algorithm computes the distances correctly, it must be shown that eventually a configuration is reached in which $D_u[v_0] \leq d(u, v_0)$ also holds for each u. We supply a proof of this property that uses an assumed weak fairness assumption, namely, that each message that is sent is eventually received in each computation. It is also possible to give a proof that does not rely on this assumption, but it is rather complicated.

Theorem 4.12 *In each computation of Algorithm 4.7 a configuration is reached in which, for each node u, $D_u[v_0] \leq d(u, v_0)$.*

Proof. Fix an optimal sink tree T for v_0 and number the nodes other than v_0 by v_1 through v_{N-1} in such a way that if v_i is the father of v_j, then $i < j$. Let C be a computation; it will be shown by induction on j that for each $j \leq N - 1$ a configuration is reached in which, for each $i \leq j$, $D_{v_i}[v_0] \leq d(v_i, v_0)$. Observe that $D_{v_i}[v_0]$ never increases in the algorithm; so if $D_{v_i}[v_0] \leq d(v_i, v_0)$ holds in some configuration, it holds in all subsequent configurations as well.

The case $j = 0$: $d(v_0, v_0) = 0$, and $D_{v_0}[v_0] = 0$ after the execution of the initialization part by v_0, , so $D_{v_0}[v_0] \leq d(v_0, v_0)$ holds after this execution.

The case $j + 1$: Assume a configuration is reached in which for each $i \leq j$, $D_{v_i}[v_0] \leq d(v_i, v_0)$, and consider node v_{j+1}. There is a shortest path $v_{j+1}, v_i, \ldots, v_0$ of length $d(v_{j+1}, v_0)$ from v_{j+1} to v_0, where v_i is the father of v_{j+1} in T, hence $i \leq j$. Consequently, by the induction hypothesis, a configuration is reached in which $D_{v_i}[v_0] \leq d(v_i, v_0)$. Whenever $D_{v_i}[v_0]$ decreases, v_i sends $\langle \mathbf{mydist}, v_0, D_{v_i}[v_0] \rangle$ messages to its neighbors, hence a $\langle \mathbf{mydist}, v_0, d \rangle$ message is sent to v_{j+1} at least once with $d \leq d(v_i, v_0)$.

By assumption, this message is received in C by v_{j+1}. The algorithm implies that after receipt of this message $D_{v_{j+1}}[v_0] \leq d + \omega v_{j+1} v_i$ holds, and the choice of i implies that $d + \omega v_{j+1} v_i \leq d(v_{j+1}, v_0)$.

$\square$

The full algorithm also includes a mechanism by which the nodes can detect that the computation has been completed; compare with the remark about the Netchange algorithm at the beginning of Subsection 4.3.3. The mechanism to detect this completion is a variation of the Dijkstra–Scholten algorithm discussed in Subsection 8.2.1.

The algorithm differs from the Merlin–Segall algorithm in two respects. First, there is no "father" of a node u that is excepted from being sent messages of the type $\langle \mathbf{mydist}, ., . \rangle$. This feature of the algorithm of Merlin and Segall ensures that the tables are always cycle-free, even during computation and in the presence of topological changes. Second, the exchange of $\langle \mathbf{mydist}, ., . \rangle$ messages is not coordinated in rounds, but takes place completely arbitrarily, which influences the complexity in a unfavorable way. The algorithm may require an exponential number of messages to compute the paths toward a single destination v_0. If all channel costs are assumed to be equal (i.e., minimum-hop routing is considered) all shortest paths towards v_0 are computed using $\mathrm{O}(N \cdot |E|)$ messages (of $\mathrm{O}(W)$ bits each), leading to the following result.

Theorem 4.13 *The algorithm of Chandy and Misra computes minimum-hop routing tables by exchanging* $O(N^2)$ *messages and* $O(N^2 W)$ *bits per channel, and* $O(N^2 \cdot |E|)$ *messages and* $O(N^2 \cdot |E| \cdot W)$ *bits in total.*

An advantage of the algorithm of Chandy and Misra over that of Merlin and Segall is its simplicity, its smaller space complexity, and its lower time complexity.

4.3 The Netchange Algorithm

Tajibnapis' Netchange algorithm [Taj77] computes routing tables that are optimal according to the "minimum-hop" measure. The algorithm can be compared to the Chandy–Misra algorithm, but maintains additional information that allows the tables to be updated with only a *partial* recomputation after the failure or repair of a channel. The presentation of the algorithm in this section follows Lamport [Lam82]. The algorithm relies on the following assumptions.

N1. The nodes know the size of the network (N).
N2. The channels satisfy the fifo assumption.
N3. Nodes are notified of failures and repairs of their adjacent channels.
N4. The cost of a path equals the number of channels in the path.

The algorithm can handle the failure and repair or addition of channels, but it is assumed that a node is notified when an adjacent channel fails or recovers. The failure and recovery of nodes is not considered; instead it is assumed that the failure of a node is observed by its neighbors as the failure of the connecting channel. The algorithm maintains in each node u a table $Nb_u[v]$, giving for each destination v a neighbor of u to which packets for v will be forwarded. It cannot be required that the computation of these tables terminates within a finite number of steps in all cases because the repeated failure or repair of channels may ask for recomputation indefinitely. The requirements of the algorithm are as follows.

R1. If the topology of the network remains constant after a finite number of topological changes, then the algorithm terminates after a finite number of steps.
R2. When the algorithm terminates the tables $Nb_u[v]$ satisfy
   (a) if $v = u$ then $Nb_u[v] = local$;
   (b) if a path from u to $v \neq u$ exists then $Nb_u[v] = w$, where w is the first neighbor of u on a shortest path from u to v;
   (c) if no path from u to v exists then $Nb_u[v] = udef$.

var $Neigh_u$: set of nodes ;   (* The neighbors of u *)
   D_u : array of 0.. N ;   (* $D_u[v]$ estimates $d(u, v)$ *)
   Nb_u : array of nodes ;   (* $Nb_u[v]$ is preferred neighbor for v *)
   $ndis_u$: array of 0.. N ;   (* $ndis_u[w, v]$ estimates $d(w, v)$ *)

Initialization:
   begin forall $w \in Neigh_u$, $v \in V$ **do** $ndis_u[w, v] := N$;
        forall $v \in V$ **do**
               begin $D_u[v] := N$; $Nb_u[v] := udef$ **end** ;
        $D_u[u] := 0$; $Nb_u[u] := local$;
        forall $w \in Neigh_u$ **do** send $\langle$ **mydist**, $u, 0 \rangle$ to w
  end

Procedure *Recompute* (v):
   begin if $v = u$
        then begin $D_u[v] := 0$; $Nb_u[v] := local$ **end**
        else begin (* Estimate distance to v *)
               $d := 1 + \min\{ndis_u[w, v] : w \in Neigh_u\}$;
               if $d < N$ **then**
                   begin $D_u[v] := d$;
                            $Nb_u[v] := w$ with $1 + ndis_u[w, v] = d$
                   end
               else begin $D_u[v] := N$; $Nb_u[v] := udef$ **end**
        end ;
      if $D_u[v]$ has changed **then**
        forall $x \in Neigh_u$ **do** send $\langle$ **mydist**, $v, D_u[v] \rangle$ to x
  end

Algorithm 4.8 THE NETCHANGE ALGORITHM (PART 1, FOR NODE u).

4.3.1 Description of the Algorithm

Tajibnapis' Netchange algorithm is given as Algorithms 4.8 and 4.9. The steps of the algorithm will first be motivated by an informal description of the operation of the algorithm, and subsequently the correctness of the algorithm will be proved formally. For sake of clear exposition the modeling of topological changes is simplified as compared to [Lam82] by assuming that the notification of the change is processed simultaneously in the two nodes affected by the change. It is indicated in Subsection 4.3.3 how asynchronous processing of these notifications is treated.

The selection of a neighbor to which packets for destination v will be forwarded is based on estimates of the distance of each node to v. The preferred neighbor is always the neighbor with the lowest estimate of this distance. Node u maintains an estimate $D_u[v]$ of $d(u, v)$ and estimates $ndis_u[w, v]$ of $d(w, v)$ for each neighbor w of u. The estimate $D_u[v]$ is

Processing a $\langle \mathbf{mydist}, v, d \rangle$ message from neighbor w:
  { A $\langle \mathbf{mydist}, v, d \rangle$ is at the head of Q_{wv} }
  begin receive $\langle \mathbf{mydist}, v, d \rangle$ from w ;
    $ndis_u[w, v] := d$; *Recompute* (v)
  end

Upon failure of channel uw:
  begin receive $\langle \mathbf{fail}, w \rangle$; $Neigh_u := Neigh_u \setminus \{w\}$;
    forall $v \in V$ **do** *Recompute* (v)
  end

Upon repair of channel uw:
  begin receive $\langle \mathbf{repair}, w \rangle$; $Neigh_u := Neigh_u \cup \{w\}$;
    forall $v \in V$ **do**
      begin $ndis_u[w, v] := N$;
        send $\langle \mathbf{mydist}, v, D_u[v] \rangle$ to w
      end
  end

Algorithm 4.9 THE NETCHANGE ALGORITHM (PART 2, FOR NODE u).

computed from the estimates $ndis_u[w, v]$, and the estimates $ndis_u[w, v]$ are obtained via communication with the neighbors.

The computation of the estimates $D_u[v]$ proceeds as follows. If $u = v$ then $d(u, v) = 0$ so $D_u[v]$ is set to 0 in this case. If $u \neq v$, a shortest path from u to v (if such a path exists) consists of a channel from u to a neighbor, concatenated with a shortest path from this neighbor to v, and consequently

$$d(u, v) = 1 + \min_{w \in Neigh_u} d(w, v).$$

Following this equation, node $u \neq v$ estimates $d(u, v)$ by applying this formula to the *estimated* values of $d(w, v)$, found in the tables as $ndis_u[w, v]$. As there are N nodes, a minimum-hop path has length at most $N - 1$. A node may suspect that no path exists if it computes an estimated distance of N or more; the value N is used in the table to represent this.

The algorithm requires a node to have an estimate of its neighbors' distances to v. These are obtained from these nodes because they communicate them in $\langle \mathbf{mydist}, ., . \rangle$ messages as follows. If node u computes the value d as an estimate of its distance to v ($D_u[v] = d$), this information is sent to all neighbors in a message $\langle \mathbf{mydist}, v, d \rangle$. Upon receipt of a message $\langle \mathbf{mydist}, v, d \rangle$ from neighbor w, u assigns $ndis_u[w, v]$ the value d. As a result of a change in $ndis_u[w, v]$ u's estimate of $d(u, v)$ can change and therefore the estimate is recomputed every time the $ndis_u$ table changes. If the estimate indeed changes, to d' say, this is of course communicated to the neighbors using $\langle \mathbf{mydist}, v, d' \rangle$ messages.

The algorithm reacts to failures and repairs of channels by modifying the local tables, and sending a $\langle \mathbf{mydist}, ., . \rangle$ message if distance-estimates change. We assume that the notification that nodes receive about channel ups and downs (assumption N3) is in the form of $\langle \mathbf{fail}, . \rangle$ and $\langle \mathbf{repair}, . \rangle$ messages. The channel between nodes u_1 and u_2 is modeled by two queues, $Q_{u_1u_2}$ for the messages from u_1 to u_2 and $Q_{u_2u_1}$ for the messages from u_2 to u_1. When a channel fails these queues are removed from the configuration (effectively causing all messages in both queues to be lost) and the nodes at both ends of the channel receive a $\langle \mathbf{fail}, . \rangle$ message. If the channel between u_1 and u_2 fails, u_1 receives a $\langle \mathbf{fail}, u_2 \rangle$ message and u_2 receives a $\langle \mathbf{fail}, u_1 \rangle$ message. When a channel is repaired (or a new channel is added to the network) two empty queues are added to the configuration and the two nodes connected by the channel receive a $\langle \mathbf{repair}, . \rangle$ message. If the channel between u_1 and u_2 comes up u_1 receives a $\langle \mathbf{repair}, u_2 \rangle$ message and u_2 receives a $\langle \mathbf{repair}, u_1 \rangle$ message.

The reaction of the algorithm to the failures and repairs is as follows. When the channel between u and w fails, w is removed from $Neigh_u$ and vice versa. The distance estimate for each destination is recomputed and, of course, sent to all remaining neighbors if it has changed. This is the case if the best route previously was via the failed channel and there is no other neighbor w' with $ndis_u[w', v] = ndis_u[w, v]$. When the channel is repaired (or a new channel is added) w is added to $Neigh_u$, but u has as yet no estimate of the distance $d(w, v)$ (and vice versa). The new neighbor w is immediately informed about $D_u[v]$ for all destinations v (by sending $\langle \mathbf{mydist}, v, D_u[v] \rangle$ messages). Until u receives similar messages from w, u uses N as an estimate for $d(w, v)$, i.e., it sets $ndis_u[w, v]$ to N.

Invariants of the Netchange algorithm. We shall prove a number of assertions to be invariants; the assertions are given in Figure 4.10. The assertion $P(u, w, v)$ states that if u has finished processing $\langle \mathbf{mydist}, v, . \rangle$ messages from w then u's estimate of $d(w, v)$ equals w's estimate of $d(w, v)$. Let the predicate $up(u, w)$ be true if and only if a (bidirectional) channel between u and w exists and is operating. The assertion $L(u, v)$ states that u's estimate of $d(u, v)$ is always in agreement with u's local knowledge, and $Nb_u[v]$ is set accordingly.

The computation of the algorithm terminates when there are no more messages of the algorithm in transit in any channel. These configurations are not terminal for the whole system, because the system's computation

$$P(u, w, v) \equiv$$
$$up(u, w) \iff w \in Neigh_u \tag{1}$$
$$\wedge \; up(u, w) \wedge Q_{wu} \text{ contains a } \langle \mathbf{mydist}, v, d \rangle \text{ message}$$
$$\Rightarrow \text{ the last such message satisfies } d = D_w[v] \tag{2}$$
$$\wedge \; up(u, w) \wedge Q_{wu} \text{ contains no } \langle \mathbf{mydist}, v, d \rangle \text{ message}$$
$$\Rightarrow ndis_u[w, v] = D_w[v] \tag{3}$$

$$L(u, v) \equiv$$
$$u = v \Rightarrow (D_u[v] = 0 \wedge Nb_u[v] = local) \tag{4}$$
$$\wedge \; (u \neq v \wedge \exists w \in Neigh_u : ndis_u[w, v] < N - 1)$$
$$\Rightarrow (D_u[v] = 1 + \min_{w \in Neigh_u} ndis_u[w, v] = 1 + ndis_u[Nb_u[v], v]) \tag{5}$$
$$\wedge \; (u \neq v \wedge \forall w \in Neigh_u : ndis_u[w, v] \geq N - 1)$$
$$\Rightarrow (D_u[v] = N \wedge Nb_u[v] = udef) \tag{6}$$

Figure 4.10 THE INVARIANTS $P(u, w, v)$ AND $L(u, v)$.

may later continue, starting with a channel failure or repair (to which the algorithm must react). We shall call message-less configurations *stable*, and define the predicate **stable** by

$$\mathbf{stable} \equiv \forall u, w : up(u, w) \Rightarrow Q_{wu} \text{ contains no } \langle \mathbf{mydist}, ., . \rangle \text{ message.}$$

It must be assumed that initially the variables $Neigh_u$ correctly reflect the existence of working communication channels, i.e., that (1) holds initially. To prove the invariance of the assertions three types of transition must be considered.

(1) The receipt of a $\langle \mathbf{mydist}, ., . \rangle$ message. The entire execution of the resulting code fragment is assumed to occur atomically and is considered a single transition. Note that in this transition a message is received and possibly a number of messages is sent.

(2) The failure of a channel and the processing of a $\langle \mathbf{fail}, . \rangle$ message by the nodes at both ends of the channel.

(3) The repair of a channel and the processing of a $\langle \mathbf{repair}, . \rangle$ message by the two connected nodes.

Lemma 4.14 *For all u_0, w_0, and v_0, $P(u_0, w_0, v_0)$ is an invariant.*

Proof. Initially, i.e., after the execution of the initialization procedure by each node, (1) holds by assumption. If initially we have $\neg up(u_0, w_0)$, (2) and (3) trivially hold. If initially we have $up(u_0, w_0)$, then $ndis_{u_0}[w_0, v_0] = N$. If $w_0 = v_0$ then $D_{w_0}[w_0] = 0$ but a message $\langle \mathbf{mydist}, v_0, 0 \rangle$ is in $Q_{w_0 u_0}$, so (2) and (3) are true. If $w_0 \neq v_0$ then $D_{w_0}[v_0] = N$ and no message is in the queue, which also implies that (2) and (3) hold. We consider the three types of state transition mentioned above in turn.

Type (1). Assume that u receives a $\langle \mathbf{mydist}, v, d \rangle$ message from w.

This causes no topological change and no change in the $Neigh$ sets, hence (1) remains true. If $v \neq v_0$ this receipt does not change anything in $P(u_0, w_0, v_0)$.

If $v = v_0$, $u = u_0$, and $w = w_0$ the value of $ndis_{u_0}[w_0, v_0]$ may change. However, if another $\langle \mathbf{mydist}, v_0, . \rangle$ message is still in the channel then the value of this message continues to satisfy (2), so (2) is preserved and (3) also because its premise is false. If the received message was the last one in the channel of this type then $d = D_{w_0}[v_0]$ by (2), which implies that the conclusion of (3) becomes true and (3) is preserved. The premise of (2) becomes false, so (2) is preserved.

If $v = v_0$, $u = w_0$ (and u_0 is a neighbor of u) the conclusion of (2) or (3) may be falsified if the value $D_{w_0}[v_0]$ changes as a result of the execution of $Recompute(v)$ in w_0. In this case, however, a message $\langle \mathbf{mydist}, v_0, . \rangle$ with the new value is sent to u_0, which implies that the premise of (3) is falsified, and the conclusion of (2) becomes true, so both (2) and (3) are preserved. This is also the only case in which a $\langle \mathbf{mydist}, v_0, . \rangle$ message is added to $Q_{w_0 u_0}$, and it always satisfies $d = D_{w_0}[v_0]$.

If $v = v_0$ and $u \neq u_0, w_0$ nothing changes in $P(u_0, w_0, v_0)$.

Type (2). Assume that channel uw fails.

If $u = u_0$ and $w = w_0$ this failure falsifies the premise of (2) and (3) so these clauses are preserved. (1) is preserved because w_0 is removed from $Neigh_{u_0}$ and vice versa. The same happens if $u = w_0$ and $w = u_0$.

If $u = w_0$ but $w \neq u_0$ the conclusion of (2) or (3) may be falsified because the value $D_{w_0}[v_0]$ changes. In this case the sending of a $\langle \mathbf{mydist}, v_0, . \rangle$ message by w_0 again falsifies the premise of (3) and makes the conclusion of (2) true, hence (2) and (3) are preserved.

In all other cases nothing changes in $P(u_0, w_0, v_0)$.

Type (3). Assume that channel uw is added.

If $u = u_0$ and $w = w_0$ this makes $up(u_0, w_0)$ true, but by the addition of w_0 to $Neigh_{u_0}$ (and vice versa) this preserves (1).

The sending of $\langle \mathbf{mydist}, v_0, D_{w_0}[v_0] \rangle$ by w_0 makes the conclusion of (2) true and the premise of (3) false, so $P(u_0, w_0, v_0)$ is preserved.

In all other cases nothing changes in $P(u_0, w_0, v_0)$.

□

Lemma 4.15 *For each u_0 and v_0, $L(u_0, v_0)$ is an invariant.*

Proof. Initially $D_{u_0}[u_0] = 0$ and $Nb_{u_0}[u_0] = local$. For $v_0 \neq u_0$, initially $ndis_{u_0}[w, v_0] = N$ for all $w \in Neigh_u$, and $D_{u_0}[v_0] = N$ and $Nb_{u_0}[v_0] = udef$.

Type (1). Assume that u receives a $\langle \textbf{mydist}, v, d \rangle$ message from w.

If $u \neq u_0$ or $v \neq v_0$ no variable mentioned in $L(u_0, v_0)$ changes.

If $u = u_0$ and $v = v_0$ the value of $ndis_{u_0}[w, v_0]$ changes, but $D_{u_0}[v_0]$ and $Nb_{u_0}[v_0]$ are recomputed exactly so as to satisfy $L(u_0, v_0)$.

Type (2). Assume that channel uw fails.

If $u = u_0$ or $w = u_0$ then $Neigh_{u_0}$ changes, but again $D_{u_0}[v_0]$ and $Nb_{u_0}[v_0]$ are recomputed exactly so as to satisfy $L(u_0, v_0)$.

Type (3). Assume that channel uw is added.

If $u = u_0$ then $Neigh_{u_0}$ changes by the addition of w, but as u sets $ndis_{u_0}[w, v_0]$ to N this preserves $L(u_0, v_0)$.

$\square$

4.3.2 Correctness of the Netchange Algorithm

The two correctness requirements for the algorithm will now be proved.

Theorem 4.16 *When a stable configuration is reached, the tables $Nb_u[v]$ satisfy*

(1) *if $u = v$ then $Nb_u[v] = local$;*

(2) *if a path from u to $v \neq u$ exists then $Nb_u[v] = w$, where w is the first neighbor of u on a shortest path from u to v;*

(3) *if no path from u to v exists then $Nb_u[v] = udef$.*

Proof. When the algorithm terminates, the predicate **stable** holds in addition to $P(u, w, v)$ for all u, v, and w, and this implies that for all u, v, and w

$$up(u, w) \Rightarrow ndis_u[w, v] = D_w[v]. \tag{4.2}$$

Applying also $L(u, v)$ for all u and v we obtain

$$D_u[v] = \begin{cases} 0 & \text{if } u = v \\ 1 + \min\limits_{w \in Neigh_u} D_w[v] & \text{if } u \neq v \wedge \exists w \in Neigh_u : D_w[v] < N - 1 \\ N & \text{if } u \neq v \wedge \forall w \in Neigh_u : D_w[v] \geq N - 1 \end{cases} \tag{4.3}$$

which is sufficient to prove that $D_u[v] = d(u, v)$ if u and v are in the same connected component of the network, and $D_u[v] = N$ if u and v are in different connected components.

First it is shown by induction on $d(u, v)$ that if u and v are in the same connected component then $D_u[v] \leq d(u, v)$.

Case $d(u, v) = 0$: this implies $u = v$ and hence $D_u[v] = 0$.

Case $d(u, v) = k + 1$: this implies that there exists a node $w \in Neigh_u$ with $d(w, v) = k$. By induction $D_w[v] \leq k$, which by (4.3) implies $D_u[v] \leq k + 1$.

Now it will be shown by induction on $D_u[v]$ that if $D_u[v] < N$ then there is a path between u and v and $d(u, v) \leq D_u[v]$.

Case $D_u[v] = 0$: Formula (4.3) implies that $D_u[v] = 0$ only for $u = v$, which gives the empty path between u and v, and $d(u, v) = 0$.

Case $D_u[v] = k + 1 < N$: Formula (4.3) implies that there is a node $w \in Neigh_u$ with $D_w[v] = k$. By induction there is a path between w and v and $d(w, v) \leq k$, which implies there is a path between u and v and $d(u, v) \leq k + 1$.

It follows that if u and v are in the same connected component then $D_u[v] = d(u, v)$, otherwise $D_u[v] = N$. This, Formula (4.2), and $\forall u, v : L(u, v)$ imply the stated result about $Nb_u[v]$. $\qquad\square$

To prove that a stable situation is eventually reached if topological changes cease, a norm function with respect to **stable** will be defined. Define, for a configuration γ of the algorithm,

$$t_i = \quad \text{(the number of } \langle \mathbf{mydist}, ., i \rangle \text{ messages)} \\ + \text{(the number of ordered pairs } u, v \text{ s.t. } D_u[v] = i)$$

and the function f by

$$f(\gamma) = (t_0, t_1, \ldots, t_N).$$

$f(\gamma)$ is an $(N + 1)$-tuple of natural numbers, on which a lexicographic order (denoted $\leq_l$) is assumed. Recall that $(\mathbb{N}^{N+1}, \leq_l)$ is a well-founded set (Exercise 2.5).

Lemma 4.17 *The processing of a* $\langle \mathbf{mydist}, ., . \rangle$ *message decreases* f.

Proof. Assume node u with $D_u[v] = d_1$ receives a $\langle \mathbf{mydist}, v, d_2 \rangle$ message, and after recomputation the new value of $D_u[v]$ is d. The algorithm implies that $d \leq d_2 + 1$.

Case $d < d_1$: Now $d = d_2 + 1$ which implies that t_{d_2} is decreased by one (and t_{d_1} as well), and only t_d with $d > d_2$ is increased. This implies that the value of f is decreased.

Case $d = d_1$: No new $\langle \mathbf{mydist}, ., . \rangle$ messages are sent by u, and the only effect on f is that t_{d_2} is decreased by one, so the value of f is decreased.

Case $d > d_1$**:** Now t_{d_1} is decreased by one (and t_{d_2} as well), and only t_d with $d > d_1$ is increased. This implies that the value of f is decreased.

$\square$

Theorem 4.18 *If the topology of the network remains constant after a finite number of topological changes, then the algorithm reaches a stable configuration after a finite number of steps.*

Proof. If the network topology remains constant only further processing of $\langle \mathbf{mydist}, ., . \rangle$ messages takes place, and, by the previous lemma, the value of f decreases with every such transition. It follows from the well-foundedness of the domain of f that only a finite number of these transitions can take place; hence the algorithm reaches a configuration satisfying **stable** after a finite number of steps. $\square$

4.3.3 Discussion of the Algorithm

The formal correctness results of the algorithm, guaranteeing the convergence to correct tables within finite time after the last topological change, are not very indicative about the actual behavior of the algorithm. The predicate **stable** may in practice be false most of the time (namely, if topological changes are frequent) and when **stable** is false nothing is known about the routing tables. They may contain cycles or even give erroneous information about the reachability of a destination node. The algorithm can therefore only be used in applications where topological changes are so infrequent that the convergence time of the algorithm is small compared with the average time between (bursts of) topological changes. This is all the more the case because **stable** is a global property, and stable configurations of the algorithm are indistinguishable from non-stable ones for the nodes. This means that a node never knows whether its routing table correctly reflects the network topology, and cannot defer forwarding data packets until a stable configuration is reached.

Asynchronous processing of notifications. It has been assumed in this section that the notifications of topological changes are processed atomically together with the change in a single transition. The processing takes place at both sides of the removed or added channel simultaneously. Lamport [Lam82] has carried out the analysis in a little more detail to allow a delay in processing these notifications. The communication channel from w to u is modeled as the concatenation of three queues.

(1) OQ_{wu}, the output queue of w;

(2) TQ_{wu}, the queue of messages (and data packets) currently being transmitted;

(3) IQ_{wu}, the input queue of u.

Under the normal operation of a channel w sends a message to u by appending it to OQ_{wu}, messages move from OQ_{wu} to TQ_{wu} and from TQ_{wu} to IQ_{wu}, and u receives them by deleting them from IQ_{wu}. When the channel fails the messages in TQ_{wu} are thrown away and messages in OQ_{wu} are thereafter also thrown away rather than appended to TQ_{wu}. The $\langle \mathbf{fail}, w \rangle$ message is placed at the end of IQ_{wu}, and when normal operation is resumed the $\langle \mathbf{repair}, w \rangle$ message is also placed at the end of IQ_{wu}. The predicates $P(u, w, v)$ take a slightly more complicated form, but the algorithm remains the same.

Shortest-path routing. It is possible to assign a weight to each channel and modify the algorithm so as to compute shortest paths rather than minimum-hop paths. The procedure *Recompute* of the Netchange algorithm takes the weight of channel uw into account when estimating the length of the shortest path via w if the constant 1 is replaced by ω_{uw}. The constant N in the algorithm must be replaced by an upper bound on the diameter of the network.

It is fairly easy to show that when the modified algorithm reaches a stable configuration the routing tables are indeed correct and give optimal paths (all cycles in the network must have positive weight). The proof that the algorithm eventually reaches such a configuration requires a more complicated norm function.

It is even possible to extend the algorithm to deal with varying channel weights; the reaction of node u to a change in a channel weight is the recomputation of $D_u[v]$ for all v. The algorithm would be practical, however, only in situations where the average time between channel-cost changes is large compared to the convergence time, which is a quite unrealistic assumption. In these situations an algorithm should be preferred that guarantees cycle-freedom also during convergence, for example the Merlin–Segall algorithm.

4.4 Routing with Compact Routing Tables

The routing algorithms discussed so far all require that each node maintains a routing table with a separate entry for each possible destination. When a packet is forwarded through the network these tables are accessed in each

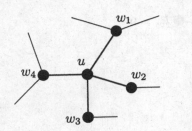

dest.	chan.
v_1	w_2
u	-
v_j	w_3
v_N	w_1

chan.	destinations
w_1	..., v_N
w_2	v_1, ...
w_3	..., v_j, ...
w_4	

Figure 4.11 REDUCING THE SIZE OF ROUTING TABLES.

node of the path (except the destination). In this section some routing table organizations that decrease the storage and table lookup overheads of routing mechanisms will be studied. How these routing tables can be computed by a distributed algorithm will not be considered here. For simplicity of presentation it is assumed throughout this section that the network is connected.

The strategy for obtaining smaller tables in each of the three routing mechanisms discussed in this section is easily explained as follows. If the routing tables of a node store the outgoing channel for each destination separately, the routing table necessarily has length N; hence the tables require $\Omega(N)$ bits, no matter how compactly the outgoing channel is encoded for each destination. Now consider a reorganization of the table, in which the table contains for each *channel* of the node an entry telling which destinations must be routed via this channel; see Figure 4.11. The table now has "length" *deg* for a node with *deg* channels; the actual saving in storage of course depends on how compactly the set of destinations for each channel can be represented. In order to keep a table-lookup efficient the table must be organized in such a way that the outgoing channel for a given destination can be retrieved quickly from the table.

4.4.1 The Tree-labeling Scheme

The first compact routing method was proposed by Santoro and Khatib [SK85]. The method is based on a labeling of the nodes with integers from 0 to $N - 1$, in such a way that the set of destinations for each channel is an interval. Let $\mathbb{Z}_N$ denote the set $\{0, 1, \ldots, N - 1\}$. In this section all arithmetic in this set is done modulo N, i.e., $(N - 1) + 1 \equiv 0$, but the order is as in $\mathbb{Z}$.

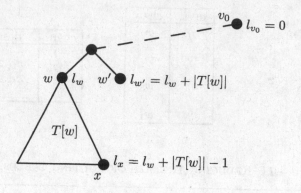

Figure 4.12 PREORDER TREE TRAVERSAL.

Definition 4.19 *The cyclic interval* $[a, b)$ *in* $\mathbb{Z}_N$ *is the set of integers defined by*

$$[a, b) = \begin{cases} \{a, a+1, \ldots, b-1\} & \text{if } a < b \\ \{0, \ldots, b-1, a, \ldots, N-1\} & \text{if } a \geq b \end{cases}$$

Observe that $[a, a) = \mathbb{Z}_N$, and for $a \neq b$ the complement of $[a, b)$ is $[b, a)$. The cyclic interval $[a, b)$ is called *linear* if $a < b$.

Theorem 4.20 *The nodes of a tree* T *can be numbered in such a way that for each outgoing channel of each node the set of destinations that must be routed via that channel is a cyclic interval.*

Proof. Pick an arbitrary node v_0 as the root of the tree and for each w let $T[w]$ denote the subtree of T rooted at w. It is possible to number the nodes in such a way that for each w the numbers assigned to the nodes in $T[w]$ form a linear interval, for example, by a preorder traversal of the tree as in Figure 4.12. In this order, w is the first node of $T[w]$ to be visited and after w all nodes of $T[w]$ are visited before a node not in $T[w]$ is visited; hence the nodes in $T[w]$ are numbered by the linear interval $[l_w, l_w + |T[w]|)$ (l_w is the label of w).

Let $[a_w, b_w)$ denote the interval of numbers assigned to the nodes in $T[w]$. A neighbor of w is either a son or the father of w. Node w forwards to a son u the packets with destinations in $T[u]$, i.e., the nodes with numbers in $[a_u, b_u)$. Node w forwards to its father the packets with destinations not in $T[w]$, i.e., the nodes with numbers in $\mathbb{Z}_N \setminus [a_w, b_w) = [b_w, a_w)$. $\qquad\square$

(* A packet with address d was received or generated at node u *)
if $d = l_u$
    then deliver the packet locally
    else begin select α_i s.t. $d \in [\alpha_i, \alpha_{i+1})$;
                 send packet via the channel labeled with α_i
    end

Algorithm 4.13 INTERVAL FORWARDING (FOR NODE u).

A single cyclic interval can be represented using only $2 \log N$ bits by giving the start point and end point. Because in this application a collection of disjoint intervals with union $\mathbb{Z}_N$ must be stored (by adding u to one of the intervals in node u), $\log N$ bits per interval are sufficient. Only the start point of the interval corresponding to each channel is stored; the corresponding end point is equal to the next begin point of an interval in the same node. The begin point of the interval corresponding with channel uw at node u is given by

$$\alpha_{uw} = \begin{cases} l_w & \text{if } w \text{ is a son of } u, \\ l_u + |T[u]| & \text{if } w \text{ is the father of } u. \end{cases}$$

Assuming that the channels of node u of degree deg_u are labeled with $\alpha_1, \ldots, \alpha_{deg_u}$, where $\alpha_1 < \cdots < \alpha_{deg_u}$, the forwarding procedure is as given in Algorithm 4.13. The channel-labels partition the set $\mathbb{Z}_N$ into deg_u segments, each corresponding to one channel; see Figure 4.14. Observe that there is (at most) one interval that is not linear. If the labels are sorted at the node, the correct label is found in $O(\log deg_u)$ steps using binary search. The index i is counted modulo deg_u, i.e., $\alpha_{deg_u+1} = \alpha_1$.

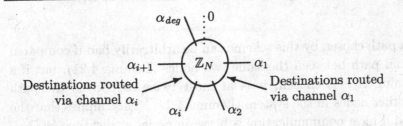

Figure 4.14 THE PARTITION OF $\mathbb{Z}_N$ IN A NODE.

The tree labeling scheme routes optimally on trees, because in a tree there exists only one simple path between each two nodes. The scheme can also be used if the network is not a tree. A fixed spanning tree T of the network is chosen, and the scheme is applied to this tree. Channels not belonging to the spanning tree are never used; each is labeled with a special symbol in the routing table to indicate that no packet is routed via this channel.

To compare the path lengths chosen by this scheme with the optimal paths, let $d_T(u, v)$ denote the distance from u to v in T and $d_G(u, v)$ the distance from u to v in G. Let D_G denote the *diameter* of G, defined as the maximum over u and v of $d_G(u, v)$.

Lemma 4.21 *There is no uniform bound on the ratio between $d_T(u, v)$ and $d_G(u, v)$. This holds already in the special case of the hop measure for paths.*

Proof. Choose G to be the ring on N nodes, and observe that a spanning tree of G is obtained by removing one channel, say xy, from G. Now $d_G(x, y) = 1$ and $d_T(x, y) = N-1$, so the ratio is $N-1$. The ratio can be made arbitrarily large by choosing a large ring. □

The following lemma relies on the symmetry of channel costs, i.e., it is assumed that $\omega_{uw} = \omega_{wu}$. This implies that $d_G(u, v) = d_G(v, u)$ for all u and v.

Lemma 4.22 *T can be chosen in such a way that for all u and v, $d_T(u, v) \leq 2D_G$.*

Proof. Choose T to be the optimal sink tree for a node w_0 (as in Theorem 4.2). Then

$$
\begin{aligned}
d_T(u, v) &\leq d_T(u, w_0) + d_T(w_0, v) \\
&= d_T(u, w_0) + d_T(v, w_0) \quad \text{by symmetry of } \omega \\
&= d_G(u, w_0) + d_G(v, w_0) \quad \text{by the choice of } T \\
&\leq D_G + D_G \qquad\qquad\qquad \text{by definition of } D_G.
\end{aligned}
$$

□

Concluding, a path chosen by this scheme can be arbitrarily bad if compared with an optimal path between the same two nodes (Lemma 4.21), but if a suitable spanning tree is chosen, it is at most twice as bad as the path between two other nodes in the system (Lemma 4.22). This implies that the scheme is good if most communication is between nodes at distance $\Theta(D_G)$, but should not be used if most communication is between nodes at a short distance (in G) from each other.

Besides the factor concerning the lengths of the chosen paths, the tree routing scheme has the following disadvantages.

(1) Channels not belonging to T are not used, which is a waste of network resources.
(2) Traffic is concentrated on a tree, which may lead to congestion.
(3) Each single failure of a channel of T partitions the network.

4.4.2 Interval Routing

Van Leeuwen and Tan [LT87] extended the tree labeling scheme to non-tree networks in such a way that (almost) every channel is used for packet traffic.

Definition 4.23 *An interval labeling scheme (ILS) for a network is*

(1) *an assignment of different labels from $\mathbb{Z}_N$ to the nodes of the network, and,*
(2) *for each node, an assignment of different labels from $\mathbb{Z}_N$ to the channels of that node.*

The interval routing algorithm assumes that an ILS is given, and forwards packets as in Algorithm 4.13.

Definition 4.24 *An interval labeling scheme is valid if all packets forwarded in this way eventually reach their destination.*

It will be shown that a valid interval labeling scheme exists for every connected network G (Theorem 4.25); for arbitrary connected networks, however, the scheme is usually not very efficient. The optimality of the paths chosen by interval routing schemes will be studied after the existence proof.

Theorem 4.25 *For each connected network G a valid interval labeling scheme exists.*

Proof. A valid interval labeling scheme is constructed by an extension of the tree labeling scheme of Santoro and Khatib, applied to a spanning tree T of the network. Given a spanning tree, a *frond edge* is an edge that does not belong to this spanning tree. Furthermore, v is an *ancestor* of u iff $u \in T[v]$. As the main problem of the construction is how to assign labels to frond edges (the tree edges will be labeled as in the tree labeling scheme), a spanning tree is chosen in such a way that all frond edges take a restricted form, as we will show.

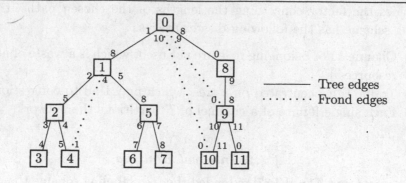

Figure 4.15 A DEPTH-FIRST SEARCH ILS.

Lemma 4.26 *There exists a spanning tree such that all frond edges are between a node and an ancestor of that node.*

Proof. Each spanning tree that is obtained by a depth-first search through the network has this property; see [Tar72] and Section 6.4. □

In the sequel, let T be a fixed depth-first search spanning tree of G.

Definition 4.27 *A depth-first search ILS for G (with respect to T) is a labeling scheme for which the following rules are satisfied.*

(1) *The node labels are assigned as in a preorder traversal of T, i.e., the nodes in subtree $T[w]$ are labeled with the numbers in $[l_w, l_w+|T[w]|)$. Write $k_w = l_w + |T[w]|$.*

(2) *The label of edge uw at node u is called α_{uw}.*

    (a) *If uw is a frond edge then $\alpha_{uw} = l_w$.*

    (b) *If w is a son of u (in T) then $\alpha_{uw} = l_w$.*

    (c) *If w is the father of u then $\alpha_{uw} = k_u$ unless $k_u = N$ and u has a frond to the root.*
    (In the latter situation, the frond edge is labeled 0 at u by the rule (a), so assigning the label k_u would violate the requirement that all edge labels at u are different. Labels are regarded as modulo N, so $N \equiv 0$.)

    (d) *If w is the father of u, u has a frond to the root, and $k_u = N$, then $\alpha_{uw} = l_w$.*

An example of a depth-first search ILS is given in Figure 4.15. Observe that all frond edges are labeled according to rule (2a), the father-edges of nodes

4, 8, and 10 are labeled according to rule (2c), and the father-edge of node 9 is labeled according to rule (2d).

It will now be shown that a depth-first search ILS is a valid scheme. Observe that $v \in T[u] \iff l_v \in [l_u, k_u)$. The following three lemmas concern the situation where node u forwards a packet with destination v to node w (a neighbor of u) using Algorithm 4.13. This implies that $l_v \in [\alpha_{uw}, \alpha)$ for some label α in u, and that there is no label $\alpha' \neq \alpha_{uw}$ in node u such that $\alpha' \in [\alpha_{uw}, l_v)$.

Lemma 4.28 *If $l_u > l_v$ then $l_w < l_u$.*

Proof. First, consider the case where $\alpha_{uw} \leq l_v$. Node w is not a son of u because in that case $\alpha_{uw} = l_w > l_u > l_v$. If uw is a frond then also $l_w = \alpha_{uw} < l_v < l_u$. If w is the father of u then $l_w < l_u$ holds in any case. Second, consider the case where α_{uw} is the largest edge label in u, and there is no label $\alpha' \leq l_v$ (i.e., l_v is in the lower part of a non-linear interval). In this case the edge to u's father is not labeled with 0, but with k_u (because $0 \leq l_v$, and there is no label $\alpha' \leq l_v$). The label k_u is the largest label in this case; an edge to a son or downward frond w' has $\alpha_{uw'} = l_{w'} < k_u$, and a frond to an ancestor w' has $\alpha_{uw'} = l_{w'} < l_u$. So w is the father of u in this case, which implies $l_w < l_u$. $\qquad\square$

The next two lemmas concern the case where $l_u < l_v$. We deduce that either $v \in T[u]$ or $l_v \geq k_u$, and in the latter case $k_u < N$ holds so that the edge to the father of u is labeled with k_u.

Lemma 4.29 *If $l_u < l_v$ then $l_w \leq l_v$.*

Proof. First consider the case where $v \in T[u]$; let w' be the son of u such that $v \in T[w']$. We have $\alpha_{uw'} = l_{w'} \leq l_v$ and this implies that $\alpha_{uw'} \leq \alpha_{uw} \leq l_v < k_{w'}$. We deduce that w is not the father of u, hence $l_w = \alpha_{uw}$, which implies $l_w \leq l_v$.

Second, consider the case where $l_v \geq k_u$. In this case w is the father of u; this can be seen as follows. The edge to the father is labeled with k_u, and $k_u \leq l_v$. The edge to a son w' of u is labeled with $l_{w'} < k_u$, the edge to a downward frond w' is labeled with $l_{w'} < k_u$, and the edge to an upward frond w' is labeled with $l_{w'} < l_u$. Because w is the father of u, $l_w < l_u < l_v$. $\qquad\square$

A norm function with respect to delivery at v can be defined as follows. The *lowest common ancestor* of two nodes u and v is the lowest node in the tree that is an ancestor of both u and v. Let $\mathrm{lca}(u, v)$ denote the label of the

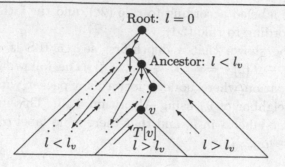

Figure 4.16 ROUTING OF PACKETS FOR v IN THE DEPTH-FIRST SEARCH ILS.

lowest common ancestor of u and v, and define

$$f_v(u) = (-\mathrm{lca}(u, v),\ l_u).$$

Lemma 4.30 *If $l_u < l_v$ then $f_v(w) < f_v(u)$.*

Proof. First consider the case where $v \in T[u]$, which implies $\mathrm{lca}(u, v) = l_u$. If w' is the son of u such that $v \in T[w']$, we have (as in the previous lemma) that $l_{w'} \le l_w < k_{w'}$, hence $w \in T[w']$, which implies $\mathrm{lca}(w, v) \ge l_{w'} > l_u$. So $f_v(w) < f_v(u)$.

Second, consider the case that $l_v \ge k_u$. As in the previous lemma, w is the father of u, and because $v \notin T[u]$, $\mathrm{lca}(w, v) = \mathrm{lca}(u, v)$. But now $l_w < l_u$, so $f_v(w) < f_v(u)$.   □

It can now be shown that each packet reaches its destination. The flow of packets towards v is indicated in Figure 4.16. Let a packet for v be generated in node u. By Lemma 4.28, the node label decreases at every hop, until, within a finite number of hops, the packet is received by a node w with $l_w \le l_v$. Every node to which the packet is forwarded after w also has a label $\le l_v$, by Lemma 4.29. Within a finite number of hops the packet is received by v, because in each hop f_v decreases or the packet arrives at v, by Lemma 4.30. This completes the proof of Theorem 4.25.   □

Efficiency of interval routing: the general case. Theorem 4.25 states that a valid ILS exists for each network, but does not imply anything about the efficiency of the paths chosen by the scheme. It should be clear that depth-first search ILSs are used to demonstrate the *existence* of a scheme for each network, but that they are not necessarily the best possible schemes. For example, if the depth-first search scheme is applied to a ring of N nodes, there are nodes u and v with $d(u, v) = 2$, and the scheme uses $N - 2$ hops to deliver a packet from u to v (Exercise 4.8). There exists an ILS for the same ring that delivers each packet via a minimum-hop path (Theorem 4.34).

In order to analyze the quality of the routing method in this respect, the following definitions are first made.

Definition 4.31 *An ILS is* optimal *if it forwards all packets via optimal paths.*
An ILS is neighborly *if it delivers a packet from one node to a neighbor of that node in one hop.*
An ILS is linear *if the interval corresponding with each edge is linear.*

We shall call an ILS *minimum-hop* (or *shortest-path*) if it is optimal with respect to the minimum-hop (or shortest-path, respectively) cost measure. It is easily seen that if a scheme is minimum hop then it is neighborly. It is also easy to verify that an ILS is linear if and only if in each node u with $l_u \neq 0$ there is an edge labeled 0, and in the node with label 0 there is an edge with label 0 or 1. It turns out that for general networks the quality of the routing method is poor, but for several classes of special network topology the quality of the scheme is very good. This makes the method suitable for processor networks with a regular structure, such as those used for the implementation of parallel computers with a virtual global shared memory.

It is not known exactly how, for an arbitrary network, the best interval labeling scheme compares with an optimal routing algorithm. Some lower bounds for the path lengths, implying that an optimal ILS does not always exist, were given by Ružička.

Theorem 4.32 [Ruž88] *There exists a network G such that for each valid ILS of G there exist nodes u and v such that a packet from u to v is delivered only after at least $\frac{3}{2} D_G$ hops.*

It is also not known how the best depth-first search ILS for a network compares with the overall best ILS for the same network. Exercise 4.7 gives a very bad depth-first search ILS for a network that actually admits an optimal ILS (by Theorem 4.37), but there may be a better depth-first search ILS for the same network.

In situations where most of the communication is between neighbors, being neighborly is a sufficient requirement for the ILS. As can be seen from Figure 4.15 a depth-first search ILS is not necessarily neighborly; node 4 forwards packets for node 2 via node 1.

Multiple interval routing schemes. The efficiency of the routing method can be improved by allowing more than one label to be assigned to each edge; we speak of *multiple interval routing* in this case. Indeed, this defines the set of destinations for this edge to be the union of several intervals and by increasing the number of intervals even optimal routing can be achieved for arbitrary networks. To see this, first consider optimal routing tables, such as computed by the Netchange algorithm for example, and observe that the set of destinations routed through any particular edge can be written as the union of cyclic intervals. With this elementary approach one finds at most $N/2$ labels per edge, and at most N labels altogether in any node; the storage of such a table takes as much space as the storage of classical, full routing tables.

It is now possible to trade storage complexity against routing efficiency; the natural question arises how many labels are really necessary in any network to achieve optimal routing. Pioneering work of Flammini *et al.* [FLMS95] developed a method for finding schemes and proving lower bounds, showing that in the general case $\Theta(N)$ labels per link may be required for optimality. But allowing just a small compromise in the length of the paths, a large reduction in table size can be achieved; results regarding this tradeoff are summarized by Ružička [Ruž98].

Linear interval routing schemes. It is essential for the applicability of the interval routing method that cyclic intervals are considered. Although some networks do have valid, and even optimal, linear-interval labeling schemes, it is not possible to label every network validly with linear intervals. The applicability of linear-interval labeling schemes was investigated by Bakker, Van Leeuwen, and Tan [BLT91].

Theorem 4.33 *There exists a network for which no valid linear-interval labeling scheme exists.*

Proof. Consider a spider graph with three legs of length two, as depicted in Figure 4.17. The smallest label (0) and largest label (6) are assigned to two nodes, and as there are three legs, there is (at least) one leg that contains neither the smallest nor the largest label. Let x be the first node from the center in this leg. Node x forwards packets addressed to 0 and 6 to the center, and the only linear interval that contains both 0 and 6 is the entire set $\mathbb{Z}_N$. Consequently, x also forwards packets for its other neighbor towards the center, and these packets never reach their destination. □

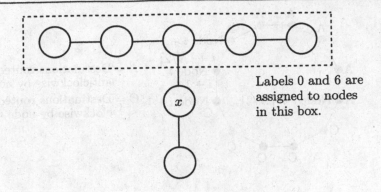

Labels 0 and 6 are assigned to nodes in this box.

Figure 4.17 THE SPIDER GRAPH WITH THREE LEGS.

Bakker, Van Leeuwen and Tan completely characterize the class of network topologies that admit a shortest-path linear ILS, and present a number of results concerning the classes of graph topologies that admit adaptive and minimum-hop linear ILSs. Networks that allow a linear scheme at all were characterized by Fragniaud and Gavoille [FG94]; Eilam *et al.* [EMZ96] showed that the path lengths obtained with linear schemes in these networks can be as big as $O(D^2)$.

Optimality of interval routing: special topologies. It turns out that there are optimal interval labeling schemes for several classes of networks having a regular structure. Networks of these structures are used, for example, in the implementation of parallel computers.

Theorem 4.34 [LT87] *There exists a minimum-hop ILS for a ring of N nodes.*

Proof. The node labels are assigned from 0 to $N-1$ in clockwise order. For node i the clockwise channel is assigned the label $i+1$ and the anticlockwise channel is assigned $(i + \lceil N/2 \rceil) \bmod N$; see Figure 4.18. With this labeling scheme the node with label i sends packets for nodes $i+1, \ldots, (i+\lceil N/2 \rceil)-1$ via the clockwise channel and packets for nodes $(i + \lceil N/2 \rceil), \ldots, i - 1$ via the anticlockwise channel, which is optimal. □

As the ILS in the proof of Theorem 4.34 is optimal, it is neighborly; it is not linear.

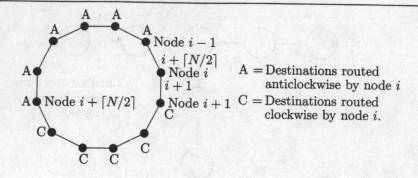

Figure 4.18 OPTIMAL ILS FOR A RING.

Theorem 4.35 [LT87] *There exists a minimum-hop ILS for an $n \times n$ grid.*

Proof. The node labels are assigned in row major order, i.e., the ith node on the jth row is labeled $(j-1)n + (i-1)$. The up-channel of this node is labeled 0, the left-channel of this node is labeled $(j-1)n$, the right-channel of this node is labeled $(j-1)n + i$, and the down-channel of this node is labeled $j \cdot n$; see Figure 4.19.

It is now easy to verify that when node u forwards a packet to node v,

Case 1: if v is in a row higher than u, then u sends the packet via its up-channel;

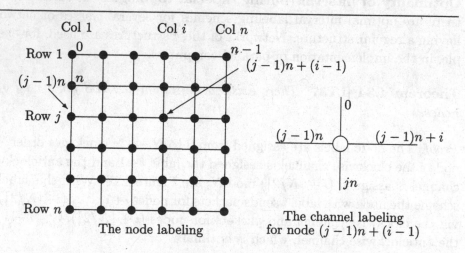

Figure 4.19 OPTIMAL ILS FOR AN $n \times n$ GRID.

Case 2: if v is in a row lower than u, then u sends the packet via its down-channel;

Case 3: if v is in the same row as u but to the left, then u sends the packet via its left-channel; and

Case 4: if v is in the same row as u but to the right, then u sends the packet via its right-channel.

In all cases, u sends the packet to a node closer to v, which implies that the chosen path is optimal. $\qquad\qquad\square$

As the ILS in the proof of Theorem 4.35 is optimal, it is neighborly; the scheme is also linear.

We state the following two results without proof; the construction of labeling schemes as claimed in the theorems is left as an exercise for the reader.

Theorem 4.36 *There exists a minimum-hop linear ILS for the Hypercube.*

Theorem 4.37 [FJ88] *There exists a shortest-path ILS for outerplanar networks with arbitrary channel weights.*

Interval routing has a number of attractive advantages, as follows, over classical routing mechanisms based on storing a preferred outgoing channel for each destination separately.

(1) *Low space complexity.* The routing tables can be stored in $O(deg \cdot \log N)$ bits for a node of degree deg.

(2) *Efficient computation of routing tables.* Routing Tables for a depth-first search ILS can be computed using a distributed depth-first search traversal of the network, which can be done using $O(E)$ messages in $O(N)$ time; see Section 6.4.

(3) *Optimality.* The routing method is able to choose optimal paths for several classes of network, cf. Theorems 4.34 through 4.37.

These advantages make the method suitable for processor networks with a regular topology. As Transputers are often used to construct such topologies, the Inmos C104 routing chips (see Subsection 1.1.5) are designed to use interval routing.

Unfortunately, for applications in networks of arbitrary topology, when the method uses a depth-first search ILS there are a number of disadvantages, as follows.

(1) *Poor robustness.* It is not possible to adapt a depth-first search ILS slightly if a channel or node is added to or removed from the network.

The depth-first search tree on which the ILS is based may no longer satisfy the requirement that there are fronds only between a node and its ancestor. As a result, a minor modification of the topology may require a complete recomputation of the routing tables, including the assignment of new addresses (labels) to each node.

(2) *Non-optimality*. A depth-first search ILS may route packets via paths of length $\Omega(N)$, even in cases of networks of small diameter; see Exercise 4.7.

Many variants of interval routing were discussed in the literature. Multiple interval routing, already discussed earlier, appears to be a quite practical method because the cost of having extra labels is not prohibitive with modern memory techniques. A multi-dimensional variant was described by Flammini *et al.* [FGNT98]. The node names and labels are points and intervals in a multi-dimensional space rather than $\mathbb{Z}_N$ and the method brings advantages in networks that have a multi-dimensional structure, such as product graphs.

A more flexible way to exploit structure of a network is *boolean routing* introduced by Flammini *et al.* [FGS93]. Here node names are bitstrings, and node labels are predicates; a message with destination label λ can be sent over a link labeled with $\mathcal{L}$ iff $\mathcal{L}(\lambda)$ holds. The method allows fairly complicated network structures to be used efficiently, but of course there is considerable complexity in the interpretation of the labels.

4.4.3 Prefix Routing

To overcome the disadvantages of interval routing, Bakker, Van Leeuwen, and Tan [BLT93] designed a routing method for which the tables can be computed using arbitrary spanning trees. The use of non-restricted spanning trees can increase both the robustness and the efficiency. If a channel is added between two existing nodes, the spanning tree remains a spanning tree and the new channel is a frond. If a new node is added together with a number of channels connecting it to existing nodes, the spanning tree is extended using one of these channels and the new node, and the other channels are fronds. The optimality can be improved by choosing a small-depth spanning tree as in Lemma 4.22.

The node and channel labels used in prefix routing are strings rather than the integers used in interval routing. Let Σ be an alphabet; in the sequel a label will be a string over Σ, ϵ denotes the empty string, and Σ^* the set of strings over Σ. To select a channel in which to forward a packet, the

(* A packet with address d was received or generated at node u *)
if $d = l_u$
    then deliver the packet locally
    else begin $\alpha_i :=$ the longest channel-label s.t. $\alpha_i \lhd d$;
                send packet via the channel labeled with α_i
    end

Algorithm 4.20 PREFIX FORWARDING (FOR NODE u).

---

algorithm considers all channel labels that are a *prefix* of the destination address. The longest of these labels is selected, and the corresponding channel is used to forward the packet. For example, assume a node has channels labeled with **aabb**, **abba**, **aab**, **aabc**, and **aa**, and must forward a packet with address **aabbc**. The channel labels **aabb**, **aab**, and **aa** are prefixes of **aabbc**, and the longest of these three labels is **aabb**, hence the node forwards the packet via the channel labeled **aabb**. The forwarding algorithm is given as Algorithm 4.20. We write $\alpha \lhd \beta$ to denote that α is a prefix of β.

Definition 4.38 *A prefix labeling scheme (over Σ) for a network G is*

(1) *an assignment of different strings from Σ^* to the nodes of G; and*
(2) *for each node, an assignment of different strings to the channels of that node.*

The prefix routing algorithm assumes that a prefix labeling scheme (PLS) is given, and forwards packets as in Algorithm 4.20.

Definition 4.39 *A prefix labeling scheme is valid if all packets forwarded in this way eventually reach their destination.*

Theorem 4.40 *For each connected network G a valid PLS exists.*

Proof. We shall define a class of prefix labeling schemes and prove, as in Theorem 4.25, that the schemes in this class are valid. Let T denote an arbitrary rooted spanning tree of G.

Definition 4.41 *A tree PLS for G (with respect to T) is a prefix labeling scheme in which the following rules are satisfied.*

(1) *The node label of the root is ϵ.*
(2) *If w is a son of u then l_w extends l_u by one letter; i.e., if $u_1, \ldots, u_k$ are the sons of u in T then $l_{u_i} = l_u.a_i$, where $a_1, \ldots, a_k$ are k different letters from Σ.*

    (3) *If uw is a frond then $\alpha_{uw} = l_w$.*

    (4) *If w is a son of u then $\alpha_{uw} = l_w$.*

    (5) *If w is the father of u then $\alpha_{uw} = \epsilon$ unless u has a frond to the root;*
        in that case, $\alpha_{uw} = l_w$.

In a tree PLS each node except the root has a channel labeled ϵ, and this channel connects the node to an ancestor (the father of the node or the root of the tree). Observe that for every channel uw, $\alpha_{uw} = l_w$ or $\alpha_{uw} = \epsilon$. For all u and v, v is an ancestor of u if and only if $l_v \lhd l_u$.

It must first be shown that a packet never gets "stuck" in a node different from its destination, that is, each node different from the destination can forward the packet using Algorithm 4.20.

Lemma 4.42 *For all nodes u and v such that $u \neq v$ there is a channel in u labeled with a prefix of l_v.*

Proof. If u is not the root of T then u has a channel labeled ϵ, which is a prefix of l_v. If u is the root then v is not the root, and $v \in T[u]$ holds. If w is the son of u such that $v \in T[w]$ then by construction $\alpha_{uw} \lhd l_v$. $\square$

The following three lemmas concern the situation where node u forwards a packet for node v to a node w (a neighbor of u) using Algorithm 4.20.

Lemma 4.43 *If $u \in T[v]$ then w is an ancestor of u.*

Proof. If $\alpha_{uw} = \epsilon$ then w is an ancestor of u as mentioned above. If $\alpha_{uw} = l_w$ then, since $\alpha_{uw} \lhd l_v$, also $l_w \lhd l_v$. This implies that w is an ancestor of v, and also of u. $\square$

Lemma 4.44 *If u is an ancestor of v then w is an ancestor of v, closer to v than u.*

Proof. Let w' be the son of u such that $v \in T[w']$ then $\alpha_{uw'} = l_{w'}$ is a non-empty prefix of l_v. As α_{uw} is the longest prefix (in u) of l_v, it follows that $\alpha_{uw'} \lhd \alpha_{uw} \lhd l_v$, so w is an ancestor of v below u. $\square$

Lemma 4.45 *If $u \notin T[v]$, then w is an ancestor of v or $d_T(w, v) < d_T(u, v)$.*

Proof. If $\alpha_{uw} = \epsilon$ then w is the father of u or the root; the father of u is closer to v than u because $u \notin T[v]$, and the root is an ancestor of v. If $\alpha_{uw} = l_w$ then, as $\alpha_{uw} \lhd l_v$, w is an ancestor of v. $\square$

Let the value *depth* be the depth of T, i.e., the number of hops of the longest simple path from the root to any leaf. It can be seen that each packet with destination v arrives at its destination in at most $2 \cdot depth$ hops. If the packet is generated in an ancestor of v then v is reached within *depth* hops by Lemma 4.44. If the packet is generated in the subtree $T[v]$ then an ancestor of v is reached within *depth* hops by Lemma 4.43, after which v is reached within another *depth* hops by the previous observation. (Because the path contains only ancestors of the source in this case, its length is actually bounded by *depth* also.) In all other cases an ancestor of v is reached within *depth* hops by Lemma 4.45, after which v is reached within another *depth* hops. (Thus, in this case the length of the path is bounded by $2 \cdot depth$.) This concludes the proof of Theorem 4.40 □

Corollary 4.46 *For each network G with diameter D_G (measured in hops) there exists a prefix labeling scheme that delivers all packets in at most $2D_G$ hops.*

Proof. Use a tree PLS with respect to a tree chosen as in Lemma 4.22. □

We conclude the discussion of the tree labeling scheme with a brief analysis of its space requirement. As before, let *depth* be the depth of T, and let k be the maximal number of sons of any node of T. Then the longest label consists of *depth* letters, and as Σ must contain (at least) k letters, a label can be stored in $depth \cdot \log k$ bits. The routing table of a node with *deg* channels is stored in $O(deg \cdot depth \cdot \log k)$ bits.

Several other prefix labeling schemes have been proposed by Bakker *et al.* [BLT93]. Their paper also characterizes the class of topologies that allows *optimal* prefix labeling schemes when the weight of links may change dynamically.

4.5 Hierarchical Routing

A way of reducing the various cost parameters of a routing method is the use of a *hierarchical division* of the network and an associated hierarchical routing method. The goal in most cases is to exploit the fact that much communication in computer networks is local, i.e., between nodes at relatively small distances from each other. Some of the cost parameters of a routing method depend on the size of the entire network rather than the length of the chosen path, as we now explain.

(1) *The length of addresses.* As each of the N nodes has a different address, each address consists of at least $\log N$ bits; more bits may even be required if information is encoded in addresses, such as in prefix routing.

(2) *The size of the routing table.* In the routing methods described in Sections 4.2 and 4.3, the table contains an entry for each node, and thus has a linear size.

(3) *The cost of table lookups.* The cost of a single table lookup is likely to be larger for a large routing table or for larger addresses. The total table-lookup time for the delivery of a single message also depends on the number of times the tables must be accessed.

In a hierarchical routing method, the network is divided into clusters, each cluster being a connected subset of nodes. If the source and destination of a packet are in the same cluster, the cost of forwarding the message is low, because to route within the cluster, the cluster is treated as a smaller isolated network. For the method described in Subsection 4.5.1, in each cluster there is a fixed single node (the cluster *center*) that can make the more complicated routing decisions necessary to send packets to other clusters. Thus, longer routing tables and the manipulation of long addresses are only necessary in the centers. Each cluster itself can be divided into subclusters in order to obtain a multi-level division of the nodes.

It is not necessarily desirable that each communication between clusters must take place via a cluster center; this type of design has the disadvantage that the entire cluster becomes vulnerable to failure of the center. Lentfert *et al.* [LUST89] describe a hierarchical routing method in which each node is equally able to send messages outside the cluster. Yet the method uses only small tables, because entire clusters to which a node does not belong are treated as a single node. Awerbuch *et al.* [ABNLP90] use the paradigm of hierarchical routing to construct a class of routing schemes that allows a trade-off between the efficiency and space requirements.

4.5.1 Reducing the Number of Routing Decisions

All the routing methods discussed so far require that routing decisions are made at each intermediate node, which means that for a route of length l the routing tables must be accessed l times. For minimum-hop strategies l is bounded by the diameter of the network, but for general, cycle-free routing strategies (such as interval routing) $N-1$ is the best bound one can give. In this subsection we shall discuss a method by which the number of table-lookups can be decreased.

We make use of the following lemma, which concerns the existence of a suitable division of the network into connected clusters.

Lemma 4.47 *For each $s \leq N$ there exists a division of the network into clusters $C_1, \ldots, C_m$ such that*

(1) *each cluster is a connected subgraph,*
(2) *each cluster contains at least s nodes, and*
(3) *each cluster has radius at most $2s$.*

Proof. Let $D_1, \ldots, D_m$ be a maximal collection of disjoint connected subgraphs such that each D_i has radius $\leq s$ and contains at least s nodes. Every node not in $\cup_{i=1}^m D_i$ is connected to one of the subsets by a path of length at most s, otherwise the path could be added as a separate cluster. Form the clusters C_i by including every node not in $\cup_{i=1}^m D_i$ in a cluster closest to it. The extended clusters still contain at least s nodes each, they are still connected and disjoint, and they have radius at most $2s$. $\qquad\square$

The routing method assigns a color to each packet, and it is assumed that only a few colors are used. Nodes now act as follows. Depending on its color, a packet is either forwarded immediately over a fixed channel (corresponding to the color) or a more complex routing decision is called for. It is allowed that nodes have different protocols for handling packets.

Theorem 4.48 [LT86] *For every network of N nodes there is a routing method that requires at most $O(\sqrt{N})$ routing decisions for each packet, and uses three colors.*

Proof. Assume that a division as implied by Lemma 4.47 is given and observe that each C_i contains a node c_i such that $d(v, c_i) \leq 2s$ for each $v \in C_i$, because C_i has radius at most $2s$. Let T be a minimum-size subtree of G connecting all the c_i. Because T is minimal it contains at most m leaves, hence it contains at most $m-2$ branch points (nodes of degree larger than 2); see Exercise 4.9. We refer to the nodes of T as *centers* (the c_i), branch points, and path nodes (the remaining nodes).

The routing method first sends a packet to the center c_i of the cluster of its source node (green phase), then via T to the center c_j of the cluster of its destination node (blue phase), and finally within C_j to the destination itself (phase red). The green phase uses a fixed sink tree for the center of each cluster, and requires no routing decisions. The path nodes of T have two incident tree channels, and forward each blue packet via the tree channel through which they did not receive the packet. Branch points and centers in T must make routing decisions. For the red phase a shortest-path routing strategy within the cluster can be used, which bounds the number of decisions in this phase to $2s$. This bounds the number of routing decisions to $2m - 2 + 2s$, which is at most $2N/s - 2 + 2s$. Choosing $s \approx \sqrt{N}$ gives the bound $O(\sqrt{N})$. □

Theorem 4.48 establishes a bound on the overall number of routing decisions necessary to deliver each packet, but does not rely on any particular algorithm by which these decisions are taken. The routing method used in T can be the tree routing scheme of Santoro and Khatib, but it is also possible to apply the principle of clustering to T itself to reduce the number of routing decisions even further.

Theorem 4.49 [LT86] *For every network of N nodes and every positive integer $f \leq \log N$ there is a routing method that requires at most $O(f \cdot N^{1/f})$ routing decisions for each packet, and uses $2f + 1$ colors.*

Proof. The argument is similar to the proof of Theorem 4.48, but instead of choosing $s \approx \sqrt{N}$ the construction is applied recursively to the tree T (with the same cluster size s). The tree is a connected network, essentially of $< 2m$ nodes because the path nodes of T only pass on packets from one fixed channel to the other, and can be ignored.

The clustering is repeated f times. The network G has N nodes. The tree obtained after one level of clustering has at most N/s centers and N/s branch points, i.e., $N(2/s)$ essential nodes. If the tree obtained after i levels of clustering has m_i essential nodes, then the tree obtained after $i + 1$ levels of clustering has at most m_i/s centers and m_i/s branch points, i.e., $m_i(2/s)$ essential nodes. The tree obtained after f levels of clustering has at most $m_f = N(2/s)^f$ essential nodes.

Each level of clustering increases the number of colors by two, hence with f levels of clustering $2f + 1$ colors are used. At most $2m_f$ decisions are needed in the highest level, and s decisions are needed at each level of clustering in the destination cluster, which brings the number of routing decisions to $2m_f + fs$. Choosing $s \approx 2N^{1/f}$ gives $m_f = O(1)$, hence the number of routing decisions is bounded by $f \cdot s = O(f \cdot N^{1/f})$. □

The use of approximately $\log N$ colors leads to a routing method that requires $O(\log N)$ routing decisions. The inspection of the color of a packet also becomes a kind of routing decision in this case, but it involves small tables (of length $O(\log N)$ at most) and is actually required only in a small fraction of the nodes.

Exercises to Chapter 4
Section 4.1

Exercise 4.1 *Assume that routing tables are updated after each topological change in such a way that they are cycle-free even during updates. Does this guarantee that packets are always delivered even when the network is subject to a possibly infinite number of topological changes?*

Prove that no routing algorithm can guarantee delivery of packets under continuing topological changes.

Section 4.2

Exercise 4.2 *A student proposes to omit the sending of $\langle \mathbf{nys}, w \rangle$ messages from Algorithm 4.6; he argues that a node knows that a neighbor is not a son in T_w if no $\langle \mathbf{ys}, w \rangle$ message is received from that neighbor.*

Is it possible to modify the algorithm in this way? What happens to the complexity of the algorithm?

Exercise 4.3 *Prove that the following assertion is an invariant of the Chandy–Misra algorithm for computing paths towards v_0 (Algorithm 4.7).*

$$\forall u, w : \langle \mathbf{mydist}, v_0, d \rangle \in M_{wu} \quad \Rightarrow \quad d(w, v_0) \leq d$$
$$\wedge \; \forall u : d(u, v_0) \leq D_u[v_0]$$

Give an example of an execution for which the number of messages is exponential in the number of channels of the network.

Section 4.3

Exercise 4.4 *Give the values of all variables in a terminal configuration of the Netchange algorithm when the algorithm is applied to a network of the following topology:*

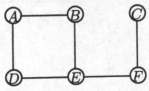

After a terminal configuration has been reached, a channel between A and F is added. What messages does F send to A when processing the $\langle \mathbf{repair}, A \rangle$

*notification? What messages does A send upon receipt of these messages
from F?*

Section 4.4

Exercise 4.5 *Give an example to demonstrate that Lemma 4.22 does not
hold for networks with asymmetric channel cost.*

Exercise 4.6 *Does there exist an ILS that does not use all channels for
routing? Does there exist a valid one? An optimal one?*

Exercise 4.7 *Give a graph G and a depth-first search tree T of G such that
G has $N = n^2$ nodes, the diameter of G and the depth of T are $O(n)$, and
there are nodes u and v such that a packet from u to v is delivered after
$N - 1$ hops with the depth-first search ILS.
(The graph can be chosen in such a way that G is outerplanar, which implies
(by Theorem 4.37) that G actually has an optimal ILS.)*

Exercise 4.8 *Give the depth-first search ILS for a ring of N nodes. Find
nodes u and v such that $d(u, v) = 2$, and the scheme uses $N - 2$ hops to
deliver a packet from u to v.*

Section 4.5

Exercise 4.9 *Prove that the minimality of the tree T in the proof of Theorem 4.48 implies that it has at most m leaves. Prove that any tree with m
leaves has at most $m - 2$ branch points.*

5

Deadlock-free Packet Switching

Messages (packets) traveling through a packet-switched communication network must be stored at each node before being forwarded to the next node on the path to their destination. Each node of the network reserves some buffer space for this purpose. As the amount of buffer space is finite in each node, situations may occur where no packet can be forwarded because all buffers in the next node are occupied, as illustrated by Figure 5.1. Each of the four nodes has B buffers, each capable of containing exactly one packet. Node s has sent B packets with destination v to t, and node v has sent B packets with destination s to u. All buffers in u and v are now occupied, and consequently none of the packets stored in t and u can be forwarded towards its destination.

Situations where a group of packets can never reach their destination because they are all waiting for the use of a buffer currently occupied by another packet in the group are referred to as *store-and-forward deadlocks*. (Other types of deadlock will be discussed briefly at the end of this chapter.) An important problem in the design of packet-switching networks is how to deal with store-and-forward deadlocks. In this chapter we shall treat several

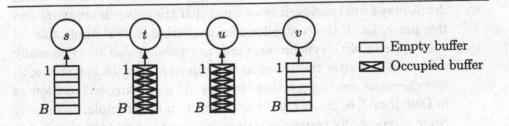

Figure 5.1 AN EXAMPLE OF A STORE-AND-FORWARD DEADLOCK.

methods, referred to as *controllers*, that can be used to avoid the possibility of store-and-forward deadlocks by introducing restrictions on when a packet can be generated or forwarded. Methods of avoiding store-and-forward deadlocks are found in the network layer of the OSI reference model (Subsection 1.2.2).

Two kinds of method will be discussed, based on *structured* and *unstructured* buffer pools. Methods using structured buffer pools (Section 5.2) will identify for a node and a packet a specific buffer that must be taken if a packet is generated or received. If this buffer is occupied, the packet cannot be accepted. In methods using unstructured buffer pools (Section 5.3) all buffers are equal; the method only prescribes whether or not a packet can be accepted, but does not determine in which buffer it must be placed. Some notations and definitions are introduced in Section 5.1, and we conclude the chapter with a discussion of further issues in Section 5.4.

5.1 Introduction

As usual, the network is modeled by a graph $G = (V, E)$; the distance between nodes is measured in hops. Each node has B buffers for temporarily storing packets. The set of all buffers is denoted $\mathcal{B}$, and the symbols b, c, b_u, etc., are used to denote buffers.

The handling of packets by the nodes is described by the following three types of moves that can occur in the network.

(1) *Generation.* A node u "creates" a new packet p (actually by accepting the packet from a higher level protocol) and places it in an empty buffer in u. The node u is called the *source* of p in this case.

(2) *Forwarding.* A packet p is forwarded from a node u to an *empty* buffer in the next node w on its route (the route is determined by the routing algorithm used). As a result of the move the buffer previously occupied by p becomes empty. Although the controllers that we shall define may forbid moves, it is assumed that the network always allows this move, i.e., if the controller does not forbid it, it is applicable.

In systems with synchronous message passing this move is easily seen to be a single transition as in Definition 2.7. In systems with asynchronous message passing the move is not a single transition as in Definition 2.6, but it can be implemented, for example, as follows. Node u repeatedly transmits p to w, but does not discard the packet from the buffer as long as no acknowledgement is received. When node w receives the packet it decides whether it will accept the packet in one of its buffers. If so, the packet is placed in the buffer and an acknowledgement is sent to u, otherwise the packet is simply ignored. Of course, more efficient protocols can be designed to implement the move, for example those where u does not transmit p until u knowns that w will accept p. In either case the move consists of several transitions of the types mentioned in Definition 2.6, but it will be considered as a single step for the purpose of this chapter.

(3) *Consumption.* A packet p occupying a buffer in its destination node is removed from the buffer. It is assumed that the network always allows this move.

Denote by $\mathcal{P}$ the collection of all paths followed by the packets. This collection is determined by the routing algorithm (see Chapter 4); how it is determined need not concern us here. Let k be the number of hops in the longest path in $\mathcal{P}$. It is not assumed that k equals the diameter of G; k may exceed the diameter if the routing algorithm does not select minimum-hop paths, and k may be smaller than the diameter if all communication in G is between nodes at limited distances.

As is seen from the example given at the beginning of this chapter, deadlocks may arise if all moves are allowed to occur unrestrictedly (barring the trivial restriction that u must have an empty buffer if a packet is generated in u and w must have an empty buffer if a packet is forwarded to w). We shall now define a controller as an algorithm that permits or forbids various moves in the network, subject to the following requirements.

(1) The consumption of a packet (at its destination) is always allowed.
(2) The generation of a packet in a node where all buffers are empty is always allowed.
(3) The controller uses only local information, i.e., the decision whether a packet can be accepted in node u depends only on information known to u or contained in the packet.

The second requirement excludes trivial solutions that avoid deadlocked packets (see Definition 5.2) by refusing to accept any packet in the network. As in Chapter 2, let Z_u denote the set of states of node u, and $\mathcal{M}$ the set of possible messages (packets).

Definition 5.1 *A controller for the network $G = (V, E)$ is a collection of pairs* **con** $= \{Gen_u, For_u\}_{u \in V}$, *where $Gen_u \subseteq Z_u \times \mathcal{M}$ and $For_u \subseteq Z_u \times \mathcal{M}$. If $c_u \in Z_u$ is a state of u where all buffers of u are empty, then for all $p \in \mathcal{M}$, $(c_u, p) \in Gen_u$.*

The controller **con** allows the generation of a packet p in node u, where the state of u is c_u, if and only if $(c_u, p) \in Gen_u$, and allows the forwarding of packet p from u to w if and only if $(c_w, p) \in For_w$. The formal definition of a controller does not include conditions for the consumption of packets, because the consumption of a packet (at its destination) is always allowed. The moves of the network under controller **con** are exactly those moves of the network that are permitted by **con**.

A packet in the network is deadlocked if it can never reach its destination in any sequence of moves of the network.

Definition 5.2 *Given a network G, a controller **con** for G, and a configuration γ of G, a packet p (occurring in configuration γ) is deadlocked if there is no sequence of moves under **con**, applicable in γ, in which p is consumed. A configuration is called a deadlock configuration if it contains deadlocked packets.*

As the example of Figure 5.1 shows, deadlock configurations exist for every controller. The task of the controller is of course to avoid that the network ever enters such a configuration. The initial configurations of the network are configurations in which there are no packets in the network.

Definition 5.3 *A controller is deadlock-free if no deadlock configuration is reachable under the controller from an initial configuration.*

5.2 Structured Solutions

We shall now discuss a class of controllers relying on so-called buffer graphs, introduced by Merlin and Schweitzer [MS80a]. The principle of these buffer graphs is based on the observation that (in the absence of a controller) a deadlock is due to a cyclic wait situation. In a cyclic wait situation there exists a sequence $p_0, \ldots, p_{s-1}$ of packets, such that for each i, p_i wants to move to a buffer occupied by p_{i+1} (index counted modulo s). Cyclic waits are avoided by moving the packets along paths in an acyclic graph (the buffer graph). In Subsection 5.2.1 buffer graphs and the related class of controllers will be defined and two simple examples of buffer graphs are presented. In Subsection 5.2.2 a more sophisticated construction of buffer graphs will be given, again with two examples.

5.2.1 Buffer Graphs

Let a network G with a set $\mathcal{B}$ of buffers be given.

Definition 5.4 *A buffer graph (for G, $\mathcal{B}$) is a directed graph BG on the buffers of the network, i.e., $BG = (\mathcal{B}, \vec{BE})$, such that*

(1) *BG is acyclic (contains no directed cycle);*

(2) *$bc \in \vec{BE}$ implies that b and c are buffers in the same node, or buffers in two nodes connected by a channel in G; and*

(3) *for each path $P \in \mathcal{P}$ there exists a path in BG whose image (see below) is P.*

The second requirement induces a mapping from paths in BG to paths in G; if b_0, b_1, ..., b_s is a path in BG, then, if u_i is the node where buffer b_i resides, u_0, u_1, ..., u_s is a sequence of nodes such that for each $i < s$ either $u_i u_{i+1} \in E$ or $u_i = u_{i+1}$. The path in G obtained from this sequence by omitting successive duplications is called the *image* of the original path b_0, b_1, ..., b_s in BG.

A packet cannot be placed in an arbitrarily chosen buffer; it must be placed in a buffer from which it can still reach its destination via a path in BG, i.e., a buffer that is suitable for the packet according to the following definition.

Definition 5.5 *Let p be a packet in node u with destination v. A buffer b in u is suitable for p if there is a path in BG from b to a buffer c in v, whose image is a path that p can follow in G.*
One such a path in BG will be designated as the guaranteed path and $nb(p, b)$ denotes the next buffer on the guaranteed path. For each newly generated packet p in u there exists a designated suitable buffer $fb(p)$ in u.

Here fb and nb are acronyms for first buffer and next buffer. Observe that the buffer $nb(p, b)$ is always suitable for p. In all buffer graphs used in this section $nb(p, b)$ resides in a node different from the node where b resides. The use of "internal" edges in BG, i.e., edges between two buffers in the same node, will be discussed later.

The buffer-graph controller. A buffer graph BG can be used to implement a deadlock-free controller $\mathbf{bgc}_{BG}$ provided that the buffer $nb(p, b)$ is encoded in each packet and/or the state of the node where p resides.

Definition 5.6 *The controller $\mathbf{bgc}_{BG}$ is defined as follows.*

(1) *The generation of a packet p in u is allowed if and only if the buffer $fb(p)$ is free. If the packet is generated it is placed in this buffer.*

(2) *The forwarding of a packet p from a buffer in u to a buffer in w*

(possibly $u = w$) is allowed if and only if $nb(p, b)$ (in w) is free. If the forwarding takes place p is placed in $nb(p, b)$.

Theorem 5.7 *The controller* $\mathbf{bgc}_{BG}$ *is a deadlock-free controller.*

Proof. If u is a node with all buffers empty the generation of any packet in u is allowed, which implies that $\mathbf{bgc}_{BG}$ is a controller.

For each $b \in \mathcal{B}$, define the *buffer class* of b as the length of the longest path in BG that ends in b. Observe that the buffer classes of buffers on a path in BG (in particular, on a guaranteed path) are strictly increasing, i.e., the buffer class of $nb(p, b)$ is larger than the buffer class of b.

As the controller allows placement of packets only in suitable buffers and as there are no packets initially, each reachable configuration of the network under $\mathbf{bgc}_{BG}$ contains only packets in suitable buffers. It can be easily shown by a downward induction on the buffer classes that no buffer of buffer class r contains a deadlocked packet in such a configuration. Let R be the highest buffer class.

Case $r = R$: A buffer b in node u with the highest possible buffer class has no outgoing edges in BG. Consequently, a packet for which b is suitable has destination u and can be consumed when it is in b. It follows that no buffer of class R contains a deadlocked packet.

Case $r < R$: The induction hypothesis is that for each r' with $r < r' \leq R$, no buffer of buffer class r' contains a deadlocked packet (in a reachable configuration).

Let γ be a reachable configuration with a packet p in a buffer b of class $r < R$ in node u. If u is the destination of p then p can be consumed and consequently is not deadlocked. Otherwise, let $nb(p, b) = c$ be the next buffer on the guaranteed path from b, and observe that the buffer class r' of c exceeds r. By the induction hypothesis c does not contain a deadlocked packet, hence there is a configuration δ, reachable from γ, in which c is empty. In δ p can move to c, and by the induction hypothesis p is not deadlocked in the resulting configuration δ'. Consequently, p is not deadlocked in γ.

$\square$

It can be seen from the proof that if the guaranteed path contains "internal" edges of the buffer graph (edges between two buffers in the same node) then the controller must allow additional moves by which a packet is placed in a different buffer in the same node. Usually the guaranteed path does not contain such edges. They are only used as optional moves to increase the efficiency of the forwarding, for example in the following situation. Packet p resides in buffer b_1 of node u and buffer $nb(p, b_1)$ in node w is occupied. There exists, however, a free buffer b_2 in u, which is suitable for p; furthermore $nb(p, b_2)$ in node w is empty. In this case the packet can be moved via b_2 and $nb(p, b_2)$.

Two examples of the use of buffer graphs, namely the destination scheme and the hops-so-far scheme, will now be discussed.

The destination scheme. The destination scheme uses N buffers in each node u, with a buffer $b_u[v]$ for each possible destination v. Node v is called the *target* of buffer $b_u[v]$. It must be assumed for this scheme that the routing algorithm forwards all packets with destination v via a directed tree T_v rooted towards v. (Actually this assumption can be relaxed; it suffices that the channels used for routing towards v form an acyclic subgraph of G.)

The buffer graph is defined by $BG_{\mathbf{d}} = (\mathcal{B}, \vec{BE})$, where $b_u[v_1] b_w[v_2] \in \vec{BE}$ if and only if $v_1 = v_2$ and uw is an edge of T_{v_1}. To see that $BG_{\mathbf{d}}$ is acyclic, observe that no edges exist between buffers with different targets and that the buffers with the same target v form a tree isomorphic to T_v. Each path $P \in \mathcal{P}$ with endpoint v is a path in T_v, and by construction there exists a path in $BG_{\mathbf{d}}$ of buffers with target v whose image is P. This path is chosen as the guaranteed path. This means that for a packet p with destination v, generated in node u, $fb(p) = b_u[v]$, and if this packet must be forwarded to w then $nb(p, b) = b_w[v]$.

Definition 5.8 *The controller* **dest** *is defined as* $\mathbf{bgc}_{BG_{\mathbf{d}}}$, *with fb and nb as defined in the previous paragraph.*

Theorem 5.9 *There exists a deadlock-free controller for arbitrary connected networks that uses N buffers in each node and allows packets to be routed via arbitrarily chosen sink trees.*

Proof. **dest** is a deadlock-free controller using this number of buffers. $\qquad\square$

As was mentioned earlier the requirement that routing is via sink trees can be relaxed to the requirement that packets towards one destination are sent via channels that form an acyclic graph. It is not sufficient that $\mathcal{P}$ contains only simple paths, as is shown by the example given in Figure 5.2. Here packets from u_1 for v are routed via the simple path $\langle u_1, w_1, u_2, \ldots, v \rangle$, and packets from u_2 for v are sent via the simple path $\langle u_2, w_2, u_1, \ldots, v \rangle$.

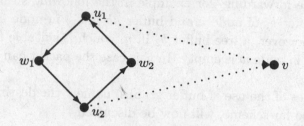

Figure 5.2 Forbidden routing for the controller **dest**.

Each path in $\mathcal{P}$ is simple; the collection of all channels used for routing packets to v contains the cycle $\langle u_1, w_1, u_2, w_2, u_1 \rangle$. See Exercise 5.2.

The controller **dest** is very simple to use, but has the disadvantage that a large number of buffers is required in each node, namely N. A dual *source* scheme can be defined in which the buffers indexed by v_i are used to store packets *generated in* v_i.

The hops-so-far scheme. In the hops-so-far scheme node u contains $k+1$ buffers $b_u[0], \ldots, b_u[k]$. It is assumed that each packet contains a *hop count* indicating how many hops the packet has made from its source.

The buffer graph is defined by $BG_{\mathbf{h}} = (\mathcal{B}, \vec{BE})$, where $b_u[i]\, b_w[j] \in \vec{BE}$ if and only if $i + 1 = j$ and $uw \in E$. To see that $BG_{\mathbf{h}}$ is acyclic, observe that the index of buffers increases strictly along each edge of $BG_{\mathbf{h}}$. As each path in $\mathcal{P}$ is at most k hops long, there is a corresponding path in the buffer graph; if $P = u_0, \ldots, u_l$ $(l \le k)$ then

$$b_{u_0}[0], \ b_{u_1}[1], \ \ldots, \ b_{u_l}[l]$$

is a path in $BG_{\mathbf{h}}$ with image P. This guaranteed path is described by $fb(p) = b_u[0]$ (for p generated in u) and $nb(p, b_u[i]) = b_w[i+1]$ for a packet that must be forwarded from u to w.

Definition 5.10 *The controller* **hsf** *is defined as* $\mathbf{bgc}_{BG_{\mathbf{h}}}$, *with* fb *and* nb *as defined in the previous paragraph.*

Theorem 5.11 *There exists a deadlock-free controller for arbitrary connected networks that uses $D + 1$ buffers in each node (where D is the diameter of the network), and requires packets to be sent via minimum-hop paths.*

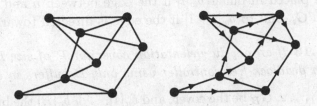

Figure 5.3 A GRAPH AND AN ACYCLIC ORIENTATION.

Proof. The use of minimum-hop paths gives $k = D$. Then **hsf** is a deadlock-free controller using $D + 1$ buffers in each node. (The number of buffers may be even smaller if packets need not be exchanged between nodes at large distances.) □

In the hops-so-far scheme the buffers indexed i are used to store packets that have traveled i hops so far. A dual *hops-to-go* scheme can be designed, in which buffers indexed i are used to store packets that have i more hops to travel towards their destination; see Exercise 5.3.

5.2.2 Orientations of G

In this subsection a method for constructing sophisticated buffer graphs, requiring only a few buffers per node, will be considered. In the hops-so-far controller the index of the buffer in which a packet is stored increases with every hop. We shall now allow a slower growth of the buffer index (thus saving on the total number of buffers in each node) by assuming an increase in the buffer index (not to be confused with the buffer class) with certain, but not necessarily all, hops. To avoid cycles in the buffer graph the channels that can be traversed without increasing the buffer index form an acyclic graph.

Definition 5.12 *An acyclic orientation of G is a directed acyclic graph obtained by directing all edges of G; see Figure 5.3.*
A sequence $G_1, \ldots, G_B$ of acyclic orientations of G is an acyclic orientation cover of size B for the collection $\mathcal{P}$ of paths if each path $P \in \mathcal{P}$ can be written as the concatenation of B paths $P_1, \ldots, P_B$, where P_i is a path in G_i.

When an acyclic orientation cover of size B is available a controller using only B buffers per node can be constructed. A packet is always generated in node u in buffer $b_u[1]$. A packet in buffer $b_u[i]$ that must be forwarded to node w is placed in buffer $b_w[i]$ if the edge between u and w is directed towards w in G_i, and to $b_w[i+1]$ if the edge is directed towards u in G_i.

Theorem 5.13 *If an acyclic orientation cover for $\mathcal{P}$ of size B exists, then there exists a deadlock-free controller using only B buffers in each node.*

Proof. Let $G_1, \ldots, G_B$ be the cover, and $b_u[1], \ldots, b_u[B]$ the buffers of node u. Write $uw \in \vec{E}_i$ if edge uw is directed towards w in G_i, and $wu \in \vec{E}_i$ if edge uw is directed towards u in G_i. A buffer graph is defined by $BG_\mathbf{a} = (\mathcal{B}, \vec{BE})$, where $b_u[i] b_w[j] \in \vec{BE}$ if and only if $uw \in E$ and $(i = j \wedge uw \in \vec{E}_i)$ or $(i + 1 = j \wedge wu \in \vec{E}_i)$. To see that this graph is acyclic, note that no cycle exists containing buffers with different indices because there is no edge from a given buffer to another with a smaller index. There is no cycle of buffers with the same index i because these buffers are arranged according to the acyclic graph G_i.

It is left to the reader (see Exercise 5.4) to demonstrate that for each $P \in \mathcal{P}$ there is a guaranteed path with image P, and that such a path is described by the following definitions:

$$fb(p) = b_u[1]$$
$$nb(p, b_u[i]) = \begin{cases} b_w[i] & \text{if } uw \in \vec{E}_i \\ b_w[i+1] & \text{if } wu \in \vec{E}_i \end{cases}$$

Having defined a buffer graph with B buffers per node, we may conclude the existence of a controller using B buffers in each node, which proves the theorem.   □

We refer to the resulting class of controllers as *acyclic orientation cover controllers*, or *AOC controllers*, for short. We shall now proceed to demonstrate the ease of controller design using acyclic orientation covers.

Packet switching on a ring. Acyclic orientation covers can be used to give deadlock-free controllers for several classes of networks. We shall first present a controller for rings, using only three buffers per node. For the following theorem it is assumed that channel weights are symmetric, i.e., $\omega_{uw} = \omega_{wu}$.

Theorem 5.14 *There exists a deadlock-free controller for a ring network that uses only three buffers per node and allows packets to be routed via shortest paths.*

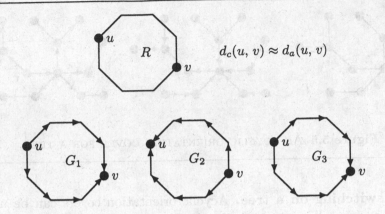

Figure 5.4 AN ACYCLIC ORIENTATION COVER FOR A RING.

Proof. By Theorem 5.13 it suffices to give an acyclic orientation cover of size three for a collection of paths that includes a shortest path between each pair of nodes.

The following notation is used. For nodes u and v, $d_c(u, v)$ denotes the length of the clockwise path from u to v and $d_a(u, v)$ the length of the anticlockwise path; $d_c(v, u) = d_a(u, v)$ and $d(u, v) = \min(d_c(u, v), d_a(u, v))$ hold. The sum of all channel weights is called C (the *circumference* of the ring) and obviously $d_c(u, v) + d_a(u, v) = C$ for all u, v, so $d(u, v) \leq C/2$.

First consider the simple case where there exist nodes u and v with $d(u, v) = C/2$. G_1 and G_3 are obtained by directing all edges towards v, and G_2 is obtained by directing all edges towards u; see Figure 5.4.

A shortest path from u to v is contained in G_1 or G_3, and a shortest path from v to u is contained in G_2. Let x, y be a pair of nodes not equal to the pair u, v. Then, as $d(x, y) \leq C/2$, there exists a shortest path P between x and y that does not contain both u and v. If P contains neither u nor v it is contained completely in either G_1 or G_2. If P contains v it is the concatenation of a path in G_1 and a path in G_2; if P contains u it is the concatenation of a path in G_2 and a path in G_3.

If there does not exist a pair u, v with $d(u, v) = C/2$, choose a pair for which $d(u, v)$ is as close to $C/2$ as possible. It can now be shown that if there is a pair x, y such that no shortest path is found as the concatenation of paths in the orientations of the cover, then $d(x, y)$ is closer to $C/2$ than $d(u, v)$.   □

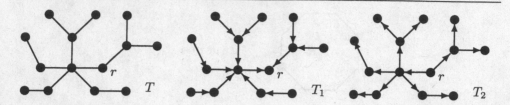

Figure 5.5 AN ACYCLIC ORIENTATION COVER FOR A TREE.

Packet switching on a tree. Acyclic orientation covers can be used to construct a controller using only two buffers per node for a network that is a tree.

Theorem 5.15 *There exists a deadlock-free controller for a tree network which uses only two buffers per node.*

Proof. By Theorem 5.13, it suffices to give an acyclic orientation for a tree that covers all simple paths. Choose an arbitrary node r, and obtain T_1 by orienting all edges towards r and T_2 by orienting all edges away from r; see Figure 5.5. A simple path from u to v is the concatenation of a path from u to the lowest common ancestor, which is in T_1, and a path from the lowest common ancestor to v, which is in T_2. $\qquad\square$

Because the scheme described here can be applied to (minimum depth) spanning trees of arbitrary networks, we have in fact shown that in every network deadlock free routing is possible with 2 buffers per node. The paths used for routing would not be optimal in general.

Application of the AOC controllers. As the ring example has demonstrated, the use of the AOC controllers may require a specific collection of paths to be used for routing messages. This poses several questions, which have been addresses by research over the past years.

Is it possible to use the minimal number of buffers and simultaneously route packets through optimal paths, and if not, what buffer/efficiency trade-offs are possible? Štefankovič [Ste99] demonstrated that AOC controllers are *less* efficient in buffer usage; he gave a class of networks that allows deadlock-free optimal routing with constant number of buffers per node, but the best optimal AOC controller requires $\Omega(\lg N/\lg\lg N)$ buffers. How big the gap between the best AOC controller and the best controller can be is unknown.

Is it possible to encode the paths used in an AOC controller with compact routing schemes such as interval routing? For the hypercube it is known that (1) there exists an optimal interval labeling scheme, (2) there exists a controller that uses optimal paths and requires 2 buffers per node, but (3) there exists *no* AOC controller that requires 2 buffers and uses optimal paths that can be coded in an interval labeling scheme. A lot of research in this area is still going on.

5.3 Unstructured Solutions

We shall now discuss a class of controllers proposed by Toueg and Ullman [TU81]. These controllers do not prescribe in which buffer a packet must be placed, and they use only simple local information such as the hop count or the number of occupied buffers in a node.

5.3.1 Forward-count and Backward-count Controllers

The forward-count controller. For a packet p, let s_p be the number of hops it still has to make to its destination; of course, $0 \leq s_p \leq k$ holds. It is not always necessary to maintain s_p in the packet, because many routing algorithms store this information in each node; see e.g. the Netchange algorithm of Section 4.3. For a node u, f_u denotes the number of free buffers in u. Of course, $0 \leq f_u \leq B$ holds always.

Definition 5.16 *The controller* **FC** *(Forward-count) accepts a packet p in node u if and only if $s_p < f_u$.*

The controller accepts a packet if the node contains more free buffers than the packet has hops to go.

Theorem 5.17 *If $B > k$ then* **FC** *is a deadlock-free controller.*

Proof. To show that generation of a packet is allowed in an empty node, observe that if all buffers of u are empty, $f_u = B$. A new packet has at most k hops to go, so $B > k$ implies that the packet is accepted.

Deadlock-freedom of **FC** will be shown by contradiction; assume γ is a reachable deadlock configuration of the controller. Obtain configuration δ by applying to γ a maximal sequence of forwarding and consumption moves. No packet can move in δ, and as γ is a deadlock configuration there is at least one packet left in configuration δ. Let p be a packet in δ with minimal distance to its destination, i.e., s_p is the smallest value of any packet in δ.

Let u be the node where p resides. As u is not the destination of p (p could be consumed in δ otherwise) there is a neighbor w of u to which p must be forwarded. As this move is not allowed by **FC**,

$$s_p - 1 \geq f_w.$$

Because $s_p \leq k$ and by assumption $k < B$, this implies $f_w < B$, which means that there is at least one packet residing in w in configuration δ. Of the packets in w, let q be the one most recently accepted by w, and let f'_w denote the number of free buffers in w just before the acceptance of q by w. Because packet q now occupies one of these f'_w buffers and (by the choice of q) all packets accepted by w after q have thereafter been removed from w, $f'_w \leq f_w + 1$.

The acceptance of q by w implies $s_q < f'_w$, and combining the three derived inequalities we obtain

$$s_q < f'_w \leq f_w + 1 \leq s_p,$$

which contradicts the choice of p. ☐

The backward-count controller. A controller that is a "dual" to **FC** is obtained when the decision to accept a packet is based on the number of steps a packet has already made. Let, for a packet p, t_p be the number of hops it has made from its source. Of course, $0 \leq t_p \leq k$ holds always.

Definition 5.18 *The controller* **BC** *(Backward-Count) accepts a packet p in node u if and only if $t_p > k - f_u$.*

The proof that **BC** is a deadlock-free controller (Exercise 5.6) is very similar to the proof of Theorem 5.17.

5.3.2 Forward-state and Backward-state Controllers

By using more detailed information about the packets residing in a node, a controller can be given that is very similar to the forward count controller, but allows more moves.

The forward-state controller. Use the notation s_p as in the previous subsection. For node u define (as a function of the state of u) the *state vector* as $\langle j_0, \ldots, j_k \rangle$, where j_s is the number of packets p in u with $s_p = s$.

Definition 5.19 *The controller* **FS** *(Forward-State) accepts a packet p in node u with state vector* $\langle j_0, \ldots, j_k \rangle$ *if and only if*

$$\forall i, 0 \le i \le s_p : i < B - \sum_{s=i}^{k} j_s.$$

Theorem 5.20 *If* $B > k$ *then* **FS** *is deadlock-free.*

Proof. It is left to the reader to show that an empty node accepts every packet. Assume there exists a reachable deadlock configuration γ, and obtain configuration δ by applying a maximal sequence of forward and consumption moves. No packet can move and there is at least one packet left in δ. Choose a packet p with a minimal value of s_p, and let u be the node where p resides and w the node to which p must be forwarded. Let $\langle j_0, \ldots, j_k \rangle$ be the state vector of w in δ.

If w contains no packets then $\sum_{s=0}^{k} j_s = 0$, which implies that w can accept p, and this is not the case. Consequently, w contains at least one packet; of the packets in w, let q be a packet that is closest to its destination, i.e., $s_q = \min\{s : j_s > 0\}$. It will be shown that $s_q < s_p$, which is a contradiction.

Of the packets in w, let r be the one that was most recently accepted by w; of course, $s_q \le s_r$ holds. Let $\langle j'_0, \ldots, j'_k \rangle$ be the state vector of w just before the acceptance of r. The acceptance of r implies

$$\forall i, 0 \le i \le s_r : i < B - \sum_{s=i}^{k} j'_s.$$

When $\langle j'_0, \ldots, j'_k \rangle$ was the state vector of w, r was accepted by w. Since then packets may have moved from w, but all packets accepted into w later than r have been removed (by the choice of r). This implies

$$j_s \le j'_s \qquad \text{for } s \ne s_r$$
$$j_{s_r} \le j'_{s_r} + 1$$

But this means that

$$\forall i, 0 \le i \le s_r : i < B - \sum_{s=i}^{k} j_s + 1.$$

Thus, taking $i = s_q$,

$$s_q \le B - \sum_{s=s_q}^{k} j_s.$$

Now use the fact that p is not accepted by w, i.e.,

$$\exists i_0, 0 \le i_0 \le s_p - 1 : i_0 \ge B - \sum_{s=i_0}^{k} j_s.$$

This gives the inequality

$$
\begin{aligned}
s_p &> s_p - 1 \\
&\ge i_0 && \text{see above} \\
&\ge B - \textstyle\sum_{s=i_0}^{k} j_s && \text{see above} \\
&\ge B - \textstyle\sum_{s=0}^{k} j_s && \text{because } j_s \ge 0 \text{ (and } i_0 \ge 0) \\
&\ge B - \textstyle\sum_{s=s_q}^{k} j_s && \text{because } j_s = 0 \text{ for } s < s_q \\
&\ge s_q,
\end{aligned}
$$

which is the required contradiction.   □

The backward-state controller. There is also a controller, "dual" to the forward-state controller, that uses more detailed information than the backward-count controller and allows more moves. Let t_p be as before, and define the state vector as $\langle i_0, \ldots, i_k \rangle$, where i_t equals the number of packets in node u that have made t hops.

Definition 5.21 *The controller* **BS** *(Backward-State) accepts a packet p in node u with state vector $\langle i_0, \ldots, i_k \rangle$ if and only if*

$$\forall j, t_p \le j \le k : j > \sum_{t=0}^{j} i_t - B + k.$$

The proof that **BS** is deadlock-free is very similar to the proof of Theorem 5.20.

Comparison between controllers. The forward-state controller is more liberal then the forward-count controller in the sense that it allows more moves:

Lemma 5.22 *Each move allowed by* **FC** *is also allowed by* **FS**.

Proof. Assume the acceptance of p by u is allowed by **FC**. Then $s_p < f_u = B - \sum_{s=0}^{k} j_s$, so for $i \le s_p$, $i < B - \sum_{s=i}^{k} j_s$ follows, which implies that the move is allowed by **FS**.   □

It was shown in [TU81] that **FC** is more liberal then **BC**, **FS** is more liberal then **BS**, and **BS** is more liberal then **BC**. It was also shown that each of these four controllers is the most liberal possible, of the controllers using the same information.

5.4 Further Issues

In the results of this chapter the number of buffers needed by a controller has always played a role. It is usually the case that the throughput is increased if more buffers are available. In the unstructured solutions only a lower bound on the number of buffers is given; a larger number can be used without any modification. In the structured solutions additional buffers must somehow be inserted into the buffer graph, which can be done either *statically* or *dynamically*. If this is done statically each buffer has a fixed location in the buffer graph, i.e., the buffer graph is constructed to be "wider" than in the examples provided in Section 5.2. Instead of a single buffer $fb(p)$ or $nb(p, b)$ usually several buffers are specified as the possible beginning or continuation of a path through the buffer graph. If the insertion of additional buffers is done dynamically the buffer graph is first constructed containing as few buffers as possible; we refer to the buffers in the graph as *logical* buffers. During operation each actual buffer (referred to as a *physical* buffer) may be used as any of the logical buffers, where it must always be ensured that for each logical buffer there is at least one physical buffer assuming its role. With such a scheme only a small number of buffers must be reserved in order to avoid deadlocks, while the rest of the buffers can be used freely in a very flexible manner.

It was assumed in this chapter that packets are of fixed size: the buffers are equally large and each buffer can contain exactly one packet. The problem can also be considered under the assumption that each packet may have a different size. The solutions of Section 5.3 have been adapted to this assumption by Bodlaender; see [Bod86].

5.4.1 Topological Changes

Up to this point we have not explicitly considered the possibility of the occurrence of topological changes in the network during a packet's travel from source to destination. After the occurrence of such a change the routing tables of each node will be updated and the packet is then forwarded using the changed values of these tables. As a result of the modification of the tables a packet may follow a path that would never have been followed if no changes had occured; it may even be the case that the ultimate route of a packet now contains cycles.

The impact of this on the deadlock-avoidance methods treated in this chapter is rather counter-intuitive. The **dest** controller, whose correctness relies on the property that $\mathcal{P}$ contains only simple paths, can still be used without any modification. The controllers that only assume an upper bound on the number of hops of a path require extra care when used in this case.

The controller dest. Within a finite time after the occurrence of the last topological change the routing tables have converged to cycle-free tables. Even though a cyclic wait situation may have existed *during* the computation of the tables, when the computation has been completed the buffer graph is again acyclic, and all packets are stored in suitable buffers. Consequently, when the routing tables have converged the resulting configuration contains no deadlocked packets.

Hop-counting controllers. Consider a controller that relies on the assumption that a packet must make at most k hops. It is possible to choose k sufficiently large in order to guarantee *with large probability* that each packet reaches its destination within k hops, even if some topological changes occur during its travel from source to destination. For all packets that reach their destination within k hops the hops-so-far, backward-count and backward-state controllers can be used without any modification. It is always possible, however, that a packet has not reached its destination after k hops due to an unlucky pattern of topological changes and table updates. If this is the case the packet is stored in an unsuitable buffer, and it will forever be blocked in a node different from its destination.

Situations of this kind can only be resolved in cooperation with protocols in higher levels of the protocol hierarchy. The simplest solution is to discard the packet. Seen from the viewpoint of the end-to-end transport protocol the packet is now lost; but this loss can be dealt with by the transport layer protocol as was seen in Section 3.2.

Discarding packets is necessary also to implement the assumption made in Section 3.2, that a packet has a maximum packet lifetime μ. If forwarding a packet takes at least time μ_0, a bound of μ on the end-to-end lifetime of a packet implies a bound of $k = \mu/\mu_0$ on the number of hops a packet can go.

5.4.2 Other Types of Deadlock

Only store-and-forward deadlocks have been considered in this chapter. If the assumptions made in Section 5.1 are valid store-and-forward deadlocks are the only deadlock types that can occur. In practical networks, however, these assumptions may not always be justified and, as pointed out by Merlin and Schweitzer [MS80b], this may introduce other types of deadlock. Merlin and Schweitzer consider four types, namely progeny deadlock, copy-release deadlock, pacing deadlock, and reassembly deadlock, and show how these types of deadlock can be avoided by an extension of the buffer-graph method.

Progeny deadlock may arise when a packet p in the network can create another packet q, for example a failure report to the source if a failed channel is encountered. This would impose a causal relation between the generation of a new packet (q) and the forwarding or consumption of an already existing one (p), which violates the assumption in Section 5.1 that the network always allows forwarding and consumption of a packet.

Progeny deadlock can be avoided by having two copies of the buffer graph, one for original messages and one for secondary messages (the progeny). If the progeny may again create a next generation of progeny, multiple levels of the buffer graph must be used.

Copy-release deadlock may arise when the source holds a copy of the packet until an (end-to-end) acknowledgement for the packet is received from the destination. (Compare the timer-based protocol of Section 3.2, and assume the that sequence in_p is stored in the same memory space as is used by the routing mechanism for the interim storage of packets.) This violates our assumption (in Section 5.1) that a buffer becomes empty when the packet occupying it is forwarded.

Two extensions of the buffer-graph principle are given by which copy-release deadlock can be avoided. The first solution relies on the assumption that a copy-release deadlock situation always arises due to the cyclic waiting of the original *and* acknowledgement messages. The solution is to treat the acknowledgements as progeny and store them in a separate copy of the buffer graph. In a second solution, which requires fewer buffers in most cases, newly generated packets are placed in dedicated *source buffers*, in which forwarded packets may not be placed.

Pacing deadlock may arise when the network contains nodes, with limited internal storage, that may refuse to consume messages until some other messages have been generated. For example, a teletype terminal must first output some characters before it can accept the next characters for displaying. This violates our assumption that a packet at its destination can always be consumed.

Pacing deadlock can be avoided by making a distinction between paceable packets and pacing responses, such that packets in the first type may be unconsumable until a packet of the second type has been generated. Different copies of the buffer graph are used for the two types of message.

Reassembly deadlock may arise in networks where large messages are divided into smaller packets for transmission and no packet can be removed from the network until all packets of the message have reached the destination. (Compare the sliding-window protocol of Section 3.1, where words are removed from out_p only if all words with smaller index have also been received.) This violates our assumption that the consumption of a packet at its destination is always possible.

Reassembly deadlocks can be avoided by using separate groups of buffers for packet forwarding and reassembly.

5.4.3 Livelock

The definition of deadlocked packets (Definition 5.2) implies that under a deadlock-free controller there exists for each packet at least one computation in which the packet is consumed. Because in general a large number of different computations are possible, this does not imply that each packet is eventually delivered at its destination, even in an infinite computation, as is illustrated by Figure 5.6. Assume that u has an infinite stream of packets to send to v, and each time a buffer in w becomes empty the next packet from u is accepted. Node s has a packet for t, which is not deadlocked because each time a buffer in w becomes empty there is a *possible* continuation of the computation in which the packet is accepted by w and forwarded to t. Although this continuation is possible, it is not enforced, and the packet may remain in s forever. A situation of this kind is referred to as *livelock*.

The controllers discussed in this chapter can be extended so as to avoid livelock situations as well.

Definition 5.23 *Given a network, a controller* **con**, *and a configuration* γ, *packet p is livelocked if there exists an infinite sequence of moves, applicable in γ, in which p is not consumed.*
Configuration γ is a livelock configuration if it contains livelocked packets.
A controller is livelock-free if no livelock configuration is reachable from a configuration having no packets under the moves of the controller.

In the remainder of this subsection livelock-freeness of the buffer graph controllers will be proved; the extensions for the unstructured solutions are briefly mentioned at the end.

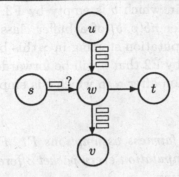

Figure 5.6 AN EXAMPLE OF LIVELOCK.

The buffer-graph controller. It can be demonstrated that the controllers of Section 5.2 are livelock-free without further modification if their moves in an infinite sequence satisfy a number of fairness assumptions. F1 and F2 are strong fairness assumptions and F3 is a weak fairness assumption.

F1. If the generation of a packet p is continuously attempted then each infinite computation in which $fb(p)$ is free in infinitely many configurations contains the generation of p.

F2. If in configuration γ packet p must be forwarded from u to w then each infinite computation starting in γ in which $nb(p, b)$ is free in infinitely many configurations contains the forwarding of p.

F3. If a packet p is in its destination in configuration γ then each infinite computation starting in γ contains the consumption of p.

Lemma 5.24 *If the fairness assumptions F2 and F3 are satisfied then in each infinite computation of* **bgc** *each buffer is free infinitely often.*

Proof. The proof is by downward induction on the buffer classes. As in the proof of Theorem 5.7, let R be the largest buffer class. Remember that in configurations reachable under **bgc** all packets reside in suitable buffers.

Case $r = R$: A buffer of class R has no outgoing edges, and consequently a packet in such a buffer has reached its destination. Hence, by assumption F3, after each configuration in which such a buffer is occupied there will be a configuration in which it is empty. This implies that it is empty in infinitely many configurations.

Case $r < R$: Let γ be a configuration in which buffer b of class $r < R$ is occupied by packet p. If p has reached its destination there will be a later configuration in which b is empty by F3. Otherwise, p must be forwarded to a buffer $nb(p, b)$ of a buffer class $r' > r$. By induction, in each infinite computation starting in γ this buffer is empty infinitely often. This implies by F2 that p will be forwarded and hence that there will be a configuration after γ in which b is empty.

$\square$

Theorem 5.25 *If the fairness assumptions F1, F2, and F3 are satisfied then in each infinite computation every packet offered to the network will be consumed in its destination.*

Proof. By Lemma 5.24 all buffers are empty in infinitely many configurations. By F1 this implies that each packet that is continuously offered to the network will be generated. By F2 it will be forwarded until it reaches its destination. By F3 it will be consumed in its destination. $\square$

One may simply assume that the mechanism for making non-deterministic choices in the distributed system ensures that the three fairness assumptions are satisfied. Alternatively the assumptions can be *enforced* by adding to the controller a mechanism that ensures that when a buffer becomes empty older packets are allowed entry with higher priority.

The unstructured solutions. The controllers of Section 5.3 must be modified in order to make them livelock-free. This can be seen by the construction of an infinite computation in which a continuous flow of packets cause the controller to forbid the forwarding of some packet. Toueg [Tou80b] gives such a computation (for **FC**) and presents a modification of **FS** (which is similar to the one presented here for the buffer-graph controllers) which is livelock-free.

Exercises to Chapter 5
Section 5.1

Exercise 5.1 *Show that there exists no deadlock-free controller that uses only one buffer per node and allows each node to send packets to at least one other node.*

Section 5.2

Exercise 5.2 *Show that* **dest** *is not deadlock-free if packet routing is as in Figure 5.2.*

Exercise 5.3 *(The hops-to-go scheme) Give the buffer graph and the* fb *and* nb *functions for a controller that uses buffer* $b_u[i]$ *to store packets that have* i *more hops to travel towards their destination.*
What is the buffer class of $b_u[i]$ *? Is it necessary to maintain a hop count in each packet?*

Exercise 5.4 *Complete the proof that the graph* BG_a *(defined in the proof of Theorem 5.13) is indeed a buffer graph, i.e., for each path* $P \in \mathcal{P}$ *there exists a guaranteed path with image* P *. Show that, as claimed,* fb *and* nb *do indeed describe a path in* BG_a *.*

Project 5.5 *Prove that there exists a deadlock-free controller, for packet switching on a hypercube, which uses only two buffers in each node and allows packets to be routed via minimum-hop paths.*
Is it possible to obtain the collection of used paths by means of the interval routing algorithm (Subsection 4.4.2)? Is it possible to use a linear interval labeling scheme?

Section 5.3

Exercise 5.6 *Prove that* **BC** *and* **BS** *are deadlock-free controllers.*

Exercise 5.7 *Prove that each move allowed by* **BC** *is also allowed by* **FC***.*

Part Two

Fundamental Algorithms

6

Wave and Traversal Algorithms

In the design of distributed algorithms for various applications several very general problems for process networks appear frequently as subtasks. These elementary tasks include the broadcasting of information (e.g., a start or terminate message), achieving a global synchronization between processes, triggering the execution of some event in each process, or computing a function of which each process holds part of the input. These tasks are always performed by passing messages according to some prescribed, topology-dependent scheme that ensures the participation of all processes. Indeed, as will become more evident to the reader in later chapters, these tasks are so fundamental that solutions to more complicated problems such as election (Chapter 7), termination detection (Chapter 8), or mutual exclusion can be given in which communication between processes occurs only via these message passing schemes.

The importance of message-passing schemes, called wave algorithms from now on, justifies a separate treatment of them in isolation from a particular application algorithm in which the schemes can be embedded. This chapter formally defines wave algorithms (Subsection 6.1.1) and proves some general results about them (Subsection 6.1.2). The observation that the same algorithms can be used for all of the fundamental tasks listed above, i.e., broadcasting, synchronization, and computing global functions, will be made rigorous (Subsections 6.1.3 through 6.1.5). Section 6.2 presents some widely used wave algorithms. Section 6.3 considers traversal algorithms, which are wave algorithms with the additional property that the events of a computation of the algorithm are *totally* ordered by causality. Section 6.4 gives several algorithms for a distributed depth-first search.

The treatment of wave algorithms as a separate issue, even though they are usually employed as subroutines in more involved algorithms, is useful for two reasons. First, the introduction of the concept facilitates the later treatment of more involved algorithms because the properties of their subroutines have already been studied. Second, certain problems in distributed computing can be solved by generic constructions that yield a specific algorithm when parametrized with a specific wave algorithm. The same construction can then be used to give algorithms for different network topologies or for different assumptions about the initial knowledge of processes.

6.1 Definition and Use of Wave Algorithms

Unless stated otherwise, it is assumed throughout in this chapter that the network topology is fixed (no topological changes occur), undirected (each channel carries messages in both directions), and connected (there is a path between any two processes). The set of all processes is denoted by $\mathbb{P}$, and the set of channels by E. As in earlier chapters, it is assumed that the system uses asynchronous message passing and that there is no notion of global time or real-time clocks. The algorithms of this chapter can also be used with synchronous message passing (possibly with some small modifications to avoid deadlocks) or with global clocks if these are available. However, some of the more general theorems are not true in these cases; see Exercise 6.1.

6.1.1 Definition of Wave Algorithms

As was observed in Chapter 2, a distributed algorithm usually allows a large collection of possible computations, due to non-determinism in the processes as well as the communication subsystem. A computation is a collection of events, partially ordered by the causal precedence relation $\preceq$ as defined following Definition 2.20. The number of events of computation C is denoted $|C|$ and the subset of the events that occur in process p is denoted C_p. It is assumed that there is a special type of internal event called a *decide* event; in the algorithms in this chapter such an event is simply represented by the statement *decide*. A wave algorithm exchanges a finite number of messages and then makes a decision, which depends causally on some event in each process.

Definition 6.1 *A wave algorithm is a distributed algorithm that satisfies the following three requirements.*

(1) **Termination.** *Each computation is finite:*

$$\forall C : |C| < \infty.$$

(2) **Decision.** *Each computation contains at least one decide event:*

$$\forall C : \exists e \in C : e \text{ is a decide event.}$$

(3) **Dependence.** *In each computation each decide event is causally preceded by an event in each process:*

$$\forall C : \forall e \in C : (e \text{ is a decide event} \Rightarrow \forall q \in \mathbb{P} \; \exists f \in C_q : f \preceq e).$$

A computation of a wave algorithm is called a *wave*. As an additional notation, in a computation of an algorithm a distinction is made between *initiators*, also called *starters*, and *non-initiators*, also called *followers*. A process is an initiator if it starts the execution of its local algorithm spontaneously, i.e., triggered by some condition internal to the process. A non-initiator becomes involved in the algorithm only when a message of the algorithm arrives and triggers the execution of the process algorithm. The first event of an initiator is an internal or send event, the first event of a non-initiator is a receive event.

A variety of wave algorithms exists because algorithms may differ in many respects. As a rationale for the treatment of a large number of algorithms in this chapter and as an aid in selecting one algorithm for a particular purpose a list of aspects in which wave algorithms differ from each other is given here; see also Table 6.19.

(1) *Centralization.* An algorithm is called *centralized* if there must be exactly one initiator in each computation, and *decentralized* if the algorithm can be started spontaneously by an arbitrary subset of the processes. Centralized algorithms are also called *single-source* algorithms, and decentralized algorithms are called *multi-source* algorithms. Centralization has an important influence on the complexity of wave algorithms, as can be seen from Table 6.20.

(2) *Topology.* An algorithm may be designed for a specific topology, such as a ring, tree, clique, etc.; see Subsection 2.4.1 and Section B.2.

(3) *Initial Knowledge.* An algorithm may assume the availability of various types of initial knowledge in the processes; see Subsection 2.4.4. Examples of prerequired knowledge include the following:

   (a) *Process identity.* Each process initially knows its own unique name.

   (b) *Neighbors' identities.* Each process initially knows the names of its neighbors.

   (c) *Sense of direction.* See Section B.3.

(4) *Number of Decisions.* In all wave algorithms in this chapter at most one decision occurs in each process. The number of processes that execute a *decide* event may vary; in some algorithms only one process decides, in others all processes decide. The tree algorithm (Subsection 6.2.2) causes a decision in exactly two processes.

(5) *Complexity.* The complexity measures considered in this chapter are the number of exchanged messages, the number of exchanged bits, and the time needed for one computation (as defined in Section 6.4). See also Subsection 2.4.5.

Each wave algorithm in this chapter will be given with the variables it uses and, if necessary, the information exchanged in its messages. Most of these algorithms send "empty messages", without any actual information: the messages carry causality, not information. Algorithms 6.9, 6.11, 6.12, and 6.18 use the messages to carry non-trivial information. Algorithms 6.15 and 6.16/6.17 use different message types; this requires that each message contains one or two bits to distinguish messages of different types.

When a wave algorithm is applied there are generally more variables and other information may be included in the message. Many applications rely on the simultaneous or sequential propagation of several waves; in this case information about the wave to which a message belongs must be included in messages. Also a process may keep additional variables to administer the wave or waves in which it is currently active.

An important subclass of wave algorithm is formed by centralized wave algorithms having the following two additional properties: the initiator is the only process that decides; all events are ordered totally by the causal order. Wave algorithms with these properties are called *traversal algorithms* and considered in Section 6.3.

6.1.2 Elementary Results about Wave Algorithms

In this subsection some lemmas that provide more insight in the structure of a wave computation are proved, and two trivial lower bounds on the message complexity of wave algorithms are presented.

Structural properties of waves. First, each event in a computation is preceded by an event in an initiator.

Lemma 6.2 *For each event $e \in C$ there exists an initiator p and an event f in C_p such that $f \preceq e$.*

Proof. Choose for f a minimal element in the history of e, i.e., $f \preceq e$ and there is no event $f' \prec f$. Such an f exists because the history of each event is finite. It remains to show that the process, p, where f takes place is an initiator. First, note that f is the first event of p, otherwise the earlier events of p would precede f. The first event of a non-initiator is a receive event, which would be preceded by the corresponding send event, contradicting the minimality of f. Hence p is an initiator. $\qquad\square$

A wave with one initiator defines a spanning tree of the network when for each non-initiator the channel is selected through which the first message is received.

Lemma 6.3 *Let C be a wave with one initiator p and, for each non-initiator q, let $father_q$ be the neighbor of q from which q received a message in its first event. Then the graph $T = (\mathbb{P}, E_T)$, with $E_T = \{qr : q \neq p \wedge r = father_q\}$ is a spanning tree directed towards p.*

Proof. As the number of nodes of T exceeds the number of edges by one it suffices to show that T contains no cycle. This follows because, with e_q the first event in q, $qr \in E_T$ implies $e_r \preceq e_q$, and $\preceq$ is a partial order. $\qquad\square$

The event f in the third clause of Definition 6.1 can be chosen to be a send event for all q other than the process where the *decide* event takes place.

Lemma 6.4 *Let C be a wave and $d_p \in C$ a decide event in process p. Then*

$$\forall q \neq p : \exists f \in C_q : (f \preceq d_p \wedge f \text{ is a send event}).$$

Proof. As C is a wave there exists an $f \in C_q$ that causally precedes d_p; choose f to be the *last* event of C_q that precedes d_p. To show that f is a send event, observe that the definition of causality (Definition 2.20) implies that there exists a sequence (causality chain)

$$f = e_0, e_1, \ldots, e_k = d_p,$$

such that for each $i < k$, e_i and e_{i+1} are either consecutive events in the same process or a corresponding send–receive pair. As f is the last event in q that precedes d_p, e_1 occurs in a process different from q, hence f is a send event. $\qquad\square$

Lower bounds on the complexity of waves. Lemma 6.4 immediately implies a lower bound of $N-1$ on the number of messages that are exchanged in a wave. If a *decide* event occurs in the only initiator of a wave (which

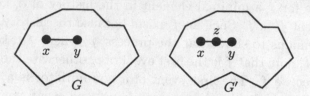

Figure 6.1 INSERTION OF A PROCESS INTO AN UNUSED CHANNEL.

is always the case in a traversal algorithm) the bound is N messages, and wave algorithms for arbitrary networks use at least $|E|$ messages.

Theorem 6.5 *Let C be a wave with one initiator p, such that a decide event d_p occurs in p. Then at least N messages are exchanged in C.*

Proof. By Lemma 6.2 each event in C is preceded by an event in p and using a causality sequence such as that in the proof of Lemma 6.4 it is easily shown that at least one send event occurs in p. By Lemma 6.4 a send event also occurs in each other process, which brings the number of send events to N. □

Theorem 6.6 *Let A be a wave algorithm for arbitrary networks without initial knowledge of the neighbors' identities. Then A exchanges at least $|E|$ messages in each computation.*

Proof. Assume A has a computation C in which less than $|E|$ messages are exchanged; there is a channel, say xy, that carries no message in C; see Figure 6.1. Consider network G' obtained by inserting one node z on the channel between x and y. As the nodes have no knowledge of the neighbors' identity, the initial state of x and y in G' is identical to the initial state in G. The same holds of course for all other nodes of G. Consequently all events of C can be applied, in the same order, starting from in the initial configuration of G', but now the *decide* event is not preceded by an event in z. □

In Chapter 7 a better lower bound will be proved on the message complexity of *decentralized* wave algorithms for rings and arbitrary networks without neighbor knowledge; see Corollaries 7.14 and 7.16.

6.1.3 Propagation of Information with Feedback

In this subsection it will be shown that wave algorithms are precisely the algorithms one needs when some information must be broadcast to all processes and certain processes must receive a notification of when the broadcast is complete. This requirement, for the propagation of information with feedback (PIF) is the following problem [Seg83]. A subset of processes is formed by those that have a message M (all of these have the *same* message), which must be broadcast, i.e., all processes must receive and accept M. Certain processes must be *notified* of termination of the broadcast; that is, they must execute a special *notify* event, with the requirement that a *notify* event may be executed only when all processes have already received the message M. The algorithm must use finitely many messages.

Notification by the PIF algorithm is considered as a *decide* event.

Theorem 6.7 *Every PIF algorithm is a wave algorithm.*

Proof. Let P be a PIF algorithm. It is required that each computation of P is finite and that in each computation a notification event (*decide*) occurs. If in some computation of P a notification d_p occurs that is not preceded by any event in a process q, then by Theorem 2.21 and Fact 2.23 an execution of P exists in which the notification occurs *before* q has accepted any message, which contradicts the requirements. □

We must bear in mind that Theorem 2.21 only holds for systems with asynchronous message passing; see Exercise 6.1.

Theorem 6.8 *Every wave algorithm can be employed as a PIF algorithm.*

Proof. Let A be a wave algorithm. To employ A as a PIF algorithm, processes initially knowing M are starters of A. The information M is appended to each message of A. This is possible because by construction starters of A know M initially and followers do not send a message before having received one, thus also knowing M. A *decide* event in the wave is preceded by an event in each process; hence when the former occurs each process knows M and it is considered the required *notify* of the PIF algorithm. □

The constructed PIF algorithm has the same message complexity as A and also shares with A all the other properties mentioned in Subsection 6.1.1, except the bit complexity. The bit complexity can be reduced by appending M only to the first message sent over each channel. If w is the number of bits of M, the bit complexity of the resulting algorithm exceeds the bit complexity of A by $w.|E|$.

6.1.4 Synchronization

In this subsection it will be shown that wave algorithms are precisely the algorithms one needs when a global synchronization between the processes must be achieved. The requirement for synchronization (SYN) is stated in the following problem [Fin79]. In each process q an event a_q must be executed, and in some processes an event b_p must be executed, such that the execution of all a_q events must have taken place temporally before any of the b_p events is executed. The algorithm must use finitely many messages.

In a SYN algorithm the b_p events will be considered as *decide* events.

Theorem 6.9 *Every SYN algorithm is a wave algorithm.*

Proof. Let S be a SYN algorithm. It is required that each computation of S is finite and that in each computation an event b_p (*decide*) occurs. If in some computation of S an event b_p occurs that is not causally preceded by a_q, then (again by Theorem 2.21 and Fact 2.23) there is an execution of S in which b_p occurs before a_q. □

Theorem 6.10 *Every wave algorithm can be employed as a SYN algorithm.*

Proof. Let A be a wave algorithm. To employ A as a SYN algorithm, each process q is required to execute a_q before q sends any message of A or decides in A. The event b_p takes place after a *decide* event in p. By Lemma 6.4 each *decide* event is causally preceded by a_q for each q. □

The constructed SYN algorithm has the same message complexity as A and also shares with A all other properties mentioned in Subsection 6.1.1.

6.1.5 Computation of Infimum Functions

In this subsection it will be shown that wave algorithms are precisely the algorithms one needs when a function must be computed whose value depends essentially on the input of every process. As a representative class of such functions algorithms will be considered that compute the *infimum* over all inputs, which must be drawn from a partially ordered set.

If $(X, \leq)$ is a partial order, then c is called the *infimum* of a and b if $c \leq a$, $c \leq b$, and $\forall d : (d \leq a \wedge d \leq b \Rightarrow d \leq c)$. Assume that X has the property that an infimum always exists; the infimum is unique in this case and is denoted $a \curlywedge b$. Now $\curlywedge$ is a binary operator and as it is commutative (i.e., $a \curlywedge b = b \curlywedge a$) and associative (i.e., $a \curlywedge (b \curlywedge c) = (a \curlywedge b) \curlywedge c$) the operation can be generalized to finite sets:

$$\inf\{j_1, \ldots, j_k\} = j_1 \curlywedge \cdots \curlywedge j_k.$$

Infimum computation (INF) is stated in the following problem. Each process q holds an input j_q, which is an element of a partially ordered set X. It is required that certain processes compute the value of $\inf\{j_q : q \in \mathbb{P}\}$ and that these processes know when the computation is terminated. They *write* the outcome of the computation as a variable *out* and are not allowed to change this variable thereafter.

The write event, which sets a value to *out*, is considered a *decide* event in an INF algorithm.

Theorem 6.11 *Every INF algorithm is a wave algorithm.*

Proof. Let I be an INF algorithm and assume there is a computation C of I with initial configuration γ, in which p *writes* the value J to out_p and this write event is not preceded by any event in q. Consider an initial configuration γ', which is equal to γ except that q has a different input j_q', chosen such that $J \not\leq j_q'$. Since no use of q's input causally precedes p's write event in C, all events of C that precede this write event are applicable in the same order starting from γ'. In the resulting computation p writes the erroneous result J as in C. $\qquad\square$

Theorem 6.12 *Every wave algorithm can be used to compute an infimum.*

Proof. Let a wave algorithm A be given. Give each process q an extra variable v_q, which is initialized to j_q. During a wave this variable is assigned as follows. Whenever process q sends a message of A, the current value of v_q is included in the message. Whenever process q receives a message of A, with the value v included, v_q is set to the value $v_q \curlywedge v$. When a *decide* event is executed in p, the current value of v_p is written to out_p.

It must now be shown that the correct value is written. Call the correct answer J, i.e., $J = \inf\{j_q : q \in \mathbb{P}\}$. For an event a in process q, denote by $v^{(a)}$ the value of v_q directly after the execution of a. Because v_q is initialized to j_q and only decreases during the wave, $v^{(a)} \leq j_q$ holds for each event a in q. The assignments to v imply that for events a and b, $a \preceq b \Rightarrow v^{(a)} \geq v^{(b)}$. Also because v is always computed as the infimum of two already existing values, $J \leq v$ holds for all values during the wave. Thus, if d is a *decide* event in p, the value $v^{(d)}$ satisfies $J \leq v^{(d)}$, and, because d is preceded by at least one event in each process q, $v^{(d)} \leq j_q$ for all q. This implies $J = v^{(d)}$.

$\square$

The constructed INF algorithm shares all properties with A except the bit complexity, because an element of X is appended to each message of A. The notion of an infimum function may seem rather abstract, but in fact many functions can be expressed as infima, as shown in [Tel91b, Theorem 4.1.1.2].

Fact 6.13 (Infimum theorem) *If $\star$ is a binary operator on a set X such that*

(1) $\star$ *is commutative, i.e., $a \star b = b \star a$,*
(2) $\star$ *is associative, i.e., $(a \star b) \star c = a \star (b \star c)$, and*
(3) $\star$ *is idempotent, i.e., $a \star a = a$*

then there is a partial order $\leq$ on X such that $\star$ is the infimum function.

Operators that satisfy these three criteria include the logical conjunction or disjunction, the minimum or maximum of integers, the greatest common divisor or lowest common multiple of integers, and the intersection or union of sets.

Corollary 6.14 $\wedge$, $\vee$, min, max, gcd, lcm, $\cap$, *and* $\cup$ *of values local to the processes can be computed in a single wave.*

The computation of operators that are commutative and associative, but not idempotent, is considered in Subsection 6.5.2.

6.2 A Collection of Wave Algorithms

A collection of wave and traversal algorithms will be presented in the next three sections. In all cases the algorithm text is given for the process p.

6.2.1 The Ring Algorithm

In this subsection a wave algorithm for a ring network will be given. The same algorithm can be used for Hamiltonian networks in which one fixed Hamiltonian cycle is encoded in the processes. Assume that for each process p a dedicated neighbor $Next_p$ is given such that all channels selected in this way form a Hamiltonian cycle.

The algorithm is centralized; the initiator sends a message $\langle \mathbf{tok} \rangle$ (called the *token*) along the cycle, each process passes it on, and when it returns to the initiator the initiator decides; see Algorithm 6.2.

For the initiator:
  begin send $\langle$**tok**$\rangle$ to $Next_p$; receive $\langle$**tok**$\rangle$; *decide* **end**

For non-initiators:
  begin receive $\langle$**tok**$\rangle$; send $\langle$**tok**$\rangle$ to $Next_p$ **end**

Algorithm 6.2 THE RING ALGORITHM.

Theorem 6.15 *The ring algorithm (Algorithm 6.2) is a wave algorithm.*

Proof. Call the initiator p_0. As each process sends at most one message the algorithm exchanges at most N messages altogether.

Within a finite number of steps the algorithm reaches a terminal configuration. In this configuration p_0 has already sent the token, i.e., has passed the send statement in its program. Furthermore, no $\langle$**tok**$\rangle$ message is in transit in any channel, otherwise it could be received and the configuration would not be terminal. Also no process other then p_0 "holds" the token (i.e., has received, but not sent $\langle$**tok**$\rangle$), otherwise this process could send $\langle$**tok**$\rangle$ and the configuration is not terminal. Concluding, (1) p_0 has sent the token, (2) for each p that has sent the token, $Next_p$ has received the token, and (3) for each $p \neq p_0$ that has received the token, p has sent the token. From this and the property of $Next$ it follows that each process has sent and received the token. As p_0 has received the token and the configuration is terminal, p_0 has executed the *decide* statement.

The receipt and sending of $\langle$**tok**$\rangle$ by each process $p \neq p_0$ precedes the receipt by p_0, hence the dependence condition is satisfied. $\qquad\square$

6.2.2 The Tree Algorithm

In this subsection a wave algorithm for a tree network will be given. The same algorithm can be used in an arbitrary network if a spanning tree of the network is available. It is assumed that all leaves of the tree initiate the algorithm. Each process sends exactly one message in the algorithm. If a process has received a message via each of its incident channels except one (this condition is initially true for leaves), the process sends a message via the remaining channel. If a process has received a message via all of its incident channels it decides; see Algorithm 6.3.

To prove that this algorithm is a wave algorithm, a few notations are introduced. Let f_{pq} be the event where p sends a message to q, and g_{pq} the event where q receives a message from p. T_{pq} denotes the subset of

var $rec_p[q]$ for each $q \in Neigh_p$: boolean **init** false ;
    (* $rec_p[q]$ is true if p has received a message from q *)

begin while $\#\{q : rec_p[q]$ is false$\} > 1$ **do**
          begin receive $\langle$ **tok** $\rangle$ from q ; $rec_p[q] := true$ **end** ;
    (* Now there is *one* q_0 with $rec_p[q_0]$ is false *)
    send $\langle$ **tok** $\rangle$ to q_0 with $rec_p[q_0]$ is false ;
  x: receive $\langle$ **tok** $\rangle$ from q_0 ; $rec_p[q_0] := true$;
    decide
    (* Inform other processes of decision:
        forall $q \in Neigh_p, q \neq q_0$ **do** send $\langle$ **tok** $\rangle$ to q *)
end

Algorithm 6.3 The tree algorithm.

---

the processes that are reachable from p without crossing the edge pq (the processes "on p's side of the edge"); see Figure 6.4. The connectivity of the network implies (see Figure 6.4)

$$T_{pq} = \bigcup_{r \in Neigh_p \setminus \{q\}} T_{rp} \cup \{p\} \quad \text{and} \quad \mathbb{P} = \{p\} \cup \bigcup_{r \in Neigh_p} T_{rp}.$$

The **forall** statement within comment signs in Algorithm 6.3 will be discussed at the end of this subsection; the next theorem is about the algorithm apart from this statement.

Theorem 6.16 *The tree algorithm (Algorithm 6.3) is a wave algorithm.*

Proof. As each process sends at most one message the algorithm uses at most N messages altogether. This implies that the algorithm reaches a terminal configuration γ after a finite number of steps; it will be shown that in γ at least one process has executed a *decide* event.

Let F be the number of *rec* bits with value false in γ and let K be the number of processes that have already sent a message in γ. As there are no messages in transit in γ (otherwise γ would not be terminal), $F = (2N - 2) - K$; the total number of *rec* bits is $2N - 2$, and K of these are true.

Assume that no process has decided in γ. The $N - K$ processes that have not yet sent a message in γ have at least two false *rec* bits each; otherwise they could send a message, contradicting that γ is terminal. The K processes that have sent a message in γ have at least one false *rec* bit each; otherwise they could decide, contradicting that γ is terminal. So $F \geq 2(N - K) + K$,

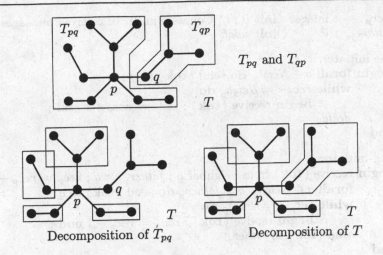

T_{pq} and T_{qp}

T

Decomposition of T_{pq} Decomposition of T

Figure 6.4 THE SUBTREES T_{pq}.

and $(2N - 2) - K \geq 2(N - K) + K$ implies $-2 \geq 0$; a contradiction, hence at least one decision has taken place in γ. See Exercise 6.5.

Finally it must be shown that a decision is preceded by an event in each process. Again let f_{pq} be the event where p sends a message to q, and g_{pq} the event where q receives a message from p. It is proved by induction on the receive events that

$$\forall s \in T_{pq} \; \exists e \in C_s : e \preceq g_{pq}.$$

Assume this is true for all receive events preceding g_{pq}. Now g_{pq} is preceded by f_{pq} (in process p) and the program of p implies that for all $r \in Neigh_p$ with $r \neq q$, f_{pq} is preceded by g_{rp}. The induction hypothesis now implies that for all such r, and for all $s \in T_{rp}$, there is an event $e \in C_s$ with $e \preceq g_{rp}$, hence $e \preceq g_{pq}$.

A decision d_p in p is preceded by g_{rp} for all $r \in Neigh_p$, which implies that $\forall s \in \mathbb{P} \exists e \in C_s : e \preceq d_p$. $\qquad \square$

The reader may simulate a computation of the algorithm on a small tree (e.g., the tree of Figure 6.4), and convince himself of the truth of the following remarks. In Algorithm 6.3 there are *two* processes that receive a message via each of their channels and decide; all others are still waiting for a message with their program counter pointing at x in the terminal configuration. If the **forall** statement (within comment signs in Algorithm 6.3) is added to the program all processes decide and in a terminal configuration each

var rec_p : integer   **init** 0 ; (* Counts number of received messages *)
    $father_p$: $\mathbb{P}$ **init** *udef*;

For the initiator:
    begin forall $q \in Neigh_p$ **do** send $\langle \textbf{tok} \rangle$ to q ;
        while $rec_p < \#Neigh_p$ **do**
            begin receive $\langle \textbf{tok} \rangle$; $rec_p := rec_p + 1$ **end** ;
       decide
    end

For non-initiators:
    begin receive $\langle \textbf{tok} \rangle$ from neighbor q ; $father_p := q$; $rec_p := rec_p + 1$;
       forall $q \in Neigh_p$, $q \neq father_p$ **do** send $\langle \textbf{tok} \rangle$ to q ;
       while $rec_p < \#Neigh_p$ **do**
           begin receive $\langle \textbf{tok} \rangle$; $rec_p := rec_p + 1$ **end** ;
       send $\langle \textbf{tok} \rangle$ to $father_p$
    end

Algorithm 6.5 THE ECHO ALGORITHM.

process is in a terminal state. The modified program uses $2N - 2$ messages altogether.

6.2.3 The Echo Algorithm

The echo algorithm is a centralized wave algorithm for networks of arbitrary topology. It was first presented in isolation by Chang [Cha82] and therefore sometimes called Chang's echo algorithm. A slightly more efficient version was given by Segall [Seg83] and this version is presented here.

The algorithm floods $\langle \textbf{tok} \rangle$ messages to all processes, thus defining a spanning tree as defined in Lemma 6.3. Tokens are "echoed" back via the edges of this tree very much like the flow of messages in the tree algorithm. The algorithm is given as Algorithm 6.5. The initiator sends messages to all its neighbors. Upon receipt of the first message a non-initiator forwards messages to all its neighbors except the one from which the message was received; when a non-initiator has received messages from all its neighbors an echo is sent to the father. When the initiator has received a message from all its neighbors it decides.

Theorem 6.17 *The echo algorithm (Algorithm 6.5) is a wave algorithm.*

Proof. As each process sends at most one message via each incident channel, the number of messages exchanged in each computation is finite. Let γ be the terminal configuration reached in a computation C with initiator p_0.

For this configuration, define (similarly to the definition in Lemma 6.3) a graph $T = (\mathbb{P}, E_T)$ by $pq \in E_T \iff father_p = q$. To show that this graph is a tree it must be shown that the number of edges is one less than the number of nodes (Lemma 6.3 claims that T is a tree, but assumes that the algorithm is a wave algorithm, which is what we still have to prove here). Observe that each process that participates in C sends messages to all its neighbors, except (if the process is not the initiator) the neighbor from which it received the first message. This implies that each of its neighbors receives at least one message in C and also participates in C. From this, it follows that $father_p \neq udef$ for all $p \neq p_0$. That T contains no cycle is shown as in the proof of Lemma 6.3.

The tree is rooted towards p_0; denote by T_p the set of nodes in the subtree of p. The edges of the network not belonging to T are called frond edges. In γ each process p has at least sent messages to all its neighbors except its father $father_p$, hence each frond edge has carried a message in both directions in C. Let f_p be the event in which p sends a message to its father (if it occurs in C) and g_p the event in which p's father receives a message from p (if it occurs). By induction on the nodes in the tree it can be shown that

(1) C contains the event f_p for each $p \neq p_0$;

(2) for all $s \in T_p$ there is an event $e \in C_s$ such that $e \preceq g_p$.

We consider the following two cases.

p **is a leaf.** p has received in C a message from its father and from all other neighbors (because all other channels are fronds). Thus the sending of $\langle \mathbf{tok} \rangle$ to p's father was applicable, and as γ is terminal it has taken place. T_p contains only p, and obviously $f_p \preceq g_p$.

p **is not a leaf.** p has received in C a message from its father and via all frond edges. By induction, C contains $f_{p'}$ for each son p' of p, and as γ is terminal, C contains $g_{p'}$ as well. Hence the sending of $\langle \mathbf{tok} \rangle$ to p's father was applicable, and as γ is terminal it has taken place. T_p consists of the union of $T_{p'}$ over the sons of p and p itself. The induction hypothesis can be used to show that in each process of this set there is an event preceding g_p.

It follows also that p_0 has received a message from each neighbor and that p_0 has executed a *decide* event, which is preceded by an event in each process. □

The spanning tree constructed in a computation of Algorithm 6.5 is some-

---

var rec_p : integer   **init** 0 ;   (* for initiator only *)

For the initiator:
    begin forall $q \in Neigh_p$ **do** send ⟨ **tok** ⟩ to qf ;
        while $rec_p < \#Neigh_p$ **do**
            begin receive ⟨ **tok** ⟩ ; $rec_p := rec_p + 1$ **end** ;
       decide
    end

For non-initiators:
    begin receive ⟨ **tok** ⟩ from q ; send ⟨ **tok** ⟩ to q **end**

Algorithm 6.6 THE POLLING ALGORITHM.

---

times employed in a subsequently executed algorithm. (For example, the Merlin–Segall algorithm for computing shortest-path routing tables assumes that a spanning tree rooted towards v_0 is initially given; see Subsection 4.2.3. The initial spanning tree can be computed using the echo algorithm.) In the last configuration of the algorithm each process (other than p_0) has recorded which neighbor is its father in the tree, but not which neighbors are its sons in the tree. In the algorithm identical messages are received from the father, via frond edges, and from the sons. If knowledge of the sons in the tree is required, the algorithm can be slightly modified so as to send a *different* message to the father (the last send operation for non-initiators). The sons of a process are then those neighbors from which the different message was received.

6.2.4 The Polling Algorithm

In clique networks a channel exists between each pair of processes. A process can decide if it has received a message from each neighbor. In the *polling algorithm*, given as Algorithm 6.6, the initiator asks each neighbor to reply with a message, and decides after receipt of all messages.

Theorem 6.18 *The polling algorithm (Algorithm 6.6) is a wave algorithm.*

Proof. The algorithm sends two messages via each channel that is incident to the initiator. Each neighbor of the initiator replies once to the original poll, hence the initiator receives $N - 1$ replies. This is exactly the number it needs to decide, which implies that the initiator will decide, and that its decision is preceded by an event in each process.   □

Polling can also be used in a star network in which the initiator is the center.

6.2.5 The Phase Algorithm

In this subsection the phase algorithm, which is a decentralized algorithm for networks of arbitrary topology will be presented; the algorithm is given in [Tel91b, Section 4.2.3]. This algorithm can be used as a wave algorithm for directed networks.

The algorithm requires that the processes know the diameter of the network, used as a constant D in the algorithm text. The algorithm is also correct (although less efficient) if the processes use instead of D a constant D' larger than the network diameter. Thus, in order to apply this algorithm, it is not necessary that the diameter is known exactly; it suffices if an upper bound (e.g., $N - 1$) on the network diameter is known. All processes must use the *same* constant D'. Peleg [Pel90] augmented the algorithm so that the diameter is computed during the execution, but this extension requires unique identities to be available.

The general case. The algorithm can be used in arbitrary *directed* networks, where channels can carry messages in one direction only. In this case the neighbors of node p are *in-neighbors* (processes that can send messages to p) and *out-neighbors* (processes to which p can send messages). The in-neighbors of p are stored in the set In_p and the out-neighbors in the set Out_p.

In the phase algorithm each process sends exactly D messages to each out-neighbor. Only after i messages have been received from each in-neighbor is the $(i+1)$th message sent to each out-neighbor; see Algorithm 6.7.

Indeed it is observed immediately from the algorithm text that at most D messages are sent through each channel (that at least D messages are sent through each channel is shown below). If an edge pq exists, let $f_{pq}^{(i)}$ be the ith event in which p sends to q, and $g_{pq}^{(i)}$ be the ith event in which q receives from p. If the channel between p and q satisfies the fifo assumption these events correspond and $f_{pq}^{(i)} \preceq g_{pq}^{(i)}$ is trivially satisfied. The causal relation between $f_{pq}^{(i)}$ and $g_{pq}^{(i)}$ also holds if the channel is not fifo, as proved in the following lemma.

Lemma 6.19 $f_{pq}^{(i)} \preceq g_{pq}^{(i)}$ *holds, also if the channel is not fifo.*

Proof. Define m_h such that $f_{pq}^{(m_h)}$ is the send event corresponding to $g_{pq}^{(h)}$,

cons D : integer   = the network diameter ;
var $Rec_p[q]$: $0..D$ **init** 0, for each $q \in In_p$;
                       (* Number of messages received from q *)
        $Sent_p$: $0..D$ **init** 0 ;
                       (* Number of messages sent to each out-neighbor *)

begin if p is initiator **then**
       begin forall $r \in Out_p$ **do** send $\langle$ **tok** $\rangle$ to r ;
          $Sent_p := Sent_p + 1$
     end ;
    while $\min_q Rec_p[q] < D$ **do**
       begin receive $\langle$ **tok** $\rangle$ (from neighbor q_0) ;
          $Rec_p[q_0] := Rec_p[q_0] + 1$;
          if $\min_q Rec_p[q] \geq Sent_p$ **and** $Sent_p < D$ **then**
            begin forall $r \in Out_p$ **do** send $\langle$ **tok** $\rangle$ to r ;
              $Sent_p := Sent_p + 1$
          end
       end ;
   decide
end

Algorithm 6.7 THE PHASE ALGORITHM.

i.e., in its hth receive event q receives p's m_hth message. The definition of causality gives $f_{pq}^{(m_h)} \preceq g_{pq}^{(h)}$.

As each message is received once in C, all m_h are different, which implies that at least one of the numbers $m_1, \ldots, m_i$ is greater than or equal to i. Choose $j \leq i$ such that $m_j \geq i$. Now $f_{pq}^{(i)} \preceq f_{pq}^{(m_j)} \preceq g_{pq}^{(j)} \preceq g_{pq}^{(i)}$. $\square$

Theorem 6.20 *The phase algorithm (Algorithm 6.7) is a wave algorithm.*

Proof. As each process sends at most D messages through each channel the algorithm terminates after a finite number of steps. Let γ be the terminal configuration of a computation C of the algorithm, and assume there is at least one initiator in C (there may be more initiators).

To demonstrate that in γ each process has decided it will first be shown that each process has sent messages at least once. Because there are no messages in the channels in γ, for each channel qp it is the case that $Rec_p[q] = Sent_q$. Also, because each process sends messages at the latest when a message is received, $Rec_p[q] > 0 \Rightarrow Sent_p > 0$. The assumption that there is at least one initiator p_0, for which $Sent_{p_0} > 0$, implies that $Sent_p > 0$ for each p.

Subsequently it will be shown that each process has decided. Let p be a process with minimal value of the variable $Sent$ in γ, i.e., for all q, $Sent_q \geq$ $Sent_p$ in γ. In particular this holds if q is an in-neighbor of p, and using $Rec_p[q] = Sent_q$ this implies that $\min_q Rec_p[q] \geq Sent_p$. But this implies $Sent_p = D$; otherwise, p would have sent additional messages the last time it received a message. Consequently, $Sent_p = D$ for all p, and hence also $Rec_p[q] = D$ for all qp, which implies indeed that each process has decided.

It now remains to show that each decision is preceded by an event in each process. If $P = p_0, p_1, \ldots, p_l$, with $l \leq D$, is a path in the network then, by Lemma 6.19,

$$f_{p_i p_{i+1}}^{(i+1)} \preceq g_{p_i p_{i+1}}^{(i+1)}$$

for $0 \leq i < l$ and, by the algorithm,

$$g_{p_i p_{i+1}}^{(i+1)} \preceq f_{p_{i+1} p_{i+2}}^{(i+2)}$$

for $0 \leq i < l - 1$. Consequently, $f_{p_0 p_1}^{(1)} \preceq g_{p_{l-1} p_l}^{(l)}$. Because the network diameter is D, for each q and p there exists a path $q = p_0, p_1, \ldots, p_l = p$ of length at most D. Thus for each q there is an $l \leq D$ and an in-neighbor r of p such that $f_{qq'}^{(1)} \preceq g_{rp}^{(l)}$; by virtue of the algorithm, $g_{rp}^{(l)}$ precedes d_p. $\square$

The algorithm sends D messages through each channel, which gives a message complexity of $|E|.D$. It should be noted, however, that in this expression $|E|$ stands for the number of *directed* channels. If the algorithm is used in an undirected network each channel counts for two directed channels, which brings the message complexity to $2|E|.D$.

The phase algorithm in cliques. If the network is a clique the diameter is 1; in this case exactly one message must be received from each neighbor, and it suffices in this case for each process to count the overall number of messages that have been received, rather than counting the messages for each in-neighbor separately; see Algorithm 6.8. The message complexity is $N(N-1)$ in this case and the algorithm uses only $O(\log N)$ bits of internal storage.

6.2.6 Finn's Algorithm

Finn's algorithm [Fin79] is another wave algorithm that can be used in arbitrary, directed networks. It does not require the diameter of the network to be known in advance, but relies on the availability of unique identities for the processes. Sets of process identities are exchanged in messages, which causes the bit complexity of the algorithm to be rather high.

var Rec_p : $0..N - 1$ **init** 0 ;
             (* Number of messages received *)
      $Sent_p$: $0..1$ **init** 0 ;
             (* Number of messages sent to each neighbor *)

begin if p is initiator **then**
       begin forall $r \in Neigh_p$ **do** send $\langle \textbf{tok} \rangle$ to r ;
              $Sent_p := Sent_p + 1$
       end ;
       while $Rec_p < \#Neigh_p$ **do**
              begin receive $\langle \textbf{tok} \rangle$;
                     $Rec_p := Rec_p + 1$;
                     if $Sent_p = 0$ **then**
                            begin forall $r \in Neigh_p$ **do** send $\langle \textbf{tok} \rangle$ to r ;
                                   $Sent_p := Sent_p + 1$
                            end
              end ;
         decide
end

Algorithm 6.8 THE PHASE ALGORITHM FOR CLIQUES.

Process p maintains two sets of process identities, Inc_p and $NInc_p$. Informally speaking, Inc_p is the set of processes q such that an event in q precedes the most recent event in p, and $NInc_p$ is the set of processes q such that for all neighbors r of q an event in r precedes the most recent event in p. This relation is maintained as follows. Initially $Inc_p = \{p\}$ and $NInc_p = \varnothing$. Process p sends messages, including Inc_p and $NInc_p$, each time one of the sets has increased. When p receives a message, including an Inc set and a $NInc$ set, these received identities are inserted into p's versions of these sets. When p has received a message from all in-neighbors, p is inserted into $NInc_p$. When the two sets become equal, p decides; see Algorithm 6.9. The informal meaning of the two sets now implies that, for each process q such that an event in q precedes d_p, for each neighbor r of q also an event in r precedes d_p, which implies the dependence of the algorithm.

It is demonstrated in the correctness proof that this will happen for each p, and that the equality of the two sets implies that the decision is preceded by an event in each process.

Theorem 6.21 *Finn's algorithm (Algorithm 6.9) is a wave algorithm.*

Proof. Observe that the two sets maintained by each process can only grow. As the size of the two sets sum up to at least 1 in the first message sent

var Inc_p : set of processes   **init** $\{p\}$;
    $NInc_p$: set of processes   **init** $\varnothing$;
    $rec_p[q]$: boolean for $q \in In_p$ **init** false ;
          (* indicates whether p has already received from q *)

begin if p is initiator **then**
      forall $r \in Out_p$ **do** send $\langle$ **sets**, $Inc_p, NInc_p \rangle$ to r ;
    while $Inc_p \neq NInc_p$ **do**
      begin receive $\langle$ **sets**, $Inc, NInc \rangle$ from q_0 ;
        $Inc_p := Inc_p \cup Inc$; $NInc_p := NInc_p \cup NInc$;
        $rec_p[q_0] := true$;
        if $\forall q \in In_p : rec_p[q]$ **then** $NInc_p := NInc_p \cup \{p\}$;
        if Inc_p or $NInc_p$ has changed **then**
          forall $r \in Out_p$ **do** send $\langle$ **sets**, $Inc_p, NInc_p \rangle$ to r
      end ;
    decide
end

Algorithm 6.9 FINN'S ALGORITHM.

over each channel, and at most $2N$ in the last message, the total number of messages is bounded by $2N.|E|$.

Let C be a computation in which there is at least one initiator, and let γ be the last configuration, which is a terminal configuration. As in the proof of Theorem 6.20 it can be shown that if process p has sent messages at least once (to each neighbor), and q is an out-neighbor of p, then q has also sent messages at least once. This implies that each process has sent at least one message (through each channel).

It will now be shown that in γ each process has decided. First, if an edge pq exists, then $Inc_p \subseteq Inc_q$ in γ. Indeed, after the last change of Inc_p process p sent a $\langle$ **sets**, $Inc_p, NInc_p \rangle$ message, and after its receipt $Inc_q := Inc_q \cup Inc_p$ was executed by q. The strong connectivity of the network implies that $Inc_p = Inc_q$ for all p and q. As $p \in Inc_p$ holds, and each Inc set only contains process identities, $Inc_p = \mathbb{P}$ holds for each p.

Second, it can be shown similarly that $NInc_p = NInc_q$ for each p and q. As every process has sent at least one message via each channel, each process p satisfies $\forall q \in In_p : rec_p[q]$, and consequently $p \in NInc_p$ holds for each p. Also, the $NInc$ sets contain only process identities, which implies that $NInc_p = \mathbb{P}$ for each p. From $Inc_p = \mathbb{P}$ and $NInc_p = \mathbb{P}$ it follows that $Inc_p = NInc_p$, hence each process p has decided in γ.

It must now be shown that a decision d_p in process p is preceded by an event in each process. For an event e in process p, let $Inc^{(e)}$ (or $NInc^{(e)}$, respectively) denote the value of Inc_p (or $NInc_p$, respectively) directly after the execution of e (cf. the proof of Theorem 6.12). The following two claims formalize the informal description of the sets at the beginning of this subsection.

Claim 6.22 *If there is an event* $e \in C_q : e \preceq f$, *then* $q \in Inc^{(f)}$.

Proof. As in the proof of Theorem 6.12 it is shown that $e \preceq f \Rightarrow Inc^{(e)} \subseteq Inc^{(f)}$, and with $e \in C_q \Rightarrow q \in Inc^{(e)}$ the result follows. $\square$

Claim 6.23 *If* $q \in NInc^{(f)}$, *then for all* $r \in In_q$ *there is an event* $e \in C_r :$ $e \preceq f$.

Proof. Let a_q be the internal event of q that is the first execution of $NInc_q :=$ $NInc_q \cup \{q\}$ by process q. Event a_q is the only event with $q \in NInc^{(a_q)}$ that is not preceded by another event a' satisfying $q \in NInc^{(a')}$; so $q \in NInc^{(f)} \Rightarrow$ $a_q \preceq f$.
The algorithm implies that for each $r \in In_q$ there is an event $e \in C_r$ preceding a_q. This implies the result. $\square$

Process p decides only when $Inc_p = NInc_p$; we write $Inc^{(d_p)} = NInc^{(d_p)}$. It is now the case that

(1) $p \in Inc^{(d_p)}$; and
(2) $q \in Inc^{(d_p)}$ implies $q \in NInc^{(d_p)}$ implies $In_q \subseteq Inc^{(d_p)}$.

The strong connectivity of the network gives the required result $Inc^{(d_p)} = \mathbb{P}$.
            $\square$

6.3 Traversal Algorithms

In this section a special class of wave algorithms will be discussed, namely, wave algorithms in which all events of a wave are *totally* ordered by the causality relation and in which the last event occurs in the same process as the first event.

Definition 6.24 *A traversal algorithm is an algorithm with the following three properties.*

(1) *In each computation there is one initiator, which starts the algorithm by sending out exactly one message.*
(2) *A process, upon receipt of a message, either sends out one message or decides.*

var rec_p : integer **init** 0 ; (* for initiator only *)

For the initiator:
    (* Write $Neigh_p = \{q_1, q_2, \ldots, q_{N-1}\}$ *)
    begin while $rec_p < \#Neigh_p$ **do**
                   begin send ⟨**tok**⟩ to q_{rec_p+1} ;
                          receive ⟨**tok**⟩; $rec_p := rec_p + 1$
             end ;
        decide
  end

For non-initiators:
    begin receive ⟨**tok**⟩ from q ; send ⟨**tok**⟩ to q **end**

Algorithm 6.10 THE SEQUENTIAL POLLING ALGORITHM.

The first two properties imply that in each finite computation exactly one process decides. The algorithm is said to *terminate* in the single process that decides.

(3) *The algorithm terminates in the initiator and when this happens, each process has sent a message at least once.*

In each reachable configuration of a traversal algorithm there is either exactly one message in transit, or exactly one process that has just received a message and not (yet) sent a message in reply. In a more abstract view the messages of a computation taken together can be seen as a single object (a *token*) that is handed from process to process and so "visits" all processes. In Section 7.4, traversal algorithms are used to construct election algorithms and for this construction it is important to know not only the overall number of token passes in one wave, but also how many token passes are necessary to visit the first x processes.

Definition 6.25 *An algorithm is an f-traversal algorithm (for a class of networks) if*

(1) *it is a traversal algorithm (for this class); and*
(2) *in each computation at least $\min(N, x+1)$ processes have been visited after $f(x)$ token passes.*

The ring algorithm (Algorithm 6.2) is a traversal algorithm, and because $x + 1$ processes have handled the token after x steps (for $x < N$) and all processes have handled it after N steps, it is an x-traversal algorithm for ring networks.

6.3.1 Traversing Cliques

A clique can be traversed by *sequential polling*; the algorithm is very much like Algorithm 6.6, but only one neighbor of the initiator is polled at a time. Only when a reply of one neighbor has been received is the next neighbor polled; see Algorithm 6.10.

Theorem 6.26 *The sequential polling algorithm (Algorithm 6.10) is a 2x-traversal algorithm for cliques.*

Proof. It is easily seen that when the algorithm terminates in the initiator each process has sent a reply. The $(2x - 1)$th message is the poll for q_x and the $2x$th message is its reply. Hence, when $2x$ messages have been exchanged the $x + 1$ processes $p, q_1, \ldots, q_x$ have been visited. $\qquad\square$

6.3.2 Traversing Tori

The $n \times n$ *torus-graph* is the graph $G = (V, E)$, where

$$V = \mathbb{Z}_n \times \mathbb{Z}_n = \{(i, j) : 0 \leq i, j < n\}$$

and

$$E = \{(i, j)(i', j') : (i = i' \land j = j' \pm 1) \lor (i = i' \pm 1 \land j = j')\};$$

see Section B.2.4. (Addition and subtraction here is mod n.) It is assumed that the torus has a sense of direction (see Section B.3), i.e., in node (i, j) the channel to $(i, j + 1)$ is labeled with *Up*, the channel to $(i, j - 1)$ with *Down*, the channel to $(i + 1, j)$ with *Right*, and the channel to $(i - 1, j)$ with *Left*. The coordinate pairs (i, j) are a convenient means of defining the network topology and its sense of direction, but we assume that the processes do not know these coordinates; the topological knowledge is restricted to the channel labels.

The torus is a Hamiltonian graph, i.e., there exists a Hamiltonian cycle in the torus (of arbitrary size) and the token is sent along such a cycle using Algorithm 6.11. After the kth step of the token it is sent upwards if $n|k$ (n divides k), otherwise it is sent to the right.

Theorem 6.27 *The torus algorithm (Algorithm 6.11) is an x-traversal algorithm for the torus.*

Proof. As is easily seen from the algorithm, a decision is taken after the token has been passed n^2 times. If the token moves from process p to process q by making U *Up*-moves and R *Right*-moves, then $p = q$ if and only

For the initiator, execute once:
    send $\langle\,\mathbf{num}, 1\,\rangle$ to Up

For each process, upon receipt of the token $\langle\,\mathbf{num}, k\,\rangle$:
    begin if $k = n^2$ **then** *decide*
                else if $n \mid k$ **then** send $\langle\,\mathbf{num}, k+1\,\rangle$ to Up
                           else send $\langle\,\mathbf{num}, k+1\,\rangle$ to $Right$
    end

Algorithm 6.11 Traversal algorithm for the torus.

---

if $(n \mid U \wedge n \mid R)$. Let the initiator be p_0 and let p_k be the process that receives the token $\langle\,\mathbf{num}, k\,\rangle$.

Of the n^2 steps of the token, n steps are upwards and the remaining $n^2 - n$ steps are rightwards. As both n and $n^2 - n$ are multiples of n, it follows that $p_{n^2} = p_0$, hence the algorithm terminates in the initiator.

It will next be shown that each of the processes p_0 through p_{n^2-1} is different; as there are n^2 processes this implies that each process was visited. Assume $p_a = p_b$ for $0 \leq a < b < n^2$. Between p_a and p_b the token has made some Up steps and some $Right$ steps, and because $p_a = p_b$ the number of both is a multiple of n. By inspection of the algorithm it is seen that this implies that

$$\#\{k : a \leq k < b \wedge n \mid k\} \text{ is a multiple of } n$$

and

$$\#\{k : a \leq k < b \wedge n \nmid k\} \text{ is a multiple of } n.$$

The sizes of the two sets sum up to $b-a$, from which it follows that $n \mid (b-a)$. Write $(b-a) = l.n$, then the set $\{k : a \leq k < b\}$ contains l multiples of n. This implies $n \mid l$, so $n^2 \mid (b-a)$, which is a contradiction.

Because all processes p_0 through p_{n^2-1} are different, $x+1$ processes have been visited after x token passes. $\square$

6.3.3 Traversing Hypercubes

The n-dimensional hypercube is a graph $G = (V, E)$ where

$$V = \{(b_0, \ldots, b_{n-1}) : b_i = 0, 1\}$$

and

$$E = \{(b_0, \ldots, b_{n-1}), (c_0, \ldots, c_{n-1}) : b \text{ and } c \text{ differ in one bit}\};$$

For the initiator, execute once:
  send ⟨**num**, 1⟩ through channel $n - 1$.

For each process, upon receipt of the token ⟨**num**, k⟩:
  begin if $k = 2^n$ **then** *decide*
          else begin let l the largest number s.t. $2^l | k$;
                      send ⟨**num**, $k + 1$⟩ through channel l
          end
  end

Algorithm 6.12 TRAVERSAL ALGORITHM FOR THE HYPERCUBE.

---

see Subsection B.2.5. It is assumed that the hypercube has a sense of direction, (see Section B.3), i.e., the channel between nodes b and c, where b and c differ in bit number i, is labeled with "i" in both nodes. It is assumed that the node labels are not known to the processes; their topological knowledge is restricted to the channel labels.

Like the torus, the hypercube is Hamiltonian, and a Hamiltonian cycle is traversed using Algorithm 6.12. The correctness proof for the algorithm is almost the same as the proof for Algorithm 6.11.

Theorem 6.28 *The hypercube algorithm (Algorithm 6.12) is an x-traversal algorithm for the hypercube.*

Proof. As is easily seen from the algorithm a decision is taken after 2^n hops of the token. Let the initiator be p_0 and let p_k be the process that receives the token ⟨**num**, k⟩. For each $k < 2^n$, the labels of p_k and p_{k+1} differ in one bit, of which the index is denoted by $l(k)$, satisfying

$$l(k) = \begin{cases} n - 1 & \text{if } k = 0 \\ \text{the largest } l \text{ with } 2^l | k \text{ if } k > 0. \end{cases}$$

Because for each $i < n$ there are an *even* number of $k \in \{0, \ldots, 2^n\}$ with $l(k) = i$, $p_0 = p_{2^n}$, the decision takes place in the initiator. With an argument similar to that used in the proof of Theorem 6.27 it can be shown that $p_a = p_b$ implies that $2^n | (b - a)$, which implies that all $p_0, \ldots, p_{2^n-1}$ are different.

From this it follows that all processes have been visited when termination occurs, and that $x + 1$ processes have been visited after x token passes.   ☐

var $used_p[q]$: boolean   **init** false for each $q \in Neigh_p$;

                                      (* Indicates whether p has already sent to q *)

     $father_p$: process   **init** $udef$;

For the initiator only, execute once:

     begin $father_p := p$; choose $q \in Neigh_p$;

               $used_p[q] := true$; send $\langle \mathbf{tok} \rangle$ to q

     end

For each process, upon receipt of $\langle \mathbf{tok} \rangle$ from q_0:

     begin if $father_p = udef$ **then** $father_p := q_0$;

           if $\forall q \in Neigh_p : used_p[q]$

              then *decide*

           else if $\exists q \in Neigh_p : (q \neq father_p \wedge \neg used_p[q])$

              then begin choose $q \in Neigh_p \setminus \{father_p\}$

                           with $\neg used_p[q]$;

                           $used_p[q] := true$; send $\langle \mathbf{tok} \rangle$ to q

               end

              else begin $used_p[father_p] := true$;

                         send $\langle \mathbf{tok} \rangle$ to $father_p$

              end

     end

Algorithm 6.13 TARRY'S TRAVERSAL ALGORITHM.

6.3.4 Traversing Connected Networks

A traversal algorithm for arbitrary connected networks was given by Tarry in 1895 [T1895]. The algorithm is formulated in the following two rules; see Algorithm 6.13.

R1. A process never forwards the token twice through the same channel.

R2. A non-initiator forwards the token to its *father* (the neighbor from which it first received the token) only if there is no other channel possible according to rule R1.

Theorem 6.29 *Tarry's algorithm (Algorithm 6.13) is a traversal algorithm.*

Proof. Because the token is sent at most once in each direction through each channel, it is passed at most $2|E|$ times before the algorithm terminates. Because each process sends the token through each channel at most once, each process receives the token through each channel at most once. Each time the token is held by a non-initiator p, process p has received the token once more often than p has sent the token. This implies that the number of channels incident to p exceeds the number of used channels of p by at least one, so p does not decide, but forwards the token. It follows that the decision takes place in the initiator.

It will be proved in three steps that when the algorithm terminates each process has forwarded the token.

(1) *All channels incident to the initiator have been used once in each direction.* Each channel has been used by the initiator to send the token, otherwise the algorithm would not terminate. The initiator has received the token exactly as often as it has sent the token; because it has been received through a different channel each time, it follows that the token has been received once through each channel.

(2) *For each visited process p, all channels incident to p have been used once in each direction.* Assuming this is not the case, choose p to be the earliest visited process for which this property is not true, and observe that by (1) p is not the initiator. By the choice of p, all channels incident to $father_p$ have been used once in each direction, which implies that p has sent the token to its father. This implies that p has used all incident channels to send the token; but as the token ends in the initiator, p has received the token exactly as often as p has sent the token, so p has received the token once through each incident channel. This is a contradiction.

(3) *All processes have been visited and each channel has been used once in both directions.* If there are unvisited processes, there are neighbors p and q such that p has been visited and q has not been visited, contradicting that each channel of p has been used in both directions. So all processes were visited, and all channels are used once in both directions by point (2).

$\square$

Each computation of Tarry's algorithm defines a spanning tree of the network by shown in Lemma 6.3. The root of this tree is the initiator, and each non-initiator p has stored its father in the tree in the variable $father_p$ at the end of the computation. If it is desired that each process should also know (at the end of the computation) which of its neighbors are its sons in the tree, this can be achieved by sending a special message to $father_p$.

6.4 Time Complexity: Depth-first Search

The processes in Tarry's algorithm are given sufficient freedom, in choosing a neighbor to which to forward the token, to allow a large class of spanning trees to arise as a result. In this section algorithms will be discussed that compute spanning trees with the additional property that each frond edge connects two nodes, one of which is an ancestor of the other. A frond edge is an edge that does not belong to the spanning tree. Given a rooted spanning tree T of G, for each p, $T[p]$ denotes the set of processes in the subtree of p, and $A[p]$ denotes the ancestors of p, i.e., the nodes on the path in T between the root and p. Observe that $q \in T[p] \iff p \in A[q]$.

Definition 6.30 *A rooted spanning tree T of G is a depth-first search tree if, for each frond edge pq, $q \in T[p] \vee q \in A[p]$.*

Depth-first search trees are used in many graph algorithms, such as those for testing planarity, for testing biconnectivity, and for the construction of interval labeling schemes (see Subsection 4.4.2). It will be demonstrated in Section 6.4.1 that a minor modification of Tarry's algorithm (namely, a restriction of the freedom of choice of the processes) enables the algorithm to compute depth-first search trees. The resulting algorithm will be referred to as the *classical depth-first search algorithm*. In Subsection 6.4.2 two algorithms will be discussed that compute depth-first search trees in less *time* than the classical algorithm. To this end the time complexity of distributed algorithms will be defined below. In Subsection 6.4.3 a depth-first search algorithm will be presented for networks with initial knowledge of neighbors' identities. In this case Theorem 6.6 does not apply, and in fact an algorithm using only $2N - 2$ messages can be given.

The time complexity of distributed algorithms. Transmission times in asynchronous networks are unknown, and we don't want to make analyses dependent on system-specific parameters. Recall that in sequential computing, time complexity is not expressed in physical time units, but in number of instructions; here we shall do the same. The time unit to measure the duration of a distributed execution is taken to be the longest message delay in that execution. The time unit is then defined by the axiom that each message delay is bounded by the time unit, so T2 below is not really an assumption about the computation, but a statement about the time unit.

Definition 6.31 *The time complexity of a distributed algorithm is the maximum time taken by a computation of the algorithm under the following assumptions.*

T1. A process can execute any finite number of events in zero time.

T2. The time between sending and receipt of a message is at most one time unit.

The time complexities of all wave algorithms of this chapter are listed in Table 6.19. It is left as an exercise to the reader to verify the values given in this table that are not proved in this chapter. Alternative definitions of time complexity are discussed in Subsection 6.5.3.

Lemma 6.32 *For traversal algorithms the time complexity equals the message complexity.*

Proof. The messages are exchanged serially, and each may take one time unit. □

6.4.1 Distributed Depth-first Search

The classical depth-first search algorithm is obtained when the freedom to choose a neighbor to forward the token in Tarry's algorithm is restricted by adopting the following third rule; see Algorithm 6.14.

R3. When a process receives the token it sends it back through the same channel if this is allowed by rules R1 and R2.

Theorem 6.33 *The classical depth-first search algorithm (Algorithm 6.14) computes a depth-first search spanning tree using $2|E|$ messages and $2|E|$ time units.*

Proof. As the algorithm implements Tarry's algorithm, it is a traversal algorithm and computes a spanning tree T. It has already been shown that each channel carries two messages (one in each direction), which proves the message complexity, and the time complexity follows because the $2|E|$ messages are exchanged one after the other, each taking at most one time unit. It remains to show that rule R3 implies that the resulting tree is a depth-first search tree.

First, rule R3 implies that the first traversal of a frond is immediately followed by the second traversal, in the reverse direction. Assume pq is a frond and p is the first process to use the frond. When q receives the token from p, q has been visited already (otherwise q would set $father_q$ to p and the edge was not a frond) and $used_q[p]$ is false (because by assumption p was the first of the two processes to use the edge). Consequently, by R3, q sends the token back to p immediately.

It can now be shown that if pq is a frond, first used by p, then $q \in A[p]$.

var $used_p[q]$: boolean   **init** false for each $q \in Neigh_p$;
                               (* Indicates whether p has already sent to q *)
     $father_p$: process   **init** $udef$;

For the initiator only, execute once:
    begin $father_p := p$; choose $q \in Neigh_p$;
          $used_p[q] := true$; send $\langle$ **tok** $\rangle$ to q
    end

For each process, upon receipt of $\langle$ **tok** $\rangle$ from q_0:
    begin if $father_p = udef$ **then** $father_p := q_0$;
        if $\forall q \in Neigh_p : used_p[q]$
          then *decide*
        else if $\exists q \in Neigh_p : (q \neq father_p \wedge \neg used_p[q])$
          then begin if $father_p \neq q_0 \wedge \neg used_p[q_0]$
                then $q := q_0$
                else choose $q \in Neigh_p \setminus \{father_p\}$
                         with $\neg used_p[q]$) ;
              $used_p[q] := true$; send $\langle$ **tok** $\rangle$ to q
          end
        else begin $used_p[father_p] := true$;
              send $\langle$ **tok** $\rangle$ to $father_p$
        end
    end

Algorithm 6.14 THE CLASSICAL DEPTH-FIRST SEARCH ALGORITHM.

Consider the path followed by the token until it is sent via pq. As pq is a frond, q has been visited before the token reached q via this edge:

$$\ldots, q, \ldots, p, q$$

Obtain from this path a possibly shorter path by replacing all patterns r_1, r_2, r_1, where $r_1 r_2$ is a frond, by r_1. By the previous observation all frond edges have now been now removed, which implies that the resulting path is a path in T, consisting only of edges used before the first use of pq. If q is not an ancestor of p this implies that the edge from q to $father_q$ was used before the edge qp was used, contradicting rule R2 of the algorithm.   □

The message complexity of classical distributed depth-first search equals $2|E|$, which is optimal (barring a constant factor 2) by Theorem 6.6 if the identities of neighbors are not known initially. The time complexity is also $2|E|$, which is the best possible for traversal algorithms in this case by Lemma 6.32. A distributed version of the depth-first search was first given by Cheung [Che83].

In Subsection 6.4.2 two algorithms will be considered that construct a depth-first search tree in networks without knowledge of the neighbors' identity in $O(N)$ time units. Consequently, these algorithms are not traversal algorithms. In Subsection 6.4.3 knowledge of neighbors will be exploited to arrive at an algorithm with message and time complexity $O(N)$.

6.4.2 Depth-first Search Algorithms Using Linear Time

The reason for the high time complexity of the classical depth-first search algorithm is that all edges, tree edges as well as fronds, are traversed serially. The token message $\langle \mathbf{tok} \rangle$ traverses all frond edges and returns immediately as shown in the proof of Theorem 6.33. All solutions with lower time complexity are based on the principle that the token message only traverses tree edges; clearly this takes linear time because there are only $N-1$ tree edges.

Awerbuch's solution. The algorithm now includes a mechanism that prevents the transmission of the token through a frond edge. In the algorithm of Awerbuch [Awe85b] it is ensured that each process knows, at the moment when it must forward the token, which of its neighbors have been visited already. The process then chooses an unvisited neighbor, or sends the token to its own father if no such neighbor exists.

When process p is first visited by the token (for the initiator this occurs when the algorithm is started) p informs each neighbor r, except its father, of the visit by sending a $\langle \mathbf{vis} \rangle$ message to r. The forwarding of the token is suspended until p has received an $\langle \mathbf{ack} \rangle$ message from each neighbor. This ensures that each neighbor r of p knows, at the moment p forwards the token, that p has been visited. When, later, the token arrives at r, r will not forward the token to p, unless p is r's father; see Algorithm 6.15.

The exchange of $\langle \mathbf{vis} \rangle$ messages causes, in most cases, $used_p[father_p]$ to be true even when p has not yet sent the token to its father. It must therefore be programmed explicitly in the algorithm that only the initiator may decide; a non-initiator p for which $used_p[q]$ is true for all neighbors q forwards the token to its father.

Theorem 6.34 *Awerbuch's algorithm (Algorithm 6.15) computes a depth-first search tree in $4N - 2$ time units and uses $4.|E|$ messages.*

Proof. The token is sent essentially through the same channels as in Algorithm 6.14, except that sending through frond edges is omitted. As transmissions through frond edges do not influence the final value of $father_p$ for any process p, the resulting tree is always a possible result of Algorithm 6.14.

var $used_p[q]$: boolean   **init** false for each $q \in Neigh_p$;
                                    (* Indicates whether p has already sent to q *)
      $father_p$: process   **init** *udef* ;

For the initiator only, execute once:
    begin $father_p := p$; choose $q \in Neigh_p$;
        forall $r \in Neigh_p$ **do** send $\langle$ **vis** $\rangle$ to r ;
        forall $r \in Neigh_p$ **do** receive $\langle$ **ack** $\rangle$ from r ;
        $used_p[q] := true$; send $\langle$ **tok** $\rangle$ to q
    end

For each process, upon receipt of $\langle$ **tok** $\rangle$ from q_0:
    begin if $father_p = udef$ **then**
            begin $father_p := q_0$;
                forall $r \in Neigh_p \setminus \{father_p\}$ **do** send $\langle$ **vis** $\rangle$ to r ;
                forall $r \in Neigh_p \setminus \{father_p\}$ **do** receive $\langle$ **ack** $\rangle$ from r
            end ;
        if p is the initiator **and** $\forall q \in Neigh_p : used_p[q]$
        then *decide*
        else if $\exists q \in Neigh_p : (q \neq father_p \wedge \neg used_p[q])$
          then begin if $father_p \neq q_0 \wedge \neg used_p[q_0]$
                  then $q := q_0$
                  else choose $q \in Neigh_p \setminus \{father_p\}$
                          with $\neg used_p[q]$;
                    $used_p[q] := true$; send $\langle$ **tok** $\rangle$ to q
          end
          else begin $used_p[father_p] := true$;
                    send $\langle$ **tok** $\rangle$ to $father_p$
          end
    end

For each process, upon receipt of $\langle$ **vis** $\rangle$ from q_0:
    begin $used_p[q_0] := true$; send $\langle$ **ack** $\rangle$ to q_0 **end**

Algorithm 6.15 AWERBUCH'S DEPTH-FIRST SEARCH ALGORITHM.

The token traverses serially each of the $N-1$ tree edges twice, which costs $2N - 2$ time units. At each node the token waits at most once, before it can be forwarded, for the exchange of $\langle$ **vis** $\rangle$/$\langle$ **ack** $\rangle$ messages, which gives rise to a delay of at most two time units at each node.

Each frond carries two $\langle$ **vis** $\rangle$ messages and two $\langle$ **ack** $\rangle$ messages. Each tree edge carries two $\langle$ **tok** $\rangle$ messages, one $\langle$ **vis** $\rangle$ (sent from father to son), and one $\langle$ **ack** $\rangle$ (from son to father). Consequently, $4.|E|$ messages are exchanged.   □

The sending of a $\langle$ **vis** $\rangle$ message can be omitted for the neighbor to which

var $used_p[q]$: boolean   **init** false for each $q \in Neigh_p$;
    $father_p$: process   **init** $udef$;
    mrs_p : process   **init** $udef$;

For the initiator only, execute once:
  begin $father_p := p$; choose $q \in Neigh_p$;
    forall $r \in Neigh_p$ **do** send $\langle \mathbf{vis} \rangle$ to r ;
    $used_p[q] := true$; $mrs_p := q$; send $\langle \mathbf{tok} \rangle$ to q
  end

For each process, upon receipt of $\langle \mathbf{vis} \rangle$ from q_0:
  begin $used_p[q_0] := true$;
    if $q_0 = mrs_p$ **then** (* Interpret as $\langle \mathbf{tok} \rangle$ message *)
     forward $\langle \mathbf{tok} \rangle$ message as upon receipt of $\langle \mathbf{tok} \rangle$ message
  end

Algorithm 6.16 CIDON'S DEPTH-FIRST SEARCH ALGORITHM (PART 1).

---

a process forwards the token. This improvement (not carried out in Algorithm 6.15) saves two messages per tree edge and hence reduces the message complexity by $2N - 2$ messages.

Cidon's solution. The algorithm of Cidon [Cid88] improves on the time complexity of Awerbuch's algorithm, by not sending the $\langle \mathbf{ack} \rangle$ messages used in Awerbuch's algorithm. In Cidon's modified algorithm, the token is forwarded immediately, i.e., without the two time unit delay introduced in Awerbuch's algorithm by waiting for the acknowledgements. The same algorithm was proposed by Lakshmanan *et al.* [LMT87]. The following situation may occur in Cidon's algorithm. Process p has been visited by the token and has sent a $\langle \mathbf{vis} \rangle$ message to its neighbor r. The token later visits r, but at the moment r receives the token the $\langle \mathbf{vis} \rangle$ message of p has not yet reached r. In this case r may forward the token to p, actually sending it via a frond edge. (Observe how the $\langle \mathbf{ack} \rangle$ messages in Awerbuch's algorithm prevent this scenario from taking place.)

To handle this situation, process p records (in variable mrs_p) to which neighbor it most recently sent the token. When the token only traverses tree edges p receives it the next time from the same neighbor mrs_p. In the scenario defined above p receives the $\langle \mathbf{tok} \rangle$ message from a different neighbor, namely from r; *the token is ignored in this case*, but p marks the edge rp as used, just as if a $\langle \mathbf{vis} \rangle$ message had been received from r. Process r receives p's $\langle \mathbf{vis} \rangle$ message after sending the token to p, i.e., r receives a $\langle \mathbf{vis} \rangle$ message from neighbor mrs_r. In this case r acts as if it had not yet

For each process, upon receipt of $\langle \textbf{tok} \rangle$ from q_0:
    begin if $mrs_p \neq udef$ **and** $mrs_p \neq q_0$
        (* This is a frond edge, interpret as $\langle \textbf{vis} \rangle$ message *)
        then $used_p[q_0] := true$
        else (* Act as in previous algorithm *)
            begin if $father_p = udef$ **then**
                begin $father_p := q_0$;
                    forall $r \in Neigh_p \setminus \{father_p\}$ **do**
                        send $\langle \textbf{vis} \rangle$ to r
                end ;
            if p is the initiator **and** $\forall q \in Neigh_p : used_p[q]$
            then *decide*
            else if $\exists q \in Neigh_p : (q \neq father_p \wedge \neg used_p[q])$
            then begin if $father_p \neq q_0 \wedge \neg used_p[q_0]$
                    then $q := q_0$
                    else choose $q \in Neigh_p \setminus \{father_p\}$
                        with $\neg used_p[q]$;
                  $used_p[q] := true$; $mrs_p := q$;
                  send $\langle \textbf{tok} \rangle$ to q
                end
            else begin $used_p[father_p] := true$;
                    send $\langle \textbf{tok} \rangle$ to $father_p$
            end
        end
    end

Algorithm 6.17 CIDON'S DEPTH-FIRST SEARCH ALGORITHM (PART 2).

sent the token to p; r selects a next neighbor and forwards the token; see Algorithm 6.16/6.17.

Theorem 6.35 *Cidon's algorithm (Algorithm 6.16/6.17) computes a DFS tree in $2N - 2$ time units using $4.|E|$ messages.*

Proof. Again the tour of the token is similar to the tour followed by Algorithm 6.14. Either transmission through frond edges is omitted (as with Algorithm 6.15) or the token crosses a $\langle \textbf{vis} \rangle$ message in the frond. In the last case the process receiving the $\langle \textbf{vis} \rangle$ message continues forwarding the token, which has the same effect as if the token had been sent back through the frond immediately.

The time between two successive transmissions of the token through a tree edge is bounded by one time unit. If the token is sent along a tree edge to p at time t, then at time t all $\langle \textbf{vis} \rangle$ messages of previously visited neighbors q of p have been sent, and consequently these messages arrive at the latest at time $t + 1$. So, even though p may have sent the token through a frond edge several times before $t + 1$, at time $t + 1$ at the latest p has recovered from all these mistakes and forwarded the token through a tree edge. As $2N - 2$ tree edges must be traversed, the algorithm terminates in $2N - 2$ time units.

At most two $\langle \mathbf{vis} \rangle$ messages and two $\langle \mathbf{tok} \rangle$ messages are transmitted through each channel, which proves that the message bound is $4.|E|$. $\quad\square$

In many cases the algorithm will send fewer messages than Awerbuch's algorithm. The analysis of the number of messages in Cidon's algorithm assumes the most pessimistic case, namely, that the token message is sent through each frond in both directions. It may be expected that the $\langle \mathbf{vis} \rangle$ messages are successful in avoiding many of these undesirable transmissions, in which case only two or three messages will be transmitted through each channel.

Cidon observes that, even though the algorithm may send the token to previously visited nodes, it has a better time (and communication) complexity than Algorithm 6.15, which prevents such undesirable transmissions. This suggests that less time and fewer messages may be spent in recovering from unnecessary actions than in avoiding these actions. Cidon leaves it as an open question whether a DFS algorithm exists that achieves the message complexity of the classical algorithm, i.e., $2|E|$, and that uses $O(N)$ time units.

6.4.3 Depth-first Search with Neighbor Knowledge

If processes know the identity of their neighbors the traversal of fronds by the token can be avoided by including a list of visited processes in the token. Process p, receiving the token with an included list L, does not forward the token to a process in L. The variables $used_p[q]$ can be omitted, because if p has previously forwarded the token to q, then $q \in L$; see Algorithm 6.18.

Theorem 6.36 *The DFS algorithm with neighbor knowledge is a traversal algorithm and computes a depth-first search tree using $2N - 2$ messages in $2N - 2$ time units.*

The bit complexity of this algorithm is high; if w is the number of bits needed to represent one identity, the list L may require up to $N.w$ bits; see Exercise 6.14.

var *father$_p$* : process **init** *udef* ;

For the initiator only, execute once:
> **begin** *father$_p$* := *p* ; choose *q* ∈ *Neigh$_p$* ;
>> send ⟨ **tlist**, {*p*} ⟩ to *q*
>
> **end**

For each process, upon receipt of ⟨ **tlist**, *L* ⟩ from *q$_0$*:
> **begin if** *father$_p$* = *udef* **then** *father$_p$* := *q$_0$* ;
>> **if** ∃*q* ∈ *Neigh$_p$* \ *L*
>>> **then begin** choose *q* ∈ *Neigh$_p$* \ *L* ;
>>>> send ⟨ **tlist**, *L* ∪ {*p*} ⟩ to *q*
>>>
>>> **end**
>>
>> **else if** *p* is initiator
>>> **then** *decide*
>>> **else** send ⟨ **tlist**, *L* ∪ {*p*} ⟩ to *father$_p$*
>
> **end**

Algorithm 6.18 DEPTH-FIRST SEARCH WITH NEIGHBOR KNOWLEDGE.

6.5 Remaining Issues

6.5.1 Overview of Wave Algorithms

Table 6.19 presents a list of the wave algorithms considered in this chapter. The column headed Number gives the number of the algorithm in this chapter; the column headed C/D indicates whether the algorithm is centralized (C) or decentralized (D); the column marked T indicates whether the algorithm is traversal; the column headed M gives the message complexity; the column headed Time gives the time complexity. In these columns N is the number of processes, $|E|$ the number of channels, and D the diameter of the network (in hops).

The complexity of waving in networks of most topologies depends considerably on whether a centralized or decentralized algorithm is required. Table 6.20 lists the message complexity of centralized and decentralized wave algorithms for rings, arbitrary networks, and trees. In the same fashion the dependence of the complexity on other parameters, such as neighbor knowledge or sense of direction (Section B.3), can be studied.

6.5.2 Computing Sums

It was shown in Subsection 6.1.5 that a single wave can compute an infimum over the inputs of all processes. The computation of an infimum can be used

Algorithm	Number	Topology	C/D	T	M	Time
Section 6.2: General algorithms						
Ring	6.2	ring	C	yes	N	N
Tree	6.3	tree	D	no	N	O(D)
Echo	6.5	arbitrary	C	no	$2|E|$	O(N)
Polling	6.6	clique	C	no	$2N - 2$	2
Phase	6.7	arbitrary	D	no	$2D.|E|$	$2D$
Phase on cliques	6.8	clique	D	no	$N(N-1)$	2
Finn	6.9	arbitrary	D	no	$\leq 4.N.|E|$	O(D)
Section 6.3: Traversal algorithms						
Sequential polling	6.10	clique	C	yes	$2N - 2$	$2N - 2$
Torus	6.11	torus	C	yes	N	N
Hypercube	6.12	hypercube	C	yes	N	N
Tarry	6.13	arbitrary	C	yes	$2|E|$	$2|E|$
Section 6.4: Depth-first search algorithms						
Classic	6.14	arbitrary	C	yes	$2|E|$	$2|E|$
Awerbuch	6.15	arbitrary	C	no	$4.|E|$	$4N - 2$
Cidon	6.16/6.17	arbitrary	C	no	$4.|E|$	$2N - 2$
with neighbor knowledge	6.18	arbitrary	C	yes	$2N - 2$	$2N - 2$

Remark: the phase algorithm (6.7) and Finn's algorithm (6.9) are suitable for directed networks.

Table 6.19 THE WAVE ALGORITHMS OF THIS CHAPTER.

Topology	C/D	Complexity	Reference
Ring	C	N	Algorithm 6.2
	D	O($N \log N$)	Algorithm 7.7
Arbitrary	C	$2|E|$	Algorithm 6.5
	D	O($N \log N + |E|$)	Section 7.3
Tree	C	$2(N - 1)$	Algorithm 6.5
	D	O(N)	Algorithm 6.3

Table 6.20 INFLUENCE OF CENTRALIZATION ON MESSAGE COMPLEXITY.

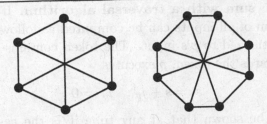

Figure 6.21 Two NETWORKS OF DIAMETER TWO AND DEGREE THREE.

to compute a commutative, associative, idempotent operator extended over the input, such as a minimum, maximum, etc. (see Corollary 6.14). A large number of functions are not computable in this way, these include the sum over all inputs, because the sum operator is not idempotent. Summing inputs can be used to count processes with a certain property (by setting the input to 1 if a process has the property and to 0 otherwise), and the results of this subsection can also be used for other operators that are commutative and associative, such as the product of integers or the union of multisets.

It turns out that there does not exist a general method for computing sums using a wave algorithm, but in special cases the computation of a sum is possible. This is the case when the algorithm is a traversal algorithm, when the processes have identities, or when the algorithm induces a spanning tree that can be used.

Impossibility of a general construction. It is not possible to give a general construction for computing sums using an arbitrary wave algorithm, similar to the construction used in Theorem 6.12 for computing infimums. This can be seen as follows. There exists a wave algorithm for the class of networks including all undirected anonymous networks of diameter two, namely the phase algorithm (with parameter $D = 2$). There does not exist an algorithm that can compute the sum of all inputs and that is correct for all undirected anonymous networks of diameter two. The class of networks includes the two networks depicted in Figure 6.21. Assuming each process has input 1, the answer is 6 for the left network and 8 for the right network. Using the techniques introduced in Chapter 9 it can be shown that any algorithm will output the same result in each of the two networks and hence is not correct in both networks. The elaboration of this argument is left to the reader as Exercise 9.7.

Computing the sum with a traversal algorithm. If A is a traversal algorithm the sum of all inputs can be computed as follows. Process p has a variable j_p, initialized to p's input. The token contains an extra field s. Whenever p forwards the token, p executes

$$s := s + j_p \; ; \quad j_p := 0$$

and it can then be shown that at any time it is the case that for each previously visited process p, $j_p = 0$, and s equals the sum of the inputs of all previously visited processes. Consequently, when the algorithm terminates, s equals the sum over all inputs.

Computing the sum using a spanning tree. Some wave algorithms make available for each decision event d_p in process p a spanning tree rooted at p, via which messages are sent towards p. In fact, each computation of any wave algorithm contains such spanning trees; however, it may be the case that a process q sends several messages, and does not know which of its outgoing edges belongs to one such a tree. If the processes are aware of which outgoing edge is the edge to their father in such a tree, the tree can be used to compute the sums. Each process sends to its father in the tree the sum of all inputs in its subtree.

This principle can be applied to the tree algorithm, the echo algorithm, and the phase algorithm for cliques. The tree algorithm is easily adapted to include the sum over the inputs in T_{pq} in the message sent from p to q. A deciding process computes the final result by summing the values contained in the two messages that cross on one edge. The phase algorithm for cliques is adapted by sending, in each message from q to p, the input of q. The process p adds all received values and its own input, and the result is the correct answer when p decides. In the echo algorithm the inputs can be added using the spanning tree T constructed explicitly during the computation; see Exercise 6.15.

Computing the sum using identities. Assume each process has a unique identity. The sum over all inputs can be computed as follows. Each process labels its input with its identity by forming the pair (p, j_p); observe that no two processes form the same pair. The algorithm ensures that when a process decides it knows each individual input; $S = \{(p, j_p) : p \in \mathbb{P}\}$ is the union over all p of the sets $S_p = \{(p, j_p)\}$, and can be computed in a single wave. From this set the desired result is computed by local operations.

This solution requires the availability of unique identities for each process, and it increases the bit complexity considerably. Each message of the wave algorithm includes a subset of S, which, if w bits are needed to represent one identity and an input, takes up to $N.w$ bits; see Exercise 6.16.

6.5.3 Alternative Definitions of Time Complexity

The time complexity of distributed algorithms can be defined in several ways. In this book Definition 6.31 is always used when time complexities are considered, but other possible definition are discussed here.

Definitions based on more restrictive timing assumptions. The time consumed by distributed computations can be estimated using more restrictive assumptions about the timing of events in the system.

Definition 6.37 *The one-time complexity of an algorithm is the maximum time of a computation of the algorithm under the following assumptions.*

O1. A process can execute any finite number of events in zero time.
O2. The time between the sending and receipt of a message is exactly one time unit.

Compare this definition with Definition 6.31 and observe that assumption O1 is the same as T1. Because the transmission times assumed under T2 are *at most* equal to the times assumed under O2 one may be trapped into think that the one-time complexity is always at least equal to the time complexity. To this end one might argue that each computation runs at least as fast under T2 as it does under O2, and consequently the computation with the maximum time also does no worse under T2 than it does under O2. The flaw in this argument is that the variations in transmission time allowed under T2 make a larger class of computations possible, including perhaps computations with poor time behavior. Recall that T2 is not a restriction on executions to be measured but a definition of the time unit; O2 actually restricts the set of executions to those in which all messages have the same delay. The point is illustrated below for the echo algorithm.

In fact the reverse is true: the time complexity of an algorithm equals at least the one-time complexity of that algorithm. Each computation allowed under assumptions O1 and O2 is also allowed under assumptions T1 and T2, and takes the same amount of time under the latter assumptions. Consequently, the worst-case behavior of an algorithm under O1 and O2 is included in Definition 6.31, and is a lower bound for the time complexity.

Theorem 6.38 *The one-time complexity of the echo algorithm is* $O(D)$. *The time complexity of the echo algorithm is* $\Theta(N)$, *even in networks with diameter* 1.

Proof. To analyze the one-time complexity, assume O1 and O2. A process at hop distance d from the initiator receives the first $\langle \mathbf{tok} \rangle$ message *exactly* d time units after the start of the computation and has depth d in the resulting tree T. (This can be shown by induction on d.) Let D_T denote the depth of T; then $D_T \leq D$ and a process with depth d in T sends the $\langle \mathbf{tok} \rangle$ message to its father at the latest at $(2D_T + 1) - d$ time units after the start of the computation. (This can be shown by a backward induction on d.) It follows that the initiator decides at the latest at $2D_T + 1$ time units after the start of the computation.

To analyze the time complexity, assume T1 and T2. A process at hop distance d from the initiator receives the first $\langle \mathbf{tok} \rangle$ message *at the latest* at d time units after the start of the computation. (This can be shown by induction on d.) Assume the spanning tree is completed F time units after the start of the computation, then $F \leq D$. It is not necessarily the case that the depth D_T of the spanning tree is bounded by the diameter (as will be shown in the computation below), but as there are N processes the depth is bounded by $N - 1$. A process with depth d in T sends the $\langle \mathbf{tok} \rangle$ message to its father at the latest at $(F + 1) + (D_T - d)$ time units after the start of the computation. (This can be shown by a backward induction on d.) It follows that the initiator decides at the latest at $(F + 1) + D_T$ time units after the start of the computation, and this is $O(N)$.

To show that $\Omega(N)$ is a lower bound on the time complexity, a computation on the clique of N processes is constructed that uses time N. Fix in the clique a spanning tree of depth $N - 1$ (actually a linear chain of nodes). Assume that all $\langle \mathbf{tok} \rangle$ messages sent downward via tree edges are received $1/N$ time units after they are sent, and $\langle \mathbf{tok} \rangle$ messages via frond edges are received after one time unit. These delays are allowed according to assumption T2 and in this computation the complete tree is formed within one time unit but has a depth of $N - 1$. Assume now that all messages sent upward via tree edges also suffer a delay of one time unit; in this case the decision takes place exactly N time units after the start of the computation. $\square$

One may argue about the question which of the two definitions should be preferred when discussing the time complexity of a distributed algorithm. The one-time complexity suffers from the disadvantage that some computations are not considered, although they are possible under the algorithm. Among the computations ignored there may be some that are extremely time-consuming. The assumptions made in Definition 6.31 do not exclude a single computation; the definition only defines a time measure for each computation. The time complexity suffers from the disadvantage that the result is determined by computations (such as in the proof of Theorem 6.38) that, although possible, are considered to be extremely unlikely to occur. Indeed, in this computation a single message is "bypassed" by a chain of $N - 1$ serially transmitted messages.

As a compromise between the two definitions one may consider the *alpha-time complexity*, which is determined under the assumption that the delay of each message is between α and 1 (α is a constant ≤ 1). Unfortunately this compromise suffers from the disadvantages of both alternatives. The reader may want to show himself that the α-time complexity of the echo algorithm is $O(\min(N, D/\alpha))$.

The most precise measure of time complexity is obtained when a probability distribution of the message delays can be assumed, from which the expected time of a computation of the algorithm can be computed. This option suffers from two major disadvantages. First, the analysis of an algorithm would be too system-dependent, because in each distributed system the distribution of message delays is different. Second, the analysis would be far too complicated to carry out in most cases.

Definition based on message chains. The time consumption of a distributed computation can be defined using structural properties of the computation rather than idealized timing assumptions. Let C be a computation.

Definition 6.39 *A message chain in C is a sequence $m_1, m_2, \ldots, m_k$ of messages, such that for each i, $0 \leq i < k$, the receipt of m_i causally precedes the sending of m_{i+1}.*
The chain-time complexity of a distributed algorithm is the length of the longest message chain in any computation of the algorithm.

This definition, like Definition 6.31, considers all possible executions of an algorithm in order to define its time complexity, but assigns a different measure to the computations. Consider the situation (as occurs in the computation defined in the proof of Theorem 6.38) that a single message is bypassed by a chain of k messages. The time complexity of this (sub)computation is 1, while the chain-time complexity of the same (sub)computation is k. In systems in which an upper bound on message delays is guaranteed (as is assumed in the definition of time complexity), the time complexity is the right measure. In systems in which most messages are delivered after an "average" delay but a small fraction of the messages may suffer from a much larger delay, the chain-time complexity is a better choice.

Exercises to Chapter 6
Section 6.1

Exercise 6.1 *Give an example of a PIF algorithm for systems with synchronous message passing that does not allow computation of infima (compare Theorem 6.7 and 6.12). Your example may be suitable for a particular topology only.*

Exercise 6.2 *In a partial order $(X, \leq)$ an element b is called a bottom if for all $c \in X$, $b \leq c$.*
It is used in the proof of Theorem 6.11 that the partial order $(X, \leq)$ does not contain a bottom. Where?
Can you give an algorithm that computes infima in a partial order with bottom, and is not a wave algorithm?

Exercise 6.3 *Give two partial orders on the natural numbers for which the infimum function is (1) the greatest common divisor, and (2) the least common ancestor.*
Give partial orders on the collection of subsets of a universe U for which the infimum function is (1) the intersection of sets, and (2) the union of sets.

Exercise 6.4 *Prove the Infimum Theorem (Theorem 6.13).*

Section 6.2

Exercise 6.5 *Show that in each computation of the tree algorithm (Algorithm 6.3) exactly two processes decide.*

Exercise 6.6 *Use the echo algorithm (Algorithm 6.5) to write an algorithm that computes a prefix labeling scheme (see Subsection 4.4.3) for an arbitrary network using $2|E|$ messages and $O(N)$ time units.*
Can you give an algorithm that computes the labeling scheme in $O(D)$ time? (D is the diameter of the network.)

Exercise 6.7 *Show that the relationship in Lemma 6.19 also holds if messages can get lost in the channel pq, but not if messages can be duplicated. What step in the proof fails if messages can be duplicated?*

Exercise 6.8 *Apply the construction of Theorem 6.12 to the phase algorithm so as to obtain an algorithm that computes the maximum over the (integer) inputs of all processes.*
What are the message, time, and bit complexities of your algorithm?

Exercise 6.9 *Suppose you want to use a wave algorithm in a network where duplication of messages may occur.*

(1) *What modifications should be made to the echo algorithm?*
(2) *What modifications should be made to Finn's algorithm?*

Section 6.3

Exercise 6.10 *A complete bipartite graph is a graph $G = (V, E)$ where $V = V_1 \cup V_2$ with $V_1 \cap V_2 = \varnothing$ and $E = V_1 \times V_2$.*
Give a 2x-traversal algorithm for complete bipartite networks.

Project 6.11 *It was shown [DRT98] that traversal and broadcast are possible in a hypercube also without sense of direction. For what f is the algorithm an f-traversal?*

Section 6.4

Exercise 6.12 *Give an example of a computation of Tarry's algorithm in which the resulting tree T is not a DFS tree.*

Exercise 6.13 *Write an algorithm that computes the depth-first search interval labeling scheme (see Subsection 4.4.2) for an arbitrary connected network.*
Can it be done in $O(N)$ time units? Can it be done using $O(N)$ messages?

Exercise 6.14 *Assume that the depth-first search algorithm with neighbor knowledge is used in a system where each process knows not only the identities of its neighbors but also the set of all process identities ($\mathbb{P}$). Show that messages of N bits each are sufficient in this case.*

Section 6.5

Exercise 6.15 *Adapt the echo algorithm (Algorithm 6.5) to compute the sum over the inputs of the processes.*

Exercise 6.16 *Assume the processes in the networks depicted in Figure 6.21 have unique identities and each process has an integer input. Simulate on both networks a computation of the phase algorithm, computing the set $S = \{(p, j_p) : p \in \mathbb{P}\}$ and the sum over the inputs.*

Exercise 6.17 *What is the chain-time complexity of the phase algorithm for cliques (Algorithm 6.8)?*

7

Election Algorithms

In this chapter the problem of *election*, also called *leader finding*, will be discussed. The election problem was first posed by LeLann [LeL77], who also proposed the first solution; see Subsection 7.2.1. The problem is to start from a configuration where all processes are in the same state, and arrive at a configuration where exactly one process is in state *leader* and all other processes are in the state *lost*.

An election under the processes must be held if a centralized algorithm is to be executed and there is no a priori candidate to serve as the initiator of this algorithm. For example, this could be the case for an initialization procedure that must be executed initially or after a crash of the system. Because the set of active processes may not be known in advance it is not possible to assign one process once and for all to the role of leader.

A large number of results about the election problem (algorithms as well as more general theorems) exist. The results in this chapter were selected for inclusion with the following criteria in mind.

(1) Synchronous systems, anonymous processes, and fault tolerant algorithms are discussed in other chapters. In this chapter it is always assumed that processes and channels are reliable, the system is fully asynchronous, and the processes are distinguished by unique identities.

(2) The election problem has taken the role of a "benchmarking problem" to compare the efficiency of different computation models. We shall therefore treat some results necessary for this comparison, and return to this problem frequently in later chapters (9, 12, 11).

(3) We concentrate on results concerning message complexity; algorithms with improved time complexity or results implying a trade-off between time and message complexity are not discussed.

227

7.1 Introduction

The election problem requires that, starting from a configuration where each process is in the same state, a configuration is reached where exactly one process is in a special the state *leader*, while all other processes are in the state *lost*. The process in state *leader* at the end of the computation is called the *leader* and is said to be elected by the algorithm.

Definition 7.1 *An election algorithm is an algorithm that satisfies the following properties.*

(1) *Each process has the same local algorithm.*
(2) *The algorithm is decentralized, i.e., a computation can be initialized by an arbitrary non-empty subset of the processes.*
(3) *The algorithm reaches a terminal configuration in each computation, and in each reachable terminal configuration there is exactly one process in the state leader and all other processes are in the state lost.*

The last property is sometimes weakened to require only that exactly one process is in the state *leader*. It is then the case that the elected process is aware that it has won the election, but the losers are not (yet) aware of their loss. If an algorithm satisfying this weaker requirement is given, it can easily be extended by a flooding, initiated by the leader, in which all processes are informed of the result of the election. This additional notification is omitted in some algorithms in this chapter.

In all algorithms in this chapter process p has a variable $state_p$, having possible values that include *leader* and *lost*. We will sometimes assume that the value of $state_p$ is *sleep* before p has executed any step of the algorithm, and *cand* if p has joined the computation but is not yet aware whether it has lost or won the election. Some algorithms use additional states, such as *active*, *passive*, etc., which will be indicated within the algorithm.

7.1.1 Assumptions Made in this Chapter

The election problem has been studied in this chapter under assumptions that we now review.

(1) *The system is fully asynchronous.* It has been assumed that the processes have no access to a common clock and that the message transmission times can be arbitrarily long or short.

It turns out that the assumption of synchronous message passing (i.e., that the sending and receipt of a message are considered to be a single transition) hardly influences the results obtained for the election problem. The reader may convince himself that the algorithms given in this chapter can be applied in systems with synchronous message passing, and that the lower-bound results can also be adapted to this case.

A global timing assumption, such as the assumption that processes can observe real time and that message delay is bounded, does have an important impact on solutions to the election problem.

(2) *Each process is identified by a unique name, its* identity, *which is known to the process initially.* For simplicity it has been assumed that the identity of process p is just p. The identities are drawn from a totally ordered set $\mathcal{P}$, i.e., a relation $\leq$ on identities is available. The number of bits that represent an identity is w.

The importance of unique identities in the election problem is that they can be used not only for addressing messages, but also for breaking the symmetry between processes. When designing an election algorithm one may, for example, postulate that the process with the smallest (or, alternatively, the largest) identity must win the election. The problem then becomes one of finding the smallest identity with a decentralized algorithm. In this case the election problem is referred to as the *extrema-finding* problem.

Although some of the algorithms discussed in this chapter were originally formulated so as to elect the largest process, we shall in fact formulate most of these algorithms so as to elect the smallest process; in each case an algorithm to elect the largest process is of course obtained by reversing the order of comparisons between identities.

(3) *Some results in this chapter concern comparison algorithms.* Comparison algorithms are algorithms that use the comparison as the only operation on identities. As can be seen by inspection of the algorithms, all algorithms presented in this chapter are comparison algorithms. Whenever a lower-bound result is presented, we state explicitly whether it concerns comparison algorithms.

It was shown (e.g., by Bodlaender [Bod91b] for the case of ring networks) that in asynchronous networks arbitrary algorithms achieve no better complexity than comparison algorithms. This is not the case in synchronous systems, as will be shown in Chapter 12; in these systems arbitrary algorithms may achieve a better complexity than comparison algorithms.

(4) *Each message may contain* O(w) *bits.* Each message may contain only up to a constant number of process identities. This assumption is

made in order to allow a fair comparison between the communication complexities of different algorithms.

7.1.2 Elections and Waves

It has already been remarked that the process identities can be used to break symmetry between processes; one may design an election algorithm in such a way that the process with the smallest identity will be the process elected. According to the results in Subsection 6.1.5 the smallest identity can be computed by the processes in a single wave; this suggests that an election can be held by executing a wave in which the smallest identity is computed, after which the process with this identity becomes leader. Because an election algorithm must be decentralized this principle can only be applied to decentralized wave algorithms (see Table 6.19).

Election with the tree algorithm. If the network topology is a tree, or a spanning tree of the network is available, an election can be held using the tree algorithm (Subsection 6.2.2). In the tree algorithm it is required that at least all leaves are initiators of the algorithm. To obtain progress in the algorithm in case only some processes are initiators also, a *wake-up* phase is added. Processes that want to start the election flood a message ⟨**wakeup**⟩ to all processes. The boolean variable ws is used to make every process send ⟨**wakeup**⟩ messages at most once, and the wr variable is used to count the number of ⟨**wakeup**⟩ messages a process has received. When a process has received a ⟨**wakeup**⟩ message through each channel, it starts Algorithm 6.3, which is augmented (as in Theorem 6.12) to compute the smallest identity and to make each process decide. When a process decides it knows the identity of the leader; if this identity equals the identity of the process, it becomes *leader*, otherwise *lost*; see Algorithm 7.1.

Theorem 7.2 *Algorithm 7.1 solves the election problem on trees using* $O(N)$ *messages and* $O(D)$ *time units.*

Proof. When at least one process initiates the algorithm, all processes send ⟨**wakeup**⟩ messages to all neighbors their, and each process starts the execution of the tree algorithm after receipt of the ⟨**wakeup**⟩ message from every neighbor. All processes terminate the tree algorithm with the same value of v, namely, the smallest identity of any process. The (unique) process with this identity will end in the state *leader* and all other processes in state *lost*.

Two ⟨**wakeup**⟩ messages and two ⟨**tok**, r⟩ messages are sent via each

```
var ws_p     : boolean                          init false ;
    wr_p     : integer                          init 0 ;
    rec_p[q] : boolean for each q ∈ Neigh_p     init false ;
    v_p      : P                                init p ;
    state_p  : (sleep, leader, lost)            init sleep ;

begin if p is initiator then
        begin ws_p := true ;
                forall q ∈ Neigh_p do send ⟨wakeup⟩ to q
        end ;
      while wr_p < #Neigh_p do
        begin receive ⟨wakeup⟩ ; wr_p := wr_p + 1 ;
              if not ws_p then
                begin ws_p := true ;
                        forall q ∈ Neigh_p do send ⟨wakeup⟩ to q
                end
        end ;
      (* Now start the tree algorithm *)
      while #{q : ¬rec_p[q]} > 1 do
        begin receive ⟨tok, r⟩ from q ; rec_p[q] := true ;
              v_p := min(v_p, r)
        end ;
      send ⟨tok, v_p⟩ to q_0 with ¬rec_p[q_0] ;
      receive ⟨tok, r⟩ from q_0 ;
      v_p := min(v_p, r) ; (* decide with answer v_p *)
      if v_p = p then state_p := leader else state_p := lost ;
      forall q ∈ Neigh_p, q ≠ q_0 do send ⟨tok, v_p⟩ to q
end
```

Algorithm 7.1 ELECTION ALGORITHM FOR TREES.

---

channel, which brings the message complexity to $4N - 4$. Within D time units after the first process starts the algorithm, each process has sent ⟨**wakeup**⟩ messages, hence within $D+1$ time units each process has started the wave. It is fairly easy to see that the first decision takes place within D time units after the start of the wave and the last decision takes place within D time units after the first one, which brings the total time to $3D + 1$. A more careful analysis reveals that the algorithm always terminates within $2D$ time units, but this is left to the reader; see Exercise 7.2. □

If messages can be reordered in a channel (i.e., the channel is not fifo) a process may receive a ⟨**tok**, r⟩ message from a neighbor *before* it receives a ⟨**wakeup**⟩ message from that neighbor. In that case the ⟨**tok**, r⟩ message can be temporarily stored or processed similarly to later-arriving $\langle \mathbf{tok}, r \rangle$ messages.

The number of messages can be reduced by two modifications. First, it may be arranged that a non-initiator does not send a $\langle \mathbf{wakeup} \rangle$ message to the process from which it received the first $\langle \mathbf{wakeup} \rangle$ message. Second, the $\langle \mathbf{wakeup} \rangle$ message sent by a leaf can be combined with the $\langle \mathbf{tok}, r \rangle$ message sent by that leaf. With these modifications, the number of messages required by the algorithm is reduced to $3N - 4 + k$, where k is the number of non-leaf starters [Tel91b, p. 139].

Election with the phase algorithm. The phase algorithm can be used for elections by letting it compute the smallest identity in a single wave, as in Theorem 6.12.

Theorem 7.3 *Using the phase algorithm (Algorithm 6.7) elections can be held in arbitrary networks using* $O(D.|E|)$ *messages and* $O(D)$ *time units.*

Peleg's algorithm [Pel90] is based on the phase algorithm; it uses $O(D.|E|)$ messages and $O(D)$ time, but does not require knowledge D because it includes on-line computation of the diameter.

Election with Finn's algorithm. Finn's algorithm (Algorithm 6.9) does not require the diameter of the network to be known in advance. The $O(N.|E|)$ messages used by Finn's algorithm are much longer than allowed for in the assumptions of this chapter; hence each message of Finn's algorithm must be counted as $O(N)$ messages, which brings the message complexity to $O(N^2.|E|)$.

7.2 Ring Networks

In this section some election algorithms for *unidirectional* rings are considered. The election problem was first posed for the context of ring networks by LeLann [LeL77], who also gave a solution with message complexity $O(N^2)$. This solution was improved by Chang and Roberts [CR79], who gave an algorithm with a worst case complexity of $O(N^2)$, but an average case complexity of only $O(N \log N)$. The solutions by LeLann and Chang–Roberts solutions are discussed in Subsection 7.2.1. The existence of an algorithm with an $O(N \log N)$ worst-case complexity remained open until 1980, when such an algorithm was given by Hirschberg and Sinclair [HS80]. Unlike earlier solutions, the Hirschberg–Sinclair algorithm required channels to be bidirectional. It was conjectured for a while that $\Omega(N^2)$ messages was a

```
var List_p        : set of P      init {p} ;
    state_p ;

begin if p is initiator then
        begin state_p := cand ; send ⟨tok, p⟩ to Next_p ; receive ⟨tok, q⟩ ;
              while q ≠ p do
                    begin List_p := List_p ∪ {q} ;
                          send ⟨tok, q⟩ to Next_p ; receive ⟨tok, q⟩
                    end ;
              if p = min(List_p) then state_p := leader
                                  else state_p := lost
        end
    else while true do
              begin receive ⟨tok, q⟩ ; send ⟨tok, q⟩ to Next_p ;
                    if state_p = sleep then state_p := lost
              end
end
```

Algorithm 7.2 LeLann's election algorithm.

lower bound for unidirectional rings, but Petersen [Pet82] and Dolev, Klawe, and Rodeh [DKR82] independently proposed an $O(N \log N)$ solution for the unidirectional ring. Their solution is treated in Subsection 7.2.2.

The algorithms were complemented by matching lower bounds at about the same time. A worst case lower bound of $\approx 0.34 N \log N$ messages for bidirectional rings was proved by Bodlaender [Bod88]. Pachl, Korach, and Rotem [PKR84] proved lower bounds of $\Omega(N \log N)$ for the average-case complexity, both for bidirectional and unidirectional rings. Their lower-bound result will be treated in Subsection 7.2.3.

7.2.1 The Algorithms of LeLann and of Chang and Roberts

In the algorithm of LeLann [LeL77] each initiator computes a list of the identities of all initiators, after which the initiator with the smallest identity is elected. Each initiator sends a token, containing its identity, via the ring, and this token is forwarded by all processes. It is assumed that the channels are fifo and that an initiator must generate its token before the token of any other initiator is received. (When a process receives a token, it will not initiate the algorithm thereafter.) When an initiator p receives its own token back, the tokens of all initiators have passed p, and p becomes elected if and only if p is the smallest among the initiators; see Algorithm 7.2.

Theorem 7.4 *LeLann's algorithm (Algorithm 7.2) solves the election problem for rings using* $O(N^2)$ *messages and* $O(N)$ *time units.*

Proof. Because the order of the tokens on the ring is preserved (by the fifo assumption) and initiator q sends out $\langle \mathbf{tok}, q \rangle$ *before* q receives $\langle \mathbf{tok}, p \rangle$, initiator p receives $\langle \mathbf{tok}, q \rangle$ before p receives $\langle \mathbf{tok}, p \rangle$ back. It follows that each initiator p ends up with $List_p$ equal to the set of all initiators, and the initiator with smallest identity is the only process that becomes elected. There are at most N different tokens and each makes N steps, which brings the message complexity to $O(N^2)$. At $N - 1$ time units at the latest after the first initiator has sent out its token, each initiator has done so, and each initiator receives its token back within N time units after the generation of that token. This implies that the algorithm terminates within $2N - 1$ time units.   □

The non-initiators all enter the *lost* state, but remain waiting for more $\langle \mathbf{tok}, r \rangle$ messages forever. The waiting can be aborted if the leader sends a special token around the ring to announce that the election is over.

The algorithm of Chang and Roberts [CR79] improves on LeLann's algorithm by removing from the ring all tokens of processes for which it can be seen that they will lose the election. That is, initiator p removes token $\langle \mathbf{tok}, q \rangle$ from the ring if $q > p$. Initiator p becomes *lost* when a token with identity $q < p$ is received, and *leader* when the token with identity p is received; see Algorithm 7.3.

Theorem 7.5 *The Chang–Roberts algorithm (Algorithm 7.3) solves the election problem for rings using* $\Theta(N^2)$ *messages in the worst case and* $O(N)$ *time units.*

Proof. Let p_0 be the initiator with the smallest identity. Each process is either a non-initiator or an initiator with an identity larger than p_0, so all processes forward the token $\langle \mathbf{tok}, p_0 \rangle$ emitted by p_0. Consequently, p_0 receives its token back and becomes elected.

Non-initiators do not become elected, but they all enter the state *lost*, at the latest when p_0's token is forwarded. Initiator p with $p > p_0$ does not become elected; p_0 does not forward the token $\langle \mathbf{tok}, p \rangle$, so p never receives its own token. Such an initiator p enters the state *lost*, at the latest when $\langle \mathbf{tok}, p_0 \rangle$ is forwarded. This proves that the algorithm solves the election problem.

At most N different tokens are used, and each token is forwarded by at most N hops, which proves an $O(N^2)$ bound on the message complexity.

var $state_p$;

begin if p is initiator **then**
        begin $state_p := cand$; send $\langle \mathbf{tok}, p \rangle$ to $Next_p$;
           while $state_p \neq leader$ **do**
               begin receive $\langle \mathbf{tok}, q \rangle$;
                      if $q = p$ **then** $state_p := leader$
                      else if $q < p$ **then**
                            begin if $state_p = cand$ **then** $state_p := lost$;
                                  send $\langle \mathbf{tok}, q \rangle$ to $Next_p$
                      end
               end
        end
      else while *true* **do**
               begin receive $\langle \mathbf{tok}, q \rangle$; send $\langle \mathbf{tok}, q \rangle$ to $Next_p$;
                    if $state_p = sleep$ **then** $state_p := lost$
               end
end
(* Only the leader terminates the program. It floods a message to all
processes to inform them of the leader's identity and to terminate *)

Algorithm 7.3 THE CHANG–ROBERTS ELECTION ALGORITHM.

To show that $\Omega(N^2)$ messages may indeed be used, consider an initial configuration where the identities are arranged in increasing order around the ring (cf. Figure 7.4) and each process is an initiator. The token of each process is removed from the ring by process 0, so the token of process i is forwarded by $N - i$ hops, which brings the number of message passes to $\sum_{i=0}^{N-1} (N - i) = \frac{1}{2} N(N + 1)$. □

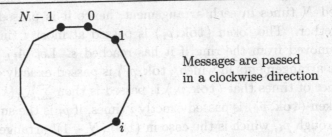

Figure 7.4 WORST-CASE SCENARIO FOR THE CHANG–ROBERTS ALGORITHM.

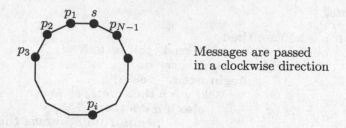

Messages are passed
in a clockwise direction

Figure 7.5 Arrangement of identities on the ring.

The Chang–Roberts algorithm is no improvement over LeLann's when the time complexity or the worst-case message complexity is considered. There is an improvement when the *average* case is considered, where the average is taken over all possible arrangements of the identities around the ring.

Theorem 7.6 *The Chang–Roberts algorithm requires only* $O(N \log N)$ *message passings in the average case when all processes are initiators.*

Proof. (This proof is based on a suggestion by Friedemann Mattern.)

Assuming all processes are initiators, we compute the average number of token passings over all circular arrangements of the N different identities. Consider a fixed set of N identities, and let s be the smallest identity. There are $(N - 1)!$ different circular arrangements of the identities; in a given circular arrangement, let p_i be the identity occurring i steps *before* s; see Figure 7.5.

To compute the total number of token passings over all arrangements, we compute first the total number of times that the token $\langle \mathbf{tok}, p_i \rangle$ is passed in all arrangements, and subsequently sum over i. The token $\langle \mathbf{tok}, s \rangle$ is passed N times in each arrangement, hence it is passed $N(N - 1)!$ times altogether. The token $\langle \mathbf{tok}, p_i \rangle$ is passed at most i times because it will be removed from the ring if it has reached s. Let $A_{i,k}$ be the number of cyclic arrangements in which $\langle \mathbf{tok}, p_i \rangle$ is passed exactly k times. The total number of times that $\langle \mathbf{tok}, p_i \rangle$ is passed is then $\sum_{k=1}^{i} (k \cdot A_{i,k})$.

Token $\langle \mathbf{tok}, p_i \rangle$ is passed exactly i times, if p_i is the smallest of identities p_1 through p_i, which is the case in $(1/i).(N - 1)!$ arrangements; so

$$A_{i,i} = \frac{1}{i}(N - 1)!.$$

Token $\langle \mathbf{tok}, p_i \rangle$ is passed *at least* k times (here $k \le i$), if process p_i is followed by $k - 1$ processes with an identity larger than p_i. Of course, the number of arrangements in which p_i is the smallest of the k identities $p_{i-k+1}, \ldots, p_i$ is a fraction $1/k$ of all arrangements, i.e., $(1/k).(N - 1)!$. Now, for $k < i$, $\langle \text{tok}, p_i \rangle$ is passed *exactly* k times, if it is passed at least k times, but not more, i.e., at least k times but *not* at least $k + 1$ times. Consequently, the number of arrangements in which this happens is

$$\frac{1}{k}(N - 1)! - \frac{1}{k+1}(N - 1)!,$$

that is,

$$A_{i,k} = \frac{1}{k(k+1)}(N - 1)! \qquad \text{(for } k < i\text{)}.$$

We find that the total number of times $\langle \text{tok}, p_i \rangle$ is passed in all arrangements is

$$\sum_{k=1}^{i-1} k \left(\frac{1}{k(k+1)}(N - 1)! \right) + i\frac{1}{i}(N - 1)!,$$

which equals $(\sum_{k=1}^{i} 1/k)(N - 1)!$. The sum $(\sum_{k=1}^{i} 1/k)$ is known as the ith *harmonic number*, denoted $\mathbf{H}_i$. It is left as Exercise 7.3 to prove the identity

$$\sum_{i=1}^{m} \mathbf{H}_i = (m + 1)\mathbf{H}_m - m.$$

Next we sum the token passes over i to obtain the total number of token passings (excluding those for $\langle \text{tok}, s \rangle$) in all arrangements. This total is

$$\sum_{i=1}^{N-1} [\mathbf{H}_i.(N - 1)!] = (N\mathbf{H}_{N-1} - (N - 1))(N - 1)!.$$

Adding the $N.(N - 1)!$ token passings for $\langle \text{tok}, s \rangle$, we arrive at a total number of token passings of

$$(N.\mathbf{H}_{N-1} + 1)(N - 1)! = (N.\mathbf{H}_N).(N - 1)!.$$

As this is for $(N - 1)!$ different arrangements, the average over the arrangements is clearly $N\mathbf{H}_N$, which is $\approx 0.69N \log N$ (see Exercise 7.4). $\square$

7.2.2 The Peterson/Dolev–Klawe–Rodeh Algorithm

The Chang–Roberts algorithm achieves an $O(N \log N)$ message complexity in the average case, but not in the worst case. An algorithm with an $O(N \log N)$ worst-case complexity was given by Franklin [Fra82], but this

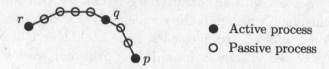

Figure 7.6 PROCESS p OBTAINS CURRENT IDENTITIES OF q AND r.

algorithm requires that channels are bidirectional. Peterson [Pet82] and Dolev, Klawe, and Rodeh [DKR82] independently developed a very similar algorithm, solving the problem using only $O(N \log N)$ messages in the worst case for unidirectional rings. The algorithm requires that channels are fifo.

The algorithm first computes the smallest identity and makes it known to each process, then the process with that identity becomes leader and all others are defeated. The algorithm is more easily understood if one first considers it as if it were an algorithm executed by the *identities* rather than by the processes. Initially each identity is *active*, but in each round some identities become *passive* as will be shown later. In a round an *active* identity compares itself with the two neighboring *active* identities in clockwise and anticlockwise directions; if it is a local minimum, it survives the round, otherwise it becomes *passive*. Because all identities are different, an identity next to a local minimum is not a local minimum, which implies that at least half of the identities do not survive the round. Consequently, after at most $\log N$ rounds only one *active* identity remains, which is the winner.

This principle can be elaborated in a straightforward manner in bidirectional networks, as is done in Franklin's algorithm [Fra82]. In directed rings messages can be sent only clockwise, which makes it difficult to obtain the next active identity in the clockwise direction; see Figure 7.6. Identity q must be compared with r and p; identity r can be sent to q, but identity p would have to travel against the direction of the channels in order to arrive at q. To make a comparison with both r and p possible, identity q is sent (in the direction of the ring) to the process holding identity p and r is forwarded not only to the process holding q but also, further, to the process holding p. If q is the only *active* identity at the beginning of a round, the first identity that q encounters on its tour equals q (i.e., $p = q$ in this case). When this situation occurs this identity is the winner of the election.

The algorithm for processes in a unidirectional ring is given as Algorithm 7.7. Process p is *active* in a round if it holds an *active* identity ci_p at the beginning of the round. Otherwise, p is *passive* and simply relays all

```
var ci_p   : P   init p ;        (* Current identity of p *)
    acn_p  : P   init udef ;     (* Id of anticlockwise active neighbor *)
    win_p  : P   init udef ;     (* Id of winner *)
    state_p: (active, passive, leader, lost) init active ;

begin if p is initiator then state_p := active else state_p := passive ;
      while win_p = udef do
            begin if state_p = active then
                  begin send ⟨ one, ci_p ⟩ ; receive ⟨ one, q ⟩ ; acn_p := q ;
                        if acn_p = ci_p then (* acn_p is the minimum *)
                              begin send ⟨ smal, acn_p ⟩ ; win_p := acn_p ;
                                    receive ⟨ smal, q ⟩
                              end
                        else (* acn_p is current id of neighbor *)
                              begin send ⟨ two, acn_p ⟩ ; receive ⟨ two, q ⟩ ;
                                    if acn_p < ci_p and acn_p < q
                                    then ci_p := acn_p
                                    else state_p := passive
                              end
                  end
            else (* state_p = passive *)
                  begin receive ⟨ one, q ⟩ ; send ⟨ one, q ⟩ ;
                        receive m ; send m ;
                        (* m is either ⟨ two, q ⟩ or ⟨ smal, q ⟩ *)
                        if m is a ⟨ smal, q ⟩ message then win_p := q
                  end
            end ;
      if p = win_p then state_p := leader else state_p := lost
end
```

Algorithm 7.7 The Peterson/Dolev–Klawe–Rodeh algorithm.

messages it receives. An *active* process sends its current identity to the next *active* process and obtains the current identity of the previous *active* process using ⟨ **one**, . ⟩ messages. The received identity is stored (in the variable acn_p) and if the identity survives the round it will be the current identity of p in the next round. To determine whether the identity acn_p survives the round it is compared with both ci_p and the active identity obtained in a ⟨ **two**, . ⟩ message. Process p sends a ⟨ **two**, acn_p ⟩ message to make this decision possible in the next active process. An exception occurs when $acn_p = ci_p$; in this case the identity is the only remaining active one and it is announced to all processes in a ⟨ **smal**, acn_p ⟩ message.

Theorem 7.7 *Algorithm 7.7 solves the election problem for unidirectional rings using* $O(N \log N)$ *messages.*

Proof. We say a process is in the ith round when it executes the main loop for the ith time. The rounds are not globally synchronized; it is possible that one process is several rounds ahead of another process in a different part of the ring. But, as each process sends and receives exactly two messages in each round and channels are fifo, a message is always received in the same round as it is sent. In the first round all initiators are *active* and each *active* process holds a different "current identity".

Claim 7.8 *If round i starts with $k > 1$ active processes, and each process holds a different ci, then at least one and at most $k/2$ processes survive the round. At the end of the round again all current identities of active processes are different and include the smallest identity.*

Proof. By the exchange of $\langle \mathbf{one}, q \rangle$ messages, which are relayed by the *passive* processes, each *active* process obtains the current identity of its first anticlockwise *active* neighbor, which is in all cases different from the own identity. Consequently, each *active* process continues the round with the exchange of $\langle \mathbf{two}, q \rangle$ messages, by which each active process also obtains the current identity of the second anticlockwise *active* neighbor. Each *active* process now holds a different value of acn, which implies that the survivors of the round all have a different identity at the end of the round. At least the identity that was the smallest at the beginning of the round survives, so there is at least one survivor. An identity next to a local minimum is not a local minimum, which implies that the number of survivors is at most $k/2$.   □

Claim 7.8 implies that there will be a round, with number $\leq \lfloor \log N \rfloor + 1$, that begins with exactly one active identity, namely the smallest identity of any initiator.

Claim 7.9 *If a round starts with exactly one active process p, with current identity ci_p, the algorithm terminates after that round with $win_q = ci_p$ for each q.*

Proof. The $\langle \mathbf{one}, ci_p \rangle$ message of p is relayed by all processes and finally received by p. Process p obtains $acn_p = ci_p$ and sends a $\langle \mathbf{smal}, acn_p \rangle$ message around the ring, which causes each process q to exit the main loop with $win_q = acn_p$.   □

The algorithm terminates in each process and and all processes agree on the identity of the leader (in the variable win_q); this process is in the state *leader* and all other processes are in the state *lost*.

There are at most $\lfloor \log N \rfloor + 1$ rounds, in each of which exactly $2N$ messages are exchanged, which proves that the message complexity is bounded by $2N \log N + O(N)$. This proves Theorem 7.7.   □

Dolev *et al.* were able to improve their algorithm to $1.5N \log N$, after which Peterson found an algorithm using only $1.44N \log N$ messages, which was again improved by Dolev *et al.* to $1.356N \log N$. The $1.356N \log N$ upper bound for elections on rings was for more than 10 years the best known, but was improved to $1.271N \log N$ by Higham and Przytycka [HP93].

7.2.3 A Lower-bound Result

In this subsection a lower bound on the complexity of election on unidirectional rings will be proved. Because an election can be held in a single execution of a decentralized wave algorithm, a lower bound on the complexity of decentralized wave algorithms for rings is obtained as a corollary.

The result is due to Pachl, Korach, and Rotem [PKR84] and is obtained under the following assumptions.

(1) The bound is shown for algorithms that compute the smallest identity. If a leader is available the smallest identity can be computed in N messages and if the smallest identity is known to at least one process the process with this identity can be elected in N messages. Consequently, the problems of election and of computing the smallest identity differ by at most N messages in complexity.

(2) The ring is unidirectional.

(3) The processes do not know the ring size.

(4) It is assumed that channels are fifo. This assumption does not weaken the results because non-fifo algorithms can have no better complexity than fifo algorithms.

(5) It is assumed that all processes are initiators. This assumption does not weaken the results because it describes a possible situation for each decentralized algorithm.

(6) It is assumed that algorithms are message driven; that is, after sending some messages when the algorithm is initialized, a process sends further messages only when a message is received. As *asynchronous* systems are considered, general algorithms achieve no better complexity than message-driven algorithms. Indeed, if A is an asynchronous algorithm, then a message-driven algorithm B can be constructed as

follows. After initialization and after receipt of any message, B sends a maximal sequence of messages that is allowed to be sent by A without receiving a message, and only then receives the next message. Not only is algorithm B message driven, but also each computation of B is a possible computation of A (possibly under a rather pessimistic distribution of the transmission delays of messages).

The latter three assumptions eliminate non-determinism from the system. Under these assumptions each computation starting from a given initial configuration contains the same set of events.

In this subsection $s = (s_1, \ldots, s_N)$, t, etc., stand for sequences of different process identities. The set of all such sequences is denoted D, i.e.,

$$D = \{(s_1, \ldots, s_k) : s_i \in \mathcal{P} \text{ and } i \neq j \Rightarrow s_i \neq s_j\}.$$

The length of a sequence s is denoted $len(s)$ and the concatenation of sequences s and t is denoted st. A *cyclic shift* of s is a sequence $s's''$, where $s = s''s'$; it is of the form $s_i, \ldots, s_N, s_1, \ldots, s_{i-1}$. $CS(s)$ is the set of cyclic shifts of s, and of course $|CS(s)| = len(s)$.

The ring is said to be *labeled with* the sequence $(s_1, \ldots, s_N)$ if the process identities s_1 through s_N appear in this order on the ring (which is of size N). The ring labeled with s is also called the s-ring. If t is a cyclic shift of s, the t-ring is of course the same ring as the s-ring.

With each message, sent in the algorithm, a sequence of process identities will be associated, called the *trace* of the message. If m is a message sent by process p before p has received a message, the trace of m is (p). If m is a message sent by process p after p has received a message with trace $s = (s_1, \ldots, s_k)$ then the trace of m is $(s_1, \ldots, s_k, p)$. A message with trace s is called an s-message. The lower bound will be derived from the properties of the set of all traces of messages that can be sent by an algorithm.

Let E be a subset of D. The set E is *exhaustive* if

(1) E is prefix closed, i.e., $tu \in E \Rightarrow t \in E$; and
(2) E cyclicly covers D, i.e., $\forall s \in D : CS(s) \cap E \neq \emptyset$.

It will be shown below that the set of all traces of an algorithm is exhaustive; in order to derive from this fact a lower bound on the complexity of the algorithm two measures of a set E are defined. A sequence t appears as a consecutive sequence of identities in the s-ring if t is a prefix of any $r \in CS(s)$. $M(s, E)$ is the number of sequences of E that occur in that way in the s-ring, and $M_k(s, E)$ is the number of these strings of length k:

$$M(s, E) = |\{t \in E : t \text{ is a prefix of some } r \in CS(s)\}|$$

and

$$M_k(s, E) = |\{t \in E : t \text{ is a prefix of some } r \in CS(s) \text{ and } len(t) = k\}|.$$

In what follows, let A be an algorithm that computes the smallest identity and define E_A to be the set of sequences s such that an s-message is sent when algorithm A is executed in the s-ring.

Lemma 7.10 *If both t and u contain s as a substring and an s-message is sent when algorithm A is executed on the t-ring, then an s-message is also sent when A is executed on the u-ring.*

Proof. The sending by process s_k of the s-message, where $s = (s_1, \ldots, s_k)$, causally depends only on the processes s_1 through s_k. Their initial state in the u-ring is the same as in the t-ring (here we remember that the ring size is unknown), and consequently, the collection of events preceding the sending of the message is applicable in the u-ring also. □

Lemma 7.11 E_A *is an exhaustive set.*

Proof. To show that E_A is prefix closed, observe that if A sends an s-message when executed on the s-ring, then, for each prefix t of s, A first sends a t-message on the s-ring. By Lemma 7.10 A sends a t-message on the t-ring, hence $t \in E_A$.

To show that E_A cyclicly covers D, consider a computation of A on the s-ring. At least one process decides on the smallest identity, which implies (by an argument similar to the one used in Theorem 6.11) that this process has received a message with a trace of length $len(s)$. This trace is a cyclic shift of s and is in E. □

Lemma 7.12 *In a computation on the s-ring, algorithm A sends at least $M(s, E_A)$ messages.*

Proof. Let $t \in E_A$ be a prefix of a cyclic shift r of s. By definition of E_A, A sends a t-message in a computation on the t-ring, hence also on the r-ring, which equals the s-ring. Hence for each t in

$$\{t \in E : t \text{ is a prefix of some } r \in CS(s)\}$$

at least one t-message is sent in the computation on the s-ring, which proves that the number of messages in that computation is at least $M(s, E)$. □

For a finite set I of process identities, let $Per(I)$ denote the set of all permutations of I. Let $\text{ave}_A(I)$ denote the average number of messages used by A in all rings labeled with identities from I, and $\text{wor}_A(I)$ the worst-case number of messages. The previous lemma implies that if I has N elements,

(1) $\text{ave}_A(I) \geq \dfrac{1}{N!} \displaystyle\sum_{s \in Per(I)} M(s, E_A)$; and

(2) $\text{wor}_A(I) \geq \displaystyle\max_{s \in Per(I)} M(s, E_A)$.

The lower bound is now shown by an analysis of arbitrary exhaustive sets.

Theorem 7.13 *The average-case complexity of a unidirectional smallest-identity-finding algorithm is at least $N \cdot \mathbf{H}_N$.*

Proof. Averaging over all initial configurations labeled with the set I, we find

$$\text{ave}_A(I) \geq \frac{1}{N!} \sum_{s \in Per(I)} M(s, E_A)$$

$$= \frac{1}{N!} \sum_{s \in Per(I)} \sum_{k=1}^{N} M_k(s, E_A)$$

$$= \frac{1}{N!} \sum_{k=1}^{N} \sum_{s \in Per(I)} M_k(s, E_A)$$

We fix k and observe that for each $s \in Per(I)$ there are N prefixes of cyclic shifts of s of length k. The $N!$ permutations in $Per(I)$ give rise to $N \cdot N!$ such prefixes, which can be grouped into $N \cdot N!/k$ groups, each containing the k cyclic shifts of one sequence. Because E_A cyclically covers D, E_A intersects each group, hence

$$\sum_{s \in Per(I)} M_k(s, E_A) \geq \frac{N \cdot N!}{k}.$$

This implies

$$\text{ave}_A(I) \geq \frac{1}{N!} \sum_{k=1}^{N} \frac{N \cdot N!}{k} = N \cdot \mathbf{H}_N.$$

$\square$

This result shows that the Chang–Roberts algorithm is optimal if the average case is considered. The worst-case complexity is at least equal to the average case, which implies that the best achievable worst-case complexity is between $N \cdot \mathbf{H}_N \approx 0.69 N \log N$ and $\approx 1.356 N \log N$.

The proof given in this subsection essentially relies on the assumptions that the ring is unidirectional and that the size of the ring is unknown. A lower bound of $\frac{1}{2}N \cdot \mathbf{H}_N$ was proved by Bodlaender [Bod88] for the average-case complexity of election algorithms on *bidirectional* rings where the size of the ring is not known. To eliminate non-determinism from a bidirectional ring, computations are considered in which each process starts at the same time and each message has the same transmission delay. For the case where the size of the ring is known, Bodlaender [Bod91a] showed a lower bound of $\frac{1}{2}N \log N$ for unidirectional rings and $(\frac{1}{4} - \epsilon)N\mathbf{H}_N$ for the bidirectional ring (both for the average case).

Summarizing, it turns out that the complexity of election on a ring is insensitive to almost all the assumptions one can make. Whether the ring size is known or not, whether the ring is bidirectional or unidirectional, and whether worst-case or average-case complexity is considered, the complexity is $\Theta(N \log N)$ in all cases. It is essential that the ring is asynchronous; for networks where global time is available the message complexity is lower, as will be seen in Chapter 12.

As a leader can be elected in a single computation of a decentralized wave algorithm, the lower bound on election implies a lower bound for wave algorithms as well.

Corollary 7.14 *Any decentralized wave algorithm for ring networks exchanges at least $\Omega(N \log N)$ messages, in the average as well as the worst case.*

7.3 Arbitrary Networks

The election problem will now be studied for networks of arbitrary, unknown topology without neighbor knowledge. A lower bound of $\Omega(N \log N + |E|)$ messages will be shown below; the proof combines the idea of Theorem 6.6 and the result of the previous subsection. In Subsection 7.3.1 a simple algorithm will be given that has a low time complexity, but a high message complexity in the worst case. In Subsection 7.3.2 a worst-case optimal algorithm will be presented.

Theorem 7.15 *Any comparison election algorithm for arbitrary networks has a (worst-case and average-case) message complexity of at least $\Omega(|E| + N \log N)$.*

Proof. The $\Omega(N \log N)$ term is a lower bound because arbitrary networks include rings, for which an $\Omega(N \log N)$ lower bound holds. To see that $|E|$ messages is a lower bound, even in the best of all computations, assume

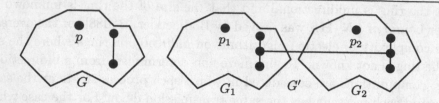

Figure 7.8 A COMPUTATION WITH TWO LEADERS.

that an election algorithm A has a computation C on network G in which fewer than $|E|$ messages are exchanged; see Figure 7.8. Construct a network G' by connecting two copies of G with one edge between nodes inserted on an edge that is not used in C. The identities in both parts of the network have the same relative order as in G. Computation C can be simulated simultaneously in both parts of G', yielding a computation in which two processes become elected.   □

Corollary 7.16 *A decentralized wave algorithm for arbitrary networks without neighbor knowledge has a message complexity of at least $\Omega(|E| + N \log N)$.*

7.3.1 Extinction and a Fast Algorithm

An algorithm for leader election can be obtained from an arbitrary centralized wave algorithm by the application of a construction called *extinction*. In the resulting election algorithm each initiator starts a separate wave; the messages of the wave initiated by process p must all be tagged with p in order to distinguish them from the messages of different waves. The algorithm ensures that, no matter how many waves are started, only one wave will run to a decision, namely, the wave of the smallest initiator. All other waves will be aborted before a decision can take place.

For a wave algorithm A, the election algorithm $Ex(A)$ is as follows. Each process is active in at most one wave at a time; this wave is its *currently active wave*, denoted caw, with initial value *udef*. Initiators of the election act as if they initiate a wave and set caw to their own identity. If a message of some wave, say the wave initiated by q, arrives at p, p processes the message as follows. If $q > caw_p$, the message is simply ignored, effectively causing q's wave to fail. If $q = caw_p$, the message is treated exactly according to the wave algorithm. If $q < caw_p$ or caw_p is *udef*, p joins the execution of q's wave

```
var caw_p       : P        init udef ;    (* Currently active wave *)
    rec_p       : integer  init 0 ;       (* Number of ⟨tok, caw_p⟩ received *)
    father_p    : P        init udef ;    (* Father in wave caw_p *)
    lrec_p      : integer  init 0 ;       (* Number of ⟨ldr, .⟩ received *)
    win_p       : P        init udef ;    (* Identity of leader *)

begin if p is initiator then
        begin caw_p := p ;
            forall q ∈ Neigh_p do send ⟨tok, p⟩ to q
        end ;
        while lrec_p < #Neigh_p do
        begin receive msg from q ;
            if msg = ⟨ldr, r⟩ then
                begin if lrec_p = 0 then
                    forall q ∈ Neigh_p do send ⟨ldr, r⟩ to q ;
                    lrec_p := lrec_p + 1 ; win_p := r
                end
            else (* a ⟨tok, r⟩ message *)
                begin if r < caw_p then (* Reinitialize algorithm *)
                    begin caw_p := r ; rec_p := 0 ; father_p := q ;
                        forall s ∈ Neigh_p, s ≠ q
                            do send ⟨tok, r⟩ to s
                    end ;
                    if r = caw_p then
                    begin rec_p := rec_p + 1 ;
                        if rec_p = #Neigh_p then
                            if caw_p = p
                            then forall s ∈ Neigh_p
                                        do send ⟨ldr, p⟩ to s
                            else send ⟨tok, caw_p⟩ to father_p
                    end
                    (* If r > caw_p, the message is ignored *)
                end
        end ;
        if win_p = p then state_p := leader else state_p := lost
end
```

Algorithm 7.9 EXTINCTION APPLIED TO THE ECHO ALGORITHM.

by resetting its variables to their initial values and setting $caw_p := q$. When the wave initiated by q executes a decision event (in most wave algorithms this decision always takes place in q), q will be elected. If the wave algorithm is such that the decider is not necessarily equal to the initiator, the decider informs the initiator via the spanning tree as defined in Lemma 6.3. This takes at most $N - 1$ messages; we ignore these in the next theorem.

Theorem 7.17 *If A is a centralized wave algorithm using M messages per wave, the algorithm Ex(A) elects a leader using at most NM messages.*

Proof. Let p_0 be the smallest initiator. The wave initiated by p_0 is joined immediately by every process that receives a message of this wave, and every process completes this wave because there is no wave with smaller identity for which the process would abort the execution of the wave of p_0. Consequently, the wave of p_0 runs to completion, a decision will take place and p_0 becomes leader.

If p is a non-initiator, no wave with identity p is ever initiated, hence p does not become leader. If $p \neq p_0$ is an initiator, a wave with identity p will be started but a decision in this wave is preceded by a send event (for this wave) by p_0, or takes place in p_0 (Lemma 6.4). As p_0 never executes a send or internal event of the wave with identity p, such a decision does not take place, and p is not elected.

At most N waves are started, and each wave uses at most M messages, which brings the overall complexity to NM.   □

It is a more delicate question to estimate the time complexity of $Ex(A)$. In many cases it will be of the same order of magnitude as the time complexity of A, but in some unlucky cases it may occur that the initiator with smallest identity starts its wave very late. In the general case a time complexity of $O(N.t)$ can be shown (where t is the time complexity of the wave algorithm), because within t time units after initiator p starts its wave, p's wave decides or another wave is started.

If extinction is applied to the ring algorithm, the Chang–Roberts algorithm is obtained; see Exercise 7.9. Algorithm 7.9 gives the election algorithm obtained from the echo algorithm. To simplify the description it is assumed that $udef > q$ for all $q \in \mathcal{P}$. When examining the code, the reader should note that upon receipt of a $\langle \mathbf{tok}, r \rangle$ message with $r < caw_p$, the **if** statement with condition $r = caw_p$ is also executed, owing to the earlier assignment to caw_p. When process p becomes elected (has received a $\langle \mathbf{tok}, p \rangle$ from each neighbor) p floods a $\langle \mathbf{ldr}, p \rangle$ message to all processes, informing them that p is leader and causing them to terminate the algorithm.

7.3.2 The Gallager–Humblet–Spira Algorithm

The election problem in arbitrary networks is closely related to the problem of computing a spanning tree with a decentralized algorithm, as the following argument reveals. Let C_E be the message complexity of the election problem, and C_T the complexity of computing a spanning tree. Theorem 7.2 implies that $C_E \leq C_T + O(N)$, and if a leader is available, a spanning tree can be computed with $2|E|$ messages with the echo algorithm, which implies that $C_T \leq C_E + 2|E|$. The lower bound on C_E (Theorem 7.15) implies that the two problems are of the same order of magnitude, namely, that they require at least $\Omega(N \log N + E)$ messages.

This subsection presents the Gallager–Humblet–Spira (GHS) algorithm for computing a (minimal) spanning tree using $2|E| + 5N \log N$ messages. This shows that C_E and C_T are $\Theta(N \log N + E)$. This algorithm was published in [GHS83]. The algorithm can be easily modified (as will be indicated at the end of this subsection) to elect a leader in the course of a computation, so that a separate election as indicated in the above argument is not necessary.

The GHS algorithm relies on the following assumptions.

(1) Each edge e has a unique weight $\omega(e)$. It will be assumed here that $\omega(e)$ is a real number, but integers are also possible as edge weights.

   If unique edge weights are not available a priori, each edge can be given a weight that is formed from the identities of the nodes connected by the edge, the smaller of the two first. Computing the edge weight thus requires that a node knows the identities of its neighbors, which costs an additional $2|E|$ messages in the initialization phase of the algorithm.

(2) All nodes though initially asleep awaken before they start the execution of the algorithm. Some nodes awaken spontaneously (if execution of the algorithm is triggered by circumstances occurring in these nodes), others may receive a message of the algorithm while they are still asleep. In the latter case the receiving node first executes the local initialization procedure, then processes the message.

Minimal spanning tree. Let $G = (V, E)$ be a weighted graph, where $\omega(e)$ denotes the weight of edge e. The weight of a spanning tree T of G equals the sum of the weights of the $N - 1$ edges contained in T, and T is called a *minimal spanning tree*, or MST, (sometimes minimal-weight spanning tree) if no tree has a smaller weight than T. It is assumed in this subsection that each edge has a unique weight, i.e., different edges have different weights, and it is a well-known fact that in this case there is a unique minimal spanning tree.

Proposition 7.18 *If all edge weights are different, there is only one MST.*

Proof. Assume, to the contrary, that both T_1 and T_2 (where $T_1 \neq T_2$) are minimal spanning trees. Let e be the lowest-weight edge that is in one of the trees, but not in both; such an edge exists because $T_1 \neq T_2$. Assume, without loss of generality, that e is in T_1 but not in T_2. The graph $T_2 \cup \{e\}$ contains a cycle, and as T_1 contains no cycle, at least one edge of the cycle, e' say, is not in T_1. The choice of e implies $\omega(e) < \omega(e')$, but then the tree $T_2 \cup \{e\} \setminus \{e'\}$ has a smaller weight than T_2, which contradicts that T_2 is an MST.   □

Proposition 7.18 considerably faciliates the distributed construction of a minimal spanning tree, because no choice from a collection of legitimate answers need be (distributively) made. On the contrary, every node that locally selects edges that belong to any minimal spanning tree thereby contributes to the construction of the globally unique MST.

All algorithms to compute the minimal spanning tree are based on the notion of a *fragment*, which is a subtree of the MST. An edge e is an *outgoing edge* of fragment F if one endpoint of e is in F and the other is not. The algorithms start with fragments consisting of a single node and incrementally enlarge fragments until the MST is complete, relying on the following observation.

Proposition 7.19 *If F is a fragment and e is the least-weight outgoing edge of F, then $F \cup \{e\}$ is a fragment.*

Proof. Assume $F \cup \{e\}$ is not part of the MST; then e forms a cycle with some edges of the MST, and one of the MST edges in this cycle, say f, is an outgoing edge of F. From the choice of e, $\omega(e) < \omega(f)$, but then deleting f from the MST and inserting e would give a tree with smaller weight than the MST, which is a contradiction.   □

Well-known sequential algorithms for computing an MST are the algorithms of Prim and Kruskal. Prim's algorithm [CLR90, Section 24.2] starts with a single fragment and enlarges it in each step with the lowest-weight outgoing edge of the current fragment. Kruskal's algorithm [CLR90, Section 24.2] starts with a collection of single-node fragments and merges fragments by adding the lowest-weight outgoing edge of some fragment. Because Kruskal's algorithm allows several fragments to proceed independently, it is more suitable for implementation in a distributed algorithm.

7.3.3 Global Description of the GHS Algorithm.

We will first describe how the algorithm operates in a global fashion, i.e., from the fragments point of view. We then describe the local algorithm that each node must execute in order to obtain this global operation of the fragments.

A computation of the GHS algorithm proceeds according to the following steps.

(1) A collection of fragments is maintained, such that the union of all fragments contains all nodes.
(2) Initially this collection contains each node as a one-node fragment.
(3) The nodes in a fragment cooperate to find the lowest-weight outgoing edge of the fragment.
(4) When the lowest-weight outgoing edge of a fragment is known, the fragment will be combined with another fragment by adding the outgoing edge, in cooperation with the other fragment.
(5) The algorithm terminates when only one fragment remains.

The efficient implementation of these steps requires the introduction of some notation and mechanisms.

(1) *Fragment name.* To determine the lowest-weight outgoing edge it must be possible to see whether an edge is an outgoing edge or leads to a node in the same fragment. To this end each fragment will have a name, which will be known to the processes in that fragment. Processes test whether an edge is internal or outgoing by a comparison of their fragment names.
(2) *Combining large and small fragments.* When two fragments are combined, the fragment name of the processes in at least one of the fragment changes, which requires an update to take place in every node of at least one of the two fragments. To keep this update efficient, the combining strategy is based on the idea that *the smaller of two fragments* combines into *the larger of the two* by adopting the fragment name of the larger fragment.
(3) *Fragment levels.* A little thinking reveals that the decision about which of two fragments is the larger should *not* be based on the number of nodes in the two fragments. This would make it necessary to update the fragment size in every process of *both* the larger *and* the smaller constituent fragment, thus spoiling the desirable property that an update is necessary only in the smaller. Instead, each

fragment is assigned a *level*, which is 0 for an initial one-node fragment. It is allowed that a fragment F_1 combines into a fragment F_2 with higher level, after which the new fragment $F_1 \cup F_2$ has the level of F_2. The new fragment also has the fragment name of F_2, so no updates are necessary for the nodes in F_2. It must also be possible for two fragments of the same level to combine; in this case the new fragment has a new name and its level is one higher than the level of the combining fragments. The new name of the fragment is the weight of the edge by which the two fragments are combined, and this edge is called the *core edge* of the new fragment. The two nodes connected by the core edge are called the *core nodes*.

Lemma 7.20 *If these combining rules are obeyed, the number of times a process changes its fragment name or level is at most $N \log N$.*

Proof. The level of a process never decreases, and only when it increases does the process change its fragment name. A fragment of level L contains at least 2^L processes, so the maximum level is $\log N$, which implies that each individual process increases its fragment level at most $\log N$ times. Hence, the overall total number of fragment name and level changes is bounded by $N \log N$. $\qquad\square$

Summary of combining strategy. A fragment F with name FN and level L is denoted as $F = (FN, L)$; let e_F denote the lowest-weight outgoing edge of F.

Rule A. If e_F leads to a fragment $F' = (FN', L')$ with $L < L'$, F combines into F', after which the new fragment has name FN' and level L'. These new values are sent to all processes in F.

Rule B. If e_F leads to a fragment $F' = (FN', L')$ with $L = L'$ and $e_{F'} = e_F$, the two fragments combine into a new fragment with level $L+1$ and name $\omega(e_F)$. These new values are sent to all processes in F and F'.

Rule C. In all other cases (i.e., $L > L'$ or $L = L'$ and $e_{F'} \neq e_F$) fragment F must wait until rule A or B applies.

7.3.4 Detailed Description of the GHS Algorithm

Node and link status. Node p maintains the variables as indicated in Algorithm 7.10, including the channel status $stach_p[q]$ for each channel pq. This status is *branch* if the edge is known to be in the MST, *reject* if it is known not to be in the MST, and *basic* if the edge is still unused. The

var $state_p$: $(sleep, find, found)$;
  $stach_p[q]$: $(basic, branch, reject)$ for each $q \in Neigh_p$;
  $name_p, bestwt_p$: real ;
  $level_p$: integer ;
  $testch_p, bestch_p, father_p$: $Neigh_p$;
  rec_p : integer ;

(1) As the first action of each process, the algorithm must be initialized:
  begin let pq be the channel of p with smallest weight ;
      $stach_p[q] := branch$; $level_p := 0$;
      $state_p := found$; $rec_p := 0$;
      send $\langle$**connect**$, 0 \rangle$ to q
  end

(2) Upon receipt of $\langle$**connect**$, L \rangle$ from q:
  begin if $L < level_p$ **then** (* Combine with Rule A *)
        begin $stach_p[q] := branch$;
            send $\langle$**initiate**$, level_p, name_p, state_p \rangle$ to q
        end
      else if $stach_p[q] = basic$
          then (* Rule C *) process the message later
          else (* Rule B *) send $\langle$**initiate**$, level_p + 1, \omega(pq), find \rangle$ to q
  end

(3) Upon receipt of $\langle$**initiate**$, L, F, S \rangle$ from q:
  begin $level_p := L$; $name_p := F$; $state_p := S$; $father_p := q$;
      $bestch_p := udef$; $bestwt_p := \infty$;
      forall $r \in Neigh_p : stach_p[r] = branch \wedge r \neq q$ **do**
          send $\langle$**initiate**$, L, F, S \rangle$ to r ;
      if $state_p = find$ **then begin** $rec_p := 0$; $test$ **end**
  end

Algorithm 7.10 THE GALLAGER–HUMBLET–SPIRA ALGORITHM (PART 1).

communication in a fragment to determine the lowest-weight outgoing edge takes place via the *branch* edges in the fragment. For process p in the fragment, $father_p$ is the edge leading to the core edge of the fragment. The state of node p, $state_p$, is *find* if p is currently engaged in the fragment's search for the lowest-weight outgoing edge and *found* otherwise. The algorithm is given as Algorithm 7.10/7.11/7.12. Sometimes the processing of a message must be deferred until a local condition is satisfied. It is assumed that in this case the message is stored, and later retrieved and treated as if it had been received at that moment. If a process receives a message while it is still in the state *sleep*, the algorithm is initialized in that node (by executing action (1)) before the message is processed.

(4) **procedure** *test*:
    begin if $\exists q \in Neigh_p : stach_p[q] = basic$ **then**
        begin $testch_p := q$ with $stach_p[q] = basic$ and $\omega(pq)$ minimal ;
            send $\langle \mathbf{test}, level_p, name_p \rangle$ to $testch_p$
    end
      else begin $testch_p := udef$; *report* **end**
  end

(5) Upon receipt of $\langle \mathbf{test}, L, F \rangle$ from q:
    begin if $L > level_p$ **then**   (* Answer must wait! *)
        process the message later
      else if $F = name_p$ **then** (* internal edge *)
        begin if $stach_p[q] = basic$ **then** $stach_p[q] := reject$;
            if $q \neq testch_p$
              then send $\langle \mathbf{reject} \rangle$ to q
              else *test*
        end
        else send $\langle \mathbf{accept} \rangle$ to q
  end

(6) Upon receipt of $\langle \mathbf{accept} \rangle$ from q:
    begin $testch_p := udef$;
      if $\omega(pq) < bestwt_p$
        then begin $bestwt_p := \omega(pq)$; $bestch_p := q$ **end** ;
      report
  end

(7) Upon receipt of $\langle \mathbf{reject} \rangle$ from q:
    begin if $stach_p[q] = basic$ **then** $stach_p[q] := reject$;
      test
  end

Algorithm 7.11 THE GALLAGER–HUMBLET–SPIRA ALGORITHM (PART 2).

Finding the lowest-weight outgoing edge. The nodes in a fragment cooperate to find the lowest-weight outgoing edge of the fragment, and when the edge is found a $\langle \mathbf{connect}, L \rangle$ message is sent through it; L is the level of the fragment. If the fragment consists of a single node, as is the case after the initialization of this node, the required edge is simply the lowest-weight adjacent edge of this node; see (1). A $\langle \mathbf{connect}, 0 \rangle$ message is sent via this edge.

Next consider the case that a new fragment is formed by combining two fragments, connection being by edge $e = pq$. If the two combined fragments were of the same level, L, both p and q will have sent a $\langle \mathbf{connect}, L \rangle$ message via e, and will have received a $\langle \mathbf{connect}, L \rangle$ message in return while

(8) **procedure** *report*:
    begin if $rec_p = \#\{q : stach_p[q] = branch \land q \neq father_p\}$
            and $testch_p = udef$ **then**
            begin $state_p := found$; send $\langle$ **report**, $bestwt_p \rangle$ to $father_p$ **end**
  end

(9) Upon receipt of $\langle$ **report**, $\omega \rangle$ from q:
    begin if $q \neq father_p$
        then (* reply for **initiate** message *)
            begin if $\omega < bestwt_p$ **then**
                begin $bestwt_p := \omega$; $bestch_p := q$ **end** ;
              $rec_p := rec_p + 1$; report
            end
        else (* pq is the core edge *)
            if $state_p = find$
              then process this message later
              else if $\omega > bestwt_p$
                  then *changeroot*
                  else if $\omega = bestwt_p = \infty$ **then stop**
  end

(10) **procedure** *changeroot*:
    begin if $stach_p[bestch_p] = branch$
        then send $\langle$ **changeroot** $\rangle$ to $bestch_p$
        else begin send $\langle$ **connect**, $level_p \rangle$ to $bestch_p$;
            $stach_p[bestch_p] := branch$
        end
  end

(11) Upon receipt of $\langle$ **changeroot** $\rangle$:
    begin *changeroot* **end**

Algorithm 7.12 THE GALLAGER–HUMBLET–SPIRA ALGORITHM (PART 3).

---

the status of e is *branch*; see action (2). Edge pq becomes the core edge of the fragment, and p and q exchange an $\langle$ **initiate**, $L + 1, N, S \rangle$ message, giving the new level and name of the fragment. The name is $\omega(pq)$ and the status *find* causes each process to start searching for the lowest-weight outgoing edge; see action (3). The message $\langle$ **initiate**, $L + 1, N, S \rangle$ is flooded to each node in the new fragment. If the level of p was smaller than the level of q, p will have sent a $\langle$ **connect**, $L \rangle$ message via e, and will have received an $\langle$ **initiate**, $L', N, S \rangle$ message in return from q; see action (2). In this case, L' and N are the current fragment level and name of q, and the name and level of the nodes on q's side of the edge do not change. On p's side of the edge the initiate message is flooded to all the nodes (see action (3)), causing every process to update its fragment name and level. If q is currently searching for the lowest-weight outgoing edge ($S = find$) the processes in p's fragment join the search by calling *test*.

Each process in the fragment searches through its edges (if it has any, see (4), (5), (6), and (7)) to see if there is one leading out of the fragment, and if so, chooses the one of lowest weight. The lowest-weight outgoing edge is reported for each subtree using $\langle$**report**, $\omega\rangle$ messages; see (8). Node p counts the number of $\langle$**report**, $\omega\rangle$ messages it receives, using the variable rec_p, which is set to 0 when the search starts (see (3)) and incremented with each receipt of a $\langle$**report**, $\omega\rangle$ message; see (9). Each process sends a $\langle$**report**, $\omega\rangle$ message to its father when it has received such a message from each of its sons and has finished the local search for an outgoing edge.

The $\langle$**report**, $\omega\rangle$ messages are sent in the direction of the core edge by each process, and the messages of the two core nodes cross on the edge; both receive the message from their *father*; see (9). Each core node waits until it has sent a $\langle$**report**, $\omega\rangle$ message itself before it processes the message of the other process. When the two $\langle$**report**, $\omega\rangle$ messages of the core nodes have crossed, the core nodes know the weight of the lowest-weight outgoing edge. The algorithm terminates at this point if no outgoing edge was reported at all (both messages report the value ∞).

If an outgoing edge was reported, the best edge is found by following the *bestch* pointer in each node, starting from the core node on whose side the best edge was reported. A $\langle$**connect**, $L\rangle$ message must be sent through this edge, and all *father* pointers in the fragment must point in this direction; this is done by sending a $\langle$**changeroot**$\rangle$ message. The core node on whose side the lowest-weight outgoing edge is located sends a $\langle$**changeroot**$\rangle$ message, which is sent via the tree to the lowest-weight outgoing edge; see (10) and (11). When the $\langle$**changeroot**$\rangle$ message arrives at the node incident to the lowest-weight outgoing edge, this node sends a $\langle$**connect**, $L\rangle$ message via the lowest-weight outgoing edge.

Testing the edges. To find its lowest-weight outgoing edge, node p inspects its *basic* edges one by one in increasing order of weight; see (4). The local search for an edge ends either when no edge remains (all edges are *reject* or *branch*), see (4), or when one edge is identified as outgoing; see (6). Because of the order in which p inspects the edges, if p identifies one edge as outgoing, this must be the lowest-weight edge outgoing from p.

To inspect edge pq, p sends a $\langle$**test**, $level_p$, $name_p\rangle$ message to q and waits for an answer, which can be a $\langle$**reject**$\rangle$, $\langle$**accept**$\rangle$, or $\langle$**test**, $L, F\rangle$ message. A $\langle$**reject**$\rangle$ message is sent by process q (see (5)) if q finds that p's fragment name, as in the test message, coincides with q's fragment name; node q also rejects the edge in this case. On receipt of the $\langle$ **reject** $\rangle$ message p rejects edge pq and continues the local search; see (7). The $\langle$ **reject** $\rangle$ message is omitted if the edge pq was just used by q also to send a $\langle$ **test**, L, F $\rangle$ message; in this case q's $\langle$ **test**, L, F $\rangle$ message serves as the reply to p's message; see (5). If the fragment name of q differs from p's, an $\langle$ **accept** $\rangle$ message is sent. On receipt of this message p terminates its local search for outgoing edges with edge pq as the best local choice; see (6).

The processing of a $\langle$ **test**, L, F $\rangle$ message by p is deferred if $L > level_p$. The reason is that p and q may actually belong to the same fragment, but the $\langle$ **initiate**, L, F, S $\rangle$ message has not yet reached p. Node p could erroneously reply to q with an $\langle$ **accept** $\rangle$ message.

Combining the fragments. After the lowest-weight outgoing edge of a fragment $F = (name, level)$ has been determined, a $\langle$ **connect**, $level$ $\rangle$ message is sent via this edge, and is received by a node belonging to a fragment $F' = (name', level')$. Call the process sending the $\langle$ **connect**, $level$ $\rangle$ message p and the process receiving it q. Node q has earlier sent an $\langle$ **accept** $\rangle$ message to p in reply to a $\langle$ **test**, $level, name$ $\rangle$ message, because the search for the best outgoing edge in p's fragment has terminated. The waiting introduced before answering test messages (see (5)) implies that $level' \geq level$.

According to the combining rules discussed earlier, the $\langle$ **connect**, $level$ $\rangle$ is answered with an $\langle$ **initiate**, L, F, S $\rangle$ message in two cases.

Case A: If $level' > level$, p's fragment is absorbed; the nodes in this fragment are informed about their new fragment name and level by a message $\langle$ **initiate**, $level', name', S$ $\rangle$, which is flooded to all nodes in fragment F. The entire absorbed fragment F becomes a subtree of q in the spanning tree of fragment F' and if q is currently engaged in a search for the best outgoing edge of fragment F', all processes in F must participate. This is why q includes its state (*find* or *found*) in the $\langle$ **initiate**, $level', name', S$ $\rangle$ message.

Case B: If the two fragments have the same level and the best outgoing edge of fragment F' is also pq, a new fragment is formed, of which the level is one higher and the name is the weight of edge pq; see (2). This case occurs if the two levels are equal and the connect message is received via a branch edge; observe that the status of an edge becomes *branch* if a connect message is sent through it.

If neither of these two cases occurs, fragment F must wait until either q

sends a $\langle \textbf{connect}, L \rangle$ message or the level of q's fragment has increased sufficiently to make Case A applicable.

Correctness and complexity. From the detailed description of the algorithm it should be clear that the edge through which a fragment sends a $\langle \textbf{connect}, L \rangle$ message is indeed the lowest-weight outgoing edge of the fragment. Together with Proposition 7.19 this implies that the MST is computed correctly if each fragment indeed sends such a message and joins the other fragment, in despite of the waiting induced by the algorithm. The most complex message contains one edge weight, one level (up to $\log N$) and a constant number of bits to indicate message type and node state.

Theorem 7.21 *The Gallager–Humblet–Spira algorithm (Algorithm 7.10/ 7.11/7.12) computes the minimal spanning tree, using at most $5N \log N + 2|E|$ messages.*

Proof. Deadlock potentially arises in situations where nodes or fragments must wait until some condition occurs in another node or fragment. The waiting introduced for $\langle \textbf{report}, \omega \rangle$ messages on the core edge does not lead to a deadlock because each core node eventually receives reports from all sons (unless the fragment as a whole waits for another fragment), after which the message will be processed.

Consider the case where a message of fragment $F_1 = (level_1, name_1)$ arrives at a node of fragment $F_2 = (level_2, name_2)$. A $\langle \textbf{connect}, level_1 \rangle$ message must wait if $level_1 \geq level_2$ and no $\langle \textbf{connect}, level_2 \rangle$ message has been sent through the same edge by fragment F_2; see (2). A $\langle \textbf{test}, level_1, name_1 \rangle$ message must wait if $level_1 > level_2$; see (5). In all cases where F_1 waits for F_2, one of the following holds.

(1) $level_1 > level_2$;

(2) $level_1 = level_2 \wedge \omega(e_{F_1}) > \omega(e_{F_2})$;

(3) $level_1 = level_2 \wedge \omega(e_{F_1}) = \omega(e_{F_2})$ and F_2 is still searching for its lowest-weight outgoing edge. (As e_{F_1} is an outgoing edge of F_2 it is not possible that $\omega(e_{F_2}) > \omega(e_{F_1})$.)

Thus no deadlock cycle can occur.

Each edge is rejected at most once and this requires two messages, which bounds the number of reject messages plus test messages leading to rejections to $2|E|$. At any level, a node receives at most one initiate and one accept message, and sends at most one report, one changeroot *or* connect message, and one test message not leading to a rejection. At level zero no accept messages are received and no report or test messages are sent. At the highest level each node only sends a report message and receives one initiate message. The total number of messages is therefore bounded by $2|E| + 5N \log N$. $\square$

7.3.5 Discussion and Variants of the GHS Algorithm

The Gallager–Humblet–Spira algorithm is one of the most sophisticated wave algorithms, requiring only local knowledge and having optimal message complexity. The algorithm can easily be extended so that it elects a leader, using only two more messages. The algorithm terminates in two nodes, namely core nodes of the last fragment (spanning the entire network). Instead of executing **stop**, the core nodes exchange their identities and the smaller of them becomes leader.

A number of variations and related algorithms have been published. The GHS algorithm may require $\Omega(N^2)$ time if some nodes start the algorithm very late. If an additional wake-up procedure is used (taking at most $2|E|$ more messages) the time complexity of the algorithm is $5N \log N$; see Exercise 7.11. Awerbuch [Awe87] has shown that the time complexity of the algorithm can be improved to $O(N)$, while keeping the message complexity order optimal, i.e., $O(|E| + N \log N)$.

Afek *et al.* [ALSY90] have adapted the algorithm to compute a spanning forest with favorable properties, namely that the diameter of each tree and the number of trees are $O(\sqrt{N})$. Their algorithm distributively computes a clustering of the network as indicated in Lemma 4.47 and a spanning tree and a center for each cluster.

One may ask if the construction of arbitrary spanning trees can be done more efficiently than the construction of the minimal spanning trees, but Theorem 7.15 implies a lower bound of $\Omega(N \log N + |E|)$ on the construction of arbitrary spanning trees as well. Johansen *et al.* [JJN+87] give an algorithm for computing an arbitrary spanning tree that uses $3N \log N + 2.|E| + O(N)$ messages, thus improving on the GHS algorithm by a constant factor if the network is sparse. Bar-Ilan and Zernik [BIZ89] presented an algorithm that computes *random* spanning trees, where each possible spanning tree is chosen with equal probability. The algorithm is randomized and uses an expected number of messages that is between $O(N \log N + |E|)$ and $O(N^3)$, depending on the topology of the network.

While the construction of arbitrary and of minimal spanning trees is of equal complexity in arbitrary networks, this is not true in cliques. Korach, Moran and Zaks [KMZ85] have shown that the construction of a minimal spanning tree in a weighted clique requires the exchange of $\Omega(N^2)$ messages.

This result indicates that knowledge of the topology does not help to reduce the complexity of finding an MST below the bound of Theorem 7.15. An arbitrary spanning tree of a clique can be constructed in $O(N \log N)$ messages as we shall show in the next section; see also [KMZ84].

7.4 The Korach–Kutten–Moran Algorithm

Many results have been obtained for the election problem, not only for the case of ring networks and arbitrary networks, but also for the case of other specialized topologies, such as clique networks, etc. In several cases the best known algorithms have an $O(N \log N)$ message complexity and in some cases this result is matched by an $\Omega(N \log N)$ lower bound. Korach, Kutten, and Moran [KKM90] have shown that there is a close relation between election and the traversal of networks. Their main result is a general construction of an efficient election algorithm for a class of networks, given a traversal algorithm for this class.

The construction yields $O(N \log N)$ election algorithms for many classes of network; because $O(x)$ (linear) traversal is the best possible, no better algorithm can be obtained with this technique. In contrast, many classes of network with sense of direction do allow better election algorithms, as will be seen in Chapter 11. Also, the time complexity of the Korach–Kutten–Moran algorithm equals its message complexity, and in some cases other algorithms with the same message complexity and lower time complexity are known. The interest of the construction is its generality and the relation that is made between traversal as a "module" in the solution of a higher-level problem, election.

7.4.1 The Modular Construction

The Korach–Kutten–Moran algorithm uses the ideas of both the extinction construction (Subsection 7.3.1) and the Peterson/Dolev–Klawe–Rodeh algorithm (Subsection 7.2.2). The resemblance to the extinction construction is that initiators of the election start a network traversal with a token labeled with their identity. If the traversal completes (decides), the initiator of that traversal becomes elected; the algorithm implies that this happens for exactly one traversal. In this subsection the algorithm is described for the case where the channels satisfy the fifo assumption, but by maintaining a little more information in each token and in each process the algorithm can be adapted for the non-fifo case; see [KKM90].

To deal with the situation of more than one initiator, the algorithm operates in *levels* that can be compared to the rounds of the Peterson/Dolev–Klawe–Rodeh algorithm. If at least two traversals are started, the tokens will arrive at a process that has already been visited by another token. If this situation arises the traversal by the arriving token will be aborted. The goal of the algorithm now becomes to bring two tokens together in one process, where they will be killed and a new traversal initiated. Compare this with the Peterson/Dolev *et al.* algorithm, where at most one of each two identities survives a round and continues to the next round. The notion of rounds is replaced in the Korach–Kutten–Moran algorithm by the notion of levels; two tokens will give rise to a new traversal only if they have the same level, and the newly generated token has a level that is one higher. If a token meets with a token of higher level, or arrives at a node already visited by a token of higher level, the arriving token is simply killed without influencing the token at higher level.

The algorithm is given as Algorithm 7.13. In order to bring tokens of the same level together in one process, each token can be in one of three modes: *annexing*, *chasing*, or *waiting*. A token is represented by (q, l), where q is the initiator of the token and l its level. The variable lev_p gives the level of process p and the variable cat_p gives the initiator of the last annexing token forwarded by p (the *currently active traversal* of p). The variable $wait_p$ is *udef* if no token is waiting at p and its value is q if a token (q, lev_p) is waiting at p. The variable $last_p$ is used for tokens in chasing mode: it gives the neighbor to which p forwarded an annexing token of level lev_p, unless a chasing token was already sent after it; in this case $last_p = udef$. The algorithm interacts with the traversal algorithm by a call to the function *trav*: this function returns either the neighbor to which the token must be forwarded, or *decide* if the traversal terminates.

A token (q, l) is initiated in *annexing* mode and in this mode it obeys the traversal algorithm (as in case IV of Algorithm 7.13) until one of the following situations occurs.

(1) The traversal algorithm terminates: q becomes leader in this case (see Case IV in Algorithm 7.13).

(2) The token arrives at node p of level $lev_p > l$: the token is killed in this case. (This case is implicit in Algorithm 7.13; the conditions in that algorithm all require $l > lev_p$ or $l = lev_p$.)

(3) The token arrives in a node where a token of level l is waiting: the two tokens are killed in this case and a new traversal is started from that node (see Case II in Algorithm 7.13).

(4) The token arrives at a node with level l that has been most recently

```
var levₚ            : integer      init −1 ;
    catₚ, waitₚ     : P            init udef ;
    lastₚ           : Neighₚ       init udef ;

begin if p is initiator then
        begin levₚ := levₚ + 1 ; lastₚ := trav(p, levₚ) ;
              catₚ := p ; send ⟨ annex, p, levₚ ⟩ to lastₚ
        end ;
     while ... (* Termination condition, see text *) do
        begin receive token (q, l) ;
              if token is annexing then t := A else t := C ;
              if l > levₚ then (* Case I *)
                 begin levₚ := l ; catₚ := q ;
                       waitₚ := udef ; lastₚ := trav(q, l) ;
                       send ⟨ annex, q, l ⟩ to lastₚ
                 end
              else if l = levₚ and waitₚ ≠ udef then (* Case II *)
                 begin waitₚ := udef ; levₚ := levₚ + 1 ;
                       lastₚ := trav(p, levₚ) ; catₚ := p ;
                       send ⟨ annex, p, levₚ ⟩ to lastₚ
                 end
              else if l = levₚ and lastₚ = udef then (* Case III *)
                 waitₚ := q
              else if l = levₚ and t = A and q = catₚ then (* Case IV *)
                 begin lastₚ := trav(q, l) ;
                       if lastₚ = decide
                          then p announces itself leader
                          else send ⟨ annex, q, l ⟩ to lastₚ
                 end
              else if l = levₚ and ((t = A and
                 q > catₚ) or t = C) then (* Case V *)
                 begin send ⟨ chase, q, l ⟩ to lastₚ ; lastₚ := udef end
              else if l = levₚ then (* Case VI *)
                 waitₚ := q
        end
end
```

Algorithm 7.13 THE KORACH–KUTTEN–MORAN ALGORITHM.

visited by a token of identity $cat_p > q$ (see Case VI) or a *chasing* token (see Case III): the token becomes *waiting* in that node.

(5) The token arrives at a node of level l that has been most recently visited by an *annexing* token with identity $cat_p < q$: the token becomes *chasing* in this case and is sent via the same channel as the previous token (see Case V).

A *chasing* token (q, l) is forwarded in each node via the channel through which the most recently passed token was sent, until one of the following situations occurs.

(1) The token arrives in a process of level $lev_p > l$: the token is killed in this case.
(2) The token arrives in a process with a *waiting* token of level l: the two tokens are removed and a new traversal is started by this process (see Case II).
(3) The token arrives at a process of level l where the most recently passed token was *chasing*: the token becomes *waiting* (see Case III).

A *waiting* token resides in a process until one of the following situations occurs.

(1) A token of higher level arrives at the same process: the waiting token is killed (see Case I).
(2) A token of equal level arrives: the two tokens are removed and a traversal of higher level is started (see Case II).

In Algorithm 7.13 the variables and token information used by the traversal algorithm are ignored. Observe that if p receives a token of level higher than lev_p, this is an annexing token of which p is not the initiator. If a traversal terminates in p, p becomes leader and floods a message to all processes, causing them to terminate.

Correctness and complexity. In order to demonstrate the correctness of the Korach–Kutten–Moran algorithm it will be shown that the number of tokens generated at each level decreases until, at some level, only one token is generated, of which the initiator will be elected.

Lemma 7.22 *If $k > 1$ tokens are generated at level l, at least one and at most $k/2$ tokens are generated at level $l + 1$.*

Proof. At most $k/2$ tokens are generated at level $l + 1$ because when such a token is generated, two tokens of level l are killed at the same time.

Assume that there is a level l such that $k > 1$ tokens are generated at level l, but no token is generated at level $l + 1$. Let q be the process with *maximal* identity that generates a token at level l. The token (q, l) does not complete the traversal, because it will be received by a process p that has already forwarded a different token of level l. When this happens for the first time, (q, l) becomes chasing or, if p has already forwarded a chasing token, (q, l) becomes waiting. In either case, there are chasing tokens at level l.

Let (r, l) be the token with *minimal* identity after which a chasing token is sent. Token (r, l) is itself not chasing, because a token only chases tokens with smaller identity. We may therefore assume that (r, l) became waiting when it first arrived at a process p' that had already forwarded a different token of level l. Let p'' be the *last* process on the path followed by (r, l) that received, after it forwarded (r, l), an annexing token that turned into a token chasing r. This chasing token either meets (r, l) in p', or abandons the chase if a waiting token was found before the token reached p'. In both cases a token at level $l + 1$ is generated, a contradiction. $\square$

Theorem 7.23 *The Korach–Kutten–Moran algorithm (Algorithm 7.13) is an election algorithm.*

Proof. Assume that at least one process initiates the algorithm. By the previous lemma, the number of tokens generated in each level decreases, and there will be a level, l say, at which exactly one token, say (q, l) is generated. No token of level $l' < l$ completes the traversal, hence none of these tokens causes a process to become elected. The unique token at level l only encounters processes at levels smaller than l, or with $cat = q$ (if it arrives at a process it has already visited), and is forwarded in both cases. Hence the traversal of this token completes and q is elected. $\square$

A function f is said to be *convex* if $f(a) + f(b) \leq f(a + b)$. The complexity of the algorithm is analyzed here under the assumption that an $f(x)$-traversal algorithm (see Section 6.3) is used, where f is a convex function.

Theorem 7.24 *If an $f(x)$-traversal algorithm is used, where f is convex, the KKM election algorithm uses at most $(1 + \log k)[f(N) + N]$ messages if initiated by k processes.*

Proof. If the algorithm is initiated by k processes, at most $2^{-l} k$ tokens are generated at level l, which implies that the highest level is at most $\lfloor \log k \rfloor$.

Each process sends annexing tokens of at most one identity in each level. If in some level l there are tokens with identities $p_1, \ldots, p_j$ and there are N_i processes that have forwarded the annexing token (p_i, l), then it follows that $\sum_{i=1}^{j} N_i \leq N$. Because the traversal algorithm is an $f(x)$-traversal algorithm, annexing token (p_i, l) has been sent at most $f(N_i)$ times, which brings the total number of messages carrying annexing tokens of level l to at most $\sum_{i=1}^{j} f(N_i)$, which is at most $f(N)$ because f is convex. Each process sends at most one chasing token at each level, which gives at most N chasing tokens per level.

So there are at most $(1 + \log k)$ different levels, and at most $f(N) + N$ messages are sent in each level, which proves the result. □

Attiya's construction. A different construction of election algorithm from traversal algorithms was given by Attiya [Att87]. In this construction, the traversal by one token, with identity q say, is not aborted as soon as the token arrives at a process r already visited by another token, of process p say. Instead, the annexing token waits at r but sends out a "hunter" token to chase the token of p and then return to r if p can be successfully defeated. If the hunter returns it is not necessary to start a new traversal, but the current traversal by q's token is continued, thus potentially saving on message complexity. To allow the hunter to return to process r it must be assumed that the network is bidirectional. If an $f(x)$-traversal algorithm is used, the resulting election algorithm has a message complexity of approximately $3. \sum_{i=1}^{N} f(N/i)$.

7.4.2 Applications of the KKM Algorithm

If an $f(x)$-traversal algorithm for a class of networks exists, this class is said to be $f(x)$-traversable. Because many classes of network are $O(x)$-traversable, the construction gives election algorithms with message complexity $O(N \log N)$, and these are the best that can be obtained from the result. In some cases, when sense of direction exists, better algorithms are possible (see Chapter 11).

Election in rings. Rings are x-traversable, hence the KKM algorithm elects a leader in a ring using $2N \log N$ messages. We already know from Theorem 7.13 that this is the best possible.

Election in cliques. Cliques are $2x$-traversable, also without sense of direction, hence the KKM algorithm elects a leader in a clique using $3N \log N$ messages according to Theorem 7.24. A more careful analysis of the algorithm reveals that the complexity is actually $2N \log N + O(N)$ in this case. Each token is chased using at most three chasing messages, so the total number of chase messages in a computation is bounded by $3. \sum_{i=0}^{\log N+1} 2^{-i} N = O(N)$. No election algorithm for cliques with a complexity better than $2N \log N + O(N)$ is known to date. A lower bound of $\Omega(N \log N)$ was proved by Korach, Moran, and Zaks [KMZ84].

These results are only true for cliques without sense of direction; with sense of direction a linear algorithm exists.

Election in tori. Torus networks with sense of direction are x-traversable (see Algorithm 6.11), hence the KKM algorithm elects a leader in a torus using $2N \log N$ messages. Without sense of direction Tarry's algorithm can be used for traversal, and this algorithm operates linearly on the torus. Peterson [Pet85] has given an election algorithm for grids and tori that uses $O(N)$ messages and does not require the edges to be labeled.

Exercises to Chapter 7
Section 7.1

Exercise 7.1 *Prove that a comparison election algorithm for arbitrary networks is a wave algorithm if the event in which a process becomes leader is regarded as a decision event.*

Exercise 7.2 *Show that the time complexity of Algorithm 7.1 is 2D.*

Section 7.2

Exercise 7.3 *Prove the identity $\sum_{i=1}^{m} \mathbf{H}_i = (m+1)\mathbf{H}_m - m$ used in Subsection 7.2.1.*

Exercise 7.4 *Show that $\ln(N+1) < \mathbf{H}_N < \ln(N) + 1$.* (*ln denotes the natural logarithm.*)

Exercise 7.5 *Consider the Chang–Roberts algorithm under the assumption that every process is an initiator. For what distribution of identities over the ring is the message complexity minimal and exactly how many messages are exchanged in this case?*

Exercise 7.6 *What is the average case complexity of the Chang–Roberts algorithm if there are exactly S initiators, where each choice of S processes is equally likely to be the set of initiators?*

Exercise 7.7 *Give an initial configuration for Algorithm 7.7 for which the algorithm actually requires $\lfloor \log N \rfloor + 1$ rounds. Also give an initial configuration for which the algorithm requires only two rounds, regardless of the* *number of initiators. Is it possible for the algorithm to terminate in one round?*

Exercise 7.8 *Determine the set E_{CR} (as defined before Lemma 7.10) for the Chang–Roberts algorithm.*

Section 7.3

Exercise 7.9 *Apply extinction to the ring algorithm and compare the algorithm with the Chang–Roberts algorithm. What is the difference and what is the effect of this difference?*

Exercise 7.10 *Determine, for each of the seven message types used in the Gallager/Humblet/Spira algorithm, whether a message of this type can be sent to a node in the sleep state.*

Exercise 7.11 *Assume that the GHS algorithm uses an additional wake-up procedure that guarantees that each node starts the algorithm within N time units.*
Prove by induction that after most $5Nl - 3N$ time units each node is at level l.
Prove that the algorithm terminates within $5N \log N$ time units.

Section 7.4

Exercise 7.12 *Show that an $O(N \log N)$ algorithm for election in planar networks exists.*

Exercise 7.13 *Show that there exists an $O(N \log N)$ election algorithm for tori without a sense of direction. (Hint: analyse the performance of Tarry's algorithm in tori.)*

Exercise 7.14 *Show that there exists an $O(N \log N)$ election algorithm for hypercubes without a sense of direction.*

Exercise 7.15 *Show that there exists an $O(N(\log N + k))$ election algorithm for networks with bounded degree k (i.e., networks where each node has at most k neighbors).*

8

Termination Detection

A computation of a distributed algorithm terminates when the algorithm has reached a *terminal configuration*; that is, a configuration in which no further steps of the algorithm are applicable. It is not always the case that in a terminal configuration each process is in a *terminal state*; that is, a process state in which there is no event of the process applicable. Consider a configuration where each process is in a state that allows the receipt of messages, and all channels are empty. Such a configuration is terminal, but the processes' states could also occur as intermediate states in the computation. In this case, the processes are not aware that the computation has terminated; and the termination of the computation is said to be *implicit*. Termination is said to be *explicit* in a process if the state of that process in the terminal configuration is a terminal state of the process. Implicit termination of the computation is also called *message termination* because no more messages are exchanged when a terminal configuration has been reached. Explicit termination is also called *process termination* because the processes have terminated if an algorithm explicitly terminates.

It is usually easier to design an algorithm that terminates implicitly than one that terminates explicitly. Indeed, during the design of an algorithm all aspects regarding the proper termination of processes can be ignored; the design concentrates on bounding the overall number of events that can take place. On the other hand, the application of an algorithm may require that processes terminate explicitly. Only after explicit termination can the results of a computation be regarded as final, and variables used in the computation discarded. Also, a *deadlock* of a distributed algorithm results in a terminal configuration; in this case the computation must be restarted when a terminal configuration is reached.

In this chapter general methods will be investigated for transforming message-terminating algorithms into process-terminating ones. Given such a method, an algorithm can be designed by taking only message termination into account (i.e., ensuring that the algorithm allows finite computations only), after which the algorithm is made process-terminating using one of these methods. The methods consist of two additional algorithms that interact with the given message-terminating algorithm and with each other. One of these algorithms observes the computation and will detect somehow that the computation has reached a terminal configuration of the underlying algorithm. It then calls the second algorithm, which floods a termination message to all processes, causing them to enter a terminal state.

The most difficult part of the transformation turns out to be the algorithm that detects the termination. The flooding procedure is rather trivial and will be discussed briefly in Subsection 8.1.3. It will be shown in this chapter that termination detection is possible for all classes of networks for which a wave algorithm can be given. These classes include networks where a leader is available, networks where processes have identities, tree networks, and networks where topological information is available, such as the diameter or the number of processes. On the other hand, it will be shown in Chapter 9 that for anonymous networks of unknown size there exists an implicitly terminating algorithm, but no explicitly terminating algorithm for computing the maximum over the inputs of the processes. Consequently, termination detection is not possible in anonymous networks where the size is not known.

For those cases where termination detection is possible, we shall establish lower bounds on the number of messages exchanged by the termination-detection algorithm. It will be shown that there exist algorithms that match these bounds. Section 8.1 introduces the problem formally by giving a model for the behavior of a distributed computation, and gives the lower bound and the flooding procedure. Section 8.2 presents several solutions based on maintaining a tree (or forest) of processes, including at least all processes that are still computing. The solutions in this section are not very difficult and match the lower bounds of Section 8.1. These first two sections contain all the fundamental results concerning the existence and complexity of termination-detection algorithms. For a variety of reasons one termination-detection algorithm may be more suitable for a particular application than another algorithm. Therefore, Sections 8.3 and 8.4 present a number of other solutions.

8.1 Preliminaries

8.1.1 Definitions

In this subsection a model of distributed computations will be defined that treats the problem of terminating distributed computations. The model is derived from the model in Chapter 2, but all aspects irrelevant to the termination problem are ignored.

The state set Z_p of process p is partitioned into two subsets, the *active* and the *passive* states. A state c_p of p is active if an internal or send event of p is applicable in c_p, and passive otherwise. In a passive state c_p only receipts are applicable, or no event is applicable at all, in which case c_p is a terminal state of p. Process p is simply said to be active if it is in an active state, and process p is said to be passive otherwise. Clearly, a message can be sent only by an active process, and a passive process can become active only when a message is received. An active process can become passive when it enters a passive state. Some assumptions are made in order to simplify the description of the algorithms in this chapter.

(1) *An active process becomes passive only in an internal event.* Any process can easily be modified to satisfy this assumption. Let (c, m, d) be a send (or receive) event of p, in which d is a passive state. Replace this event of p by (c, m, d'), where d' is a new state, and the only event applicable in d' is the internal event (d', d). As d' is an active state, p becomes passive in the internal event (d', d).

(2) *A process always becomes active when a message is received.* Any process can easily be modified to satisfy this assumption. Let (c, m, d) be a receive event of p, in which d is a passive state. Replace this event of p by (c, m, d'), where d' is a new state, and the only event applicable in d' is the internal event (d', d). As d' is an active state, p becomes active in the receive event and passive in its next event (d', d).

(3) *The internal events in which p becomes passive are the only internal events of p.* Internal events in which p moves from one active state to another active state are ignored, because the termination-detection algorithm must be *oblivious*; it is not allowed to use information about how the local computation of a process will proceed All active states are therefore identical for the termination detection algorithm.

Of p's state it is only relevant whether it is active or passive; this will be represented in the variable $state_p$. All transitions of the computation are

var $state_p$: $(active, passive)$;

S_p: { $state_p = active$ }
  begin send $\langle \mathbf{mes} \rangle$ **end**

R_p: { A message $\langle \mathbf{mes} \rangle$ has arrived at p }
  begin receive $\langle \mathbf{mes} \rangle$; $state_p := active$ **end**

I_p: { $state_p = active$ }
  begin $state_p := passive$ **end**

Algorithm 8.1 THE BASIC DISTRIBUTED ALGORITHM.

---

given in Algorithm 8.1. As usual, initial configurations are assumed to have no messages in transit. Processes can be either active or passive initially.

In order to distinguish this algorithm from the termination detection algorithm, it is often called the *basic algorithm*, and its computation is then called the *basic computation* or *underlying computation*. The termination-detection algorithm is referred to as the *control* or *superimposed algorithm*, and its computation as the *control* or *superimposed* computation. Likewise, messages are referred to as either *basic messages* or *control messages*.

The predicate **term** is defined to be true in every configuration where no event of the basic computation is applicable; according to the following theorem, this is the case if all processes are passive and no basic messages are in transit.

Theorem 8.1

$$\mathbf{term} \iff \quad (\forall p \in \mathbb{P} : state_p = passive)$$
$$\land (\forall pq \in E : M_{pq} \ does\ not\ contain\ a\ \langle \mathbf{mes} \rangle\ message).$$

Proof. If all processes are passive, no internal or send event is applicable. If, moreover, no channel contains a $\langle \mathbf{mes} \rangle$ message, no receive event is applicable, hence no basic event is applicable at all.

If some process is active, a send or internal event is possible in that process, and if some channel contains a $\langle \mathbf{mes} \rangle$ message the receipt of this message is applicable. $\qquad \square$

In a terminal configuration of the basic algorithm each process is waiting to receive a message and remains waiting forever. The problem discussed in this chapter is that of adding a control algorithm to the system that brings the processes into a terminal state after the basic computation has reached a terminal configuration. For the combined algorithm (basic plus control algorithm) a configuration satisfying **term** is not necessarily terminal; in general there will be applicable events of the control algorithm. The control algorithm exchanges (control) messages, and these can be sent by passive processes and do not make a passive process active when they are received.

The control algorithm consists of a *termination-detection* algorithm and a *termination-announcement* algorithm. The termination detection algorithm calls *Announce*, and this announcement algorithm brings the processes in a terminated state. The detection algorithm must satisfy the following three requirements.

(1) **Non-interference.** It must not influence the computation of the basic algorithm.
(2) **Liveness.** If **term** holds, *Announce* must be called within a finite number of steps.
(3) **Safety.** If *Announce* is called, the configuration must satisfy **term**.

The termination detection problem was first stated by Francez [Fra80]. Francez proposed a solution that does not satisfy non-interference; the solution first "freezes" the basic computation by disabling all events, then inspects the configuration to see if it is terminate. If so, *Announce* is called; otherwise, the basic computation is "unfrozen" and the procedure is repeated some time later. The above-mentioned requirements exclude this solution and ask that the detection algorithm works "on-the-fly", i.e., while the basic computation proceeds. In the correctness proofs of termination detection in this chapter, no reference to non-interference is made because it is usually clear from the description of the algorithm that this requirement is satisfied.

The basic computation is called centralized if in each initial state there is exactly one active process and decentralized if the number of active processes in an initial configuration is arbitrary. Centralized basic computations are frequently referred to as *diffusing computations* in the literature about termination detection. The control computation is said to be centralized if there is one special process for the control computation, and decentralized if the processes all execute exactly the same control algorithm.

8.1.2 Two Lower Bounds

The complexity of a termination-detection algorithm is expressed using as before the parameters N and $|E|$ and the number M of messages exchanged by the basic computation. The complexity of termination detection is also related to the cost of executing a wave algorithm; let W denote the message complexity of the best wave algorithm. W of course depends on characteristics of the class of networks under consideration, such as whether a leader is available, the topology, and the knowledge initially assumed for the processes.

It will be shown that the worst-case complexity of termination detection, for centralized as well as decentralized computations, is bounded from below by M. It will then be shown that the complexity of termination detection for decentralized basic computations is bounded from below by W. At the end of this subsection a lower bound of $|E|$ messages, given by Chandrasekaran and Venkatesan [CV90], will be discussed.

Theorem 8.2 *For every termination-detection algorithm there exists a basic computation that exchanges M basic messages and for which the detection algorithm exchanges at least M control messages.*

Proof. If the system can reach a configuration from which the control algorithm may exchange infinitely many control messages without a single occurrence of a basic event, the result follows trivially. Assume therefore in the remainder of this proof that the control algorithm reacts with only finitely many messages to each basic event.

Let γ be a configuration in which two processes, p and q, are active and no messages are in transit. If the basic algorithm is centralized, such a configuration can be reached from the initial configuration by exchanging one basic message; otherwise, such configurations include initial configurations.

First consider the computation where, starting from configuration γ, both processes become passive concurrently, i.e., the system reaches the configuration $\delta = \mathbf{I}_p(\mathbf{I}_q(\gamma))$. Termination must be detected within a finite number of steps; but neither p nor q can call *Announce* without first receiving a message from the other process. Otherwise, termination could erroneously be detected in a configuration where the other process is still active. (If termination is detected by a third process at least two messages are necessary.) Consequently, at least one control message must be exchanged in configuration δ before termination can be detected.

Without loss of generality, assume p will send a control message in configuration δ. Consider a computation in which, starting from γ, only p becomes passive, i.e., the system reaches the configuration $\gamma_p = \mathbf{I}_p(\gamma)$. The state of p is the same in configurations γ_p and δ, and consequently, p also sends a control message in configuration γ_p. More activity of the control algorithm may follow, but this does not lead to detection because q is still active. After the control algorithm has stopped exchanging messages, q sends a basic message to p to return to a configuration where both p and q are active. More control activity may follow but, after finitely many steps again a configuration is reached in which both p and q are active and no messages are in transit. Summarizing,

(1) a configuration in which both p and q are active and no messages are in transit can be reached from an initial configuration by exchanging at most one basic message;

(2) the basic algorithm can move from one such a configuration to another by exchanging one message and forcing the control algorithm to exchange at least one control message; and

(3) if the basic computation terminates after such a configuration, at least one control message must be exchanged in order to detect this.

This implies the result.   □

Theorem 8.3 *Detecting the termination of a decentralized basic computation requires the exchange of at least W control messages in the worst case.*

Proof. Consider the basic computation that does not exchange any message and where each active process becomes passive as its first event. This basic computation requires the detection algorithm to be a wave algorithm if the detection (the call to *Announce*) is regarded as the decision. Indeed, a call to *Announce* must occur within a finite number of steps, which proves that the detection algorithm itself terminates and decides. If the decision is not preceded by an event in some process q, a different basic computation is considered where q does not become passive. The decision does not depend causally on any event in q, so the detection algorithm may erroneously call *Announce* while q is still active. As the detection algorithm is a wave, it exchanges at least W messages.   □

The start of the detection algorithm. Chandrasekaran and Venkatesan [CV90] have obtained a lower bound of $|E|$ control messages under the following two additional assumptions.

C1. The channels are fifo.
C2. The termination-detection algorithm may start its execution at any time after the basic computation has started, i.e., in an arbitrary configuration of the basic computation.

Under these assumptions an incorrect detection can be enforced if the detection algorithm does not send a control message through one particular edge, say pq. Just before the detection algorithm starts, the basic computation

var $SentStop_p$: boolean   **init** false ;
       $RecStop_p$: integer   **init** 0 ;

Procedure *Announce*:
     begin if not $SentStop_p$ **then**
           begin $SentStop_p := true$;
               forall $q \in Out_p$ **do** send $\langle$ **stop** $\rangle$ to q
           end
     end

{ A $\langle$ **stop** $\rangle$ message has arrived at p }
     begin receive $\langle$ **stop** $\rangle$; $RecStop_p := RecStop_p + 1$;
        Announce ;
        if $RecStop_p = \#In_p$ **then halt**
     end

Algorithm 8.2 THE ANNOUNCEMENT ALGORITHM.

---

sends one additional message via channel pq; this message is not observed by the control algorithm, from which an incorrect detection is deduced. The algorithm of Chandrasekaran and Venkatesan sends a control message through each channel, thus forcing all messages sent before the start of the control algorithm to be received before detection takes place.

With an argument similar to the one used in [CV90] it can be shown that the problem allows no solution at all if assumption C2 is in effect but assumption C1 is not. It will be assumed in this chapter that the control algorithm is started in the initial configuration of the basic computation, i.e., the basic computation performs no unnoticed event before the start of the control algorithm. If this assumption is replaced by assumption C2, the problem has a solution if and only if the channels are fifo, and the solution is found in [CV90] for this case.

8.1.3 Terminating the Processes

To announce the termination to all processes, a $\langle$ **stop** $\rangle$ message is flooded to all processes. Each process sends such a message to all neighbors, but does so at most once, either in a local call of *Announce* or upon receipt of the first $\langle$ **stop** $\rangle$ message. When a $\langle$ **stop** $\rangle$ message has been received from every neighbor a process executes the statement **stop**, causing the process to enter a terminal state. The announcement procedure is given as Algorithm 8.2.

Algorithm 8.2 can be used for arbitrary connected topologies, including directed networks, and requires no leader, no identities, and no topological knowledge at all.

8.2 Computation Trees and Forests

The solutions described in this section are based on maintaining dynamically a directed graph, called the *computation graph*, of which the nodes include all active processes and all basic messages in transit. Termination is detected when the computation graph becomes empty. The solutions of this section require that the network is undirected, i.e., messages can be sent in two directions via each channel. Subsection 8.2.1 describes a solution for centralized basic computations, in which the computation graph is a tree with the initiator as the root. Subsection 8.2.2 generalizes this solution to decentralized basic computations and uses a forest, in which each initiator of the basic computation is the root of a tree.

8.2.1 The Dijkstra–Scholten Algorithm

The algorithm of Dijkstra and Scholten [DS80] detects the termination of a *centralized* basic computation (called a *diffusing computation* in [DS80]). The initiator of the basic computation (called the *environment* in [DS80]), also plays a special role in the detection algorithm and is denoted by p_0.

The detection algorithm dynamically maintains a computation tree $T = (V_T, E_T)$ with the following two properties.

(1) Either T is empty, or T is a directed tree with root p_0.
(2) The set V_T includes all active processes and all basic messages in transit.

The initiator p_0 calls *Announce* when $p_0 \notin V_T$; by the first property, T is empty in this case, and by the second property, **term** holds.

To preserve the properties of the computation tree when the basic computation evolves, T must be expanded when a basic message is sent or when a process, not in the tree, becomes active. When p sends a basic message $\langle \textbf{mes} \rangle$, $\langle \textbf{mes} \rangle$ is inserted into the tree and the father of $\langle \textbf{mes} \rangle$ is p. When a process p, not in the tree, becomes active by the receipt of a message from q, q becomes the father of p. To represent the sender of a message explicitly, a basic message $\langle \textbf{mes} \rangle$ sent by q will be denoted as $\langle \textbf{mes}, q \rangle$.

The removal of nodes from T is also necessary, for two reasons. First, a basic message is deleted when it is received. Second, to ensure progress of the detection algorithm the tree must collapse within a finite number

var $state_p$: $(active, passive)$ **init if** $p = p_0$ **then** $active$ **else** $passive$;
       sc_p : integer   **init** 0 ;
       $father_p$: $\mathbb{P}$ **init if** $p = p_0$ **then** p **else** $udef$;

S_p: { $state_p = active$ }
    begin send $\langle \textbf{mes}, p \rangle$; $sc_p := sc_p + 1$ **end**

R_p: { A message $\langle \textbf{mes}, q \rangle$ has arrived at p }
    begin receive $\langle \textbf{mes}, q \rangle$; $state_p := active$;
            if $father_p = udef$ **then** $father_p := q$ **else** send $\langle \textbf{sig}, q \rangle$ **to** q
    end

I_p: { $state_p = active$ }
    begin $state_p := passive$;
            if $sc_p = 0$ **then** (* Delete p from T *)
                begin if $father_p = p$
                       then $Announce$
                       else send $\langle \textbf{sig}, father_p \rangle$ **to** $father_p$;
                    $father_p := udef$
                end
    end

A_p: { A signal $\langle \textbf{sig}, p \rangle$ arrives at p }
    begin receive $\langle \textbf{sig}, p \rangle$; $sc_p := sc_p - 1$;
            if $sc_p = 0$ **and** $state_p = passive$ **then**
                begin if $father_p = p$
                       then $Announce$
                       else send $\langle \textbf{sig}, father_p \rangle$ **to** $father_p$;
                    $father_p := udef$
                end
    end

Algorithm 8.3 The Dijkstra–Scholten algorithm.

---

of steps after termination. Messages are leaves of T; processes maintain a variable that counts the number of their sons in T. The deletion of a son of process p occurs in a different process q; it is either the receipt of a son message, or the deletion of the son process q. To prevent corruption of p's son count, a signal message $\langle \textbf{sig}, p \rangle$ can be sent to p when a son of p is deleted. This message replaces the deleted son of p, and its deletion, i.e., its receipt, occurs in process p and p decrements its son count when it receives a signal.

The algorithm is given as Algorithm 8.3. Each process p has a variable $father_p$, which is $udef$ if $p \notin V_T$, equal to p if p is the root, and the father of p if p is a non-root in T. The variable sc_p gives the number of sons of p in T.

The correctness proof rigorously establishes that the graph T, as defined, is a tree and that it becomes empty only after termination of the basic computation. For any configuration γ of Algorithm 8.3, define

$$V_T = \{p : father_p \neq udef\} \cup \{\langle \mathbf{mes}, p \rangle \text{ in transit }\} \cup \{\langle \mathbf{sig}, p \rangle \text{ in transit }\}$$

and

$$
\begin{aligned}
E_T = \quad & \{(p, father_p) : father_p \neq udef \wedge father_p \neq p\} \\
& \cup \{(\langle \mathbf{mes}, p \rangle, p) : \langle \mathbf{mes}, p \rangle \text{ in transit }\} \\
& \cup \{(\langle \mathbf{sig}, p \rangle, p) : \langle \mathbf{sig}, p \rangle \text{ in transit }\}.
\end{aligned}
$$

The safety of the algorithm will follow from the assertion P, defined by

$$
\begin{aligned}
P \equiv \quad & state_p = active \Rightarrow p \in V_T & (1) \\
& \wedge (u, v) \in E_T \Rightarrow u \in V_T \wedge v \in V_T \cap \mathbb{P} & (2) \\
& \wedge sc_p = \#\{v : (v, p) \in E_T\} & (3) \\
& \wedge V_T \neq \varnothing \Rightarrow T \text{ is a tree with root } p_0 & (4) \\
& \wedge (state_p = passive \wedge sc_p = 0) \Rightarrow p \notin V_T & (5)
\end{aligned}
$$

The meaning of this invariant is as follows. By definition, the node set of T includes all messages (basic as well as control messages), and by (1) it also includes all active processes. Clause (2) is rather technical; it states that T is indeed a graph and all edges are directed towards processes. Clause (3) expresses the correctness of the son count of each process, and clause (4) states that T is a tree and p_0 is the root. Clause (5) is used to show that the tree indeed collapses if the basic computation terminates. For the correctness proof, note that P implies that $father_p = p$ holds only for $p = p_0$.

Lemma 8.4 *P is an invariant of the Dijkstra–Scholten algorithm.*

Proof. Initially $state_p = passive$ for all $p \neq p_0$ and $father_{p_0} \neq udef$, which proves (1). Also, $E_T = \varnothing$, which proves (2). As $sc_p = 0$ for each p, (3) is satisfied. $V_T = \{p_0\}$ and $E_T = \varnothing$, so T is a tree with root p_0, which proves (4). The only process in V_T is p_0, and p_0 is active.

$\mathbf{S}_p$: No process becomes active in $\mathbf{S}_p$ and no process is deleted from V_T, so (1) is preserved.

The applicability of the action implies that p, the father of the new node $\langle \mathbf{mes}, p \rangle$, is in V_T, which proves that (2) is preserved.

As a result of the action, V_T is extended with $\langle \mathbf{mes}, p \rangle$ and E_T with $(\langle \mathbf{mes}, p \rangle, p)$, which implies that T remains a tree, and sc_p is correctly incremented to reflect the new son of p, hence (3) and (4) are preserved.

No process becomes a passive leaf and no process is inserted in V_T, so (5) is preserved.

$\mathbf{R}_p$: Either p was in V_T already ($father_p \neq udef$) or p is inserted into V_T in the action, so (1) is preserved.

If a value is assigned to $father_p$, its new value is q, and if a signal is sent by p its father is also q, and q is in V_T, so (2) is preserved.

The number of sons of q does not change, because the son $\langle \mathbf{mes}, q \rangle$ of q is replaced either by the son p or the son $\langle \mathbf{sig}, q \rangle$, so sc_q remains correct, which preserves (3).

The structure of the graph does not change, so (4) is preserved.

Process p is in V_T after the action in any case, so (5) is preserved.

$\mathbf{I}_p$: Making p passive preserves (1), (2), (3), and (4). That p was previously active implies that p was in V_T. If $sc_p = 0$, p is removed from V_T, so (5) is preserved.

We next consider what happens if p is removed from T, i.e., if p turns out to be a passive leaf of T.

If a signal is sent by p, the father of the signal is the last father of p, which is in V_T, hence (2) is preserved. In this case, the signal replaces p as a son of $father_p$, hence sc_{father_p} remains correct and (3) is preserved. The structure of the graph is not changed, hence (4) is preserved.

Otherwise, i.e., if $father_p = p$ was true, $p = p_0$ and p being a leaf implies that p was the only node of T, so its removal makes T empty, which preserves (4).

$\mathbf{A}_p$: The receipt of the signal decreases the number of sons of p by one and the assignment to sc_p ensures (3) is preserved. That p was the father of the signal implies that p was in V_T. If $state_p = passive$ and after the receipt $sc_p = 0$ holds, p is removed, so (5) is preserved.

If p is removed from V_T, the invariant is preserved by the same argument as used for action $\mathbf{I}_p$.

$\square$

Theorem 8.5 *The Dijkstra–Scholten algorithm (Algorithm 8.3) is a correct termination-detection algorithm and uses M control messages.*

Proof. Define S to be the sum of all sun-counts, i.e., $S = \sum_{p \in \mathbb{P}} sc_p$. Initially S is zero, S is incremented when a basic message is sent (in $\mathbf{S}_p$), S is decremented when a control message is received (in $\mathbf{A}_p$), and S is never negative (from (3)). This implies that the number of control messages never exceeds the number of basic messages in any computation.

To prove liveness of the algorithm, assume that the basic computation has terminated. After termination only actions $\mathbf{A}_p$ can take place and because S decreases by one in every such transition, the algorithm reaches a terminal configuration. Observe that in this configuration, V_T contains no messages. Also, by (5), V_T contains no passive leaves. Consequently, T has no leaves, which implies that T is empty. The tree became empty when p_0 removed itself, and the program is such that p_0 called *Announce* in this step.

To prove the safety, note that only p_0 calls *Announce*, and does so when it removes itself from V_T. By (4), T is empty when this happens, which implies **term**.   □

The Dijkstra–Scholten algorithm achieves an attractive balance between the control communication and the basic communication; for each basic message sent from p to q the algorithm sends exactly one control message from q to p. The control communication equals the lower bound given in Theorem 8.2, so the algorithm is a worst-case optimal algorithm for termination detection of centralized computations.

In the description in this subsection, all messages carry their father explicitly, but this will usually not be necessary because the father of a basic (or control, respectively) message is always its sender (or destination, respectively).

8.2.2 The Shavit–Francez Algorithm

The Dijkstra–Scholten algorithm was generalized to decentralized basic computations by Shavit and Francez [SF86]. In their algorithm, the computation graph is a *forest* of which each tree is rooted at an initiator of the basic computation. The tree rooted at p is denoted T_p.

The algorithm maintains a graph $F = (V_F, E_F)$, such that (1) either F is empty or F is a forest of which each tree is rooted in an initiator; and (2) V_F includes all active processes and all basic messages. As in the Dijkstra–Scholten algorithm termination is detected when the graph becomes empty. Unfortunately, in the case of a forest it is not trivial to see whether the graph is empty. Indeed, the property of the computation tree that it is rooted at p_0 implies that emptiness of the tree is observed by p_0, which calls *Announce* when the tree is empty. In the case of a forest, each initiator only observes the emptiness of its own tree, but this does not imply the emptiness of the forest.

The verification that all trees have collapsed is done by a single wave. The forest is maintained with the additional property that if the tree T_p has become empty, it remains empty thereafter. Note that this does not prevent p from becoming active; but if p becomes active after the collapse of its tree, p is inserted in the tree of another initiator. Each process participates in the wave only if its tree has collapsed; when the wave decides, *Announce* is called. (Calling *Announce* is superfluous if the chosen wave algorithm generates a decision in every process; in this case, a process simply halts after deciding and completing the wave algorithm.)

The algorithm is given as Algorithm 8.4, in which the wave algorithm is not shown explicitly. Each process p has a variable $father_p$, which is *udef* if $p \notin V_F$, equal to p if p is a root, and the father of p if p is a non-root in F. The variable sc_p gives the number of sons of p in F. The boolean variable $empty_p$ is true if and only if p's tree is empty.

The correctness proof of the algorithm is very similar to the proof of the Dijkstra–Scholten algorithm. For any configuration γ of Algorithm 8.4, define

$$V_F = \{p : father_p \neq udef\} \cup \{\langle \mathbf{mes}, p \rangle \text{ in transit }\} \cup \{\langle \mathbf{sig}, p \rangle \text{ in transit }\}$$

and

$$\begin{aligned}
E_F = \quad & \{(p, father_p) : father_p \neq udef \wedge father_p \neq p\} \\
\cup \; & \{(\langle \mathbf{mes}, p \rangle, p) : \langle \mathbf{mes}, p \rangle \text{ in transit }\} \\
\cup \; & \{(\langle \mathbf{sig}, p \rangle, p) : \langle \mathbf{sig}, p \rangle \text{ in transit }\}.
\end{aligned}$$

The safety of the algorithm will follow from the assertion Q, defined below. It is an invariant of the algorithm, and the proof of the invariance is of course very similar to the proof of Lemma 8.4. The meaning of the clauses (1) through (5) of Q is the same as that for the invariant of the Dijkstra–Scholten algorithm and clause (6) expresses that each process correctly records whether it is still the root of a tree in the forest. Of course, the forest is empty if no process is a root.

$$\begin{aligned}
Q \iff \quad & state_p = active \Rightarrow p \in V_F & (1) \\
\wedge \; & (u, v) \in E_F \Rightarrow u \in V_F \wedge v \in V_F \cap \mathbb{P} & (2) \\
\wedge \; & sc_p = \#\{v : (v, p) \in E_F\} & (3) \\
\wedge \; & V_F \neq \varnothing \Rightarrow F \text{ is a forest} & (4) \\
\wedge \; & (state_p = passive \wedge sc_p = 0) \Rightarrow p \notin V_F & (5) \\
\wedge \; & empty_p \iff T_p \text{ is empty} & (6)
\end{aligned}$$

Lemma 8.6 *Q is an invariant of the Shavit–Francez algorithm.*

Proof. Initially $state_p = passive$ for every non-initiator p, and $father_p = p$

for every initiator p, which proves (1). Also, $E_F = \varnothing$, which proves (2). As $sc_p = 0$ for each p, (3) is satisfied. $V_F = \{p : p \text{ is an initiator}\}$ and $E_F = \varnothing$, so F is a forest consisting of a one-node tree for each initiator, which proves (4). The processes in V_F are initiators, which are active; this proves (5). Initially $empty_p$ equals (p is non-initiator) and T_p is indeed empty if and only if p is not an initiator, which proves (6).

$\mathbf{S}_p$: No process becomes active in $\mathbf{S}_p$ and no process is deleted from V_F, so (1) is preserved.

The applicability of the action implies that p, the father of the new node, is in V_F, so (2) is preserved.

As a result of the action, V_F is extended with $\langle \mathbf{mes}, p \rangle$ and E_F with $(\langle \mathbf{mes}, p \rangle, p)$, which implies that F remains a forest, and sc_p is correctly incremented to reflect the new son of p, so (3) and (4) are preserved.

No process becomes a passive leaf and no process is inserted in V_F, so (5) is preserved.

As the new leaf is added to a non-empty tree, no tree becomes non-empty, and as no $empty$ variable changes, (6) is preserved.

$\mathbf{R}_p$: Either p was in V_F already ($father_p \neq udef$) or p is inserted in the action, so (1) is preserved.

If a value is assigned to $father_p$, its new value is q, and if a signal is sent, its father is also q, and q is in V_T, so (2) is preserved.

The number of sons of q does not change, because the son $\langle \mathbf{mes}, q \rangle$ of q is replaced either by the son p or the son $\langle \mathbf{sig}, q \rangle$, so sc_q remains correct (3).

The structure of the graph does not change, so (4) is preserved.

No process becomes a passive leaf and no process is inserted in V_F, so (5) is preserved.

No tree becomes empty or becomes non-empty, hence (6) is preserved.

$\mathbf{I}_p$: Making p passive preserves (1), (2), (3), and (4). That p was previously active implies that p was in V_F. If $sc_p = 0$, p is removed from V_F, so (5) is preserved.

We next consider what happens if p is removed from F, i.e., if p turns out to be a passive leaf of F. If a signal is sent, the father of the signal is the last father of p, which is in V_F, hence (2) is preserved. In this case, the signal replaces p as a son of $father_p$, hence sc_{father_p} remains correct and (3) is preserved. The structure of the graph is not changed, hence (4) is preserved. No tree becomes empty, so (6) is preserved. Otherwise, i.e., if $father_p = p$ was true, p was a root and

var $state_p$: $(active, passive)$ **init if** p is initiator **then** $active$ **else** $passive$;
      sc_p : integer   **init** 0 ;
      $father_p$: $\mathbb{P}$ **init if** p is initiator **then** p **else** $udef$;
      $empty_p$: boolean   **init if** p is initiator **then** false **else** true ;

S_p: $\{ state_p = active \}$
     begin send $\langle \textbf{mes}, p \rangle$; $sc_p := sc_p + 1$ **end**

R_p: $\{$ A message $\langle \textbf{mes}, q \rangle$ has arrived at p $\}$
     begin receive $\langle \textbf{mes}, q \rangle$; $state_p := active$;
             if $father_p = udef$ **then** $father_p := q$ **else** send $\langle \textbf{sig}, q \rangle$ to q
     end

I_p: $\{ state_p = active \}$
     begin $state_p := passive$;
          if $sc_p = 0$ **then** (* Delete p from F *)
             begin if $father_p = p$
                 then $empty_p := true$
                 else send $\langle \textbf{sig}, father_p \rangle$ to $father_p$;
               $father_p := udef$
             end
     end

A_p: $\{$ A signal $\langle \textbf{sig}, p \rangle$ arrives at p $\}$
     begin receive $\langle \textbf{sig}, p \rangle$; $sc_p := sc_p - 1$;
          if $sc_p = 0$ **and** $state_p = passive$ **then**
             begin if $father_p = p$
                 then $empty_p := true$
                 else send $\langle \textbf{sig}, father_p \rangle$ to $father_p$;
               $father_p := udef$
             end
     end

The processes concurrently execute a wave algorithm in which sending or deciding by p is allowed only if $empty_p$ is true and in which *decide* calls *Announce*.

Algorithm 8.4 THE SHAVIT–FRANCEZ ALGORITHM.

---

that p is a leaf implies that p was the only node of T_p, so its removal makes T_p empty, and the assignment to $empty_p$ preserves (6).

A_p: The receipt of the signal decreases the number of sons of p by one and the assignment to sc_p ensures that (3) is preserved. That p was the father of the signal implies that p was in V_F. If $state_p = passive$ and if after the receipt of the signal $sc_p = 0$ holds, p is removed, so (5) is preserved.

If p is removed from V_F, the invariant is preserved by the same argument as used under action $\mathbf{I}_p$.

$\square$

Theorem 8.7 *The Shavit–Francez algorithm (Algorithm 8.4) is a correct termination-detection algorithm and uses $M + W$ control messages.*

Proof. As in Theorem 8.5 it can be shown that the number of signals does not exceed the number of basic messages. Besides signals, the control algorithm only sends messages for one wave. It follows that at most $M + W$ control messages are sent.

To prove liveness of the algorithm, assume that the basic computation has terminated. Within a finite number of steps the termination-detection algorithm reaches a terminal configuration, and as in Theorem 8.5 it can be shown that in this configuration F is empty. Consequently, all events of the wave are enabled in every process, and that the configuration is terminal now implies that all events of the wave have been executed, including at least one decision, which caused a call to *Announce*.

To prove the safety, note that *Announce* is called when a decision occurs in the wave algorithm. This implies that each process p has sent a wave message or has decided, and the algorithm implies that $empty_p$ was true when p did so. No action makes $empty_p$ false again, so (for each p) $empty_p$ is true when *Announce* is called. By (6), V_F is empty, which implies **term**.

$\square$

The number of control messages exchanged by the Shavit–Francez algorithm matches in order of magnitude the lower bounds proved in Theorems 8.2 and 8.3. The algorithm is a worst-case optimal algorithm for termination detection of decentralized computations (if an optimal wave algorithm is supplied).

Application of the algorithms considered in this section requires that communication channels are bidirectional; for each basic message sent from p to q a signal must be sent from q to p. The average-case complexity equals the worst-case complexity; each execution requires one signal message per basic message and, in the case of the Shavit–Francez algorithm, exactly one wave execution.

8.3 Wave-based Solutions

For two reasons it is useful to consider some other algorithms for termination detection apart from the two algorithms given in Section 8.2. First, the algorithms given there can only be used when channels are bidirectional. Second, although the message complexity of these algorithms is optimal in the *worst case*, there exist algorithms that have a better complexity in the average case. The algorithms of the previous section use their worst-case number of messages in every execution.

In this section some algorithms based on the repeated execution of a wave algorithm will be studied; at the end of each wave, either termination is detected, or a new wave is started. Termination is detected if a local condition turns out to be satisfied in each process.

We shall first consider concrete instances of the algorithms, where in all cases the wave algorithm is the ring algorithm. A ring is supposed to be embedded as a subtopology of the network for this purpose; but the exchange of basic messages is not restricted to the channels belonging to the ring. The processes are numbered p_0 through p_{N-1}, and the ring algorithm is initiated by p_0 by sending the token to p_{N-1}. Process p_{i+1} (for $i < N - 1$) forwards the token to process p_i. The token tour ends when the token is received back by process p_0.

The first solution discussed in this class is the algorithm by Dijkstra, Feijen, and Van Gasteren (Subsection 8.3.1); this algorithm detects the termination of computations with synchronous message passing. Several authors have generalized the algorithm to computations with asynchronous message passing; the main problem here is to verify that the communication channels are empty. We discuss the solution by Safra (Subsection 8.3.2), which counts in each process the number of messages that are sent and received; by comparing the counts it can indeed be certified that the channels are empty. It is also possible to use acknowledgements for this purpose (Subsection 8.3.3); but this solution again requires that channels are bidirectional and that the number of control messages at least equals the number used by the Shavit–Francez algorithm.

In Subsection 8.3.4 the detection principle will be generalized to the use of an arbitrary wave algorithm.

8.3.1 The Dijkstra–Feijen–Van Gasteren Algorithm

The algorithm of Dijkstra, Feijen, and Van Gasteren [DFG83] detects termination of a basic computation using *synchronous* message passing; the actions of such a computation are given as Algorithm 8.5. In these computations, termination is described by

$$\mathbf{term} \iff \forall p : state_p = passive$$

---

var $state_p$: $(active, passive)$;

C_{pq}: { $state_p = active$ }
     begin (* p sends a basic message, which is received by q *)
               $state_q := active$
     end

I_p: { $state_p = active$ }
      begin $state_p := passive$ **end**

Algorithm 8.5 THE BASIC ALGORITHM WITH SYNCHRONOUS MESSAGES.

Compare the algorithm and **term** with Algorithm 8.1 and Theorem 8.1.

The algorithm is developed in a series of small steps, each easy to understand, and its correctness will follow from an invariant, which is developed together with the algorithm. The treatment here is taken from [DFG83]. In the following, t denotes the number of the process that holds the token or, if the token is in transit, the number of the process to which the token is under way. Forwarding of the token can only be done by process p_t, and decreases t by 1. The wave ends when $t = 0$; hence the invariant, P, must be chosen such that termination can be concluded from P, $t = 0$, and other information in p_0. The invariant must hold when p_0 initiates the wave, i.e., when $t = N - 1$.

As a first attempt, set $P = P_0$, where

$$P_0 \quad \equiv \quad \forall i \ (N > i > t) : state_{p_i} = passive.$$

Indeed, P_0 is true when $t = N - 1$, and if $t = 0$ and $state_{p_0} = passive$, termination can be concluded from this assertion. The forwarding of the token preserves P_0 if only passive processes forward the token, hence we adopt the following rule.

Rule 1. A process only handles the token when it is passive.

Under this regime, P is preserved by token forwarding and also by internal actions; unfortunately, P is *not* preserved by communication actions. The predicate P_0 can be falsified when a process p_j is activated by a process p_i, where $j > t$ and $i \leq t$; see Exercise 8.4. Because P_0 can be falsified, P is replaced by a weaker assertion $(P_0 \vee P_1)$, where P_1 is chosen such that after each falsification of P_0, P_1 is true. We provide each process with a *color*, which is either *white* or *black*, and let $P = (P_0 \vee P_1)$ where

$$P_1 \quad \equiv \quad \exists j \ (t \geq j \geq 0) : color_{p_j} = black.$$

Each falsification of P_0 ensures that P_1 is or becomes true if a sending process colors itself black.

Rule 2. A sending process becomes *black*.

As $(P \wedge color_{p_0} = white \wedge t = 0) \Rightarrow \neg P_1$, it is still possible to detect termination with the new invariant, namely, by whether p_0 is white (and passive) when it processes the token.

Weakening P is successful in preventing falsification by communication events; but the weaker assertion can be falsified by token forwarding, namely if process t is the only black process and forwards the token. The situation is saved by a further weakening of P. The token is now supposed to have a color (white or black) also, and P is weakened to $(P_0 \vee P_1 \vee P_2)$, where

$$P_2 \equiv \text{the token is black.}$$

Token forwarding preserves P_2 if black processes forward the token black.

Rule 3. When a black process other than p_0 forwards the token, the token becomes black.

Because (the token is white) $\Rightarrow \neg P_2$, termination can still be detected by p_0, namely, by whether it receives a white token (and is white itself, and passive).

Indeed, it can now be verified that internal actions, basic communication, and token forwarding preserve P. The blackening of the token has introduced the phenomenon of *unsuccessful waves*; termination cannot be concluded by p_0 if the returning token is black. If the wave ends unsuccessfully, a new one must be started.

Rule 4. When the wave ends unsuccessfully, p_0 initiates a new one.

The next wave would certainly be as unsuccessful as its predecessor if there was no way for black processes to become white again; indeed, the black processes would blacken the token when forwarding it, causing the next wave to fail as well.

Observe that whitening process p_i does not falsify P if $i > t$, and that P always becomes true when p_0 initiates the wave by sending the token to p_{N-1}. This implies that whitening can safely take place upon forwarding the token.

Rule 5. Each process turns white immediately after sending the token.

This whitening regime suffices to guarantee the eventual success of a wave

var $state_p$: $(active, passive)$;
$\qquad color_p$: $(white, black)$;

$\mathbf{C}_{pq}$: { $state_p = active$ }
$\qquad$ **begin** (* p sends a basic message, which is received by q *)
$\qquad\qquad color_p := black$;   (* Rule 2 *)
$\qquad\qquad state_q := active$
$\qquad$ **end**

$\mathbf{I}_p$:   { $state_p = active$ }
$\qquad$ **begin** $state_p := passive$ **end**

Start the detection, executed once by p_0:
$\qquad$ **begin** send $\langle$ **tok**, $white$ $\rangle$ to p_{N-1} **end**

$\mathbf{T}_p$:   (* Process p handles the token $\langle$ **tok**, c $\rangle$ *)
$\qquad$ { $state_p = passive$ }   (* Rule 1 *)
$\qquad$ **begin if** $p = p_0$
$\qquad\qquad$ **then if** $(c = white \wedge color_p = white)$
$\qquad\qquad\qquad$ **then** *Announce*
$\qquad\qquad\qquad$ **else** send $\langle$ **tok**, $white$ $\rangle$ to p_{N-1} (* Rule 4 *)
$\qquad\qquad$ **else if** $(color_p = white)$ (* Rule 3 *)
$\qquad\qquad\qquad$ **then** send $\langle$ **tok**, c $\rangle$ to $Next_p$
$\qquad\qquad\qquad$ **else** send $\langle$ **tok**, $black$ $\rangle$ to $Next_p$;
$\qquad\qquad color_p := white$ (* Rule 5 *)
$\qquad$ **end**

Algorithm 8.6 THE DIJKSTRA–FEIJEN–VAN GASTEREN ALGORITHM.

after termination of the basic computation. The algorithm is given as Algorithm 8.6.

Theorem 8.8 *The Dijkstra–Feijen–Van Gasteren algorithm (Algorithm 8.6) is a correct termination-detection algorithm for basic computations using synchronous message passing.*

Proof. The predicate $P \equiv (P_0 \vee P_1 \vee P_2)$ and the algorithm have been designed in such a way that P is an invariant of the algorithm. Termination is detected when the passive, white p_0 handles the white token. Indeed, when this happens, the color of the token implies $\neg P_2$, the color of p_0 and $t = 0$ imply $\neg P_1$, and then P_0 and the state of p_0 imply **term**. Hence the algorithm is safe.

To show liveness, assume the basic computation terminates. From then on, all processes forward the token without delay when they receive it. When the token completes its first full tour started after termination, all processes are *white* and when the token completes its next tour, termination is detected. □

We shall now attempt to estimate the number of control messages used by the algorithm. The basic computation used in the proof of Theorem 8.2 forces the algorithm to use at least one tour of the token for each two basic messages; hence the worst case complexity of the algorithm is $\frac{1}{2}N.M$ control messages; see Exercise 8.5.

The algorithm may use far fewer messages in an "average" basic computation. Assume the basic computation has time complexity T. Because the token is always forwarded sequentially, it is not unreasonable to assume that the token is forwarded approximately T times before the basic computation terminates. (Even this estimate may be pessimistically large because token forwarding is suspended in active processes.) As the token is forwarded fewer than $3N$ times after termination, the algorithm exchanges $T + 3N$ control messages in this case. The complexity of the basic computation is at least T (namely, its time complexity), but if the computation contains sufficient parallelism its message complexity can be as high as $\Omega(N.T)$. If the parallelism allows each process to send a constant number of α messages per time unit, the message complexity of the basic computation is $N.T.\alpha$, i.e., $\Omega(N.T)$. The number of control messages,r which is $O(N + T)$, is then much better than one may expect from the worstr- case complexity of the termination detection problem.

8.3.2 Counting Basic Messages: Safra's Algorithm

The synchronous message passing assumed for the basic computation in the Dijkstra–Feijen–Van Gasteren algorithm is a serious limitation on its general applicability. Several authors have generalized this algorithm to computations with asynchronous message passing (cf. Algorithm 8.1). In the present subsection Safra's solution [Dij87] will be discussed; it has the property that its average-case complexity is comparable with that of the Dijkstra–Feijen–Van Gasteren algorithm.

Define, for each configuration, the number of messages in transit as B. Now **term** is equivalent to

$$(\forall p : state_p = passive) \land B = 0.$$

Again an invariant P will be developed such that termination can be concluded from P, $t = 0$, and other information in p_0. The invariant must hold when p_0 initiates the wave, i.e., when $t = N - 1$.

To make information about B available in the processes (albeit in a distributed fashion), process p is equipped with a message counter mc_p and the processes will maintain P_m as an invariant, where

$$P_m \quad \equiv \quad B = \sum_{p \in \mathbb{P}} mc_p.$$

The invariance of P_m is obtained when initially $mc_p = 0$ for each p, and processes obey the following rule.

Rule M. When process p sends a message, it increments its message counter; when process p receives a message, it decrements its message counter.

The invariant must allow p_0 to decide that **term** holds when it receives the token ($t = 0$). Because **term** now also includes a restriction on the value of B, the token will be used to carry an integer q to compute the sum of the message counters of the processes that have forwarded it. As a first attempt, set $P = P_m \wedge P_0$, where

$$P_0 \quad \equiv \quad (\forall i \ (N > i > t) : state_{p_i} = passive) \wedge \left(q = \sum_{N > i > t} mc_{p_i} \right).$$

Indeed, P_0 is true when $t = N - 1$ and $q = 0$, and if $t = 0$ then P implies

$$(\forall i > 0 : state_{p_i} = passive) \wedge (mc_{p_0} + q = B),$$

so p_0 can conclude termination if $state_{p_0} = passive$ and $mc_{p_0} + q = 0$.

Assertion P_0 is established when p_0 initiates the wave by sending the token to p_{N-1} with $q = 0$. The forwarding of the token preserves P_0 if only passive processes forward the token and add the value of their message counter; hence we adopt the following rule.

Rule 1. A process only handles the token when it is passive, and when a process forwards the token it adds the value of its message counter to q.

Under this regime, P is preserved by token forwarding and also by internal actions; unfortunately, P is *not* preserved by the receipt of a message by process p_i with $i > t$. The falsification of P_0 takes place in a receipt, i.e., it is applicable only when $B > 0$. Because P_0 holds before its falsification, this implies that P_1 holds, where

$$P_1 \quad \equiv \quad \left(\sum_{i \leq t} mc_{p_i} + q \right) > 0.$$

Assertion P_1 remains true under a receipt by p_i with $i > t$; consequently, the

var $state_p$: $(active, passive)$;
  $color_p$: $(white, black)$;
  mc_p : integer **init** 0 ;

$\mathbf{S}_p$: { $state_p = active$ }
  begin send $\langle \mathbf{mes} \rangle$;
    $mc_p := mc_p + 1$ (* Rule M *)
  end

$\mathbf{R}_p$: { A message $\langle \mathbf{mes} \rangle$ has arrived at p }
  begin receive $\langle \mathbf{mes} \rangle$; $state_p := active$;
    $mc_p := mc_p - 1$; (* Rule M *)
    $color_p := black$ (* Rule 2 *)
  end

$\mathbf{I}_p$: { $state_p = active$ }
  begin $state_p := passive$ **end**

Start the detection, executed once by p_0:
  begin send $\langle \mathbf{tok}, white, 0 \rangle$ to p_{N-1} **end**

$\mathbf{T}_p$: (* Process p handles the token $\langle \mathbf{tok}, c, q \rangle$ *)
  { $state_p = passive$ } (* Rule 1 *)
  begin if $p = p_0$
    then if $(c = white) \wedge (color_p = white) \wedge (mc_p + q = 0)$
      then *Announce*
      else send $\langle \mathbf{tok}, white, 0 \rangle$ to p_{N-1} (* Rule 4 *)
    else if $(color_p = white)$ (* Rules 1 and 3 *)
      then send $\langle \mathbf{tok}, c, q + mc_p \rangle$ to $Next_p$
      else send $\langle \mathbf{tok}, black, q + mc_p \rangle$ to $Next_p$;
    $color_p := white$ (* Rule 5 *)
  end

Algorithm 8.7 SAFRA'S ALGORITHM.

weaker assertion P, defined by $P_m \wedge (P_0 \vee P_1)$, is preserved under message reception by p_i with $i > t$.

This modified assertion still allows the detection of termination by p_0 under the same conditions, because if $t = 0$, P_1 reads $mc_{p_0} + q > 0$, so since $mc_{p_0} + q = 0$ (this is already required for detection), $\neg P_1$ holds. Token-forwarding preserves P_1, and so does the sending of a basic message. Unfortunately, P_1 can be falsified by the receipt of a message by p_i with $i \leq t$. As in Subsection 8.3.1, this situation is remedied by giving each process a color, adopting the rule

Rule 2. A receiving process becomes black.

and replacing P by $P_m \wedge (P_0 \vee P_1 \vee P_2)$, where

$$P_2 \quad \equiv \quad \exists j \ (t \geq j \geq 0) : color_{p_j} = black.$$

Each receipt that falsifies P_1 makes P_2 true, so P is not falsified by any basic action. As $(P \wedge color_{p_0} = white \wedge t = 0) \Rightarrow \neg P_2$, it is still possible to detect termination with the new assertion, namely, by whether p_0 is white (and passive) when it processes the token.

Weakening P was successful in preventing falsification by basic events; but the weaker assertion can be falsified by token forwarding, namely, if process t is the only black process and forwards the token. The situation is saved by a further weakening of P. The token is again supposed to have a color (white or black) also, and P is weakened to $P_m \wedge (P_0 \vee P_1 \vee P_2 \vee P_3)$, where

$$P_3 \quad \equiv \quad \text{the token is black.}$$

Token forwarding preserves P_3 if black processes forward the token black.

Rule 3. When a black process forwards the token, the token becomes black.

Because (the token is *white*) $\Rightarrow \neg P_3$, termination can still be detected by p_0, namely, by whether it receives a white token (and is white itself, and passive).

Indeed, it can now be verified that internal actions, basic communication, and token forwarding preserve P. A wave ends unsuccessfully if, when the token returns to p_0, the token is black, p_0 is black, or $mc_{p_0} + q \neq 0$. If the wave ends unsuccessfully, a new one must be started.

Rule 4. When the wave ends unsuccessfully, p_0 initiates a new one.

The next wave would be as unsuccessful as its predecessor if there were no way for black processes to become white again; indeed, the black processes would blacken the token when forwarding it, causing the next wave to fail as well.

Observe that whitening process p_i does not falsify P if $i > t$, and that P always becomes true when p_0 initiates the wave by sending the token to p_{N-1}. This implies that whitening can safely take place upon forwarding the token.

Rule 5. Each process turns white immediately after sending the token.

This whitening regime suffices to guarantee the eventual success of a wave after termination of the basic computation. The algorithm is given as Algorithm 8.7.

Theorem 8.9 *Safra's algorithm (Algorithm 8.7) is a correct termination-detection algorithm for computations with asynchronous message passing.*

Proof. The algorithm has been designed so that the predicate P, defined by $P_m \wedge (P_0 \vee P_1 \vee P_2 \vee P_3)$, is an invariant of the algorithm.

To show the safety, observe that termination is detected when $t = 0$, $state_{p_0} = passive$, $color_{p_0} = white$, and $mc_{p_0} + q = 0$. These conditions imply $\neg P_3$, $\neg P_2$, and $\neg P_1$, hence $P_m \wedge P_0$, which together with $state_{p_0} = passive$ and $mc_{p_0} + q = 0$ implies **term**.

To show liveness, observe that after termination of the basic computation the message counters are constant and their sum equals 0. A wave started in such a configuration ends with $mc_{p_0} + q = 0$ and with all processes colored white, after which the next wave is guaranteed to be successful. $\square$

Unlike the Dijkstra–Feijen–Van Gasteren algorithm, Safra's algorithm does not have a bounded worst-case complexity; the token may be passed an unbounded number of times while all processes are passive, but some basic messages remain in transit for a long period of time. As for the Dijkstra–Feijen–Van Gasteren algorithm, a performance of $\Theta(T + N)$ messages may be expected for a basic computation with time complexity T.

The vector-counting algorithm. Mattern [Mat87] has proposed an algorithm comparable with Safra's algorithm, but which maintains a separate message count for each destination. For process p the message count is an array $mc_p[\mathbb{P}]$. When p sends to q, p updates the count with $mc_p[q] := mc_p[q] + 1$ and when p receives, p updates the count with $mc_p[p] := mc_p[p] - 1$. The token carries an array of counts also, and when p handles the token, mc_p is added to the token and reset to $\vec{0}$ (the array with each entry equal to 0). Termination is detected when the token equals $\vec{0}$.

The vector-counting algorithm has some advantages over Safra's algorithm, but also suffers from some serious disadvantages. One advantage of the algorithm is that termination is detected faster, namely within one round of the token after the occurrence of termination. A second advantage is that as long as the computation has not terminated, the token is suspended more often, which may reduce the number of control messages exchanged by the algorithm. In Safra's algorithm, each passive process forwards the token; in vector-counting algorithms such a process p will not forward the token if the information contained in the token implies that a message is still under way to p.

A major disadvantage of vector-counting algorithms is that the token contains a large amount of information (namely, an integer for each process),

var $state_p$: $(active, passive)$;
    $color_p$: $(white, black)$;
    $unack_p$: integer **init** 0 ;

S_p: { $state_p = active$ }
    begin send $\langle \mathbf{mes} \rangle$; $unack_p := unack_p + 1$;   (* Rule A *)
        $color_p := black$ (* Rule B *)
    end

R_p: { A message $\langle \mathbf{mes} \rangle$ from q has arrived at p }
    begin receive $\langle \mathbf{mes} \rangle$; $state_p := active$;
        send $\langle \mathbf{ack} \rangle$ to q (* Rule A *)
    end

I_p: { $state_p = active$ }
    begin $state_p := passive$ **end**

A_p: { An acknowledgement $\langle \mathbf{ack} \rangle$ has arrived at p }
    begin receive $\langle \mathbf{ack} \rangle$; $unack_p := unack_p - 1$ **end**   (* Rule A *)

Start the detection, executed once by p_0:
    begin send $\langle \mathbf{tok}, white \rangle$ to p_{N-1} **end**

T_p: (* Process p handles the token $\langle \mathbf{tok}, c \rangle$ *)
    { $state_p = passive \wedge unack_p = 0$ }
    begin if $p = p_0$
            then if $c = white \wedge color_p = white$
                then *Announce*
                else send $\langle \mathbf{tok}, white \rangle$ to p_{N-1}
        else if $(color_p = white)$
                then send $\langle \mathbf{tok}, c \rangle$ to $Next_p$
                else send $\langle \mathbf{tok}, black \rangle$ to $Next_p$;
        $color_p := white$ (* Rule B *)
    end

Algorithm 8.8 TERMINATION DETECTION USING ACKNOWLEDGEMENTS.

---

which must be passed in every control message. This disadvantage may not be too serious if the number of processes is small. Another disadvantage is that knowledge of other processes' identities is required. If the vector is represented as an array, each process must know the entire collection of process identities in advance, but this requirement can be relaxed if the vector is represented as a collection of identity–integer pairs. Initially each process must know at least the identities of its neighbors (in order to increment the count correctly), and the other identities will be learned during the computation.

8.3.3 Using Acknowledgements

Safra's algorithm counts the basic messages that are sent and received in order to establish that no basic messages are under way. It is also possible to guarantee this using acknowledgements; several authors have proposed such an augmentation of the Dijkstra–Feijen–Van Gasteren algorithm, see, e.g., Naimi [Nai88]. This variation of the principle is discussed only briefly because the resulting algorithm is not in any respect an improvement on the Shavit–Francez algorithm, and has therefore become obsolete.

First, observe that *no message is in transit* is equivalent to *for all p, no message sent by p is in transit*. Each process is responsible for the messages it has sent, i.e., it must prevent the call to *Announce* until it can be certain that all basic messages sent by that process have been received. The detection method defines for each process p a local condition $quiet(p)$ in such a way that

$$quiet(p) \Rightarrow (state_p = passive \land \text{no basic message sent by } p \text{ is in transit})$$

is satisfied. Then $(\forall p : quiet(p)) \Rightarrow$ **term**.

In order to establish that no message sent by p is in transit, each message is acknowledged and each process maintains a count of the number of acknowledgements it must still receive. Formally, the assertion P_a defined by

$$P_a \equiv \forall p : (unack_p = \quad \#(\text{messages in transit with sender } p) \\ + \#(\text{acknowledgements in transit to } p))$$

is maintained invariant by the following rule.

Rule A. When sending a message, p increments $unack_p$; when receiving a message from q, p sends an acknowledgement to q; when receiving an acknowledgement, p decrements $unack_p$.

The requirement set above for *quiet* (namely, that $quiet(p)$ implies that p is passive and no basic message sent by p is in transit) is now satisfied if *quiet* is defined by

$$quiet(p) \equiv (state_p = passive \land unack_p = 0).$$

The derivation of the detection algorithm proceeds in approximately the same steps as the Dijkstra–Feijen–Van Gasteren algorithm and starts by considering the assertion P_0, defined by

$$P_0 \equiv \forall i \ (N > i > t) : quiet(p).$$

The introduction of P_1 needs some care, because the activation of process

p_j with $j > t$ by p_i with $i \leq t$ does not take place in the same event as the sending of a message by p_i. It is the case, however, that when p_j is activated (thus falsifying P_0), $unack_{p_i} > 0$. Hence if the assertion P_b, defined by

$$P_b \equiv \forall p : (unack_p > 0 \Rightarrow color_p = black),$$

is maintained by observing

Rule B. When a process sends it becomes black; a process becomes white only when it is quiet.

the conclusion is again justified that when P_0 is falsified, P_1 holds, hence $(P_0 \vee P_1)$ is not falsified.

The resulting algorithm is given as Algorithm 8.8, and its invariant is $P_a \wedge P_b \wedge (P_0 \vee P_1 \vee P_2)$, where

$$
\begin{aligned}
P_a &\equiv &&\forall p : (unack_p = &&\#(\text{messages in transit with sender } p) \\
& && && + \#(\text{acks. in transit with destination } p)) \\
P_b &\equiv &&\forall p : (unack_p > 0 \Rightarrow color_p = black) \\
P_0 &\equiv &&\forall i \ (N > i > t) : quiet(p) \\
P_1 &\equiv &&\exists i \ (t \geq i \geq 0) : color_{p_i} = black \\
P_2 &\equiv &&\text{the token is black.}
\end{aligned}
$$

Theorem 8.10 *Algorithm 8.8 is a correct termination-detection algorithm for computations with asynchronous message passing.*

Proof. Termination is announced when p_0 is quiet and processes the white token. These conditions imply that $\neg P_2$ and $\neg P_1$, and hence $P_a \wedge P_b \wedge P_0$ holds. This implies with $quiet(p_0)$ that all processes are quiet, hence **term** holds.

When the basic computation terminates, within some time all acknowledgements are received and all processes become quiet. The first wave that starts when all processes are quiet terminates with all processes white, and termination is announced at the end of the next wave.   □

A solution based on bounded message delay. In [Tel91b, Section 4.1.3] a class of solutions for termination detection (and other problems) is described based on the assumption that the delay of a message is bounded by a constant μ (see also Section 3.2). In these solutions, a process remains unquiet for a μ-time interval after the emission of its most recent message and a process also remains black as long as it is unquiet, as in the solution using acknowledgements described above. Process p becomes quiet if (1) the most recent sending by p is at least μ time units ago, and (2) p is passive. The complete formal derivation of the algorithm is left to the reader.

8.3.4 Termination Detection with Waves

All termination-detection algorithms discussed so far in this section use a ring subtopology for control communication; the algorithms are all based on the wave algorithm for rings. Similar solutions have been proposed for other topologies; for example, Francez and Rodeh [FR82] and Topor [Top84] gave an algorithm using a rooted spanning tree for control communication. Tan and Van Leeuwen [TL86] gave decentralized solutions for ring networks, for tree networks, and for arbitrary networks. Inspection of these solutions reveals that they are almost similar, except for the wave algorithm on which they rely.

This subsection sketches a derivation of a termination-detection algorithm (and its invariant) based on an arbitrary wave algorithm, rather than a specific algorithm (the ring algorithm). For each wave, the first event in which a process sends a message for the wave or decides, is called the *visit* to that process. It is assumed that, if necessary, the process can suspend the visit until the process satisfies a local condition. Later events of the same wave in that process are never suspended.

This subsection presents the derivation only for the case of synchronous message passing of the basic computation (as for the derivation in Subsection 8.3.1). This derivation can be generalized to the asynchronous case in a way similar to that of Subsections 8.3.2 and 8.3.3.

The invariant of the algorithm must allow termination to be detected when the wave decides; therefore, as a first attempt, we set $P = P_0$, where

$$P_0 \quad \equiv \quad \text{all visited processes are passive.}$$

Indeed, as all processes have been visited when the decision occurs, this assertion allows termination detection when the wave decides. Moreover, P_0 is established when the wave is initiated (no process has been visited yet). The activity of the wave algorithm preserves P_0 if rule 1 below is observed.

Rule 1. Only passive processes are visited by the wave.

Unfortunately, P_0 is falsified when a visited process is activated by an unvisited process. Therefore, each process is provided with a color, and P is weakened to $(P_0 \vee P_1)$, where

$$P_1 \quad \equiv \quad \text{there is an unvisited black process.}$$

The weaker invariant is preserved under rule 2.

Rule 2. A sending process becomes black.

The weaker assertion can be falsified by the wave if a visit is made to the only unvisited black process. The situation is saved by a further weakening of P. Each process submits a color, either white or black, as input to the wave. The wave is modified so as to compute the *darkest* of the submitted colors; recall that waves can compute infima, and "the darkest" is an infimum. When the wave decides, the darkest of all submitted colors will be computed; this will be white if all processes submitted white and black if at least one process submitted black. During the wave, the wave will be called white if no process has yet submitted black; and black if at least one process has already submitted black. Thus a process, when it is visited, either submits white, which leaves the color of the wave unchanged, or submits black, which colors the wave black.

P is weakened to $(P_0 \lor P_1 \lor P_2)$, where

$$P_2 \quad \equiv \quad \text{the wave is black.}$$

This assertion is preserved under the following rule.

Rule 3. A process, when visited, submits its current color to the wave.

Indeed, all basic communication as well as wave activity preserves this assertion, which is therefore an invariant. A wave ends unsuccessfully if the processes decide for black, but in this case a new wave is simply initiated. The new wave can only be successful if processes can become *white*, and this happens immediately after the visit of the wave.

Rule 4. A decider in a black wave initiates a new wave.

Rule 5. Each process turns white immediately after each visit of a wave.

These rules guarantee the eventual success of a wave after the termination of the basic computation. Indeed, if the basic computation has terminated, the first wave started after termination makes all processes white, and the next wave terminates successfully.

In this algorithm only one wave may be running at any time. If two waves, say A and B, run concurrently, the whitening of a process after a visit of B may violate the invariant for wave A. Therefore, if the detection algorithm must be decentralized, a decentralized wave algorithm must be used so that all initiators of the detection algorithm cooperate in the same wave. It is also possible to use a different detection principle, in which different waves can compute concurrently without violating the correct operation of the detection algorithm; see Subsection 8.4.2.

8.4 Other Solutions

Two more solutions to the termination-detection problem are discussed in this section: the credit-recovery algorithm and the timestamp algorithm.

8.4.1 The Credit-recovery Algorithm

Mattern [Mat89a] has proposed an algorithm that detects termination very fast, namely, within one time unit after its occurrence (under the idealized timing assumptions of Definition 6.31). The algorithm detects the termination of a centralized computation and assumes that each process can send a message to the initiator of the computation directly (i.e., the network contains a star with the initiator as the center).

In the algorithm each message and each process are assigned a *credit* value, which is always between 0 and 1 (inclusive), and the algorithm maintains the following assertions as invariants.

S1. The sum of all credits (in messages and processes) equals 1.
S2. A basic message has a positive credit.
S3. An active process has a positive credit.

Processes holding a positive credit when this is not prescribed according to these rules (i.e., passive processes) send their credit to the initiator. The initiator acts as a bank, collecting all credits sent to it in a variable *ret* (for *returned*).

When the initiator owns all the credits, the requirement for active processes and basic messages to have a positive credit implies that there are no such processes and no such messages; hence **term** holds.

Rule 1. When $ret = 1$, the initiator calls *Announce*.

In order to fulfill the liveness requirement, it must be ensured that if termination occurs, all credits are eventually transferred to the initiator. If the basic computation has terminated, there are no basic messages any more, and we only need to concern ourselves with the credits held by processes.

Rule 2. When a process becomes passive, it sends its credit to the initiator.

In the initial configuration only the initiator is active and has a positive credit, namely 1, and $ret = 0$, which implies that S1 through S3 are satisfied. The invariant must be maintained during the computation; this is taken care of by the following rules. First, each basic message must be given a positive credit when it is sent; fortunately, its sender is active, and hence has a positive credit.

var $state_p$: $(active, passive)$ **init if** $p = p_0$ **then** *active* **else** *passive* ;
     $cred_p$: fraction   **init if** $p = p_0$ **then** 1 **else** 0 ;
     ret : fraction   **init** 0 ;   for p_0 only

S_p: $\{ state_p = active \}$ (* Rule 3 *)
     begin send $\langle \mathbf{mes}, cred_p/2 \rangle$; $cred_p := cred_p/2$ **end**

R_p: $\{$ A message $\langle \mathbf{mes}, c \rangle$ has arrived at $p \}$
     begin receive $\langle \mathbf{mes}, c \rangle$; $state_p := active$;
          $cred_p := cred_p + c$ (* Rules 4 and 5b *)
     end

I_p: $\{ state_p = active \}$
     begin $state_p := passive$;
          send $\langle \mathbf{ret}, cred_p \rangle$ to p_0 ; $cred_p := 0$ (* Rule 2 *)
     end

A_{p_0}: $\{$ A $\langle \mathbf{ret}, c \rangle$ message has arrived at $p_0 \}$
     begin receive $\langle \mathbf{ret}, c \rangle$; $ret := ret + c$;
          if $ret = 1$ **then** *Announce*   (* Rule 1 *)
     end

Algorithm 8.9 THE CREDIT-RECOVERY ALGORITHM.

Rule 3. When the active process p sends a message, its credit is divided among p and the message.

A process must be given a positive credit when it is activated; fortunately, the message it receives at that point contains a positive credit.

Rule 4. When a process is activated it is given the credit of the message activating it.

The only situation not covered by these rules is the receipt of a basic message by an already active process. The process already has a positive credit, hence does not need the credit of the message in order to satisfy S3; however, the credit may not be destroyed as this would lead to a violation of S1. The receiving process may handle the credit in two different ways, both giving rise to a correct algorithm.

Rule 5a. When an active process receives a basic message, the credit of that message is sent to the initiator.

Rule 5b. When an active process receives a basic message, the credit of that message is added to the credit of the process.

The algorithm is given as Algorithm 8.9. In this algorithm, it is assumed that each process knows the name of the initiator (at least when it first becomes passive) and the algorithm implements Rule 5b. When the initiator becomes passive, it sends a message to itself.

Theorem 8.11 *The credit-recovery algorithm (Algorithm 8.9) is a correct termination-detection algorithm.*

Proof. The algorithm implements rules 1 through 5, which implies that $S_1 \wedge S_2 \wedge S_3$ is an invariant, where

$$S_1 \equiv 1 = \left(\sum_{\langle \mathbf{mes}, c \rangle} c \right) + \left(\sum_{p \in \mathbb{P}} cred_p \right) + \left(\sum_{\langle \mathbf{ret}, c \rangle} c \right) + ret$$

$$S_2 \equiv \forall \langle \mathbf{mes}, c \rangle \text{ in transit} : c > 0$$

$$S_3 \equiv \forall p \in \mathbb{P} : (state_p = passive \Rightarrow cred_p = 0)$$

$$\wedge \ (state_p = active \Rightarrow cred_p > 0).$$

Termination is detected when $ret = 1$, which together with the invariant implies that **term** holds.

To show liveness, observe that after termination no basic actions occur, hence only receipts of $\langle \mathbf{ret}, c \rangle$ messages occur and each receipt decreases the number of messages in transit by one. Consequently, the algorithm reaches a terminal configuration. In such a configuration there are no basic messages (by **term**), $cred_p = 0$ for all p (by **term** and S_3), and there are no $\langle \mathbf{ret}, c \rangle$ messages (the configuration is terminal). Consequently, $ret = 1$ (from S_1), and termination is detected. □

If rule 5a is implemented, the number of control messages equals the number of basic messages plus one. (Here we also count messages sent by p_0 to itself upon becoming passive.) If rule 5b is implemented, the number of control messages equals the number of internal events in the basic computation plus one, which is *at most* equal to the number of basic messages plus one. It would appear that rule 5b is to be preferred from the viewpoint of the message complexity of the control algorithm. The situation is different when the bit complexity is considered. Under rule 5a, each amount of credit in the system except ret is a negative power of 2 (i.e., equal to 2^{-i} for some natural number i). Representing the credit by its negative logarithm reduces the number of bits to be transmitted.

The credit-recovery algorithm is the only algorithm in this chapter that requires additional information (namely, the credit) to be included in basic messages. Adding information to basic messages is called *piggybacking*. If piggybacking is not desirable, the credit of a message can be transmitted in a control message, sent immediately after the basic message. (The algorithm of the next subsection also requires piggybacking if it is implemented using Lamport's logical clock.)

A problem may arise if the credits (of messages and processes) are stored in a fixed number of bits. In this case there exists a smallest positive credit, and it is not possible to divide this amount of credit into two. When a credit with the smallest possible value must be divided, the basic computation is suspended while the process acquires additional credit from the initiator. The initiator subtracts this amount from ret (ret may become negative as a result) and transmits it to the requesting process, which resumes the basic computation upon its receipt. This credit raising introduces a blocking of the basic computation, contradicting the requirement that a termination-detection algorithm should not influence the basic computation. Fortunately, these operations are rare.

8.4.2 Solutions Using Timestamps

This subsection discusses solutions to the termination-detection problem based on the use of timestamps. The processes are assumed to be equipped with clocks (Subsection 2.3.3) for this purpose; hardware clocks as well as Lamport's logical clock (Subsection 2.3.3) can be used. The detection principle was proposed by Rana [Ran83].

Like the solutions of Subsection 8.3.3, Rana's solution is based on a local predicate $quiet(p)$ for each process p, where

$$quiet(p) \Rightarrow state_p = passive \land \text{no basic message sent by } p \text{ is in transit,}$$

which implies $(\forall p\ quiet(p)) \Rightarrow \textbf{term}$. As before, $quiet$ is defined by

$$quiet(p) \equiv (state_p = passive \land unack_p = 0).$$

The algorithm aims to check whether, for a certain point in time t, all processes were quiet at time t; termination at time t follows. This is done by a wave, which asks each process to confirm that it was quiet at that time and later; a process that was not quiet does not respond to messages of the wave, effectively extinguishing the wave.

Unlike the solutions in Section 8.3 the visit of a wave to process p does not affect the variables of process p used for termination detection. (The visit of the wave may affect variables of the wave algorithm and, if Lamport's logical clock is used, the clock of the process.) As a consequence the correct operation of the algorithm is not disturbed by the concurrent execution of several waves.

var $state_p$: $(active, passive)$;
    θ_p : integer **init** 0 ;   (* Logical clock *)
    $unack_p$: integer **init** 0 ;   (* Number of unacknowledged messages *)
    qt_p : integer **init** 0 ;   (* Time of most recent transition to *quiet* *)

$\mathbf{S}_p$: { $state_p = active$ }
    begin $\theta_p := \theta_p + 1$; send $\langle$**mes**, $\theta_p\rangle$; $unack_p := unack_p + 1$ **end**

$\mathbf{R}_p$: { A message $\langle$**mes**, $\theta\rangle$ from q has arrived at p }
    begin receive $\langle$**mes**, $\theta\rangle$; $\theta_p := \max(\theta_p, \theta) + 1$;
            send $\langle$**ack**, $\theta_p\rangle$ to q ; $state_p := active$
    end

$\mathbf{I}_p$: { $state_p = active$ }
    begin $\theta_p := \theta_p + 1$; $state_p := passive$;
            if $unack_p = 0$ **then** (* p becomes quiet *)
                begin $qt_p := \theta_p$; send $\langle$**tok**, $\theta_p, qt_p, p\rangle$ to $Next_p$ **end**
    end

$\mathbf{A}_p$: { An acknowledgement $\langle$**ack**, $\theta\rangle$ has arrived at p }
    begin receive $\langle$**ack**, $\theta\rangle$; $\theta_p := \max(\theta_p, \theta) + 1$;
         $unack_p := unack_p - 1$;
         if $unack_p = 0$ **and** $state_p = passive$ **then** (* p becomes quiet *)
            begin $qt_p := \theta_p$; send $\langle$**tok**, $\theta_p, qt_p, p\rangle$ to $Next_p$ **end**
    end

$\mathbf{T}_p$: { A token $\langle$**tok**, $\theta, qt, q\rangle$ has arrived at p }
    begin receive $\langle$**tok**, $\theta, qt, q\rangle$; $\theta_p := \max(\theta_p, \theta) + 1$;
         if $quiet(p)$ **then**
            if $p = q$ **then** *Announce*
            else if $qt \geq qt_p$ **then** send $\langle$**tok**, $\theta_p, qt, q\rangle$ to $Next_p$
    end

Algorithm 8.10 RANA'S ALGORITHM.

Rana's algorithm is decentralized; each process executes exactly the same detection algorithm. A decentralized algorithm could also be obtained by providing the algorithm of Subsection 8.3.4 with a decentralized wave algorithm. In Rana's solution the processes can initiate private waves, which run concurrently.

Process p, when becoming quiet, stores the time qt_p at which this happens, and starts a wave to check whether all processes have been quiet since qt_p. If this is the case, termination is detected. Otherwise, there will be a process that becomes quiet later, and a new wave will be started. Algorithm 8.10 implements this principle, using Lamport's clock and using the ring algorithm as a wave.

Theorem 8.12 *Rana's algorithm (Algorithm 8.10) is a correct termination-detection algorithm.*

Proof. To prove the liveness of the algorithm, assume **term** holds in a configuration γ where a acknowledgements are still in transit. From then on, only A_p and T_p actions occur. As each A_p action decreases the number of $\langle \textbf{ack}, \theta \rangle$ messages in transit by one, only a finite number of these steps occurs. Each process becomes quiet at most once; hence a token is generated at most N times, and each token is passed at most N times. Hence within $a + N^2$ steps the termination-detection algorithm reaches a terminal configuration δ, in which **term** still holds.

Let p_0 be a process with the maximal value of qt in δ, i.e., in the terminal configuration $qt_{p_0} \geq qt_p$ for each process p. When p_0 became quiet for the last time (i.e., at time qt_{p_0}), it sent out a token $\langle \textbf{tok}, qt_{p_0}, qt_{p_0}, p_0 \rangle$. This token was passed all the way around the ring and returned to p_0. Indeed, each process p must have been quiet and have satisfied $qt_p \leq qt_{p_0}$ when it received this token. If not, p would have set its clock to a value greater than qt_{p_0} upon receipt of the token and become quiet later than p_0, contradicting the choice of p_0. When the token returned to p_0, p_0 was still quiet, and hence called *Announce*.

To prove the safety of the algorithm, assume process p_0 calls *Announce*; this occurs when p_0 is quiet and receives back its token $\langle \textbf{tok}, \theta, qt, p_0 \rangle$, which has been forwarded by all processes. The proof continues by contradiction. Assume that **term** does not hold when p_0 detects termination; this implies that there is a process p such that p is not quiet. In this case p has become unquiet *after* forwarding p_0's token; indeed, p was quiet when it forwarded this token. Let q be the *first* process that became unquiet after forwarding the token $\langle \textbf{tok}, \theta, qt, p_0 \rangle$. This implies that q was activated by the receipt of a message from a process, say r, that had not yet forwarded p_0's token. (Otherwise r would have become unquiet after forwarding the token, but before q became unquiet, contradicting the choice of q.)

Now after forwarding the token, $\theta_q > qt_{p_0}$ continues to hold. This implies that the acknowledgement for the message that made q unquiet, sent to r, carries a timestamp $\theta_0 > qt_{p_0}$. Thus, when r became quiet, after the receipt of this acknowledgement, $\theta_r > qt_{p_0}$ holds, and hence $qt_r > qt_{p_0}$ holds when r receives the token. According to the algorithm r does not forward the token; this is a contradiction. □

A correctness proof using invariants and a norm function was given by Van Wezel [WT94]. A presentation of this algorithm that does not rely on the ring topology, was given by Huang [Hua88].

Exercises to Chapter 8
Section 8.1

Exercise 8.1 *Characterize the active and passive states of Algorithm A.2. Where are these states found in Algorithm A.1?*

Section 8.2

The *time complexity* of a termination-detection algorithm is defined as the worst-case number of time units (under the idealized assumptions of Definition 6.31) between the termination of the basic computation and the call to *Announce*.

Exercise 8.2 *What is the time complexity of the Dijkstra–Scholten algorithm?*

Exercise 8.3 *The Shavit–Francez algorithm is applied in an arbitrary network with unique identities, and to keep control-message overheads low the Gallager–Humblet–Spira algorithm is used as the wave algorithm. The time complexity of the detection is $\Omega(N \log N)$.*
Can you improve the time complexity to $O(N)$ at the cost of exchanging $O(N)$ additional control messages?

Section 8.3

Exercise 8.4 *Why is the predicate P_0 in the derivation of the Dijkstra–Feijen–Van Gasteren algorithm not falsified if p_j is activated by p_i, where $j \leq t$ or $i > t$?*

Exercise 8.5 *Show that for each m there exists a basic computation that exchanges m messages and forces the Dijkstra–Feijen–Van Gasteren algorithm to exchange $m \cdot (N - 1)$ control messages.*

Section 8.4

Exercise 8.6 *What modifications must be made in Algorithm 8.9 to implement rule 5a of the credit-recovery algorithm, instead of rule 5b?*

Exercise 8.7 *It is assumed in Rana's algorithm that processes have identities. Now assume instead that processes are anonymous, but have a means of sending messages to their successors in the ring, and that the number of processes is known. Modify Algorithm 8.10 to work under this assumption.*

Exercise 8.8 *Show the correctness of Rana's algorithm (Algorithm 8.10) from an invariant of the algorithm.*

Exercise 8.9 *Rewrite Rana's algorithm (Algorithm 8.10) so as to use an arbitrary wave algorithm for communication, rather than the ring algorithm.*

9

Anonymous Networks

In earlier chapters the assumption was usually made that unique identities are available to distinguish the processes of a distributed system. This assumption is valid in most of the existing distributed systems; the identity of a process is often taken as the address used to send messages to the process. For the latter purpose, however, it is also possible for processes to be identified via *indirect addressing* (Subsection 2.4.4), where each process distinguishes between its neighbors by locally known channel names.

A different use of identities was made in Chapter 7, where the identities of processes were employed to break the symmetry between processes. A typical example of this phenomenon is already found in a simple algorithm like that of Chang and Roberts (Algorithm 7.3), when it is initiated by two processes, p and q. In this computation, p receives q's token and q receives p's token; the situation would be completely symmetric if no ordering on process identities were available. The symmetry is broken by this ordering; the smaller of the two processes survives, the larger becomes defeated. More complicated examples of symmetry breaking by means of identity comparisons are found in other algorithms in Chapter 7.

Globally unique identities have also been used to detect termination, e.g., in Finn's algorithm (Algorithm 6.9). A process detects that it has indirectly received information about all processes if two collections of names coincide, where collection *Inc* includes the names of all neighbors of processes in *NInc* (for details, see Subsection 6.2.6). A similar use of identities was made, but in a much more sophisticated way, in the Gallager–Humblet–Spira algorithm (Subsection 7.3.2).

This chapter compares the power of *anonymous* networks with the power of *named* networks; what kind of problems solvable on named networks are also solvable on anonymous networks? This question is a relevant one, albeit mainly from a theoretical point of view because even though most distributed systems do provide unique names for the processes. But also in practice we may encounter anonymous networks, when cheap (eg., embedded) devices are combined into a network. The Lego MindStorm toys serve as an example here: multiple controllers can be put together in a Lego model and communicate, but the controllers are series-produced chips and all identical. First, the results in this chapter indicate classes of problems that cannot be solved without actually using the process names; a perhaps unexpected example is the implementation of synchronous message passing (see Subsection 9.1.4). Second, the results imply that certain conditions must be satisfied if networks are to be constructed from identical processors, such as Transputer or Lego MindStorm chips. The components must be equipped with a random-number generator in order to execute probabilistic algorithms and the size of the network must be known to the processors, or a centralized initialization of the network must be applied. Indeed the MindStorm controllers do provide random numbers.

It is shown in this chapter that it is possible to break the symmetry in anonymous networks but that it is not possible to detect termination unless the size of the network is known. Breaking the symmetry is possible by using *probabilistic algorithms*. In such algorithms processes repeatedly "flip a coin" until their outcomes differs; when this happens, the symmetry is broken. Needless to say, the distributed algorithm for comparing and repeating the tosses turns out to be more complicated than this concise statement of the principle (see Section 9.3). Termination detection is possible if the network size is known; the number of processes agreeing on the result is counted, and termination is detected when the count equals the network size. It is not possible to detect termination by using coin tosses because, with a very small probability, processes will draw identical results when tossing, after which termination may be concluded erroneously (see Subsection 9.4).

It was mentioned that probabilistic algorithms can fruitfully be used in anonymous networks to break the symmetry; they are introduced formally in Section 9.1. They give rise to several probabilistic notions of correctness, also defined in that section. Besides their importance in anonymous networks, probabilistic algorithms are of interest in other fields of distributed computing: they also play an important role in obtaining fault resilience in distributed systems, as will be seen in Chapter 14. Further, for some problems solvable by deterministic algorithms, probabilistic solutions with a lower complexity exist; but we shall not discuss this issue further in this book.

9.1 Preliminaries

An *anonymous network* is a network in which unique identities are not available to distinguish the processes. It is also assumed that a leader is not a priori available. Consequently, all processes with the same degree are identical. Angluin [Ang80] proposed the term *line of processors* for an infinite sequence P_1, P_2, ... of processes, where P_i has degree i (i.e., is connected to i channels). The term *symmetric system* is also found to indicate networks where all processes are equal (i.e., symmetric).

9.1.1 Definitions

In this subsection it will be indicated how the model of distributed systems presented in Chapter 2 can be extended to cover algorithms that rely on randomization. Randomization is the use of "electronic coin flipping" and random-number generators to obtain a random behavior of a process, where each of several behaviors occurs with known probability. Randomization differs from the non-determinism that results from the unpredictability of relative speeds and the possibility that a process may continue its execution with different events. It is a programming tool that introduces a probability distribution on the collection of the computations of a system, and allows us to make statements about properties of the algorithm with a certain probability. Inherent non-determinism is not controllable and therefore an algorithm designer should always cope with the worst case over all choices that arise from inherent non-determinism.

Probabilistic algorithms. A *probabilistic process* is modeled as a process that tosses a coin with every step it executes. The collection of applicable steps depends not only on the state of the process, but also on the outcome of the coin toss in the previous step of the process. The first step of the process depends on a toss made in the initial state.

Non-probabilistic processes (or algorithms) are usually referred to as *deterministic processes* (or algorithms); but this term does not exclude the possibility that networks of non-probabilistic processes proceed non-deterministically. Such networks behave non-deterministically as according to the models of Chapter 2, but the choices depend on the scheduling of events in the computation and no probabilistic analysis is possible for these choices. The choices introduced through randomization are subject to probabilistic analysis, which introduces a probability distribution on the computations of a system. To make the distribution explicit, it is assumed in the formal model that the entire sequence of tosses made by the process during its execution is given prior to the execution.

In order to understand the formal definition, we first consider processes having only internal events. A *probabilistic process* is defined by a quadruple $p = (Z, I, \vdash^0, \vdash^1)$, where Z and I are as in Definition 2.4, and $\vdash^0$ and $\vdash^1$ are binary relations on Z. The ith step of the process must be according to $\vdash^0$ if the ith coin flip is a zero, and according to $\vdash^1$ otherwise. Let $\rho = (\rho_0, \rho_1, \ldots)$ be an infinite sequence of coin flips, i.e., of zeros and ones. A ρ-*execution* of p is a maximal sequence of states $c_0, c_1, \ldots$, such that $c_0 \in I$ and $(c_i, c_{i+1}) \in \vdash^{\rho_i}$. Observe that the inherent non-determinism is still there, because different events may be possible, given the outcome of the coin flip. However, no probabilistic assumptions about the latter choice can be made. About the probabilistic choices the assumption is made that for each $k \geq 0$, each sequence of k bits has the same probability (namely, 2^{-k}) of occurring as a prefix of ρ. Given a sequence ρ, the probabilistic process behaves like a deterministic process, which can be seen as a particular instantiation of the probabilistic process.

To introduce communication between processes, a process is defined as an octuple consisting of a set of states, a set of initial states, and six event relations, namely for send, receive, and internal events, both for a coin flip of zero and for a coin flip of one. A *probabilistic distributed algorithm* is modeled as a collection $\mathbb{P}$ of probabilistic processes. Rather than giving a complete formal definition, we indicate here how the definition differs from the definitions of Section 2.1.2. A *configuration* of a probabilistic distributed algorithm consists of a state and an integer for each process, and a collection of messages if the algorithm uses asynchronous message passing. The integer for each process counts the number of events that the process has executed. The transitions of the system are as in Section 2.1.2, with the addition that each transition concerning process p increments by one the count of the number of steps of p.

If ρ is an assignment of an infinite sequence ρ_p of zeros and ones to each process p, a ρ-*computation* of the system is a computation in which the ith transition concerning process p is in the event relation specified by the ith element of ρ_p. Given a collection ρ of sequences, the probabilistic algorithm behaves like a deterministic distributed algorithm, which can be seen as a particular instantiation of the probabilistic distributed algorithm. The probabilistic assumption is made that, for each $k > 0$, each collection of N sequences of k bits has equal probability (namely, 2^{-kN}) of occurring as the prefixes of the sequences of ρ. A consequence of this assumption is that in an instantiation of the probabilistic algorithm, each process executes a *different* local algorithm with probability one.

Probabilistic correctness and complexity. In this chapter we shall consider problems whose correctness is captured by a *postcondition* ψ; the aim of an algorithm is to reach a terminal configuration in which ψ is satisfied. The postcondition depends on the problem under consideration; for the election problem ψ reads "one process is in the state *leader* and other processes are in the state *lost*", while for an algorithm for the computation of the network size ψ reads "for each p, $size_p$ equals N". The terminal configuration is either message terminated (the processes are all waiting to receive a message) or process terminated (the processes are in a terminal state).

For deterministic algorithms correctness is expressed as in Section 2.2. A deterministic algorithm is *terminating* if a terminal configuration is reached in every computation. A deterministic algorithm is *partially correct* (with respect to postcondition ψ) if each terminal configuration of the algorithm satisfies ψ. A deterministic algorithm is *correct* if it is both terminating and partially correct.

For probabilistic algorithms correctness is defined via the correctness of the instantiations obtained by specifying ρ. A probabilistic algorithm is ρ-*terminating* if a terminal configuration is reached in every ρ-computation. A probabilistic algorithm is ρ-*partially correct* (with respect to postcondition ψ) if each terminal configuration of a ρ-computation satisfies ψ. A probabilistic algorithm is ρ-*correct* if it is both ρ-terminating and ρ-partially correct.

A probabilistic algorithm is *terminating* if it is ρ-terminating for every ρ. A probabilistic algorithm is *partially correct* if it is ρ-partially correct for every ρ. A probabilistic algorithm is *correct* if it is ρ-correct for every ρ.

A probabilistic algorithm is *terminating with probability* P if the probability that the algorithm is ρ-terminating is at least P. A probabilistic algorithm is *partially correct with probability* P if the probability that the algorithm is ρ-partially correct is at least P. A probabilistic algorithm is *correct with probability* P if the probability that the algorithm is ρ-correct is at least P.

Termination (or partial correctness or correctness) with probability one is not equivalent to termination (or partial correctness or correctness). A probabilistic algorithm may fail for a non-empty collection of assignments, where the probability of ρ being in that collection is zero.

The ρ-*message complexity* of a probabilistic algorithm is the maximal number of messages exchanged in any ρ-computation. The *average message complexity* of a probabilistic algorithm is the expected value of the ρ-message complexity. The time and bit complexity of a probabilistic algorithm are defined similarly.

Proving negative results. In this chapter some negative results will be proved, i.e., results that state that no algorithm exists that will achieve a certain postcondition. For deterministic algorithms such a proof is generally easier to obtain; it suffices to construct a single computation that does not terminate with a configuration satisfying ψ. A typical example of such a proof is found in Theorem 9.5.

The construction of a single infinite computation does not prove the non-existence of a probabilistic algorithm; such an algorithm may have infinite computations, and still terminate with probability one. To prove the impossibility of probabilistic solutions an incorrect computation can be constructed from an assumed correct computation starting from a different initial configuration. Examples of such proofs are found in Theorems 9.12 and 9.13.

9.1.2 Classification of Probabilistic Algorithms

Probabilistic algorithms are classified in *Las Vegas*, *Monte Carlo*, and *Sherwood* algorithms according to the degree of correctness guaranteed by the algorithm. A probabilistic algorithm can be correct (i.e., partially correct and terminating), or only correct with a certain probability, as explained in Subsection 9.1.1.

Sherwood algorithms. Correct probabilistic algorithms are called *Sherwood algorithms* [BB88]. As we are concerned with computability of problems (and not primarily with complexity), Sherwood algorithms are only of minor interest, due to the following observation.

Theorem 9.1 *If there exists a correct probabilistic algorithm that achieves a postcondition ψ, then there exists a correct deterministic algorithm that achieves ψ.*

Proof. Let PA be a probabilistic algorithm that is correct. PA is ρ-correct for *every* ρ, in particular for that in which only zeros are assigned to every process; let $\rho^{(0)}$ be this assignment.

Consider algorithm DA, which acts as PA when each coin flip produces the value zero (i.e., every call to the coin-flip is replaced by "0" in the program). This algorithm is deterministic, and it is correct because PA is $\rho^{(0)}$-correct. □

This result does not imply that Sherwood algorithms are useless; their average complexity may compare favourably with the (worst-case) complexity of the best deterministic algorithm. As an example, consider the Chang–Roberts election algorithm (Algorithm 7.3), whose message complexity is $\Theta(N^2)$ in the worst case but only $\Theta(N \log N)$ in the average case. In a randomized version, each process expands its name with a randomly chosen bitstring; this randomly chosen part is most significant in comparisons. Regardless of the distribution of the original identities, the expected complexity of the modified algorithm is the average case complexity of the original algorithm, i.e., $\Theta(N \log N)$ messages.

We shall not be concerned with Sherwood algorithms in this book.

Las Vegas and Monte Carlo algorithms. As a consequence of Theorem 9.1, the best one can achieve for a problem that cannot be solved deterministically is a probabilistic algorithm that is correct with probability P ($0 \le P \le 1$). Usually, either the termination or the partial correctness is satisfied in every execution.

Definition 9.2 *A Las Vegas algorithm is a probabilistic algorithm that*

    (1) *terminates with positive probability and*

    (2) *is partially correct.*

A Monte Carlo algorithm is a probabilistic algorithm that

    (1) *terminates and*

    (2) *is partially correct with positive probability.*

The probability of termination of a Las Vegas algorithm is often one; infinite executions do exist, but occur only if an unfavorable pattern of random bits is selected infinitely often. This means in practice that a Las Vegas algorithm always terminates, although only an *expected* number of steps can be given, no upper bound on the number of steps taken by the algorithm. An example of a Las Vegas algorithm is the election algorithm by Itai and Rodeh (Algorithm 9.4).

The probability of failure of a Monte Carlo algorithm (if it is not a Sherwood algorithm) is always smaller than 1. In an erroneous finite execution only finitely many random bits have been selected, hence the probability of the execution is positive. Usually an upper bound on the number of steps taken by a Monte Carlo algorithm can be given. An example of a Monte

Carlo algorithm is the algorithm by Itai and Rodeh to compute the ring size (Algorithm 9.5).

Under some additional constraints it is possible to obtain a Las Vegas algorithm from a Monte Carlo algorithm and vice versa; see Exercises 9.1 and 9.2.

Summary of relevant aspects. The algorithms in this chapter can be classified according to the following four criteria; we briefly indicate what type of algorithm is considered more attractive.

(1) *Network size known or unknown.* Algorithms not relying on knowledge of N are more attractive because they are more general.

(2) *Process- or message-termination.* Process-terminating algorithms are more attractive, because they terminate explicitly so processes can use the computed result.

(3) *Deterministic or probabilistic.* Deterministic algorithms are more attractive because no random number generator is required, and the correctness properties are stronger than those satisfied by Las Vegas or Monte Carlo algorithms.

(4) *Las Vegas or Monte Carlo.* Las Vegas algorithms are usually considered more attractive because their probabilistic termination is hardly distinguishable from termination in practical situations.

9.1.3 The Problems Considered in this Chapter

It is not our aim to present a complete theory of computing on anonymous networks, including the numerous results that have been obtained for these networks. Rather we intend to investigate the computational power of such networks when considering problems relating to election and computation of functions, including the network size.

These problems turn out to be fundamental. If a leader can be elected, the anonymous network is as powerful as a named network, because names can be assigned by a centralized algorithm as is demonstrated below. In Section 9.3 it will be shown that a leader can be elected by a probabilistic algorithm if the network size is known, which indicates the importance of computing the network size. Because the network size is easily computed by a centralized algorithm (as demonstrated below) election and computing the size are equivalent problems. It will be seen that the network size cannot be computed probabilistically and the election problem is unsolvable if the network size is not known.

var rec_p : integer   **init** 0 ; (* Counts number of received messages *)
     $father_p$: $\mathbb{P}$ **init** *udef* ;
     $size_p$: integer   **init** 1 ; (* Size of subtree of p *)

For the initiator:
     begin forall $q \in Neigh_p$ **do** send $\langle \mathbf{tok}, 0 \rangle$ to q ;
           while $rec_p < \#Neigh_p$ **do**
               begin receive $\langle \mathbf{tok}, s \rangle$; $rec_p := rec_p + 1$;
                     $size_p := size_p + s$
               end   (* The network size is $size_p$ *)
     end

For non-initiators:
     begin receive $\langle \mathbf{tok}, s \rangle$ from neighbor q ; $father_p := q$; $rec_p := rec_p + 1$;
           forall $r \in Neigh_p$, $r \neq father_p$ **do** send $\langle \mathbf{tok}, 0 \rangle$ to r ;
           while $rec_p < \#Neigh_p$ **do**
               begin receive $\langle \mathbf{tok}, s \rangle$; $rec_p := rec_p + 1$;
                     $size_p := size_p + s$
               end ;
           send $\langle \mathbf{tok}, size_p \rangle$ to $father_p$
     end

Algorithm 9.1 CENTRALIZED COMPUTATION OF THE NETWORK SIZE.

Centralized computations. The size of the network can easily be computed by a single computation of the echo algorithm if a unique starter process (a *leader*) is available. Each message sent upwards in the spanning tree induced by the computation reports the number of processes in the subtree of the sender; see Algorithm 9.1.

To assign unique names, the network size is first computed with Algorithm 9.1, after which the interval $\{0, \ldots, N - 1\}$ is divided among the processes, and each subtree receives an interval the length of which corresponds to its size.

Theorem 9.3 *There exists a deterministic centralized algorithm to compute the size of the network, which exchanges $2|E|$ messages and has time complexity $O(N)$. There exists a deterministic centralized algorithm to assign unique names, which exchanges $2|E| + (N - 1)$ messages and has time complexity $O(N)$.*

A more efficient algorithm for name assignement exists; see Exercise 9.3. A consequence of Theorem 9.3 is that, with only a small overhead, the availability of a leader can compensate for the absence of unique names.

Therefore it is assumed in the study of anonymous networks, in addition to the absence of names, that no leader is available.

9.1.4 Synchronous Versus Asynchronous Message Passing

The results concerning elections on anonymous cliques turn out to be sensitive to whether communication is by synchronous or asynchronous message passing. Under synchronous message passing two processes cooperate in a single transition of the system, in which the symmetry between the two processes can be broken.

Theorem 9.4 *There exists a deterministic, process terminating algorithm for election in a network of two processes that communicate by synchronous message passing.*

Proof. Each process has three states, namely *sleep*, *leader*, and *lost*, and the initial state is *sleep*. Each process can either send and enter the terminal state *leader*, or receive and enter the terminal state *lost*.

Consequently, the system has nine configurations, but only three are reachable; from the initial configuration (*sleep, sleep*) the system can move to (*leader, lost*) and (*lost, leader*). Both configurations are process terminated and contain exactly one process in the state *leader* and one process in the state *lost*.   □

This algorithm is taken from Angluin [Ang80]; she also generalized the algorithm to cliques of arbitrary size. There exists no deterministic algorithm for this problem if communication is by asynchronous message passing; this can be shown by an argument similar to the one that will be used in Theorem 9.5. We do not want to consider solutions in which the symmetry is broken by the communication mechanism; therefore we consider only systems where communication is by asynchronous message passing.

The solution provided by Angluin is quite topology specific and will not work in rings, for example. The impossibility results of this chapter will generalize to systems with synchronous message passing of arbitrary or ring topology.

The symmetry between two processes can be broken deterministically if messages are passed synchronously, but not if messages are passed asynchronously. A consequence is that there is no deterministic algorithm to implement synchronous message passing in an anonymous network that passes messages asynchronously.

9.2 Deterministic Algorithms

This section contains some results concerning deterministic algorithms. The most important result is negative; it is not possible to elect a leader deterministically, not even in a ring network when the size is known. It will also be proved that functions can be computed if the ring size is known, but not if the ring size is not known.

9.2.1 Deterministic Election: Negative Results

It will be shown in this subsection that no deterministic election is possible in anonymous networks. The proof uses the concept of *symmetric configurations*. It is shown that there exists a computation that starts in a symmetric configuration and reaches a symmetric configuration after every N steps. The impossibility of a deterministic solution follows from the observation that a correct algorithm does not terminate in a symmetric configuration.

Theorem 9.5 *There exists no deterministic algorithm for election in an anonymous ring of known size.*

Proof. The result is proved for the case of unidirectional rings, but it is fairly easy to obtain the proof for the bidirectional case when this proof is understood. Let the processes p_0 through p_{N-1} be arranged in a ring such that for $i < N-1$, p_i can send messages to p_{i+1} and p_{N-1} can send messages to p_0. For a configuration of the ring, let c_i denote the state of p_i and let M_i denote the collection of messages with destination p_i.

A configuration is called *symmetric* if all states are equal and the same set of messages is in transit to each process, i.e.,

$$\forall i, j : (c_i = c_j \ \wedge \ M_i = M_j).$$

For any algorithm for the ring, a computation $C = (\gamma_0, \gamma_1, \ldots)$ is constructed such that each configuration γ_{kN} in C is symmetric. Let γ_0 be a symmetric initial configuration. Such a configuration exists because each process has the same set of initial states, and initially all M_i are equal to $\varnothing$.

If configuration γ_{kN} is terminal, the construction is completed; the computation C terminates with a symmetric configuration. Otherwise, γ_{kN} is a symmetric configuration in which at least one event is applicable, say event e_i in p_i. The symmetry of the configuration now implies that the same event is applicable in every process. Theorem 2.19 implies that it can be executed by all processes concurrently, and after the execution of these N transitions a symmetric configuration results. Indeed, all processes move from the same state to the same state. If a message is received in the event, it is removed from each of the identical collections M_i, and if a message is sent it is added to each of the identical collections M_i. Hence the computation is extended by N steps, after which a symmetric configuration $\gamma_{(k+1)N}$ results.

It follows that each algorithm for the anonymous ring has a computation that is either infinite or ends in a symmetric terminal configuration. In a symmetric configuration either all processes are in the state *leader*, or no process is, so that in a symmetric configuration there is not exactly one process in the state *leader*. For a deterministic election algorithm, all computations end in a terminal configuration with one process in the state *leader*; consequently, no such algorithm exists.   □

Theorem 9.5 implies that the more general problem of election in arbitrary networks or rings of unknown size is also unsolvable by deterministic algorithms.

9.2.2 Computing Functions on the Ring

The impossibility of election raises the question whether there are "easier" problems that can be solved even when elections are impossible. In this subsection the problem of function evaluation on a directed anonymous ring is considered. Assume process p_i has an input $x_i \in X$, and let SX denote the set of all sequences of elements from X. A function f on SX is *cyclic* if it is invariant under cyclical shifts in input, i.e., $f(y) = f(x)$ for all cyclic shifts y of x. Examples of cyclic functions include: the sum, minimum or maximum of integers; conjunction, disjunction, or exclusive-or of booleans, length of the input; and so on. Assume that process p has a variable $result_p$; the postcondition of an algorithm to compute f reads "$result_p = f(x_0, \ldots, x_{N-1})$".

The results of this subsection indicate the importance of knowledge of the ring size, as well as the importance of the difference between message and process termination.

The ring size is known. If the ring size is known each cyclic function can be computed by a deterministic algorithm by collecting all inputs in every process, a solution known as *input collection*. Input collection costs $N(N-1)$ messages, and this is also the lower bound for computing some functions by a deterministic algorithm.

Theorem 9.6 *Any cyclic function f can be computed by a process-terminating deterministic algorithm using $N(N-1)$ messages if the ring size is known.*

Proof. To keep the argument simple, assume the channels are fifo. The algorithm sends messages in $N - 1$ phases. In the first phase, each process sends its own input to its clockwise neighbor and receives the input of its counterclockwise neighbor. In each next phase, each process sends the value it received in the previous round to its clockwise neighbor and receives a new value from its anticlockwise neighbor. As each input is passed one process further in every round, a process receives in the ith phase the input of its ith anticlockwise neighbor, and has collected all inputs (in the order in which they appear in the ring) after $N-1$ phases. After the communication rounds each process computes the value of f locally and terminates. □

Theorem 9.7 *Any deterministic process-terminating algorithm for computing AND, OR, or SUM exchanges at least $N(N - 1)$ messages in the worst case.*

Proof. Let a deterministic process-terminating algorithm A for one of these problems be given. Similarly to the definition in Subsection 7.2.3 the *trace* of a message is defined as follows. If p sends a message before it has received any message, the trace of this message is (p). If p sends a message m when the longest trace of any message it has received so far is $(p_1, \ldots, p_k)$, the trace of m is $(p_1, \ldots, p_k, p)$.

The three problems mentioned in the theorem have in common that, at least for one symmetric initial configuration, a process must receive a trace of length $N - 1$ before it can terminate. For the SUM problem this is the case for every initial configuration. For AND this is the case for the situation where each process has input *true*, and for OR this is the case for the situation where each process has input *false*. To see that a message with a trace of length $N - 1$ must be received, consider the evaluation of AND in the situation where each process has input *true*; the answer is *true* in this case. Assume a process terminates with output *true* when the longest trace of any message it has received has length $k < N - 1$. The event in which the process terminates causally depends only on events in $k + 1$ processes, and consequently it can also occur in a computation starting from an initial configuration where these k processes have input *true* and others have input *false*.

Again, call a configuration symmetric if each process is in the same state and each channel contains the same set of messages. As in the proof of Theorem 9.5 a computation is constructed in which a symmetric configuration is reached after every N steps, and in which every process executes the same set of events. The initial configuration can be chosen to force the algorithm to send at least one message with a trace of length $N - 1$. In the computation at least one message is sent with a trace of length i, for each $i \leq N - 1$. But as each process executes the same set of events, the number of messages sent with a trace of length i is a multiple of N, and hence is at least N. Consequently, the number of messages is at least $N.(N - 1)$. $\quad \square$

The ring size is not known. If the ring size is not known, non-constant functions cannot be computed by a process-terminating deterministic algorithm. The proof of this result uses the technique of replaying a (correct) computation of the algorithm in different parts of the ring. If f is a constant function (i.e., $f(x) = c$ for every x), its computation is trivially done by an algorithm that immediately terminates in every process p with $result_p = c$; the negative results concern non-constant functions only.

Theorem 9.8 *There exists no deterministic process-terminating algorithm for computing a non-constant function f if the ring size is not known.*

Proof. Because f is non-constant, there exist inputs $x = (x_0, \ldots, x_{k-1})$ and $y = (y_0, \ldots, y_{l-1})$ such that $f(x) \neq f(y)$; say $f(x) = a$ and $f(y) = b$. Let A be a deterministic, process-terminating algorithm such that there is a computation C_x, on the ring with input x, in which there is a process p that terminates with $result_p = a$ and there is a computation C_y, on the ring with input y, in which there is a process q that terminates with $result_q = b$.

Let the longest trace of any message received by p in C_x have length K; it is possible that $K > k$ because A may circle messages around the ring several times before p terminates. Consider a (larger) ring that contains a segment S of $K + 1$ processes with the following property. The last process of S (i.e., the process at the clockwise end of the segment) is given the same input as process p in computation C_x; call this process p'. The ith anticlockwise neighbor of p' is given the same input as the ith anticlockwise neighbor of p in computation C_x. The correspondence of processes in S to processes in the ring with input x is depicted in Figure 9.2.

Algorithm A, when executed on a ring that contains segment S, has a computation with the following property. For each $i \leq K$, the ith anticlockwise neighbor of process p' sends all messages having traces of length $\leq K + 1 - i$ that are sent by the ith anticlockwise neighbor of p in computation C_x. This is shown by a downward induction on K.

Case $i = K$: The Kth anticlockwise neighbor of p' has the same initial state as the Kth anticlockwise neighbor of p in C_x, and hence there is a

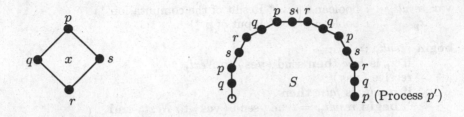

Figure 9.2 Construction of an incorrect computation.

computation in which it sends the same collection of messages having a trace of length one.

Inductive step: Assume that in some computation the $(i+1)$th anticlockwise neighbor of p' sends all the messages with traces of length $\leq K - i$ that are sent by the ith anticlockwise neighbor of p in computation C_x. In this computation, the ith anticlockwise neighbor of p' has the same initial state as the ith anticlockwise neighbor of p in C_x, and receives the same collection of messages having traces of length $\leq K - i$. Therefore there is a computation in which it sends the same collection of messages having traces of length $\leq K + 1 - i$ as the ith anticlockwise neighbor of p in C_x.

In the constructed computation, p' receives the same collection of messages as p does in C_x, and p' has the same initial state as p; consequently, there is a computation in which p' terminates with $result_{p'} = a$.

The constructed computation "fools" process p' into terminating with the outcome $result_{p'} = f(x)$, while actually the input is a longer sequence x', different from x. The computation would still give the correct answer if it were the case that $f(x') = f(x)$. To arrive at a contradiction, consider a ring that contains also a segment in which processes simulate computation C_y and a process q' terminates with $result_{q'} = b$. For this ring there is a computation in which two processes terminate with a different value of $result$; a contradiction because at most one answer is correct. □

Theorem 9.9 *OR and AND are computable by a deterministic message terminating algorithm in a ring of unknown size using at most N messages.*

Proof. The value of OR is *true* if at least one process has input *true* and the value is *false* if all processes have input *false*. Upon initialization, process p assigns $result_p := x_p$ and, if x_p is *true*, sends a ⟨**yes**⟩ message to its

var $result_p$: boolean ;   (* Result of the computation *)
     x_p : boolean ;   (* Input of p *)

begin $result_p := x_p$;
       if x_p is *true* **then** send $\langle$ **yes** $\rangle$ to $Next_p$;
       receive $\langle$ **yes** $\rangle$;
       if $result_p$ is *false* **then**
           begin $result_p := true$; send $\langle$ **yes** $\rangle$ to $Next_p$ **end**
end

Algorithm 9.3 DETERMINISTIC COMPUTATION OF OR.

---

clockwise neighbor. When such a message is received by process p, it is ignored if $result_p$ has the value *true*, and otherwise $result_p$ is set to *true* and the message is forwarded; see Algorithm 9.3.

First consider the case where each process has input *false*. Each process p assigns to $result_p$ the value *false* and starts waiting for a message. As no process sends a message, the configuration in which every process waits is terminal, and moreover, $result_p$ contains the correct answer (*false*) in this case.

Next consider the case where there are processes with input *true*. A process p with input *true* assigns to $result_p$ the value *true* and sends a message $\langle$ **yes** $\rangle$ to the next process. As each process sends at most one message (see the algorithm), a terminal configuration is reached in this case also. If in a terminal configuration $result_p = true$, then also $result_{Next_p} = true$, because the message sent by p is received by $Next_p$. As $result_p = true$ for at least one process p, it follows that $result_p = true$ for every process p, hence also in this case the algorithm terminates with the correct answer in every process.

The computation of AND is similar, but with all occurrences of *true* and *false* reversed. $\square$

Partial knowledge of the ring size. As a compromise between known and unknown ring size one may consider the situation where N is not known exactly, but is known to be between certain bounds. The following results are easily proved by modifying the proofs given in this subsection.

(1) There does not exist a deterministic algorithm for computing SUM that is correct for two different ring sizes.

(2) There does not exist a deterministic algorithm for computing XOR that is correct for both an even and an odd ring size.

(3) If an upper bound of S is known on the ring size, AND and OR can be computed deterministically using $N.(S-1)$ messages.

Other topologies. Replay arguments can also be given for other classes of network topology, but it requires that a small graph can be "unrolled" several times over a larger class of the graph. The required type of mapping from one graph to another is called a *cover*.

Algorithms for computing functions on anonymous networks have also been given for other topologies. Beame and Bodlaender [BB89] have shown that deterministic input collection is possible in $O(n^3)$ messages on an $n \times n$ torus, and that $\Omega(n^3)$ messages is a lower bound for some functions, including AND and OR. Kranakis and Krizanc showed that input collection is possible on an n-dimensional hypercube using $O(2^n.n^4)$ bits [KK90].

9.3 A Probabilistic Election Algorithm

If the network size is known, partially correct election algorithms can be given that terminate with probability one, i.e., the algorithms are of the Las Vegas type. As no deterministic algorithms exist (cf. Theorem 9.5), a Las Vegas algorithm is the best possible. An algorithm for election on anonymous rings of known size, proposed by Itai and Rodeh [IR81], will be presented here. The algorithm relies on the principles used in the Chang–Roberts algorithm (Algorithm 7.3), but to apply this algorithm some adaptations must be made.

First, because the Chang–Roberts algorithm relies on the availability of identities, any (anonymous) process p that acts as an initiator selects an identity id_p randomly from the set $\{1, \ldots, N\}$. This makes comparisons between the tokens of different processes possible, but also raises some new difficulties, due to the possibility that several processes may draw the same identity. In the Chang–Roberts algorithm, a process knows that it has received its own token when the identity in the token coincides with the identity of the process and this is a sufficient condition for the process to become *leader*.

Because several processes may select the same identity, a hop counter in the token is used by processes to recognize the receipt of their own token; p receives its own token when the hop count equals N. The receipt of the token implies that no process has selected a smaller identity; but this is not a sufficient condition to become *leader*, as there may be another process with the same identity. To detect this situation, each token also carries a boolean value *un*, which is true when the token is generated, but set to false

var $state_p$: (*sleep, cand, leader, lost*)   **init** *sleep* ;
  $level_p$: integer   **init** 0 ;
  id_p : integer ;
  $stop_p$: boolean   **init** false ;

begin if p is initiator **then**
      begin $level_p := 1$; $state_p := cand$; $id_p := \text{rand}(\{1, \ldots, N\})$;
           send $\langle \textbf{tok}, level_p, id_p, 1, true \rangle$ to $Next_p$
      end ;
    while not $stop_p$ **do**
      begin receive a message ; (* Either a token or a ready message *)
        if it is a token $\langle \textbf{tok}, level, id, hops, un \rangle$ **then**
          if $hops = N$ **and** $state_p = cand$ **then**
            if un **then** (* Become elected *)
              begin $state_p := leader$; send $\langle \textbf{ready} \rangle$ to $Next_p$;
                   receive $\langle \textbf{ready} \rangle$; $stop_p := true$
              end
            else (* There are more winners for this level *)
              begin $level_p := level_p + 1$; $id_p := \text{rand}(\{1, \ldots, N\})$;
                   send $\langle \textbf{tok}, level_p, id_p, 1, true \rangle$ to $Next_p$
              end
          else if $level > level_p$ **or** ($level = level_p$ **and** $id < id_p$) **then**
            begin $level_p := level$; $state_p := lost$;
                 send $\langle \textbf{tok}, level, id, hops + 1, un \rangle$ to $Next_p$
            end
          else if $level = level_p$ **and** $id = id_p$ **then**
              send $\langle \textbf{tok}, level, id, hops + 1, false \rangle$ to $Next_p$
            else skip (* Purge the token *)
        else (* The message is $\langle \textbf{ready} \rangle$ *)
            begin send $\langle \textbf{ready} \rangle$ to $Next_p$; $stop_p := true$ **end**
      end
end

Algorithm 9.4 THE ITAI–RODEH ELECTION ALGORITHM.

if it is forwarded by a process with the same identity. A process can thus become *leader* when it receives its own token with $un = true$.

The last difficulty concerns the situation where a process receives its own token, but with $un = false$; this indicates that the process does have minimal identity but that there exists another process with the same identity. All processes with minimal identity may receive their own token and "win" the Chang–Roberts algorithm. If this situation occurs, each "winner" of the Chang–Roberts algorithm starts a new round by initiating the Chang–Roberts algorithm again, but at a higher level. To prevent another tie, at the new level, a new identity must be chosen by each process that initiates the next level. The level is also indicated in the token, and tokens of some level abort all activity of smaller levels.

Summarizing, p's receipt of its own token makes it win the Chang–Roberts algorithm if it is still in state *cand*. If p is the only winner, it becomes *leader*, otherwise p initiates the Chang–Roberts algorithm at the next level. The receipt of another process's token causes p to become *lost* if this token has a higher level or the same level and a smaller identity; the token is forwarded. A token with equal level and identity is forwarded, but with *un* set to false. A token of lower level or of the same level but with larger identity is purged (i.e., its forwarding is aborted); see Algorithm 9.4. We shall continue by proving that the algorithm is partially correct, and that it terminates with probability one.

Lemma 9.10 *If at least one process generates a token at level l, either one process becomes elected at that level and no process generates a token at level $l + 1$, or at least one process generates a token at level $l + 1$.*

Proof. A token at level $l + 1$ can be generated by process p if p receives its own token (of level l).

Assume that process p generates a token at level l but its identity is not minimal among the identities chosen at level l. The token does not return to p in this case; if it is not purged by a process at a higher level, it is received by a process at the same level but with smaller identity, where it is purged. (Observe that all processes that generate a token at level l do so before the receipt of p's token of level l.) It follows that only a process that chose the minimal identity at level l can become elected at that level or generate a token at level $l + 1$.

Assume that p generates a token at level l and its identity is minimal among the identities chosen at level l. If the token is not purged by a process at a higher level (in which case at least one process generated a token at level $l + 1$) this token returns to p. Two cases arise: either p was the only process that chose the minimal identity at level l, or there are more processes that chose this identity. In the first case, the token returns with $un = true$ and p becomes elected. In the second case, the token returns with $un = false$ and a token at level $l + 1$ is generated. $\square$

Theorem 9.11 *The Itai–Rodeh algorithm (Algorithm 9.4) is an election algorithm for rings of known size that is partially correct and terminates with probability one.*

Proof. The partial correctness, i.e., that if the algorithm terminates there is exactly one leader, is proved using Lemma 9.10. Let l be the highest level at which a token was generated; l is defined because by assumption a finite computation is considered. No process was elected at a level smaller than l, and that no token was generated at level $l + 1$ implies that exactly one process was elected at level l.

It remains to show that the algorithm terminates with probability one. If for some level l there are $k > 1$ processes that generate a token at level l, there is a probability $P_k > 0$ that exactly one process chooses the minimal identity for this level, in which case the algorithm terminates. Let P be the minimum over k of P_k; now, if tokens are generated at level l, the probability that tokens will be generated also at level $l+1$ is at most $(1-P)$. Consequently, the probability that the algorithm has *not* terminated after l levels is bounded by $(1 - P)^l$, which has the limit zero if l goes to infinity.

□

A probabilistic analysis (given in [IR81]) reveals that the expected number of levels is bounded by $e.N(N - 1)$. The expected number of messages per level is bounded by $O(N \log N)$ (this is shown by an argument similar to the one used in Theorem 7.6), which implies that the expected complexity of the algorithm is $O(N \log N)$ messages.

Arbitrary networks. Using very similar ideas, an algorithm can be given for election in arbitrary networks. The algorithm is based on Algorithm 7.9 rather than on the Chang–Roberts algorithm. A process "wins" in a level of this algorithm if it has initiated the echo algorithm and receives an echo from all neighbors. As in the Itai–Rodeh algorithm this is not a sufficient condition for becoming leader, because it is possible that several processes with the same identity have initiated an election. To detect this, the size of the tree constructed by the echo algorithm is computed as in Algorithm 9.1; if there are several initiators with the same identity, each of the echo invocations constructs a tree containing only a subset of the processes. When a process completes the echo algorithm (by receiving an echo from every neighbor) it knows the size of the tree it has generated. If this size equals N, the process becomes elected; otherwise, the echo algorithm is initiated at a higher level.

The resulting algorithm is partially correct and terminates with probability one; its complete description is found in [Tel94]. Other algorithms for election are found in [SS89], [MA89].

9.4 Computing the Network Size

Various results in this chapter have indicated the importance of knowledge of the network size. In this section the problem of computing the size of an anonymous ring will be considered. The ring size can be computed only by a message-terminating algorithm and with a non-zero probability of arriving at a wrong answer.

9.4.1 Negative Results

This subsection contains two impossibility results concerning computation of the ring size. The proofs use the idea in the proof of Theorem 9.8, namely, the replay of a given (presumably correct) computation in different parts of a larger ring. For probabilistic algorithms it must be demonstrated that such a replay has a non-zero probability, but this follows from the fact that in a finite execution a process uses only a finite prefix of its sequence of random bits.

Theorem 9.12 *There exists no process-terminating algorithm for computing the ring size that is correct with probability $r > 0$.*

Proof. Assume that A is a probabilistic algorithm that has a ρ-computation C_N on a ring of size N and in C_N each process p terminates with $result_p = N$. Select one process p and let the longest trace of a message received by p in C_N have length K. Each process executes only finitely many steps in C_N; let L be the largest number of steps executed by any process in computation C_N.

Consider a larger ring that contains a segment of $K + 1$ processes; let p_0 be the last process, and let p_i bethe ith anticlockwise neighbor of p_0. Let ρ' be an assignment of bit sequences to the processes of this ring with the following property. The first L bits of ρ'_{p_0} are the same as the first L bits of ρ_p. The first L bits of ρ'_{p_i}, for $i \leq K$, are the same as the first L bits of ρ_q, where q is the ith anticlockwise neighbor of p in the N ring. When a segment of length $K + 1$ is fixed, the probability of such an assignment is very small, namely, $2^{-(K+1)L}$.

There exists a ρ'-computation C of A on the larger ring in which process p_i sends exactly the same messages with traces of length $\leq K + 1 - i$ as the ith anticlockwise neighbor of p in C_N. This is proved exactly as in Theorem 9.8. It is seen that for any fixed segment of length $K + 1$ there is a probability of at least $2^{-(K+1)L}$ that the processes in the segment replay computation C_N, in which case process p_0 terminates with $result_{p_0} = N$, which is incorrect.

The probability that this occurs on one fixed segment is extremely small; but by making the ring size very large the probability that it happens somewhere on the ring can be made arbitrary large. Let a probability $r > 0$ be given. Choose a natural number R such that $(1 - 2^{-(K+1).L})^R < r$ and consider a ring of size $R.(K+1)$. This ring has R disjoint segments of length $K+1$, and for each of these segments the probability is at most $1 - 2^{-(K+1).L}$ that its last process cannot terminate with an incorrect answer. It follows that the probability that no process can terminate with an incorrect answer is smaller than r.   □

Using the same argument it is in fact established that no non-constant function can be computed by a message-terminating algorithm that is correct with probability $r > 0$. The next impossibility result cannot be generalized to arbitrary non-constant functions. It states that no message terminating Las Vegas algorithm exists, so the best we can achieve is a message terminating Monte Carlo algorithm.

Theorem 9.13 *There exists no message-terminating algorithm for computing the ring size that is correct with probability one.*

Proof. Assume A is a probabilistic algorithm that has a ρ-computation C_N on the ring of size N, which message-terminates with $result_p = N$ for some p. Each process executes only finitely many steps in C_N; let L be the largest number of steps executed by any process in computation C_N. Number the processes of the size-N ring as p_0 through p_{N-1}.

Now consider a size-$2N$ ring of which the processes are numbered q_0 through q_{2N-1} and an assignment ρ' of bitstrings such that the first L bits of ρ'_{q_i} and $\rho'_{q_{i+N}}$ are the same as the first L bits of ρ_{p_i} for all $i < N$. A ρ'-computation of A on the size-$2N$ ring is constructed as follows. Each step of p_i in C_N is executed concurrently by q_i and by its antipode q_{i+N}. Since the last configuration of C_N is terminal, so is the last computation of C_{2N}, and in this configuration there are at least two processes q with $result_q = N$, which is an incorrect result in this case.

The probability of such an assignment ρ' is 2^{-2NL}, which is positive and shows that A does not compute ring sizes correctly with probability larger than $1 - 2^{-2NL}$.   □

The difference in the probabilities with which process- or message-terminating algorithms can be correct can be explained informally as follows.

A process-terminating algorithm gives an incorrect result if certain unlucky random choices are made *somewhere* in the ring. By making the ring size large, the probability that this happens increases. In a message-terminating algorithm the processes that made unlucky choices always have the possibility of recovering from their incorrect answer, namely, if they receive information from other processes. Consequently, a message-terminating algorithm gives an incorrect result if certain unlucky random choices are made *everywhere* in the ring. Although this can never be excluded, the probability that this happens is bounded, and in fact decreases when the ring size becomes large.

9.4.2 An Algorithm to Compute the Ring Size

This subsection presents a message-terminating Monte Carlo algorithm for computing the ring size. It will be shown that when the algorithm terminates, $est_p = N$ for all p with a probability that can be made arbitrarily large by choosing a parameter R of the algorithm. The algorithm is similar to the algorithm given by Itai and Rodeh [IR81], but slightly simplified.

Process p maintains a local *estimate*, est_p, of the ring size, for which it is guaranteed that at any time this estimate is conservative, i.e., $est_p \leq N$. Initially $est_p = 2$. Whenever p receives information that implies that est_p is not equal to the ring size, p increments its estimate.

In order to gain confidence in the correctness of its estimate, process p generates a token and sends it over a distance of est_p hops over the ring. If the estimate turns out to be correct, p receives its own token and if this happens, p will be (temporarily) satisfied and not take further actions. Process p receives a similar token in the case where N is in fact larger than est_p, but the (est_p)th anticlockwise neighbor of p has the same estimate and has initiated a token as well.

This situation (i.e., where p receives a token that is not its own) can be detected with high probability; each process chooses a random label from $\{1, \ldots, R\}$ and includes it in the token. The label of p remains unchanged as long as p's estimate is not incremented. If a token is received from another process, the included label differs from p's label with probability $1 - 1/R$, and if a process receives its own token the two labels certainly coincide.

Process p increases its estimate in the following two situations.

(1) *A token is received that contains an estimate est with est > est_p.* As it is ensured that all estimates are conservative, the receipt of this token implies that $N > est_p$.

```
cons R        : integer      ;   (* Determines correctness probability *)

var  est_p   : integer ;
     lbl_p   : integer ;

begin est_p := 2 ; lbl_p := rand({1, ..., R}) ;
      send ⟨test, est_p, lbl_p, 1⟩ to Next_p ;
      while true do
         begin receive ⟨test, est, lbl, h⟩ ;
               if est > est_p then      (* p's estimate must increase *)
                  if est = h then      (* est is also too low *)
                     begin est_p := est + 1 ; lbl_p := rand({1, ..., R}) ;
                           send ⟨test, est_p, lbl_p, 1⟩ to Next_p
                     end
                  else     (* forward token and increase est_p *)
                     begin send ⟨test, est, lbl, h + 1⟩ to Next_p ;
                           est_p := est ; lbl_p := rand({1, ..., R}) ;
                           send ⟨test, est_p, lbl_p, 1⟩ to Next_p
                     end
               else if est = est_p then
                  if h < est then send ⟨test, est, lbl, h + 1⟩ to Next_p
                  else (* This token has made est hops *)
                     if lbl ≠ lbl_p then
                        begin est_p := est + 1 ;
                              lbl_p := rand({1, ..., R}) ;
                              send ⟨test, est_p, lbl_p, 1⟩ to Next_p
                        end
                     else skip     (* Possibly p's token returned *)
               else (* est < est_p *) skip
         end
end
```

Algorithm 9.5 PROBABILISTIC COMPUTATION OF THE RING SIZE.

(2) *A token with estimate $est = est_p$ is received, this token has made est hops, but the included label differs from p's label.* This token was generated by p's (est)th anticlockwise neighbor, and this latter process has a label different from p. Consequently, p's (est)th anticlockwise neighbor is different from p and hence $N \neq est$.

A token with $est < est_p$ is purged (i.e, its propagation is aborted); see Algorithm 9.5.

Lemma 9.14 *The algorithm message-terminates after exchanging* $O(N^3)$ *messages. In the terminal configuration all est_p are equal, and their common value is bounded by N, i.e., for all p and q, $est_p = est_q \leq N$.*

Proof. The crucial step in proving termination is to demonstrate that the estimates indeed remain conservative. Observe that est_p never decreases, and that lbl_p changes only when est_p increases. This implies that as long as p's token $\langle \text{test}, est, lbl, h \rangle$ circulates and $est = est_p$, also $lbl_p = lbl$. Using this it can be shown inductively that all estimates that are computed are conservative.

Because the estimates found in tokens are estimates of processes, it suffices to consider the computation of estimates by processes, which takes place in three situations.

(1) Process p may increase est_p to est upon receipt of a token with estimate est; but as this estimate was computed earlier, it may be assumed by induction that it is conservative.

(2) Process p may increase est_p to $est + 1$ upon receipt of a token with estimate est and hop count est. In this case est is conservative by induction, and $N \neq est$ because the initiator of the token is est hops away and is not equal to p.

(3) Finally, process p may increase est_p to $est + 1$ upon receipt of a token with $est = h = est_p$, but $lbl \neq lbl_p$. The initiator of this token is est hops away and in this case $lbl \neq lbl_p$ implies that the initiator is not equal to p. Again this implies $N \neq est$, and the conservativity of est implies $N > est$.

Each process generates less than N different tokens, namely with estimates 2 through N, and a token with estimate e is forwarded at most e hops; this implies the $O(N^3)$ bound on messages. If process p increases est_p, say to e, p sends to $Next_p$ a token that includes the value of e. After receipt of this token, est_{Next_p} has at least the value e, so in a terminal configuration $est_{Next_p} \geq est_p$. This holds for all p, which implies that all estimates are equal. It has already been shown that they are bounded by N. $\qquad \square$

Theorem 9.15 *Algorithm 9.5 terminates, and upon termination $est_p = N$ for all p with probability at least $1 - (N-2).(1/R)^{N/2}$.*

Proof. According to Lemma 9.14 the algorithm terminates in a configuration in which all estimates are equal; call their common value e and assume $e < N$. Name the processes in clockwise order p_0 through p_{N-1}.

Process p_i chose a label lbl_{p_i} and generated a token $\langle \text{test}, e, lbl_{p_i}, h \rangle$ when the value of est_{p_i} was set to e. This token was forwarded e hops and reached the eth clockwise neighbor of p_i, p_{i+e}, which accepted the token without increasing its estimate further. This implies that $lbl_{p_i} = lbl_{p_{i+e}}$ for all i. Let

$f = \gcd(N, e)$; using the equalities $lbl_{p_i} = lbl_{p_{i+e}}$, it follows that when i and j differ by a multiple of f, the labels chosen by p_i and p_j are equal, i.e.,

$$f \,|\, (j - i) \Rightarrow lbl_{p_i} = lbl_{p_j}.$$

The processes p_0 through p_{N-1} are partitioned into f groups of N/f processes each, where all processes in one group have the same label.

But as the labels are chosen randomly from $\{1, \ldots, R\}$, the probability that all processes in one group chose the same label is $(1/R)^{N/f-1}$ and the probability that this happens in all f groups is only $(1/R)^{f(N/f-1)} = (1/R)^{N-f}$. For all possible values of e, f is at most $N/2$, and summing the probabilities of terminating with all possible incorrect answers (from 2 to $N - 1$), the probability of a correct answer is at least $1 - (N - 2)(1/R)^{N/2}$.

$\square$

Exercises to Chapter 9
Section 9.1

Exercise 9.1 *Let ψ be some postcondition and assume that are given*

   (1) *a process terminating Monte Carlo algorithm A to establish ψ; and*
   (2) *a deterministic, process terminating verification algorithm B that tests if ψ holds or not.*

Show how to construct a Las Vegas algorithm C to establish ψ.

Exercise 9.2 *Let ψ be some postcondition and assume that a Las Vegas algorithm A to establish ψ is given and the expected number of messages exchanged by A is known, namely K. Construct a Monte Carlo algorithm to establish ψ with parameterizable failure probability ϵ (i.e., the algorithm must terminate and be correct with probability $1 - \epsilon$).*

Exercise 9.3 *Give a deterministic, centralized name assignment algorithm that uses $2|E|$ messages and $O(D)$ time units.*

Exercise 9.4 [**Ang80**] *Give a deterministic algorithm for election in a clique where communication is by synchronous message passing.*

Exercise 9.5 *Give deterministic, message-terminating algorithms for computing MAX for rings and arbitrary networks of unknown size.*

Exercise 9.6 *Consider the election problem for anonymous trees of un-known size, where communication is by asynchronous message passing.*

    (1) *Give a randomized algorithm that is partially correct, process-term-inates with probability one, and has an expected message complexity of $O(N)$ messages. (Actually, an expected message complexity of $N+1$ messages is achievable.)*

    (2) *Does a deterministic algorithm exist for this case?*

Section 9.2

Exercise 9.7 *Prove that there exists no deterministic algorithm that com-putes the number of processes and that is correct for all anonymous networks of diameter at most two.*
Hint: exploit the symmetry in the networks of Figure 6.21.

Exercise 9.8 *Prove that there exists no deterministic algorithm for election in rings of known, even size where communication is by synchronous message passing.*
Generalize the proof to show the impossibility of election for all composite ring sizes.

Exercise 9.9 *Define the function f on strings $x = (x_1, \ldots, x_k)$ of integers, where $f(x)$ is true if all x_i are equal and false otherwise. Is f determinis-tically computable by a process-terminating algorithm in rings of unknown size? Is f deterministically computable by a message-terminating algorithm in rings of unknown size?*

Exercise 9.10 *The same questions as in Exercise 9.9, but for the case where $g(x)$ is true if x has a nondecreasing cyclic shift, i.e., there exists a cyclic shift z of x such that $i < j \Rightarrow z_i \leq z_j$.*

Section 9.3

Exercise 9.11 *Give a process-terminating Monte Carlo algorithm for elec-tion on anonymous rings of known size. What is the message complexity and what is the success probability of your algorithm?*
Is it possible to achieve a success probability that is arbitrarily close to one?

A *pseudo-anonymous network* is a network where the processes have iden-tities, but the identities are not necessarily all distinct. A pseudo-anonymous ring (of processes p_0 through p_{N-1} say) is *periodic* if there exists a number $k < N$ such that $id_i = id_{i+k}$ for all i.

Exercise 9.12 *Show that there exists a deterministic, process terminating algorithm for election on non-periodic pseudo-anonymous rings of known size.*

Exercise 9.13 *Show that there exists no probabilistic, process terminating algorithm for election on non-periodic pseudo-anonymous rings of unknown size that is correct with positive probability.*

Section 9.4

Exercise 9.14 *Define the function g as in Exercise 9.10. Give a probabilistic, message-terminating algorithm for computing g in a ring of unknown size that is correct with probability $1 - \epsilon$.*

Exercise 9.15 *Is it possible to detect termination of the Itai–Rodeh algorithm (Algorithm 9.5) using Safra's termination-detection algorithm (Algorithm 8.7)?*
Can you think of an other termination-detection algorithm discussed earlier that can be used for this purpose?

10

Snapshots

The algorithms we have considered so far (with the exception of those in Chapter 8) perform tasks related to the network structure or global network functionality. In this chapter we shall discuss algorithms whose task is to analyze properties of *computations*, usually arising from other algorithms. It is, however, surprisingly hard to observe the computation of a distributed system from *within* the same system. An important building block in the design of algorithms operating on system computations is a procedure for computing and storing a single configuration of this computation, a so-called *snapshot*.

According to Definition 2.22, a distributed computation is described by different sequences of configurations, containing different collections of configurations. Therefore it is not obvious which configurations are considered as configurations of a computation. This question will be addressed in Section 10.1, where the notions of cuts, consistent cuts, and snapshots are tied together. These notions are closely related to the notion of causality defined in Chapter 2.

The construction of snapshots is motivated by several applications, of which we list three here.

First, properties of the computation, as far as they are reflected within a single configuration, can be analyzed *off-line*, i.e., by an algorithm that inspects the (fixed) snapshot rather than the (varying) actual process states. These properties include *stable properties*; a property P of configurations is stable if

$$P(\gamma) \wedge \gamma \rightsquigarrow \delta \Rightarrow P(\delta).$$

In words, if a computation ever reaches a configuration γ for which P holds, P remains true in every configuration δ from then on. Consequently, if P is found to be true for a snapshot of the configuration, the truth of P can be

335

concluded for all configurations from then on. Examples of stable properties include termination, deadlock, loss of tokens, and non-reachability of objects in dynamic memory structures. In Section 10.4 we shall apply snapshots to the deadlock detection problem.

Second, a snapshot can be used instead of the initial configuration if the computation must be restarted due to a process failure. To this end, the local state c_p for process p, captured in the snapshot, is restored in that process, after which the operation of the algorithm is continued.

Third, snapshots are a useful tool in *debugging* distributed programs. An off-line analysis of a configuration taken from an erroneous execution may reveal why a program does not act as expected.

10.1 Preliminaries

Let C be a computation of a distributed system, consisting of a set $\mathbb{P}$ of processes; the set of events of the computation is denoted Ev. We make the weak fairness assumption that every message will be received in finite time, and it is assumed that the network is (strongly) connected. The local computation of process p consists of a sequence $c_p^{(0)}, c_p^{(1)}, \ldots$ of process states, where $c_p^{(0)}$ is an initial state of process p. The transition from state $c_p^{(i-1)}$ to $c_p^{(i)}$ is marked by the occurrence of an *event* $e_p^{(i)}$ in p; see Figure 10.1. Thus, $Ev = \cup_{p \in \mathbb{P}} \{e_p^{(1)}, e_p^{(2)}, \ldots\}$.

On the events of process p a *local causal order* is defined by

$$e_p^{(i)} \preceq_p e_p^{(j)} \iff i \leq j.$$

Each of the events can be either a *send, receive,* or *internal* event, cf. the definitions in Chapter 2. To simplify the representation of the algorithms and theorems in this chapter, we shall assume for the time being that the entire communication history of a process is reflected in its state. That is, if a channel from p to q exists, then the state $c_p^{(i)}$ of p includes a list $sent_{pq}^{(i)}$ of messages that p has sent to q in the events $e_p^{(1)}$ through $e_p^{(i)}$. Also, the state $c_q^{(i)}$ of q includes a list $rcvd_{pq}^{(i)}$ of messages that q has received from p in the events $e_q^{(1)}$ through $e_q^{(i)}$. To avoid explicit storage of communication histories in applications of the algorithms, it will be shown in Subsection 10.3.1 how to lift this assumption.

The aim of a snapshot algorithm is to construct explicitly a system configuration composed from local states (snapshot states) of each process. Process p takes a *local snapshot* by storing one local state c_p^*, called the *snapshot state* of p. If the snapshot state is $c_p^{(i)}$, i.e., p takes its snapshot between $e_p^{(i)}$

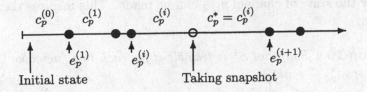

Figure 10.1 COMPUTATION OF PROCESS p.

and $e_p^{(i+1)}$, the events $e_p^{(j)}$ with $j \leq i$ are called the *preshot events* of p and the events with $j > i$ are called the *postshot events* of p. In time diagrams the taking of a local snapshot is depicted by placing an open circle on the process state that becomes a snapshot state; see Figures 10.1 and 10.2.

A (global) snapshot S^* consists of a snapshot state c_p^* for each process p in $\mathbb{P}$; we write $S^* = (c_{p_1}^*, \ldots, c_{p_N}^*)$. Because local states include communication histories, a snapshot S^* defines a configuration γ^* if the state of channel pq is defined to be the set of messages sent by p (according to c_p^*) but not received by q (according to c_q^*). In other words, the state of channel pq in snapshot S^* is defined to be the set of messages $sent_{pq}^* \setminus rcvd_{pq}^*$. The configuration consisting of the snapshot states and the defined channel states will be denoted γ^*.

Some anomalies in the construction of the configuration arise if $rcvd_{pq}^*$ is not a subset of $sent_{pq}^*$; see Figure 10.2. According to state $c_{p_1}^*$ in the collected snapshot, a message was sent by p_1 to p_3, but according to $c_{p_3}^*$ no message was received from p_1. Thus, the channel $p_1 p_3$ contains one message in the snapshot, and this message is said to be "in transit" in the snapshot. Now consider the message sent from p_1 to p_2. The sending of this message is a postshot event, while its receipt is a preshot event. Thus, according to $c_{p_1}^*$, no message was sent on channel $p_1 p_2$, but according to $c_{p_2}^*$ a message was received via this channel. Because $rcvd_{p_1 p_2}^* \not\subseteq sent_{p_1 p_2}^*$, no meaningful

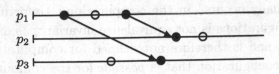

Figure 10.2 AN INCONSISTENT SNAPSHOT.

choice for the state of channel p_1p_2 can be made. This inspires the following definition.

Definition 10.1 *Snapshot S^* is feasible if for each two (neighbor) processes p and q, $rcvd^*_{pq} \subseteq sent^*_{pq}$.*

The feasibility of a snapshot implies that in the construction of the implied configuration no messages "remain" in $rcvd^*_{pq}$ that cannot be deleted from $sent^*_{pq}$. We shall call a message a *preshot message* (or *postshot message*, respectively) if it is sent in a preshot event (or postshot event, respectively).

There is a one-to-one correspondence between snapshots and finite *cuts* in the event collection of the computation. A cut is a collection of events that is left-closed with respect to local causality.

Definition 10.2 *A cut of Ev is a set $L \subseteq Ev$ such that*

$$e \in L \wedge e' \preceq_p e \;\Rightarrow\; e' \in L.$$

Cut L_2 is said to be later than cut L_1 if $L_1 \subseteq L_2$.

On the one hand, for each snapshot S^* the collection L of preshot events is easily seen to be a finite cut. On the other hand, let L be a finite cut. For each process p, either no event in p is included in L (let $m_p = 0$ in this case), or there is a maximal event $e_p^{(m_p)}$ contained in L, and all events $e \preceq_p e_p^{(m_p)}$ are also contained in L. Therefore, L is exactly the set of preshot events of the snapshot defined by $S^* = (c_{p_1}^{(m_{p_1})}, \ldots, c_{p_N}^{(m_{p_N})})$.

A snapshot will be used to derive information about the computation from which it is taken, but an arbitrarily taken snapshot provides little information about this computation. As an example, consider an algorithm based on the passing of a single token, such as the traversal algorithms of Section 6.3. Assume that process p takes its snapshot while it has the token, and some time later process q also takes its snapshot while it has the token. In the constructed configuration two processes have the token, which is a situation that never occurs in any computation of the algorithm.

Intuitively, we would like the snapshot algorithm to compute a configuration that "actually occurs" in the computation. Unfortunately, the set of occurring configurations is not equivalence invariant, as demonstrated in Subsection 2.3.2, and is therefore not defined for computations. Thus we shall accept any configuration that is *possible* for the computation (i.e., occurs in some execution of the computation) as a meaningful output of the algorithm.

Definition 10.3 *Snapshot S^* is meaningful in computation C if there exists an execution $E \in C$ such that γ^* is a configuration of E.*

We require the snapshot algorithm to coordinate the registration of the local snapshots in such a way that the resulting global snapshot is meaningful. The timeliness of snapshots is discussed in Subsection 10.3.2.

The feasibility of a snapshot imposes relations only between local snapshots of neighbors, while meaningfulness is a global property of the snapshot. Yet it will be shown below (Theorem 10.5) that feasible snapshots are meaningful and vice versa, and also that these snapshots correspond to *consistent cuts*. A cut is consistent if it is left-closed with respect to causality.

Definition 10.4 *A consistent cut of Ev is a set $L \subseteq Ev$ such that*

$$e \in L \wedge e' \preceq e \Rightarrow e' \in L.$$

Theorem 10.5 *Let S^* be a snapshot and L the cut implied by S^*. The following three statements are equivalent.*

(1) S^* *is feasible.*

(2) L *is a consistent cut.*

(3) S^* *is meaningful.*

Proof. We show that (1) implies (2), (2) implies (3), and (3) implies (1).

(1) implies (2). Assume S^* is feasible. To show that L is consistent, take $e \in L$ and $e' \preceq e$. By the definition of $\preceq$ it suffices to show that $e' \in L$ in the following two cases.

    (1) $e' \preceq_p e$ (where p is the process where e' and e take place): in this case $e' \in L$ follows because L is a cut.

    (2) e' is a send event and e is the corresponding receive event: let p be the process where e' takes place, q the process where e takes place, and m the message exchanged in these events. Now:

$$e \in L \Rightarrow m \in rcvd^*_{pq} \text{ because } e \text{ is preshot}$$
$$\Rightarrow m \in sent^*_{pq} \text{ because } S^* \text{ is feasible}$$
$$\Rightarrow e' \in L$$

(2) implies (3). The gist of the proof is to construct an execution in which all preshot events occur before all postshot events.

Let $f = (f_0, f_1, \ldots)$ be an enumeration of Ev defined as follows. First f lists all preshot events of Ev, in any order consistent with $\preceq$; then f lists the postshot events in any order consistent with $\preceq$; see Figure 10.3.

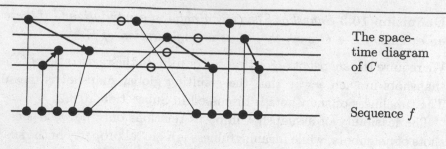

The space-
time diagram
of C

Sequence f

Figure 10.3 THE EXECUTION F.

In order to apply Theorem 2.21, it must be shown that the entire sequence f is consistent with $\preceq$. Let $f_i \preceq f_j$; if f_i and f_j are both preshot events, $i \leq j$ follows because f enumerates preshot events in an order consistent with $\preceq$. The same holds if f_i and f_j are both postshot events. If f_i is a preshot event and f_j is a postshot event, $i \leq j$ follows because f contains all preshot events before all postshot event. The situation that f_j is a preshot event and f_i is a postshot event is excluded by the assumption that the cut L is consistent; if $f_j \in L$ and $f_i \preceq f_j$, $f_i \in L$, i.e., f_i is a preshot event. We conclude that f is consistent with $\preceq$.

By Theorem 2.21 there exists an execution F that consists of the events of Ev, appearing in the order f. Execution F contains configuration γ^* immediately after the execution of all preshot events.

(3) implies (1). If S^* is meaningful, γ^* occurs in an execution of C; in each execution a message is sent before it is received, and this implies that $rcvd_{pq}^* \subseteq sent_{pq}^*$ for each p and q. Hence S^* is feasible.

$\square$

10.2 Two Snapshot Algorithms

By Theorem 10.5, it suffices to coordinate the local snapshots so as to guarantee that the resulting snapshot is feasible. This simplifies the requirements of the snapshot algorithm to the following two properties.

(1) The taking of a local snapshot must be triggered in each process.
(2) No postshot message is received in a preshot event.

In all snapshot algorithms it is ensured that a process takes its snapshot before the receipt of a postshot message. The two algorithms that are treated in this section differ in how these messages are recognized and how it is ensured that each process takes a snapshot.

var $taken_p$: boolean   **init** $false$;

To initiate the algorithm:
    begin record the local state ; $taken_p := true$;
        forall $q \in Neigh_p$ **do** send $\langle \mathbf{mkr} \rangle$ to q
    end

If a marker has arrived:
    begin receive $\langle \mathbf{mkr} \rangle$;
        if not $taken_p$ **then**
            begin record the local state ; $taken_p := true$;
                forall $q \in Neigh_p$ **do** send $\langle \mathbf{mkr} \rangle$ to q
            end
    end

Algorithm 10.4 THE CHANDY–LAMPORT SNAPSHOT ALGORITHM.

To distinguish the messages of the snapshot algorithm from the messages of the computation proper, the former are called control messsages and the latter are called basic messages..

10.2.1 The Algorithm of Chandy and Lamport

In this subsection the additional assumption is used that channels are fifo, that is, messages sent via any single channel are received in the same order as they were sent. In the algorithm of Chandy and Lamport [CL85], processes inform each other about the snapshot construction by sending special $\langle \mathbf{mkr} \rangle$ messages (markers) via each channel. Each process sends markers exactly once, via each adjacent channel, when the process takes its local snapshot; the markers are control messages. The receipt of a $\langle \mathbf{mkr} \rangle$ message by a process that has not yet taken its snapshot causes this process to take a snapshot and send $\langle \mathbf{mkr} \rangle$ messages as well; see Algorithm 10.4, which is executed concurrently with the computation C.

Lemma 10.6 *If at least one process initiates the algorithm, all processes take a local snapshot within finite time.*

Proof. Because each process takes a snapshot and sends $\langle \mathbf{mkr} \rangle$ messages at most once, the activity of the snapshot algorithm ceases within finite time. If p is a process that has taken a snapshot by then, and q is a neighbor of p, then q has taken a snapshot as well. This is so because the $\langle \mathbf{mkr} \rangle$ message, sent by p, has been received by q and has caused it to take a snapshot if it had not already done so. Because at least one process initiated the algorithm, at least one process has taken a snapshot; the connectivity of the network implies that all processes have taken a snapshot.   □

Observe that the algorithm must be initiated by *at least* one process, but it works correctly if initiated by any arbitrary non-empty set of processes.

Theorem 10.7 *The algorithm of Chandy and Lamport (Algorithm 10.4) computes a meaningful snapshot within finite time after its initialization by at least one process.*

Proof. By the previous lemma, the algorithm computes a snapshot in finite time. It remains to show that the resulting snapshot is feasible, i.e., that each postshot (basic) message is received in a postshot event. Let m be a postshot message sent from p to q. Before sending m, p took a local snapshot and sent a $\langle \mathbf{mkr} \rangle$ message to all its neighbors, including q. Because the channel is fifo, q received this $\langle \mathbf{mkr} \rangle$ message before m and, by the algorithm, q took its snapshot upon receipt of this message or earlier. Consequently, the receipt of m is a postshot event.   □

The Chandy–Lamport algorithm requires the exchange of $2.|E|$ $\langle \mathbf{mkr} \rangle$ messages and the storage of a single bit (plus, of course, the recorded snapshot state) in each process; its time complexity is $O(D)$.

10.2.2 The Algorithm of Lai and Yang

The algorithm of Lai and Yang [LY87] does not rely on the fifo property of channels. Therefore, it is not possible to "separate" preshot and postshot messages by markers as is done in the algorithm of Chandy and Lamport. Instead, each individual basic message is tagged with information revealing whether it is preshot or postshot; to this end, process p, sending a message of C, appends the value of $taken_p$ to it. Because the contents of the messages of C are not of concern here, we denote these messages simply as $\langle \mathbf{mes}, c \rangle$, where c is the value of $taken$ included by the sending process. The snapshot algorithm inspects incoming messages and records the local state as it is before receipt of the first postshot message; see Algorithm 10.5.

Algorithm 10.5 exchanges no control messages, but it does not ensure that each process eventually records its state, which it may indeed fail to do. Consider process p, which is not an initiator of the snapshot algorithm, and assume that the neighbors of p do not send messages to p after taking their local snapshots. In this situation p never records its state, and the snapshot algorithm terminates with an incomplete snapshot.

var *taken_p* : boolean   **init** *false* ;

To initiate the algorithm:
    begin record the local state ; *taken* := *true* **end**

To send a message of *C*:
    send ⟨ **mes**, *taken_p* ⟩

If a message ⟨ **mes**, *c* ⟩ has arrived:
    begin receive ⟨ **mes**, *c* ⟩ ;
            if *c* **and not** *taken_p* **then**
                begin record the local state ; *taken* := *true* **end** ;
            change state as in the receive event of *C*
   end

Algorithm 10.5 THE LAI–YANG SNAPSHOT ALGORITHM.

The solution to this problem depends on what is known about the computation *C*; if eventual communication with every process is guaranteed, a complete snapshot will always be taken. Otherwise, the algorithm may be augmented with the initial exchange of control messages between all processes, as in Algorithm 10.4. These messages then ensure only that each process eventually records its state (as proved in Lemma 10.6), but play no role in proving the feasibility of the resulting snapshot. In either way, computation of a complete snapshot is guaranteed.

Theorem 10.8 *The algorithm of Lai and Yang (Algorithm 10.5) only computes meaningful snapshots.*

Proof. Consider a snapshot computed by the algorithm, and let $m = $ ⟨ **mes**, *c* ⟩ be a postshot message sent from *p* to *q*. This implies that *c* = *true*, hence *q* takes its snapshot at the latest upon receipt of *m*. Thus, the state recorded by *q* occurs before the receipt of $\dot{m}$, and the receipt of *m* is a postshot event. (Recall that it only matters which local state is recorded, not when it is recorded; in this case, recording may take place simultaneously with the first postshot event.) □

The use of inhibition (freezing). The algorithm of Chandy and Lamport (Algorithm 10.4) uses markers to distinguish between preshot and postshot messages, and hence requires the fifo property of channels. The algorithm of Lai and Yang (Algorithm 10.5) explicitly includes in basic messages whether they are preshot or postshot, hence requires the possibility to *piggyback* information in basic messages. Taylor [Tay89] has shown that if the channels are not fifo and piggybacking is not used, any solution to the snapshot problem must be *inhibitory*, i.e., temporarily suspend the basic computation. A classification of different types of inhibition and a characterization of the necessary inhibition under various assumptions about communications is found in Critchlow and Taylor [CT90].

10.3 Using Snapshot Algorithms
10.3.1 Computation of the Channel State

It has so far been assumed that the state of each process contains the communication history of the process, so that the state of a channel in the snapshot can be computed from the states of the adjacent processes. In most cases, however, it is too costly to store explicitly all the messages a process has ever sent and received. We shall now demonstrate how the construction of the channel state may proceed more efficiently.

Reduction to relevant information. Depending on the purpose of the snapshot, it may be sufficient to store only a limited amount of relevant information about the communication history. For example, we may wish to construct a snapshot of a token-exchange algorithm (such as the Korach–Kutten–Moran algorithm) to determine how many token traversals are still active. In order to determine the *number* of tokens in each channel it suffices that each process stores the number of tokens it has sent and received. As a second example, the snapshot may be constructed to test whether the computation has terminated (see Chapter 8). It need only be determined whether the channels are empty or not, and again it suffices to count messages rather than store them explicitly. (In both examples, the recorded state of each process also can be limited to a small amount of relevant information, namely, the number of tokens residing in the process, or whether the process is active or passive, respectively.)

Explicit construction of the channel state. The channel state can be constructed explicitly by relying on the following lemma.

Lemma 10.9 *In a feasible snapshot, $sent^*_{pq} \setminus rcvd^*_{pq}$ equals the set of messages sent by p in a preshot event and received by q in a postshot event.*

Proof. On the one hand, it is easily seen that a message $m \in sent^*_{pq} \setminus rcvd^*_{pq}$ is sent preshot and received postshot. On the other hand, if m is sent preshot and received postshot, it is by definition included in $sent^*_{pq}$ but not in $rcvd^*_{pq}$, consequently it is in $sent^*_{pq} \setminus rcvd^*_{pq}$.   □

Process q constructs the state of channel pq by recording all preshot messages that are received postshot. As all these messages are received after q takes its snapshot, q starts recording messages after recording its state and recording should stop when all preshot messages have arrived.

The Chandy–Lamport algorithm. All preshot messages from p to q are received before the $\langle \mathbf{mkr} \rangle$ message sent from p to q; moreover, *only* preshot messages are received before the marker. The construction of the channel state in this case is therefore extremely simple: the state of channel pq is the collection of messages, received by q after recording its state but before receipt of p's $\langle \mathbf{mkr} \rangle$ message.

The Lai–Yang algorithm. If the channels are not fifo, process q may receive preshot and postshot messages alternatingly; the receipt of a postshot message does not imply that all preshot messages have been received. Thus, although it is clear which messages should be recorded by q (namely, messages tagged with *false* are preshot), it is not clear when q has constructed the complete channel state and can stop recording.

As a solution to this, it was proposed by Mattern [Mat89c] that p may count the total number of preshot messages sent to q, and inform q about this number (either in a separate message, or by piggybacking the number on postshot messages). Process q counts the number of preshot messages received (both those received in a preshot event and those received in a postshot event) and terminates the construction of the channel state when sufficiently many preshot messages have been received.

10.3.2 Timeliness of the Snapshot

The snapshots constructed by algorithms in this chapter are guaranteed to be meaningful in the computation from which they are taken. In addition, we want the snapshots to be recent in the sense that information derived from the snapshot is not very old. As a notion of time is needed in order to express how recent information is, we shall relate a snapshot to configurations occurring in a distributed *execution*. In an execution, the computed snapshot is "between" the configurations in which recording started and ended, as expressed in the following theorem.

Theorem 10.10 *Let E be an execution, S^* a feasible snapshot taken during this execution, and γ^* the implied system configuration. Let γ_s be the config-*

uration in which the first process recorded its state, and γ_e the configuration in which the last process recorded its state.

Then $\gamma_s \rightsquigarrow \gamma^* \rightsquigarrow \gamma_e$.

Proof. We shall strengthen the argument used in the proof of Theorem 10.5. Construct a sequence f of events by first enumerating the preshot events of E in the order in which they occur in E, and then enumerating the postshot events of E in the order in which they occur in E. This enumeration is consistent with the causal order of E, hence defines an execution F.

F contains the configurations γ_s, γ^*, and γ_e, in this order, which shows the desired result. F contains γ_s because all events preceding γ_s in E are preshot events, and hence f starts with exactly these events and in the same order. F contains γ_e, because collection of events preceding γ_e in execution E contains all preshot events. Hence f starts with these events (though possibly in a different order), and F contains γ_e by Theorem 2.21. $\square$

10.3.3 Detection of Stable Properties

Let P be a stable property of configurations; once an execution reaches a configuration in which P holds, P thereafter holds forever. Stable properties include:

(1) *Termination.* If γ is a terminal configuration and $\gamma \rightsquigarrow \delta$, then $\gamma = \delta$, hence δ is a terminal configuration. Consequently, the termination-detection problem (Chapter 8) may be solved by computing a snapshot and inspecting it for active processes and basic messages in this snapshot. However, the specialized solutions in Chapter 8 are usually more efficient.

(2) *Deadlock.* If in configuration γ a subset S of processes is blocked because all processes in S are waiting for other processes in S, the same holds in later configurations, even though processes outside S may have changed state. The problem of detecting deadlocks is considered in Section 10.4.

(3) *Loss of tokens.* Consider an algorithm that circulates tokens among processes, and processes may consume tokens. The property "There are at most k tokens" is stable, because tokens may be consumed, but not generated.

(4) *Garbage.* In an object-oriented programming environment a collection of objects is created, each of which may hold a *reference* to other objects. An object is called *reachable* if a path can be found from some designated object to this object by following references, and

---

var *detect*   : boolean   **init** *false* ;

while not *Pholds* **do**
        begin compute a global snapshot γ^* ;
               compute *Pholds* $:= P(\gamma^*)$
        end ;
detect $:= true$

Algorithm 10.6 STABLE-PROPERTY-DETECTION ALGORITHM.

---

garbage otherwise. References may be added and deleted, but a reference to a garbage object is never added. Therefore, once an object has become garbage, it will remain garbage forever. (The garbage-collection problem has created a vast amout of literature, but is not treated in this book. Interested readers may consult [TM93] and the references of that paper.)

In order to take appropriate action when P becomes true, the truth of P may be detected by means of an additional algorithm that observes the computation and triggers the action when P is found to be true.

A very general detection mechanism is given as Algorithm 10.6. The algorithm requires a test of whether P holds for a snapshot configuration, but this can usually be done by a relatively simple distributed procedure. While the task of the detection algorithm is to observe the dynamic behavior of a distributed computation, this procedure only analyzes static data (which happens to represent a configuration). The computation of *Pholds* can be done either in a centralized way or distributively. In a centralized computation, each process sends its snapshot state to a particular process, which constructs the complete configuration and computes *Pholds*. In a distributed computation all processes cooperate in this computation.

Algorithm 10.6 satisfies a safety property and a liveness property as expressed in the following two theorems; these properties are exactly those required from a detection algorithm. Assume Algorithm 10.6 observes a distributed algorithm that generates an execution E.

Theorem 10.11 (Safety) *If Algorithm 10.6 assigns true to detect while the system is in the configuration δ, then $P(\delta)$ holds.*

Proof. Let γ^* be the last snapshot computed, and let γ_e be the configuration of E in which the last local snapshot of γ^* was taken. By the algorithm,

$P(\gamma^*)$ holds. By Theorem 10.10, $\gamma^* \rightsquigarrow \gamma_e$, and because *detect* is assigned after completion of γ^*, $\gamma_e \rightsquigarrow \delta$. By the stability of P, $P(\delta)$ is implied.   □

Theorem 10.12 (Liveness) *If E reaches a configuration in which P holds, Algorithm 10.6 assigns true to detect within finite time.*

Proof. Assume δ is the first configuration of E that satisfies P. Let γ_s be the first configuration after δ (or equal to it) in which the computation of a snapshot is started by Algorithm 10.6, and γ^* the snapshot whose computation starts in γ_s. As $\delta \rightsquigarrow \gamma_s \rightsquigarrow \gamma^*$, $P(\gamma^*)$ holds, and the detection algorithm terminates after this round.   □

Algorithm 10.6 can be used to solve all stability-detection problems, but the following remarks can be made concerning its use.

(1) For a particular property P, the (distributed) evaluation of $P(\gamma^*)$ may require a fairly complicated algorithm. This is the case for some models of the deadlock-detection problem; see Section 10.4 for an algorithm to test deadlock in a given configuration.

(2) In some cases the method may not be feasible due to space limitations. This is the case for the garbage collection problem; storing all references and messages of a snapshot would more than double the space requirements of the algorithm, and this price is too high to pay.

Earlier garbage-collection algorithms suspend the basic computation while the garbage predicate is being evaluated; this solution is fairly elementary, but is usually rejected because suspending the basic computation is felt to be unacceptable. More recent algorithms work "on-the-fly"; rather than operating on a single configuration they cooperate with the basic computation, and do not fall into the category of algorithms relying on snapshot computations. See [Tel91b, Chapter 5] and [TM93].

(3) Even in cases where solutions based on Algorithm 10.6 are simple and efficient, they may not be the most simple and most efficient. This situation occurs for the termination-detection problem, for which quite elementary solutions were presented in Chapter 8.

Snapshots may also be used to evaluate *monotonic functions* of the system configuration; a function f is monotonic if

$$\gamma \rightsquigarrow \delta \Rightarrow f(\gamma) \leq f(\delta).$$

If a snapshot γ^* is computed and $f^* = f(\gamma^*)$ is evaluated, $f(\delta) \geq f^*$ holds for every configuration δ thereafter. An example of a monotonic function is the global virtual time (GVT) of a distributed discrete-event simulator (see, e.g., [Tel91b, Chapter 4] or [CBT97]).

10.4 Application: Deadlock Detection

In some distributed programs processes are temporarily blocked while waiting for messages from other processes. Examples include transactions in database systems and processes that compete for several resources. Deadlocks, if they occur and are not appropriately dealt with, seriously endanger the performance and usefulness of a distributed system. First, the processes involved in the deadlock will never complete their task, and second, the resources occupied by these processes are no longer available to other processes. Clearly, the appropriate handling of deadlocks is of utmost importance in the implementation of distributed systems.

10.4.1 Model of the Basic Computation and Problem Statement

Consider a set $\mathbb{P}$ of processes, executing a *basic computation* of which the purpose and working are of no concern here. A process may have to suspend its local computation because it is waiting for messages from other processes; this is modeled by the *active* state of a process being replaced by a *blocked* state.

When process p becomes blocked (action $\mathbf{B}_p$ of Algorithm 10.7), it sends request messages to a collection of processes denoted $Reqs_p$. To become active again (action $\mathbf{F}_p$), p must receive grant messages from processes in $Reqs_p$, but not necessarily from all. The subsets of $Reqs_p$ from which the grants suffice to make p active again are those that satisfy the predicate $Free_p$. Requests received by p (action $\mathbf{R}_p$) are stored in a set $Pend_p$ and replies can be given to them (action $\mathbf{G}_p$) when p is itself active. The request numbers issued by process p are attached to every request and grant message and enable p to discard grant messages sent in reply to obsolete requests (see $\mathbf{F}_p$).

We illustrate the use of $Free_p$ with several examples. First, if p needs replies to all request messages, $Free_p$ is true only for $Reqs_p$. Second, if a single grant suffices for p, $Free_p$ is true for every non-empty set. Third and finally, assume p needs 1000 Mega-bytes of free storage capacity and sends requests to disks A (with 900 Mega-bytes free), B (with 600 Mega-bytes free), C (with 300 Mega-bytes free), and D (with 100 Mega-bytes free). If A and any of the other disks become available, p can continue. Also, if B, C, and D become available, p can continue. Here $Free_p(S)$ could be expressed

---

var $state_p$: $(active, blocked)$ **init** $active$;
      v_p : integer   **init** 0 ;   (* Request number *)
      $Reqs_p$: set of processes ;   (* Request set *)
      $Grant_p$: set of processes ;   (* Received grants *)
      $Pend_p$: set of requests   **init** $\varnothing$;   (* Pending requests *)
      $Free_p$: predicate ;   (* Freeing constraints *)

$\mathbf{B}_p$: { $state_p = active$ }
      begin determine $Reqs_p$ and $Free_p$; $v_p := v_p + 1$;
             forall $q \in Reqs_p$ **do** send $\langle \mathbf{req}, v_p \rangle$ to q ;
             $Grant_p := \varnothing$; $state_p := blocked$
      end

$\mathbf{R}_p$: { A message $\langle \mathbf{req}, v \rangle$ arrives from q }
      begin receive $\langle \mathbf{req}, v \rangle$ from q ; $Pend_p := Pend_p \cup \{(q, v)\}$ **end**

$\mathbf{G}_p$: { $state_p = active \ \wedge \ (q, v) \in Pend_p$ }
      begin send $\langle \mathbf{grant}, v \rangle$ to q ; $Pend_p := Pend_p \setminus \{(q, v)\}$ **end**

$\mathbf{F}_p$: { A message $\langle \mathbf{grant}, v \rangle$ arrives from q }
      begin receive $\langle \mathbf{grant}, v \rangle$ from q ;
             if $state_p = blocked$ **and** $v = v_p$ **then**
                 begin $Grant_p := Grant_p \cup \{q\}$;
                        if $Free_p(Grant_p)$ **then** $state_p := active$
                 end
      end

Algorithm 10.7 The basic algorithm.

---

as

$$(\#S \geq 2 \wedge A \in S) \vee (\#S \geq 3).$$

The predicate $Free_p$ may be different each time p becomes blocked, but always satisfies the following two assumptions.

D1. $Free_p(\varnothing)$ is false and $Free_p(Reqs_p)$ is true.
D2. $Free_p(A)$ and $A \subseteq B$ imply $Free_p(B)$.

According to D1, p does not become active before receiving any grant, and does become active when grants are received from all processes in $Reqs_p$. According to D2, p may still become active if more grants have been received than any minimal collection of grants.

Given the basic algorithm, we can now define a deadlocked process or deadlock configuration.

Definition 10.13 *Process p is alive in configuration γ if there is a config-*

uration δ, *reachable from* γ, *in which* p *is active; process* p *is deadlocked if it is not alive.*

Configuration γ *is a deadlock configuration if there are deadlocked processes in* γ.

Clearly, deadlock is a *stable* property; if p is deadlocked in γ_1 and $\gamma_1 \rightsquigarrow \gamma_2$, then p is deadlocked in γ_2. A sequence of events of the basic computation that brings the system from configuration γ to configuration δ is called a *continuation* from γ to δ of the basic computation.

The deadlock detection problem is to design a control algorithm that can be superimposed on the basic computation and satisfies the following three requirements.

(1) *Non-interference.* The control algorithm does not influence the basic computation.

(2) *Liveness.* If a deadlock occurs, it will be detected by the control algorithm.

(3) *Safety.* The algorithm detects deadlock only if there is a deadlock.

The control algorithm may require the exchange of additional messages, referred to as *control messages*, which can be sent by active as well as blocked processes. In addition to reporting that a deadlock has occurred, it is usually required that the control algorithm identifies one or more deadlocked processes to be used for the resolution of the deadlock.

10.4.2 The Global-marking Algorithm

In this subsection we propose an algorithm, called the *global-marking algorithm*, for deadlock detection and identification of all deadlocked processes. The algorithm repeatedly computes a snapshot and applies Algorithm 10.8 to the constructed snapshot configuration. The values $state_p^*$, v_p^*, $Reqs_p^*$, $Grant_p^*$, $Pend_p^*$, $Free_p^*$, and $(sent_{qp}^* \setminus rcvd_{qp}^*)$, are used as constants (they are computed by the snapshot algorithm). The algorithm simulates the exchange of grants and the freeing of processes in a continuation from γ^* to determine which processes are alive.

The ariable $alive_p$ is initially false, but set to true when p detects that it is alive in the snapshot. This is the case when p is in the active state in the snapshot, but also if the set of $\langle \mathbf{grant}, v_p^* \rangle$ and $\langle \mathbf{Alive} \rangle$ messages received so far satisfies $Free_p^*$. Variable $GrRec_p$ contains the set of grants (for the current request) already received or in transit in the snapshot, and the $\langle \mathbf{Alive} \rangle$ messages received by p.

var $alive$: boolean   **init** $false$;
       $GrRec$: set of $\mathbb{P}$ **init** $Grant_p^* \cup \{q : \langle \mathbf{grant}, v_p^* \rangle \in sent_{qp}^* \setminus rcvd_{qp}^* \}$;

$\mathbf{M}_p$: (* Start marking in active process *)
     $\{ \neg alive_p \;\wedge\; (state_p^* = active \;\vee\; Free_p^*(GrRec_p)) \}$
     begin $alive_p := true$;
         forall $q \in Pend_p^* \cup \{q : \langle \mathbf{req}, v \rangle \in (sent_{qp}^* \setminus rcvd_{qp}^*)\}$
            do send $\langle \mathbf{Alive} \rangle$ to q
     end

$\mathbf{P}_p$: (* Propagate marking in freed processes *)
     $\{$ An $\langle \mathbf{Alive} \rangle$ message arrives from q $\}$
     begin receive $\langle \mathbf{Alive} \rangle$ from q ; $GrRec_p := GrRec_p \cup \{q\}$;
         if not $alive_p$ **and** $Free_p^*(GrRec_p)$ **then**
            begin $alive_p := true$;
                forall $q \in Pend_p^* \cup \{q : \langle \mathbf{req}, v \rangle \in (sent_{qp}^* \setminus rcvd_{qp}^*)\}$
                   do send $\langle \mathbf{Alive} \rangle$ to q
         end
     end

Algorithm 10.8 THE GLOBAL-MARKING ALGORITHM

Theorem 10.14 *The global-marking algorithm terminates, and upon termination, $alive_p$ is true if and only if p is alive in γ^*.*

Proof. Process p sets $alive_p$ to $true$ (and sends the associated $\langle \mathbf{Alive} \rangle$ messages) at most once, hence only finitely many messages are exchanged.

The marking algorithm simulates a possible continuation of the basic algorithm from γ^*, where the processes that become active are those that set $alive$ to $true$, and grant messages are the $\langle \mathbf{Alive} \rangle$ messages. In the simulated continuation, a process immediately grants all pending requests when it becomes active. Process p executing $\mathbf{M}_p$ is active in γ^* or becomes active as a result of receiving the messages in transit in γ^*, hence is alive in γ^*. Process p setting $alive_p$ to $true$ in action $\mathbf{P}_p$ becomes active in the simulated continuation as a result of receiving a grant message that was sent in the continuation, but this also implies that the process is alive in γ^*. Consequently, all processes p with $alive_p = true$ when the marking algorithm terminates are alive in γ^*.

It remains to show that, conversely, if p is alive in γ^* then $alive_p$ is set to $true$. Let p be alive in γ^* and $(f_1, \ldots, f_l)$ a continuation from γ^* that results in a configuration δ in which p is active. Call the sequence of configurations in this schedule $(\gamma_0, \gamma_1, \ldots, \gamma_l)$, where $\gamma_0 = \gamma^*$ and $\gamma_l = \delta$.

We show by induction on i that if γ_i is the first configuration (among γ_0

through γ_l) in which process q is active, then $alive_q$ is set to *true* during marking.

Case $i = 0$: As q is active in γ^*, action $\mathbf{M}_q$ is applicable, setting $alive_q$ to *true*.

Case $i > 0$: Process q was blocked in γ_0 through γ_{i-1} and becomes active in event f_i. Clearly, f_i is the receipt of a $\langle \mathbf{grant}, v_q^* \rangle$ message that increases $Grant_q$ to a collection G satisfying $Free_q^*(G)$. We shall show that for each $r \in G$, r is eventually included in $GrRec_q$ in the marking algorithm; we consider two cases.

(1) The $\langle \mathbf{grant}, v_q^* \rangle$ message was in transit from r to q in γ^*. In this case r has been included in $GrRec_q$ already, during its initialization to $Grant_q^* \cup \{r : \langle \mathbf{grant}, v_q^* \rangle \in sent_{rq}^* \setminus rcvd_{rq}^* \}$.

(2) The $\langle \mathbf{grant}, v_q \rangle$ message was sent in one of the events f_1 through f_{i-1}. In this case, $(q, v_q) \in Pend_r$ or $\langle \mathbf{req}, v_q \rangle$ is in transit to r in configuration γ, and r is active in one of the configurations γ_0 through γ_{i-2}. By induction, $alive_r$ is set to *true* by the marking algorithm,, and when this happens, r sends an $\langle \mathbf{Alive} \rangle$ message to q; after its receipt, $r \in GrRec_q$ holds.

If $GrRec_q$ contains G after initialization, $\mathbf{M}_q$ is applicable and will set $alive_q$i to *true*; otherwise, $alive_q$ will be set to *true* (at the latest) when the $\langle \mathbf{Alive} \rangle$ message completing G is received.

In particular, $alive_p$ is set to *true*. $\qquad\square$

The termination of Algorithm 10.8 is implicit, but can be detected by applying a termination detection algorithm (Chapter 8). When termination of the global marking algorithm is detected, precisely those processes p with $alive_p = false$ are deadlocked in γ^*.

10.4.3 Deadlock Detection in Restricted Models

The model of the basic computation used in this section is the most general model used for studying the deadlock-detection problem, and not many algorithms are known for detecting deadlocks in this model.

One algorithm, also based on simulating a continuation of the basic algorithm, was proposed by Brzezinski, Hélary, and Raynal [BHR92]. Their algorithm concentrates all control communication on an embedded ring, circulating a token containing the set of processes not yet known to be alive. Keeping all information centralized in the token facilitates termination detection of the marking; when the token has made one full tour without a change in the set, termination is detected.

The deadlock-detection problem is often studied under more restricted assumptions concerning the activation of processes, allowing a graph-theoretical characterization of deadlocks. See, e.g., Knapp's article [Kna87] for an overview of several models and algorithms. The most common models are those in which a process must obtain grants from all processes in its request set in order to become active (the AND model), and those in which a single grant suffices (the OR model).

Resource deadlocks: the AND model. A distributed database consists of a collection of files, dispersed over a number of sites (computers). The database management system allows users to access this data, either just to read it, or to modify the data. Accessing the data occurs in a structured way by means of database *transactions*, which usually address data at different sites. Due to the dispersion of data items, care must be taken to avoid certain interleavings of steps taken by different transactions, and correct operation of the database is usually ensured by means of *locking* the data items on which the transaction operates. Of course, if the required data is already locked by another transaction, the transaction must wait.

To become active, a transaction must obtain all the locks it has requested, i.e., $Free_p(G) \equiv (G = Reqs_p)$. The restricted model of deadlocks where all requests must be granted before a process becomes active is referred to as the *AND model*.

It can be shown that in the AND model a deadlock is equivalent to the occurrence of a cycle in the *wait-for graph*; this is a graph on the processes with an edge pq if p is blocked waiting for q. Algorithms to check for cycles in this graph have been proposed by, e.g., Chandy, Misra, and Haas [CMH83], Menasce and Muntz [MM79], and Mitchell and Merritt [MM84].

Communication deadlocks: the OR model. A process cooperating with other processes in a distributed algorithm may enter a blocked state, in which the only possible events are communications with other processes. The execution of any communication event brings the process into another state, from which it may continue its computation. Hence to become active it suffices that a single request of a process is granted, i.e., $Free_p$ is true for every non-empty subset of $Reqs_p$. The restricted model of deadlocks where a single grant suffices for a process to become active is referred to as the *OR model*.

In the OR model, a deadlock is equivalent to the occurrence of a knot in the wait-for graph. Algorithms for this model have been proposed by, e.g., Chandy, Misra, and Haas [CMH83] and Natarajan [Nat86].

Exercises to Chapter 10
Section 10.1

Exercise 10.1 *Consider the registration of the local snapshot of p as an additional internal event a_p. Prove that*

$$S^* \text{ is meaningful} \iff \forall p, q : a_p \parallel a_q.$$

Section 10.3

Exercise 10.2 *Give a full description of the Lai–Yang algorithm, including mechanisms to enforce completion of the snapshot and construction of the channel states.*

Exercise 10.3 *Professor Przlwytszkowsky writes:*
"Reading Chapter 10 improved my understanding of the algorithms of Chapter 8. In Safra's algorithm (Algorithm 8.7), for example, the handling of the token by p should be seen as defining p's snapshot state. In the constructed snapshot all processes are passive, because the token is only handled by passive processes. So the computation of *Pholds* only requires a check of whether all channels are empty, to which end the token collects the sum of the message counts.
I do not understand, however, the role of the colors white and black, and how the meaningfulness of the snapshot is guaranteed."
Can you help the professor?

11

Sense of Direction and Orientation

Networks of regular structure, such as the torus or the hypercube, usually have the links labeled with their direction. We now discuss some recent research evaluating the benefits of such a labeling, called *Sense of Direction* or SoD. The availability of sense of direction strengthens the model and allows processors to communicate more efficiently with each other, and to exploit topological properties of the network algorithmically.

Sense of direction has been shown to reduce the complexity of some problems, but the number of problems for which this applies is surprisingly small. Indeed, for many problems, more efficient or easier algorithms are known if the edge labeling can be exploited. However, in many non-trivial cases good lower bounds for the unlabeled case are not available, and moreover some surprisingly efficient algorithms exist in unlabeled graphs.

The chapter attempts to follow the scientific struggle, started by Santoro [San84], to establish cases in favor of sense of direction in two areas: broadcasting and election.

We shall define sense of direction for several specific classes of network, and show how the election problem on rings can be solved more efficiently if chords and a sense of direction are available. We shall show that elections can be performed with linear complexity in hypercubes and cliques if SoD is available, but also that a randomized algorithm can achieve the same complexity without using SoD. Algorithms to compute an SoD in networks where none is given will also be discussed.

Chapter overview. Section 11.1 introduces some general notions and problems further discussed in later sections. Subsection 11.1.1 provides the formal definitions of sense of direction, and Subsection 11.1.2 illustrates its use. Subsection 11.1.3 describes how a message can be broadcast efficiently using a *uniform* sense of direction. Then Section 11.2 presents some results regarding elections in rings and chordal rings with sense of direction; this includes a demonstration that sense of direction helps to reduce election complexity in cliques.

Section 11.3 studies the benefits of sense of direction in hypercubes. For several years, very efficient algorithms for labeled hypercubes have been known; the algorithms for unlabeled hypercubes were less efficient, and research was focussed on proving matching lower bounds. Recently, more efficient algorithms were proposed for unlabeled hypercubes, indicating that the efficiency gain is intrinsic in the topology, not the edge labeling.

Section 11.4 discusses various topics related to complexity, including algorithms to compute a sense of direction in unlabeled networks. We end the chapter with discussion and open questions (Section 11.5).

11.1 Introduction and Definitions

As usual we model a processor network by a graph with N nodes and m edges. The edges of each processor are locally named so a processor can distinguish from which edge it has received information, and can choose through which edge to send information. Processors have distinct identities, but these identities are uninterpreted numbers, and have no topological significance. We assume an asynchronous network.

11.1.1 Definition and Characterization of Sense of Direction

Although sense of direction has received quite a bit of attention in recent years, no easy definition of what it is has been agreed upon. Several instances were defined [Tel94], and classes of sense of direction were identified [FMS98].

The group definition. We shall follow a group-theoretical approach and therefore we recall some group theory notions first. For some students, unfamiliar with this theory, some of the definitions may appear mysterious, but we shall give clear examples for concrete structures where possible.

A commutative or abelian *group* is a set G with special *zero* element 0 and a binary operator +, satisfying the following requirements.

(1) *Closure:* For all $x, y \in G$, $(x + y) \in G$.
(2) *Identity:* For all $x \in G$, $0 + x = x + 0 = x$.
(3) *Inverse:* For all $x \in G$ there exists a $y \in G$ such that $x + y = y + x = 0$.
(4) *Associativity:* For all $x, y, z \in G$, $(x + y) + z = x + (y + z)$.
(5) *Commutativity:* For all x, y, $x + y = y + x$.

Because of associativity we may omit parentheses in summations; we write $-x$ for x's inverse, and if $s \in \mathbb{Z}$, $s \cdot x$ denotes the sum of s x's.

The number of elements in G is called its *order*; $\mathrm{ord}(G)$ is assumed finite for use in sense of direction. In finite groups, for each x there are positive numbers k such that $k \cdot x = 0$; the smallest such number is the *order* of x, and it always divides the order of the group.

For elements g_1 through g_k, consider the set of elements that can be written as a sum of g_i:

$$S = \left\{ x \ : \ \exists s_1, ..., s_k : \ x = \sum_{i=1}^{k} s_i \cdot g_i \right\}.$$

This set is itself a group, called the *subgroup generated by g_1 through g_k* and denoted by $\langle g_1, ..., g_k \rangle$. For $y \in G$, the set $T = S + y = \{y + x : x \in S\}$ is called an *orbit* of S or of g_1 through g_k. All orbits of S are of the same size, and orbits $S + y_1$ and $S + y_2$ are either equal or disjoint, hence the orbits of S partition G.

The group is *cyclic* if it is generated by one single element, i.e., there is a g such that $G = \langle g \rangle$. The generator is not unique (except in the case of the group of order 2), but we usually fix a generator and call it 1, and write i for $i \cdot 1$; the cyclic group of order k is called $\mathbb{Z}_k$.

Thus, $\mathbb{Z}_k$ is simply the group of numbers modulo k: its elements are the numbers 0 through $k - 1$. Another group deserving special attention is the group $(\mathbb{Z}_k)^d$: its elements are vectors of length d, and the group operation adds them pointwise modulo k.

Networks and labelings. In the sequel, let G denote a commutative group and for neighboring processors p and q, let $\mathcal{L}_p(q)$ denote the name of link pq at p. The idea behind group sense of direction is that the topology of the network matches the structure of the group.

Definition 11.1 *The edge labeling $\mathcal{L}$ is a sense of direction (based on G) if the edge labels are elements of G, and there exists an injection $\mathcal{N}$ from the nodes to G such that for all neighbors p and q, $\mathcal{N}_q = \mathcal{N}_p + \mathcal{L}_p(q)$.*

Given a sense of direction $\mathcal{L}$, a node labeling as specified in the definition is called a *witnessing labeling* or *witness* for $\mathcal{L}$. The processors know the link labels $\mathcal{L}$, but a witnessing node labeling is not required or assumed to be known to the processors and is *not* part of the sense of direction. It can easily be shown [Tel95] that witnessing node labelings are not unique; any given witnessing labeling can be modified by adding a fixed element $s \in G$

to every label and hence the number of witnessing labelings for a sense of direction is exactly ord(G).

Sense of direction can also be characterized without reference to a node labeling, namely by properties of closed paths; see Exercise 11.1.

Observe that an SoD does not contain the label 0 as an edge label (because node labels of neighbors differ) and that an SoD satisfies the *anti-symmetry* property $\mathcal{L}_p(q) + \mathcal{L}_q(p) = 0$, or, equivalently, $\mathcal{L}_p(q) = -\mathcal{L}_q(p)$. It is usually the case that the order of the group equals the number of nodes, hence the witnessing labelings are bijective. This property is not essential in most of the algorithms we give, but we often assume it implicitly.

Given a network of N processors and a group G of order N, a sense of direction can be constructed easily. If first the nodes are labeled arbitrarily with distinct elements of G, and then $\mathcal{L}_p(q)$ is taken as $\mathcal{N}_q - \mathcal{N}_p$ for each edge pq, a sense of direction is obtained.

The resulting labeling already allows a significant reduction in complexity for certain tasks, as will be shown later, but most of the labelings that have turned out to be very efficient satisfy an additional property: uniformity.

Uniformity. The processors in a parallel computer are usually connected in a structure that is symmetric (i.e., the graph "looks the same" from all processors) and known; both symmetry and topological knowledge are implicit in uniform sense of direction.

Definition 11.2 *A sense of direction is* uniform *if each processor has the same collection of local labels.*

Let L be the common set of link labels; some properties of uniform sense of direction are immediate.

(1) If $g \in L$, then so is $-g$: a link labeled g is labeled $-g$ at the other end.
(2) L generates G, because for each $g \in G$ a path P with $SUM_\mathcal{L}(P) = g$ exists.
(3) For a $g \in G$ a shortest path P with $SUM_\mathcal{L}(P) = g$ can be locally computed by a generalized version of the *coin exchange problem*. It suffices to compute a minimal sequence of labels in L with sum g and, because every processor has these labels, this sequence defines a path in the network.

We describe a network with uniform sense of direction by the set of labels in a processor, often omitting inverses.

Examples. Several examples of sense of direction are found in the literature, most of which are instances of our definition. Flocchini *et al.* [FMS98]
define *chordal* sense of direction as any sense of direction over $\mathbb{Z}_N$. Of special
interest are uniform chordal SoD where 1 (or any other generator) is among
the labels. A *chordal ring* of size N is like the ring, but has in each node
extra "short cuts" to nodes at certain numbers of steps further in the ring.

Definition 11.3 *A chordal ring* $C_N(c_1, \ldots, c_k)$ *is a network for which there
exists a uniform chordal sense of direction with*

$$L = \{-c_k, \ldots, -c_1, -1, 1, c_1, \ldots, c_k\};$$

here k is called the number of chords.

The requirement that a generator of the group occurs as a label is crucial; a
$k \times l$ torus, for example, with wraparound and k and l coprime has a uniform
chordal sense of direction, but it is not a chordal ring. We now redefine some
already known topologies in the group framework.

Definition 11.4 *An* $n \times n$ *torus is a network for which there exists a uniform
SoD over* $(\mathbb{Z}_n)^2$ *and* $L = \{(0,1), (0,-1), (1,0), (-1,0)\}$. *(The labels are
conveniently referred to as* N, S, E, W.)

Definition 11.5 *An n-dimensional hypercube is a network for which there
exists a uniform sense of direction with base* $(\mathbb{Z}_2)^n$ *and n labels denoted by*
$i = (0, ..., 1, ..., 0)$ *for* $i = 0, ..., n-1$.

Definition 11.6 *A clique is a network for which there exists a uniform SoD
with base* $\mathbb{Z}_N$ *and* $L = \mathbb{Z}_N \setminus \{0\}$.

11.1.2 Exploiting Sense of Direction

We shall now give a few key techniques that underlie the exploitation of sense
of direction. Later in the chapter complete algorithms will be presented to
illustrate and clearify these techniques.

Path comparison. Given two paths π_1 and π_2 originating from the same
node, it can be decided from the labels on the paths if they end in the same
node or not. Indeed, all we need to do is to add the labels on the paths; if
and only if the sums of the labels are the same, the endpoints of the paths
are the same.

This gives sense of direction a strength equal to neighbor knowledge, and allows a depth-first search traversal with $O(N)$ messages as in Subsection 6.4.3. The sense of direction need not be uniform to allow this technique.

The possibility of path comparison is so fundamental to sense of direction, that Flocchini *et al.* [FMS98] have proposed it to be the *definition* of sense of direction. In their approach, the labeling proper is accompanied with explicit translation functions to compute the relative position of the endpoint of a path. On the one hand, this definition is more general because it describes a larger class of labelings. The advantage of this is limited, however: the larger class includes neighbor knowledge (in our definition *not* an instance of sense of direction) and some labelings rarely exploited in the design of distributed algorithms. On the other hand, the group approach compactly obtains the translation functions (as addition of group elements), thus allowing one to concentrate on more advanced usages of sense of direction.

Path compression. If the sense of direction is uniform, it also implies full knowledge of the network topology; indeed, in this case the availability of sense of direction cannot be considered independently from full topological awareness. Uniform sense of direction allows efficient routing to any node of which the relative position in the network is known, using the generalized coin exchange problem as mentioned above.

Network structure. Uniform sense of direction allows the group structure of the network to be exploited for guiding the overall progress of the algorithm. This will be exemplified in the algorithm for broadcasting (Algorithm 11.2) and the one for election in hypercubes (Subsection 11.3.2).

11.1.3 Broadcasting with Sense of Direction

Because one of our main directives is to compare complexity of broadcasting with and without sense of direction, we shall now demonstrate that sense of direction allows a broadcast within $O(N)$ messages. If no topological information is available, a broadcast requires the exchange of at least one message through every channel (Theorem 6.6), hence has $\Omega(|E|)$ message complexity.

Depth-first search exploiting sense of direction. It was observed by Mans and Santoro that the depth-first search algorithm using neighbor knowledge (Subsection 6.4.3) can easily be generalized to networks with

var $father_p$: process   **init** $udef$;

For the initiator only, execute once:
    begin $father_p := p$; choose $q \in Neigh_p$;
        send $\langle \mathbf{tlist}, \{0\} \rangle$ to q
    end

For each process, upon receipt of $\langle \mathbf{tlist}, L \rangle$ through link λ:
    begin forall $x \in L$ **do** $x := x + \lambda$;
        if $father_p = udef$ **then** $father_p := \lambda$;
        if $\exists q \in Neigh_p \setminus L$
           then begin choose $q \in Neigh_p \setminus L$;
                send $\langle \mathbf{tlist}, L \cup \{0\} \rangle$ to q
           end
        else if p is initiator
           then *decide*
           else send $\langle \mathbf{tlist}, L \cup \{0\} \rangle$ to $father_p$
    end

Algorithm 11.1 Depth-first search with SoD.

---

a sense of direction. Recall that Algorithm 6.18 circulates a token that contains a list of the names of processors already visited. Sending the token through backedges can be completely avoided, because a processor forwarding the token will inspect the list to see if the name of the neighbor is in the list in the token.

Algorithm 11.1 shows how sense of direction is used instead of neighbor knowledge. The list circulated in the token contains no longer processor *names* (these are not assumed to be available), but an indication of the position of a processor relative to the holder of the message. The algorithm uses the "path comparison" capability: a processor q adding itself to the list always inserts the number 0 in the list. After forwarding this list over a path π with label sum σ to a processor, say p, the 0 has changed into $-\sigma$. Observe at this moment that $\mathcal{L}_q(p) = \sigma$ and $\mathcal{L}_p(q) = -\sigma$, so the label on edge pq is now found in the list.

The only addition to Algorithm 6.18 is that upon receipt of the list, the relative positions are updated by adding the label of the link through which they were received.

This algorithm not only can be used for broadcasting, but also can be used in the election algorithm of Kutten *et al.* (Section 7.4) in which it yields an algorithm using $O(N \log N)$ messages. As a result we obtain a first success for sense of direction, because for broadcasting and election *without SoD* we have nice lower bounds (Theorems 6.6 and 7.15). We emphasize that the sense of direction need not be uniform, hence exploitation of the path comparison capability suffices to obtain this result.

Corollary 11.7 *In networks without topological awareness, the availability of a sense of direction decreases the complexity of broadcast from $\Theta(m)$ to $\Theta(N)$ and the complexity of election from $\Theta(N \log N + m)$ to $\Theta(N \log N)$.*

A structural algorithm for uniform SoD. Uniform sense of direction allows the processors to determine a spanning tree of the network "on the fly" and send the broadcast message through it, achieving the broadcast in exactly $N - 1$ messages. This number is optimal, because each of the $N - 1$ processors different from the initiator of the broadcast must learn the information by receiving a message.

We first give an elementary example of this algorithm: assume the network is an $n \times n$ torus with the edges labeled by North, East, etcetera. Broadcasting is done as follows. The initiator sends the message to the East, and the message is forwarded over $n - 1$ hops in the eastern direction. The initiator and every node receiving the message from the West subsequently forward the message to the North, and the message will travel exactly $n - 1$ steps in that direction.

It is easily seen that this strategy works and uses exactly $N - 1$ messages; by adding another $N - 1$ acknowledgement messages, the algorithm implements broadcast with feedback (PIF). Should we forward the message one step further to the East, the initiator would be the next recipient and this is superfluous. Should the message be forwarded one step further to the North, it would be received by the processor that originally sent it to the North, which is also superfluous.

The example shows how uniform sense of direction locally provides information about the entire network structure, and this information is used by the algorithm. We continue with a general formulation of this algorithm, where the group underlying the network is arbitrary. Call the labels g_1 through g_k (omitting inverses) in any order, and define n_1 through n_k as follows. First, n_1 is the order of g_1. Then, let n_2 be the order of g_2 in $G/\langle g_1 \rangle$; this is the smallest number for which $n_2 \cdot g_2$ is a multiple of g_1. Further, let n_i be the order of g_i in $G/\langle g_1, ..., g_{i-1} \rangle$; this is the smallest number for which g_i can be written as a sum of elements from $\{g_1, ..., g_{i-1}\}$. The n_i have the following properties: their product equals N, and each g in G can

For the initiator:
> **for** $i = 1$ **to** k
> > **do if** $n_i > 1$ **then** send $\langle \textbf{info}, n_i - 1 \rangle$ via link g_i

Upon receiving $\langle \textbf{info}, s \rangle$ via link $-g_j$:
> **if** $s > 1$ **then** send $\langle \textbf{info}, s - 1 \rangle$ via link g_j ;
> **for** $i = j + 1$ **to** k
> > **do if** $s_i > 1$ **then** send $\langle \textbf{info}, s_i - 1 \rangle$ via link g_i

Algorithm 11.2 BROADCASTING WITH UNIFORM SENSE OF DIRECTION.

---

be *uniquely* written as

$$g = \sum_{i=1}^{k} s_i \cdot g_i \quad \text{with } 0 \le s_i < n_i.$$

Algorithm 11.2 sends the information in direction g_1 over $n_1 - 1$ hops, serving all processors that differ from the initiator by a multiple of g_1. The initiator and all processors receiving the message from direction $-g_1$ send it in direction g_2 over $n_2 - 1$ hops, serving all processors that differ from the initiator by a multiple of g_1 plus a multiple of g_2. In general, the initiator and all processors receiving the information through direction $-g_1$ through $-g_{i-1}$ forward it in direction g_i over $n_i - 1$ hops. Because every processor different from the initiator receives the information exactly once, Algorithm 11.2 exchanges exactly $N - 1$ messages.

If such is required, $N - 1$ additional feedback messages can turn this algorithm into a PIF algorithm.

If such is required, the non-initiators can store the link through which they received the message to build a spanning tree of the network with the initiator as the root. The tree can be used for sending information back to the initiator; see Subsection 11.3.2. The depth of the spanning tree employed by the algorithm is $\sum_{i=1}^{k}(n_i - 1)$; if required the depth can be influenced by the order in which $g_1, ..., g_k$ lists the labels in L. We shall not pursue this issue (which is related to the *time complexity* of the broadcast) further here.

11.2 Election in Rings and Chordal Rings

The election problem on rings and chordal rings has a long history, see Section 7.2. Subsection 11.2.1 presents Franklin's solution [Fra82], which was improved by Attiya *et al.* [ALSZ89] by using chords added (uniformly) to the ring. Their algorithm exploits the path compression capabilities and

$state_p := active$;
while $state_p = active$ **do**
    begin send $\langle$ **name**$, p \rangle$ to left ; send $\langle$ **name**$, p \rangle$ to right ;
            receive $\langle$ **name**$, x \rangle$ from right ; receive $\langle$ **name**$, y \rangle$ from left ;
            if $x = p$ **and** $y = p$ **then** $state_p := elected$;
            if $x > p$ **or** $y > p$ **then** $state_p := relay$
    end

Algorithm 11.3 FRANKLIN'S RING ELECTION ALGORITHM.

a linear complexity is possible with a very small number of chords as will be shown in Subsections 11.2.2 and 11.2.3. However, this algorithm only uses path compression but leaves the network structure unexploited. We show in Subsection 11.2.4 that even fewer chords are needed to get a linear algorithm if the network structure is exploited as well.

11.2.1 Franklin's Algorithm

Franklin's algorithm distinguishes *active* and *relay* processors and uses a succession of rounds. Before the first round, every processor is active. A round starting with *more than one* active processor will turn at least half of them, and at most all but one of them, into relay processors, and will be followed by another round. A round starting with one active processor elects this processor and is the last round. Thus, the number of rounds is at most $\lfloor \log N \rfloor + 1$, and because each round takes exactly $2N$ messages, the message complexity is approximately $2N \log N$ in the worst case.

In each round, active processors exchange their name with the nearest active processor to the left and to the right. If a processor is its own "nearest active processor", it is the only active processor and becomes elected. Otherwise it survives the round only if its name is larger than both its right and left "active neighbors", a condition that is true in at least one processor (the largest active processor) and at most half of them (because it fails in both neighbors of a "survivor"). An active processor with a larger nearest active neighbor becomes a relay. Relay processors forward all messages they receive in the opposite direction; this is not shown in Algorithm 11.3.

11.2.2 Attiya's Amelioration

The number of messages sent by *active* processors in Franklin's algorithm is linear, and Algorithm 11.4 eliminates as many messages by relay processors as possible.

As the number of active processors halves in each round, the *sum over the* $\lg N$ *rounds* of the number of active processors participating in it is bounded by $2N$. Because an active processor sends two messages in a round, the number of messages sent by active processors is linear: $4N$. However, the messages are relayed over successively larger distances, because after round i, successive active processors are spaced at least 2^i positions apart. Concluding, the relaying of messages by passive processors accounts for almost the entire message complexity.

In a ring network, this is unavoidable; even if the active processors know the distance to the next one, the message must be forwarded through the nodes in the ring as this is the shortest path. Attiya's algorithm preserves the basic control structure of Franklin, but ensures that the active processors know the distance to the next one and uses chords and path compression to forward the $\langle \mathbf{name}, p \rangle$ messages quickly. The chords are not used to modify the basic competition structure of the algorithm.

We now consider a chordal ring with sense of direction. At the beginning of each round an active processor knows the relative position of its nearest active colleagues to the left and the right, and sends its name, but exploiting the chords. We assume the path compression to be implemented in primitives $Send(message, g)$ and $Receive(message, g)$. The first primitive forwards *message* via a path with $SUM_{\mathcal{L}} = g$, and the latter one receives such a message. A possible implementation is *greedy routing*, where a message is always sent through the largest chord that doesn't "overshoot" the destination; see Algorithm 11.5. Of course more sophisticated selection of edges could be used, but this would probably influence the complexity of the resulting election algorithms only marginally.

Initially the relative positions of the left and right active neighbors are -1 and $+1$, respectively. At the end of a round the surviving active processors find the relative position of the closest active processors by passing a $\langle \mathbf{pos}, . \rangle$ message through a chain of processors that became relays in this round. Leadership is detected at the end of the round with one survivor, by the processor finding it is its own neighbor ($Left = 0$).

The new algorithm differs from Franklin's only in the way active processors communicate; the sum over the rounds of the number of active processors is still $2N$. Now the number of messages sent in each round by active

$state_p := active$; $Left_p := -1$; $Right_p := +1$;
while $state_p = active$ **do**
   begin $Send(\langle \mathbf{name}, p \rangle, Left)$; $Send(\langle \mathbf{name}, p \rangle, Right)$;
         $Receive(\langle \mathbf{name}, x \rangle, Right)$; $Receive(\langle \mathbf{name}, y \rangle, Left)$;
         if $p \geq x$ **and** $p \geq y$ **then**
            begin $Send(\langle \mathbf{pos}, 0 \rangle, Left)$; $Send(\langle \mathbf{pos}, 0 \rangle, Right)$;
                $Receive(\langle \mathbf{pos}, r \rangle, Right)$; $Right := Right + r$;
                $Receive(\langle \mathbf{pos}, l \rangle, Left)$; $Left := Left + l$;
                if $Left_p = 0$ **then** $state_p := elected$
         end
        else
            begin (* relay the $\langle \mathbf{pos}, . \rangle$ messages *)
                $Receive(\langle \mathbf{pos}, r \rangle, Right)$; $Send(\langle \mathbf{pos}, r + Right \rangle, Left)$;
                $Receive(\langle \mathbf{pos}, l \rangle, Left)$; $Send(\langle \mathbf{pos}, l + Left \rangle, Right)$
            end
  end

Algorithm 11.4 ATTIYA'S CHORDAL RING ELECTION ALGORITHM.

processors is 4, so the number of *Send* operations in the entire algorithm is bounded by $8N$.

We first discuss the special case of a clique; the algorithm for this case was proposed earlier by Loui *et al.* [LMW86]. Because the network is fully connected, the *Send* operation routes the message directly, which costs a single message pass, and the overall complexity is bounded by $8N$ messages. This is again fortunate, because Korach *et al.* [KMZ84] have given an $\Omega(N \log N)$ lower bound for election in a clique without sense of direction.

---

procedure $Send(m, g)$:
  begin if $g = 0$
        then deliver message m to waiting *Receive*
        else begin $ch :=$ the largest of g_i s.t. $ch \leq g$;
                send $\langle m, g - g_i \rangle$ through link ch
        end
  end

Upon receipt of $\langle m, g \rangle$:
  $Send(m, g)$

Algorithm 11.5 THE GREEDY ROUTING STRATEGY.

Corollary 11.8 *The availability of sense of direction in a clique decreases the complexity of election from* $\Theta(N \log N)$ *to* $\Theta(N)$.

For the general case of a chordal ring Attiya defines the *message cost function* F as the smallest monotone and convex function for which $Send(m, g)$ requires at most $F(g)$ message exchanges. (Informally, F is the cost of sending a message to a processor g ring hops away.) In the worst case, round i starts with $N/(2^{i-1})$ active processors spaced 2^{i-1} hops apart, and thus uses $\frac{N}{2^{i-1}} \times 4 \times F(2^{i-1})$ messages.

Lemma 11.9 *Algorithm 11.4 uses* $4N \cdot \sum_{i=0}^{n-1} \frac{F(2^i)}{2^i}$ *messages in the worst case.*

The lemma expresses how the overall complexity of the election depends on the cost of sending messages over the ring. As special cases, the complexity in a ring (where $F(g) = g$) and a clique (where $F(g) = 1$) can be found to be $O(N \log N)$ and $O(N)$, respectively. Attiya *et al.* showed that a logarithmic number of chords suffices to bound the sum by a constant, for example in the chordal ring $C_N(2, 3, 4, ..., \lg N)$; we shall not repeat the computation here.

11.2.3 Minimizing the Number of Chords

Attiya's result determined the complexity of election on chordal rings to be linear; attention focussed on the minimal number of chords necessary to obtain this complexity. In this section we shall determine the number of chords needed asymptotically by Attiya's algorithm using "backward graph engineering" from mathematical formulae. The results illustrate a trend in algorithmic research to become less "algorithmic" and more focussed on analysis. Indeed, once the algorithmic aspects of the election are handled, and the relation between chords and complexity "encapsulated" in formulae (Lemma 11.9), work concentrates on formula manipulation.

The sum is a geometric series. As a geometric series (with growth rate smaller than 1) has a bounded sum we shall first investigate how many chords we need to bound $\frac{F(2^i)}{2^i}$ by some c^i for $c < 1$.

Consider the sequence of chords $L = \{2, 4, 16, 256, ...\}$, where each successive chord is the square of the previous one; the sequence ends when the next number exceeds N. Chords are of the form 2^{2^i} and the number of chords is $\log \log N$.

Lemma 11.10 $F(d) \leq 2 \cdot \sqrt{d}$.

Proof. By induction on d; the proof uses *greedy* routing, where a path of sum d starts with the *largest chord l* that fits in d, and proceeds with a path of length $d - l$. First, $F(1) = 1 \leq 2\sqrt{1}$.

Now assume $d > 0$ but the result is true for $d' < d$. The chord construction implies that the longest chord that fits in d has length l s.t. $\sqrt{d} < l \leq d$ and we find $F(d) \leq 1 + F(d - l) \leq 1 + 2\sqrt{d - l} < 1 + 2\sqrt{d - \sqrt{d}} < 2\sqrt{d}$. $\square$

So $\frac{F(2^i)}{2^i}$ is bounded by $2 \cdot (\frac{1}{\sqrt{2}})^i$, and the summation in Lemma 11.9 becomes a geometric series and has bounded sum. We have shown that linear election is possible with $O(\log \log N)$ chords. It turns out that $\Omega(\log \log N)$ chords are also necessary (if greedy routing is used) to make the summation a geometric series!

Lemma 11.11 *If there is a constant $c < 1$ such that with greedy routing $\frac{F(2^i)}{2^i} < c^i$, then the number of chords is $\Omega(\log \log N)$.*

Proof. For each $i < \log N$, $F(2^i) < c^i \cdot 2^i$, which implies that a chord of length at least $(1/c)^i$ is used, and by the greedy routing strategy this chord is at most 2^i. Consequently, for each i there is a chord with length in the interval $[(1/c)^i \ldots 2^i]$; observe that if $i' = i \cdot ({}^{1/c}\log 2)$ the intervals for i and i' are disjoint. Consequently, for the ${}^{(1/c}\log 2)} \log({}^2\log N)$ different values $i_r = ({}^{1/c}\log 2)^r$ (here $r < {}^{(1/c}\log 2)} \log({}^2\log N)$) we have a collection of disjoint intervals $[(1/c)^{i_r} \ldots 2^{i_r}]$, each containing a chord length. $\square$

Allowing other routing strategies probably does not improve this result any more than by a constant factor; the proof of this is left as an open question. Determining F from L is related to the *coin exchange problem*, asking to pay some amount using coins from a given set of denominations. General routing strategies mean allowing the use of coin returns in the coin exchange problem.

More slowly decreasing summations. We saw that a geometric series in Lemma 11.9 gives a linear complexity, but requires $\Theta(\log \log N)$ chords to implement. So we select a sequence that decreases more slowly, but still has a bounded sum; the square-harmonic series $\sum(1/i^2)$.

Assume the collection $L = \{36, 64, 256, 65\,536, \ldots\}$ of chords, where $g_{i+1} = 2^{\sqrt{g_i}}$; 36 is the smallest number for which this formula gives a larger power of 2. As $g_i = \log^2(g_{i+1})$, there is, for each d, a chord of length between $\log^2 d$ and d.

Lemma 11.12 *There are less than $2 \log^* N$ chords in L.*

Proof. As $g_{i+2} = 2^{\sqrt{2\sqrt{g_i}}} = 2^{(\sqrt{2}\sqrt{g_i})} > 2^{g_i}$, the sequence $g_0, g_2, g_4, g_6, \ldots$ grows faster than $2, 2^2, 2^{2^2}, 2^{2^{2^2}}, \ldots$ and exceeds N within $\log^* N$ terms. □

To route messages efficiently over short distances ($d < 36$) some short chords are added, but this is only a constant number.

Lemma 11.13 $F(d) \leq 2 \cdot \frac{d}{\log^2 d}$.

Proof. For large d, the greedy routing algorithm first chooses a chord l larger than $\log^2 d$ and achieves

$$F(d) = 1 + F(d-l) \leq 1 + 2 \cdot \frac{d-l}{\log^2(d-l)} < 1 + 2 \cdot \frac{d - \log^2 d}{\log^2(d - \log^2 d)} < 2 \cdot \frac{d}{\log^2 d}.$$

□

The calculations imply that $\Theta(\log^* N)$ chords are sufficient for obtaining a linear complexity for election; a matching lower bound on the number of chords will now be given. The proof is based on a summation that decreases even more slowly and has unbounded sum: the harmonic series $\sum(1/i)$. It is known that the first $\log n$ terms of this sequence sum to $\Theta(\log \log N)$, yet it requires $\Omega(\log^* N)$ chords to achieve it!

Lemma 11.14 *If, with greedy routing, $\frac{F(2^i)}{2^i} < 1/i$, then there are at least $\log^* N$ chords.*

Proof. Similar to the previous lower bound; for each i there must be a chord between i and 2^i. □

Concluding:

(1) $O(\log^* N)$ chords suffice to have the *convergent* square-harmonic series (Lemma 11.13);
(2) $\Omega(\log^* N)$ chords are required to have the *divergent* harmonic series (Lemma 11.14).

In order to obtain a linear complexity the sum in Lemma 11.9 must be bounded, hence decrease more rapidly than the harmonic series and thus use at least $\Omega(\log^* N)$ chords. This implies that $\Theta(\log^* N)$ chords are necessary and sufficient for Attiya's algorithm to have linear complexity.

11.2.4 One-chord Linear Algorithm

This subsection presents a linear chordal ring election algorithm that needs only one chord. We have already seen that with Attiya's algorithm this is not possible; that algorithm only exploits the path compression capability, and leaves the network structure unexploited.

Now assume a chordal ring with only one chord of length t, and assume t is approximately $\sqrt{N}$. A chordal ring with a single chord of length close to $\sqrt{N}$ is topologically very reminiscent of a torus, and our algorithm is adapted from Peterson's [Pet85] torus algorithm.

When starting a round, an active processor attempts to find, or *see*, another active processor of the same round; a processor sees at most one other processor, but can be seen by more than one processor. There are two ways in which an active processor can be promoted to the next round.

The first is very similar to the "local maxima" promotion in Franklin's algorithm: if a processor sees a smaller one and *is seen by* a smaller processor, it can be promoted. At most half of the processors can be promoted by this rule, because if a processor is promoted, at least one smaller processor that saw it isn't.

It would be too costly to have each active processor search the network until another active processor is seen; therefore an active processor searches only a restricted subset of the network, and the search may terminate without seeing another active processor. The second promotion rule states that the searching processor is promoted to the next round in this case!

The crucial achievement of the algorithm is to design the search procedure in such a way that (i) the search area is sufficiently large to have only few processors promoted by the second rule; and (ii) the search is sufficiently efficient to have a good overall complexity. Now imagine we draw larger and larger squares in an infinite grid and observe that the number of points on the border grows more slowly than the number of points in the interior.

Squares and boundaries, search procedure. For $g \in \mathbb{Z}_N$, define the *l-square* of g as the set $S_{g,l} = \{g + i \cdot 1 + j \cdot t : 0 \le i \le l, \, 0 \le j \le l\}$. The set $S_{g,l}$ is the set of (at most) $(l+1)^2$ processors reachable from g by crossing at most l 1-edges and at most l t-edges. An active processor searches for other active processors in an l-square, but not by sending messages to all processors in the square because this would be too expensive.

Define the *boundary* $B_{g,l}$ as the set of points where at least one of the inequalities is an equality, i.e., $B_{g,l} = \{g + i \cdot 1, \, g + i \cdot 1 + l \cdot t, \, g + i \cdot t, \, g + l \cdot 1 + i \cdot t : 0 \le i \le l\}$, and the *internal* $I_{g,l} = S_{g,l} \setminus B_{g,l}$. The boundary $B_{g,l}$ contains (at most) $4l$ processors and, if $S_{g,l}$ and $S_{h,l}$ intersect, then $B_{g,l}$

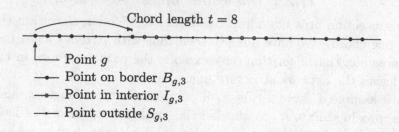

Figure 11.6 SQUARE AND BOUNDARY.

and $B_{h,l}$ intersect. Figure 11.6 exemplifies a 3-square in a chordal ring with a chord of length 8.

A processor in round i starts looking for other processors by sending an explorer token along the boundary of an l-square. This token attempts to make l steps in direction 1, l steps in direction t, l steps in direction -1, and l steps in direction $-t$. The length of the square depends on the round number; in round i the length is chosen as $l_i = \alpha^i$ (where α is a constant slightly larger than 1). Traversing the entire boundary takes $4l$ messages, but the traversal can be interrupted for several reasons.

If the token of p enters a processor already visited by a token of a larger round number, traversal is aborted; p will never receive its explorer back and it will never enter a subsequent round. If the token enters for the first time a processor already visited by a (different) token (of q, say) of the same round, p "sees" q. If q is smaller than p, processor p must become aware because seeing q is essential for p in order to be promoted by rule one. If q is larger than p, p's chances of being promoted are gone, but q must be informed because being seen by p could be essential for q in order to be promoted by rule one. So either the token goes back to p, or a chasing token is sent to q, via the boundary traversed by q's token, to inform q that it was seen by a smaller processor. Now, as it suffices for q to be informed about one smaller processor that saw it, a processor that already forwarded a chasing token to q will not forward p's chasing token any more.

The procedures descibed for token handling imply the following local conditions for promotion of p to the next round. First, p's explorer token returns having seen a smaller processor, *and* a chasing token arrives reporting p was seen by a smaller processor. Second, p's explorer returns without having seen another processor.

We argue that each round promotes at least one processor. If no proces-

sor sees another, all processors are promoted. If at least one process sees
another, let r be the largest processor that is seen; either r sees no processor
and is promoted by the second rule, or r sees a smaller processor and is
promoted by the first rule.

Some calculations. Our algorithm is very close to Peterson's [Pet85] and
the same calculations are found there also. Let A_i be the number of active
processors starting round i; we have $A_0 \le N$. We shall first bound A_i
for all rounds in which the size of the squares is less than N, i.e., rounds
$i \le {}^\alpha \log \sqrt{N}$.

Lemma 11.15 *For the rounds $i \le {}^\alpha \log \sqrt{N}$, we have $A_i \le \frac{N}{\alpha^{2i}(2-\alpha^2)}$.*

Proof. We have seen that each processor promoted by the first promotion
rule was seen by another processor that is not promoted. So at most half
the processors that saw another processor are promoted by this rule.

Some processors may be promoted by the second rule (by not seeing another process) but we claim that if both p and q are promoted by this rule,
$S_{p,l}$ and $S_{q,l}$ are disjoint. Indeed, if the squares overlap, so do the borders
traversed by p's and q's tokens. One of the tokens arrives at the intersection
point as the first, making it impossible for the other to complete its walk
without seeing another processor. Consequently, the number of processors
promoted by this rule is less than N/l_i^2.

From the above and the earlier choice of $l_i = \alpha^i$ we can conclude that

$$A_{i+1} \le \frac{A_i + N/\alpha^{2i}}{2}.$$

Using induction on i it can be verified that this implies $A_i \le \frac{N}{\alpha^{2i}(2-\alpha^2)}$. $\square$

The lemma implies both a linear bound on the number of messages and a
constant bound on the number of processors reaching round ${}^\alpha \log \sqrt{N}$.

Corollary 11.16 *In rounds 0 through ${}^\alpha \log \sqrt{N}$, less than $\frac{8\alpha}{(\alpha-1)(2-\alpha^2)}N$
messages are exchanged.*

Proof. Lemma 11.15 already established the number of active processors in
round i. The messages are charged as follows. The explorer of an active
processor p can make $4\alpha^i$ steps, charged to p. The chasing tokens routed
towards p are also charged to p; as each processor visited by p's explorer
forwards at most one chasing token, at most $4\alpha^i$ chasing steps are charged
to p.

So each of the $\frac{N}{\alpha^{2i}(2-\alpha^2)}$ processors in round i is charged at most $8\alpha^i$

messages, and the total number of messages in round i is bounded by $\frac{8N}{2-\alpha^2} \cdot (1/\alpha)^i$. The summation over the rounds is a geometric series with sum $\frac{8N}{2-\alpha^2} \cdot \frac{\alpha}{\alpha-1}$. $\qquad\qquad\square$

Termination of the algorithm. Lemma 11.15 implies that only a constant number of processors, namely less than $1/(2-\alpha^2)$, survives round $^\alpha \log \sqrt{N}$. To elect between these processors, the algorithm continues after that round with a second phase, organized as the Chang–Roberts algorithm (Subsection 7.2.1). Each processor surviving round $^\alpha \log \sqrt{N}$ sends a token along the entire ring, i.e., N steps in direction +1. The token is eliminated by any processor with larger identity which has also survived that round already, and aborts activity of processors in the first phase of the algorithm. This second phase ensures that only the largest processor that survives round $^\alpha \log \sqrt{N}$ receives its token back; this processor is elected.

Theorem 11.17 *The algorithm elects a leader using* $O(N)$ *messages in a chordal ring with one chord (of length $\sqrt{N}$).*

Proof. As no round in the first phase kills all active processors, at least one processor makes it to the second phase. The second phase ensures that exactly one of these processors is elected, which establishes the correctness of the algorithm.

The first phase uses $O(N)$ messages by Corollary 11.16, and the second phase uses only $O(N)$ messages because at most a constant number of processors initiate a token in that phase. $\qquad\qquad\square$

11.3 Computing in Hypercubes

In this section we shall study the question whether sense of direction reduces the complexity of broadcast and election in hypercubes. The answer has long been hypothesized to be affirmative because the known algorithms using sense of direction outperformed the best known algorithms for unlabeled hypercubes. However, because there were no matching lower bounds for the unlabeled case, firm conclusions could not be drawn.

Over recent years, surprisingly efficient algorithms were proposed for unlabeled hypercubes, closing the gap between the known complexities for labeled and unlabeled cases. Subsection 11.3.1 considers the case where the network has no sense of direction, and no topological awareness; that is, we consider algorithms that are correct in every network, and study their complexity on a hypercube. In Subsection 11.3.2 we study the case where both topological awareness and sense of direction are assumed and we shall see that there are elegant, simple, and efficient algorithms there.

The hard part of the study is the case where there is topological awareness but no sense of direction: that is, the algorithm only needs to work correctly in hypercube networks, but no meaningful edge labeling is assumed. It was shown that broadcasting can be done using linear messages; Subsection 11.3.3 presents a hypercube orientation algorithm and Subsection 11.3.4 introduces the masking technique and the broadcast algorithm. Subsection 11.3.5 discusses some techniques used in a recent election algorithm for unlabeled hypercubes. We do not consider the case where there is sense of direction but no topological awareness.

11.3.1 Baseline: No Topological Awareness

In the absense of topological awareness and sense of direction, both broadcasting and election require all edges of the network to carry at least one message. Indeed, the obligation for the algorithm to work correctly in every graph allows the technique of "node insertion" as used in Theorems 6.6 and 7.15. Consequently the algorithms use $\Omega(N \log N)$ messages at least when executed on a hypercube.

On the other hand, broadcasting can be done by flooding or the echo algorithm (Algorithm 6.5) and election using the Gallager *et al.* algorithm (Algorithm 7.10/7.11/7.12). Thus, both tasks are performed in $O(N \log N)$ messages.

Theorem 11.18 *Election and broadcast in hypercubes without topological awareness cost* $\Theta(N \log N)$ *messages.*

11.3.2 The Match-making Algorithm

The match-making election algorithm for hypercubes with sense of direction uses the recursive structure of the hypercube graph. To elect a leader in a hypercube of dimension $d+1$, the algorithm first elects a leader in each of the faces of dimension d generated by all but the last generator, and then elects one of the two leaders. To avoid confusion between leadership at different stages of the algorithm, a node is called a *d-leader* if it has won the election in a d-dimensional face.

The base case of this algorithm, election in a face of dimension 0, is easy; the network consists of exactly one node, which becomes a 0-leader immediately.

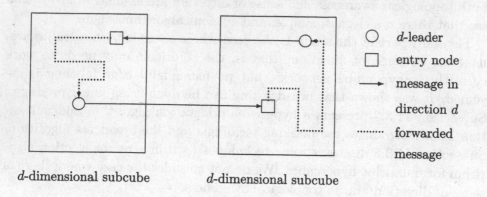

d-dimensional subcube d-dimensional subcube

Figure 11.7 Message forwarding in the tournament.

The tournament. A node that becomes d-leader (for $d < n$) engages in a tournament with the d-leader of the adjacent face in direction d. A tournament between two nodes that can communicate directly is easily organized. Each node sends the other one a message containing its name; the node receiving a larger name than its own becomes *non-leader*, the node receiving a smaller name than its own becomes *leader*.

The tournament between the two d-leaders is organized in the same way, but with the difficulty that the nodes do not know how to reach the leader in the other (or even their own) face. As a first step, node p that becomes d-leader sends a tournament message $\langle \mathbf{tour}, p, d \rangle$, containing its name and the phase number d, through its edge in direction d; it is received by a node in the other d-dimensional face. It is the responsibility of the receiving node, called the *entry* node, to forward this message to its d-leader; see Figure 11.7.

The difficulty in forwarding the message to the d-leader is that the entry node does not know the relative position of the d-leader. It is too expensive for the d-leader to announce its position to all nodes in the d-cube so that the entry node can forward the message in d steps. This announcement would cost $2^d - 1$ messages, leading to an $O(N \log N)$ overall complexity of the election. Similarly, it is too expensive to have the entry node broadcast the tournament message through the d-cube; this would also cost $2^d - 1$ messages.

Our solution uses a combination of these two basic strategies. The d-leader announces its leadership to all nodes in a $\lfloor d/2 \rfloor$-dimensional face, referred to as the leader's *row*. The entry node broadcasts the tournament message through a $\lceil d/2 \rceil$-dimensional face called its *column*. As each row intersects each column in exactly one node (as will be shown below), there is one node, called the *match node*, that receives both the announcement from the *d*-leader and the tournament message. The match node forwards the tournament message further to the *d*-leader via the spanning tree induced by the announcement messages.

Definition 11.19 *Consider the hypercube of dimension d.*
A row *is a face w.r.t. generators* 0 *through* $\lfloor d/2 \rfloor - 1$;
a column *is a face w.r.t. generators* $\lfloor d/2 \rfloor$ *through* $d - 1$.

The tournament between the two *d*-leaders is organized as follows.

(1) A *d*-leader p sends a $\langle \mathbf{tour}, p, d \rangle$ message via link d.

(2) A *d*-leader broadcasts its leadership in its row using Algorithm 11.2. The nodes in the row store the link through which they receive the broadcast message, thus computing a spanning tree of the row. (The broadcast algorithm takes a simple form because the generators are independent, and each n_i is equal to 1. The hop counter in the messages can be suppressed.)

(3) An entry node (i.e., a node receiving $\langle \mathbf{tour}, p, d \rangle$ via link d) broadcasts the message through its column using Algorithm 11.2.

(4) A non-*d*-leader q in the row of the leader (i.e., q has received an $\langle \mathbf{ann}, d \rangle$ message) receiving a $\langle \mathbf{tour}, p, d \rangle$ message sends the message to its father.

(5) A *d*-leader q receiving a $\langle \mathbf{tour}, p, d \rangle$ message compares p with q; if $q > p$, q becomes $(d+1)$-leader, and q becomes non-leader otherwise.

The communication complexity. Let $T(d)$ be the number of messages exchanged in a tournament between two *d*-leaders and $E(n)$ the number of messages used by the election algorithm (on a hypercube of dimension n). As an election requires two elections on smaller cubes and one tournament, we find the recursion

$$E(n) = \begin{cases} 0 & \text{if } n = 0, \\ 2 \cdot E(n-1) + T(n-1) & \text{otherwise.} \end{cases}$$

In the analysis of the message complexity we need the well-known sum of the infinite geometric series (with $\alpha < 1$) and its derivative with respect to α:

$$\sum_{c=0}^{\infty} \alpha^c = \frac{1}{1-\alpha} \quad \text{and} \quad \sum_{c=0}^{\infty} c \cdot \alpha^{c-1} = \frac{1}{(1-\alpha)^2}.$$

Counting the number of messages exchanged in each of the steps of the tournament between two d-leaders, we find:

Step 1: 2 messages.
Step 2: $2 \cdot (2^{\lfloor d/2 \rfloor} - 1)$ messages.
Step 3: $2 \cdot (2^{\lceil d/2 \rceil} - 1)$ messages.
Step 4: at most $2 \cdot \lfloor d/2 \rfloor$ messages.

Summing up, we find $T(d) \leq 2 \cdot (2^{\lfloor d/2 \rfloor} + 2^{\lceil d/2 \rceil} + \lfloor d/2 \rfloor - 1)$.

For even d we have $\lfloor d/2 \rfloor = \lceil d/2 \rceil = d/2$, and for odd d we have $\lfloor d/2 \rfloor = (d/2) - \frac{1}{2}$ and $\lceil d/2 \rceil = (d/2) + \frac{1}{2}$; using this we find

$$
\begin{aligned}
T(2c) &= 2 \cdot (2^c + 2^c + c - 1) &= 4 \cdot 2^c + 2c - 2, \\
T(2c+1) &= 2 \cdot (2^c + 2^{c+1} + c - 1) &= 6 \cdot 2^c + 2c - 2.
\end{aligned}
$$

Subsequently we write $F(n) = E(n)/2^n$, and using the recursion for E we find

$$
F(n) = \begin{cases}
0 & \text{if } n = 0, \\
F(n-1) + \dfrac{T(n-1)}{2^n} & \text{otherwise,}
\end{cases}
$$

which allows us to write $F(n)$ as a sum and bound it by an infinite series:

$$
F(n) = \sum_{d=0}^{n-1} \frac{T(d)}{2^{d+1}} < \sum_{d=0}^{\infty} \frac{T(d)}{2^{d+1}}.
$$

Now we use the expression for T above for odd and even d, sort the terms with exponential, linear, and constant numerator, and find:

$$
\sum_{d=0}^{\infty} \frac{T(d)}{2^{d+1}} = \sum_{c=0}^{\infty} \frac{T(2c)}{2^{2c+1}} + \sum_{c=0}^{\infty} \frac{T(2c+1)}{2^{2c+2}}
$$

$$
= \sum_{c=0}^{\infty} \frac{4 \cdot 2^c + 2c - 2}{2^{2c+1}} + \sum_{c=0}^{\infty} \frac{6 \cdot 2^c + 2c - 2}{2^{2c+2}}
$$

$$
= \sum_{c=0}^{\infty} \left(\frac{4 \cdot 2^c}{2^{2c+1}} + \frac{6 \cdot 2^c}{2^{2c+2}} \right) + \sum_{c=0}^{\infty} \left(\frac{2c}{2^{2c+1}} + \frac{2c}{2^{2c+2}} \right)
$$

$$
- \sum_{c=0}^{\infty} \left(\frac{2}{2^{2c+1}} + \frac{2}{2^{2c+2}} \right)
$$

$$= 3\frac{1}{2} \cdot \left(\sum_{c=0}^{\infty} \frac{1}{2^c} \right) + \frac{3}{8} \cdot \left(\sum_{c=0}^{\infty} \frac{c}{4^{c-1}} \right)$$

$$- \frac{3}{2} \cdot \left(\sum_{c=0}^{\infty} \frac{1}{4^c} \right)$$

$$= 3\frac{1}{2} \cdot 2 \qquad + \frac{3}{8} \cdot \frac{16}{9} \qquad - \frac{3}{2} \cdot \frac{4}{3}$$

$$= 7 + \frac{2}{3} - 2 = 5\frac{2}{3}.$$

It follows that $E(n) < 5\frac{2}{3} \cdot N$.

11.3.3 The Multi-path Flow Algorithm

As a stepping stone in the development of a linear broadcasting algorithm, we now present an algorithm to compute sense of direction in a hypercube of dimension n. The algorithm assumes a processor is designated as initiator of the algorithm (leader) and that the links of the leader are arbitrarily labeled with numbers $0, ..., n - 1$. The initiator's labeling uniquely defines a sense of direction as expressed in the following theorem (given here without proof).

Theorem 11.20 *Let w be a node and $\mathcal{P}$ a labeling of w's edges with numbers 0 through $n - 1$. There exists exactly one orientation $\mathcal{L}$ which satisfies $\mathcal{L}_w(v) = \mathcal{P}(v)$ for each neighbor of w.*

The algorithm computes exactly this orientation, and, moreover, the unique witnessing node labeling in which the leader is labeled with $(0, ..., 0)$. The algorithm uses three types of messages. The leader sends to each of its neighbors the label of the connecting link in $\langle \mathbf{dmn}, i \rangle$ messages. Non-leaders send their node label to other processors in $\langle \mathbf{iam}, nla \rangle$ message. Non-leaders inform their neighbors about the label of connecting links in $\langle \mathbf{labl}, i \rangle$ messages.

The algorithm is given as Algorithm 11.8 (for the leader) and Algorithm 11.9 (for non-leaders). It consists of two phases, where in the first phase messages flow away from the leader, and in the second phase messages flow towards the leader. A *predecessor* of node p is a neighbor q of p for which $d(q, w) < d(p, w)$, and a *successor* of node p is a neighbor q of p for which $d(q, w) > d(p, w)$. In a hypercube node p has no neighbor q

begin $num\_rec_p := 0$; $dis_p := 0$; $lbl_p := (0, ..., 0)$;
    for $l = 0$ **to** $n - 1$ **do** (* Send for phase 1 *)
      begin send $\langle \mathbf{dmn}, l \rangle$ via link l ;
        $\pi_p[l] := l$
    end ;
    while $num\_rec_p < n$ **do** (* Receive for phase 2 *)
      begin receive $\langle \mathbf{labl}, l \rangle$;   (* necessarily via link l *)
        $num\_rec_p := num\_rec_p + 1$
    end
end

Algorithm 11.8 ORIENTATION OF HYPERCUBE (INITIATOR).

---

for which $d(q, w) = d(p, w)$ and a node at distance d from the leader has d predecessors and $n - d$ successors.

The leader initiates the algorithm by sending a $\langle \mathbf{dmn}, i \rangle$ message over the link labeled i. When a non-leader processor p has learned its distance dis_p from the leader and has received the messages from its predecessors, p is able to compute its node label nla_p. Processor p forwards this label in an $\langle \mathbf{iam}, nla_p \rangle$ message to its successors. To show that p is indeed able to do so, first consider the case where p receives a $\langle \mathbf{dmn}, i \rangle$ message via link l. As the message is sent by the leader, $dis_p = 1$, and all other neighbors are successors. The node label of p has a 1 in position i, and the other bits are 0. (The label of link l becomes i in this case.) Then p forwards $\langle \mathbf{iam}, nla_p \rangle$ via all links $k \neq l$.

Next, consider the case where p receives an $\langle \mathbf{iam}, label \rangle$ message. The distance d of the sender of this message from the leader is derived from the message (the number of 1's in $label$). The $\langle \mathbf{iam}, label \rangle$ messages are sent only to successors, thus the sender is a predecessor of p and $dis_p = d+1$. This also reveals the number of predecessors, and p waits until dis_p $\langle \mathbf{iam}, label \rangle$ messages have been received. Then p computes its node label as the logical disjunction of the node labels received, and forwards it to the neighbors from which no $\langle \mathbf{iam}, label \rangle$ was received, as these are the successors.

In the first phase, each non-leader processor p computes its node label. In the second phase, each non-leader processor p learns from its successors the orientation of the links to the successors, and computes the orientation of the links to its predecessors. This information is sent over the link in $\langle \mathbf{labl}, i \rangle$ messages. A processor sends $\langle \mathbf{labl}, i \rangle$ messages to its predecessors as soon as it has received these messages from all successors, and then terminates.

```
begin num_rec_p := 0 ; dis_p := n + 1 ; lbl_p := (0, ..., 0) ;
      forall l do nei_p[l] := nil ;
      while num_rec_p < dis_p do (* Receive for phase 1 *)
          begin receive msg via link l ; num_rec_p := num_rec_p + 1 ;
                (* msg is a ⟨dmn, i⟩ or ⟨iam, nla⟩ message *)
                if msg is ⟨dmn, i⟩ then
                    begin dis_p := 1 ;
                          nei_p[l] := (0, ..., 0) ; lbl_p[i] := 1
                          (* So now lbl_p = (0, .., 1, .., 0), with one 1 *)
                    end
                else
                    begin dis_p := 1 + # of 1's in nla ;
                          lbl_p := (lbl_p or nla) ;
                          nei_p[l] := nla
                    end
          end ;
      (* Send for phase 1 *)
      forall l with nei_p[l] = nil do
          send ⟨iam, lbl_p⟩ via link l ;
      while num_rec_p < n do (* Receive for phase 2 *)
          begin receive ⟨labl, i⟩ via link l ;
                num_rec_p := num_rec_p + 1 ; π_p[l] := i
          end ;
      (* Send for phase 2 *)
      forall l with nei_p[l] ≠ nil do
          begin π_p[l] := bit in which lbl_p and nei_p[l] differ ;
                send ⟨labl, π_p[l]⟩ via link l
          end
end
```

Algorithm 11.9 ORIENTATION OF A HYPERCUBE (NON-INITIATOR).

The leader terminates when ⟨labl, i⟩ messages have been received from all neighbors.

The variables for processor p are: num_rec_p, the number of messages already received; dis_p, the distance to the leader (computed when the first message arrives, initialized to $n + 1$); lbl_p, the node label computed by p; $nei_p[0..n − 1]$, an array holding the node labels of the predecessors of p; and $π_p[0..n − 1]$, to store the sense of direction.

Lemma 11.21 *The algorithm terminates in every processor.*

Proof. Using induction on d it is easily verified that all processors at distance at most d eventually send the messages for phase 1. For $d = 0$, only the leader itself has distance d from the leader and it may send the messages without receiving other messages first. Assume all processors at distance d from the leader send all messages for phase 1, and consider a processor p at distance $d+1$ from the leader. As all predecessors of p eventually send the phase 1 messages to p, p eventually receives one of these messages, and sets $dis_p := d+1$. When p has received the phase 1 messages from all of its $d+1$ predecessors, p sends phase 1 messages itself (to its successors).

Similarly it is shown that all processors send the messages of phase 2 and terminate. $\square$

Lemma 11.22 *After termination π is an orientation. For neighbors p and q connected via link l, lbl_p and lbl_q differ exactly in bit $\pi_p[l]$ (which is equal to $\pi_q[l]$).*

Proof. According to Theorem 11.20 there exist exactly one orientation $\mathcal{L}$ and a witnessing node labeling $\mathcal{N}$ such that $\mathcal{L}_w(p) = \mathcal{P}_w(p)$ and $\mathcal{N}(w) = (0, ..., 0)$.

In phase 1 the processors compute the node labeling $\mathcal{N}$, as is seen by using induction on the distance from the leader. Node w sets lbl_w to $(0, ..., 0)$, which is $\mathcal{N}(w)$. Neighbor p of w sets lbl_p with b_i is 1 if the link from w to p is labeled i in w, and 0 otherwise. Thus $lbl_p = \mathcal{N}(p)$.

Now assume all nodes q at distance d from w compute $lbl_q = \mathcal{N}(q)$ and consider node p at distance $d+1$ from w. $\mathcal{N}(p)$ is a string of $d+1$ 1's and $n-d-1$ 0's. Node p has $d+1$ predecessors, and $\mathcal{N}(q)$ is found for predecessor q by changing one 1 in $\mathcal{N}(p)$ into a 0. Thus the disjunction of the $d+1$ labels $\mathcal{N}(q)$ is indeed $\mathcal{N}(p)$.

After phase 1, for predecessor q of p connected via link l, $nei_p[l] = lbl_q$. In phase 2, p computes $\pi_p[l]$ as the bit in which lbl_p and $nei_p[l]$ differ, so that lbl_p and lbl_q differ exactly in bit $\pi_p[l]$. The same label is used by q for the link, after q receives p's $\langle \mathbf{labl}, \pi_p[l] \rangle$ message. $\square$

Concluding, Algorithm 11.8/11.9 orients a hypercube with leader, exchanging $2 \cdot |E|$ messages. The message complexity is asymptotically optimal; see Corollary 11.27.

11.3.4 Efficient Hypercube Algorithms by Masking

Algorithm 11.8/11.9 can be used to perform other tasks on unlabeled hypercubes [DRT98] and one can even use fewer messages by excluding some processors from sending messages. This is done by defining a *mask*, which is a subset of the bitstrings of length n. Upon computing its node label, a processor will check if this label is in the mask (the mask is predefined and known to all processors). *If and only if* the label is in the mask, the processor will send messages, the same as specified in Algorithm 11.8/11.9.

Explanation of the mask algorithm. In the sequel, M is a subset of $\mathbb{Z}_2^n$, that is, a set of bitstrings of length n, and we denote by M_k the subset M of strings that contain exactly k 1's. Understandably, the mask must satisfy some requirements, and a few more modifications must be made to the algorithm, but this will be explained now. In the first place, the string $00\ldots00$ will always be in M and neighbors of the initiator will be able to compute their label upon receipt of the $\langle \mathbf{dmn}, i \rangle$ message. Other nodes in the mask must be able to compute their label by receiving messages from at least two predecesors. Thus, for string $v \in M_k$ (where $k \geq 2$) there must be at least two predecessors x and y in M_{k-1}.

A technical detail is now to be explained: as x and y are predecessors of v, v is a common successor of x and y, but x and y also have a common predecessor, let us say w. There are exactly two processors that receive the messages of both x and y, and these are the processors v and w. We shall require that the common predecessor of x and y has computed its label *before x and y send* by assuming that w is also in the mask.

Definition 11.23 *A mask is a subset $M \subseteq \mathbb{Z}_2^n$ satisfying*

(1) $0^n \in M$;

(2) *For $v \in M_k$ where $k \geq 2$, there are x, $y \in M_{k-1}$ that are predecessors of v;*

(3) *If v and its two predecessors x and y are in M, then the common predecessor of x and y is in M.*

Given a (commonly known) mask M, the operation of the algorithm is as follows.

(1) The initiator sends $\langle \mathbf{dmn}, i \rangle$ over link i where $00\ldots1\ldots00 \in M$ (the 1 is in the ith position).

(2) Upon receipt of such a message: the processor computes its label $lbl_p = 00\ldots1\ldots00$ and (because it is in M) sends $\langle \mathbf{iam}, lbl_p \rangle$ messages through all other edges.

(3) Upon receipt of *two* $\langle \mathbf{iam}, l \rangle$ messages that contain the same number of 1's in the string, a node can compute the label v that is the common successor of the two labels.
   If this label is *not* in M: ignore all further messages.
   If this label is in M: await the receipt of $\langle \mathbf{iam}, l \rangle$ from all predecessors of v that are in M, then send $\langle \mathbf{iam}, v \rangle$ through all links.

Observe that the algorithm computes less information than the "full" orientation algorithm 11.8/11.9: it computes the node label only for processors where the node label is in M, and computes the link label only if both endpoints are in M. But it also uses fewer messages: we can bound the number by $n \cdot |M|$ because only nodes with label in M send, and they send at most n messages each.

Small masks for sending and broadcast. We can now observe a phenomenon similar to Subsection 11.2.3: fine-tuning of the algorithm does not concentrate on algorithmical issues, but is a combinatorial exercise with properties of masks.

The first task we consider is *FarSend*, where the initiator wants to send a message to a specific node at distance d, w.l.o.g. we can assume its label to be $1^d 0^{n-d}$. This address is to be interpreted in the "private" sense of direction of the initiator, that is, the local link labeling of the initiator, which need not of course coincide with the orientation at other nodes. Recall that at the beginning, no node except the initiator has any knowledge of its node or link labels!

Lemma 11.24 *There exists a mask of size* $1 + \frac{d(d+1)}{2}$ *that contains* $1^d 0^{n-d}$.

Proof. The set $M = \{0^i 1^k 0^{n-i-k} \; : \; i + k \leq d\}$ satisfies all required properties. $\qquad\square$

Consequently, *FarSend* costs only $O(d^2 n)$ messages on unlabeled hypercubes. The size of this mask was shown to be optimal [DRT98]. The mask for *FarSend*ing a message to the node labeled v will be denoted by F_v.

The broadcast task would be solved with any mask that *covers* the entire network, that is, each node is contained in the mask or adjacent to a node in the mask. However, in order to have a linear complexity, the mask should contain at most $O(N/n)$ nodes and it is not known if a covering mask of this size exists. The broadcasting algorithm therefore uses *FarSend* to transfer the message to a sparser set of selected nodes, from which it is then flooded over a bounded number of hops. Because it takes $O(n^3)$ messages to *FarSend* to a single node, the number of "chiefs" in our algorithm is N/n^3.

Proposition 11.25 *There exists a set* $C \subseteq \mathbb{Z}_2^n$ *such that*
(1) $|C| = O(\frac{N}{n^3})$;
(2) *For each* $x \in \mathbb{Z}_2^n$, $d(x, C) \leq 3$.

The broadcast algorithm uses a set as specified in the proposition; its members are called *chiefs*. In the first phase, each chief receives the message from the originator by *FarSend*. In the second phase, each chief floods the message over distance 3, that is, sends the message to each neighbor, the neighbors forward it to their neigbors, and the latter forward it one step further to their neighbors.

Now observe that because of the second property of C, each node receives the message in phase 2. Next, consider the complexity. Because each chief is reached with $O(n^3)$ messages, the size bound of C implies that phase 1 costs linear messages. Because a chief has n neighbors and (less than) n^2 neighbors-of-neighbors, and each of these nodes sends n messages in the second phase, phase 2 costs linear messages as well.

Another application: FarOrient. The mask algorithm can be used to orient one node with respect to the other; assume node v wants to orient a specific node at distance d, that is, this node must relabel all its edges consistently with the edge labeling at v. Node u starts the mask algorithm with a mask M that contains all neighbors of v; as v will receive an $\langle \mathbf{iam}, l \rangle$ message through each link, it will be able to compute the direction of each link. It was shown [DRT98] that such masks exist of size close to $n \cdot d$ and this is optimal; hence *FarOrient* can be done with $O(n^3)$ messages.

11.3.5 Election in Unlabeled Hypercubes

The most efficient hypercube election algorithm is based on the principle of merging trees, as used in the Galleger–Humblet–Spira algorithm (Subsection 7.3.2). Topological properties of the hypercube are exploited to reduce the complexity. This section attempts to describe the most important techniques, but a full description of the algorithm is not given here; see [Dob99].

Recall that the GHS algorithm has a message complexity of $\Theta(N \log N + m)$, and this is optimal (without topological awareness). The two terms have different origins. One ingredient of the algorithm is the search for an edge leaving the current subtree: the GHS algorithm tests each edge for a possible merge with another tree. Only a linear number of these attempts is successful, while in most cases the edge is found to lead back to a member of the same subtree and these *unsuccessful* attempts contribute to the m-term in the complexity. Another part of the algorithm is concerned with merging two subtrees of sizes n_1 and n_2 into a single subtree of size $n_1 + n_2$. The GHS algorithm relabels the smaller tree and hence achieves the merge in $\min(n_1, n_2)$ messages and this keeps the total cost for merging at $\Theta(N \log N)$.

To keep the cost of the election low, we need to bound the number of edges that are tried unsuccessfully, and we must reduce the cost of merging subtrees. In the first stage of Dobrev's algorithm, nodes initiate the construction of a subtree of constant depth (5) according to the breadth-first search method. The hypercube topology implies a bound on the number of unsuccessful explore attempts; indeed, a node at distance 5 from the root has exactly five neighbors at level 4 in the tree, hence is "found" exactly five times, a constant number. Hence, BFS trees of depth 5 can be constructed at acceptably low cost.

If a tree contains all nodes at distance 5 and less from some center node, a different expansion strategy is used. Because at most $O(N/n^5)$ trees remain, a cost of n^5 messages per merge is acceptable. In a tree center, the tree is represented by a list of relative positions, but expressed in the "private" sense of direction; that is, the sense of direction that would result if the local edge labeling of the center were extended to the entire graph.

Having the entire tree available in this format allows the center to decide on a position where the tree must be extended: a point at distance 5 from the tree. If no such point exists, the center becomes leader; the condition implies that nowhere in the hypercube there is a ball of radius 5 belonging to a distinct subtree. The chosen point will be approached using *FarOrient* and from there the tree is extended, either by a BFS for five levels, or by merging with another subtree.

To merge two trees, the list of positions in one center is translated to the sense of direction of the other center; this is done by *FarOrient*, which orients the two nodes consistently w.r.t. each other. The resulting algorithm is far from simple; its analysis is a subject of current research.

11.4 Complexity-related Issues

The main themes concerning sense of direction and topological awareness were developed in the previous sections; we now continue with some other, less interrelated issues, some of which are central in current research.

11.4.1 Orienting a Clique or Arbitrary Graph

Knowing that sense of direction reduces the complexity of some tasks, the question arises if sense of direction can be computed in networks where it is not given. Risking confusion with a graph operation in which edges of the graph are directed, we call the problem of computing sense of direction *orienting* the network. In this section we shall prove a lower bound on the message complexity of orienting a graph, and present several algorithms for network orientation.

Lower bound on orientation. Because orienting a network requires placing a label on every edge, it requires using every edge, as demonstrated in the first theorem.

Theorem 11.26 *Any orientation algorithm exchanges at least $m - \frac{1}{2}N$ messages in every execution.*

Proof. For a link labeling $\mathcal{P}$, let $\mathcal{P}^{u,v,w}$ (where v and w are neighbors of u) be the labeling defined by $\mathcal{P}_u^{u,v,w}(v) = \mathcal{P}_u(w)$, $\mathcal{P}_u^{u,v,w}(w) = \mathcal{P}_u(v)$, and all other labels of $\mathcal{P}^{u,v,w}$ as in $\mathcal{P}$. ($\mathcal{P}^{u,v,w}$ is obtained by exchanging $\mathcal{P}_u(w)$ and $\mathcal{P}_u(v)$.) If $\mathcal{L}$ is an orientation, $\mathcal{L}_u[v] = -\mathcal{L}_v[u]$ but $\mathcal{L}_u^{u,v,w}[v]$ is different, hence $\mathcal{L}^{u,v,w}$ is *not* an orientation.

Consider an execution of an orientation algorithm, with initial labeling $\mathcal{P}$, that terminates with a permutation π_v for each node (where $\mathcal{L} = \pi(\mathcal{P})$ is an orientation). Assume furthermore that in this execution some node u did not send or receive any message to or from its two neighbors v and w. As u has not communicated with v, or with w, the same execution is possible if the network is initially labeled with $\mathcal{P}^{u,v,w}$, and all processors terminate with the same permutation. However, $\mathcal{L}' = \pi(\mathcal{P}^{u,v,w}) = \mathcal{L}^{u,v,w}$ is *not* an orientation, and the algorithm is not correct.

It follows that in every execution, every node must communicate with at least all its neighbors except one. □

Corollary 11.27 *The orientation of the N clique requires the exchange of $\Omega(N^2)$ messages. The orientation of the n-dimensional hypercube requires the exchange of $\Omega(n2^n)$ messages. The orientation of the $n \times n$ torus requires the exchange of $\Omega(n^2)$ messages.*

Orienting a clique. The clique orientation algorithm (Algorithm 11.10) assigns each processor a unique number in the range $0, ..., N-1$; each processor computes its rank in the set of all names, after receiving the name of each neighbor. The rank of each neighbor is computed similarly, and the link label is found as the difference of the neighbor's and its own rank.

The algorithm relies on the availability of distinct identities in the nodes, but is easily adapted to use a leader instead. In that case, the leader starts to send the numbers 1 through $N-1$ to its neighbors, and then these numbers are used as the identities. Handing out these distinct number is cheap (N

```
begin for l = 1 to N − 1 do send ⟨name, p⟩ via l ;
      rec_p := 0 ;
      while rec_p < N − 1 do
         begin receive ⟨name, n⟩ via link l ;
               rec_p := rec_p + 1 ; nei_p[l] := n
         end ;
      (* Compute node label *)
      lbl_p := #{k : nei_p[k] < p} ;
      for l = 1 to N − 1 do
         begin (* Compute neighbor's node label and link label *)
               ll := #{k : nei_p[k] < nei_p[l]} ;
               if p < nei_p[l] then ll := ll + 1 ;
               π_p[l] := (ll − lbl_p) mod N
         end
  end
```

Algorithm 11.10 ORIENTATION OF CLIQUES.

---

messages) compared to finding the link labels, which must cost a quadratic number of messages according to Theorem 11.26.

Chordal sense of direction in arbitrary networks. In an arbitrary network the nodes can be numbered by a token traversing the network, for example by a depth-first search traversal, provided that a node is distinguished as starting node. The traversal uses $2m$ messages (one message crosses each edge in each direction) and nodes will be assigned a number in the order in which they are visited. During the traversal, the processors learn their own, but also their neighbors', numbers, and are then able to compute a chordal sense of direction. (The number of nodes must be known; if this is not a priori the case, the number nodes can be counted during traversal and broadcast from the initiator using an additional $N − 1$ messages.)

11.4.2 Bit complexity and Multi-path Flow Algorithm

We shall now evaluate the complexity on a more detailed level by considering the bit complexity of orientation on the hypercube. Theorem 11.26 already implies a bound on the number of messages, but can be extended to bound the bit complexity.

Lemma 11.28 *In the orientation of the n-dimensional hypercube, each node communicates at least $\Omega(n \log n)$ bits.*

Proof. It was already explained that the node must communicate at least $n - 1$ messages to be able to distinguish between its n links. In order to really distinguish between the links, these messages must be different, which implies they contain at least $\Omega(\log n)$ bits. □

The messages used in the multi-path flow algorithm (Subsection 11.3.3) contain a node label, which is n bits. It will now be shown that the algorithm can be implemented using only messages of $O(\log n)$ bits.

The algorithm does not need all information contained in the $\langle \mathbf{iam}, label \rangle$ messages; there is a lot of redundancy. It suffices to transmit the number of 1's, the smallest index at which there is a 1, and the sum modulo n of the indexes for which there is a 1. For a node label $label$ define the weight, low, and index sum as $wgt(label) = \#\{i : b_i = 1\}$; $low(label) = \min\{i : b_i = 1\}$; $ixs(label) = (\sum_{b_i=1} i) \bmod n$. Finally, the *summary* is the tuple $smy(label) = (wgt(label),\ low(label),\ ixs(label))$. The summary of a node is the summary of its node label.

Lemma 11.29 *Let p be a node at distance $d + 1 \geq 2$ from w.*
(1) We have that $dis_p = d + 1$ can be derived from one summary of a predecessor of p.
(2) The summary of p can be computed from the $d + 1$ summaries of p's predecessors.
(3) The node label of p can be computed from the summary of p and the $d+1$ summaries of p's predecessors.
(4) The node label of a predecessor q of p can be computed from the node label of p and the summary of q.

Proof. (1) The computation of dis_p is trivial as $wgt(\mathcal{N}(q))$ equals $d(q, w)$.

(2) Now let $d + 1$ summaries of predecessors of p be given. Then d of the $d + 1$ summaries have low equal to $low(\mathcal{N}(p))$, while one summary has a higher low (the predecessor whose label is found by flipping the *first* 1 in $\mathcal{N}(p)$). This gives $low(\mathcal{N}(p))$, but also identifies the index sum ixs_0 of a node label which differs from $\mathcal{N}(p)$ in position low. Thus $ixs(\mathcal{N}(p)) = (ixs_0 + low(\mathcal{N}(p))) \bmod n$. This completes the computation of $smy(\mathcal{N}(p))$.

(3) The $d+1$ positions of a 1 in $\mathcal{N}(p)$ are found as $ixs(\mathcal{N}(p)) - ixs(\mathcal{N}(q)) \bmod n$ for the $d + 1$ choices of q as a predecessor of p.

(4) For a predecessor q of p, $\mathcal{N}(q)$ is found by flipping the bit indexed $(ixs(\mathcal{N}(p)) - ixs(\mathcal{N}(q))) \bmod n$ from 1 to 0 in $\mathcal{N}(p)$. □

cons K (* Safety parameter *)

var $state : (sleep, awake, leader)$ **init** $sleep$;
         $maxid_p$;   (* Highest identity seen *)

To start an election:
        begin $i := p$; $s := 0$; $maxid_p := i$;
                if $s < K$
                        then send $\langle \textbf{walk}, i, s + 1 \rangle$ through a *random* edge
                        else $state_p := leader$
        end

Upon arrival of token $\langle \textbf{walk}, i, s \rangle$:
        begin if $state_p = sleep$ **then** start an election ;
                receive $\langle \textbf{walk}, i, s \rangle$; $maxid_p := \max(maxid_p, i)$;
                if $i = maxid_p$
                        then if $s < K$
                                        then send $\langle \textbf{walk}, i, s + 1 \rangle$ through a *random* edge
                                        else $state_p := leader$
                        else (* Kill token *) **skip**
        end

Algorithm 11.11 THE ELECTION ALGORITHM (FOR PROCESSOR p).

It follows from Lemma 11.29 that it suffices in the orientation algorithm to send the summary of a node label instead of the full label, and hence the algorithm can be implemented with messages of $O(\log n)$ bits.

11.4.3 Verweij's Random Walk Algorithm

We now present Verweij's [VT95] randomized, Monte Carlo algorithm for the election problem; it works for any topology and does *not* use sense of direction because it is based on competing random walks.

Initially each processor is in state *sleep*. Upon becoming *awake* (this happens spontaneously or upon receipt of a message in the *sleep* state) the processor generates a token containing its identity and a hop counter. Tokens are forwarded through the network in a *random walk* and are removed from the network by a processor already visited by a token with larger identity. When a token has completed K steps without being removed, the processor holding it becomes elected; see Algorithm 11.11.

How does it work? The largest token initiated is not killed; consequently, this token completes K steps and causes a process to become leader; this is called a *correct* leader claim. This property implies that the algorithm can only fail by choosing multiple leaders, but *not* by choosing no leader at all.

The algorithm fails (i.e., elects more than one leader) if any non-maximal token succeeds in completing K steps without entering a processor already visited by a larger token. The resulting leader claim is termed a *false* one. The probability of false claims is reduced by increasing K, but because tokens can make as many as K steps, increasing K also increases the message complexity.

For $K = 0$ every token generated results in a false claim. Thus the failure probability is high (1), but the message complexity is low (0). On the other hand, if K runs to ∞ the error probability converges to 0 because no non-maximal token can make infinitely many steps and still avoid the largest processor with positive probability.

Fortunately the choice of K is not very critical for the correctness or complexity properties of the algorithm. First, even with small K, the message complexity is at least linear in N because every processor may generate a token. Second, choosing K larger than necessary for the desired reliability generates additional token steps, but (with high probability) only for the maximal token! It follows from this discussion that the asymptotic expected number of messages is not influenced by K as long as it exceeds the minimal value by a linear amount.

A mathematical analysis of the complexity and the necessary value of K are not known; this is an open problem. In the sequel we shall sketch why this is difficult and that a full, competitive analysis can only be expected in combination with timing assumptions.

Timing assumptions. The optimal value of K and the performance of the algorithm are influenced by the relative speeds of the tokens. The following discussion refers to the case where the network is a clique, i.e., each successive step of the token leads to a completely random node.

On the one extreme, consider the case where the largest token is infinitely slow as compared to the second largest one. Here the second token is killed only when entering the maximal processor, and, for example, in the clique, a linear value of K would be necessary to ensure this with probability close to 1.

Considering message complexity, the worst timing arises when any token is received only when all tokens with smaller identities have been killed. Then every token is killed only by being received by a processor with larger identity, and for the $(i + 1)$th largest identity this happens only after an expected number of $\Omega(N/i)$ steps. The discussion implies that in a fully asynchronous clique the message complexity is $\Omega(N \log N)$.

On the other hand, consider the case of synchronous cliques, where at any moment, each of the surviving tokens has made equally many steps. After $O(\sqrt{N})$ steps, the largest token has visited $O(\sqrt{N})$ processors, and after another $O(\sqrt{N})$ steps the second token enters one of these with probability close to 1. Consequently $K = O(\sqrt{N})$ suffices to kill the second largest token with high probability; the probability of false leader claims by smaller tokens is very small.

Simulation study of complexity. The algorithm was simulated to establish its complexity empirically [VT95] on cliques and hypercubes, and a message complexity of about $3N$ messages was found. It can be seen that this measurement is far better than the complexity that can be argued in the fully asynchronous case. This implies that, in order to derive the complexity analytically, timing assumptions (cf. the Archimedean assumption) must be taken into account.

11.5 Conclusions and Open Questions

We have seen that sense of direction allows for efficient exploitation of the network topology and for more direct communication between processors. Studying the properties of sense of direction is the topic of the annual SIROCCO (Structural InfoRmatiOn and Communication COmplexity) meeting. Proceedings of the SIROCCO meeting are published by Carleton University Press.

11.5.1 Use of Sense of Direction

It was pointed out in Subsection 11.1.2 that sense of direction can be useful in various ways. The path comparison capability makes it possible to circumvent the $\Omega(m)$ lower bound on broadcast and election algorithms, because it is no longer necessary to send a message over an edge to verify if the neighbor was already reached by the algorithm. Path comparison opens the possibility for linear broadcast and $O(N \log N)$ elections in arbitrary networks.

Path compression makes it possible to reach nodes with known position through shortest paths. Section 11.2 demonstrated its use in election algorithms for chordal rings, where the amount of path compression can be fine-tuned by choosing various settings for the chords. It was shown that

Task	Network	No SoD No TA	No SoD TA	SoD and TA	Improvement due to
BC	Arbitrary	m	(1)	N	Yes: SD
	Chord. Ring (2)	$c \cdot N$	unknown	N	Yes (3)
	Torus	N	N	N	No
	HyperCube	$N \cdot n$	N	N	Yes: TA
	Clique	N^2	N	N	Yes: TA
El.	Arbitrary	$N \log N + m$	(1)	$N \log N$	Yes: SD
	Chord. Ring (2)	$N \log N$	N	N	Yes: TA
	Torus	$N \log N$	N	N	Yes: TA
	HyperCube	$N \log N$	??	N	Yes: TA or SD
	Clique	N^2	$N \log N$	N	Yes: TA+SD

Remarks:
(1) Topological awareness is not relevant for this class.
(2) c is the number of chords; assume $c \leq \log N$.
(3) Unknown if improvement can be achieved with TA only.

Table 11.12 STRUCTURAL KNOWLEDGE AND COMPLEXITY.

path compression may lead to linear election algorithms even if only a modest amount of chords are available. The use path compression requires that the sense of direction is uniform.

Section 11.2 also compares path compression to a third capability of sense of direction: exploitation of the topological knowledge that is implicit in uniform sense of direction. It was shown that fewer chords are necessary to obtain a linear election algorithm if this knowledge is exploited in the algorithm.

11.5.2 Complexity Reduction

Table 11.12 summarizes many of the findings reported in this chapter. It gives the message complexity for broadcast and election on various network classes, considering three assumptions. First, neither topological awareness nor sense of direction is assumed; because the algorithm does not "know" in what topology it is, both tasks require the algorithm to send through every edge. Second, topological awareness is assumed; this allows the algorithm to exploit properties of the network graph, but the directions of the edges is not known. Third, both topological awareness and sense of direction are given.

The rightmost column reports whether structural information helps to reduce the complexity of the task. We see that in all cases except broad-casting on a torus (which can be done with linear messages even without knowing the network is a torus), structural information reduces the message complexity. In most cases, however, the reduction is due to the availability of topological awareness. Barring the reduction achieved in arbitrary net-works, election in cliques has remained the only task for which directing the edges provably reduces message complexity.

If it isn't in asymptotic message complexity, sense of direction brings other advantages: simpler algorithms, smaller implicit constants, and better time complexities.

11.5.3 Current Research

Here are some directions of the current research on this topic.

(1) Prove Lemmas 11.11 and 11.14 for general routing strategies.
(2) For what values of the chord length t can the one-chord algorithm (Subsection 11.2.4) be adapted, and still have a linear message com-plexity?
(3) Compute the expected complexity of the random walk election algo-rithm (for cliques, hypercubes, and tori).
(4) Generalize the results in this chapter for sense of direction based on non-commutative groups. Such a generalization would be of interest, for example, w.r.t. the cube connected cycles network, defined using a permutation group.

Exercises to Chapter 11
Section 11.1

Exercise 11.1 *Let $\mathcal{L}$ be a labeling of edges with elements of group G and denote by $SUM(P)$ the sum of labels found on path P. Prove that the following two are equivalent.*

(1) $\mathcal{L}$ *is a sense of direction.*
(2) *A path P is closed iff $SUM(P) = 0$.*

Section 11.2

Project 11.2 *Show that* $\Omega(\log \log N)$ *chords are necessary with any routing strategy to make the summation in Lemma 11.9 a geometric series. (Compare Lemma 11.11.)*

Section 11.3

Exercise 11.3 *What is the time complexity of the match-making algorithm (Subsection 11.3.2)?*

12

Synchrony in Networks

In this chapter we investigate how the theory of distributed computing is affected by the assumption that there exists a global time, to which processes have access. A global time frame is part of the physical reality that surrounds us; this reality includes the processes of a distributed system and the design of distributed algorithms may profit from exploiting time. The results of this chapter show that time can be exploited to reduce the communication complexity of distributed algorithms if processing and communication times are bounded.

However, problems that are unsolvable without using time remain unsolvable after its introduction; thus, introducing synchrony improves the compexity but not the computability of distributed systems. This situation differs from the impact of synchronism in networks that are subject to failures; in Chapters 14 and 15 it will be shown that larger classes of failures can be handled deterministically if synchronism is exploited. Synchronism has already been used in Section 3.2 to overcome transmission failures.

In this chapter global time will mainly be studied in an idealized form, namely, where the entire network operates in discrete steps called *pulses*, as explained in Subsection 12.1.1. Each process performs local computations in each pulse, and it is ensured that a message that is sent in one pulse is received before the next pulse. This globally synchronized operation is also referred to as a *lockstep* operation. Lockstep operation is fairly easy to implement if clocks are available and an upper bound on transmission delay is assumed; see Subsection 12.1.3.

A network operating in lockstep is usually referred to as a *synchronous network*. A synchronous network must not be confused with a network where messages are passed synchronously, as defined in Section 2.1.3. In the latter there is no global synchronism. Only when two processes communicate do they synchronize temporarily in the message exchange; they do not synchronize with all processes and the synchrony is broken immediately after the message exchange.

Globally synchronized networks are able to solve distributed problems using less communication than fully asynchronous networks. This will be demonstrated by providing synchronous algorithms (for the election problem) with a complexity below the proven lower bounds for asynchronous algorithms for the same problem; see Section 12.2. That synchronous algorithms cannot solve more problems than asynchronous algorithms will be shown by providing so called *synchronizer* algorithms, by which asynchronous networks simulate synchronous networks; see Section 12.3.

The design of distributed algorithms is often easier for synchronous networks, because less non-determinism has to be taken into account. An asynchronous algorithm may be designed by first giving a synchronous algorithm and then combining it with the simulation techniques of Section 12.3. Despite the overhead introduced by the synchronizer, the resulting algorithm may still compare favorably with algorithms designed directly for asynchronous networks. As an application of synchronizers the construction of breadth-first search trees will be considered in Section 12.4.

Even if clocks are not available, some very weak timing assumptions may be justified, for example that the ratio between the execution speeds of the fastest and the slowest component in the system is bounded. This assumption, referred to as the *Archimedean assumption* [Vit85], is discussed briefly in Section 12.5. It has been argued that it is generally better to rely on fully asynchronous algorithms and not to exploit timing assumptions, for several reasons. In the Archimedean framework, algorithms are designed so that their correctness does not rely on timing assumptions, while their complexity profits from such assumptions.

12.1 Preliminaries

12.1.1 Synchronous Networks

In a *synchronous* distributed system the operation of each process takes place in a (possibly infinite) sequence of discrete steps, called *pulses*. In a pulse a process first sends (zero or more) messages, then receives (zero or more) messages, and finally performs local computations (changing the state). Messages are received in the same pulse as that in which they are sent; i.e., if p sends a message to q in its ith pulse, then the message is received by q in its ith pulse and before q's computation in that pulse.

The pulses can be thought of as the ticks ("pulses") of a global clock.

Computation is performed at the clock pulses, and a message sent at one pulse is guaranteed to be received before the next pulse. The system configuration after i pulses is defined to be the tuple consisting of the state of each process after the ith pulse.

To define synchronous systems formally, let $\mathcal{M}$, as in Chapter 2, be a set of messages and let $\mathcal{PM}$ denote the collection of multisets of messages. The definition of a process in a synchronous system differs from that of a process in an asynchronous system, because collections of messages are sent and received in a single system transition. To avoid confusion we shall refer to processes of a synchronous system as *synchronous processes*.

Definition 12.1 *A synchronous process is a four-tuple* $p = (Z, I, \mathcal{MG}, \vdash)$ *where*

(1) Z *is a set of states,*

(2) I *is a subset of Z of initial states,*

(3) $\mathcal{MG} : Z \to \mathcal{PM}$ *is a message-generation function, and*

(4) $\vdash$ *is a relation on $Z \times \mathcal{PM} \times Z$. We write $(c, M) \vdash d$ for $(c, M, d) \in \vdash$.*

A process starts its computation in a state $c_0 \in I$. When the process starts a pulse in state $c \in Z$, it sends the collection $\mathcal{MG}(c)$ of messages. Before the next pulse, it receives the collection of messages, say M, sent to it in this pulse and enters a state d such that $(c, M) \vdash d$.

Under this definition the collection of messages sent by the process is fully determined by the state at the beginning of the pulse; all internal non-determinism of the process is in the relation $\vdash$. It is possible to allow non-determinism in $\mathcal{MG}$ as well ($\mathcal{MG}$ is then a relation rather than a function), but the non-deterministic choice can equally well be modeled in the relation $\vdash$.

A synchronous system is a collection $\mathbb{P}$ of synchronous processes, and a configuration of a synchronous system is a tuple consisting of a state of each process. An initial configuration is a configuration in which each process is in an initial state. The state changes of all processes are synchronized in one global transition of the system, where the state change of each process is influenced by the collection of messages sent to it in the current configuration.

Definition 12.2 *The synchronous system consisting of (synchronous) processes* $\mathbb{P} = (p_1, \ldots, p_N)$ *(where p_i is the process $(Z_i, I_i, \mathcal{MG}_i, \vdash_i)$) is a transition system* $S = (\mathcal{C}, \to, \mathcal{I})$, *where*

(1) $\mathcal{C} = \{(c_1, c_2, \ldots, c_N) : \forall i, c_i \in Z_i\}$,

(2) $\rightarrow$ *is the relation defined by* $(c_1, \ldots, c_N) \rightarrow (d_1, \ldots, d_N)$ *if, for each*
    $p_i \in \mathbb{P}$; $(c_i, \{m \in (\cup_{p_j \in \mathbb{P}} \mathcal{MG}_j(c_j)) : m$ *has destination* $p_i\}) \vdash_i d_i$;

(3) $\mathcal{I} = \{(c_1, c_2, \ldots, c_N) : \forall i, c_i \in I_i\}$.

A *synchronous computation* of a system is a maximal sequence $\gamma_0, \gamma_1, \ldots$
of configurations, such that γ_0 is an initial configuration and, for all $i \geq 0$,
$\gamma_i \rightarrow \gamma_{i+1}$. The message complexity of this computation is the number of
messages exchanged, and the time complexity equals the index of the last
configuration (assuming the computation is finite).

12.1.2 Increased Efficiency through Synchronism

Where useful it will be assumed implicitly in the algorithms of this chapter
that the state of a process includes a pulse counter, indicating the number of
pulses executed by the process. In this subsection we shall discuss a number
of paradigms that can be used in synchronous networks in order to decrease
the communication complexity of distributed algorithms.

Coding in time. It is possible to save on the number of bits exchanged by
sending an arbitrary message using only two bits. To this end, the contents
of the message will be "coded" in the time (number of pulses) between the
sending of the two bits.

Assume process p must send a message to process q. It is assumed here
that the message contents can be represented as an integer m. To transmit
the value m, two messages, $\langle\text{start}\rangle$ and $\langle\text{stop}\rangle$, are used. Process p sends a
$\langle\text{start}\rangle$ message in pulse i, the pulse in which the transmission is initiated,
and a $\langle\text{stop}\rangle$ message in pulse $i + m$. Process q receives a $\langle\text{start}\rangle$ and a
$\langle\text{stop}\rangle$ message, say in pulses a and b, respectively, and accepts the message
$b - a$ in pulse b. Coding in time causes message transmission to be time
consuming; q accepts the message m pulses later than the pulse in which
p initiated its transmission. Message transmission can be made less time
consuming at the expense of sending more bits; see Exercise 12.1.

Implicit messages. In asynchronous systems a process can obtain information from a neighbor only by receiving a message from this neighbor. In
synchronous systems, if a process receives no message from a given neighbor
in some pulse, the neighbor did not send a message in this pulse; thus, the
process has obtained information about the state of its neighbor.

As an example, consider Toueg's algorithm for the all-pairs shortest-paths
problem (Algorithm 4.6). In the pivot round for pivot w, each process must
learn which of its neighbors are sons in the tree T_w, to which end a $\langle\text{ys}, w\rangle$ or

⟨**nys**, w⟩ message is exchanged via each channel. In a synchronous network only ⟨**ys**, w⟩ messages need be sent; if no such message is received (in the pulse in which the exchange of these messages takes place) from a neighbor, this neighbor is not a son. Making the ⟨**nys**, w⟩ messages implicit reduces the complexity of computing the sons of each process from $2|E|$ to at most $N - 1$ messages. (Sending the ⟨**nys**, w⟩ messages can be avoided in asynchronous systems as well, but at the cost of a more complicated algorithm and increased space complexity.)

Selective delay. We have met distributed algorithms that start several subcomputations one of which is guaranteed to produce the desired result, while the results of all other subcomputations are ignored. Examples of such algorithms include election algorithms obtained by applying the extinction principle (Subsection 7.3.1) to a centralized wave algorithm.

Each particular subcomputation can be slowed down by a different factor in order to reduce the message complexity. In the asynchronous case it cannot be avoided (at least in the worst case) that non-successful subcomputations run to completion, which brings the communication complexity to the number of subcomputations times the complexity of each individual subcomputation. In the synchronous case the number of steps taken by a non-successful subcomputation is bounded by the completion time of the successful subcomputation divided by the slow-down factor of this subcomputation. The selective delay produced by carefully chosen slow-down factors will be analyzed in Subsection 12.2.2.

12.1.3 Asynchronous Bounded-delay Networks

The assumption underlying synchronous networks, namely, that all state changes of processes are globally synchronized, is a very strong one. A more moderate assumption is that processes are equipped with (not necessarily synchronized) physical clocks, and that there is an upper bound on the message delivery time. This model was used in Section 3.2 and after Chou *et al.* [CCGZ90] such networks are referred to as *asynchronous bounded-delay networks* or shortly *ABD networks*.

Definition 12.3 *An asynchronous bounded-delay network is a distributed system where the following assumptions hold.*

(1) *The execution of an event in a process takes zero time units.*

(2) *Each process has a clock to measure physical time; if $CLOCK_p^{(t)}$ denotes the value of p's clock at time t, and p does not assign a value*

to its clock between t_1 and t_2, then

$$CLOCK_p^{(t_2)} - CLOCK_p^{(t_1)} = t_2 - t_1.$$

(3) *The physical time between the sending and the receipt of a message is bounded by μ, i.e., if a message is sent at time σ and received at time τ, then*

$$\sigma < \tau < \sigma + \mu.$$

It is not difficult to implement a synchronous network on an ABD network, using only a small overhead in messages and time. A mechanism to implement synchronous networks is called a *synchronizer*; see also Section 12.3. The main difficulty in the design of synchronizers is to ensure that a process receives all messages of pulse i before changing state and starting pulse $i+1$.

ABD synchronizers. The principle of synchronizers for ABD networks is that the clocks of processes are synchronized as accurately as possible, say with precision δ, and each process executes a next pulse after $\delta + \mu$ time units of its clock. Algorithms for clock synchronization are discussed in Section 15.3. We now present some elementary results by Tel *et al.* [TKZ94].

The ABD synchronizer of Tel *et al.* consists of two parts, namely, a *clock-synchronization phase* and a *simulation phase*, together given as Algorithm 12.1. In the clock-synchronization phase each process resets its clock to zero and sends ⟨ **start** ⟩ messages to each of its neighbors. By the assumptions underlying ABD networks, the resetting and sending of the ⟨ **start** ⟩ messages takes zero time. A process executes these steps either to initiate the synchronous algorithm (spontaneously) or when the first ⟨ **start** ⟩ message is received. As a result of the synchronization phase, the clocks of neighboring processes are synchronized with precision μ.

Theorem 12.4 *At each time t after the execution of the initialization procedure init by neighbors p and q, the clocks of p and q satisfy*

$$|CLOCK_p^{(t)} - CLOCK_q^{(t)}| < \mu.$$

Proof. Let w_p (or w_q) denote the time at which p (or q, respectively) executes the procedure *init*. As p sends to q a ⟨ **start** ⟩ message at time w_p, and q executes *init* at the latest when this message is received, $w_q < w_p + \mu$. By reversing p and q in this argument, $|w_p - w_q| < \mu$ is obtained. Because p and q do not assign values to their clocks after the execution of *init*, we have for $t \geq \max(w_p, w_q)$,

$$|CLOCK_p^{(t)} - CLOCK_q^{(t)}|$$

```
var CLOCK_p    : clock ;
    state_p    : Z_p ;
    pulse_p    : integer ;
```

procedure *init*:   (* Can be executed spontaneously *)
    begin if not $started_p$ **then**
            begin $CLOCK_p := 0$;
                forall $q \in Neigh_p$ **do** send $\langle$ **start** $\rangle$ to q
        end
    end

$\mathbf{I}_p$: { A $\langle$ **start** $\rangle$ message has arrived at p }
    begin receive $\langle$ **start** $\rangle$; *init* **end**

$\mathbf{P}_p^{(i)}$:{ The start of the ith pulse at p }
    when $CLOCK_p = 2i\mu$ **do**
        begin (* End previous pulse, compute $state_p^{(i-1)}$ *)
            if $i = 1$
                then $state_p :=$ initial state
                else (* M is the collection of $(i-1)$-messages received *)
                    $state_p := d_p$ satisfying $(state_p, M) \vdash d_p$;
            $pulse_p := i$;
            (* send the messages of pulse i *)
            $M' = \mathcal{MG}(state_p)$; send all messages of M'
        end

$\mathbf{M}_p$:{ A basic i-message has arrived *)
    begin receive and store the message **end**

Algorithm 12.1 THE ABD SYNCHRONIZER.

$$= \|[CLOCK_p^{(w_p)} + (t - w_p)] - [CLOCK_q^{(w_q)} + (t - w_q)]\|$$
$$= \|[0 + (t - w_p)] - [0 + (t - w_q)]\|$$
$$= |w_q - w_p| < \mu.$$

□

In the simulation phase the processes execute the pulses (state changes) dictated by the synchronous algorithm. A message that is exchanged by the synchronous algorithm in pulse i will be referred to as an i-*message*. The ith pulse is started when the local clock reads $2i\mu$, after a state change using the $(i-1)$-messages received so far. The approximate synchronization and the upper bound on the message delay imply that all messages of a pulse have arrived at a process before this process starts the next pulse, and that the system behaves as a synchronous system. Let $state_p^{(i)}$ denote the state of process p after $i + 1$ state changes, i.e., after the start of the $(i + 1)$th pulse, and write γ_i for the tuple $(state_{p_1}^{(i)}, \ldots, state_{p_N}^{(i)})$. The reader should note that this tuple does not necessarily occur as a configuration of the ABD network, because it may be the case that the processes are never in these states simultaneously.

Theorem 12.5 *The sequence $C = (\gamma_0, \gamma_1, \ldots)$ is a computation of the synchronous algorithm.*

Proof. It is shown by induction on i that the sequence $(\gamma_0, \gamma_1, \ldots, \gamma_i)$ is the prefix of a computation. For $i = 0$, observe that γ_0 is an initial configuration for the synchronous algorithm because for each p, $state_p^{(0)}$ is an initial state of p in the synchronous algorithm.

Assume that $(\gamma_0, \gamma_1, \ldots, \gamma_i)$ is a prefix of a computation of the synchronous algorithm. Process p ends pulse $i + 1$ and changes its state to $state_p^{(i+1)}$ when its clock reads $2(i + 2)\mu$, using the set $M_p^{(i+1)}$ of $(i + 1)$-messages it has received so far. To show that the configuration defined by $(state_{p_1}^{(i+1)}, \ldots, state_{p_N}^{(i+1)})$ extends the computation, it suffices to demonstrate that $M_p^{(i+1)}$ equals the set of messages sent to p in pulse $i + 1$.

Assume that q sends a message to p in pulse $i + 1$, i.e., when q's clock reads $2(i+1)\mu$. Let σ be the (global) time at which this message is sent, and τ the (global) time at which it is received by p. As $CLOCK_q^{(\sigma)} = 2(i+1)\mu$ and q is a neighbor of p, $CLOCK_p^{(\sigma)} < 2(i+1)\mu + \mu$ (by Theorem 12.4). As $\tau - \sigma < \mu$, $CLOCK_p^{(\tau)} < 2(i+1)\mu + \mu + \mu = 2(i+2)\mu$, i.e., p receives the message before p ends pulse $i + 1$. $\qquad\square$

It is possible that a process receives a message of pulse i before starting that pulse itself. The message must then be stored and processed only in the next pulse. It must be possible for a process to decide, for each message received, in which pulse it must be processed; this is possible if the pulse number modulo 2 is sent with each message; see Exercise 12.3. No additional information is necessary if each process stores the clock time at which the ⟨start⟩ message of each neighbor is received; see Exercise 12.4 or [TKZ94].

Complexity of synchronization. The complexity of a synchronization mechanism is measured in communication and in time, where both the initialization of the synchronizer and the overhead per simulated pulse are considered; see also Section 12.3.

The initialization phase requires the exchange of $2|E|$ messages and takes $O(D)$ time units. The simulation phase requires no additional messages (only the messages of the simulated synchronous algorithm are sent) and the processes complete one pulse every 2μ time units. The time between pulses is called the *pulse time*.

Tel *et al.* [TKZ94] have studied the class of all synchronizers for ABD networks that use $2|E|$ messages in the initialization phase and no additional messages during simulation. They have shown that a pulse time of 2μ is optimal for arbitrary networks, for rings, and for hypercubes. Stars can be synchronized with a pulse time of $(3/2)\mu$ and cliques with a pulse time of $(2 - 1/N)\mu$, and all these pulse times are optimal.

Clock drift and non-negligible processing time. In order to use results for ABD networks in practical situations the assumptions in Definition 12.3 must be relaxed. In practice the clocks of processors suffer from drift, and the time for processing a message is not equal to zero.

Drifting clocks can be dealt with by increasing the pulse time gradually during the simulation phase to compensate for the possibly growing difference between the clock readings of neighboring processes. If the pulse time would thus become too large (after simulating many pulses), it is possible to re-execute the synchronization phase after a predetermined number of pulses; see [Tel91b, Chapter 2].

If the time necessary for processing the messages of one pulse and starting the next pulse is not negligible but bounded by a constant π, the synchronizer can easily be adapted by increasing the pulse time by π.

12.2 Election in Synchronous Networks

The aim of this section is to show that synchronous networks require a strictly smaller message complexity for the sloution of certain problems than do asynchronous networks. In Chapter 7 lower bounds on the number of messages exchanged by an asynchronous network in electing a leader were proved. The synchronous algorithms given in this section have a message complexity that is below these bounds. The time complexity (i.e., the number of the pulse in which a leader is elected) depends heavily on whether the size of the network is known or not.

The algorithms assume that the identities of the processes are distinct integers; if the identities are taken from an arbitrary countable set, they can be converted into integers using a fixed enumeration of this set. It is also assumed that all initiators of the algorithm start the election in the same pulse (pulse 0). The case where initiators do not necessarily start the algorithm in the same pulse is briefly discussed in Subsection 12.2.3.

12.2.1 The Network Size is Known

The algorithms considered in this subsection rely on knowledge of an upper bound D on the network diameter. If the number of processes, N, is known, the value $N - 1$ can always be used as an upper bound on the diameter.

The algorithm. Process p can flood a message by sending it to each neighbor, after which each process other than p that receives a message for the first time sends it to each of its neighbors in the next pulse. Flooding a message in this way costs $2|E|$ messages and if a process initiates the flooding of a message in pulse i_0, each process receives this message at the latest in pulse $i_0 + (D - 1)$. This implies that if a process has not received a flooded message in pulse $i + (D - 1)$ or earlier, no process has initiated a flooding in pulse i or earlier.

In the election algorithm exactly one message is flooded, namely, by the process p_0 with the smallest identity, and this flooding is initiated in pulse $p_0 D$. Process p_0 knows there is no process with an identity smaller than p_0 if it has received no flooded message in or before pulse $p_0 D - 1$. By not initiating the flooding of a message, all processes have implicitly flooded the message "my identity exceeds $p_0 - 1$".

Summarizing, process p waits until either a message arrives, or the pulse number reaches pD before p has received a message. In the latter case p initiates the flooding of a message and becomes the leader. The algorithm was proposed by Santoro and Rotem [SR85]. The message complexity is $O(|E|)$ and the time complexity is $p_0 D + (D - 1)$, where p_0 is the smallest identity of any process. Observe that the time complexity is not bounded by a function of N.

Extensions and variants. The algorithm can easily be extended to compute a spanning tree of which the leader is the root. Each process chooses as its father one of the processes from which it received a message in the earliest pulse in which it received any message.

As no information need be exchanged in messages, the bit complexity of these algorithms equals their message complexity.

If topological knowledge is available the flooding can be done more efficiently. Of course, if the topology is arbitrary and unknown at least one message must be sent through each channel, as is shown by an argument similar to the one used in Theorem 7.15. If the topology is known to be a clique, torus, or hypercube the number of messages can be reduced by using more efficient flooding algorithms; see Exercise 12.6.

Van Leeuwen *et al.* [LSUZ87] have shown that the time complexity can be reduced at the expense of exchanging more messages. By allowing a flooding to take place k times (giving rise to a message complexity of $O(k.|E|)$), the smallest identity can be found in $O(p_0^{1/k}D)$ pulses.

12.2.2 The Network Size is Not Known

In the case where the network size and diameter are not known, an efficient election algorithm is obtained by applying extinction (Subsection 7.3.1) to a *traversal* algorithm, using a selective delay.

If process p is an initiator of the election algorithm, p initiates a traversal algorithm and labels the token by p. The token is forwarded according to the traversal algorithm, until either it is purged by a process that has already seen a smaller identity, or it terminates its traversal in process p. If the latter situation occurs, p becomes *leader*. The token of initiator p is delayed by 2^p pulses in each hop, i.e., if a process receives p's token in pulse i, it forwards the token in pulse $i + 2^p$.

The correctness of the resulting algorithm is proved similarly to Theorem 7.17; let p_0 be the initiator with smallest identity. Process p_0 receives its token back and becomes elected, and no token of an other initiator terminates the traversal because it is purged by p_0 or another initiator.

It remains to be shown how the selective delay bounds the complexity to $O(W)$ messages, where W is the complexity of the traversal algorithm. Process p_0 is elected in pulse $2^{p_0}W$, because the token makes W hops, each taking 2^{p_0} pulses. In pulse $2^{p_0}W$ each process has seen the identity p_0, hence no other token is forwarded in or after that pulse. The token of an initiator $p \neq p_0$ is forwarded at most $(2^{p_0}W)/2^p$ times, because it is not forwarded after pulse $2^{p_0}W$ and is forwarded at most $P/2^p$ times before pulse P. Let S be the set of initiators. The total number of message passings is bounded by W (the number of hops for the token of p_0) plus the number of hops by tokens other than p_0's token:

$$\text{complexity} = W + \sum_{p \in S \backslash \{p_0\}} (\text{hops by } p\text{'s token})$$

$$\leq W + \sum_{p \in S \backslash \{p_0\}} \frac{2^{p_0}W}{2^p}$$

$$< W + \sum_{i>0} \frac{W}{2^i} = 2W.$$

The contents of the message can be coded in time, so that each token can be transmitted using two messages of one bit each. This proves that the bit complexity of election is bounded by O(W). In this case, coding in time does not increase the time complexity further, because the delay that a token suffers in each node exceeds the time needed for its transmission. The time complexity of this algorithm is also not bounded by a function of N, and is in fact *exponential* in p_0, the smallest identity of any process.

12.2.3 Additional Results

Comparison algorithms. The algorithms described in this section are not comparison algorithms. In a comparison algorithm the only operation allowed on process identities is comparison, so counting pulses until an identity-dependent value is reached is not allowed.

Frederickson and Lynch [FL84] have shown that comparison algorithms for election on synchronous rings exchange at least $\Omega(N \log N)$ messages, that is, the asynchronous lower bounds hold for synchronous comparison algorithms. Also, Frederickson and Lynch have shown that if the time complexity is bounded by a function on N and the size of the set of possible identities is not bounded, each algorithm behaves like a comparison algorithm in the worst case, which implies that at least $\Omega(N \log N)$ messages are necessary.

This shows that the reduction in message complexity can be achieved only at the cost of increasing the time complexity to a value not bounded by a function of N. It is still an open question whether a synchronous election algorithm exists for networks of unknown size and having the same message complexity as the algorithm given above and a time complexity that is *polynomial* in the smallest identity.

Non-simultaneous start. The election problem becomes harder if it is not assumed (as we implicitly did) that each process initiates the election in the same pulsei (i.e., all processes start counting in pulse 0). By flooding wake-up messages when some processes start it can be ensured that all initiators start the algorithm within D pulses, which is sufficient for (adapted versions of) the algorithms in this section. Flooding costs O($|E|$) messages, however.

Election in cliques. With the algorithms of this section a leader can be elected in a clique using O(N) messages. These algorithms require, however, that all processes start the algorithm in the same pulse. The addition of an initialization phase in which a wake-up message is flooded increase the message complexity by $2|E|$, making it $\Omega(N^2)$. The complexity of election in cliques was analyzed by Afek and Gafni [AG91], who proved that $\Theta(N \log N)$ messages are required and sufficient if simultaneous start is not assumed.

They presented an algorithm with this message complexity and an $O(\log N)$ time complexity.

12.3 Synchronizer Algorithms

In this section we shall consider several synchronizers for fully asynchronous networks. The complexity of these synchronizers is measured by the following four parameters:

M_{init},   the message complexity of the initialization phase;
T_{init},   the time complexity of the initialization phase;
M_{pulse}, the message complexity of simulating each pulse;
T_{pulse}, the time complexity of simulating each pulse.

A process is said to simulate a certain pulse when it sends the messages of that pulse. The time complexity of the initialization phase is measured as the maximal time between the first step of any process and the last simulation of the first pulse. The time complexity of a pulse is the maximal time between the last simulation of one pulse and the last simulation of the next pulse. In both cases the time complexity is measured under the idealized timing assumptions of Definition 6.31. The message complexity of the pulse only counts additional messages, not the messages of the simulated algorithm.

A synchronous algorithm with message complexity M and time complexity T can be simulated using $M_{\text{init}} + M + M_{\text{pulse}}T$ messages in $T_{\text{init}} + T_{\text{pulse}}T$ time units. Table 12.3 presents an overview of the synchonizer algorithms of this chapter.

12.3.1 A Simple Synchronizer

In all synchronizers of this chapter a process certifies that all messages of the current pulse have been received; when this is the case all messages are processed and the next pulse is started. In the ABD synchronizer the certification is based on the use of clocks, but in synchronizers for fully asynchronous systems this is not possible. As all asynchronous algorithms can be written in message-driven form, each process must receive a message to trigger the next pulse, which implies that at least N messages are needed to simulate each pulse.

In the simplest synchronizer each process sends exactly one message to each neighbor in each pulse. If the simulated algorithm does not send a message in some pulse, the synchronizer adds an "empty" message. If the simulated algorithm sends more than one message, these messages are packed

var $pulse_p$: integer ;
$state_p$: Z_p ;
$wait_p$: integer   **init** $|Neigh_p|$;
$nwait_p$: integer   **init** $|Neigh_p|$;

To initiate the algorithm:
    begin (* start first pulse spontaneously *)
        $state_p :=$ initial state ; $pulse_p := 1$;
        forall $q \in Neigh_p$ **do**
            begin $M_p[q] := \{m \in \mathcal{MG}_p(state_p) :$
                        m has destination $q\}$;
                send $\langle$ **pack**, $M_p[q], pulse_p \rangle$ to q
            end
    end

{ A message $\langle$ **pack**, $(m_1, ..), i \rangle$ has arrived }
    begin receive and store message ;
        if $i = pulse_p$ **then** $wait_p := wait_p - 1$
                else $nwait_p := nwait_p - 1$;
        while $wait_p = 0$ **do**
            begin (* M is the set of received messages of this pulse *)
                $state_p := d_p$ with $(state_p, M) \vdash d_p$;
                $pulse_p := pulse_p + 1$;
                $wait_p := nwait_p$; $nwait_p := |Neigh_p|$;
                forall $q \in Neigh_p$ **do**
                    begin $M_p[q] := \{m \in \mathcal{MG}_p(state_p) :$
                              m has destination $q\}$;
                      send $\langle$ **pack**, $M_p[q], pulse_p \rangle$ to q
                end
        end
    end

Algorithm 12.2 A SIMPLE SYNCHRONIZER.

in one message of the synchronizer. Each process must receive exactly one message from each neighbor in every pulse; when a pulse-i message has been received from every neighbor, all messages are processed and pulse $i + 1$ is started; see Algorithm 12.2. The initialization is executed spontaneously by starters, and upon receipt of the first message by followers.

Process p with $pulse_p = i$ can only receive the messages of pulses i and $i + 1$. All messages of earlier pulses have already been received, and no neighbor of p can send messages of pulses higher than $i + 1$ before p has sent its messages of pulse $i + 1$. Therefore p only maintains knowledge of the number of messages still to be expected for the current ($wait_p$) and the next ($nwait_p$) pulse, and it suffices to transmit pulse numbers modulo 2.

No additional messages are necessary to initiate the simulation; each process sends the messages of the initial pulse either spontaneously or when a message is received. When at least one process starts the simulation, all processes join in within D time units. Consequently, $M_{\text{init}} = 0$ and $T_{\text{init}} = D$.

Each pulse requires the exchange of exactly $2|E|$ messages, and in the worst case all these messages are additional messages; hence $M_{\text{pulse}} = 2|E|$. If the last simulation of pulse i occurs at time t, all pulse-i messages have been received at time $t + 1$, and hence the last simulation of pulse $i + 1$ occurs at the latest at time $t + 1$. Consequently, $T_{\text{pulse}} = 1$.

Application of the simple synchronizer requires no leader, and no knowledge of the network size or other topological information; neither does it require the network to be named. The generality of the simple synchronizer shows that all synchronous algorithms can be simulated by asynchronous networks. Consequently, all problems that can be solved by synchronous algorithms can be solved in asynchronous systems.

12.3.2 The α, β, and γ Synchronizers

In the simple synchronizer each process communicates with each of its neighbors in every pulse, leading to a message complexity of $\Theta(|E|)$ for the simulation of each pulse. The message complexity can be reduced (at the cost of an increased time complexity) if communication takes place via a subtopology. The aim of the communication induced by a synchronizer is to let a process know that all messages sent by its neighbors in the current pulse have been received.

Process p becomes *safe* for its current pulse some time after the receipt of all messages sent by p in that pulse. An acknowledgement is sent for each message of the simulated algorithm, and when p has received an acknowledgement for each message, it becomes safe. The synchronizer must now provide the interprocess communication by which a process learns that all its neighbors are safe. When process p has verified that all its neighbors are safe for pulse i, p processes the messages of pulse i, changes state, and starts pulse $i + 1$.

The α and β synchronizers presented below are two special cases of the γ synchronizer presented thereafter. These three synchronizers were proposed by Awerbuch [Awe85a].

The α synchronizer. The first synchronizer, called the α synchronizer, is very similar to the simple synchronizer. Communication in the synchronizer takes place via each channel: each process, when safe, sends an $\langle$ **iamsafe** $\rangle$ message to each neighbor. A process learns that all neighbors are safe when an $\langle$ **iamsafe** $\rangle$ message has been received from each neighbor.

No initialization procedure is necessary, and clearly $O(|E|)$ messages are sent by the synchronizer for each pulse. If the last simulation of pulse i takes place at time t, all messages of this pulse have been received by $t + 1$, and all acknowledgements have been received by $t + 2$. Thus each process is safe by $t + 2$, and the $\langle$ **iamsafe** $\rangle$ messages have all been received by $t + 3$, allowing all processes to simulate pulse $i + 1$; hence $T_{\text{pulse}} = 3$.

The β synchronizer. In the β synchronizer communication takes place via a spanning tree. A process sends a $\langle$ **ts** $\rangle$ ("tree safe") message to its father in the tree when all processes in its subtree are safe; this is the case when the process is safe itself and a $\langle$ **ts** $\rangle$ message was received from each son in the tree. When the root is safe and has received a $\langle$ **ts** $\rangle$ message from each son, all processes are safe. The root sends a $\langle$ **pulse** $\rangle$ message via the spanning tree to let each process know that all processes are safe in the current pulse. The receipt of a $\langle$ **pulse** $\rangle$ message indicates that all processes are safe; this implies that all neighbors of the receiving process are safe, hence the process proceeds to the next pulse.

This synchronizer requires an initialization phase in which a spanning tree is computed. It was shown in Section 7.3 how this can be done using $\Theta(N \log N + |E|)$ messages, provided unique identities are available. An $O(N)$ time-units solution is possible. A centralized algorithm can compute a spanning tree using $O(|E|)$ messages in $O(N)$ time units.

In addition to the acknowledgement, each pulse requires $\langle$ **ts** $\rangle$ and $\langle$ **pulse** $\rangle$ messages to be sent via each edge of the tree, to a total of $O(N)$ control messages. The time this takes is proportional to the depth of the tree, which is $\Omega(N)$ in the worst case.

The γ synchronizer. The γ synchronizer requires an initialization phase in which the network is divided into clusters. Within each cluster the algorithm operates as the β synchronizer and between clusters the algorithm operates as the α synchronizer.

Each cluster contains a cluster spanning tree and a cluster leader, which is the root of the cluster spanning tree. For each two neighboring clusters (two clusters are neighbors if there exists an edge between nodes in the clusters) one *preferred edge* between the two clusters is chosen. Synchronization takes place in five steps.

(1) A $\langle\,\mathbf{ts}\,\rangle$ message is sent by a process to its father in the cluster tree if all processes in its subtree are safe, i.e., if the process is safe and has received a $\langle\,\mathbf{ts}\,\rangle$ message from each son.

(2) If the leader of a cluster is safe and has received a $\langle\,\mathbf{ts}\,\rangle$ message from each son, all processes of the cluster are safe. A $\langle\,\mathbf{cs}\,\rangle$ ("cluster safe") message is sent via the cluster spanning tree to let each process in the cluster know that all processes in the cluster are safe.

(3) The processes of a cluster that are incident to a preferred edge leading to another cluster send messages to the other clusters to indicate that the cluster is safe. To this end an $\langle\,\mathbf{ocs}\,\rangle$ ("our cluster safe") message is sent through the preferred edge when a $\langle\,\mathbf{cs}\,\rangle$ message is received.

(4) Messages are sent upwards in each cluster tree to report that all neighboring clusters are safe. A process sends an $\langle\,\mathbf{ncs}\,\rangle$ ("neighboring clusters safe") message to its father in the cluster tree when all neighboring clusters connected by preferred edges in its spanning tree are reported to be safe. This is the case when this process has received an $\langle\,\mathbf{ocs}\,\rangle$ message via all incident preferred edges and an $\langle\,\mathbf{ncs}\,\rangle$ message from each son in the cluster tree.

(5) When the cluster leader has received an $\langle\,\mathbf{ncs}\,\rangle$ message from each son and an $\langle\,\mathbf{ocs}\,\rangle$ message from each incident preferred edge, all neighboring clusters are safe. When this is the case and the cluster itself is safe, a $\langle\,\mathbf{pulse}\,\rangle$ message is sent via the cluster tree to trigger the start of the next pulse in each process of the cluster.

When a process receives a $\langle\,\mathbf{pulse}\,\rangle$ message, its cluster and the neighboring clusters are safe; this implies that all its neighbors are safe.

To establish the complexity of this synchronizer, for a clustering c, let E_c be the number of tree edges and preferred edges in c, and H_c the maximum height of a tree in c. As the synchronizer sends four messages via each tree edge ($\langle\,\mathbf{ts}\,\rangle$, $\langle\,\mathbf{cs}\,\rangle$, $\langle\,\mathbf{ncs}\,\rangle$, and $\langle\,\mathbf{pulse}\,\rangle$) and two messages via each preferred edge (two $\langle\,\mathbf{ocs}\,\rangle$ messages) to simulate each pulse, M_{pulse} is $O(E_c)$. Let t be the time of the last simulation of pulse i. At time $t+2$ all processes are safe, at time $t+2+H_c$ all clusters are known (by their leader) to be safe, and at time $t+2+2H_c$ all processes have received a $\langle\,\mathbf{cs}\,\rangle$ message and $\langle\,\mathbf{ocs}\,\rangle$ messages are now sent via each preferred edge. At time $t+3+2H_c$ all $\langle\,\mathbf{ocs}\,\rangle$ messages have been received, at time $t+3+3H_c$ the root of each cluster knows that all neighboring clusters are safe, and at time $t+3+4H_c$ all processes have received the ⟨**pulse**⟩ message and simulate the next pulse. Therefore, T_{pulse} is $O(H_c)$.

If the entire network is taken to be one cluster, $E_c = N - 1$ and $H_c = O(N)$, and the synchronizer is the same as synchronizer β. If each single node is taken to be one cluster, $E_c = E$ and $H_c = O(1)$, and the synchronizer is the same as synchronizer α.

Computation of a suitable clustering. The complexity of the γ synchronizer depends on the clustering used in the algorithm. By a clustering we mean a particular specification of the following:

(1) a division of the network in clusters (connected subgraphs);
(2) a center (leader) and a rooted spanning tree for each cluster;
(3) and one preferred edge between each pair of neighboring clusters.

Theorem 12.6 *For each k in the range $2 \leq k < N$, there exists a clustering c such that $E_c \leq k.N$ and $H_c \leq \log N / \log k$.*

Proof. The clustering is constructed incrementally by choosing clusters $C_1, C_2, \ldots$. Assume clusters C_1 through C_r have been chosen and there are remaining nodes in the network that do not belong to any cluster C_1 through C_r.

To construct C_{r+1}, choose one of the remaining nodes p as the leader of the cluster and add nodes to the cluster layer by layer. The singleton $\{p\}$ is the first layer of the cluster. After construction of i layers of C_{r+1} let n be the number of nodes in C_{r+1} and consider the set S of neighbors of nodes in the ith layer that do not yet belong to a cluster. If the size of S is at least $(k-1)n$, the nodes in S are added to C_{r+1} as the next layer. Otherwise, i.e., if S contains fewer than $(k-1)n$ nodes, the construction of C_{r+1} is complete.

The construction of each cluster implies that a cluster of i levels (i.e., with a spanning tree of depth $i-1$) contains at least k^{i-1} nodes, and consequently H_c is bounded by $\log_k N = \log N / \log k$.

The number of tree edges of the clustering is bounded by N, because the tree edges form a spanning forest of the network. Select for each two neighboring clusters one preferred edge and charge this edge to the cluster that was created first of the two. The construction of this cluster was complete when the number of remaining neighboring nodes was less than $k-1$ times the size of the cluster. This implies that for a cluster of size n there are at most $(k-1)n$ neighboring clusters that are created later. Consequently, with this charging policy a cluster of size n is charged for at most $(k-1)n$

Synchr.	M_{init}	T_{init}	M_{pulse}	T_{pulse}	Remarks
ABD	$2|E|$	$D\mu$	0	2μ	
Simple	0	D	$2|E|$	1	
α	0	D	$2|E|$	3	Acks.
β	$\Theta(N\log N + |E|)$	$O(N)$	$2N-2$	$2N$	Acks.
γ	$O(k.N^2)$	$O(N\frac{\log N}{\log k})$	$O(k.N)$	$O(\frac{\log N}{\log k})$	$2 \le k < N$ Acks.

Table 12.3 OVERVIEW OF SYNCHRONIZERS.

preferred edges, and hence the number of preferred edges is bounded by $(k-1)N$. This proves that $E_c < k.N$.   □

A distributed algorithm for carrying out the construction was given by Awerbuch [Awe85a]. The algorithm uses $O(k.N^2)$ messages and the time complexity is $O(N\log N/\log k)$ time units.

12.4 Application: Breadth-first Search

As an application of synchronizers we shall present in this section several algorithms for computing a breadth-first search (BFS) spanning tree of a network. A spanning tree T of network G is a *breadth-first search tree* if, for each node, the tree path to the root is a minimum-hop path in G. That is, a breadth-first search tree is an optimal sink tree for its root with respect to the minimum-hop distance measure (see Theorem 4.2).

Breadth-first search trees play an important role in the design of message- and time-efficient algorithms, because they allow the message-optimal broadcast of information in minimal time. The tree-labeling scheme of Santoro and Khatib (Subsection 4.4.2) can be made to work efficiently using a BFS tree, and Frederickson [Fre85] used a BFS tree to solve the shortest-path problem efficiently.

The computation of a BFS tree is done by a centralized algorithm initiated by the root of the tree (which is assumed to be defined a priori). The complexity of breadth-first search algorithms is analyzed in this section in terms of the parameters N and $|E|$. Observe that the depth of the tree is bounded by N. A more careful analysis may establish the complexity in terms of the parameters N, $|E|$, and D; the depth of the tree is bounded by D.

It will first be demonstrated, in Subsection 12.4.1, that the computation of a BFS tree is extremely simple in synchronous networks; in fact, each execution of the echo algorithm results in a BFS tree. In Subsection 12.4.2 the synchronous algorithm will be combined with a synchronizer algorithm and a tabulated comparison between the complexity of several solutions is given. The asynchronous algorithms of Subsection 12.4.2 are easily obtained and understood, but they are less efficient then other algorithms for the problem. We shall finally discuss two asynchronous algorithms proposed by Frederickson [Fre85] (Subsection 12.4.3).

12.4.1 A Synchronous BFS Algorithm

The natural method for building a breadth-first search tree is to compute the tree level by level. Initially the root forms level 0, and after completion of level i the tree is extended to level $i + 1$ by the addition of the neighbors of level-i nodes.

In a synchronous algorithm for computing a breadth first search tree, each process will send messages to each of its neighbors in exactly one pulse. The initiator does so in pulse 1. Each other process sends messages in pulse $i + 1$ if i is the first pulse in which the process receives one or more messages. A process that receives messages for the first time in pulse i assigns itself to level i, and chooses one of the processes from which it received a message in pulse i as its father.

Theorem 12.7 *With the above algorithm, a process at distance i from the initiator sends messages in pulse $i + 1$ and, if $i > 0$, chooses a process at distance $i - 1$ from the initiator as its father.*

The choices of the father imply that the resulting tree is a breadth-first search tree, and as each process sends messages exactly once, the message complexity is $2|E|$. The time complexity is $O(N)$ because after pulse N each process has determined its father.

12.4.2 Combination with a Synchronizer

A breadth-first search algorithm for ABD or asynchronous networks is easily obtained by combining the synchronous algorithm with one of the synchronizers discussed earlier in this chapter. The complexities of the resulting asynchronous algorithms are given in Table 12.4. The algorithms obtained in this way are easy to understand, but they are not the best-known asynchronous algorithms.

Algorithm	Messages	Time
Synchronous	$2|E|$	$O(N)$
Synch+ABD	$O(|E|)$	$O(N)$
Synch+α	$O(N.|E|)$	$O(N)$
Synch+β	$O(N^2)$	$O(N^2)$
Synch+γ	$O(k.N^2)$	$O(N \frac{\log N}{\log k})$
Simple	$O(N^2 + |E|)$	$O(N^2)$
Advanced	$O(N\sqrt{|E|})$	$O(N\sqrt{|E|})$
[AG85]	$O(|E|.2^{\sqrt{\log N \log \log N}})$	$O(N.2^{\sqrt{\log N \log \log N}})$

Table 12.4 COMPLEXITY OF BREADTH-FIRST SEARCH ALGORITHMS.

12.4.3 Asynchronous BFS Algorithms

In this subsection three asynchronous algorithms for breadth-first search that have a lower complexity than the algorithms derived in the previous subsection are discussed. The reader should not conclude that it is useless to apply the concept of synchronizers in the design of asynchronous algorithms; synchronizer algorithms are implicitly used in the design of the following algorithms.

A breadth-first search tree is usually built level by level. After the completion of level i, the neighbors of the nodes in that level (in so far as they are not already nodes of the tree) are added to the tree as level $i + 1$. Consider what happens if the construction of the next level, $i + 2$, is started before the construction of level $i + 1$ is complete. Neighbors of nodes at level $i + 1$ are added to the tree at level $i + 2$; but it may turn out later that such a node is also a neighbor of a node at level i, so the level of the node should in fact be $i + 1$.

The simple algorithm given below avoids this situation by synchronizing the expansion of the tree between every two levels. The synchronization takes place according to synchronizer β, and is applied to the part of the tree that is already constructed. In the more advanced algorithm synchronization takes place after every l levels; this decreases the overhead due to synchronization, but requires that a node may be in the tree at different levels during the computation.

The level of a node in the final BFS tree equals its distance to the root in the full network. A node at level f only has neighbors at levels $f - 1$, f, and $f + 1$; see Exercise 12.9.

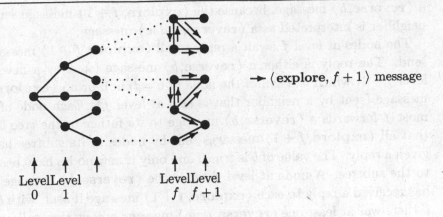

Figure 12.5 THE CONSTRUCTION OF LEVEL $f + 1$.

The simple algorithm. To start the algorithm, the initiator assigns itself level 0, after which the construction of level 0 of the BFS tree is complete. The tree is constructed level by level, and when the construction of level f is complete, each node at level f knows that it is at level f and which of its neighbors are at level $f - 1$.

Assume the construction of level f is complete, but the algorithm has not terminated. To start the construction of level $f + 1$, the initiator broadcasts a $\langle \textbf{forward}, f \rangle$ message down the tree. Node p at level f, upon receipt of the $\langle \textbf{forward}, f \rangle$ message, sends an $\langle \textbf{explore}, f + 1 \rangle$ message to those neighbors that p does not already know to be at level $f - 1$. The sending of $\langle \textbf{explore}, f + 1 \rangle$ messages is depicted in Figure 12.5.

As a result of the sending of $\langle \textbf{explore}, f + 1 \rangle$ messages by all nodes at level f, a node at distance $f + 1$ from the initiator receives such a message from each neighbor at level f. The first $\langle \textbf{explore}, f' \rangle$ message received by a node defines the level f' and the father of the node in the BFS tree and is answered by a $\langle \textbf{reverse}, true \rangle$ message. Subsequently arriving $\langle \textbf{explore}, f' \rangle$ messages are answered by a $\langle \textbf{reverse}, false \rangle$ message, and all senders of these messages are known to be at level $f' - 1$. Observe that when the construction of level $f + 1$ is complete, which implies that all $\langle \textbf{explore}, f + 1 \rangle$ messages have been answered, each process at level $f + 1$ knows which of its neighbors are at level f.

A node at level f may also receive $\langle \textbf{explore}, f + 1 \rangle$ messages, namely, from a neighbor that is also at level f. These messages are not answered by a $\langle \mathbf{reverse}, b \rangle$ message, because the $\langle \mathbf{explore}, f+1 \rangle$ message sent to this neighbor is interpreted as a $\langle \mathbf{reverse}, \mathit{false} \rangle$ message.

The nodes at level f await a reply to all $\langle \mathbf{explore}, f+1 \rangle$ messages they send. The reply is either a $\langle \mathbf{reverse}, b \rangle$ message (sent by a new node at level $f+1$, which is a son of the node iff $b = \mathit{true}$), or an $\langle \mathbf{explore}, f+1 \rangle$ message (sent by a neighbor that is also at level f). Each node of level at most f forwards a $\langle \mathbf{reverse}, b \rangle$ message to its father in the tree to report that all $\langle \mathbf{explore}, f+1 \rangle$ messages sent by nodes in its subtree have been given a reply. The value of b is true if and only if new nodes have been added to the subtree. A node at level f sends the $\langle \mathbf{reverse}, b \rangle$ message when it has received a reply to each $\langle \mathbf{explore}, f+1 \rangle$ message it sent, with $b = \mathit{true}$ if there was at least one $\langle \mathbf{reverse}, \mathit{true} \rangle$ message among the replies. A node at level smaller than f sends a $\langle \mathbf{reverse}, b \rangle$ message to its father if it has received a $\langle \mathbf{reverse}, b' \rangle$ message from each of its sons. Again the value of b is true if there has been at least one $\langle \mathbf{reverse}, \mathit{true} \rangle$ message among the received messages.

The construction of level $f+1$ terminates when the root has received a $\langle \mathbf{reverse}, b \rangle$ message from each son. If no node has been added to the tree (all received messages contained the value false) the tree construction terminates, otherwise it continues by constructing level $f+2$.

Theorem 12.8 *A breadth-first search tree can be constructed by a centralized asynchronous algorithm using* $O(N^2)$ *messages in* $O(N^2)$ *time units.*

Proof. The construction terminates after at most N levels and each tree edge carries for each level at most one forward or explore message and one reverse message sent in reply to it. A frond edge that connects two nodes at level f carries two $\langle \mathbf{explore}, f+1 \rangle$ messages during the construction of level $f+1$. A frond edge connecting a node at level f with one at level $f+1$ carries one $\langle \mathbf{explore}, f+1 \rangle$ message and one $\langle \mathbf{reverse}, \mathit{false} \rangle$ message during the construction of level $f+1$. In either case, a frond edge carries exactly two messages for the entire algorithm. The message complexity is thus bounded by $2N(N-1) + 2(|E| - (N-1)) \le 2N^2 + 2|E| = O(N^2)$. Level $f+1$ is computed in $2(f+1)$ time units, which implies that the algorithm terminates in at most $O(N^2)$ time units. $\Box$

An advanced algorithm. In the simple algorithm the exploration of each individual level is synchronized by the root (by means of reverse and forward messages). As can be seen from the complexity analysis, the synchronization messages dominate the complexity of the algorithm. If the network is *dense* (i.e., $|E|$ is almost $\Omega(N^2)$), the message complexity cannot be improved because $|E|$ is a lower bound on the number of messages. If the network is *sparse* (i.e., $|E|$ is $o(N^2)$) the synchronization overheads can be reduced by exploring several levels between synchronization rounds.

Assume the construction of level f of the tree is complete. To construct the next l levels, the initiator broadcasts a message $\langle$ **forward**, $f \rangle$ down the tree. Upon receipt of this message, nodes at level f send $\langle$ **explore**, $f + 1, l \rangle$ messages to those neighbors that are not already known to be at level $f - 1$. The first parameter of the explore message represents the new level of the receiver if the latter becomes a child of the sender. The second parameter gives the number of levels that must still be explored, starting from the sender of the message.

Initially a node is at level ∞. If an $\langle$ **explore**, $f, l \rangle$ message arrives at node p, f is compared with the current level of p, $level_p$. If $f \geq level_p$, a $\langle$ **reverse**, $false \rangle$ message is sent in reply. If $f < level_p$, p adopts the sender of the message as its father, changes its level to f, and, if $l > 1$, sends $\langle$ **explore**, $f + 1, l - 1 \rangle$ messages to those neighbors that are not already known to be at level $f + 1$. (The latter is the case if an $\langle$ **explore**, $f + 2, l \rangle$ message has previously been received from this neighbor.) The termination of the construction of levels $f + 1$ through $f + l$ is detected by a flood of reverse messages sent in reply to explore and forward messages, as for the simple algorithm.

Theorem 12.9 *If the ratio between $|E|$ and N^2 is (approximately) known, a breadth-first search tree can be constructed by a centralized asynchronous algorithm using $O(N\sqrt{E})$ messages in $O(N\sqrt{E})$ time.*

Proof. The construction terminates after approximately N/l synchronization rounds, and thus each tree edge carries at most $2N/l$ forward messages and replies to forward messages, to a total of $O(N^2/l)$. Each edge carries at most l explore messages and l replies to them, totaling to $O(l|E|)$ messages, which brings the message complexity to $O(N^2/l + l|E|)$. As levels $f + 1$ through $f + l$ are computed in $O(f + l)$ time units, the time complexity of the algorithm is $O(N^2/l)$.

The complexity bounds stated in the theorem follow by choosing l as $\sqrt{N^2/E}$. □

The Awerbuch–Gallager algorithm. By introducing more synchronization mechanisms Awerbuch and Gallager [AG85] were able to reduce the complexity of breadth-first search even further. The l levels that are explored between synchronization rounds are called a *strip*. In the Awerbuch–Gallager algorithm not only is there a global synchronization between the exploration of every two strips, but the exploration of each strip itself is also synchronized, through the spanning forest built during the exploration. The algorithm is too complicated to be explained here in detail, but its complexity is listed in Table 12.4 for the sake of completeness.

12.5 The Archimedean Assumption

Depending on the availability of physical clocks, time may or may not be observable to processes, but even if time is not observable, the so-called Archimedean assumption may be justified. Under this assumption there is a bound on the ratio between the maximum and the minimum possible times consumed in a single step of a process or the transmission of a message.

Even if a system is not equipped with devices that actually measure time, a very rough notion of clocks can be obtained by, for example, counting executed instructions for each processor and defining a clock tick for every 1000 or 10,000 instructions. The "elapsed time" in a process is then the number of clock ticks counted by that process. In the sequel, t_1 and t_2 denote instances of physical time. The times t_1 and t_2 being understood from the context, let m denote the smallest time between two consecutive clock ticks of any process between t_1 and t_2. Let u denote the maximum transmission delay of any message between t_1 and t_2, plus the largest time between two consecutive clock ticks of any process between t_1 and t_2. The ratio u/m is called the Archimedean ratio of the interval (t_1, t_2).

Definition 12.10 *The system is Archimedean (with Archimedean ratio s) if the ratio u/m is bounded (by s).*

Given t_1 and t_2, only finitely many clock ticks and messages occur between t_1 and t_2, which implies that there is an s such that the system is Archimedean with ratio s. For many systems it may be a justified assumption that there exists an s_0 such that the system is Archimedean with ratio s_0 between the start and termination of any algorithm executed by the system. This implies that a (fairly weak) synchronism assumption is verified in the system, and the question arises whether this weak form of synchronism can be exploited in the design of efficient distributed algorithms.

It has been argued that, for several reasons, it is better to use fully asynchronous algorithms and not to rely on timing assumptions.

(1) The slowest component of the system determines (together with the fastest component) the value of the Archimedean ratio. If the time complexity of an algorithm is influenced by the ratio (as it usually is), it is the slowest component that determines the speed of the entire system.

(2) The analysis of the timing assumptions may be extremely difficult, and give rise to incorrect algorithms.

(3) The introduction of arbitrary delays in the execution of algorithms (for example, in the ring algorithm when used in the termination-detection algorithm of Dijkstra, Feijen, and Van Gasteren) may invalidate the Archimedean assumption. Therefore this algorithmical technique cannot be used if algorithms rely on the Archimedean assumption.

(4) The replacement of components of the system by faster or slower ones may change the Archimedean ratio, thereby possibly causing algorithms to deliver erroneous results. Errors of this type are extremely hard to trace and repair, because the error arises from the replacement of a component by a functionally equivalent one.

In the light of these arguments, two different ways of exploiting the Archimedean assumption may be distinguished. An algorithm is called *robust* if its correctness does not rely on this assumption, i.e., the algorithm is correct in a fully asynchronous system. The Archimedean assumption is used in the complexity analysis of the algorithm, which may reveal that the algorithm performs better if the ratio is closer to one. An algorithm is called *critical* if its correctness relies on the Archimedean assumption, i.e., the algorithm may give erroneous results if the Archimedean ratio exceeds a design parameter s_0 during the execution. The techniques of "coding in time" and sending "implicit messages" are critical with respect to the Archimedean assumption, while "selective delay" is robust.

Vitányi [Vit85] shows that, using selective delay, election can be performed robustly in Archimedean systems, with a message time complexity; see Exercise 12.11. Spirakis and Tampakas [ST89] have presented several robust and critical distributed algorithms for various tasks.

Exercises to Chapter 12
Section 12.1

Exercise 12.1 *Improve the protocol for sending information by "coding* *in time" so that message m is transmitted in $O(\sqrt{m})$ time units using a constant number of bits.*

Exercise 12.2 *Theorem 9.8 states that:*

> *There exists no deterministic process-terminating algorithm for computing a non-constant function f if the ring size is not known.*

Does this theorem hold for synchronous networks as well?

Exercise 12.3 *Prove that in Algorithm 12.1 a process can receive during the execution of pulse i (the interval $(2i\mu, 2(i+1)\mu)$ on its local clock) only messages of pulses i and $i + 1$.*

(As a consequence, the pulse number of a message can be determined using its time of receipt and the parity of the pulse number.)

Exercise 12.4 *Assume the synchronization phase of Algorithm 12.1 is extended in such a way that process p records the clock time $\delta_{pq} = CLOCK_p^{(\tau)}$ at the time τ at which p receives the $\langle$start$\rangle$ message of q. ($\delta_{pq} = 0$ if this message caused the execution of init in p.) Prove that when p receives a pulse-i message of q, the value of p's clock is between $\delta_{pq} + 2i\mu - \mu$ and $\delta_{pq} + 2i\mu + \mu$.*

(As a consequence, the pulse number of a message received from q at clock time c is found as $\lfloor (c - \delta_{pq} + \mu)/2 \rfloor$; so no information concerning the message's pulse number need be included in the message.)

Exercise 12.5 *Adapt Algorithm 12.1 to handle the situation where internal processing takes nonzero time; assume instead that executing the body of $\mathbf{P}_p^{(i)}$ takes a time bounded by λ.*

Section 12.2

Exercise 12.6 *Give algorithms for flooding messages in cliques, tori, and hypercubes that require $N - 1$ messages and $O(D)$ time units. (It must be assumed that the tori and hypercubes are labeled.)*

Exercise 12.7 *Give synchronous election algorithms for networks of known size, in the case where processes do not necessarily start the election in the same pulse, but may initiate the algorithm in different pulses.*

Section 12.3

Exercise 12.8 *Determine the message complexity of the asynchronous election algorithms obtained by combining the synchronous algorithms of Section 12.2 with the synchronizers of Section 12.3.*

Section 12.4

Exercise 12.9 *Prove that a neighbor of a node of level f in the BFS tree has level $f - 1$, f, or $f + 1$.*

Exercise 12.10 *Analyze the complexity of the breadth-first search algorithms in terms of N, $|E|$, and D (the network diameter).*

Section 12.5

Exercise 12.11 [Vit85] *The aim of this exercise is to investigate the effect of selective delays in Archimedean networks. Let a network be given with Archimedean ratio s.*

Election is performed by applying extinction to a traversal algorithm with message complexity W. Each message of process p is delayed by $f(p) - 1$ clock ticks in each process. A separate wake-up procedure ensures that each process launches its traversal within Du time units after the start of the algorithm.

(1) *Prove that the algorithm terminates within $D.u + W.u.f(p_0)$ time units, where p_0 is the process with the smallest identity.*

(2) *Prove that the token of process p is sent at most $1 + t/(f(p) - 2)$ times during a time interval of length t.*

(3) *Derive a formula for the worst-case message complexity of the algorithm.*

(4) *Show, by varying f, that a linear message complexity can be obtained.*

Part Three

Fault Tolerance

13

Fault Tolerance in Distributed Systems

The earlier parts of this book studied the coordinated behavior that can be achieved in distributed systems where processes are *reliable*. For several reasons it is attractive to study what coordinated behavior of processes is possible under the assumption that processes may fail; this study is the subject of the last part of the book. Many solutions for fault tolerance are *ad hoc* and, also, in the large collection of impossibility proofs structure and underlying theory are sometimes hard to find. On the other hand, some problems have elegant and well-established theory and simple solutions whose presentation fits well in this introductory textbook.

This chapter serves as a general introduction to the later chapters. We illustrate the reasons for using fault-tolerant algorithms (Section 13.1), and subsequently introduce two main types of fault-tolerant algorithms, namely robust algorithms (Section 13.2) and stabilizing algorithms (Section 13.3).

13.1 Reasons for Using Fault-tolerant Algorithms

Increasing the number of components in a distributed system means increasing the probability that some of these components will be subject to failure during the execution of a distributed algorithm. Computers in a network may fail, processes in a system can be erroneously killed by switching off a workstation, or a machine may produce an incorrect result due to, e.g., memory malfunctioning. Modern computers are becoming more and more reliable, thereby decreasing the chance of the occurrence of such failures in any individual computer. Nonetheless, the chance of a failure occurring at some place in a distributed system may grow arbitrarily large when the number of its components increases. To avoid the necessity of restarting an algorithm each time a failure occurs, algorithms should be designed so as to deal properly with such failures.

Of course, vulnerability to failures is also a concern in sequential computations, in safety-critical applications, or if a computation runs for a long time and produces a non-verifiable result. Internal checks protect against errors of some types (e.g., modular checking against arithmetic miscalculation), but of course no protection can be achieved against the complete loss of the program or erroneous changes in its code. Therefore the possibilities of fault-tolerant computing by sequential algorithms and uni-processor computing systems are limited.

Because of the dispersion of processing resources in a distributed system, these systems have the *partial-failure* property; no matter what kind of failure occurs, it usually affects only a part of the entire system. And, while the growth of the number of components makes it extremely likely that a failure will occur in some component, it becomes extremely unlikely that a failure will occur in all components. Therefore it may be hoped that the tasks of failing processes can be taken over by the remaining components, leading to a graceful degradation rather than an overall malfunctioning. Indeed, as can be seen in the following chapters, the design of distributed algorithms for systems with defective processes is possible, and coordinated behavior can be achieved.

The partial-failure property makes the use of distributed ("replicated") architectures an attractive option for the design of computer applications that are not distributed by nature, but require high reliability. The primary computer system of the Space Shuttle aircraft serves as an example; Spector and Gifford [SG84] describe its development. Controlling the Shuttle is a task well within the capacity of a single off-the-shelf microprocessor, but the possibility of such a processor's breaking down during a flight was a serious concern in its design. The final control system used four identical processors, each performing exactly the same computation[1]; the actuators vote on the outcome, which allows perfect control even if one processor fails. (The physical realization of the actuators allows the system to survive the later failure of a second processor as well.) Although replication is an appealing option for increasing reliability, the design of the algorithms necessary to coordinate a cluster of (unreliable) processors is far from trivial. This is illustrated by the postponement of the first flight of the Shuttle (from April 8 to April 10, 1981), because of an error in the software precisely responsible for that task.

Fortunately, the study of fault-tolerant algorithms has advanced consider-

---

[1] See [SG84] for an explanation of the fifth ("hot spare") and sixth ("cold spare") processors.

ably since 1981, and reliable applications based on replication are now well within reach.

Two radically different approaches towards fault tolerance are followed in the literature, and both will be studied in this book. In *robust algorithms* each step of each process is taken with sufficient care to ensure that, in spite of failures, correct processes only take correct steps. In *stabilizing algorithms* correct processes can be affected by failures, but the algorithm is guaranteed to recover from any arbitrary configuration when the processes resume correct behavior. We shall briefly introduce robust algorithms in Section 13.2 and stabilizing algorithms in Section 13.3, and give a short comparison at the end of the chapter.

13.2 Robust Algorithms

Robust algorithms are designed to guarantee the continuous correct behavior of correctly operating processes in spite of failures occurring in other processes during their execution. These algorithms rely on strategies such as voting, whereby a process will only accept certain information when sufficiently many other processes have also declared receipt of this information. However, a process should never wait to receive information from all processes, because a deadlock may thus arise, if a process has crashed.

13.2.1 Failure Models

To determine how the correctly operating processes can protect themselves against failed processes, assumptions must be made about *how* a process might fail. In the following chapters it is always assumed that only *processes* can fail; channels are reliable. Thus, if a correct process sends a message to another correct process, receipt of the message within finite time is guaranteed. (A failing channel can be modeled by a failure in one of the incident processes, for example, an omission failure.) As an additional assumption, we always assume that each process can send to each other process.

The following *fault models* are used in this book.

(1) *Initially dead processes.* A process is called initially dead if it does not execute a single step of its local algorithm.

(2) *Crash model.* A process is said to crash if it executes its local algorithm correctly up to some moment, and does not execute any step thereafter.

(3) *Byzantine behavior.* A process is said to be Byzantine if it executes

arbitrary steps that are not in accordance with its local algorithm. In particular, a Byzantine process may send messages with an arbitrary content.

The correctness requirements set forward for robust algorithms always refer to the local state (or output) of *correct* processes only. An initially dead process never produces output and its state always equals the initial state. The output of a crashing process, if it produces any, will be correct, because up to the occurrence of the crash the process behaves correctly. Needless to say, the local state or output of a Byzantine process can be arbitrary, and no non-trivial requirement on it can be satisfied by any algorithm.

Hierarchy of fault models. A hierarchy can be defined among these three fault models. First, an initially dead process can be considered a special case of a crashing process, namely, the case where the crash occurs before the first event in that process. Second, a crashed process can be considered as a special case of a Byzantine process, because the arbitrary behavior assumed for Byzantine processes includes execution of no steps at all. It is therefore more difficult to tolerate crashes than to tolerate initially dead processes, and it is even more difficult to tolerate Byzantine processes. Stated differently, a Byzantine-robust algorithm is also crash-robust, and a crash-robust algorithm is also initially-dead-robust. On the other hand, impossibility of an initially-dead-robust algorithm implies impossibility of a crash-robust algorithm, and impossibility of a crash-robust algorithm implies impossibility of a Byzantine-robust algorithm.

An *omission failure* consists of skipping a step in the algorithm (e.g., the sending or receipt of a message), after which execution continues. Omission failures are a special case of Byzantine behavior, and a crash is a special case of omission (namely, where *all* steps after a certain moment are omitted). Therefore omission failures fit into this hierarchy between crash and Byzantine failures.

Mixed failures and timing errors. Initially dead processes and crashes are called *benign* failure types, while Byzantine failures are called *malign* failures. For several distributed problems it turns out that a collection of N processes can tolerate t benign failures if $2t < N$, while robustness against t malign failures requires $3t < N$ (in an *asynchronous* model of computation). Because malign failures often cannot be excluded in practice but are very rare compared with benign failures, Garay and Perry [GP92] extended some results to a mixed-failure model, where t processes may fail, b out of which in a malign way. Correct behavior of the remaining processes can be achieved in this model if $2b + t < N$ (in a *synchronous* model of computation).

In synchronous distributed systems there is an additional failure mode, namely, where a process executes correct steps but at the wrong time (due to a slow or fast clock of the process). This type of incorrect process behavior is called a *timing error*.

13.2.2 Decision Problems

The study of robust algorithms is centered around the solution of so-called *decision problems*, where it is required that each of the (correct) processes irreversibly writes a "decision" value to its output. The required decision value usually depends in a quite trivial manner on the input values of the processes, making these problems fairly easy to solve in a fault-free (reliable) environment.

The requirements set for the decisions are usually of three types, namely, *termination, consistency*, and *non-triviality*.

The termination requirement states that all correct processes will decide, i.e., write a value to their output, eventually. In deterministic algorithms termination is required in all computations; in probabilistic algorithms it is required to occur with probability one (see Chapter 9). The requirement that all correct processes write ia value to their output excludes any solution in which a process must wait to receive some information from more than $N - t$ processes. Indeed, the stopping of t processes causes an indefinite wait in a correct process, violating the termination requirement.

The consistency requirement imposes a relation between the decisions taken by different processes. In the simplest case, all decisions are required to be equal; we speak of a *consensus problem* in this case (which value is required may depend on the inputs). In more complicated problems a class of output vectors can be defined, and the decisions of correct processes should form a vector in this class. In the election problem (Chapter 7), for example, the requirement is that one process decides that it is *elected* ("1"), and all other processes should decide *defeated* ("0").

A termination and a consistency requirement are usually sufficient for a distributed algorithm to be useful; in cases where a task is shown to be impossible to solve, an additional requirement of a more technical nature is needed. The non-triviality requirement excludes algorithms based on a fixed output for the problem, on which every process decides without any communication. The consensus problem, for example, could be solved by an algorithm in which each process writes a "0" to the output immediately.

The non-triviality requirement states that two essentially different outputs are possible in different executions of the algorithm (i.e., in the case of consensus, that the algorithm has executions that write "0" *and* executions that write "1"; of course, within one execution all decisions are consistent).

Decision problems abstract a large number of common situations in distributed computing, as we now discuss.

(1) *Commit–Abort.* In a distributed database a transaction involving various sites must be executed in *all* involved sites or in *none* of them. Therefore, after announcing the update to these sites, each site determines whether the update can be executed locally and votes either "yes" or "no". Subsequently, all (correct) sites must decide whether to *commit* the transaction, meaning that it will be executed everywhere, or to *abort* it, meaning that it will not be executed. If all processes voted "yes" the processes must decide *commit*, if some processes vote "no" the outcome must be *abort*. Consistency here means that all decisions are equal, and the problem is non-trivial because, depending on the input, both a *commit* and an *abort* may be required.

(2) *Distributed computations: consensus on input.* In systems where a computation is replicated to increase reliability, the outcome of the various processors can be equal only if the computations are based on the same inputs. The effect of a defective sensor, sending different values to the various processors, must be eliminated by executing a consensus algorithm among the processors. The input of each processor is the value received from the sensor, and each (correct) processor must decide on the same value to be used in the subsequent computation. The output is usually required to be the value that is a majority of the inputs or, weaker, to be any value that occurs at least once as an input; in both cases the problem is non-trivial.

(3) *Election.* In the election problem (see also Chapter 7) it is required that one process decides to become a leader and all other (correct) processes decide to become a non-leader. The problem becomes non-trivial if we require that potentially different processes can become leader.

(4) *Approximate agreement.* In cases where consensus among inputs is not achievable, a weaker form of consistency may suffice for some applications. In the approximate-agreement problem each process has an integer input from a given finite range, say $1, \ldots, k$. The decisions of processes are required to differ by at most 1, and to lie

between values that actually occurred as input; see also Section 14.3 for a continuous version of the problem (ϵ-approximate agreement).

13.2.3 Overview of Chapters 14 through 16

Due to the large number of known results concerning robust algorithms it is impossible in this book to discuss completely the state-of-the-art in the field. The material presented in Chapters 14 through 16 has been selected with the following criteria in mind.

(1) Some fundamental results should be included: that there is no deterministic consensus in asynchronous systems; that probabilistic algorithms tolerate benign failures in up to one-half of the processes, or malign failures in up to one-third of the processes.

(2) A demonstration should be given of some of the techniques used to achieve robustness or to prove its impossibility.

(3) A demonstration should be included that synchronous systems can achieve more robustness than asynchronous systems. This contrasts with the results (presented in Chapter 12) that indicate that reliable synchronous systems are not more powerfull than reliable asynchronous systems.

(4) Failure detectors are a promising new paradigm, rapidly making the move to being applied technology, and should be included.

Chapter 14 studies the robustness that can be achieved in *asynchronous* systems. A fundamental result was shown by Fischer, Lynch, and Paterson [FLP85], namely, that no deterministic algorithm for consensus exists that can tolerate even a single crash failure. This result was generalized by Moran and Wolfstahl [MW87] to a wider class of decision problems (tasks) including, e.g., election, but not approximate agreement. The conclusion of these works is that crashes can be tolerated only by probabilistic algorithms (or synchronous ones). The result cannot be strengthened to apply to the weaker fault model of initially dead processes; this is shown by the existence of deterministic consensus and election algorithms for initially dead processes. Randomization does help; a randomized consensus algorithm by Bracha and Toueg [BT85], which is asynchronous and tolerates $t < N/2$ crashing processes or $t < N/3$ Byzantine processes is presented.

Chapter 15 studies the robustness that can be achieved in *synchronous* systems. Unlike in the asynchronous model, the crashing of a process can be detected by the remaining processes, because a bounded response time of a correct process is guaranteed. Consequently, a much higher degree of robustness is achievable, which is shown in the idealized model of a system operating in pulses (see Chapter 12). Deterministic algorithms can tolerate $t < N/3$ Byzantine processes, $t < N$ crashing processes, or $t < N$ Byzantine processes if message authentication is possible. This and the impossibility results of Chapter 14 imply that robust synchronizers for fully asynchronous networks do not exist. The implementation of the pulsed model on systems with limited asynchrony (physical clocks and bounded message-delay time) requires the clocks to be accurately synchronized, a problem which is the subject of the remainder of Chapter 15.

Failure detection, discussed in Chapter 16, is another way to strengthen the computational model and, like synchrony, is usually available in distributed systems in some form. Just like one can compare various models of synchrony to see how much is necessary to solve a problem, we may study models of failure detection and see how accurate their output must reflect actual failures in order to solve the consensus problem.

13.2.4 Topics not Addressed in this Book

The results in Chapter 14 and 15 give an indication about the degree of robustness achievable in distributed systems. Many problems and results remain for further study; below we indicate a few of these and give pointers to the literature.

(1) *Refinement of synchrony assumptions.* In this book only completely asynchronous and completely synchronous systems are considered, and these systems differ considerably in their achievable robustness. Dolev, Dwork, Lynch, and Stockmeyer [DDS87], [DLS88] studied the fault-tolerance of systems under intermediate assumptions about synchrony.

(2) *Determination of solvable tasks.* In this book the solvability of some tasks and the unsolvability of others is demonstrated; a precise characterization of solvable and unsolvable tasks was given by Biran, Moran, and Zaks [BMZ90].

(3) *Complexity of fault tolerance.* In addition to deciding what tasks are solvable, it is possible to study the amount of computational resources consumed by a protocol for solvable tasks. Several complexity measures can be taken into account: message complexity, bit complexity, and time complexity (often called round complexity in this context). An overview of some results and a consensus protocol meeting several lower bounds simultaneously is found in [BGP92].

(4) *Dynamic systems and group membership.* In this book it is assumed that the collection of processes is fixed (static) and known (though some processes may fail). A static collection of processes is suitable for an application that must run reliably for a fixed, finite amount of time, such as an aircraft control system, where repairs and reconfiguration take place *off-line*. Fault-tolerant operation of a system for an indefinite duration (as in, for example, an operating system or an air-traffic-control system) requires that processes can be repaired and the set of processes reconfigured *on-line*, i.e., without stopping the application. Reconfiguring the set of processes is done by executing a *group membership* protocol, in which the active processes agree on the set of processes in the system. Some results on these protocols and references are found in [RBS92].

(5) *Communication using shared variables.* In this book interprocess communication by means of message passing is considered. Some authors have studied the fault tolerance of distributed systems where communication is based on shared variables; see Taubenfeld and Moran [TM89].

(6) *Wait-free synchronization.* An even more sophisticated communication model is where processes share arbitrary objects, rather than registers. In this model the desired interaction between the processes can be formulated in terms of object methods, and algorithmical problems are formulated as implementation of objects. There is extensive theory about which objects can and which cannot be implemented; see [AW98].

13.3 Stabilizing Algorithms

Robust algorithms continuously show correct coordinated behavior even when failures occur, but the number of failures is limited and the failure model must usually be known precisely. The second approach to fault tolerance, that of stabilizing algorithms, is different. Any number of failures of arbitrary types is allowable, but correct behavior of the algorithm is suspended until some time after the repair of the failures. A *stabilizing* algorithm (sometimes called *self-stabilizing*) can be started in any system configuration, and eventually reaches an allowed state, and behaves according to its specifications from then on. Consequently, the effects of temporal failures die out, and also, there is no need to initialize the system consistently.

Stabilizing algorithms are studied in Chapter 17. The concept of stabilization was introduced as early as in 1974 [Dij74], and applied to algorithms to achieve mutual exclusion on a ring of processors. These algorithms are discussed because of their historical value and because they are elegant and insightful. Stabilizing solutions exist for a number of problems solved earlier in this book, such as data transmission, election, and the computation of routing tables and a depth-first search tree.

Robust versus stabilizing algorithms. Stabilizing algorithms offer protection against so-called *transient failures*, i.e., temporary misbehavior of system components. These failures may occur in large parts of a distributed system when the physical conditions temporarily reach extreme values, inducing erroneous behavior of memories and processors. Examples include the control system of a spacecraft when being hit by large amounts of cosmic rays, and systems in which many components are simultaneously affected by a natural disaster. When conditions return to normal, the processes resume operation according to their programs, but due to their temporal misbehavior the global state (configuration) may be an arbitrary one. The stabilizing property guarantees convergence to the required behavior.

Robust algorithms protect against the *permanent failure* of a limited number of components. The surviving processes maintain correct (though possibly less efficient) behavior during the repair and reconfiguration of the system. Therefore, robust algorithms must be used when the temporal interruption of service is unacceptable.

Publications by Gopal and Perry [GP93] and Anagnostou and Hadzilacos [AH93] study algorithms that are both robust and stabilizing. Gopal and Perry demonstrate how a robust protocol can be modified automatically (compiled) into a protocol that is both robust and stabilizing. Anagnostou and Hadzilacos show that no robust and stabilizing algorithm exists for election and computation of the ring size, and present a (randomized) protocol for assigning distinct names.

14

Fault Tolerance in Asynchronous Systems

This chapter studies the solvability of decision problems in asynchronous
distributed systems. The results are arranged around a fundamental result
by Fischer, Lynch, and Paterson [FLP85], presented in Section 14.1. Formulated as an impossibility proof for a class of decision algorithms, the result
can also be read as a list of assumptions that together exclude solutions
for decision problems. Relaxing the assumptions makes it possible to obtain practical solutions for various problems, as is shown in the subsequent
sections. See also Subsection 14.1.3 for a further discussion.

14.1 Impossibility of Consensus

In this section the fundamental theorem of Fischer, Lynch, and Paterson
[FLP85], stating that there are no asynchronous, deterministic 1-crash robust consensus protocols, is proved. The result is shown by reasoning involving fair execution sequences of the algorithms. We first introduce some
notation (in addition to that introduced in Section 2.1) and give elementary
results that are useful also in later sections.

14.1.1 Notation, Definitions, Elementary Results

The sequence $\sigma = (e_1, \ldots, e_k)$ of events is *applicable* in configuration γ if
e_1 is applicable in γ, e_2 in $e_1(\gamma)$, and so on. If the resulting configuration
is δ, we write $\gamma \leadsto^\sigma \delta$ or $\sigma(\gamma) = \delta$, to make the events leading from γ to δ
explicit. If $S \subseteq \mathbb{P}$ and σ contains only events in processes of S we also write
$\gamma \leadsto_S \delta$.

Proposition 14.1 *Let sequences σ_1 and σ_2 be applicable in configuration γ, and let no process participate in both σ_1 and σ_2. Then σ_2 is applicable in $\sigma_1(\gamma)$, σ_1 is applicable in $\sigma_2(\gamma)$, and $\sigma_2(\sigma_1(\gamma)) = \sigma_1(\sigma_2(\gamma))$.*

Proof. This follows from repeated application of Theorem 2.19.   □

Process p has a read-only input variable x_p and a write-once output register y_p with initial value b. The input configuration is completely determined by the value of x_p for each process p. Process p can *decide* on a value (usually 0 or 1) by writing it in y_p; the initial value b is *not* a decision value. It is assumed that a correct process executes infinitely many events in a fair execution; to this end, a process can always execute a (possibly void) internal event.

Definition 14.2 *A t-crash fair execution is an execution in which at least $N - t$ processes execute infinitely many events, and each message sent to a correct process is received. (A process is correct if it executes infinitely many events.)*

The maximal number of faulty processes that can be handled by an algorithm is called the *resilience* of the algorithm, and is always denoted by t. In this section the impossibility of an asynchronous, deterministic algorithm with resilience one is demonstrated.

Definition 14.3 *A 1-crash-robust consensus algorithm is an algorithm satisfying the following three requirements.*

(1) **Termination.** *In every 1-crash fair execution, all correct processes decide.*

(2) **Agreement.** *If, in a reachable configuration, $y_p \neq b$ and $y_q \neq b$ for correct processes p and q, then $y_p = y_q$.*

(3) **Non-triviality.** *For $v = 0$ and for $v = 1$ there exist reachable configurations in which, for some p, $y_p = v$.*

For $v = 0, 1$ a configuration is called *v-decided* if for some p, $y_p = v$; a configuration is called *decided* if it is 0-decided or 1-decided. In a v-decided configuration, some process has decided on v. A configuration is called *v-valent* if all decided configurations reachable from it are v-decided. A configuration is called *bivalent* if both 0-decided and 1-decided configurations are reachable from it, and *univalent* if it is either 1-valent or 0-valent. In a univalent configuration, although no decision has necessarily been taken by any process the eventual decision is implicitly determined already.

A configuration γ of a t-robust protocol is called a *fork* if there exists a set T of (at most) t processes, and configurations γ_0 and γ_1, such that $\gamma \leadsto_T \gamma_0$, $\gamma \leadsto_T \gamma_1$, and γ_v is v-valent. Informally, γ is a fork if a subset of t processes can enforce a 0-decision as well as a 1-decision. The following proposition formalizes that at any moment, the crash of at most t processes must be survived by the remaining processes.

Proposition 14.4 *For each reachable configuration of a t-robust algorithm and each subset S of at least $N - t$ processes, there exists a decided configuration δ such that $\gamma \leadsto_S \delta$.*

Proof. Let γ and S be as above, and consider an execution that reaches configuration γ and contains infinitely many events in each process of S thereafter (and no steps of processes not in S). This execution is t-crash fair, and the processes in S are correct; hence they reach a decision. $\qquad\square$

Lemma 14.5 *There exist no reachable fork.*

Proof. Let γ be a reachable configuration and T a subset of at most t processes.

Let S be the complement of T, i.e., $S = \mathbb{P} \setminus T$; S has at least $N - t$ processes, hence there exists a decided configuration δ such that $\gamma \leadsto_S \delta$ (Proposition 14.4). Configuration δ is either 0- or 1-decided; assume w.l.o.g. that it is 0-decided.

It will now be shown that $\gamma \leadsto_T \gamma'$ for no 1-valent γ'; let γ' be any configuration such that $\gamma \leadsto_T \gamma'$. As steps in T and S commute (Proposition 14.1), there is a configuration δ' that is reachable from both δ and γ'. As δ is 0-decided, so is δ', which shows that γ' is *not* 1-valent. $\qquad\square$

14.1.2 The Impossibility Proof

We shall first exploit the non-triviality of the problem to show that there exists a bivalent initial configuration (Lemma 14.6). Subsequently it will be shown that, starting from a bivalent configuration, every enabled step can be executed without moving to a univalent configuration (Lemma 14.7). This suffices to show the impossibility of consensus algorithms (Theorem 14.8). In the sequel, let A be a 1-crash-robust consensus algorithm.

Lemma 14.6 *There exists a bivalent initial configuration for A.*

Proof. As A is non-trivial (Definition 14.3), there are reachable 0- and 1-decided configurations; let δ_0 and δ_1 be initial configurations such that a v-decided configuration is reachable from δ_v.

If $\delta_0 = \delta_1$, this initial configuration is bivalent and the result holds. Otherwise, there are initial configurations γ_0 and γ_1 such that a v-decided configuration is reachable from γ_v, and γ_0 and γ_1 differ in the input of a single process. Indeed, consider a sequence of initial configurations, starting with δ_0 and ending with δ_1, in which each next initial configuration differs from the previous one in a single process. (The sequence is obtained by inverting input bits one by one.) From the first configuration in the sequence, δ_0, a 0-decided configuration is reachable, and from the last one, δ_1, a 1-decided configuration is reachable. Because a decided configuration is reachable from each initial configuration, γ_0 and γ_1 as described can be found as two subsequent configurations in the sequence. Let p be the process in which γ_0 and γ_1 differ.

Consider a fair execution starting in γ_0 in which p takes no steps; this execution is 1-crash fair and hence reaches a decided configuration β. If β is 1-decided, γ_0 is bivalent. If β is 0-decided, observe that γ_1 only differs from γ_0 in p, and p takes no steps in the execution; hence β is reachable from γ_1, showing that γ_1 is bivalent. (More precisely, a configuration β' can be reached from γ_1, where β' differs only from β in the state of p; hence β' is 0-decided.)   □

To construct a non-deciding fair execution we must show that every process can take a step, and every message can be received, without enforcing a decision. Let a *step* s denote the receipt and handling of a particular message or a spontaneous move (internal or send) by a particular process. Depending on the state of the process where the step occurs, a different event may result. The receipt of a message is applicable if it is in transit, and a spontaneous step is always applicable.

Lemma 14.7 *Let γ be a reachable bivalent configuration and s an applicable step for process p in γ. There exists a sequence σ of events such that s is applicable in $\sigma(\gamma)$, and $s(\sigma(\gamma))$ is bivalent.*

Proof. Let C be the set of configurations reachable from γ without applying s, i.e., $C = \{\sigma(\gamma) : s \text{ does not occur in } \sigma\}$; s is applicable in every configuration of C (recall that s is a step, not a particular event).

There are configurations α_0 and α_1 in C such that a v-decided configuration is reachable from $s(\alpha_v)$. To see this, observe that by the bivalence of γ, v-decided configurations β_v are reachable from γ for $v = 0, 1$. If $\beta_v \in C$

(i.e., s was not applied to reach a decided configuration), observe that $s(\beta_v)$ is still v-decided, so choose $\alpha_v = \beta_v$. If $\beta_v \notin C$ (i.e., s was applied to reach a decided configuration), choose α_v as the configuration from which s was applied.

If $\alpha_0 = \alpha_1$, $s(\alpha_0)$ is the required bivalent configuration. Assume further that $\alpha_0 \neq \alpha_1$, and consider the configurations on the paths from γ to α_0 and α_1. Two configurations on these paths are called neighbors if one is obtained from the other in a single step. Because a 0-decided configuration is reachable from $s(\alpha_0)$ and a 1-decided configuration from $s(\alpha_1)$, it follows that

(1) there is a configuration γ' on the paths such that $s(\gamma')$ is bivalent; or

(2) there are neighbors γ_0 and γ_1 such that $s(\gamma_0)$ is 0-valent and $s(\gamma_1)$ is 1-valent.

In the first case, $s(\gamma')$ is the required bivalent configuration and we are done. In the second case, one of γ_0 and γ_1 is a fork, which is a contradiction. Indeed, assume (w.l.o.g.) that γ_1 is obtained in a single step from γ_0, i.e., $\gamma_1 = e(\gamma_0)$ for event e in process q. Now $s(e(\gamma_0))$ is $s(\gamma_1)$ and hence 1-valent, but it is not the case that $e(s(\gamma_0))$ is 1-valent because $s(\gamma_0)$ is already 0-valent. So e and s do not commute, which implies (Theorem 2.19) that $p = q$, but then the reachable configuration γ_0 satisfies $\gamma_0 \leadsto_p s(\gamma_0)$ and $\gamma_0 \leadsto_p s(e(\gamma_0))$. As the former is 0-valent and the latter 1-valent, γ_0 is a fork, which is a contradiction. $\square$

Theorem 14.8 *There exists no asynchronous, deterministic, 1-crash-robust consensus algorithm.*

Proof. Assuming that such an algorithm exists, a non-deciding fair execution can be constructed, starting from a bivalent initial configuration γ_0.

When the construction is completed up to configuration γ_i, choose for s_i an applicable step that has been applicable for the longest possible number of steps. By the previous lemma, the execution can be extended in such a way that s_i is executed, and a bivalent configuration γ_{i+1} is reached.

The construction gives an infinite fair execution in which all processes are correct but a decision is never taken. $\square$

14.1.3 Discussion

The result states that there are no asynchronous, deterministic, 1-crash-robust decision algorithms for the consensus problem; this excludes algorithms for a class of non-trivial problems (see Subsection 13.2.2).

Fortunately, some assumptions underlying the result of Fischer, Lynch, and Paterson can be made explicit, and the result turns out to be very sensitive to the weakening of any of them. Despite the impossibility result, many non-trivial problems do have solutions, even in asynchronous systems and where processes may fail.

(1) *Weaker fault model.* Section 14.2 considers the fault model of initially dead processes, which is weaker than the crash model, and in this model consensus and election are deterministically achievable.

(2) *Weaker coordination.* Section 14.3 considers problems that require a less close coordination between processes than does consensus, and demonstrates that some of these problems, including renaming, are solvable in the crash model.

(3) *Randomization.* Section 14.4 considers randomized protocols, where the termination requirement is sufficiently relaxed to make solutions possible even in the presence of Byzantine failures.

(4) *Weak termination.* Section 14.5 considers a different relaxation of the termination requirement, namely where termination is required only when a given process is correct; here also Byzantine-robust solutions are possible.

(5) *Synchrony.* The influence of synchrony is further studied in Chapter 15.

Fairly trivial solutions are possible if one of the three requirements of Definition 14.3 is simply omitted; see Exercise 14.1. Omission of the assumption (implicitly used in the proof of Lemma 14.6) that all combinations of inputs are possible is studied in Exercise 14.2.

14.2 Initially Dead Processes

In the model of initially dead processes, no process can fail after having executed an event, hence in a fair execution each process executes either 0 or infinitely many events.

Definition 14.9 *A t-initially-dead fair execution is an execution in which at least $N - t$ processes are active, each active process executes infinitely many events, and each message sent to a correct process is received.*

In a t-initially-dead-robust consensus algorithm, every correct process decides in every t-initially-dead fair execution. Agreement and non-triviality are defined as for the crash model.

```
var Succ_p, Alive_p, Rcvd_p  : sets of processes      init ∅ ;

begin shout ⟨ name, p ⟩ ;
        (* that is: forall q ∈ ℙ do send ⟨ name, p ⟩ to q *)
        while #Succ_p < L
                do. begin receive ⟨ name, q ⟩ ; Succ_p := Succ_p ∪ {q} end ;
        shout ⟨ pre, p, Succ_p ⟩ ;
        Alive_p := Succ_p ;
        while Alive_p ⊄ Rcvd_p
                do begin receive ⟨ pre, q, Succ ⟩ ;
                          Alive_p := Alive_p ∪ Succ ∪ {q} ;
                          Rcvd_p := Rcvd_p ∪ {q}
                end ;
        Compute a knot in G
end
```

Algorithm 14.1 COMPUTATION OF A KNOT.

Because processes do not fail after sending a message, it is safe for a process to wait for the receipt of a message from p if it knows that p has already sent at least one message. It will be shown that consensus and election are solvable in the initially dead model as long as a minority of the processes can be faulty $(t < N/2)$. A larger number of initially dead processes cannot be tolerated (see Exercise 14.3).

Agreement on a subset of correct processes. First an algorithm by Fischer, Lynch, and Paterson [FLP85] is presented by which each of the correct processes computes *the same* collection of correct processes. The resiliency of this algorithm is $\lfloor (N-1)/2 \rfloor$; let L stand for $\lceil (N+1)/2 \rceil$, and observe that there are at least L correct processes. The algorithm works in two stages; see Algorithm 14.1.

Observe that processes send messages to themselves; this is done in many robust algorithms, and facilitates analysis. Here and in the remainder, let the operation "shout ⟨ mes ⟩" stand for

$$\text{forall } q \in \mathbb{P} \text{ do send } \langle \text{mes} \rangle \text{ to } q .$$

The processes construct a directed graph G by shouting their identity (in a ⟨ name, p ⟩ message) and waiting for the receipt of L messages. As there are at least L correct processes, each correct process receives sufficiently many messages to complete this part. The successors of p in graph G are the nodes q from which p has received a ⟨ name, q ⟩ message.

An initially dead process has not sent nor received any message, hence forms an isolated node in G; a correct process has L successors, hence is not isolated. A knot is a strongly connected component without outgoing edges, containing at least two nodes. There is a knot in G, containing correct processes, and, because each correct process has out-degree L, this knot has size at least L. Consequently, as $2L > N$, there exists exactly one knot; call it K. Finally, as the correct process p has L successors, at least one successor belongs to K, implying that all processes in K are descendants of p.

Therefore, in the second stage of the algorithm, processes construct an induced subgraph of G, containing at least their descendants, by receiving the set of successors from every process they know to be correct. Because processes do not fail after sending a message, no deadlock occurs in this stage. Indeed, p waits to receive a message from q only if in the first stage some process has received a $\langle$ **name**, $q \rangle$ message, showing that q is correct.

Upon termination of Algorithm 14.1 each correct process has received the set of successors of each of its descendants, allowing it to compute the unique knot in G.

Consensus and election. As all correct processes agree on a knot of correct processes, it is now trivial to elect a process; the process with largest identity in K is elected. It is also easy to achieve consensus. Each process broadcasts, together with its successors, its input (x). After computing K, the processes decide on a value that is a function of the collection of inputs in K (for example, the value that occurs the more often, zero in the case of a draw).

The algorithms for knot-agreement, consensus, and election exchange $O(N^2)$ messages, where a message may contain a list of L process names. More efficient election algorithms have been proposed. Itai *et al.* [IKWZ90] gave an algorithm using $O(N(t + \log N))$ messages and demonstrated that this is a lower bound. Masuzawa *et al.* [MNHT89] considered the problem for cliques with sense of direction and proposed an $O(N t)$ message algorithm, which is again optimal.

Any election algorithm choosing a correct process as leader also solves the consensus problem; the leader broadcasts its input and all correct processes decide on it. Consequently, the above-mentioned upper bounds hold for the consensus problem for initially dead processes as well. In the crash model, however, the availability of a leader does not help in solving the consensus problem; the leader itself can crash before broadcasting its input. In addition, the election problem is not solvable in the crash model as is demonstrated in the next section.

14.3 Deterministically Achievable Cases

The consensus problem studied so far requires the same value to be decided upon in each process; this section studies the solvability of tasks that require a less close coordination between processes. In Subsection 14.3.1 a solution is presented for a practical problem, namely, the renaming of a collection of processes in a smaller name space. In Subsection 14.3.2 the impossibility results given earlier are extended to cover a larger class of decision problems.

A distributed *task* is described by sets X and D of possible input and output values, and a (possibly partial) mapping

$$T : X^N \longrightarrow \mathcal{P}(D^N).$$

The interpretation of the mapping T is that if the vector $\vec{x} = (x_1, \ldots, x_N)$ describes the input of the processes, then $T(\vec{x})$ is the set of legal outputs of the algorithm, described as a decision vector $\vec{d} = (d_1, \ldots, d_N)$. If T is a partial function, not every combination of input values is allowed.

Definition 14.10 *An algorithm is a t-crash robust solution for task T if it satisfies the following.*

(1) **Termination.** *In every t-crash fair execution, all correct processes decide.*

(2) **Consistency.** *If all processes are correct, the decision vector $\vec{d}$ is in $T(\vec{x})$.*

The consistency condition implies that in executions where a subset of the processes decide, the partial vector of decisions can always be extended to a vector in $T(\vec{x})$. The set D_T denotes the collection of all output vectors, i.e., the range of T.

(1) *Example: consensus.* The consensus problem requires all decisions to be equal, i.e.,

$$D_{\mathbf{cons}} = \{(0, 0, \ldots, 0), (1, 1, \ldots, 1)\}.$$

(2) *Example: election.* The election problem requires one process to decide on 1 and the others on 0, i.e.,

$$D_{\mathbf{elec}} = \{(1, 0, \ldots, 0), (0, 1, \ldots, 0), \ldots, (0, 0, \ldots, 1)\}.$$

(3) *Example: approximate agreement.* In the ϵ-*approximate agreement* problem each process has a real input value and decides on a real output value. The maximal difference between two output values is

at most ϵ, and the outputs are required to be enclosed between two inputs.

$$D_{\textbf{approx}} = \{(d_1, \ldots, d_N) : \max(d_i) - \min(d_i) \leq \epsilon\}.$$

(4) *Example: renaming.* In the *renaming problem* each process has a distinct identity, which can be taken from an arbitrarily large domain. Each process must decide on a new name, taken from a smaller domain $1, \ldots, K$, such that all new names are different.

$$D_{\textbf{rename}} = \{(d_1, \ldots, d_N) : i \neq j \Rightarrow d_i \neq d_j\}.$$

In the *order-preserving* version of the renaming problem, the new names are required to preserve the order of the old names, i.e., $x_i < x_j \Rightarrow d_i < d_j$.

14.3.1 A Solvable Problem: Renaming

In this subsection an algorithm for renaming, by Attiya *et al.* [ABND$^+$90], will be presented. The algorithm tolerates up to $t < N/2$ crashes (t is a parameter of the algorithm) and renames in a space of size $K = (N - t/2)(t + 1)$.

An upper bound on t. We first show that no renaming algorithm can tolerate $N/2$ or more crashes; in fact, almost all crash-robust algorithms have a limit $t < N/2$ on the number of faults, and the proof below can be adapted to other problems.

Theorem 14.11 *No algorithm for renaming exists if $t \geq N/2$.*

Proof. If $t \geq N/2$, two disjoint groups of processes S and T of size $N - t$ can be formed. Owing to the possibility that t processes fail, a group must be able to decide "on its own", i.e., without interaction with processes outside the group (see Proposition 14.4). But then the groups can *independently* reach a decision in a single execution; the crux of the proof is to show that these decisions can be mutually inconsistent. We proceed with the formal argument for the case of renaming.

By Proposition 14.4, for each initial configuration γ there exists a configuration δ_S such that all processes in S have decided and $\gamma \leadsto_S \delta_S$; a similar property holds for T. The operation of the algorithm within a group of $N - t$ processes defines a relation from vectors of $N - t$ initial identities to vectors of $N - t$ new names. Because the initial name space is unbounded and the new names come from a bounded range, there are disjoint inputs

```
var V_p     : set of identities ;
    c_p     : integer ;

begin V_p := {x_p} ; c_p := 0 ; shout ⟨set, V_p⟩ ;
      while true
      do begin receive ⟨set, V⟩ ;
             if V = V_p then
                 begin c_p := c_p + 1 ;
                     if c_p = N − t and y_p = b then
                         (* V_p is stable for the first time: decide *)
                         y_p := ( #V_p , rank(V_p, x_p) )
                 end
             else if V ⊆ V_p then
                 skip     (* Ignore "old" information *)
             else   (* new input; update V_p and restart counting *)
                 begin if V_p ⊂ V then c_p := 1 else c_p := 0 ;
                     V_p := V_p ∪ V ; shout ⟨set, V_p⟩
                 end
         end
      end
end
```

Algorithm 14.2 A SIMPLE RENAMING ALGORITHM.

---

that are mapped onto overlapping outputs. That is, there are input vectors (of length $N − t$) $\vec{u}$ and $\vec{v}$ such that $u_i \neq v_j$ for all i, j, but there are corresponding output vectors $\vec{d}$ and $\vec{e}$ such that $d_i = e_j$ for some i, j.

An incorrect execution is now constructed as follows. The initial configuration γ has inputs $\vec{u}$ in group S and $\vec{v}$ in group T; observe that all initial names are different (the initial names outside both groups can be chosen arbitrarily). Let σ_T be the sequence of steps by which group T reaches, from γ, the configuration δ_T in which the processes in T have decided on the names $\vec{e}$. By Proposition 14.1, this sequence is still applicable in configuration γ_S, in which the processes in S have decided on the names $\vec{d}$. In $\sigma_T(\gamma_S)$, two processes have decided on the same name (because $d_i = e_j$), which shows that the algorithm is not consistent. □

In what follows, $t < N/2$ is assumed.

The renaming algorithm. In the renaming algorithm (Algorithm 14.2), process p maintains a set V_p of process inputs that p has seen; initially, V_p contains just x_p. Every time p receives a set of inputs including ones that are new for p, V_p is extended by the new inputs. Upon starting and every time V_p is extended, p shouts its set. It follows that the set V_p only grows during the execution, i.e., subsequent values of V_p are totally ordered by inclusion, and moreover, V_p contains at most N names. Consequently, process p shouts its set at most N times, showing that the algorithm terminates and that the message complexity is bounded by $O(N^3)$.

Further, p counts (in the variable c_p) the number of times it has received copies of its current set V_p. Initially c_p is 0, and c_p is incremented each time a message containing V_p is received. The receipt of a message $\langle \mathbf{set}, V \rangle$ may cause V_p to grow, necessitating a reset of c_p. If the new value of V_p equals V (i.e., if V is a strict superset of the old V_p), c_p is set to 1, otherwise to 0.

Process p is said to reach a *stable set* V if c_p becomes $N - t$ when the value of V_p is V. In other words, p has received for the $(N - t)$th time the current value V of V_p.

Lemma 14.12 *Stable sets are totally ordered, i.e., if q reaches the stable set V_1 and r reaches the stable set V_2, then $V_1 \subseteq V_2$ or $V_2 \subseteq V_1$.*

Proof. Assume q that reaches the stable set V_1 and r reaches the stable set V_2. This implies that q has received $\langle \mathbf{set}, V_1 \rangle$ from $N - t$ processes and r has received $\langle \mathbf{set}, V_2 \rangle$ from $N - t$ processes. As $2(N - t) > N$, there is at least one process, say p, from which q has received $\langle \mathbf{set}, V_1 \rangle$ and r has received $\langle \mathbf{set}, V_2 \rangle$. Consequently, V_1 and V_2 are both values of V_p, implying that one is included in the other.   □

Lemma 14.13 *Each correct process reaches a stable set at least once in every fair t-crash execution.*

Proof. Let p be a correct process; the set V_p can only expand, and contains at most N input names. Consequently, a maximal value V_0 is reached for V_p. Process p shouts this value, and a $\langle \mathbf{set}, V_0 \rangle$ message is received by every correct process, which shows that every correct process eventually holds a *superset* of V_0.

However, this superset is *not* strict; otherwise, a correct process would send a strict superset of V_0 to p, contradicting the choice of V_0 (as being the largest set ever held by p). Consequently, every correct process q has a value $V_q = V_0$ at least once in the execution, and hence every correct process sends a $\langle \mathbf{set}, V_0 \rangle$ message to p during the execution. All these messages are received in the execution, and as V_p is never increased beyond V_0, they are all counted and cause V_0 to become stable in p.   □

Upon reaching a stable set V for the first time, process p decides on the pair (s, r), where s is the size of V and r is the rank of x_p in V. A stable set has been received from $N - t$ processes, and hence contains at least

$N - t$ input names, showing that $N - t \leq s \leq N$. The rank in a set of size s satisfies $1 \leq r \leq s$. The number of possible decisions is therefore $K = \sum_{s=N-t}^{N} s$, which is $(N - t/2)(t + 1)$; if desired, a fixed mapping from the pairs to integers in the range $1, \ldots, K$ can be used (Exercise 14.5).

Theorem 14.14 *Algorithm 14.2 solves the renaming problem with an output name space of size $K = (N - t/2)(t + 1)$.*

Proof. Because, in any fair t-crash execution, each correct process reaches a stable set, each correct process decides on a new name. To show that the new names are all distinct, consider the stable sets V_1 and V_2 reached by processes q and r respectively. If the sets have different sizes, the decisions of q and r are different because the size is included in the decision. If the sets have the same size, then by Lemma 14.12, they are equal; hence q and r have a different rank in the set, again showing that their decisions are different. ☐

Discussion. Observe that a process does not terminate Algorithm 14.2 after deciding on its name; it continues the algorithm to "help" other processes to decide, too. Attiya *et al.* [ABND+90] show that this is necessary because the algorithm must deal with the situation that some processes are so slow that they execute their first step after some other processes have already decided.

The simple algorithm presented here is not the best in terms of the size of name space used for renaming. Attiya *et al.* [ABND+90] gave a more complicated algorithm that assigns names in the range from 1 to $N + t$. The results of the next subsection imply a lower bound of $N + 1$ on the size of the new name space for crash-robust renaming.

Attiya *et al.* also proposed an algorithm for order-preserving renaming. It renames to integers in the range 1 to $K = 2^t \cdot (N - t + 1) - 1$, which was shown to be the smallest size of name space possible for t-crash-robust order-preserving renaming.

14.3.2 Extended Impossibility Results

The impossibility result for consensus (Theorem 14.8) was generalized by Moran and Wolfstahl [MW87] to more general decision problems. The *decision graph* of task T is the graph $G_T = (V, E)$, where $V = D_T$ and

$$E = \{ (\vec{d_1}, \vec{d_2}) : \vec{d_1} \text{ and } \vec{d_2} \text{ differ in exactly one component} \}.$$

Task T is called *connected* if G_T is a connected graph, and *disconnected* otherwise. It was assumed by Moran and Wolfstahl that the input graph of T (defined similarly to the decision graph) is connected, i.e., as in the proof of Lemma 14.6 we can move between any two input configurations by changing process inputs one by one. Furthermore, the impossibility result was shown for non-trivial algorithms, i.e., algorithms that satisfy, in addition to (1) termination and (2) consistency,

(3) **Non-triviality.** For each $\vec{d} \in D_T$, there is a reachable configuration in which the processes have decided on $\vec{d}$.

Theorem 14.15 *There exists no non-trivial 1-crash-robust decision algorithm for a disconnected task T.*

Proof. Assume, to the contrary, that such an algorithm, A, exists; a consensus algorithm A' may be derived from it, which constitutes a contradiction by Theorem 14.8. To simplify the argument we assume that G_T contains two connected components, "0" and "1".

Algorithm A' first simulates A, but instead of deciding on value d, a process shouts $\langle \textbf{vote}, d \rangle$ and awaits the receipt of $N - 1$ vote messages. No deadlock arises, because all correct processes decide in A; hence at least $N - 1$ processes shout a vote message.

After receiving the messages, process p holds $N-1$ components of a vector in D^N. This vector can be extended by a value for the process from which no vote was received, in such a way that the entire vector is in D_T. (Indeed, a consistent decision was taken by this process, or is still possible.)

Now observe that different processes may compute different extensions, but that these extensions belong to the same connected component of G_T. Each process that has received $N - 1$ votes decides on the name of the connected component to which the extended vector belongs. It remains to show that A' is a consensus algorithm.

Termination. It has already been argued above that every correct process receives at least $N - 1$ votes.

Agreement. We first argue there exists a vector $\vec{d_0} \in D_T$ such that each correct process obtains $N - 1$ components of $\vec{d_0}$.

Case 1: *All processes found a decision in A.* Let $\vec{d_0}$ be the vector of decisions reached; each process obtains $N - 1$ components of $\vec{d_0}$, though the "missing" component may be different for each process.

Case 2: *All processes except one, say r, found a decision in A.* All correct processes receive the same $N - 1$ decisions, namely those of all processes except r. It is possible that r crashed, but because it is also possible that r is only slow, it must still be possible for r to reach a decision, i.e., there exists a vector $\vec{d_0} \in D_T$ which extends the decisions taken so far.

From the existence of $\vec{d_0}$ it follows that each process decides on the connected component of this vector $\vec{d_0}$.

Non-triviality. By the non-triviality of A, decision vectors in both component 0 and component 1 can be reached; by the construction of A', both decisions are possible.

Thus, A' is an asynchronous, deterministic, 1-crash-robust consensus algorithm. With Theorem 14.8 the non-existence of algorithm A follows. $\qquad\square$

Discussion. The non-triviality requirement, stating that every decision vector in D_T is reachable, is fairly strong. One may ask whether some algorithms that are trivial in this sense may nonetheless be of interest. As an example, consider Algorithm 14.2 for renaming; it is not immediately clear that it is non-trivial, i.e., *every* vector with distinct names is reachable (it is); even less clear is why non-triviality would be of interest in this case.

Inspection of the proof of Theorem 14.15 reveals that a weaker requirement of non-triviality can be used in the proof, namely, that decision vectors are reachable in at least two different connected components of G_T. This weaker non-triviality may sometimes be induced from the statement of the problem.

Fundamental work concerning the decision tasks that are solvable and unsolvable in the presence of one faulty processor was done by Biran, Moran, and Zaks [BMZ90]. They gave a complete combinatorial characterization of the solvable decision tasks.

14.4 Probabilistic Consensus Algorithms

It was shown in the proof of Theorem 14.8 that every asynchronous consensus algorithm has infinite executions in which no decision is ever taken. Fortunately, for well-chosen algorithms such executions may be sufficiently rare to have probability zero, which makes the algorithms very practical in a probabilistic sense; see Chapter 9. In this section we present two probabilistic consensus algorithms, one for the crash model and one for the Byzantine model; the algorithms were proposed by Bracha and Toueg [BT85]. In both cases an upper bound on the resilience ($t < N/2$ and $t < N/3$, respectively) is proved first, and both algorithms match the respective bound.

In the correctness requirements for these probabilistic consensus algorithms, the termination requirement is made probabilistic, i.e., replaced by the weaker requirement of convergence.

(1) **Convergence.** For every initial configuration,

$$\lim_{k \to \infty} \mathbf{Pr}[\text{ a correct process has not decided after } k \text{ steps }] = 0.$$

Partial correctness (Agreement) must be satisfied in every execution; the resulting probabilistic algorithms are of the Las Vegas class (Subsection 9.1.2).

The probability is taken over all executions starting in a given initial configuration. In order for the probabilities to be meaningful, a probability distribution over these executions must be given. This can be done by using randomization in the processes (as in Chapter 9), but here a probability distribution on message arrivals is defined instead.

The probability distribution on executions starting in a given initial configuration is defined by the assumption of *fair scheduling*. Both algorithms operate in rounds; in a round a process shouts a message and awaits the receipt of $N - t$ messages. Define $R(q, p, k)$ as the event that, in round k, process p receives the (round-k) message of q among the first $N - t$ messages. Fair scheduling means that

(1) $\exists \epsilon > 0 \; \forall p, q, k \; : \; \mathbf{Pr}[\, R(p, q, k) \,] \geq \epsilon$.
(2) For all k, and different processes p, q, r, the events $R(q, p, k)$ and $R(q, r, k)$ are independent.

Observe that Proposition 14.4 also holds for probabilistic algorithms when convergence (termination with probability one) is required. Indeed, because a reachable configuration is reached with positive probability, a decided configuration must be reachable from every reachable configuration (albeit not necessarily reached in every execution).

14.4.1 Crash-robust Consensus Protocols

In this subsection the consensus problem is studied in the crash failure model. An upper bound $t < N/2$ on the resiliency is proved first, and subsequently an algorithm with resiliency $t < N/2$ is given.

Theorem 14.16 *There is no t-crash-robust consensus protocol for $t \geq N/2$.*

Proof. The existence of such a protocol, say P, implies the following three claims.

Claim 14.17 *P has a bivalent initial configuration.*

Proof. This is similar to the proof of Lemma 14.6; details are left to the reader. □

For a subset S of processes, configuration γ is said to be S-bivalent if both a 0- and a 1-decided configuration are reachable from γ by taking steps only in S. γ is called S-0-valent if, by taking steps only in S, a 0-decided configuration, but no 1-decided configuration, can be reached, and an S-1-valent configuration is defined similarly.

Partition the processes in two groups, S and T, of size $\lfloor N/2 \rfloor$ and $\lceil N/2 \rceil$.

Claim 14.18 *For a reachable configuration γ, γ is either both S-0-valent and T-0-valent, or both S-1-valent and T-1-valent.*

Proof. Indeed, the high resilience of the protocol implies that both S and T can reach a decision independently; if *different* decisions are possible, an inconsistent configuration can be reached by combining the schedules. □

Claim 14.19 *P has no reachable bivalent configuration.*

Proof. Let a reachable bivalent configuration γ be given and assume, w.l.o.g., that γ is S-1-valent and T-1-valent (use Claim 14.18). However, γ is bivalent, so also (clearly in cooperation between the groups) a 0-decided configuration δ_0 is reachable from γ. In the sequence of configurations from γ to δ_0 there are two subsequent configurations γ_1 and γ_0, where γ_v is both S-v-valent and T-v-valent. Let p be the process causing the transition from γ_1 to γ_0. Now $p \in S$ is impossible because γ_1 is S-1-valent and γ_0 is S-0-valent; similarly $p \in T$ is impossible. This is a contradiction. □

Contradiction to the existence of the protocol P arises from Claims 14.17 and 14.19; thus Theorem 14.16 is proved. □

The crash-robust consensus algorithm of Bracha and Toueg. The crash-robust consensus algorithm proposed by Bracha and Toueg [BT85] operates in *rounds*: in round k, a process sends a message to all processes (including itself) and awaits the receipt of $N - t$ round-k messages. Waiting for this number of messages does not introduce the possibility of deadlock (see Exercise 14.10).

In each round, process p shouts a vote for either 0 or 1, together with a weight. The weight is the number of votes received for that value in the previous round (1 in the first round); a vote with a weight exceeding $N/2$ is called a *witness*. Although different processes may vote differently in a round, there are never witnesses for different values in one round, as will be shown below. If process p receives a witness in round k, p votes for its value in round $k + 1$; otherwise p votes for the majority of the received votes. A decision is taken if more than t witnesses are received in a round; the decided process exits the main loop and shouts witnesses for the next two rounds in order to enable other processes to decide. The protocol is given as Algorithm 14.3.

Votes arriving for later rounds must be processed in the appropriate round; this is modeled in the algorithm by sending this message to the process itself for later processing. Observe that in any round a process receives at most one vote from each process, to a total of $N - t$ votes; because more than $N - t$ processes may shout a vote, processes may take different subsets of the shouted votes into account. We subsequently show several properties of the algorithm that together imply that it is a probabilistic crash-robust consensus protocol (Theorem 14.24).

Lemma 14.20 *In any round, no two processes witness for different values.*

Proof. Assume that in round k, process p witnesses for v and process q witnesses for w; $k > 1$ because in round 1 no process witnesses. The assumption implies that in round $k - 1$, p received more than $N/2$ votes for v and q received more than $N/2$ votes for w. Together more than N votes are involved; consequently, the processes from which p and q received votes overlap, i.e., there is an r that sent a v-vote to p and a w-vote to q. This implies $v = w$. □

Lemma 14.21 *If a process decides, then all correct processes decide for the same value, and at most two rounds later.*

Proof. Let k be the first round in which a decision is taken, p a process deciding in round k, and v the value of p's decision. The decision implies that there were v-witnesses in round k; hence by Lemma 14.20 there were no witnesses for other values, and so no different decision is taken in round k.

In round k there were more than t witnesses for v (this follows from p's decision), hence all correct processes receive at least one v-witness in round k. Consequently, all processes that vote in round $k + 1$ vote for v (observe also that p still shouts a vote in round $k + 1$). This implies that if a decision is taken at all in round $k + 1$, it is a decision for v.

In round $k + 1$, only v-votes are submitted, hence all processes that vote in round $k + 2$ witness for v in that round (p also does so). Consequently, in

```
var value_p        : (0, 1)    init x_p      (* p's vote *)
    round_p        : integer   init 0        (* Round number *)
    weight_p       : integer   init 1        (* Weight of p's vote *)
    msgs_p[0..1]   : integer   init 0        (* Count received votes *)
    witness_p[0..1] : integer  init 0        (* Count received witnesses *)

begin
    while y_p = b do
        begin witness_p[0], witness_p[1], msgs_p[0], msgs_p[1] :=
                                    0, 0, 0, 0 ;    (* Reset counts *)
            shout ⟨ vote, round_p, value_p, weight_p ⟩ ;
            while msgs_p[0] + msgs_p[1] < N − t do
                begin receive ⟨ vote, r, v, w ⟩ ;
                    if r > round_p then        (* Future round ... *)
                        send ⟨ vote, r, v, w ⟩ to p   (* ... process later *)
                    else if r = round_p then
                        begin msgs_p[v] := msgs_p[v] + 1 ;
                            if w > N/2 then        (* Witness *)
                                witness_p[v] := witness_p[v] + 1
                        end
                    else (* r < round_p, ignore *) skip
                end ;
            (* Choose new value: vote and weight in next round *)
            if witness_p[0] > 0 then value_p := 0
            else if witness_p[1] > 0 then value_p := 1
            else if msgs_p[0] > msgs_p[1] then value_p := 0
            else value_p := 1 ;
            weight_p := msgs_p[value_p] ;
            (* Decide if more than t witnesses *)
            if witness_p[value_p] > t then y_p := value_p ;
            round_p := round_p + 1
        end ;
    (* Help other processes decide *)
    shout ⟨ vote, round_p, value_p, N − t ⟩ ;
    shout ⟨ vote, round_p + 1, value_p, N − t ⟩
end
```

Algorithm 14.3 CRASH-ROBUST CONSENSUS ALGORITHM.

---

round $k+2$ all correct processes that did not decide in earlier rounds receive $N − t$ v-witnesses, and decide on v. $\square$

Lemma 14.22 $\lim_{k \to \infty}$ **Pr**[No decision is taken in a round $\leq k$] $= 0$.

Proof. Let S be a set of $N−t$ correct processes (such a set exists) and assume that no decision was taken until round k_0. The fair-scheduling assumption implies that, for some $\rho > 0$, in any round the probability is at least ρ that every process in S receives exactly the votes of the $N - t$ processes in S. With probability at least $\psi = \rho^3$ this happens in three subsequent rounds, k_0, $k_0 + 1$, and $k_0 + 2$.

If this happens, the processes in S receive the same votes in round k_0 and hence choose the same value, say v_0, in round k_0. All processes in S vote for v_0 in round $k_0 + 1$, implying that each process in S receives $N - t$ votes for v_0 in round $k_0 + 1$. This implies that the processes in S witness for v_0 in round $k + 2$; hence they all receive $N - t > t$ witnesses for v_0 in round $k_0 + 2$, and all decide for v_0 in that round. It follows that

$\mathbf{Pr}[$ Processes in S have not decided in round $k + 2$ $]$
$\leq \psi \times \mathbf{Pr}[$ Processes in S have not decided before round k $]$,

which implies the result.   □

Lemma 14.23 *If all processes start the algorithm with input v, then all processes decide for v in round 2.*

Proof. All processes receive only votes for v in round 1, so all processes witness for v in round 2. This implies that they all decide on v in that round.   □

Theorem 14.24 *Algorithm 14.3 is a probabilistic, t-crash-robust consensus protocol for $t < N/2$.*

Proof. Convergence was shown in Lemma 14.22 and agreement in Lemma 14.21; non-triviality is implied by Lemma 14.23.   □

The dependence of the decision on the input values is further analyzed in Exercise 14.11.

14.4.2 Byzantine-robust Consensus Protocols

The Byzantine failure model is more malicious than the crash model, because Byzantine processes may execute arbitrary state transitions and may send messages that are in disaccordance with the algorithm. In the sequel, we use the notation $\gamma \rightsquigarrow \delta$ (or $\gamma \rightsquigarrow_S \delta$) to denote that there is a sequence of *correct steps*, i.e., transitions of the protocol (in processes of S), leading the system from γ to δ. Similarly, γ is reachable if there is a sequence of correct steps leading from an initial configuration to γ. The maliciousness of the Byzantine model implies a lower maximum on the resilience than for the crash model.

Theorem 14.25 *There is no t-Byzantine-robust consensus protocol for $t \geq N/3$.*

Proof. Assume, to the contrary, that such a protocol exists. Again it is left to the reader to show the existence of a bivalent initial configuration of any such protocol (exploit, as usual, the non-triviality).

The high resilience of the protocol implies that two sets S and T of processes can be chosen such that $|S| \geq N - t$, $|T| \geq N - t$, and $|S \cap T| \leq t$. In words, both S and T are sufficiently large to survive independently, but their intersection can be entirely malicious. This is exploited to show that no bivalent configurations are reachable.

Claim 14.26 *A reachable configuration γ is either both S-0-valent and T-0-valent, or both S-1-valent and T-1-valent.*

Proof. As γ is reached by a sequence of correct steps, all possibilities for choosing a set of t processes that fail are still open. Assume, on the contrary, that *different* decisions can be reached by S and T, i.e., $\gamma \rightsquigarrow_S \delta_v$ and $\gamma \rightsquigarrow_T \delta_{\bar{v}}$, where δ_v ($\delta_{\bar{v}}$) is a configuration where all processes in S (in T) have decided on v ($\bar{v}$). An inconsistent state can be reached by assuming that the processes in $S \cap T$ are malicious and combining schedules as follows. Starting from configuration γ, the processes in $S \cap T$ cooperate with the other processes in S as in the sequence leading to a v-decision in S. When this decision has been taken by the processes in S, the malicious processes restore their state as in configuration γ, and subsequently cooperate with the processes in T as in the sequence leading to an $\bar{v}$ decision in T. This results in a configuration in which correct processes have decided differently, which conflicts with the agreement requirement. $\square$

Claim 14.27 *There is no reachable bivalent configuration.*

Proof. Let a reachable bivalent configuration γ be given and assume, w.l.o.g., that γ is both S-1-valent and T-1-valent (Claim 14.26). However, γ is bivalent, so a 0-decided configuration δ_0 is also reachable (clearly in cooperation between S and T) from γ. In the sequence of configurations from γ to δ_0 there are two subsequent configurations γ_1 and γ_0, where γ_v is both S-v-valent and T-v-valent. Let p be the process causing the transition from γ_1 to γ_0. Now $p \in S$ is impossible because γ_1 is S-1-valent and γ_0 is S-0-valent; similarly $p \in T$ is impossible. This is a contradiction. $\square$

Again, the last claim contradicts the existence of bivalent initial configurations. Thus Theorem 14.25 is proved. $\square$

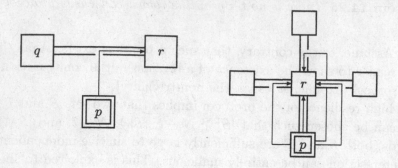

Figure 14.4 BYZANTINE PROCESS SIMULATING OTHER PROCESSES.

The Byzantine-robust consensus algorithm of Bracha and Toueg.
For $t < N/3$, t-Byzantine-robust consensus protocols do exist. It is necessary that the communication system allows a process to determine by what
process a received message was sent. If Byzantine process p can send to correct process r a message and successfully pretend that r receives the message
from q (see Figure 14.4), the problem becomes unsolvable. Indeed, process
p can simulate sufficiently many correct processes to enforce an incorrect
decision in process r.

Like the crash-robust protocol, the Byzantine-robust protocol (Algorithm
14.5) operates in rounds. In each round, every process can submit votes,
and a decision is taken when sufficiently many processes vote for the same
value. The lower resilience ($t < N/3$) eliminates the necessity to distinguish
between witnesses and non-witnesses; a process decides upon accepting more
than $(N + t)/2$ votes for the same value.

The maliciousness of the fault model necessitates, however, the introduction of a vote-verification mechanism, which is the crux of the protocol. Without such a mechanism a Byzantine process can disturb the voting
among correct processes by sending *different* votes to various correct processes. Such malicious behavior is not possible in the crash model. The
verification mechanism ensures that, although Byzantine process r can send
different votes to correct processes p and q, it cannot fool p and q into
accepting different votes for r (in some round).

The verification mechanism is based on echoing messages. A process
shouts its vote (as *initial*, **in**), and each process, upon receiving the first
vote for some process in some round, echoes the vote (as *echo*, **ec**). A process will accept a vote if more than $(N+t)/2$ echo messages for it have been

var $value_p$: $(0, 1)$ **init** x_p ;
       $round_p$: integer   **init** 0 ;
       $msgs_p[0..1]$: integer   **init** 0 ;
       $echos_p[\mathbb{P}, 0..1]$: integer   **init** 0 ;

while *true* **do**
       begin forall v, q **do begin** $msgs_p[v] := 0$; $echos_p[q, v] := 0$ **end** ;
           shout $\langle$ **vote**, **in**, p, $value_p$, $round_p \rangle$;
           (* Now accept $N - t$ votes for the current round *)
           while $msgs_p[0] + msgs_p[1] < N - t$ **do**
               begin receive $\langle$ **vote**, $t, r, v, rn \rangle$ from q ;
                  if $\langle$ **vote**, $t, r, *, rn \rangle$ has been received from q already
                     then skip   (* q repeats, must be Byzantine *)
                  else if $t = $ **in** and $q \neq r$
                     then skip   (* q lies, must be Byzantine *)
                  else if $rn > round_p$
                     then (* Process message in later round *)
                          send $\langle$ **vote**, $t, r, v, rn \rangle$ to p
                  else (* Process or echo vote message *)
                     case t **of**
                       in : shout $\langle$ **vote**, **ec**, $r, v, rn \rangle$
                       ec : **if** $rn = round_p$ **then**
                            begin $echos_p[r, v] := echos_p[r, v] + 1$;
                                if $echos_p[r, v] = \lfloor (N + t)/2 \rfloor + 1$
                                    then $msgs_p[v] := msgs_p[v] + 1$
                          end
                       else skip (* Old message *)
                 esac
              end ;
           (* Choose value for next round *)
           if $msgs_p[0] > msgs_p[1]$ **then** $value_p := 0$ **else** $value_p := 1$;
           if $msgs_p[value_p] > (N + t)/2$ **then** $y_p := value_p$;
           $round_p := round_p + 1$
     end

Algorithm 14.5 BYZANTINE-ROBUST CONSENSUS ALGORITHM.

---

received. The verification mechanism preserves the (partial) correctness of communication between correct processes (Lemma 14.28), and correct processes never accept different votes for the same process (Lemma 14.29). No deadlocks are introduced (Lemma 14.30).

We say that process p *accepts a v-vote* for process r in round k if p increments $msgs_p[v]$ upon receipt of a vote message $\langle$ **vote**, **ec**, $r, v, k \rangle$. The algorithm ensures that p passes round k only after acceptance of $N - t$ votes, and also that p accepts at most one vote for each process in each round.

Lemma 14.28 *If correct process p accepts in round k the vote v for correct process r, then r has voted for v in round k.*

Proof. Process p accepts the vote upon receipt of a $\langle \mathbf{vote}, \mathbf{ec}, r, v, k \rangle$ message from more than $(N + t)/2$ (different) processes; at least one correct process s has sent such a message to p. Process s sends the echo to p upon receipt of a $\langle \mathbf{vote}, \mathbf{in}, r, v, k \rangle$ from r, which implies, because r is correct, that r votes for v in round k.   □

Lemma 14.29 *If correct processes p and q accept a vote for process r in round k, they accept the same vote.*

Proof. Assume that in round k process p accepts a v-vote for r, and process q accepts a w-vote. Thus, p has received a $\langle \mathbf{vote}, \mathbf{ec}, r, v, k \rangle$ from more than $(N+t)/2$ processes, and q has received a $\langle \mathbf{vote}, \mathbf{ec}, r, w, k \rangle$ from more than $(N+t)/2$ processes. Because there are only N processes, more than t processes must have sent a $\langle \mathbf{vote}, \mathbf{ec}, r, v, k \rangle$ to p *and* a $\langle \mathbf{vote}, \mathbf{ec}, r, w, k \rangle$ to q. This implies that at least one correct process did so, and hence that $v = w$.   □

Lemma 14.30 *If all correct processes start round k, then all correct processes accept sufficiently many votes in that round to complete the round.*

Proof. Correct process r starting round k with $value_r = v$ shouts an initial vote for that round, which is echoed by all correct processes. Thus, for correct processes p and r, a $\langle \mathbf{vote}, \mathbf{ec}, r, v, k \rangle$ is sent to p by at least $N - t$ processes, allowing p to accept the v-vote for r in round k unless $N - t$ other votes are accepted earlier. It follows that process p accepts $N - t$ votes in this round.   □

The proof of correctness of the protocol now follows similar lines to the correctness proof of the crash-robust protocol.

Lemma 14.31 *If a correct process decides on v in round k, then all correct processes choose v in round k and all later rounds.*

Proof. Let S be the set of at least $(N+t)/2$ processes for which p accepts a v-vote in round k. Correct process q accepts, in round k, $N-t$ votes, including at least $|S| - t > (N - t)/2$ votes for processes in S. By Lemma 14.29, q accepts more than $(N-t)/2$ v-votes, which implies that q chooses v in round k.

To show that all correct processes choose v in later rounds, assume that all correct processes choose v in some round l; hence, all correct processes vote for v in round $l+1$. In round $l+1$ each correct process accepts $N-t$ votes, including more than $(N-t)/2$ votes for correct processes. By Lemma 14.28, a correct process accepts at least $(N-t)/2$ v-votes, and hence chooses v again in round $l+1$. □

Lemma 14.32 $\lim_{k\to\infty} \mathbf{Pr}[$ Correct p has not decided before round k $] = 0.$

Proof. Let S be a set of at least $N-t$ correct processes and assume that p has not decided before round k. With probability $\psi > 0$, the processes in S all accept, in round k, votes for *the same* collection of $N-t$ processes and, in round $k+1$, only votes for processes in S. If this happens, the processes in S vote equally in round $k+1$, and decide in round $k+1$. It follows that

$$\mathbf{Pr}[\text{ Correct process } p \text{ has not decided before round } k+2 \text{ }]$$
$$\leq \psi \times \mathbf{Pr}[\text{ Correct process } p \text{ has not decided before round } k \text{ }],$$

which implies the result. □

Lemma 14.33 *If all correct processes start the algorithm with input v, a decision for v is eventually taken.*

Proof. As in the proof of Lemma 14.31 it can be shown that all correct processes choose v again in every round. □

Theorem 14.34 *Algorithm 14.5 is a probabilistic, t-Byzantine-robust consensus protocol for $t < N/3$.*

Proof. Convergence was shown in Lemma 14.32 and agreement in Lemma 14.31; non-triviality is implied by Lemma 14.33. □

The dependence of the decision on the input values is further analyzed in Exercise 14.12. Algorithm 14.5 is described as an infinite loop for ease of presentation; we finally describe how the algorithm can be modified so as to terminate in every deciding process. After deciding on v in round k, process p exits the loop and shouts "multiple" votes $\langle \mathbf{vote}, \mathbf{in}, p, k^+, v \rangle$ and echoes $\langle \mathbf{vote}, \mathbf{ec}, *, k^+, v \rangle$. These messages are interpreted as initial and echoed votes for all rounds later than k. Indeed, p will vote for v in all later rounds, and so will all correct processes (Lemma 14.31). Hence the multiple messages are those that would be sent by p when continuing the algorithm, with a possible exception for the echoes of malicious initial votes.

14.5 Weak Termination

In this section the problem of an asynchronous Byzantine broadcast is studied. The goal of a broadcast is to make a value that is present in one process g, referred to as the *general*, known to all processes. Formally, the non-triviality requirement for a consensus protocol is strengthened by specifying that the decision value is the input of the general if the general is correct:

(3) **Dependence.** If the general is correct, all correct process decide on its input.

With this specification, however, the general becomes a single point of failure, implying that the problem is not solvable, as expressed in the following theorem.

Theorem 14.35 *There is no 1-Byzantine robust algorithm satisfying convergence, agreement, and dependence, even if convergence is required only if the general has sent at least one message.*

Proof. We consider two scenarios. In the first one the general is assumed Byzantine; the scenario serves to define a reachable configuration γ. A contradiction is then derived, in the second scenario.

(1) Assume that the general is Byzantine, and sends a message to initiate a broadcast of "0" to process p_0 and a message to initiate a broadcast of "1" to process p_1. Then the general stops. We call the resulting configuration γ.

By convergence, a decided configuration can be reached even if the general crashes; let $S = \mathbb{P} \setminus \{g\}$ and assume, w.l.o.g., that $\gamma \leadsto_S \delta_0$, where δ_0 is 0-decided.

(2) For the second scenario, assume that the general is correct and has input 1, and sends messages to initiate a broadcast of 1 to p_0 and p_1, after which its messages are delayed for a very long time. Now assume p_0 is Byzantine, and, after receipt of the message, changes its state to the state in γ, i.e., pretends to have received a 0-message from the general. As $\gamma \leadsto_S \delta_0$, a 0-decision can now be reached without interaction with the general, which is not allowed because the general is correct and has input 1.

$\square$

The impossibility results from the possibility that the general initiates a broadcast and halts (first scenario) without providing sufficient information about its input (as exploited in the second scenario). It will now be shown that a (deterministic) solution is possible if termination is required only in the case where the general is correct.

Definition 14.36 *A t-Byzantine-robust broadcast algorithm is an algorithm satisfying the following three requirements.*

> (1) **Weak termination.** *All correct processes decide, or no correct process decides. If the general is correct, all correct processes decide.*
>
> (2) **Agreement.** *If the correct processes decide, they decide on the same value.*
>
> (3) **Dependence.** *If the general is correct, all correct processes decide on its input.*

The resilience of an asynchronous Byzantine broadcast algorithm can be shown to be bounded by $t < N/3$ by arguments similar to those used in the proof of Theorem 14.25. The broadcast algorithm of Bracha and Toueg [BT85], given as Algorithm 14.6, uses three types of vote messages: *initial* messages (type **in**), *echo* messages (type **ec**), and *ready* messages (type **re**). Each process counts, for each type and value, how many messages have been received, counting at most one message received from every process.

The general initiates the broadcast by shouting an initial vote. Upon receipt of an initial vote from the general, a process shouts an echo vote containing the same value. When more than $(N + t)/2$ echo messages with value v have been received, a ready message is shouted. The number of required echoes is sufficiently large to guarantee that no correct processes send ready messages for different values (Lemma 14.37). The receipt of more than t ready messages for the same value (implying that at least one correct process has sent such a message) also triggers the shouting of ready messages. The receipt of more than $2t$ ready messages for the same value (implying that more than t correct processes have sent such a message) causes a decision for that value. No provision is taken in Algorithm 14.6 to prevent a correct process from shouting a ready message twice, but the message is ignored by correct processes anyway.

Lemma 14.37 *No two correct processes send ready messages for different values.*

Proof. A correct process accepts at most one initial message (from the general), and hence sends echoes for at most one value.

Let p be the first correct process to send a ready message for v, and q the first correct process to send a ready message for w. Although a ready

var $msgs_p[(\mathbf{in}, \mathbf{ec}, \mathbf{re}), 0..1]$: integer   **init** 0 ;

For the general only:
    shout $\langle \mathbf{vote}, \mathbf{in}, x_p \rangle$

For all processes:
while $y_p = b$ **do**
    begin receive $\langle \mathbf{vote}, t, v \rangle$ from q;
        if a $\langle \mathbf{vote}, t, * \rangle$ message has been received from q already
          then skip   (* q repeats, ignore *)
        else if $t = \mathbf{in}$ and $q \neq g$
          then skip   (* q mimics g, must be Byzantine *)
        else begin $msgs_p[t, v] := msgs_p[t, v] + 1$;
                case t **of**
                    in : **if** $msgs_p[\mathbf{in}, v] = 1$
                        then shout $\langle \mathbf{vote}, \mathbf{ec}, v \rangle$
                  ec : **if** $msgs_p[\mathbf{ec}, v] = \lceil (N + t)/2 \rceil + 1$
                        then shout $\langle \mathbf{vote}, \mathbf{re}, v \rangle$
                  re : **if** $msgs_p[\mathbf{re}, v] = t + 1$
                        then shout $\langle \mathbf{vote}, \mathbf{re}, v \rangle$;
                        if $msgs_p[\mathbf{re}, v] = 2t + 1$
                        then $y_p := v$
              esac
        end
    end

Algorithm 14.6 BYZANTINE-ROBUST BROADCAST ALGORITHM.

message can be sent upon receipt of sufficiently many ready messages, this is not the case for the first correct process that sends a ready message. This is so because $t + 1$ ready messages must be received before sending one, implying that a ready message from at least one correct process has been received already. Thus, p has received v-echoes from more than $(N + t)/2$ processes and q has received w-echoes from more than $(N + t)/2$ processes.

Because there are only N processes and $t < N/3$, there are more than t processes, including at least one correct process r, from which p has received a v-echo and q has received a w-echo. Because r is correct, $v = w$ is implied.

$\square$

Lemma 14.38 *If a correct process decides, then all correct processes decide, and on the same value.*

Proof. To decide on v, more than $2t$ ready messages must be received for v, which includes more than t ready messages from correct processes; Lemma 14.37 implies that the decisions will agree.

Assume correct process p decides on v; p has received more than $2t$ ready messages, including more than t messages from correct processes. A correct process sending a ready message to p sends this message to all processes, implying that all correct processes receive more than t ready messages. This in turn implies that all correct processes send a ready message, so that every correct process eventually receives $N - t > 2t$ ready messages and decides. $\square$

Lemma 14.39 *If the general is correct, all correct processes decide on its input.*

Proof. If the general is correct it sends no initial messages with values different from its input. Consequently, no correct process will send echoes with values different from the general's input, which implies that at most t processes send these bad echoes. The number of bad echoes is insufficient for correct processes to send ready messages for bad values, which implies that at most t processes send bad ready messages. The number of bad ready messages is insufficient for a correct process to send ready messages or to decide, which implies that no correct process sends a bad ready message or decides incorrectly.

If the general is correct it sends an initial vote with its input to all correct processes, and all correct processes shout an echo with this value. Consequently, all correct processes will receive at least $N - t > (N + t)/2$ correct echo messages, and will shout a ready message with the correct value. Thus, all correct processes will receive at least $N - t > 2t$ correct ready messages, and will decide correctly. $\square$

Theorem 14.40 *Algorithm 14.6 is an asynchronous t-Byzantine-robust broadcast algorithm for $t < N/3$.*

Proof. Weak termination follows from Lemmas 14.39 and 14.38, agreement from Lemma 14.38, and dependence from Lemma 14.39. $\square$

Exercises to Chapter 14
Section 14.1

Exercise 14.1 *Omission of any of the three requirements of Definition 14.3 (termination, agreement, non-triviality) for the consensus problem allows a very simple solution. Show this by presenting the three simple solutions.*

Exercise 14.2 *In the proof of Lemma 14.6 it is assumed that each of the 2^N assignments of a bit to the N processes produces a possible input configuration.*

Give deterministic, 1-crash robust consensus protocols for each of the following restrictions on the input values.

(1) *It is given that the parity of the input is even (i.e., there are an even number of processes with input 1) in each initial configuration.*

(2) *There are two (known) processes r_1 and r_2, and each initial configuration satisfies $x_{r_1} = x_{r_2}$.*

(3) *In each initial configuration there are at least $\lceil (N/2) + 1 \rceil$ processes with the same input.*

Section 14.2

Exercise 14.3 *Show that there is no t-initially-dead-robust election algorithm for $t \geq N/2$.*

Section 14.3

Exercise 14.4 *Show that no algorithm for ϵ-approximate agreement can tolerate $t \geq N/2$ crashes.*

Exercise 14.5 *Give a bijection from the set*

$$\{(s, r) \,:\, N - t \leq s \leq N \text{ and } 1 \leq r \leq s\}$$

to integers in the range $[1, \ldots, K]$.

Project 14.6 *Is Algorithm 14.2 non-trivial?*

Exercise 14.7 *Adapt the proof of Theorem 14.15 for the case that G_T consists of k connected components.*

Exercise 14.8 *In this exercise we consider the problem of* $[k, l]$*-election, which generalizes the usual election problem. The problem requires that all correct processes decide on either 0 ("defeated") or 1 ("elected"), and that the number of processes that decide 1 is between* k *and* l *(inclusive).*

  (1) *What are the uses of* $[k, l]$*-election?*

  (2) *Demonstrate that no deterministic 1-crash robust algorithm for* $[k, k]$*-election exists (if* $0 < k < N$*).*

  (3) *Give a deterministic t-crash robust algorithm for* $[k, k + 2t]$*-election.*

Section 14.4

Exercise 14.9 *Does the convergence requirement imply that the expected number of steps is bounded?*
Is the expected number of steps bounded in all algorithms of this section?

Exercise 14.10 *Show that if all correct processes start round* k *of the crash-robust consensus algorithm (Algorithm 14.3), then all correct processes will also finish round* k.

Exercise 14.11

  (1) *Prove, that if more that* $(N + t)/2$ *processes start the crash-robust consensus algorithm (Algorithm 14.3) with input* v*, then a decision for* v *is taken in three rounds.*

  (2) *Prove, that if more than* $(N - t)/2$ *processes start the algorithm with input* v*, then a decision for* v *is possible.*

  (3) *Is a decision for* v *possible if exactly* $(N - t)/2$ *processes start the algorithm with input* v*?*

  (4) *What are the bivalent input configurations of the algorithm?*

Exercise 14.12

  (1) *Prove that, if more than* $(N + t)/2$ *correct processes start Algorithm 14.5 with input* v*, a* v*-decision is eventually taken.*

  (2) *Prove that, if more than* $(N + t)/2$ *correct processes start Algorithm 14.5 with input* v *and* $t < N/5$*, a* v*-decision is taken within two rounds.*

Section 14.5

Exercise 14.13 *Prove that no asynchronous t-Byzantine-robust broadcast algorithm exists for $t \geq N/3$.*

Exercise 14.14 *Prove that during the execution of Algorithm 14.6 at most $N(3N + 1)$ messages are sent by correct processes.*

15

Fault Tolerance in Synchronous Systems

The previous chapter has studied the degree of fault tolerance achievable in completely asynchronous systems. Although a reasonable robustness is attainable, reliable systems in practice are always synchronous in the sense of relying on the use of timers and upper bounds on the message-delivery time. In these systems a higher degree of robustness is attainable, the algorithms are simpler, and the algorithms guarantee an upper bound on the response time in most of the cases.

The synchrony of the system makes it impossible for faulty processes to confuse correct processes by not sending information; indeed, if a process does not receive a message when expected, a default value is used instead, and the sender becomes suspected of being faulty. Thus, crashed processes are detected immediately and pose no difficult problems in synchronous systems; we concentrate on Byzantine failures in this chapter.

In Section 15.1 the problem of performing a broadcast in synchronous networks is studied; we present an upper bound ($t < N/3$) on the resilience, as well as two algorithms with optimal resilience. The algorithms are deterministic and achieve consensus; it is assumed that all processes know at what time the broadcast is initiated. Because consensus is not deterministically achievable in asynchronous systems (Theorem 14.8), it follows that in the presence of failures (even a single crash), synchronous systems exhibit a strictly stronger computational power than asynchronous ones.

Because crashing and not sending information are detected (and hence "harmless") in synchronous systems, Byzantine processes are only able to disturb the computation by sending erroneous information, either about their own state or by incorrectly forwarding information. In Section 15.2 it will be demonstrated that the robustness of synchronous systems can be further enhanced by providing methods for information authentication.

469

With these mechanisms it becomes impossible for a malicious process to "lie" about information received from other processes. It remains possible, though, to send inconsistent information about the process's own state. It is also shown that implementation of authentication is in practice possible using cryptographic techniques.

The algorithms in Sections 15.1 and 15.2 assume an idealized model of synchronous systems, in which the computation proceeds in pulses (also called *rounds*); see Chapter 12. The fundamentally higher resilience of synchronous systems over asynchronous systems implies the impossibility of any 1-crash-robust deterministic implementation of the pulse model in the asynchronous model. (Such an implementation, called a *synchronizer*, is possible in reliable networks; see Section 12.3).

Implementation of the pulse model is possible, however, in asynchronous bounded-delay networks (Subsection 12.1.3), where processes possess clocks and an upper bound on message delay is known. The implementation is possible even if the clocks drift and up to one-third of the processes may fail maliciously. The most difficult part of the implementation is to synchronize the process clocks reliably, a problem that will be discussed in Section 15.3.

15.1 Synchronous Decision Protocols

In this section we shall present algorithms for Byzantine-robust broadcast in synchronous (pulsed) networks; we start with a brief review of the model of pulsed networks as defined in Section 12.1.1. In a synchronous network the processes operate in pulses numbered 1, 2, 3, and so on; each process can execute an unbounded number of pulses as long as its local algorithm does not terminate. The initial configuration (γ_0) is described by the initial states of the processes, and the configuration after the ith pulse (denoted γ_i) is also described by the states of the processes. In pulse i, each process first sends a finite set of messages, depending on its state in γ_{i-1}. Subsequently each process receives all the messages sent to it in this pulse, and computes the new state from the old one and the collection of messages received in the pulse.

The pulse model is an idealized model of synchronous computations. The synchrony is reflected in

(1) the apparently simultaneous occurrence of the state transitions in the processes; and

(2) the guarantee that messages of a pulse are received before the state transitions of that pulse.

These idealized assumptions can be weakened to more realistic assumptions, namely (1) the availability of hardware clocks and (2) an upper bound on the message-delivery time. The resulting model of *asynchronous bounded delay networks* allows very efficient implementation of the pulse model (see Section 12.1.3). As shown in Chapter 12, the simultaneity of state transitions is only apparent. In an implementation of the model the state transitions may occur at different times, as long as timely receipt of all messages is guaranteed. In addition, the implementation should allow a process an unbounded number of pulses. The latter requirement excludes the implementations of Chapter 12 for use in fault-tolerant applications, because they all suffer from deadlock, most of them even in case of a single message loss. As already mentioned, robust implementation of the pulse model will be treated in Section 15.3.

Because the pulse model guarantees delivery of messages in the same pulse, a process is able to determine that a neighbor *did not send a message* to it. This feature is absent in asynchronous systems and makes a solution to the consensus problem, and even to the reliable-broadcast problem, possible in synchronous systems, as we shall see shortly.

In the Byzantine-broadcast problem, one distinct process g, called the *general*, is given an input x_g taken from a set V (usually $\{0, 1\}$). The processes different from the general are called the *lieutenants*. The following three requirements must be satisfied.

(1) **Termination.** Every correct process p will decide on a value $y_p \in V$.
(2) **Agreement.** All correct processes decide on the same value.
(3) **Dependence.** If the general is correct, all correct processes decide on x_g.

It is possible to require, in addition, **simultaneity**, i.e., that all correct processes decide in the same pulse. All algorithms discussed in this section and the following section satisfy simultaneity; see also Subsection 15.2.6.

15.1.1 A Bound on the Resilience

The resilience of synchronous networks against Byzantine failures is, as in the case of asynchronous networks (Theorem 14.25), bounded by $t < N/3$. The bound was first shown by Pease, Shostak, and Lamport [PSL80], by presenting several scenarios for an algorithm in the presence of $N/3$ or more Byzantine processes. Unlike the scenarios used in the proof of Theorem 14.25, here the correct processes receive contradictory information, allowing the conclusion that some processes are faulty. However, it turns out to be impossible

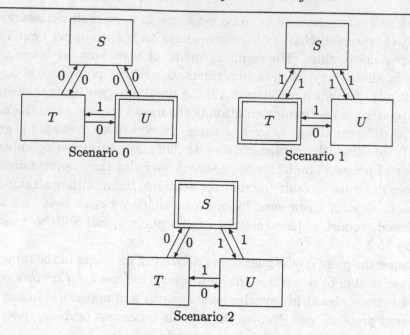

Figure 15.1 SCENARIOS FOR THE PROOF OF THEOREM 15.1.

to determine which processes are unreliable, and an incorrect decision can be enforced by the incorrect processes.

Theorem 15.1 *There is no t-Byzantine-robust broadcast protocol for* $t \geq N/3$.

Proof. As in earlier proofs, a resilience of $N/3$ or higher allows a partition of the processes into three groups (S, T, and U), each of which can be entirely faulty. The group containing the general is called S. A contradiction is derived by considering three scenarios, depicted in Figure 15.1, where the faulty group is indicated by a double box.

In scenario 0 the general broadcasts the value 0 and the processes in group U are faulty; in scenario 1 the general broadcasts a 1 and the processes in T are faulty. In pulse i of scenario 0, the processes of group U send to the processes in group T exactly those messages they would have sent (according to the protocol) in scenario 1. (That is, the messages sent in reaction to the messages received in pulse $i - 1$ of scenario 1.) To the processes in S they send the messages directed by the protocol. Processes in S and T of course send the correct messages in all pulses. Observe, that in this scenario only the processes in group U send incorrect messages, and the specifications of the protocol dictate that all correct processes, including group T, decide on 0.

Scenario 1 is defined similarly, but here the processes in T are faulty and send the messages they should have sent in scenario 0. In this scenario the processes in U decide on 1.

Finally consider scenario 2, where the processes in S are faulty and behave as follows. To the processes in T they send the messages of scenario 0 and to the processes in U they send the messages of scenario 1. It now can be shown by induction on the pulse number that the messages sent by T to U (or, from U to T) are exactly those sent in scenario 0 (or 1, respectively). Consequently, for the processes in T scenario 2 is indistinguishable from scenario 0 and for the processes in U it is indistinguishable from scenario 1. It follows that the processes in T decide on 0 and the processes in U decide on 1, a contradiction. $\square$

It is used in the proof that Byzantine processes can send the messages of a 1-scenario, even if they have only the received messages of a 0-scenario. That is, the processes can "lie" not only about their own state, but also about the messages they have received. It is exactly this possibility that can be eliminated by using authentication, as discussed in Section 15.2; this leads to a resilience of $N - 1$.

15.1.2 Byzantine-broadcast Algorithm

In this subsection it will be shown that the upper bound on the resilience, shown in the previous subsection, is sharp. Moreover, contrasting the situation in asynchronous networks, the maximal resilience is attainable using deterministic algorithms. We present a recursive algorithm, also due to Pease *et al.* [PSL80], that tolerates t Byzantine failures for $t < N/3$. The resilience is a parameter of the algorithm.

The algorithm $Broadcast(N, 0)$ is given as Algorithm 15.2; it tolerates no failures ($t = 0$), and if no failures occur all processes decide on the input of the general in pulse 1. If a failure occurs, agreement may be violated, but termination (and simultaneity) is still guaranteed.

The protocol for resilience $t > 0$ (Algorithm 15.3) makes use of recursive calls to the procedure for resilience $t - 1$. The general sends its input to all lieutenants in pulse 1, and in the next pulse each lieutenant starts a broadcast of the received value to the other lieutenants, but this broadcast has resilience $t - 1$. This reduced resilience is a subtle point in the algo-

Pulse

1:        The general sends $\langle$ **value**, x_g $\rangle$ to all processes,
          the lieutenants do not send.
          receive messages of pulse 1.
          The general decides on x_g.
          Lieutenants decide as follows:
                  if a message $\langle$ **value**, x $\rangle$ was received from g in pulse 1
                          then decide on x
                          else decide on *udef*

Algorithm 15.2 *Broadcast*$(N, 0)$.

rithm, because (if the general is correct) all t Byzantine processes may be found among the lieutenants, so the actual number of faults may exceed the resilience of the nested call of *Broadcast*. To prove the correctness of the resulting algorithm it is necessary to reason using the resilience t *and* the actual number of faulty processes f (see Lemma 15.3). In pulse $t+1$ the nested calls produce a decision, so lieutenant p decides in $N-1$ nested broadcasts. These $N-1$ decisions are stored in the array W_p, from which the decision of p is obtained by majority voting (the value received directly from the general is ignored here!). To this end a deterministic function *ma-*

Pulse

1:        The general sends $\langle$ **value**, x_g $\rangle$ to all processes,
          the lieutenants do not send.
          receive messages of pulse 1.
          Lieutenant p acts as follows.
          if a message $\langle$ **value**, x $\rangle$ was received from g in pulse 1
                  then $x_p := x$ **else** $x_p := udef$;
                  Announce x_p to the other lieutenants by acting as a general
                          in *Broadcast*$_p(N-1, t-1)$ in the next pulse

$(t+1)$:   **receive messages of pulse $t+1$.**
          The general decides on x_g.
          For lieutenant p:
          a decision occurs in *Broadcast*$_q(N-1, t-1)$ for each lieutenant q.
          $W_p[q] :=$ decision in *Broadcast*$_q(N-1, t-1)$;
          $y_p := major(W_p)$

Algorithm 15.3 *Broadcast*(N, t) (FOR $t > 0$).

jor is defined on arrays, with the property that if v has a majority in W, (i.e., more than half the entries equal v), then $major(W) = v$.

Lemma 15.2 (Termination) *If Broadcast(N, t) is started in pulse 1, every process decides in pulse $t + 1$.*

Proof. Because the protocol is recursive, its properties are proved using recursion on t.

In the algorithm $Broadcast(N, 0)$ (Algorithm 15.2), every process decides in pulse 1.

In the algorithm $Broadcast(N, t)$, the lieutenants initiate recursive calls of the algorithm, $Broadcast(N - 1, t - 1)$, in pulse 2. When started in pulse 1, this algorithm decides in pulse t (this is the induction hypothesis), hence when started in pulse 2, all nested calls decide in pulse $t + 1$. In the same pulse, the decision in $Broadcast(N, t)$ is taken. $\square$

To prove dependence (also by induction) it is assumed that the general is correct, hence all t faulty processes are found among the $N - 1$ lieutenants. As $t < (N - 1)/3$ is not necessarily true, simple induction cannot be used, and we reason using the actual number of faults, denoted f.

Lemma 15.3 (Dependence) *If the general is correct, if there are f faulty processes, and if $N > 2f + t$, then all correct processes decide on the input of the general.*

Proof. In the algorithm $Broadcast(N, 0)$, if the general is correct all correct processes decide on the value of the general's input.

Now assume the lemma holds for $Broadcast(N - 1, t - 1)$. As the general is correct, it sends its input to all lieutenants in pulse 1, so every correct lieutenant q chooses $x_q = x_g$. Now $N > 2f + t$ implies $(N - 1) > 2f + (t - 1)$, so the induction hypothesis applies to the nested calls, even now all f faulty processes are found among the lieutenants. Thus, for correct lieutenants p and q, the decision of p in $Broadcast_q(N - 1, t - 1)$ equals x_q, i.e., x_g. But, as a strict majority of the lieutenants is correct $(N > 2f + t)$, process p will end with W_p in which a majority of the values equals x_g. Hence the application of *major* by p yields the desired value x_g. $\square$

Lemma 15.4 (Agreement) *All correct processes decide on the same value.*

Proof. Because dependence implies agreement in the executions in which the general is correct, we now concentrate on the case where the general is faulty. But then at most $t - 1$ of the lieutenants are faulty, implying that the nested calls operate within the bounds of their resilience!

Indeed, $t < N/3$ implies $t - 1 < (N - 1)/3$, hence the nested calls satisfy agreement. So, all *correct* lieutenants will decide on the same value of x_q for *every* lieutenant q in the nested call $Broadcast_q(N - 1, t - 1)$. Thus, every correct lieutenant computes exactly the same vector W in pulse $t + 1$, which implies that the application of *major* gives the same result in every correct process.   ☐

Theorem 15.5 *The Broadcast(N, t) protocol (Algorithm 15.2/15.3) is a t-Byzantine-robust broadcast protocol for $t < N/3$.*

Proof. Termination was shown in Lemma 15.2, dependence in Lemma 15.3, and agreement in Lemma 15.4.   ☐

The *Broadcast* protocol decides in the $(t + 1)$th pulse, which is optimal; see Subsection 15.2.6. Unfortunately, the message complexity is exponential; see Exercise 15.1.

15.1.3 A Polynomial Broadcast Algorithm

In this section we present a Byzantine broadcast algorithm by Dolev *et al.* [DFF+82], which uses only a polynomial number of messages and bits. The time complexity is higher than for the previous protocol; the algorithm requires $2t + 3$ pulses to reach a decision. In the following description it will be assumed that $N = 3t + 1$, and the case $N > 3t + 1$ will be discussed later.

The algorithm uses two thresholds, $L = t + 1$ and $H = 2t + 1$. These numbers are chosen such that (1) each set of L processes contains at least one correct process, (2) each set of H processes contains at least L correct processes, and (3) there are at least H correct processes. Note that the assumption $N \geq 3t + 1$ is necessary and sufficient to make the choice of L and H satisfying these three properties possible.

The algorithm exchanges messages of the type $\langle \mathbf{bm}, v \rangle$, where v is either the value 1, or the name of a process. ($\mathbf{bm}$ stands for "broadcast message".) Process p maintains a two-dimensional boolean table R, where $R_p[q, v]$ is true if and only if p has received a message $\langle \mathbf{bm}, v \rangle$ from process q. Initially all entries in the table are false, and we assume that the table is updated in the receive phase of every pulse (this is not shown in Algorithm 15.4). Observe that R_p is monotone in the pulses, i.e., if $R_p[q, v]$ becomes true in some pulse, it remains true in later pulses. Furthermore, as correct processes only shout messages, we have for correct p, q, and r at the end of each pulse: $R_p[r, v] = R_q[r, v]$.

Unlike the *Broadcast* protocol of the previous subsection, the protocol of Dolev *et al.* is asymmetric in the values 0 and 1. A decision on 0 is the default value, and is chosen if insufficiently many messages are exchanged. If the general has input 1 it will shout $\langle \mathbf{bm}, 1 \rangle$ messages, and the receipt of sufficiently many echoing messages, of type $\langle \mathbf{bm}, q \rangle$, causes a process to decide on 1.

Three types of activity are relevant in the algorithm: *initiating, supporting*, and *confirming*.

(1) *Supporting.* Process p *supports* process q in pulse i if p has received sufficient evidence in earlier pulses that q has sent $\langle \mathbf{bm}, 1 \rangle$ messages; if this is the case, p will send $\langle \mathbf{bm}, q \rangle$ messages in pulse i. Process p is a *direct supporter* of q if p has received a $\langle \mathbf{bm}, 1 \rangle$ message from q. Process p is an *indirect supporter* of q if p has received a $\langle \mathbf{bm}, q \rangle$ message from at least L processes. The set S_p of processes supported by p is defined implicitly from R_p by

$$DS_p = \{q : R_p[q, 1]\}$$
$$IS_p = \{q : \#\{r : R_p[r, q]\} \geq L\}$$
$$S_p = DS_p \cup IS_p$$

The threshold for becoming an indirect supporter implies that if a correct process supports process q, then q has sent at least one $\langle \mathbf{bm}, 1 \rangle$ message. Indeed, assume some correct process supports q; let i be the first pulse in which this happens. As supporting q indirectly requires the receipt of at least one $\langle \mathbf{bm}, q \rangle$ message from a correct process in an earlier pulse, the first support for q by a correct process is direct. The direct support by a correct process implies that this process has received a $\langle \mathbf{bm}, 1 \rangle$ message from q.

(2) *Confirming.* Process p *confirms* process q upon receiving $\langle \mathbf{bm}, q \rangle$ messages from H processes, i.e.,

$$C_p = \{q : \#\{r : R_p[r, q]\} \geq H\}.$$

The choice of thresholds implies that if a correct process p confirms q, then all correct processes confirm q at most one pulse later. Indeed, assume p confirms q after pulse i. Process p has received $\langle \mathbf{bm}, q \rangle$ messages from H processes, including (by the choice of thresholds) at least L correct supporters for q. The correct supporters for q send the message $\langle \mathbf{bm}, q \rangle$ to all processes, implying that in pulse i all correct processes receive at least $L \langle \mathbf{bm}, q \rangle$ messages, and support q in pulse $i + 1$. Thus, in pulse $i + 1$ all correct processes send $\langle \mathbf{bm}, q \rangle$, and as the number of correct processes is at least H, each correct process receives sufficient support to confirm q.

(3) *Initiating.* Process p *initiates* when it has sufficient evidence for the final decision value to be 1. After initiation, process p sends $\langle \mathbf{bm}, 1 \rangle$ messages. Initiation can be caused by three types of evidence, namely (1) p is the general and $x_p = 1$, (2) p receives $\langle \mathbf{bm}, 1 \rangle$ from the general in pulse 1, or (3) p has confirmed sufficiently many *lieutenants* at the end of a later pulse. The last possibility in particular requires some attention, because the number of confirmed lieutenants that is "sufficient" increases during the execution, and a confirmed general does not count for this rule. In the first three pulses L lieutenants need be confirmed to initiate, but starting from pulse 4 the threshold is incremented every two pulses. Thus, initiating according to rule (3) requires that by the end of pulse i, $Th(i) = L + \max(0, \lfloor i/2 \rfloor - 1)$ lieutenants are confirmed. The notation $C_p^{\mathbf{L}}$ in the algorithm denotes the set of confirmed lieutenants, i.e., $C_p \setminus \{g\}$. Initiation by p is represented by the boolean variable ini_p.

If a correct lieutenant r initiates at the end of pulse i, all correct processes confirm r at the end of pulse $i+2$. Indeed, r shouts $\langle \mathbf{bm}, 1 \rangle$ in pulse $i + 1$, so all correct processes (directly) support r in pulse $i + 2$, so every process receives at least $H \langle \mathbf{bm}, q \rangle$ messages in that pulse.

The algorithm continues for $2t + 3$ pulses; if process p has confirmed at least H processes (here the general does count) by the end of that pulse, p decides 1, otherwise p decides 0. See Algorithm 15.4.

The general, being the only process that can enforce initiations (in other processes) on its own, holds a powerful position in the algorithm. It is easily seen that if the general initiates correctly, an avalanche of messages starts that causes all correct processes to confirm H processes and to decide on the value 1. Also, if it does not initiate there is no "critical mass" of messages that leads to the initiation by any correct process.

Lemma 15.6 *Algorithm 15.4 satisfies termination (and simultaneity) and dependence.*

Proof. It can be seen from the algorithm that all correct processes decide at the end of pulse $2t + 3$, which shows termination and simultaneity. To show dependence, we shall assume that the general is correct.

var $R_p[..., ...]$: boolean **init** *false* ;
      ini_p : boolean **init if** $p = g \wedge x_p = 1$ **then** *true* **else** *false* ;

Pulse i: (* Sending phase *)
     if ini_p **then** shout $\langle \mathbf{bm}, 1 \rangle$;
     forall $q \in S_p$ **do** shout $\langle \mathbf{bm}, q \rangle$;
     receive all messages of pulse i ;
     (* State update *)
     if $i = 1$ **and** $R_p[g, 1]$ **then** $ini_p := true$;
     if $\#C_p^{\mathbf{L}} \geq Th(i)$ **then** $ini_p := true$;
     if $i = 2t + 3$ **then**   (* Decide *)
        if $\#C_p \geq H$ **then** $y_p := 1$ **else** $y_p := 0$

Algorithm 15.4 RELIABLE-BROADCAST PROTOCOL.

If the general is correct and has input 1, it shouts a $\langle \mathbf{bm}, 1 \rangle$ message in pulse 1, causing every correct process q to initiate. Hence every correct process q shouts $\langle \mathbf{bm}, 1 \rangle$ in pulse 2, so that by the end of pulse 2 every correct process p supports all other correct processes. This implies that in pulse 3 every correct p shouts $\langle \mathbf{bm}, q \rangle$ for every correct q, so at the end of pulse 3 every correct process receives $\langle \mathbf{bm}, q \rangle$ from every other correct process, causing it to confirm q. Thus from the end of round 3 every correct process has confirmed H processes, implying that the final decision will be 1. (The general is supported and confirmed by all correct processes one pulse earlier than the other processes.)

If the general is correct and has input 0, it does not shout $\langle \mathbf{bm}, 1 \rangle$ in pulse 1, and neither does any other correct process. Assume no correct process has initiated in pulses 1 through $i - 1$; then no correct process sends $\langle \mathbf{bm}, 1 \rangle$ in pulse i. At the end of pulse i no correct process supports or confirms any correct process, because as we have seen earlier, this implies that the latter process has sent a $\langle \mathbf{bm}, 1 \rangle$ message. Consequently, no correct process initiates at the end of pulse i. It follows that no correct process initiates at all. This implies that no correct process ever confirms a correct process, so no correct process confirms more than t processes, and the decision at the final pulse is 0. $\square$

We continue by proving agreement, and we shall assume in the following lemmas that the general is *faulty*. A sufficient "critical mass" of messages, leading inevitably to a 1-decision, is created by the initiation of L correct processes when there are at least four pulses to go.

Lemma 15.7 *If L correct processes initiate by the end of pulse i, where $i < 2t$, then all correct processes decide on the value 1.*

Proof. Let i be the first pulse at the end of which at least L correct processes initiate, and let A denote the set of correct processes that have initiated at the end of pulse i. All processes in A are lieutenants because the general is faulty. At the end of pulse $i + 2$ all correct processes have confirmed the lieutenants in A; we show that at that time all correct processes initiate.

Case $i = 1$: All correct processes have confirmed the lieutenants of A by the end of pulse 3, and initiate because $\#A \geq L = Th(3)$.

Case $i \geq 2$: At least one process, say r, of A initiated in pulse i because it had confirmed $Th(i)$ lieutenants (initiation by receiving $\langle \mathbf{bm}, 1 \rangle$ from the general is only possible in pulse 1). Those $Th(i)$ lieutenants are confirmed by *all* correct processes at the end of pulse $i+1$, but r does not belong to these $Th(i)$ confirmed lieutenants, because r sends $\langle \mathbf{bm}, 1 \rangle$ messages for the first time in pulse $i + 1$. However, all correct processes will have confirmed r at the end of pulse $i + 2$; thus they have confirmed at least $Th(i) + 1$ lieutenants at the end of round $i + 2$. Finally, as $Th(i + 2) = Th(i) + 1$, all correct processes initiate.

Now, as all correct processes initiate by the end of round $i + 2$, they are confirmed (by all correct processes) at the end of round $i + 4$, hence all correct processes have confirmed at least H lieutenants. As $i < 2t$ was assumed, $i + 4 \leq 2t + 3$, so all correct processes decide on the value 1. □

For any correct process to decide on 1, an "avalanche" consisting of initiation by at least L correct processes is necessary. Indeed, a 1-decision requires the confirmation of at least H processes, including L correct ones, and these correct processes have initiated. The question is whether a Byzantine conspiracy can postpone the occurrence of an avalanche sufficiently long to trigger a 1-decision in some correct processes, without enforcing it in all according to Lemma 15.7. Of course, the answer is no, because there is a limit on how long a conspiracy can postpone an avalanche, and the number of pulses, $2t+3$, is chosen precisely so as to prevent this from happening. The reason is the growing threshold for the required number of confirmed processes; in the later pulses it becomes so high that already L initiated correct lieutenants have become necessary for a next correct process to initiate.

Lemma 15.8 *Assume at least L correct processes initiate during the algorithm, and let i be the first pulse at the end of which L correct processes initiate. Then $i < 2t$.*

Proof. To initiate in pulse $2t$ or higher, a correct process needs to have confirmed at least $Th(2t) = L + (t-1)$ lieutenants. As the general is faulty, there at most $t-1$ faulty lieutenants, so at least L correct lieutenants must have been confirmed, showing that already, in an earlier pulse, L correct processes must have initiated. □

Theorem 15.9 *The broadcast algorithm by Dolev et al. (Algorithm 15.4) is a t-Byzantine-robust broadcast protocol.*

Proof. Termination (and simultaneity as well) and dependence were shown in Lemma 15.6. To show agreement, assume that there is a correct process that decides on the value 1. We have observed that this implies that at least L correct processes have initiated. By Lemma 15.8, this happened for the first time in pulse $i < 2t$. But then, by Lemma 15.7, all correct processes decide on the value 1. □

To facilitate the presentation of the algorithm it has been assumed that processes repeat in every round the messages they have sent in earlier rounds. As correct processes record the messages received in earlier rounds, this is not necessary, so it suffices to send each message only once. In this way, each correct process sends each of the $N+1$ possible messages at most once to every other process, which bounds the message complexity to $\Theta(N^3)$. As there are only $N+1$ different messages, each message need contain only $O(\log N)$ bits.

If the number of processes exceeds $3t+1$, a collection of $3t$ *active lieutenants* is chosen to execute the algorithm. (The choice is done statically, e.g., by taking the $3t$ processes whose names follow g in the process name ordering.) The general and the active lieutenants inform the passive lieutenants about their decision, and the passive lieutenants decide on a value they receive from more than t processes. The message complexity of this layered approach is $\Theta(t^3 + t \cdot N)$, and the bit complexity is $\Theta(t^3 \log t + t N)$.

15.2 Authenticating Protocols

The malicious behavior considered up to now has included the incorrect forwarding of information in addition to the sending of incorrect information about the process's own state. Fortunately, this extremely malicious behavior of Byzantine processes can be restricted using cryptographic means, which would render Theorem 15.1 invalid. Indeed, in the scenarios used in its proof, faulty processes would send messages as in scenario 1, while having received only the messages of scenario 0.

In this section a means for digitally *signing* and *authenticating* messages is assumed. Process p sending message M adds to this message some additional information $S_p(M)$, called the *digital signature* of p for message M. Unlike handwritten signatures, the digital signature depends on M, which makes copying signatures into other messages useless. The signature scheme satisfies the following properties.

(1) If p is correct, only p can feasibly compute $S_p(M)$. This computation is referred to as *signing* message M.

(2) Every process can efficiently verify (given p, M, and S) whether $S = S_p(M)$. This verification is referred to as *authenticating* message M.

Signature schemes are based on *private* and *public keys*. The first assumption does not exclude that Byzantine processes conspire by revealing their secret keys to each other, allowing one Byzantine process to forge the signature of another. Only correct processes are assumed to keep their private keys secret.

We shall study the implementation of signature schemes in Subsections 15.2.2 through 15.2.5. In the next subsection, a message $\langle \mathbf{msg} \rangle$ signed by process p, i.e., the pair containing $\langle \mathbf{msg} \rangle$ and $S_p(\langle \mathbf{msg} \rangle)$, is denoted $\langle \mathbf{msg} \rangle : p$.

15.2.1 A Highly Resilient Protocol

An efficient Byzantine broadcast algorithm, using polynomially many messages and $t + 1$ pulses, was proposed by Dolev and Strong [DS83]. The authentication used in the protocol allows an unbounded resilience. We observe, though, that no more than N processes (out of N) can fail, and if N processes fail, all requirements are satisfied vacuously; hence let $t < N$. Their protocol is based on an earlier one by Lamport, Shostak, and Pease [LSP82], which is exponential in the number of messages. We present the latter protocol first.

In pulse 1 the general shouts the message $\langle \mathbf{value}, x_g \rangle : g$, containing its (signed) input.

In pulses 2 through $t+1$, processes sign and forward messages they received in the previous pulse; therefore, a message exchanged in pulse i contains i signatures. A message $\langle \mathbf{value}, v \rangle : g : p_2 : \cdots : p_i$ is called *valid* for the receiving process p if all the following hold.

(1) All i signatures are correct.

(2) The i signatures are from i different processes.

(3) p does not occur in the list of signatures.

During the algorithm, process p maintains a set W_p of values contained in valid messages received by p; initially this set is empty, and the value of each valid message is inserted in it.

The messages forwarded in pulse i are exactly the valid messages received in the previous pulse. At the end of pulse $t + 1$, process p decides based on W_p. If W_p is the singleton $\{v\}$, p decides v; otherwise, p decides a default (e.g., 0). To save on the number of messages, p forwards the message $\langle \textbf{value}, v \rangle : g : p_2 : \cdots : p_i : p$ only to the processes not occurring in the list $g, p_2, \ldots, p_i$. This modification has no influence on the behavior of the algorithm because for processes on the list the message is not valid.

Theorem 15.10 *The algorithm by Lamport, Shostak, and Pease is a correct Byzantine broadcast algorithm for $t < N$, using $t + 1$ pulses.*

Proof. All processes decide in pulse $t + 1$, implying both termination and simultaneity of the algorithm.

If the general is correct and has input v, all processes receive its message $\langle \textbf{value}, x_g \rangle : g$ in pulse 1, so all correct processes include v in W. No other value is inserted in W, because no other value is ever signed by the general. Consequently, in pulse $t + 1$ all processes have $W = \{v\}$ and decide on v, which implies dependence.

To show agreement, we shall derive that for correct processes p and q, $W_p = W_q$ at the end of pulse $t + 1$. Assume $v \in W_p$ at the end of pulse $t + 1$, and let i be the pulse in which p inserted v in W_p, on receipt of the message $\langle \textbf{value}, v \rangle : g : p_2 : \cdots : p_i$.

Case 1: If q occurs in $g, p_2, \ldots, p_i$, then q has itself seen the value v and inserted it in W_q.

Case 2: If q does not occur in the sequence $g, p_2, \ldots, p_i$ and $i \leq t$, then p forwards the message $\langle \textbf{value}, v \rangle : g : p_2 : \cdots : p_i : p$ to q in pulse $i + 1$, so q validates v at the latest in pulse $i + 1$.

Case 3: If q does not occur in $g, p_2, \ldots, p_i$ and $i = t + 1$, observe that the message received by p was signed by $t+1$ consecutive processes, including at least one correct process. This process forwarded the message to all other processes, including q, so q sees v.

As $W_p = W_q$ by the end of pulse $t + 1$, p and q decide equally. $\square$

It is not possible to terminate the algorithm earlier than in pulse $t + 1$. In all pulses up to t, a correct process could receive messages created and forwarded only by faulty processors, and not sent to other correct processes, which could lead to inconsistent decisions.

The intermediate result in the previous algorithm, namely agreement on a set of values among all correct processes, is stronger than necessary to achieve agreement on a single value. This was observed by Dolev and Strong [DS83], who proposed a more efficient modification. It is in fact sufficient that at the end of pulse $t + 1$, either (a) for every correct p the set W_p is *the same* singleton, or (b) for no correct p the set W_p is a singleton. In the first case all processes decide v, in the latter case they all decide 0 (or, if it is desired to modify the algorithm in this way, they decide "general faulty").

The weaker requirement on the sets W is achieved by the algorithm of Dolev and Strong. Instead of relaying every valid message, process p forwards at most two messages, namely one message with the first and one message with the second value accepted by p. A complete description of the algorithm is left to the reader.

Theorem 15.11 *The algorithm of Dolev and Strong as described above is a Byzantine-broadcast protocol using $t + 1$ pulses and at most $2N^2$ messages.*

Proof. Termination and simultaneity are as for the previous protocol, because each correct process decides at the end of pulse $t + 1$. Dependence also follows as in the previous protocol. If g correctly shouts v in the first pulse, all correct processes accept v in that pulse and no other value is ever accepted; hence all correct processes decide on v. The claimed message complexity follows from the fact that each (correct) process shouts at most two messages.

To show agreement, we shall show that for correct processes p and q, W_p and W_q satisfy at the end of pulse $t + 1$ the following.

(1) If $W_p = \{v\}$ then $v \in W_q$.
(2) If $\#W_p > 1$ then $\#W_q > 1$.

For (1): Assume that p accepted the value v upon receipt of the message $\langle \textbf{value}, v \rangle : g : p_2 : \cdots : p_i$ in pulse i, and reason as in the proof of Theorem 15.10:

Case 1: If q occurs among $g, \ldots, p_i$, q has clearly accepted v.
Case 2: If q does not occur among $g, \ldots, p_i$ and $i \leq t$, then p forwards the value to q, which will accept it in this case.
Case 3: If q does not occur and $i = t + 1$, at least one of the processes that signed the message, say r, is correct. Process r has forwarded the value v to q as well, implying that v is in W_q.

For (2): Assume that $\#W_p > 1$ at the end of the algorithm, and let w be the second value accepted by p. Again by similar reasoning, it can be shown that $w \in W_q$, which implies that $\#W_q > 1$. (Equality of W_p and W_q cannot be derived because process p will not forward its third accepted value or later ones.)

Having proved (1) and (2), assume that correct process p decides on $v \in W_p$, that is, $W_p = \{v\}$. Then, by (1), v is contained in all W_q for correct q, but it follows that W_q is not larger than the singleton $\{v\}$; otherwise W_p is not a singleton, by (2). Therefore, every correct process q also decides on v. Further, assume that correct process p decides on a default because W_p is not a singleton. If W_p is empty, every correct q has W_q empty by (1) and if $\#W_p > 1$, then $\#W_q > 1$ by (2); consequently, q also decides on a default. □

Dolev and Strong have further improve the algorithm and obtained an algorithm that solves the Byzantine-broadcast problem in the same number of pulses and only $O(Nt)$ messages.

15.2.2 Implementation of Digital Signatures

Because p's signature $S_p(M)$ should constitute sufficient evidence that p is the originator of the message, the signature must consist of some form of information, which

(1) can be computed efficiently by p (signed);
(2) cannot be computed efficiently by any other process than p (forged).

We should remark immediately that, for most of the signature schemes in use today, the second requirement is not proved to the extent that the problem of forgery is shown to be exponentially hard. Usually, the problem of forging is shown to be related to (or sometimes equivalent to) some computational problem that has been studied for a long time without being known to be polynomially solvable. For example, forging signatures in the Fiat–Shamir scheme allows to factor large integers; as the latter is (presumably) computationally hard, the former must also be computationally hard.

Signature schemes have been proposed based on various supposedly hard problems, such as computing the discrete logarithm, factoring large numbers, knapsack problems. Requirements (1) and (2) imply that process p must have a computational "advantage" over the other processes; this advantage is some secret information, held by p and referred to as p's *secret* (or private) *key*. So, the computation of $S_p(M)$ is efficient when the secret key is known, but (presumably) difficult without this information. Clearly, if p succeeds in keeping its key secret, this implies that only p can tractably compute $S_p(M)$.

All processes must be able to verify signatures, that is, given a message M and a signature S, it must be possible to verify efficiently that S has indeed been computed from M using p's secret key. This verification requires that some information is revealed regarding p's secret key; this information is referred to as p's *public key*. The public key should allow verification of the signature, but it should be impossible or at least computationally hard to use it to compute p's secret key or forge signatures.

The most successful signature schemes proposed up to date are based on number-theoretic computations in the arithmetic rings modulo large numbers. The basic arithmetic operations of addition, multiplication, and exponentiation can be performed in these rings in times polynomial in the length (in bits) of the modulus. Division is possible if the denominator and modulus are coprime (i.e., have no common prime factors) and can also be performed in polynomial time. Because signing and verification require computations on the message, M is interpreted as a large number.

15.2.3 The ElGamal Signature Scheme

ElGamal's signature scheme [ElG85] is based on a number-theoretic function called the *discrete logarithm*. For a large prime number P, the multiplicative group modulo P, denoted $\mathbb{Z}_P^*$, contains $P - 1$ elements and is *cyclic*. The latter means that an element $g \in \mathbb{Z}_P^*$ can be chosen such that the $P - 1$ numbers

$$g^0 = 1, \ g^1, \ g^2, \ \ldots, \ g^{P-3}, \ g^{P-2}$$

are all different and hence, enumerate all elements of $\mathbb{Z}_P^*$. Such a g is called a *generator* of $\mathbb{Z}_P^*$, or also a *primitive root* modulo P. The generator is not unique; usually there are many of them. Given fixed P and generator g, for each $x \in \mathbb{Z}_P^*$ there is a *unique* integer i modulo $P - 1$ such that $g^i = x$ (equality in $\mathbb{Z}_P^*$). This i is called the *discrete logarithm* (sometimes *index*) of x. Unlike the basic arithmetic operations mentioned above, computation of the discrete log is *not* easy. It is a well-studied problem for which no efficient general solution has been found to date, but neither has the problem been shown to be intractable; see [Odl84] for an overview of results.

The signature scheme of ElGamal [ElG85] is based on the difficulty of computing discrete logarithms. The processes share a large prime number P and a primitive root g of $\mathbb{Z}_P^*$. Process p chooses as its secret key a number

d, randomly between 1 and $P - 2$, and the public key of p is the number $e = g^d$; observe that d is the discrete log of e. The signature of p can be computed efficiently knowing the log of e, and therefore forms an implicit proof that the signer knows d.

A valid signature for message M is a pair (r, s) satisfying $g^M = e^r r^s$. Such a pair is easily found by p using the secret key d. Process p selects a random number a, coprime with $P - 1$, and computes

$$r = g^a \pmod{P}$$

and

$$s = (M - dr)a^{-1} \pmod{(P-1)}.$$

These numbers indeed satisfy

$$e^r \cdot r^s = e^r (g^a)^{(M-dr)a^{-1}}$$
$$= g^{dr} g^{M-dr} = g^M.$$

(All equalities are in $\mathbb{Z}_P^*$.) The validity of a signature $S = (r, s)$ for message M is easily verified by checking whether $g^M = e^r r^s$.

Algorithms for the discrete logarithm. Because p's secret key, d, equals the discrete logarithm of its public key, e, the scheme is broken if discrete logarithms modulo P can be computed efficiently. To date, no efficient algorithm to do this in the general case or to forge signatures in any other way is known.

A general algorithm for computing discrete logarithms was presented by Odlyzko [Odl84]. Its complexity is of the same order of magnitude as the best-known algorithms for factoring integers as big as P. The algorithm first computes several tables using only P and g, and, in a second phase, computes logarithms for given numbers. If Q is the largest prime factor of $P - 1$, the time for the first phase and the size of the tables are of the order of Q; therefore it is desirable to select P such that $P - 1$ has a large prime factor. The second phase, computing logarithms, can be performed within seconds even on very small computers. Therefore it is necessary to change P and g sufficiently often, say every month, so that the tables for a particular P are obsolete before their completion.

Randomized signing. The randomization in the signing procedure makes each one of $\phi(P - 1)$ different signatures[1] for a given message an equally likely outcome of the signing procedure. Thus, the same document signed

---

[1] The function ϕ is known as *Euler's phi function*; $\phi(n)$ is the size of $\mathbb{Z}_n^*$.

twice will almost certainly produce two different valid signatures. Randomization is essential in the signing procedure; if p signs two messages using the same value of a, p's secret key can be computed from the signatures; see Exercise 15.6.

15.2.4 The RSA Signature Scheme

If n is a large number, the product of two prime numbers P and Q, it is very hard to compute square and higher-order roots modulo n unless the factorization is known. The ability to compute square roots can be exploited to find the factors of n (see Exercise 15.7), which shows that square rooting is as hard as factoring.

In the signature scheme by Rivest, Shamir and Adleman [RSA78], the public key of p is a large number n, of which p knows the factorization, and an exponent e. The signature of p for message M is the eth root of M modulo n, which is easily verified using exponentiation. This higher-order root is found by p using exponentiation as well; when generating its key, p computes a number d such that $de = 1 \pmod{\phi(n)}$, which implies that $(M^d)^e = M$, that is, M^d is an eth root of M. The secret key of p consists only of the number d, i.e., p need not memorize the factorization of n.

In the RSA scheme, p shows its identity by computing roots modulo n, which requires (implicit) knowledge of a factorization of n; only p is supposed to have this knowledge. In this scheme, every process uses a different modulus.

15.2.5 The Fiat–Shamir Signature Scheme

A more subtle use of the difficulty of (square) rooting is made in a scheme by Fiat and Shamir [FS86]. In the RSA scheme, a process signs by showing that it is able to compute roots modulo its public key, and the ability to compute roots presumably requires knowledge of the factorization. In the Fiat–Shamir scheme the processes make use of a *common* modulus n, of which the factorization is known only to a trusted center. Process p is given the square roots of some specific numbers (depending on p's identity), and the signature of p for M provides evidence that the signer knows these square roots, but without revealing what they are.

An advantage of the Fiat–Shamir scheme over the RSA scheme is the lower arithmetic complexity and the absence of a separate public key for every process. A disadvantage is the necessity of a trusted authority that issues the secret keys. As mentioned before, the scheme uses a large integer

n, the product of two large prime numbers known only to the center. In addition there is a one-way pseudo-random function f mapping strings to $\mathbb{Z}_n$; this function is known and can be computed by every process, but its inverse cannot be computed feasibly.

The secret and public keys. As its secret key, p is given the square roots s_1 through s_k of k numbers modulo n, namely $s_j = \sqrt{v_j^{-1}}$, where $v_j = f(p, j)$. The v_j can be considered as the public keys of p, but as they can be computed from p's identity they need not be stored. To avoid some technical nuisance we assume that these k numbers are all quadratic residues modulo n. The square roots can be computed by the center, which knows the factors of n.

Signing messages: first attempt. The signature of p implicitly proves that the signer knows the roots of the v_j, i.e., can provide a number s such that $s^2 v_j = 1$. Such a number is s_j, but sending s_j itself would reveal the secret key; to avoid revealing the key, the scheme uses the following idea. Process p selects a random number r and computes $x = r^2$. Now p is the only process that can provide a number y satisfying $y^2 v_j = x$, namely, $y = r\, s_j$. Thus, p may demonstrate its knowledge of s_j without revealing it by sending a pair (x, y) satisfying $y^2 v_j = x$. As p does not send the number r, computing s_j from the pair is not possible without computing a square root.

But there are two problems with signatures consisting of such pairs. First, anybody can produce such a pair by cheating in the following way: select y *first* and compute $x = y^2 v$ subsequently. Second, the signature does not depend on the message so a process that has received a signed message from p can copy the signature onto any forged message. The crux of the signature scheme is to have p demonstrate knowledge of the root of *the product of a subset of the v_j*, where the subset depends on the message and the random number. Scrambling the message and the random number through f prevents a forger from selecting y first.

To sign message M, p acts as follows.

(1) p selects a random number r and computes $x = r^2$.
(2) p computes $f(M, x)$; call the first k bits e_1 through e_k.
(3) p computes $y = r \prod_{e_j=1} s_j$.
   The signature $S_p(M)$ consists of the tuple $(e_1, \ldots, e_k, y)$.

To verify the signature $(e_1, \ldots, e_k, y)$ of p for message M, act as follows.

(1) Compute the v_j and $z = y^2 \prod_{e_j=1} v_j$.
(2) Compute $f(M, z)$ and verify that the first k bits are e_1 through e_k.

If the signature is computed genuinely, the value of z computed in the first step of verification equals the value of x used in signing and hence the first k bits of $f(M, z)$ equal e_1 through e_k.

Forgery and final solution. We now consider a strategy for a forger to obtain a signature according to the above scheme without knowing the s_j.

(1) Choose k random bits e_1 through e_k.
(2) Choose a random number y and compute $x = y^2 \prod_{e_j=1} v_j$.
(3) Compute $f(M, x)$ and see whether the first k bits equal the values of e_1 through e_k chosen earlier. If so, $(e_1, \ldots, e_k, y)$ is the forged signature for message M.

As the probability of equality in step (3) can be assumed to be 2^{-k}, forgery succeeds after an expected number of 2^k trials.

With $k = 72$ and an assumed time of 10^{-9} seconds to try one choice of the e_j, the expected time for forgery (with this strategy) is $2^{72} \cdot 10^{-9}$ seconds or 1.5 million years, which makes the scheme very safe. However, each process must store k roots, and if k must be limited due to space restrictions, an expected 2^k forgery time may not be satisfactory. We now show how to modify the scheme so as to use k roots, and obtain a 2^{kt} expected forgery time for a chosen integer t. The idea is to use the first kt bits of an f-result to define t subsets of the v_j, and have p demonstrate its knowledge of the t products of these. To sign message M, p acts as follows.

(1) p selects random $r_1, \ldots, r_t$ and computes $x_i = r_i^2$.
(2) p computes $f(M, x_1, \ldots, x_t)$; call the first kt bits e_{ij} ($1 \le i \le t$ and $1 \le j \le k$).
(3) p computes $y_i = r_i \prod_{e_{ij}=1} s_j$ for $1 \le i \le t$. The signature $S_p(M)$ consists of $(e_{11}, \ldots, e_{tk}, y_1, \ldots, y_t)$.

To verify the signature $(e_{11}, \ldots, e_{tk}, y_1, \ldots, y_t)$ of p for message M, act as follows.

(1) Compute the v_j and $z_i = y_i^2 \prod_{e_{ij}=1} v_j$.
(2) Compute $f(M, z_1, \ldots, z_t)$ and verify that the first kt bits are e_{11} through e_{tk}.

A forger trying to produce a valid signature with the same strategy as above now has a probability of 2^{-kt} of success in its third step, implying an expected number of 2^{kt} of trials. Fiat and Shamir show in their paper that unless factoring n turns out to be easy, no essentially better forgery algorithm exists, hence the scheme can be made arbitrarily safe by choosing k and t sufficiently large.

15.2.6 Summary and Discussion

In this and the previous section it has been demonstrated that in synchronous systems there exist deterministic solutions to the Byzantine broadcast problem. The maximal resilience of such solutions is $t < N/3$ if no authentication is used (Section 15.1), and unbounded if message authentication is used (this section). In all solutions presented here synchrony has been modeled using the (rather strong) assumptions of the pulse model; fault-tolerant implementation of the pulse model is discussed in Section 15.3.

The firing-squad problem. In addition to assuming the pulse model, a second assumption underlying all solutions presented so far is that the pulse in which the broadcast starts is known to all processes (and numbered 1 for convenience). If this is not the case a priori, the problem arises of starting the algorithm simultaneously, after one or more processes (spontaneously) initiate a request for execution of the broadcast algorithm. A request may come from the general (after computing a result that must be announced to all processes) or from lieutenants (realizing that they all need information stored in the general). This problem is studied in the literature as the *firing-squad* problem. In this problem, one or more processes *initiate* (a request), but not necessarily in the same pulse, and processes may *fire*. The requirements are:

(1) **Validity.** No correct process fires unless some process has initiated.
(2) **Simultaneity.** If any correct process fires then all correct processes fire in the same pulse.
(3) **Termination.** If a correct process initiates, then all correct processes fire within finitely many pulses.

Indeed, given a solution for the firing squad problem, the first pulse of the broadcast need not be agreed upon in advance; processes requesting a broadcast initiate the firing squad algorithm, and the broadcast starts in the pulse following the firing. The techniques used in the solutions for the Byzantine-broadcast problem and the firing-squad problem can be combined to obtain more time-efficient protocols that solve the broadcast problem directly in the absence of a priori agreement about the first pulse.

The time complexity and early-stopping protocols. In this chapter we have presented protocols using $t + 1$ or $2t + 3$ pulses, or rounds of communication. It was shown by Fischer and Lynch [FL82] that $t + 1$ rounds of communication is optimal for t-robust consensus protocols, and the result was extended to cover authenticating protocols by Dolev and Strong [DS83].

A subtle point in these proofs is that in the scenarios used a process must fail in each of the pulses 1 through t, so the lower bounds are worst-case w.r.t. the number of actual failures during the execution. Because in most executions the actual number of failures is much lower than the resilience, the existence has been studied of protocols that can reach agreement earlier in those executions that have only a small number of failures. Broadcast protocols with this property are called *early stopping* protocols. Dolev, Reischuk, and Strong [DRS82] demonstrated a lower bound of $f + 2$ rounds for any protocol in an execution with f failures. A discussion of several early stopping broadcast and consensus protocols is found in [BGP92].

The early stopping protocols decide within a few pulses after correct processes conclude that there has been a pulse without new failures. It cannot be guaranteed, however, that all correct processes reach this conclusion in the same pulse. (Unless, of course, they do so in pulse $t + 1$; as at most t processes fail, there is one round among the first $t + 1$ in which no new failure occurs.) As a consequence, early stopping protocols do not satisfy simultaneity. It was shown by Coan and Dwork [CD91] that to achieve simultaneity, $t + 1$ rounds are also necessary in executions where no failures occur, even for randomized protocols and in the (very weak) crash model. This implies that authenticated protocols also need $t + 1$ pulses to agree simultaneously.

Decision problems and interactive consistency. Using a broadcast protocol as a subroutine, virtually all decision problems can be solved for synchronous systems by reaching *interactive consistency*, that is, agreement on the set of inputs. In the interactive consistency problem, processes decide on a *vector* of inputs, with one entry for each process in the system. Formally, the requirements are:

(1) **Termination.** Each correct process p decides on a vector V_p, with one entry for each process.
(2) **Agreement.** The decision vectors of correct processes are equal.
(3) **Dependence.** If q is correct, then for correct p, $V_p[q] = x_q$.

Interactive consistency can be achieved by multiple broadcasts: each process broadcasts its input, and process p places its decision in q's broadcast in

$V_p[q]$. Termination, agreement, and dependence are immediately inherited from the corresponding properties of the broadcast algorithm.

Because every correct process computes the same vector (agreement), most decision problems are easily solved using a deterministic function on the decision vector (which immediately guarantees agreement). Consensus, for example, is solved by extracting the majority value from the decision vector. Election is solved by selecting the smallest unique identity in the vector (beware; the elected process can be faulty).

15.3 Clock Synchronization

It was shown in the previous sections that (when deterministic algorithms are considered) synchronous systems have a higher resilience than asynchronous systems. The demonstration was made for the idealized model of synchrony, where processes operate in pulses. The higher resilience of the pulse model implies that it is not possible deterministically to synchronize fully asynchronous networks in a robust way. It will be shown in this section that a robust implementation of the pulse model is possible in the model of asynchronous bounded-delay networks (ABD networks).

The ABD model is characterized by the availability of local clocks and an upper bound on message delay. In the description and analysis of algorithms we make use of a *real-time frame*, which is an assignment of a time of occurrence $t \in \mathbb{R}$ to every event. According to relativistic physics, there is no standard or preferred way to make this assignment; we assume in the following that a physically meaningful assignment has been chosen. The real-time frame is not observable for processes in the system, but processes can indirectly observe time using their *clocks*, whose values are related to real time. Process p's clock is denoted C_p and can be read and written to by process p (writing to the clocks is necessary for synchronization). The value of the clock changes continuously in time when the clock is not assigned; we write $C_p(t) = T$ to denote that at real time t the clock reads T.

Capitals (C, T) are used for clock times and lower case letters (c, t) for real times. Clocks can be used for controlling the occurrence of events, as in

when $C_p = T$ **then** send message

which causes the message to be sent at time $C_p^{-1}(T)$. The function C_p^{-1} is denoted c_p.

The value of a perfect clock increases by Δ in Δ time units, i.e., it satisfies $C(t + \Delta) = C(T = t) + \Delta$. Perfect clocks, once synchronized, never need adjustment again, but unfortunately they are only a (useful) mathematical abstraction. Clocks used in distributed systems suffer a *drift*, bounded by a small known constant ρ (typically of the order of 10^{-5} or 10^{-6}). The drift of clock C is *ρ-bounded* if, for t_1 and t_2 such that no assignment to C occurs between t_1 and t_2,

$$(t_2 - t_1)(1 + \rho)^{-1} \leq C(t_2) - C(t_1) \leq (t_2 - t_1)(1 + \rho). \qquad (15.1)$$

The various clocks in distributed systems do not show the same clock time at any given real time, i.e., $C_p(t) = C_q(t)$ does not hold necessarily. The clocks are *δ-synchronized* at real time t if $|C_p(t) - C_q(t)| \leq \delta$, and they are δ-synchronized at clock time T if $|c_p(T) - c_q(T)| \leq \delta$. We shall regard these notions as equivalent; see Exercise 15.8. The goal of clock-synchronizing algorithms is to achieve and maintain a global δ-synchronization, i.e., δ-synchronization between each pair of clocks. The parameter δ is the *precision* of synchronization.

The message delay is bounded from below by $\delta_{\min}$ and from above by $\delta_{\max}$, where $0 \leq \delta_{\min} < \delta_{\max}$; formally, if a message is sent at real time σ and received at real time τ, then

$$\delta_{\min} \leq \tau - \sigma \leq \delta_{\max}. \qquad (15.2)$$

Because the choice of a real-time frame is free, assumptions (15.1) and (15.2) have regard to the time frame as well as to the clocks and the communication system.

15.3.1 Reading a Remote Clock

In this subsection the degree of precision with which process p can adjust its perfect clock to the perfect clock of a reliable server s will be studied. With a deterministic protocol the best obtainable precision is $\frac{1}{2}(\delta_{\max} - \delta_{\min})$, and this precision can be obtained by a simple protocol that exchanges only one message. Probabilistic protocols may achieve an arbitrary precision, but the message complexity depends on the desired precision and the distribution of message-delivery times.

Theorem 15.12 *There exists a deterministic protocol for synchronizing C_p to C_s with precision $\frac{1}{2}(\delta_{\max} - \delta_{\min})$, which exchanges one message. No deterministic protocol achieves a higher precision.*

Proof. We first present the simple protocol and prove that it achieves the precision claimed in the theorem. To synchronize C_p the server sends one

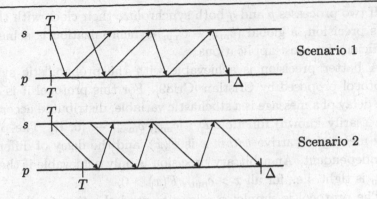

Figure 15.5 SCENARIOS FOR THE DETERMINISTIC PROTOCOL.

message, $\langle \mathbf{time}, C_s \rangle$. When p receives $\langle \mathbf{time}, T \rangle$ it adjusts its clock to $T + \frac{1}{2}(\delta_{\max} + \delta_{\min})$.

To prove the claimed precision, call the real times of sending and receiving the $\langle \mathbf{time}, T \rangle$ message σ and τ, respectively; now $T = C_s(\sigma)$. Because the clocks are perfect, $C_s(\tau) = T + (\tau - \sigma)$. At time τ, p adjusts its clock to read $C_p(\tau) = T + \frac{1}{2}(\delta_{\max} + \delta_{\min})$, so $C_s(\tau) - C_p(\tau) = (\tau - \sigma) - \frac{1}{2}(\delta_{\max} + \delta_{\min})$. Now $\delta_{\min} \leq \tau - \sigma \leq \delta_{\max}$ implies $|C_s(\tau) - C_p(\tau)| \leq \frac{1}{2}(\delta_{\max} - \delta_{\min})$.

To show the lower bound on the precision, let a deterministic protocol be given; in this protocol p and s exchange some messages, after which p adjusts its clock. Two scenarios for the protocol are considered, as depicted in Figure 15.5. In the first scenario, the clocks are equal prior to the execution, all messages from s to p are delivered after $\delta_{\min}$, and all messages from p to s are delivered after $\delta_{\max}$. If the adjustment in this scenario is Δ_1, p's clock is exactly Δ_1 ahead of C_s after the synchronization.

In the second scenario, C_p is $\delta_{\max} - \delta_{\min}$ behind C_s prior to execution, all messages from p to s are delivered after $\delta_{\min}$, and all messages from s to p are delivered after $\delta_{\max}$. Calling the adjustment in this scenario Δ_2, we find that p's clock is exactly $\delta_{\max} - \delta_{\min} - \Delta_2$ behind C_s after the synchronization.

However, neither p nor s observes the difference between the scenarios, because the uncertainty in message delay hides the difference; consequently $\Delta_1 = \Delta_2$. This implies that the worst-case precision is at best

$$\min_{\Delta} \max(|\Delta|, \ |\delta_{\max} - \delta_{\min} - \Delta|).$$

This minimum equals $\frac{1}{2}(\delta_{\max} - \delta_{\min})$ (and occurs for $\Delta = \frac{1}{2}(\delta_{\max} - \delta_{\min}))$. $\qquad\square$

If two processes p and q both synchronize their clock with the server with this precision, a global $(\delta_{max} - \delta_{min})$-synchronization is achieved, which is sufficient for most applications.

A better precision is achievable with the probabilistic synchronization protocol proposed by Cristian [Cri89]. For this protocol it is assumed that the delay of a message is a stochastic variable, distributed according to a (not necessarily known) function $F : [\delta_{min}, \delta_{max}] \rightarrow [0, 1]$. The probability for any message to arrive *within* x is $F(x)$, and the delay of different messages is independent. An arbitrary precision is only achievable if the lower bound δ_{min} is tight, i.e., for all $x > \delta_{min}$, $F(x) > 0$.

The protocol is simple; p asks s to send the time, and s responds with a $\langle \textbf{time}, T \rangle$ message immediately. Process p measures the time I between sending the request and receipt of the response; $I \geq 2\delta_{min}$ holds. The delay of the response message is at least δ_{min} and at most $I - \delta_{min}$, and hence differs by at most $\frac{1}{2}(I - 2\delta_{min})$ from $\frac{1}{2}I$. So p can set its clock to $T + \frac{1}{2}I$, and achieves a precision of $\frac{1}{2}(I - 2\delta_{min})$. Assuming the desired precision is ϵ, p sends a new request if $\frac{1}{2}(I - 2\delta_{min}) > \epsilon$, and terminates otherwise.

Lemma 15.13 *The probabilistic clock-synchronization protocol achieves precision ϵ with an expected number of messages of at most $F(\delta_{min} + \epsilon)^{-2}$.*

Proof. The probability that p's request arrives within $\delta_{min} + \epsilon$ is $F(\delta_{min} + \epsilon)$ and so is the probability that the response arrives within $\delta_{min} + \epsilon$. Consequently, the probability that p receives the response within $2\delta_{min} + 2\epsilon$ is at least $F(\delta_{min} + \epsilon)^2$, which implies a bound of $F(\delta_{min} + \epsilon)^{-2}$ on the expected number of trials before a successful message exchange. $\square$

The time complexity of the protocol is reduced if p sends a new request when no response was received $2\delta_{min} + 2\epsilon$ after sending the request. The expected time is then independent of the expected or maximal delay, namely $2(\delta_{min} + \epsilon)\, F(\delta_{min} + \epsilon)^{-2}$, and the protocol is robust against loss of messages. (Sequence numbers must be used to distinguish obsolete responses.)

15.3.2 Distributed Clock Synchronization

This section presents a t-Byzantine-robust (for $t < N/3$) distributed clock-synchronization algorithm due to Mahany and Schneider [MS85]. It was shown by Dolev, Halpern, and Strong [DHS84] that no synchronization is possible if $t \geq N/3$, unless authentication is used.

The core of the synchronization algorithm is a protocol that achieves *inexact agreement* on the average values of the clocks. The processes adjust

var x_p, y_p, $esti_p$: real ; (* Input, output, estimator of V *)
V_p, A_p : multiset of real ;

begin (* Input collection phase *)
$V_p := \varnothing$;
forall $q \in \mathbb{P}$ **do send** $\langle \textbf{ask} \rangle$ to q ;
wait $2\,\delta_{\max}$; (* Process $\langle \textbf{ask} \rangle$ and $\langle \textbf{val}, x \rangle$ messages *)
while $\#V_p < N$ **do** $insert(V_p, \infty)$;
(* Now compute acceptable values *)
$A_p := \{x \in V_p : \#\{y \in V_p : |y - x| \leq \delta\} \geq N - t\}$;
$esti_p := estimator(A_p)$;
while $\#A_p < N$ **do** $insert(A_p, esti_p)$;
$y_p := (\sum A_p)/N$
end

Upon receipt of $\langle \textbf{ask} \rangle$ from q:
send $\langle \textbf{val}, x_p \rangle$ to q

Upon receipt of $\langle \textbf{val}, x \rangle$ from q:
if no such message was received from q before
then $insert(V_p, x)$

Algorithm 15.6 THE FAST-CONVERGENCE ALGORITHM.

their clocks and achieve a high degree of synchronization. Due to drift, the precision degrades after a while, necessitating a new synchronization round after a certain interval. Assume that at real time t_0 the clocks are δ_0-synchronized; then until time $t_0 + R$, the clocks are $(\delta_0 + 2\rho R)$-synchronized. Thus, if the desired precision is δ and a synchronization round achieves precision δ_0, the rounds are repeated every $(\delta - \delta_0)/2\rho$ time units. As the time, say S, to execute a synchronization round is usually very small compared to R, the simplifying assumption is justified that during the synchronization the drift is negligible, i.e., the clocks are perfect.

Inexact agreement: the fast-convergence algorithm. In the problem of inexact agreement, used by Mahany and Schneider [MS85] to synchronize clocks, process p has a real input value x_p, where for correct p and q, $|x_p - x_q| \leq \delta$. The output of process p is a real value y_p, and the precision of the output is defined as $\max_{p,q} |y_p - y_q|$; the aim of the algorithm is to achieve a very small value of the precision.

The fast-convergence algorithm proposed by Mahany and Schneider is given as Algorithm 15.6. For a finite set $A \subset \mathbb{R}$, define two functions $intvl(A) = [\min(A), \max(A)]$ and $width(A) = \max(A) - \min(A)$. The algorithm has an input collection phase and a computation phase. In the first phase process p requests every other process to send its input (by shouting an $\langle$ **ask** $\rangle$ message) and waits for $2\delta_{max}$ time units. After that time p has received all the inputs from the correct processes, as well as answers from a subset of faulty processes. These answers are padded with (meaningless) values ∞ for processes that did not reply.

The process then applies a filter to the received values, which is guaranteed to pass all values of correct processes and only those faulty values that are sufficiently close to correct values. As correct values differ only by δ and there are at least $N - t$ correct values, each correct value has at least $N - t$ values that differ at most δ from it; A_p stores the received values with this property.

The output is then computed by averaging over the values, where all rejected values are replaced by an estimate computed by applying a deterministic function *estimator* to the surviving values. This function satisfies *estimator*$(A) \in intvl(A)$, but is otherwise arbitrary; it could be the minimum, maximum, average, or $\frac{1}{2}[\max(A) + \min(A)]$.

Theorem 15.14 *The fast-convergence algorithm achieves precision* $2t\delta/N$.

Proof. Let v_{pr} be the value included in V_p for process r when p times-out (i.e., v_{pr} is either x_r or ∞), and a_{pr} the value in A_p for process r when p computes y_p (i.e., a_{pr} is either v_{pr} or $esti_p$). The precision will be bounded by splitting the summation in the computation of the decision into summations over correct processes (C) and incorrect processes (B). For correct p and q, the difference $|a_{pr} - a_{qr}|$ is bounded by 0 if $r \in C$ and by 2δ if $r \in B$.

The first bound follows because if p and r are correct processes, $a_{pr} = x_r$. Indeed, as r replies to p's $\langle$ **ask** $\rangle$ message promptly, $v_{pr} = x_r$. Similarly, $v_{pr'} = x_{r'}$ for all correct r', and the assumption on the input implies that r's value survives the filtering by p, hence $a_{pr} = v_{pr}$.

The second bound holds because for correct p and q, $width(A_p \cup A_q) \leq 2\delta$ when p and q compute their decisions. Because the added estimates lie between accepted values, it suffices to consider the maximal difference between values a_p and a_q that passed the filters of p and q, respectively. There are at least $N - t$ processes r for which $|v_{pr} - a_p| \leq \delta$, and at least $N - t$ processes r for which $|v_{qr} - a_p| \leq \delta$. This implies that there is a *correct* r such that both $|v_{pr} - a_p| \leq \delta$ and $|v_{qr} - a_p| \leq \delta$; but as r is correct, $v_{pr} = v_{qr}$, hence $|a_p - a_q| \leq 2\delta$.

It now follows that, for correct p and q,

$$|y_p - y_q| = |(\sum A_p)/N - (\sum A_q)/N|$$

$$= \frac{1}{N} \cdot \left| \left(\sum_{r \in C} a_{pr} + \sum_{r \in B} a_{pr} \right) - \left(\sum_{r \in C} a_{qr} + \sum_{r \in B} a_{qr} \right) \right|$$

$$= \frac{1}{N} \cdot \left| \left(\sum_{r \in C} a_{pr} - \sum_{r \in C} a_{qr} \right) + \left(\sum_{r \in B} a_{pr} - \sum_{r \in B} a_{qr} \right) \right|$$

$$\leq \frac{1}{N} \cdot \left[\left(\sum_{r \in C} |a_{pr} - a_{qr}| \right) + \left(\sum_{r \in B} |a_{pr} - a_{qr}| \right) \right]$$

$$\leq \frac{1}{N} \cdot \left[(0) + \left(\sum_{r \in B} 2\delta \right) \right] \leq 2t\delta/N.$$

$\square$

An arbitrary precision can be achieved by repeating the algorithm; when iterated i times, the precision becomes $(\frac{2}{3})^i \delta$. The precision is even better if a smaller fraction (than one-third) of the processes is faulty; in the derivation of the precision, t can be understood as the actual number of faulty processes. The (worst-case) output precision of the algorithm cannot be improved by a suitable choice of the function *estimator*; indeed, a Byzantine process r can enforce to p any value $a_{pr} \in intvl(A_p)$, by simply sending this value to p. The function can be chosen suitably so as to achieve a good average precision when something is known about the most likely behavior of faulty processes.

Clock synchronization. To synchronize clocks, the fast-convergence algorithm is used to reach inexact agreement on the new value of the clocks. It is assumed that the clocks are δ-synchronized initially. The algorithm must be adapted because

(1) the message delay is not known exactly so a process cannot know the exact value of another process; and

(2) time elapses during execution of the algorithm, so the clocks do not have constant values but increase in time.

To compensate for the unknown delay a process adds $\frac{1}{2}(\delta_{\max} + \delta_{\min})$ to the received clock values (as in the deterministic protocol of Theorem 15.12),

> **var** C_p, Δ_p, $esti_p$: real ;   (* Clock, adaptation, estimator of V *)
> D_p, A_p : multiset of real ;
>
> **begin** (* Input collection phase *)
> $D_p := \varnothing$;
>   **forall** $q \in \mathbb{P}$ **do** send $\langle$**ask**$\rangle$ to q ;
>   **wait** $2\delta_{max}$; (* Process $\langle$**ask**$\rangle$ and $\langle$**val**, $x\rangle$ messages *)
>   **while** $\#D_p < N$ **do** $insert(D_p, \infty)$;
>   (* Now compute acceptable values *)
> $A_p := \{x \in D_p : \#\{y \in D_p : |y - x| \leq \delta + (\delta_{max} - \delta_{min})\} \geq N - t\}$;
> $esti_p := estimator(A_p)$;
>   **while** $\#A_p < N$ **do** $insert(A_p, esti_p)$;
> $\Delta_p := (\sum A_p)/N$;
> $C_p := C_p + \Delta_p$
> **end**
>
> Upon receipt of $\langle$**ask**$\rangle$ from q:
>   send $\langle$**val**, $C_p\rangle$ to q
>
> Upon receipt of $\langle$**val**, $C\rangle$ from q:
>   **if** no such message was received from q before
>   **then** $insert(D_p, (C + \frac{1}{2}(\delta_{max} + \delta_{min})) - C_p)$

Algorithm 15.7 FAST CONVERGENCE OF CLOCKS.

---

introducing an additional $\delta_{max} - \delta_{min}$ term in the output precision. To represent the received value as a clock value rather than as a constant, p stores the difference of the received clock value (plus $\frac{1}{2}(\delta_{max} + \delta_{min})$) and its own as Δ_{pr}. At time t, p's approximation of r's clock is $C_p(t) + \Delta_{pr}$. The modified algorithm is given as Algorithm 15.7.

Observe that in Algorithm 15.7 the filter has a wider margin, namely $\delta + (\delta_{max} - \delta_{min})$, than in Algorithm 15.6, where the margin is δ. The wider margin compensates for the unknown message delay and the threshold is motivated by the following proposition. Let d_{pr} denote the value that p has inserted in D_p for process r after the first phase of p (compare with the value v_{pr} in the previous algorithm).

Proposition 15.15 *For correct p, q, and r, after p's time-out* $|d_{pr} - d_{qr}| \leq \delta + (\delta_{max} - \delta_{min})$ *holds.*

Proof. The exchange of the $\langle$**val**, $C\rangle$ message from q to p implements the deterministic clock reading algorithm from Theorem 15.12. When p receives this message, $|C_q - [C + \frac{1}{2}(\delta_{max} + \delta_{min})]|$ is bounded by $\frac{1}{2}(\delta_{max} - \delta_{min})$, so d_{pq} differs by at most $\frac{1}{2}(\delta_{max} + \delta_{min})$ from $C_q - C_p$. Similarly, d_{pr} differs by at most $\frac{1}{2}(\delta_{\max} + \delta_{\min})$ from $C_r - C_p$. As C_q and C_r differ by at most δ, the result follows. □

Theorem 15.16 *After execution of Algorithm 15.7 the clocks are synchronized with precision*

$$(\delta_{\max} - \delta_{\min}) \ + \ \frac{2t}{N}[\delta + (\delta_{\max} - \delta_{\min})].$$

Proof. In this proof, write C_p for the unadjusted clock, and C'_p for the adjusted clock, i.e., $C'_p(t) = C_p(t) + \Delta_p$. To bound the precision of the adjusted clocks, fix a real time t that is later than the time-out by all correct processes, and let $w_{pr} = C_p + d_{pr}$. From the proof of the proposition it is seen that (for correct p, q, and r) $|w_{pr} - C_r(t)| \leq \frac{1}{2}(\delta_{\max} - \delta_{\min})$, which implies $|w_{pr} - w_{qr}| \leq (\delta_{\max} - \delta_{\min})$. For incorrect r, the difference $|w_{pr} - w_{qr}|$ is bounded by $2\delta + 3(\delta_{\max} - \delta_{\min})$, which is proved similarly to the corresponding step in the proof of Theorem 15.14.

Finally, as $C'_p(t) = C_p(t) + \Delta_p = (\sum_r w_{Pr})/N$, the precision is derived as in the proof of Theorem 15.14 by splitting the average into averages over correct processes and over incorrect processes. □

It is implicit in the description of the algorithm that all $\langle \mathbf{val}, C \rangle$ messages are sent with the *unadjusted* clock values; this can be achieved by deferring the clock adjustment until a reply has been sent to all $\langle \mathbf{ask} \rangle$ messages.

15.3.3 Implementing the Round-model

The pulse model of synchronous computations can be simulated in systems with weaker synchrony assumptions, provided that

(1) there is an upper bound $\delta_{\max}$ on the message delay;
(2) there is an upper bound γ on the time necessary for the local computation in a pulse (the time for state change plus the time for sending messages); and
(3) the processes have clocks that are δ-synchronized at every clock time T and have ρ-bounded drift.

The simulation takes $(1 + \rho)(\delta_{\max} + \delta + \gamma)$ clock time per pulse.

The simulation algorithm is very elementary; assume that execution of the simulated algorithm is supposed to start at clock time 0 (starting at a later time can be implemented by adding a fixed term T_0 to all clock times). When a process's clock reads 0, it sends its messages of pulse 1. When a process's clock reads $i(1 + \rho)(\delta_{\max} + \delta + \gamma)$, the process executes the state change of pulse i and subsequently sends the messages for pulse $(i+1)$. As the clock increases to arbitrarily high values, each correct process executes infinitely many pulses with this strategy.

It remains to show that correct process p receives all messages sent to it in pulse i (by correct processes) before it executes the state change for that pulse. Assume process q sends a message to p in pulse i. Process q started executing the state change of the previous pulse and sending messages of pulse i when its clock read $(i-1)(1+\rho)(\delta_{\max}+\delta+\gamma)$, that is, at real time $c_q[(i-1)(1+\rho)(\delta_{\max}+\delta+\gamma)]$. The assumption regarding the bound on local processing time implies that the pulse-i message is sent, at the latest, at real time

$$c_q[(i-1)(1+\rho)(\delta_{\max}+\delta+\gamma)]+\gamma\,,$$

which implies (by the bound on message delay) that it is received at the latest at real time

$$c_q[(i-1)(1+\rho)(\delta_{\max}+\delta+\gamma)]+\gamma+\delta_{\max}\,.$$

Process p starts executing the state change at local clock time $i(1+\rho)(\delta_{\max}+\delta+\gamma)$, which means at real time

$$c_p[i(1+\rho)(\delta_{\max}+\delta+\gamma)].$$

As the clocks of p and q are δ-synchronized at clock time $(i-1)(1+\rho)(\delta_{\max}+\delta+\gamma)$,

$$c_q[(i-1)(1+\rho)(\delta_{\max}+\delta+\gamma)]\leq c_p[(i-1)(1+\rho)(\delta_{\max}+\delta+\gamma)].$$

The ρ-bounded drift of p's clock implies that

$$c_p[i(1+\rho)(\delta_{\max}+\delta+\gamma)]\geq c_p[(i-1)(1+\rho)(\delta_{\max}+\delta+\gamma)]+(\delta_{\max}+\delta+\gamma)\,.$$

Combining these equations,

$$c_p[i(1+\rho)(\delta_{\max}+\delta+\gamma)]\geq c_q[(i-1)(1+\rho)(\delta_{\max}+\delta+\gamma)]+\gamma+\delta_{\max}\,,$$

which implies that p receives the message before executing the state change.

Exercises to Chapter 15

Section 15.1

Exercise 15.1 *How many messages are exchanged in the Broadcast(N, t) protocol (Algorithm 15.2 and 15.3)?*

Exercise 15.2 *What is the highest number of messages sent by correct processes in Algorithm 15.4 in executions that decide on 0? Answer both for the case where the general is correct and the case where the general is faulty.*

Section 15.2

Exercise 15.3 *How many messages are exchanged by the broadcast algorithm of Lamport, Shostak, and Pease, described in Subsection 15.2.1?*

Exercise 15.4 *Give an execution of the protocol of Dolev and Strong, described in Subsection 15.2.1, where correct processes p and q end with $W_p \neq W_q$.*

Exercise 15.5 *Show that order-preserving renaming in the range 1 through N can be solved when interactive consistency is achieved.*

Exercise 15.6 *Assume that p signs two messages M_1 and M_2 with the ElGamal signature scheme (Subsection 15.2.3), using the same value of a. Show how to find P's secret key from the two signed messages.*

Exercise 15.7 *Let n be the product of two large prime numbers, and assume that a black box is given that computes square roots. That is, given a quadratic residue y, the box outputs an x with $x^2 = y$ (equation is modulo n). Show how the box can be used to factor n.*

Section 15.3

Exercise 15.8 *Show that if clocks C_p and C_q have ρ-bounded drift and are δ-synchronized at real time t, then they are $\delta(1 + \rho)$-synchronized at clock time $T = C_p(t)$.*

Exercise 15.9 *The probabilistic clock-synchronization protocol is efficient if many messages have a delay close to $\delta_{\min}$ (that is, $F(\delta_{\min} + \epsilon)$ moves away from 0 quickly even for small ϵ).*
Give a "dual" protocol that works efficiently if many messages have a delay close to $\delta_{\max}$ (that is, if $F(\delta_{\max} - \epsilon)$ stays sufficiently far from 1 even for small ϵ). Show that the expected message complexity is bounded by $2.[1 - F(\delta_{\max} - \epsilon)]^{-2}$ and prove a bound on the expected running time.

Exercise 15.10 *Does the set A_p in Algorithm 15.6 satisfy width$(A_p) \leq \delta$ for all correct p?*

16

Failure Detection

The impossibility of solving consensus in asynchronous systems (Section 14.1) has led to weaker problem formulations and stronger models. Examples of the former include weaker coordinations and randomization, and examples of the latter include introducing synchrony. Failure detectors are now widely recognized as an alternative way to strengthen the computation model.

Studying synchronous models is practically motivated because most distributed programming environments do provide clocks and timers in some way. Theoretical studies reveal for what tasks the use of these primitives is necessary and to what degree they must be used. With failure detectors, the situation is similar: quite often the run-time support system will return error messages upon an attempt to communicate with a crashed process. However, these error messages are not always absolutely reliable. It is therefore useful to study how reliable they must be to allow a solution for the consensus problem (or other problems).

In contrast to synchrony (implemented using physical clocks), failure detectors have no straightforward intuitive implementation. This implies that non-trivial solutions must be found in order to implement them in the run-time system or as a module in the application. The implementations more often than not rely on the use of timers (see Section 16.4) and this has led to some serious critiques of the failure detector approach. It was argued that "failure detectors" as such do not solve any problems, because their implementation requires the same resources (time) that can be used to solve consensus directly.

There certainly is a point here, but the same argument applies to virtually everything that was invented in computer science over the past half century. Why use a higher order programming language if the program must still be compiled to machine language in order to be executed? We could "just

as well" write the whole program in machine language directly! Why use
device drivers to access disks and printers from an application if these drivers
are just programs themselves as well? We could "just as well" include the
driver code in our application and do without the driver. Of course we know
all the arguments for using higher order languages and drivers: they make
programming easier, improve understandability and portability, and allow
studies of the power of certain concepts. And these arguments apply to
failure detectors as well.

16.1 Model and Definitions

Failure detection, being available in many practical systems since a long
time ago, was first formulated as an abstract mechanism around 1991 by
the research goup of Sam Toueg of Cornell University. It took about five
years for a foundational paper to appear [CT96], from which most of our
definitions and results are taken.

A failure detector is a module that provides to each process a collection
of *suspected* processes; the test $j \in D$ in the program returns if process j
is suspected at the moment of evaluation. The type of failure considered in
this chapter is crashes. The modules in different processes need not agree
(that is, correct process p may suspect r while correct q doesn't) and need
not be just at any time (correct p may suspect correct r or not suspect
failed r). Of course, in order to be able to reason about programs with
failure detectors we must first express the properties of the detectors, most
notably the relation between the detector output and actual failures.

The actual failures are expressed in a *failure pattern* which we shall first
define. To circumvent the use of expressions in temporal logic we use an
explicit time variable t in our expressions; this t ranges over the set T of
all time instances, which could be the natural numbers for example. Please
note that processes can *not* observe the time t, the failure pattern F, the
sets $Crash(F)$ and $Corr(F)$, or the failure detector history! Process q *only*
"sees" the value $H(q, t)$ when it accesses its failure detector at time t.

16.1.1 Four Basic Detector Classes

The crashes occurring during an execution are modeled by a *failure pattern*,
which is a function $F : T \to \mathcal{P}(\mathbb{P})$. Here $F(t)$ is the collection of processes
that have crashed at time t, and because we do not assume restarts, $t_1 \leq t_2$
implies $F(t_1) \subseteq F(t_2)$. The collections of defective and correct processes are
defined by $Crash(F) = \cup_{t \in T} F(t)$ and $Corr(F) = \mathbb{P} \setminus Crash(F)$.

Suspicions may differ from time to time and from process to process, and are therefore modeled by a function $H : \mathbb{P} \times T \rightarrow \mathcal{P}(\mathbb{P})$. Here $H(q, t)$ is the collection of processes suspected by q at time t.

To allow failure detectors to be *non-deterministic* (i.e., with a given failure pattern, different responses are possible), we model a detector $\mathcal{D}$ as a mapping from failure patterns to *collections of* failure detector histories. That is, for a failure pattern F, an element $H \in \mathcal{D}(F)$ is a failure detector history.

Properties of histories. Understandably, in order for a failure detector to be useful, there must be a relation between its output (the failure detector histories) and its input (the failure pattern). The requirements are always of two types, namely completeness (the detector will suspect crashed processes) and accuracy (the detector will not suspect correct processes). Completeness bounds the set of suspected processes from below and accuracy from above, but in neither case is an exact match with the set of crashed processes required (such a requirement could never be met by any practically imaginable system).

We consider completeness in just one form.

Definition 16.1 *Failure detector $\mathcal{D}$ is* complete *if every crashed process will eventually be suspected by every correct process:*

$$\forall F : \forall H \in \mathcal{D}(F) : \exists t : \forall p \in Crash(F) : \forall q \in Corr(F) : \forall t' \geq t : p \in H(q, t').$$

(This property is also called strong completeness in the literature.)

We consider four different forms of accuracy. Remember that accuracy dictates that correct processes are unsuspected; in the strong form this holds for *all*, in the weak form this holds for *at least one* correct process. We further distinguish "eventual" versions, where the property need not hold initially but is required to hold from some time on.

Definition 16.2 *Failure detector $\mathcal{D}$ is* strongly accurate *if no process is ever suspected if it has not crashed:*

$$\forall F : \forall H \in \mathcal{D}(F) : \forall t : \forall p, q \notin F(t) : p \notin H(q, t).$$

Failure detector $\mathcal{D}$ is weakly accurate *if there exists a correct process that is never suspected:*

$$\forall F : \forall H \in \mathcal{D}(F) : \exists p \in Corr(F) : \forall t : \forall q \notin F(t) : p \notin H(q, t).$$

Failure detector $\mathcal{D}$ is eventually strongly accurate *if there exists a time after* *which no correct process is suspected:*

$$\forall F : \forall H \in \mathcal{D}(F) : \exists t : \forall t' \geq t : \forall p, q \in Corr(F) : p \notin H(q, t').$$

Failure detector $\mathcal{D}$ is eventually weakly accurate *if there exist a time and a correct process that is not suspected after that time:*

$$\forall F : \forall H \in \mathcal{D}(F) : \exists t : \exists p \in Corr(F) : \forall t' \geq t : \forall q \in Corr(F) : p \notin H(q, t').$$

Observe that the definition only restricts the suspicions by *non-crashed* processes q; the suspicions by crashed processes are irrelevant. Further, the definition of strong accuracy explicitly rules out that a crashing process is suspected *before* it is going to crash. For the other three forms of accuracy it makes no difference to exclude this.

It is very easy to have a failure detector that is complete (a detector that suspects everybody: $H(q, t) = \mathbb{P}$) and also to have a failure etector that is accurate (a detector that suspects nobody: $H(q, t) = \varnothing$). Interesting and useful detectors always combine a completeness and an accuracy property, and four classes are considered.

Definition 16.3 *A failure detector is* perfect *if it is complete and strongly accurate; the class of perfect detectors is denoted by $\mathcal{P}$.*
A failure detector is strong *if it is complete and weakly accurate; the class of strong detectors is denoted by $\mathcal{S}$.*
A failure detector is eventually perfect *if it is complete and eventually strongly accurate; the class of eventually perfect detectors is denoted by $\diamond\mathcal{P}$.*
A failure detector is eventually strong *if it is complete and eventually weakly accurate; the class of eventually strong detectors is denoted by $\diamond\mathcal{S}$.*

16.1.2 Use of Failure Detectors and Pitfalls

It isn't particularly difficult to imagine how failure detectors can be used in designing distributed applications.

Recall the communication operations that we encountered frequently in asynchronous distributed algorithms (Chapter 14):

(1) Each node performs a *shout*, that is, sends a message to each node.
(2) Each node collects $N - t$ of the shouted messages.

A process should never wait for the arrival of more than $N - t$ messages because this risks a deadlock in case of crashes. The construction causes no eternal blocking (see, e.g., Lemma 14.30) because at least $N - t$ processes are alive. The pitfall is that even without any crashes, the set of collected messages may differ from process to process. The set of messages collected always has the same size $(N - t)$. Waiting for a message to arrive from any *specific* process is absolutely forbidden without detectors, because it may lead to blocking if the desired sender has crashed.

The standard way of communication using failure detectors runs like this:

(1) Each node sends a message to each node.
(2) Each node waits until for each process q, a message from q has arrived or q is suspected.

The completeness of the failure detector makes this construction free of eternal blocking; indeed, each process that doesn't send the message because of having crashed will eventually be suspected. As in the case of the previous construction, there is a pitfall: there are various scenarios leading to different sets of messages collected by different correct processes.

(1) Process q crashes, but prior to its crash sends some or all of the required messages. Process p_1 receives the message before suspecting q, process p_2 doesn't, and ends its receive phase without q's message.
(2) Process q is correct and sends the message, but p_1 suspects q and doesn't collect q's message, while p_2 does not suspect q and collects the message.

Thus, a set of collected messages may include a message from a crashed process, as well as miss one from a correct processes. The size of the set may differ and, even if a bound t on the number of crashes exists, the set can be smaller than $N - t$ messages because of erroneous suspicions. Only a bound on the number of processes that can be *suspected* may bound the size of the set from below; basically this is done in the weakly accurate detectors.

With a failure detector it is possible to receive a message from a specifically mentioned process: waiting for the message will be interrupted when suspicion against the process arises. Again observe that in this way a message from a correct process to a correct process may fail to be received.

The mode of receiving messages sketched is so common that we introduce a programming shorthand for it: the statement "collect $\langle$ **message**, *par* $\rangle$ from q". The instruction waits until either a message $\langle$ **message**, *par* $\rangle$ is received from q, or q is supected; a boolean value indicating the succes of reception is returned.

```
xᵢ := input ;
for r := 1 to N
    do begin if i = r
                then forall j do send ⟨ value, xᵢ, r ⟩ to j ;
             if collect ⟨ value, x', r ⟩ from pᵣ
                then xᵢ := x'
       end ;
decide xᵢ
```

Algorithm 16.1 A ROTATING COORDINATOR ALGORITHM USING $\mathcal{S}$ (FOR p_i).

16.2 Solving Consensus with a Weakly Accurate Detector

This section presents a relatively simple consensus algorithm using failure detectors. The correctness specifications are:

(1) **Termination.** Every correct process decides once.
(2) **Agreement.** All decisions (in one execution) are equal.
(3) **Validity.** A decision equals the input of at least one process.

It is easy to see that validity implies non-triviality, and it is thus seen that we obtain a result that is impossible without failure detection (Theorem 14.8).

Algorithm 16.1 solves the problem using a weakly accurate failure detector; there exists a process that is *never* suspected, but of course the processes do not know which one! Only when the processes collect a message from this unknown process, are they all guaranteed to receive the message, hence to receive *the same* information. The algorithm avoids the difficulty of not knowing which node is unsuspected by giving a turn to each process; such an approach is called the *rotating coordinator* paradigm. The algorithm consists of N rounds, each process coordinates one of them.

We call the processes p_1 through p_N and p_j coordinates round j. In a round the coordinator shouts its value, all nodes collect a message from the coordinator, and if a node succeeds it replaces its value by the value received from the coordinator. The correctness proof is just outlined here because the details are fairly obvious.

Theorem 16.4 *Algorithm 16.1 solves consensus.*

Proof. The algorithm satisfies termination because no correct process blocks forever in a round; indeed, the coordinator is correct and sends the message, or is eventually suspected (because of the completeness of the detector).

Formally one proves with induction on i that every correct process reaches round i.

Validity is satisfied because a process can only keep its value or replace it by a value received from the coordinator, which allows us to prove (again by induction) that each process enters each round with a value that was the input of some process.

To show agreement, let p_j be the process that is never suspected. In round j every process (that completes the round) receives the value from p_j, hence all processes complete round j with *the same* value. A round that is entered with one value is also completed with one value (the same), which implies that the entire algorithm is completed with just one value. □

Observe that the resiliency t does *not* occur in the program. Actually the resiliency is $N-1$. It is currently not known how the number of rounds can be reduced if the resiliency is limited. The reason is that correct coordinators can be suspected; in this algorithm it doesn't help if processes are correct, what one needs is that they are unsuspected. The number of rounds can be reduced if the accuracy of the detector is strengthened; see Exercise 16.5.

16.3 Eventually Weakly Accurate Detectors

The weak accuracy assumed in the previous section implies that there is a round with unsuspected coordinator *among the first N rounds* of the algorithm. Thus the algorithm can be designed to terminate after N rounds. However, *eventual* weak accuracy, though it implies that a round with unsuspected coordinator will occur *at some time*, does not provide a bound on which round this will be.

Therefore, in addition to actually reaching agreement, the solution must also *detect* when agreement has been reached. This detection requires that, in addition to a failure detector, there is a bound on the resiliency of $t < N/2$; this will be shown in Subsection 16.3.1. The algorithm we present in Subsection 16.3.2 does not provide the optimal resiliency: a bound of $t < N/3$ is assumed.

16.3.1 Upper Bound on Resiliency

Failure detectors with *eventual* accuracy properties may exhibit arbitrary behavior during an arbitrarily (but finitely) long initial period of time. Put bluntly, this means that they are useless to prevent *finite* erroneous executions. In terms of impossibility proofs: results that can be obtained by constructing *finite* erroneous executions carry over to the model with eventually accurate failure detectors. This is the case, for example, for Theorem 14.16, and we extend the theorem here to models with failure detection. The theorem is stated for an eventually perfect detector; the result also holds for an eventually strong one, because this class of detectors satisfies weaker specifications.

Theorem 16.5 *There exists no consensus algorithm using $\diamond\mathcal{P}$ that allows $t \geq N/2$ crashes.*

Proof. Assume, to the contrary, that such an algorithm exists. In $\mathbb{P}$ two disjoint sets of processes S and T can be formed, both of size $N - t$. We consider two scenarios.

- In scenario 0, the processes in S all have input 0, those outside S fail immediately, and this is detected right from the start by all processes in S. Because S contains $N - t$ processes, the processes in S decide in finite time, and because all alive processes have input 0, their decision is 0.

- In scenario 1, the processes in T all have input 1, those outside T fail immediately, and this is detected right from the start by all processes in T. Because T contains $N - t$ processes, the processes in T decide in finite time, and because all alive processes have input 1, their decision is 1.

Observe that in both scenarios the failure detector behavior is in accordance with the requirements for $\diamond\mathcal{P}$. We don't expand on why the decision for 0 (or 1) is inevitable in scenario 0 (or 1, respectively).

Because S and T are disjoint, the scenarios can be combined into a new scenario, let us say scenario 2. Assume *only the processes outside $S \cup T$ fail*, the processes in S all have input 0, the processes in T all have input 1, and the failure of processes outside $S \cup T$ is detected immediately by those in S and T. Moreover, the processes in S erroneously suspect those in T right from the start, and those in T erroneously suspect those in S right from the start; the requirement of *eventual* perfectness allows this situation to last for any finite amount of time. The messages sent from S to T and vice versa are delivered very slowly.

Now scenario 2 is like scenario 0 for the processes in S and is like scenario 1 for the processes in T, hence these processes start to execute the same series of steps. Within *finite time* these processes decide on the same value as in the earlier scenario, that is, processes in S and T decide on 0 and 1. After the taking of at least one decision in each group, erroneous suspicions stop and messages from S to T and vice versa arrive.

We have thus constructed a scenario in which fewer than t processes fail, the failure detector behaves according to the definition of eventual perfection, and all messages from correct to correct processes arrive. Yet different processes take different decisions, which shows that Agreement isn't satisfied. □

The proof that consensus is not possible at all (Theorem 14.8) constructs an *infinite* non-deciding execution and we shall see in the next section that this infinite behavior can be avoided with eventually correct detectors.

16.3.2 The Consensus Algorithm

Algorithm 16.1 assumed the failure detector to be weakly accurate from the start, which implies that there is an unsuspected coordinator, and hence agreement on values, within the first N rounds. In Algorithm 16.2 the coordinator must extend its activities to also find out if agreement is already occurring. It first collects the current values of all processes and checks if they are uniform (see phase 2). Now here is a pitfall because due to erroneous suspicions the coordinator could collect effectively *less than half* of the active values and then announce a value as the unanimous outcome while it is actually supported by a minority of the processes. Here is where we use the bound on the number of failed processes: in the collection phase the coordinator does not use its detector, but awaits $N-t$ votes as in the classical approaches. The robustness t of Algorithm 16.2 is bounded by $t < N/3$. Now an observed agreement by the coordinator at least implies that a strict majority of the processes has the computed value; not necessarily all correct processes do, because some conflicting votes may be missed because the coordinator only awaits a fixed number of votes.

A decision is allowed if the coordinator has proclaimed that it chose the value v from unanimous votes, as indicated by the bit d in the message $\langle \textbf{outcome}, d, v, r \rangle$ that announces the result of round r. The processes continue their activity after a decision to help other processes decide too.

Lemma 16.6 *For each round r and correct process p, p finishes round r.*

Proof. Assume all correct processes start a round r. A correct coordinator will complete phase 1 because sufficiently many votes are sent. A correct process will complete phase 3 because the coordinator will send the message if it is correct, and eventually be suspected if it isn't. Thus, all correct processes complete the entire round. Induction completes the proof. □

$x_i :=$ input ;
$r := 0$;
while *true* **do**
         begin (* Start new round and compute coordinator*)
                 $r := r + 1$; $c := (r \bmod N) + 1$;
                 (* Phase 1: all processes send value to coordinator *)
                 send $\langle$ **value**$, x_i, r \rangle$ to p_c ;
                 (* Phase 2: coordinator evaluates outcome *)
                 if $i = c$ **then**
                     begin wait until $N - t$ mesgs. $\langle$ **value**$, v_j, r \rangle$ have been received;
                         $v :=$ majority of received values;
                         $d := (\forall j : v_j = v)$;   (* range over received messages *)
                         forall j **do** send $\langle$ **outcome**$, d, v, r \rangle$ to p_j
                 end ;
                 (* Phase 3: evaluate the round *)
                 if collect $\langle$ **outcome**$, d, v, r \rangle$ from p_c **then**
                     begin $x_i := v$;
                         if $(d \wedge (y_i = @))$
                             then decide(v)
                   end
         end

Algorithm 16.2 A ROTATING COORDINATOR ALGORITHM WITH $\diamond\mathcal{S}$.

We now proceed to show that a majority, sufficiently large to cause a decision, is persistent.

Lemma 16.7 *If at the beginning of a round $k \geq N - t$ processes have value v, then at least k processes have v at the end of that round.*

Proof. A process can suspect the coordinator and keep the same value; the only way to change value is to receive a message with that value from the coordinator. The coordinator took the majority of $N - t$ values received; at most t processes have a value different from v, so at least $N - 2t$ votes for v were received, and $N - 2t > t$. This shows that the coordinator, if it sent a value in phase 2, sent the value v and thus the number of processes with value v can only grow, not decrease.   □

Lemma 16.8 *Each correct process decides.*

Proof. Eventual accuracy implies that eventually there is a round r whose coordinator c is not suspected in round r or later. In that round all correct processes receive from the coordinator and agree on the same value, and continue to do so (Lemma 16.7). Consequently, all messages sent by

var D_p set of processes ;
      $r_p[\mathbb{P}]$ A timer for each process

Initialization of the detector:
      $D_p := \varnothing$;
      forall q **do** $r_p[q] := \sigma + \mu$

The sending process, at each multiple of σ:
      forall q **do** send $\langle$**alive**$\rangle$ to q

The receiving process, upon receipt of $\langle$**alive**$\rangle$ from q:
      $r_p[q] := \sigma + \mu$

Failure detection, when $r_p[q]$ elapses:
      $D_p := D_p \cup \{q\}$

Algorithm 16.3 PERFECT FAILURE DETECTOR.

---

coordinators after round r announce that v was unanimous ($d = true$), so a process will decide v as soon as it collects a message in phase 3. But c is never suspected any more, and is coordinator again in round $r + N$, so at the end of this round all processes have decided. $\qquad\square$

Theorem 16.9 *Algorithm 16.2 is a consensus algorithm with* $\diamond\mathcal{S}$.

Proof. It is fairly trivial (and left to the reader) to show by induction on r that if any process holds a value in round r, this value was among the inputs; this shows validity. Lemma 16.7 implies agreement, because from a deciding round there is never sufficient support to decide a different value. Finally termination is expressed in the preceding lemma. $\qquad\square$

16.4 Implementation of Failure Detectors

A definite advantage of the failure detector approach is that one has to deal only with the *properties* of the detectors, and not with their implementation. However, we do give some possible implementations to show what happens behind the curtains and as an illustration to the definitions. In most cases the detector is a wrapping with asynchronous interface around the careful use of timers.

var D_p set of processes ;
    $r_p[\mathbb{P}]$ A timer for each process ;
    me_p μ estimate, initially 1

Initialization of the detector:
    $D_p := \varnothing$;
    forall q **do** $r_p[q] := \sigma + me_p$

The sending process, at each multiple of σ:
    forall q **do** send $\langle$ **alive** $\rangle$ to q

The receiving process, upon receipt of $\langle$ **alive** $\rangle$ from q:
    if $j \in D_p$ **then**
        begin $D_p := D_p \setminus \{q\}$;
             $me_p := me_p + 1$
        end ;
    $r_p[q] := \sigma + me_p$

Failure detection, when $r[q]$ elapses:
    $D_p := D_p \cup \{q\}$

Algorithm 16.4 Eventually Perfect Failure Detector.

16.4.1 Synchronous Systems: Perfect Detection

Algorithm 16.3 for perfect failure detection assumes an upper bound of μ on the communication delay. Alive processes send $\langle$ **alive** $\rangle$ messages at σ time intervals, and not receiving a message from a process for $\sigma + \mu$ time implies the process has crashed.

16.4.2 Partially Synchronous Systems: Eventually Perfect Detection

A detector with only slightly weaker properties is possible if the upper bound on message delays is unknown or, for some reason, it is undesirable to include it in the program (e.g., portability reasons). The detector (Algorithm 16.4) starts with a small estimated value of μ. It is then possible that early time-outs take place, i.e., a process is timed out, and suspected, while actually an $\langle$ **alive** $\rangle$ message from the process is still in transit. If a message from a suspected process arrives, it is immediately deleted from D, but moreover, the estimate for μ is increased. After a fixed number of such corrections, the estimate exceeds the actual value of μ, and from then on no more erroneous suspicions occur. As the number of erroneous suspicions is finite, they all occur in a finite initial segment of the execution, which shows that the detector is eventually strongly accurate.

16.4.3 Final Remarks

This chapter has only introduced the subject of failure detectors by presenting a few elementary results that can be easily understood and presented in class. Because the subject has been introduced relatively recently and has just caught the attention of the international research community, it is not possible to make a selection of the results that is indicative of future directions of research and development. We conclude the chapter with some examples of results concerning failure detectors.

A hierarchy of failure detectors is established by the notion of *emulation* of failure detectors [CT96]. Detector $\mathcal{A}$ emulates detector $\mathcal{B}$ if there exists a distributed algorithm that uses the information provided by $\mathcal{A}$ and implements detector $\mathcal{B}$. Detector $\mathcal{B}$ is said to be weaker than $\mathcal{A}$ in this case.

A weaker form of completeness was defined: a detector is weakly complete if every crashed process is eventually permanently suspected by at least one correct process [CT96]. However, it can be easily shown that a weakly complete detector can emulate a strongly complete one (see Definition 16.1) without weakening any of the accuracy properties of Definition 16.2. Therefore, weak completeness is not often considered in the literature (or in this book).

It has been asked whether the consensus problem is solvable with a detector that is weaker than $\diamond\mathcal{S}$ (as used in Section 16.3), but this is not the case. Chandra *et al.* [CHT96] show that any detector that allows one to implement consensus can emulate $\diamond\mathcal{S}$. The work develops a lot of mathematical machinery and proof techniques surrounding failure detection.

Not all failure detectors use time outs in their implementation: a *Heartbeat* [ACT97] detector was proposed that only exchanges asynchronous messages. This detector, however, necessitates a different kind of interaction with the processes from that used in this chapter, and the problem that can be solved with it is slightly contrived. The related issues, such as what can be implemented asynchronously, what problems can be solved with asynchronously implemented detectors, etc., are too complicated and too novel to discuss here.

Exercises to Chapter 16
Section 16.1

Exercise 16.1 *Page 509 lists various possibilities for correct processes to collect different sets of messages in a receive phase. For each of the four types of detector (Definition 16.3), say if this possibility can occur.*

Exercise 16.2 *Let F be a failure pattern; prove there is a t such that $F(t) = Crash(F)$.*
Where does your proof use that $\mathbb{P}$ is finite? Show that the result doesn't hold if $\mathbb{P}$ is an infinite collection of processes.

Exercise 16.3 *The requirement of strong accuracy is stronger than the requirement that no correct process is ever suspected:*

$$\forall F : \forall H \in \mathcal{D}(F) : \forall t : \forall p \in Corr(F), q \notin F(t) : p \notin H(q, t).$$

Give an example of a failure patern and failure detector history that satisfy this property, yet are not allowed in a strongly accurate detector.

Exercise 16.4 *Process p sends a message to q and then to r; q and r collect a message from p. Show with an example that it is possible, even if detection is perfect, that r receives the message and q doesn't. In your example, q and r must be correct.*

Section 16.2

Exercise 16.5 *A failure detector is called l-accurate if in each run at least l correct processes are unsuspected. (The property implies a bound of $N - l$ on the resiliency; weak accuracy is 1-accuracy.)*
Adapt Algorithm 16.1 so as to complete in $N - l + 1$ rounds.

Exercise 16.6 *Modify Algorithm 16.2 as described for Algorithm 14.5 so as to obtain a finite algorithm, or show that this is impossible with an eventually accurate detector.*

Section 16.3

Exercise 16.7 *Give an example of an execution of Algorithm 16.2 in which decisions occur in different rounds.*

Section 16.4

Exercise 16.8 *How much time can elapse in Algorithm 16.3 between a crash and its detection?*

Exercise 16.9 *Prove the eventual perfection of Algorithm 16.4. Is the relation $me_p \geq \mu$ eventually satisfied in every execution?*

17

Stabilization

The stabilizing algorithms considered in this chapter achieve fault-tolerant behavior in a manner radically different from that of the robust algorithms studied in the previous chapters. Robust algorithms follow a *pessimistic* approach, suspecting all information received, and precede all steps by sufficient checks to guarantee the validity of all steps of correct processes. Validity must be guaranteed in the presence of faulty processes, which necessitates restriction of the number of faults and of the fault model.

Stabilizing algorithms are *optimistic*, which may cause correct processes to behave inconsistently, but guarantee a return to correct behavior within finite time after all faulty behavior ceases. That is, stabilizing algorithms protect against *transient* failures; eventual repair is assumed, and this assumption allows us to abandon failure models and a bound on the number of failures. Rather than considering processes to be faulty, it is assumed that all processes operate correctly, but the configuration can be corrupted arbitrarily during a transient failure. Ignoring the history of the computation during the failure, the configuration at which we start the analysis of the algorithm, is considered the initial one of the (correctly operating) algorithm. An algorithm is therefore called stabilizing if it eventually starts to behave correctly (i.e., according to the specification of the algorithm), regardless of the initial configuration.

The concept of stabilization was proposed by Dijkstra [Dij74], but little work on it was done until the late nineteen-eighties; hence the subject can be considered relatively new. Nonetheless, a large number of stabilizing algorithms and related results were proposed in the following years up to the date of the present text, and in this chapter a selection of this work will be presented.

The term "stabilizing" is used throughout, whereas "self-stabilizing" is frequently found in the literature.

17.1 Introduction

17.1.1 Definitions

Stabilizing algorithms are modeled as transition systems without initial configurations (compare this definition with Definition 2.1).

Definition 17.1 *A system is a pair $S = (\mathcal{C}, \rightarrow)$, where $\mathcal{C}$ is a set of configurations and $\rightarrow$ is a binary transition relation on $\mathcal{C}$. An execution of S is a maximal sequence $E = (\gamma_0, \gamma_1, \gamma_2, \ldots)$ such that for all $i \geq 0$, $\gamma_i \rightarrow \gamma_{i+1}$.*

Unlike in Definition 2.2, each (non-empty) suffix of a computation is now also a computation. The correctness of an algorithm, i.e., the desired "consistent behavior of processes", is expressed as a specification, which is a predicate (usually denoted P) on sequences of configurations.

Definition 17.2 *System S stabilizes to specification P if there exists a subset $\mathcal{L} \subseteq \mathcal{C}$, of legitimate configurations, with the following properties.*

(1) **Correctness.** *Every execution starting in a configuration in $\mathcal{L}$ satisfies P.*

(2) **Convergence.** *Every execution contains a configuration of $\mathcal{L}$.*

The set of legitimate configurations is usually closed, i.e., if $\gamma \in \mathcal{L}$ and $\gamma \rightarrow \delta$ then $\delta \in \mathcal{L}$, but as this is not used in the proof of the following result, we do not include closedness in the definition.

Theorem 17.3 *If system S stabilizes to P, then every execution of S has a non-empty suffix satisfying P.*

Proof. Every execution contains a legitimate configuration by the convergence property, and a suffix starting there satisfies P by the correctness. $\square$

Proving stabilization. The use of legitimate configurations allows us to use the standard verification techniques to show the stabilization of an algorithm. Convergence is shown by a norm function.

Lemma 17.4 *Assume that*

(1) *all terminal configurations belong to $\mathcal{L}$;*

(2) *there exists a function $f : \mathcal{C} \to W$, where W is a well-founded set, and, for each transition $\gamma \to \delta$, $f(\gamma) > f(\delta)$ or $\delta \in \mathcal{L}$ holds.*

Then $S = (\mathcal{C}, \to)$ satisfies convergence.

To show correctness, one may perform a classical algorithm analysis, considering $\mathcal{L}$ as the set of initial configurations; indeed, only executions starting in $\mathcal{L}$ are considered.

Properties of stabilizing algorithms. Stabilizing algorithms offer the following three fundamental advantages over classical algorithms.

(1) *Fault tolerance.* As was observed in the introduction to this chapter, a stabilizing algorithm offers full and automatic protection against all transient process failures, because the algorithm recovers from any configuration, no matter how much the data has been corrupted by failures.

(2) *Initialization.* The need of proper and consistent initialization of the algorithm is eliminated, because the processes can be started in arbitrary states and yet eventual coordinated behavior is guaranteed.

(3) *Dynamic topology.* A stabilizing algorithm computing a topology-dependent function (routing tables, spanning tree) converges to a new solution after the occurrence of a topological change.

A fourth advantage, namely, the possibility of "sequential" composition without the need for termination detection, is discussed in Subsection 17.3.1. Finally, many of the stabilizing algorithms known to date are simpler then their classical counterparts for the same network problem. This, however, is partly because these algorithms are not yet optimized with respect to their complexity, so this "advantage" may vanish when the study of stabilizing algorithms develops further.

On the other hand, there are the following three disadvantages.

(1) *Initial inconsistencies.* Before a legitimate configuration is reached the algorithm may show an inconsistent output.

(2) *High complexity.* The stabilizing algorithms known to date are usually far less efficient than their classical counterparts for the same problem.

(3) *No detection of stabilization.* It is not possible to observe from within the system that a legitimate configuration has been reached; hence the processes are never aware of when their behavior has become reliable.

Pseudo-stabilization. The property of stabilizing algorithms that was proved in Theorem 17.3 can be taken as an alternative definition: it is then simply required that each execution has a suffix satisfying the specification. This notion, however, is not equivalent to our definition and is referred to as *pseudo-stabilization* by Burns *et al.* [BGM93].

To show the difference, consider the system S with configurations a and b and transitions $a \rightarrow a$, $a \rightarrow b$, and $b \rightarrow b$. Specification P reads "all configurations are the same". Because S can move from a to b at most once, it is easily seen that every execution has a suffix consisting of equal configurations. Configuration a cannot be chosen as legitimate, because the execution $(a, b, b, \ldots)$ starting in it does not satisfy P. Hence the S-execution $(a, a, a, \ldots)$ (although satisfying P itself) does not contain a legitimate configuration.

Burns *et al.* show that the weaker requirement of pseudo-stabilization allows solutions for problems that have no stabilizing solution; one example is data-sequence transmission. On the other hand, in pseudo-stabilizing solutions (that are not stabilizing) there is no upper bound on the number of steps that the system can take before specification P is satisfied, while for stabilizing algorithms such a bound can be given. In this chapter we shall restrict ourselves to the study of stabilizing algorithms.

17.1.2 Communication in Stabilizing Systems

In most of the earlier chapters in this book we have assumed an asynchronous model with communication by message passing, but this model is not adequate for studying stabilizing algorithms.

Indeed, first consider an asynchronous message-passing algorithm in which there is a process p for which every state is a send state (i.e., p can send a message in every local state). This system has an execution consisting only of send actions by p, while all other processes remain frozen in their initial state, and this behavior does not satisfy any meaningful non-trivial specification.

Second, consider an algorithm in which, for every process, there are states in which the process does not send (but can only receive or do an internal step). Every configuration in which every process is in such a state and all channels are empty is a terminal configuration and therefore must satisfy the specification. Again, no non-trivial specification is satisfied by all such configurations.

A stabilizing version of the Netchange algorithm was presented in [Tel91a], using timers in each process and an upper bound on the message-delivery time. This assumption may work out well in practice, but the analysis of the algorithm is concerned mainly with technical details about timing. Therefore we shall assume the more usual model of communication by shared variables, where one process can write and other processes can read the same variable.

In *state* models a process can (atomically) read the entire state of its neighbor. In such a model every neighbor of p reads the same state, so it is not possible for a process to transfer different information to its various neighbors. In *link-register* models, communication between processes is by two registers shared between the two processes; each process can read one of these and write the other. A process can transfer different information to various neighbors by writing different values in its link registers.

We further distinguish between *read-one* and *read-all* models, in which a process can read in one atomic step the state (or link register) of one neighbor, or of all neighbors, respectively.

17.1.3 Example: Dijkstra's Token Ring

The first stabilizing algorithms were proposed by Dijkstra [Dij74] and these algorithms achieved *mutual exclusion* in a ring of processes. For this problem it is assumed that processes must sometimes execute *critical sections* of their code, but it is required that at most one process executes a critical section at any given time. Each process is provided with a local predicate that, when true, indicates that the process has the *privilege* of executing the critical section. The specification of the problem is then:

(1) In every configuration, at most one process has the privilege.
(2) Every process has the privilege infinitely often.

The problem can be solved by introducing a token that circulates over the ring and grants the privilege to the process holding it. The strength of Dijkstra's solution is that it automatically recovers (within $O(N^2)$ process steps) from situations where no token or more than one token is present in the system.

Description of the solution. The state of process i, denoted σ_i, is an integer in the range $0, ..., K-1$, where K is an integer exceeding N. Process i can read σ_{i-1} (as well as σ_i) and process 0 can read σ_{N-1}. All processes except process 0 are equal. Process $i \neq 0$ has the privilege if $\sigma_i \neq \sigma_{i-1}$, while process 0 has the privilege if $\sigma_0 = \sigma_{N-1}$. A process that has the privilege is also enabled to change its state (presumably it will do so after completing its critical section, or when it does not need to execute the latter at all).

The state change of a process always causes the loss of its privilege. Process $i \neq 0$ may set σ_i equal to σ_{i-1} (when it is enabled, i.e., $\sigma_i \neq \sigma_{i-1}$) by assigning $\sigma_i := \sigma_{i-1}$. Process 0 may set σ_0 unequal to σ_{N-1} (when it is at present equal) by assigning $\sigma_0 := (\sigma_{N-1} + 1) \bmod K$.

Proof of stabilization. The definition of privilege implies that in every configuration at least one process has the privilege (i.e., there are no terminal configurations). Indeed, if no process other than 0 has the privilege, then $\sigma_i = \sigma_{i-1}$ for every $i > 0$, which implies that $\sigma_0 = \sigma_{N-1}$ and process 0 has the privilege. Further, no step increases the number of privileged processes, because a process changing state loses its privilege and the only process that can obtain a privilege in this step is its successor.

To show stabilization, define $\mathcal{L}$ as the set of configurations in which exactly one process has the privilege.

Lemma 17.5 *Executions starting in legitimate configurations satisfy P.*

Proof. In a legitimate configuration exactly one step is possible, namely by the unique privileged process. In this step, this process loses its privilege, but, because there are no configurations without a privilege, its successor necessarily obtains the privilege. Consequently, the privilege circulates over the ring and every process holds the privilege once in every N consecutive configurations. $\square$

Lemma 17.6 *Dijkstra's token ring converges to $\mathcal{L}$.*

Proof. Again, every execution of the system is infinite by the absence of terminal configurations.

An execution contains infinitely many steps of process 0, because at most $\frac{1}{2}N(N-1)$ steps can occur without a step of process 0. Indeed, because a step of i removes i's privilege and may give a privilege only to $i + 1$, the norm function

$$F = \sum_{i \in S} (N - i)$$

where $S = \{i : i > 1 \text{ and process } i \text{ has the privilege}\}$

decreases with every step of a process other than process 0.

In the initial configuration γ_0 at most N different states occur so there are at least $K - N$ states that do not occur in γ_0. Because process 0 increments its state (modulo K) in each of its steps, it reaches a state not occurring in γ_0 after at most N steps (of process 0). All processes other than 0 only copy states, hence the first time process 0 computes such a state, its state is unique in the ring. As process 0's state is unique, it will not get the privilege again before the configuration satisfies $\sigma_1 = \sigma_2 = \ldots = \sigma_{N-1} = \sigma_0$, which describes a legitimate configuration.

As the system reaches a legitimate configuration before the $(N+1)$th step of process 0 and (at most) $\frac{1}{2}N(N-1)$ steps of other processes can occur consecutively, a legitimate configuration is reached after (at most) $(N+1)\frac{1}{2}N(N-1) + N = O(N^3)$ steps.

With a more precise analysis an $O(N^2)$ bound on the number of steps can be proved; see Exercise 17.2. □

Corollary 17.7 *Dijkstra's token ring stabilizes to mutual exclusion.*

Uniform solutions. A stabilizing algorithm is called *uniform* if all processes are equal and have no identities to distinguish between them. Finding uniform solutions to mutual exclusion and other problems has received considerable attention in recent years, and this interest can be explained mainly as due to their theoretical interest. Uniform solutions are also attractive, however, in practice, because a process identity is usually stored in memory like any other process variable, so that a corrupted configuration may violate the required uniqueness of identities.

A uniform stabilizing algorithm is also an algorithm for an anonymous network for the same problem; consequently, problems unsolvable for anonymous networks (see Chapter 9) do not have uniform stabilizing solutions. By assuming a symmetric configuration and showing that the symmetry may be preserved indefinitely, Dijkstra [Dij82] showed that no uniform (deterministic) token ring exists if the size of the ring is not prime. A uniform solution, assuming the ring size is prime and known, was proposed by Burns and Pachl [BP88].

The impossibility of deterministic uniform stabilizing algorithms for election, spanning tree, and other symmetry-breaking tasks can be shown similarly, but solutions usually become possible if randomization is allowed. As this chapter is concerned with stabilization, and not with anonymity, we shall assume freely in the sequel that unique names or a leader are available.

17.2 Graph Algorithms

If the purpose of an algorithm is to achieve a postcondition ψ, its specification may be set to "every configuration satisfies ψ". We say S stabilizes to ψ if a set $\mathcal{L}$ exists such that

(1) $\mathcal{L}$ is closed and $\gamma \in \mathcal{L}$ implies $\psi(\gamma)$; and

(2) every computation reaches a configuration of $\mathcal{L}$.

The algorithm may terminate, but this is not always the case. Subsection 17.2.1 presents a ring-orientation algorithm that may eventually go through an infinite sequence of different (but oriented) configurations. Subsection 17.2.2 presents an algorithm for finding a maximal matching, in which the legitimate configurations are terminal.

17.2.1 Ring Orientation

In the ring-orientation problem we consider an undirected ring of N processes, where each process has labeled one of its links by *succ* (successor) and the other by *pred* (predecessor). (A process immediately changes one of its labels if the two labels are equal.) Process p's label of the link pq is called l_{pq}, and no global consistency of the labels is initially assumed. The goal of an orientation algorithm is to compute a consistent sense of direction in the ring.

The orientation problem requires the system to reach the postcondition ψ, defined by "for every edge pq, l_{pq} is *succ* if and only if l_{qp} is *pred*". It was shown by Israeli and Jalfon [IJ90] that no deterministic solution is possible in the state-reading models; we present the Israeli–Jalfon algorithm for the link-register model. The presented algorithm is uniform.

The algorithm, given as Algorithm 17.1, uses, besides the link registers holding *pred* or *succ*, a variable s with values S, R, and I. In one step, process p considers its state, the state of neighbor q and the link registers, and changes state if one of the five guards is *true*. The processes circulate tokens, each process setting its successor to the direction of the last forwarded token; if two tokens meet, one is eliminated. Eventually all remaining tokens will travel in the same direction, which causes the ring to be oriented; the remaining tokens will then keep circulating.

In the S state, a process waits to forward a token (to its current successor), while in the R state a process waits to receive a token; in the I state a process is idle. A process *holds a token* if either its state is S or its state is R and its predecessor is not in state S. A token moves from p to q in action (2) of the algorithm, and is destroyed or created in p in actions (4) or (5), respectively; these steps are called *token steps*. Steps (1) and (3) have no effect on the location of tokens and are called *silent steps*. After step (1), the next step of the same process is step (3), and after step (3) the next step is step (4)

var s_p : (S, R, I) ;

(1) $\{state_p = I \land s_q = S \land l_{qp} = succ\}$
    $s_p := R$; **if** $l_{pq} = succ$ **then** *flip*

(2) $\{s_p = S \land l_{pq} = succ \land s_q = R \land l_{qp} = pred\}$
    $s_p := I$

(3) $\{s_p = R \land l_{pq} = pred \land \neg(s_q = S \land l_{qp} = succ)\}$
    $s_p := S$

(4) $\{s_p = s_q = S \land l_{pq} = l_{qp} = succ\}$
    $s_p := R$; *flip*

(5) $\{s_p = s_q = I \land l_{pq} = l_{qp} = succ\}$
    $s_p := S$

procedure *flip*: reverse *succ* and *pred* for p

Algorithm 17.1 RING-ORIENTATION ALGORITHM.

or step (2), which bounds the number of silent steps in linear relation to the number of token steps.

In action (1), if q wants to forward a token to the idle p, p agrees to accept the token (although it does not move yet) and makes q its predecessor. In action (2), p observes that its successor has agreed to accept the token it wants to transmit and becomes idle, thus moving the token. In action (3), p observes that q, from which it has accepted a token, has become idle, and starts transmitting the token to its successor. The last two actions concern the symmetric situations where (4) two tokens traversing in different directions meet, and (5) two idle processes are inconsistently oriented. In these cases, both processes are enabled, and the first process that takes a step breaks the symmetry[1]. In action (4), p accepts q's token, implicitly destroying its own. In action (5), p generates a token that will overrule q's orientation.

The effect of each action is visualized in Table 17.2, where the state and orientation of each process is compactly represented by an arrow in the direction of its successor.

A configuration is called legitimate if and only if it is oriented, i.e., all arrows point in the same direction.

---

[1] Israeli and Jalfon consider a finer grain of atomicity of action, which necessitates breaking the symmetry explicitly. In terms of [IJ90], Algorithm 17.1 works for the central demon.

Action no.	q	p		p
(1)	$\overset{\rightarrow}{\underset{\leftarrow}{S}}$	$\overleftarrow{I}$	$\longrightarrow$	$\overrightarrow{R}$
(2)	$\overrightarrow{R}$	$\overleftarrow{S}$	$\longrightarrow$	$\overleftarrow{I}$
(3)	$\neg\,\overrightarrow{S}$	$\overrightarrow{R}$	$\longrightarrow$	$\overrightarrow{S}$
(4)	$\overrightarrow{S}$	$\overleftarrow{S}$	$\longrightarrow$	$\overrightarrow{R}$
(5)	$\overrightarrow{I}$	$\overleftarrow{I}$	$\longrightarrow$	$\overleftrightarrow{S}$

Action (1) is applicable regardless of the original orientation of p.

Table 17.2 EFFECT OF THE ACTIONS OF ALGORITHM 17.1.

Lemma 17.8 $\mathcal{L}$ *is closed and* $\gamma \in \mathcal{L}$ *implies* $\psi(\gamma)$.

Proof. Legitimate configurations are oriented by the choice of $\mathcal{L}$, which immediately implies the second part. Further, only steps of the types (1), (2), and (3) occur, because steps (4) and (5) are only enabled when there are differently oriented neighbors. Steps (2) and (3) never flip the orientation of a process, and neither does (1) if p is oriented in the same direction as q, which shows the closedness of $\mathcal{L}$. □

Proposition 17.9 *A terminal configuration is legitimate.*

Proof. Let γ be terminal; no process is in state R in γ, because if $s_p = R$ then either p is enabled, by action (3), or its predecessor is enabled, by action (2).

If γ is not oriented there are two processes pointing at each other, i.e., p and q with $l_{pq} = l_{qp} = succ$. If one of p and q is idle action (1) is enabled, if both are idle action (5) is enabled, and if both are sending action (4) is enabled. It follows that a terminal configuration without receiving processes is oriented; hence all terminal configurations are oriented. □

Theorem 17.10 *The protocol converges to a legitimate state.*

Proof. Token creation occurs in a pair $\overrightarrow{I}\,\overleftarrow{I}$, and such a pair is not formed in any of the five actions, so a token is generated only in an initially idle process as the first step of that process. This implies that the overall number of tokens that exists (i.e., initial tokens plus tokens created during execution) in an execution is bounded by N.

If a token exists in a configuration during the execution and this token has already moved k times, then a sequence of $k + 1$ processes (ending in the one holding the token) is consistently oriented. All these processes have forwarded the token and adopted its direction, and no tokens that could have disturbed the orientation again have been created "behind" the token. So if one token moves $N - 1$ times all processes are oriented equally, and the configuration is legitimate.

Because there are no more than N different tokens during the execution, a legitimate configuration is reached after at most N^2 token steps.   □

17.2.2 Maximal Matching

A *matching* in a graph is a set of edges such that no node of the graph is incident to more than one of the edges. The matching is *maximal* if it cannot be extended by more edges of the graph, and a maximal matching of a graph can be constructed in a time linear in the number of edges. Each edge is considered in turn, and included in the matching if it is not incident to any edge already in the matching. This algorithm is, however, inherently sequential, and not suited for distributed execution; we shall now present a stabilizing algorithm for constructing maximal matchings, proposed by Hsu and Huang [HH92].

The matching algorithm. Process p has one variable $pref_p$, whose value belongs to $Neigh_p \cup \{nil\}$, representing p's *preferred neighbor*. If $pref_p = q$, p has selected its neighbor q to become matched with, i.e., to include edge pq in the matching; $pref_p = nil$ if p has not selected a matching partner. We distinguish five cases depending on p's preference and that of its neighbors. If p has selected q, then p is waiting (for q) if q has not made a selection yet, matched if q has selected p, and chaining if q has selected a neighbor other than p. If p has not made a selection, p is dead if all neighbors of p are matched and free if there is an unmatched neighbor. Formally,

$$
\begin{aligned}
wait(p) &\equiv pref_p = q \in Neigh_p \wedge pref_q = nil \\
match(p) &\equiv pref_p = q \in Neigh_p \wedge pref_q = p \\
chain(p) &\equiv pref_p = q \in Neigh_p \wedge pref_q = r \in Neigh_q \wedge r \neq p \\
dead(p) &\equiv pref_p = nil \wedge \forall q \in Neigh_p : match(q) \\
free(p) &\equiv pref_p = nil \wedge \exists q \in Neigh_p : \neg match(q).
\end{aligned}
$$

The required postcondition for the algorithm is

$$\psi \equiv \forall p : (match(p) \vee dead(p)).$$

Proposition 17.11 *If ψ holds, the set $M = \{(p, pref_p) : pref_p \neq nil\}$ is a maximal matching.*

var $pref_p$: $Neigh_p \cup \{nil\}$;

$\mathbf{M}_p$: $\{pref_p = nil \land pref_q = p\}$
$pref_p := q$

$\mathbf{S}_p$: $\{pref_p = nil \land \forall r \in Neigh_p : pref_r \neq p \land pref_q = nil\}$
$pref_p := q$

$\mathbf{U}_p$: $\{pref_p = q \land pref_q \neq p \land pref_q \neq nil\}$
$pref_p := nil$

Algorithm 17.3 THE MAXIMAL-MATCHING ALGORITHM.

Proof. If there is an edge $pq \in M$, then $pref_p = q$ or $pref_q = p$ by the definition of M; but because q is not waiting or chaining, the latter implies $pref_p = q$ as well. It follows that at most one edge incident to p belongs to M, hence M is a matching.

To show maximality, assume $M \cup \{pq\}$, where $pq \notin M$, is also a matching; then M contains no edge incident to p, which implies $dead(p) \lor free(p)$, and hence, by ψ, $dead(p)$. But $dead(p)$ implies $match(q)$, so M contains an edge incident to q, contradicting the possible extension of M by pq. □

The algorithm is described for the read-all state model and consists of three actions for each process p; see Algorithm 17.3. Process p matches with neighbor q (action $\mathbf{M}_p$) if p is free and q has selected p. If p is free but cannot match, it selects a free neighbor if such is possible (action $\mathbf{S}_p$), and if p is chaining it unchains (action $\mathbf{U}_p$).

Analysis of the algorithm.

Lemma 17.12 *Configuration γ is terminal if and only if $\psi(\gamma)$ holds.*

Proof. Action $\mathbf{M}_p$ is enabled for p only if neighbor q is waiting, action $\mathbf{S}_p$ requires that p is free, and action $\mathbf{U}_p$ that p is chaining, hence $\psi(\gamma)$ implies that no action is enabled in γ.

If ψ does not hold, there is a p such that p is chaining, waiting, or free; in a chaining p, $\mathbf{U}_p$ is enabled, and if p is waiting for q, $\mathbf{M}_q$ is enabled. Finally, assume p is free and q is an unmatched neighbor. Because p is not matched, q is not dead. If q is waiting, the matching action is enabled for one of its neighbors and if q is chaining $\mathbf{U}_q$ is enabled. Finally, if q is free, p and q can select each other. Hence, if ψ does not hold, the configuration is not terminal. □

Lemma 17.13 *Algorithm 17.3 reaches a terminal configuration in* $O(N^2)$ *steps.*

Proof. Define the norm function F by the pair $(c + f + w, 2c + f)$ where c, f, and w are the numbers of chaining, free, and waiting processes respectively. We show that F decreases (in the lexicographic order) with every step; first observe that a matched or dead process remains matched or dead forever, so $c + f + w$ never increases.

$\mathbf{M}_p$: This action applies when p is free and its neighbor q is waiting, and causes both to become matched, decreasing $c + f + w$ by 2. (The sum may decrease even further if some neighbors of p and q become dead.)

$\mathbf{S}_p$: This action is applicable when p is free, and causes p to become waiting, thus decreasing $2c + f$ by 1. No waiting process becomes free or chaining, because the action is applicable only if no process waits for p, and no free process becomes chaining.

$\mathbf{U}_p$: This action is applicable when p is chaining, and causes p to become free (if there are unmatched neighbors) or dead (if all neighbors are matched), thus decreasing $2c + f$ by at least 1. Chaining neighbors of p may become waiting, thus further decreasing c.

As $c + f + w$ is bounded by N and $2c + f$ by $2N$, the number of different values of F is at most $(N + 1)(2N + 1)$, so each execution terminates in $2N^2 + 3N$ steps. $\square$

Algorithm 17.3 is now easily seen to stabilize to ψ, by taking all configurations satisfying ψ as the legitimate ones.

17.2.3 Election and Spanning-tree Construction

Afek, Kutten, and Yung [AKY90] proposed a stabilizing algorithm for computing a spanning tree on a network, in which the largest process is the root. We describe the algorithm for the read-all state model (although the algorithm can also be used for the read-one model) and assume that the network is connected. In this subsection we shall use capitalized initials for process variables, and lower-case initials for predicates.

Process p maintains the variables $Root_p$, Par_p, and Dis_p to describe the tree structure; we introduce the following predicates.

$$root(p) \equiv Root_p = p \land Dis_p = 0$$
$$child(p, q) \equiv Root_p = Root_q > p \land Par_p = q \in Neigh_p \land Dis_p = Dis_q + 1$$
$$tree(p) \equiv root(p) \lor \exists q : child(p, q)$$
$$lmax(p) \equiv \forall q \in Neigh_p : Root_p \geq Root_q$$
$$sat(p) \equiv tree(p) \land lmax(p)$$

The intended postcondition of the algorithm is ψ, defined by $\forall p : sat(p)$.

Lemma 17.14 ψ *implies that the edges* $\{(p, q) : child(p, q)\}$ *form a spanning tree with the largest process as the root.*

Proof. As $lmax(p)$ is satisfied for all p and the network is connected, all processes have the same value of $Root$. The process p_0 with minimal value of Dis does not have a neighbor q with $Dis_p = Dis_q + 1$, so $root(p_0)$ holds and the common value of the $Root$ variables is p_0. But then, for all $p \neq p_0$, $child(p)$ holds, and, because $child(p, q) \Rightarrow (Dis_p > Dis_q)$, the $child$-relation is acyclic. The result follows. □

Description of the algorithm. In order to establish ψ, process p with $sat(p)$ true never changes those of its variables that describe the tree structure (see Algorithm 17.4). Process p with $sat(p)$ false attempts to establish $sat(p)$ by becoming a child of its neighbor with the highest value of $Root$ (action $\mathbf{J}_p$).

Call the value of $Root_q$ a *false root* if there is no process with that identity in the network; false roots may exist initially but are not created during execution. A main problem in the design of the algorithm is to prevent processes from becoming the child of a process with a false root infinitely often. To this end, joining q's tree by p is done in three steps. First, p becomes a root (action $\mathbf{B}_p$), then asks for join permission (action $\mathbf{A}_p$), and finally joins when q grants the permission (action $\mathbf{J}_p$).

The remaining four actions ($\mathbf{C}_p$, $\mathbf{F}_p$, $\mathbf{G}_p$, and $\mathbf{R}_p$) implement the request/reply mechanism and are only executed by processes p with $sat(p)$. Variable Req_p contains the process whose join request p is currently processing; $From_p$ is the neighbor from whom p read the request; To_p is the neighbor to which p forwards it; and Dir_p (values Ask and $Grant$) indicates

var $Root_p$, Par_p, Dis_p ;   (* Describe tree structure *)
    Req_p, $From_p$, To_p, Dir_p ;   (* Request forwarding *)

$\mathbf{B}_p$: (* Become root *)
    $\{ \neg tree(p) \}$
    $Root_p := p$; $Dis_p := 0$;
    $Req_p := p$; $To_p := q$; $Dir_p := Ask$

$\mathbf{A}_p$: (* Ask permission to join *)
    $\{ tree(p) \wedge \neg lmax(p) \}$
    Select $q \in Neigh_p$ with maximal value of $Root_q$;
    $Req_p := p$; $From_p := p$; $To_p := q$; $Dir_p := Ask$

$\mathbf{J}_p$: (* Join tree *)
    $\{ tree(p) \wedge \neg lmax(p) \wedge grant(To_p, p) \}$
    $Par_p := q$; $Root_p := Root_q$; $Dis_p := Dis_q + 1$;
    $Req_p := From_p := To_p := Dir_p := udef$

$\mathbf{C}_p$: (* Clear request variables *)
    $\{ sat(p) \wedge \neg \exists q : forw(p, q) \wedge \neg idle(p) \}$
    $Req_p := From_p := To_p := Dir_p := udef$

$\mathbf{F}_p$: (* Forward request *)
    $\{ sat(p) \wedge idle(p) \wedge asks(q, p) \}$
    $Req_p := Req_q$; $From_p := q$; $To_p := Par_p$

$\mathbf{G}_p$: (* Grant join request *)
    $\{ sat(p) \wedge root(p) \wedge forw(p, q) \wedge Dir_p = Ask \}$
    $Dir_p := Grant$

$\mathbf{R}_p$: (* Relay grant *)
    $\{ sat(p) \wedge grant(Par_p, p) \wedge Dir_p = Ask \}$
    $Dir_p := Grant$

Algorithm 17.4 THE SPANNING-TREE ALGORITHM.

---

whether the request was granted. We define the following predicates.

$$idle(p) \quad \equiv Req_p = From_p = To_p = Dir_p = udef$$
$$asks(p, q) \quad \equiv ((root(p) \wedge Req_p = p) \vee child(p, q))$$
$$\wedge To_p = q \wedge Dir_p = Ask)$$
$$forw(p, q) \equiv Req_p = Req_q \wedge From_p = q \wedge To_q = p \wedge To_p = Par_p$$
$$grant(p, q) \equiv forw(p, q) \wedge Dir_p = Grant$$

Process p clears the variables for request processing (action $\mathbf{C}_p$) if it is not currently processing a request and the variables are not undefined already. Then, if p is idle but has a neighbor q with a request for p (a root that wants to join, or a child of p forwarding a request), process p may start forwarding the request (action $\mathbf{F}_p$). If p is a root and forwards a request, it will grant it (action $\mathbf{G}_p$), and if p forwards the request to its parent and the parent grants it, then p relays the grant (action $\mathbf{R}_p$).

Correctness of the algorithm. Afek *et al.* [AKY90] argue the correctness of the algorithm by showing properties of executions using behavioral reasoning.

The request/reply mechanism ensures that a process can join a tree with a false root only finitely often, because the non-existent root does not grant requests, and only finitely many false grants exist initially. Then, no *Root* variable contains a false root forever; the process with the smallest value of *Dis* containing a false root does not satisfy *tree*, and will reset *Root* to its own identity. It follows that eventually there are no false roots, and also that eventually the process with highest identity will be a root, for this is the only way to satisfy *sat* in the absence of higher *Root* values.

A node that does not belong to the tree rooted at the highest node, but does have a neighbor in that tree, does not satisfy the *sat* predicate and will attempt to join, while nodes in the tree never leave it. As all incorrect requests eventually disappear from the tree, addition of nodes to the tree continues until the tree spans the whole network.

17.3 Methodology for Stabilization

The requirement of stabilization complicates the design of distributed algorithms considerably, but some general paradigms can be used. In Subsection 17.3.1 we discuss how stabilizing computations can be "sequentially composed", even though the stabilization of the first cannot be detected. We focus on Herman's work [Her91], but the techniques have been known and used before that. In Subsection 17.3.2 it is demonstrated that stabilizing algorithms exist for all problems that can be expressed as finding a "minimal path" in a suitably chosen measure.

17.3.1 Protocol Composition

In many cases an algorithm for achieving a desired postcondition ψ is composed of two stages; the first achieves a postcondition θ, while the second has precondition θ and achieves ψ. Examples of composed algorithms are numerous and include some algorithms treated in this book.

(1) *Routing.* Most routing methods start by computing routing tables in every node, after which packets are forwarded using these tables.

(2) *Election.* The reason for electing a leader in a network is usually the desire to subsequently execute a centralized algorithm in the network.

(3) *Deadlock detection.* The global-marking algorithm for deadlock detection (Algorithm 10.8) first computes a snapshot of the basic computation and subsequently analyses the configuration obtained.

(4) *Graph coloring.* A six-coloring of a planar graph can be computed by finding a suitable acyclic orientation of the graph (cf. Definition 5.12), after which the nodes can be colored in an order consistent with this orientation.

The natural way to guide the control switch between two classical distributed algorithms is by means of a termination-detection protocol. Such a protocol (see Chapter 8) is superimposed on the first phase, and when it indicates that the first stage is completed (i.e., θ has been established), the processes start executing the second stage. A similar method cannot be used when the designed algorithm must be stabilizing, because it is not possible to observe (in a stabilizing manner) the termination of the first stage.

Fortunately, a similar composition of stabilizing algorithms is much simpler: execution of the second stage may begin at any time, even when the first stage is not yet complete. If a classical algorithm (for the second stage) is started before its precondition has been established, it may reach a faulty state from which it does not recover; this necessitates detecting the termination of the first stage. However, if the second stage is stabilizing, it eventually establishes its postcondition in spite of erroneous steps made before its precondition has reached the value *true*.

The collateral-composition rule. These observations were formalized by Herman [Her91] in the definition of an algorithm-composition operator. Assume a program is given as a collection of variables and atomic steps on those variables.

Definition 17.15 *Let S_1 and S_2 be programs such that no variable that is written by S_2 occurs in S_1. The collateral composition of S_1 and S_2, denoted $S_1 \rhd S_2$, is the program that has all the variables and all the actions of both S_1 and S_2.*

In this definition, S_1 is the program implementing the first stage of the computation, and S_2 the program for the second stage. The restriction on

S_1 and S_2 means that no results of S_2 are used by S_1, that is, there is no "feedback" from S_2 to S_1; the variables of S_1 occur as constants in S_2.

Now let θ be a predicate over the variables of S_1, and ψ a predicate over the variables of S_2. In the composite algorithm, θ will be established by S_1 and subsequently ψ will be established by S_2; two technical conditions must be kept in mind. First, the execution of the composition must be *fair* w.r.t. both programs; this excludes executions in which all steps occur in one of the stages, preventing progress in the other stage.

Definition 17.16 *An execution of $S_1 \boxminus S_2$ is fair w.r.t. S_i if it contains infinitely many steps of S_i, or contains an infinite suffix in which no step of S_i is enabled.*

Second, we assume that the variables read by S_2 are not changed by S_1 when condition θ has been established. This excludes some (far-fetched) situations where S_1 prevents progress in S_2 by presenting with it different settings of the variables, all satisfying θ.

Theorem 17.17 *If the following four conditions hold:*

(1) *program S_1 stabilizes to θ;*
(2) *program S_2 stabilizes to ψ if θ holds;*
(3) *program S_1 does not change variables read by S_2 once θ holds; and*
(4) *all executions are fair w.r.t. both S_1 and S_2,*

then $S_1 \boxminus S_2$ stabilizes to ψ.

Proof. We establish the result by reasoning involving the execution sequences of $S_1 \boxminus S_2$. For a configuration γ of $S_1 \boxminus S_2$, let $\gamma^{(i)}$ denote the projection of γ onto the variables of S_i. For an execution $E = (\gamma_0, \gamma_1, \ldots)$ of $S_1 \boxminus S_2$, let $E^{(i)}$ denote the sequence $(\gamma_0^{(i)}, \gamma_1^{(i)}, \ldots)$ from which duplicates have been eliminated.

Let $E = (\gamma_0, \gamma_1, \ldots)$ be an execution of $S_1 \boxminus S_2$, and consider the sequence $E^{(1)}$. As S_2 does not write the variables of S_1, all changes in $\gamma^{(1)}$ are by steps of S_1, which implies that $E^{(1)}$ is an execution of S_1. The fairness of E w.r.t. S_1 implies that if $E^{(1)}$ is finite, the last configuration is terminal for S_1. Because S_1 stabilizes to θ, it follows that θ is established, i.e., that there is an i such that $\theta(\gamma_j)$ is true for every $j \geq i$.

We next consider the suffix E_i of E starting in γ_i, i.e., the sequence $(\gamma_i, \gamma_{i+1}, \ldots)$. In this suffix θ is true for every configuration, which implies (by the third assumption in the theorem) that no variable read by S_2 is changed by S_1. Hence, the sequence $(\gamma_i^{(2)}, \gamma_{i+1}^{(2)}, \ldots)$ is an execution of S_2

that, if finite, ends in a terminal configuration of S_2. Because S_2 stabilizes to ψ if θ holds, it follows that ψ is established and remains true.   □

If the stabilization of S_1 and S_2 is proved by providing adequate norm functions f_1 and f_2 (with ranges W_1 and W_2 respectively), a norm function for $S_1 \boxminus S_2$ can be given. Define the function $f(\gamma) = (f_1(\gamma^{(1)}), f_2(\gamma^{(2)}))$. When every step of S_1 decreases f_1, and a step of S_2 decreases f_2 and leaves f_1 unchanged, f decreases in the lexicographic order with every step of $S_1 \boxminus S_2$. However, if one of the programs establishes its postcondition without terminating (such as, e.g., the ring orientation program), the fairness condition is still needed to guarantee progress in both programs; see [Fra86] for a discussion of fairness issues.

Application: Six-coloring of planar graphs. As an application of the principle of protocol composition we present an algorithm that stabilizes to a six-coloring of a planar graph. Assume process p has a variable c_p, with values in $\{1, 2, 3, 4, 5, 6\}$; the graph is six-colored if neighbors are colored differently, i.e., if the predicate ψ, defined by

$$\psi \equiv (\forall pq \in E : c_p \neq c_q),$$

is true. The development of the algorithm closely follows the proof that such a coloring exists, which is based on the following fact.

Fact 17.18 *A planar graph has at least one node with degree five or less.*

Lemma 17.19 *A planar graph has an acyclic orientation in which every node has an out-degree of at most five.*

Proof. This is by induction on the number of nodes; the single-node case is trivial, so consider a graph with two or more nodes. There is at least one node, say v, with degree five or less. The graph $G - \{v\}$ is planar and has one node less, hence by induction it has an acyclic orientation in which every node has an out-degree of at most five. In the orientation of G, all edges of $G - \{v\}$ are directed as in this orientation, and the edges incident to v are directed away from v. Clearly, the resulting orientation is acyclic and no node has more than five outgoing edges.   □

Theorem 17.20 (Six-color theorem) *Planar graphs are six-colorable.*

Proof. Let G be a planar graph; consider an acyclic orientation of G in which no node has more than five outgoing edges. Because the orientation is acyclic, the nodes can be numbered v_1 through v_n such that if there is an edge directed from v_j to v_i, then $j > i$. Color the nodes in the order v_1 through v_n; the property of the numbering implies that before node v only out-neighbors of v are colored. This, and the property of the orientation, now imply that at most five neighbors of v are colored before v, hence v can be colored differently from all (already colored) neighbors. $\qquad\square$

The proof of the six-color theorem suggests the design of an algorithm for computing a six-coloring; the first stage computes an acyclic orientation as indicated in Lemma 17.19, and the second stage colors the nodes in an order consistent with the orientation. To represent an acyclic orientation, process p is given an integer variable x_p, and we define edge pq to be directed from p to q, denoted $\vec{pq}$, if

$$x_p < x_q \ \vee \ (x_p = x_q \wedge p < q).$$

Clearly, each edge is directed in exactly one way (i.e., either $\vec{pq}$ or $\vec{qp}$ holds), and the orientation is acyclic. Let $out(p)$ denote the number of outgoing edges of p, i.e.,

$$out(p) = \#\{q \in Neigh_p : \vec{pq}\}.$$

The desired postcondition of the first phase is θ, defined by

$$\theta \equiv (\forall p : \ out(p) \leq 5).$$

Program S_1, for establishing θ, consists of one operation for each process, directing all edges of p towards p if p has more than five outgoing edges:

D_p: $\{ \ out(p) > 5 \ \}$
$\qquad x_p := \max\{x_q : q \in Neigh_p\} + 1$

Theorem 17.21 *Program S_1 stabilizes to θ, and if θ holds then the value of x_p remains constant.*

Proof. A configuration is terminal if and only if θ is true; hence, if the program halts θ is established, and if θ is established the variables x_p remain constant.

To prove the termination of S_1 we use a "reference" acyclic orientation as in Lemma 17.19; this reference orientation need not be, however, the orientation computed by S_1. Lemma 17.19 implies the existence of an enumeration $v_1, v_2, \dots$ of the nodes such that every node has at most five neighbors with a higher index. An edge $v_i v_j$ is called *wrong* if it is oriented as $\vec{v_i v_j}$ while $i > j$; let $f(\gamma)$ be the list $(n_1, n_2, \dots)$, where n_i is the number of wrong edges incident to v_i. Each application of action D_p decreases f (in the lexicographic order); consider its application in node v_j, whose out-neighbor

var x_p : integer ;
$\quad c_p$: $\{1, 2, 3, 4, 5, 6\}$;

$\quad p\vec{q} \equiv x_p < x_q \;\vee\; (x_p = x_q \wedge p < q)$;
$\quad out(p) \equiv \#\{q \in Neigh_p : p\vec{q}\}$;

$\mathbf{D}_p$: $\{\; out(p) > 5 \;\}$
$\quad x_p := \max\{x_q : q \in Neigh_p\} + 1$

$\mathbf{C}_p$: $\{\; (\exists q : p\vec{q} \wedge c_p = c_q) \wedge (\forall r \text{ s.t. } p\vec{r} : c_r \neq b) \;\}$
$\quad c_p := b$

Algorithm 17.5 SIX-COLORING ALGORITHM FOR PLANAR GRAPHS.

---

with the smallest index is v_i. As v_j has at least six out-neighbors but has at most five neighbors with higher index, $i < j$ so the edge $v_i v_j$ was wrong but ceases to be so, thus decrementing n_i, while no n_k is affected for $k < i$. $\quad\square$

Program S_2, for establishing ψ, also consists of a single operation for each process, in which p adopts a color b different from its successors if c_p equals one of those colors and an unused color exists:

$\mathbf{C}_p$: $\{\; (\exists q : p\vec{q} \wedge c_p = c_q) \wedge (\forall r \text{ s.t. } p\vec{r} : c_r \neq b) \;\}$
$\quad c_p := b$

Theorem 17.22 *Program S_2 terminates, and if θ is true the final configuration satisfies ψ.*

Proof. To show termination, use that the edges are directed as in an acyclic orientation, hence there exists an enumeration of the nodes $v_1, v_2, \ldots$ such that each node has only successors with a smaller index. Define $g(\gamma) = (m_1, m_2, \ldots)$, where m_i is 0 if c_i is different from the colors of each of v_i's successors and 1 otherwise. The application of action $\mathbf{C}_p$ by node v_i changes m_i from 1 to 0, and may only change m_j from 0 to 1 for $j > i$, hence the value of g decreases in the lexicographic order.

Finally, assume θ holds and consider a configuration in which no $\mathbf{C}_p$ action is applicable. Process p has at most five successors, hence there is a color $b \in \{1, 2, 3, 4, 5, 6\}$ not used by any of its successors. As the guard of $\mathbf{C}_p$ is false, it follows that c_p differs from the color of every successor.

Finally, for every edge qr, either r is a successor of q or q is a successor of r, which now implies that $c_r \neq c_q$. $\quad\square$

The collateral composition of S_1 and S_2 is given as Algorithm 17.5.

Theorem 17.23 *Algorithm 17.5 stabilizes to ψ.*

Proof. The collateral composition can be formed because the variables written by S_2 (the c_p) do not occur in S_1. It was demonstrated above that S_1 stabilizes to θ and does not change the x_p after establishing it (Theorem 17.21) and that S_2 stabilizes to ψ if θ holds (Theorem 17.22).

In order to conclude that $S_1 \boxminus S_2$ stabilizes to ψ by Theorem 17.17 it remains to show that the composition is fair. By Theorem 17.22, there are only finitely many steps of S_2 between every two steps of S_1, which shows fairness w.r.t. S_1. By Theorem 17.21 S_1 terminates, which shows fairness w.r.t. S_2. $\qquad\square$

17.3.2 Computing Minimal Paths

This subsection presents a stabilizing algorithm for a class of problems that can be formulated as finding a minimal path in a suitably chosen cost function on paths. Examples include not only the (straightforward) computation of routing tables, but also depth-first search trees and, more surprisingly, election (see Exercise 17.12). We shall first present the minimal-path problem in an algebraic setting and present the Update algorithm (Algorithm 17.6), which stabilizes to minimal paths; applications are given at the end of this subsection.

Properties of the cost function and minimal paths. Assume a function D from paths to a totally ordered domain U is given; for a path π, the value $D(\pi)$ will be referred to as the *cost* of π. The cost of the *empty path* (p) of length 0 from p to p, is denoted c_p and assumed to be known to p. We consider cost functions for which the cost of a path can be computed incrementally, which means that the cost of non-empty paths can be computed as

$$D(p_0, \ldots, p_k, p_{k+1}) = f_{p_{k+1}p_k}(D(p_0, \ldots, p_k)).$$

Here f_{pq} is a function $f_{pq} : U \longrightarrow U$, called the *edge function*, given for each edge pq. The cost of a path $\pi = (p_0, p_1, \ldots, p_{k-1}, p_k)$ can now be computed incrementally as $f_{p_k p_{k-1}}(\ldots(f_{p_1 p_0}(c_{p_0}))\ldots)$. Denoting as $f_\pi(x)$ the value $f_{p_k p_{k-1}}(\ldots(f_{p_1 p_0}(x))\ldots)$, we can write $D(\pi)$ as $f_\pi(c_{p_0})$. The cost function (and edge functions) are presumed to satisfy the following axioms.

(1) **Monotonicity.** For every edge pq and $x \in U$, if π is a simple path to q not containing p, then $D(\pi) < x \Rightarrow f_{pq}(D(\pi)) \leq f_{pq}(x)$.
(2) **Cycle-increase.** If π is a cycle, $f_\pi(x) > x$ for all $x \in U$.

(3) **Length-increase.** There exists a number B such that for each path ρ of length B or more, each $x \in U$, and each simple path π of length $N - 1$ or less, $f_\rho(x) > D(\pi)$.

The *minimal-path problem* is to compute, for each p, the minimal cost of any path ending in p, and its predecessor q in a path of minimal cost (*nil* if the minimal path is empty). The cost of a minimal path is denoted $\kappa(p)$ and the predecessor is denoted $\phi(p)$. The existence and an important property of minimal paths are expressed in the following theorem.

Theorem 17.24

(1) *For every p there exists a simple path $\pi(p)$ ending in p, such that all paths ending in p have a cost of at least $D(\pi(p))$.*

(2) *There exists a spanning forest (called a minimal-path forest) such that for every p the (unique) path from a root to p has the cost $D(\pi(p))$.*

Proof. For (1): as there are only finitely many simple paths ending in p, we can choose $\pi(p)$ as a minimal simple path ending in p. By the choice of $\pi(p)$, all simple paths ending in p then have a cost of at least $D(\pi(p))$. The cost of a path containing a cycle is (by cycle-increase and monotonicity) higher than the cost of the simple path obtained by removing cycles, hence also bounded by $D(\pi(p))$. This shows that $\pi(p)$ witnesses the first part of the theorem.

For (2): as minimal paths need not be unique, the second part of the theorem requires some care; the graph obtained by taking all edges occurring in minimal paths need not be a forest. Like the optimal sink trees considered in Theorem 4.2, the minimal-path forest is not unique, but it is possible to construct such a forest, as follows.

Choose for every node p a father $\phi(p)$ as follows. If the empty path (p) is optimal, $\phi(p) = nil$, otherwise $\phi(p)$ is a neighbor q such that a minimal path to p with penultimate node q exists. Consider the edges $p, \phi(p)$ for which $\phi(p) \neq nil$.

By monotonicity, for every p with $\phi(p) \neq nil$, $\kappa(p) \geq f_{p\phi(p)}(\kappa(\phi(p)))$. Consequently, if C is a cycle (from p to p) in the formed graph, then $\kappa(p) \geq f_C(\kappa(p))$, which contradicts the cycle-increase property, hence the chosen edges define a forest.

Induction from the roots shows the desired property of this forest. $\square$

Observe that the length-increase property is not needed in the proof; it is only necessary to show that erroneous information in the initial configura-

var K_p : D ;
    L_p : $Neigh_p \cup \{nil\}$;

$\mathbf{C}_p$: $K_p := \min(c_p, \min\{f_{pq}(K_q) : q \in Neigh_p\})$;
    if $K_p = c_p$ **then** $L_p := nil$
        else $L_p := q$ s.t. $K_p = f_{pq}(K_q)$

Algorithm 17.6 THE UPDATE ALGORITHM FOR MINIMAL PATHS.

---

tion is eventually removed in a stabilizing algorithm for computing minimal paths.

The required postcondition of an algorithm for the minimal-path problem can now be stated:

$$\psi \equiv (\forall p : K_p = \kappa(p) \land L_p = \phi(p)).$$

A classical (non-stabilizing) algorithm for establishing ψ consists of a single operation on each edge, called *pushing* the edge:

$\mathbf{P}_{pq}$: $\{ f_{pq}(K_q) < K_p \}$
    $K_p := f_{pq}(K_q)$; $L_p := q$

The variable K_p is initialized to c_p. The assertion $K_p \geq \kappa(p)$ can be shown to be invariant. To show liveness we must assume that pushing is fair w.r.t. every edge, that is, in an infinite execution each edge is pushed infinitely often. That $K_p \leq \kappa(p)$ is established is then shown by induction of the nodes in a minimal path leading to p; the reader may compare the Chandy–Misra algorithm for minimal-path computation (Algorithm 4.7).

The Update algorithm. In order to establish ψ in a stabilizing way the information about existing paths may flow through the graph by pushing it through edges. However, it is also necessary to remove from the system erroneous information present in the initial configuration; that is, values of K_p for which no corresponding path to p exists. This is done by moving this information via longer and longer paths such that, by the length-increase property, the erroneous information will eventually be rejected in favor of information concerning an existing path.

The Update algorithm consists of a single operation for each node, in which it computes the smallest cost of the empty path and paths whose cost is stored at its neighbors; see Algorithm 17.6. In the analysis of the algorithm we shall assume, as we did for the pushing algorithm, that execution is fair w.r.t. every process; that is, in every execution each process computes infinitely often.

Theorem 17.25 *The Update algorithm stabilizes to minimal paths.*

Proof. As $\mathbf{C}_p$ is always enabled, each execution is infinite; the fairness assumption allows us to partition an execution in *rounds* as follows. Round 1 ends when every process has computed at least once. Round $i + 1$ ends when every process has computed at least once after the end of round i.

It will first be shown that eventually K_p is a lower bound for $\kappa(p)$. Define $\kappa_i(p)$ as the minimal cost of a path of length i or less to p; we claim that at any time from the end of round i, $K_p \leq \kappa_{i-1}(p)$. We establish this claim by induction on i.

Case $i = 1$: The empty path, with cost c_p, is the only path to p of length 0, and it can be seen from the code that after the first $\mathbf{C}_p$ step, $K_p \leq c_p$.

Case $i + 1$: Let π be a minimal path to p of length at most i; if π has length 0, $K_p \leq D(\pi)$ after every step by p, hence also after the end of round $i + 1$. Assume π is a non-empty path, namely the concatenation of path ρ and edge qp; the length of ρ is at most $i - 1$. By induction, $K_q \leq D(\rho)$ after the end of round i. It follows that after every step by p taken after the end of round i, $K_p \leq f_{pq}(D(\rho)) = D(\pi)$. At the end of round $i + 1$, p has taken at least one such step, showing that $K_p \leq D(\pi)$ from the end of that round.

As a minimal path contains no cycles, its length is bounded by $N - 1$, which implies $\kappa(p) = \kappa_{N-1}(p)$, hence $K_p \leq \kappa(p)$ from the end of round N.

To show that eventually K_p is an upper bound for $\kappa(p)$, we shall show that after i rounds the value K_p corresponds to an existing path or to initial information that has traveled via at least i hops. Denote the initial value of K_r by K_r^*. We claim that if $K_p = K$ then there exists a path π to p with $D(\pi) = K$ or there exists a path ρ from r to p such that $K = f_\rho(K_r^*)$. Moreover, if K is computed in round i, the length of ρ is at least i. The claim is established by induction on the steps in an execution.

Base case: Initially, $K_r = f_{(r)}(K_r^*)$, where (r) is a path of length 0; of course K_r may or may not correspond to an existing path.

Induction step: Consider the value K computed in a step by p. If $K = c_p$ it is the cost of an existing path (of length 0) to p, and we are done. Otherwise, $K = f_{pq}(K_q)$; by induction, K_q is (1) the cost of a path π to q, or (2) there exists a path ρ from r to q such that $K_q = f_\rho(K_r^*)$. In the first case, $\pi \cdot qp$ is an existing path with cost $f_{pq}(D(\pi)) = f_{pq}(K_q) = K$, and we are done. In the second case, $K = f_{pq}(f_\rho(K_r^*)) = f_{(\rho \cdot qp)}(K_r^*)$.

Moreover, if K is computed in round i then K_q was computed in round $i-1$ or later, which implies by induction that the length of ρ is at least $i-1$, so that the length of $\rho \cdot qp$ is at least i.

The result is now an application of the length-increase axiom; at the end of round B, $f_\rho(K_r^*)$ exceeds the cost of any existing simple path, which shows that K_p is bounded from below by the cost of some existing path to p. Consequently, at the end of round B, $K_p = \kappa(p)$ for every p. It is easily verified that the value of L_p satisfies the requirement set for $\phi(p)$, which implies that the edges (p, L_p) define a minimal-path forest. $\qquad\square$

The length-increase property can be enforced on path cost functions not satisfying it if the network size is known. The cost of paths is modified to include the length as well; when comparing costs, a path of length N or more is always larger than a path of length $N-1$ or less. To describe this modification formally, let a cost function D be given. Define the cost function D' by $D'(\pi) = (D(\pi), |\pi|)$; the cost of an empty path for p is given by $c_p' = (c_p, 0)$ and the edge functions are given by $f'pq(C, k) = (f_{pq}(C), k+1)$. Costs of paths are compared as follows

$$(C_1, k_1) <' (C_2, k_2) \iff (k_1 < N \wedge k_2 \geq N) \vee (C_1 < C_2).$$

All simple paths are ordered by D' exactly as they are by D, which shows that monotonicity is preserved, and the modification also preserves the cycle-increase property. As paths of length at least N have a cost larger than paths of length smaller than N, the length-increase property is satisfied.

Application: routing. A straightforward application of the Update algorithm is found in the computation of routing tables; as with the Netchange algorithm, the computation is done separately per destination. Fix a destination v and define $D(\pi)$ to be the weight of π (i.e., the sum of the weights of the edges in π) if π starts in v, and ∞ otherwise. This function can be computed incrementally by setting c_p to 0 if $p = v$ and to ∞ otherwise, and by setting $f_{pq}(C) = C + \omega_{pq}$ (where ω_{pq} is the weight of edge pq).

Monotonicity follows from the additional nature of the edge functions, and cycle-increase from the assumption that cycles in the network have positive cost. To show the length-increase property, note that there are only finitely many simple cycles and let δ be the smallest weight of a simple cycle and ω be the largest weight of any edge. A path of length $N-1$ or less has weight less than $N\omega$, while a path of length $B = N(N\omega)/\delta$ contains more than $(N\omega)/\delta$ simple cycles, and has weight more than $N\omega$.

Consequently, the distance to v (and a preferred neighbor for v, which is the first neighbor on a shortest path to v) can be computed with the Update algorithm. To build a complete routing table the algorithm is executed for each destination in parallel.

Application: depth-first search tree. It will now be shown that selecting the lexicographically smallest simple path to each process defines a depth-first search spanning tree, whose root is the smallest process in the network. Consequently, a depth-first search tree can be constructed with the Update algorithm.

Define as the cost of π the list of nodes that occur in the path, i.e., $c_p = (p)$ and $f_{pq}(\sigma) = \sigma.p$. Comparison is lexicographic, but simple paths are always smaller than paths containing cycles:

$$\sigma < \tau \iff (\ \sigma \text{ is simple and } \tau \text{ is not}) \lor (\sigma <_L \tau).$$

Monotonicity is implied by the properties of lexicographic order, and cycle-increase holds because paths containing cycles are larger than simple paths. Length-increase holds because paths of length N or more contain cycles, which makes them larger than simple paths. Consequently, the Update algorithm can compute the smallest simple path to every node. It remains to analyze the properties of the resulting minimal-path forest.

First, the forest consists of a single tree, rooted at the smallest node; call this smallest node r. Indeed, for every node p there exists a simple path from r to p; a simple path from r is smaller than a path from any other node to p, hence the minimal path to p starts in r.

Second, for neighbors p and q, either $\kappa_p \lhd q$ or $\kappa_q \lhd p$ ($\lhd$ denotes the prefix relation). Indeed, consider $\kappa(p)$ and $\kappa(q)$ and assume, w.l.o.g., that $\kappa(p) < \kappa(q)$; as the minimal paths are simple, $\kappa(p) <_L \kappa(q)$ follows. It is also implied that q does not occur in $\kappa(p)$; otherwise, its prefix up to q is a path to q, and lexicographically smaller than $\kappa(q)$, which contradicts the definition of $\kappa(q)$. But then, $\kappa(p).q$ is the cost of a *simple* path to q, which implies that $\kappa(q) \leq_L \kappa(p).q$. So $\kappa(p) <_L \kappa(q) \leq_L \kappa(p).q$, which implies that $\kappa(p) \lhd \kappa(q)$, or, equivalently, p is an ancestor of q in the minimal-path tree.

These two properties, namely

(1) that the forest consists of a single tree, and
(2) that for neighbors p and q, either $\kappa_p \lhd q$ or $\kappa_q \lhd p$,

imply that the minimal-path forest computed by the Update algorithm is a depth-first search tree. This application of the Update algorithm was proposed by Herman [Her91], who also extended the algorithm in such a way as to compute separating nodes of the network (nodes whose removal disconnects the network).

17.3.3 Conclusion and Discussion

In this section we have studied two strategies that are useful in the design of stabilizing algorithms. Collateral composition can be used to design algorithms consisting of two (or more) temporally sequential phases, and the Update algorithm can be used to solve any problem that can be formulated as finding a minimal path to every process.

There exist methods for automatically transforming arbitrary algorithms into stabilizing ones (satisfying the same specification). To achieve this goal, Katz and Perry [KP93] have proposed the following mechanism. Concurrently with the execution of a given classical algorithm P the system repeatedly computes a snapshot of the global state of P and verifies whether the constructed configuration is a reachable one for P. If this is not the case, a reset protocol will re-initialize the system to an initial configuration of P. However, implementation of this idea faces many technical problems, owing to the need for stabilizing algorithms for snapshot computation and reset.

Exercises to Chapter 17
Section 17.1

Exercise 17.1 *Prove Lemma 17.4.*

Exercise 17.2 *Prove that Dijkstra's token ring reaches a legitimate configuration in* $O(N^2)$ *steps. Shorten the analysis by giving a single norm function, quadratically bounded in N, that decreases with every step of the algorithm.*

Exercise 17.3 *Prove that Dijkstra's token ring stabilizes already if $K \geq N$ (rather than $K > N$ as assumed in the text). (See [Hoe99].)*

Section 17.2

Exercise 17.4 *Modify the ring-orientation algorithm (Algorithm 17.1) so that it will terminate after establishing its postcondition.*

Project 17.5 *Design a stabilizing algorithm to orient a torus, preferably, so that the algorithm terminates.*

Exercise 17.6 *Show that the maximal-matching algorithm can be implemented* uniformly *in the link-register read-all model.*

Exercise 17.7 *Show that the maximal-matching algorithm stabilizes in $N^2 + O(N)$ steps and show that there is an $\Omega(N^2)$ lower bound on the (worst-case) number of steps).*

Exercise 17.8 *Design a stabilizing algorithm to construct a maximal independent set and compute the maximal number of steps before stabilization.*

Project 17.9 *Give a norm function that proves the termination of Algorithm 17.4.*

Section 17.3

Project 17.10 *Prove that outerplanar graphs are three-colorable. Design a stabilizing algorithm that computes a three-coloring of an outerplanar graph.*

Project 17.11 *Design a stabilizing algorithm that computes a five-coloring of a planar graph. (See [McH90] or another text on graph algorithms.)*

Exercise 17.12 *Show that the Update algorithm can be used for election and computation of a breadth-first search spanning tree by giving an appropriate path-cost function.*

Exercise 17.13 *Give a stabilizing algorithm for computing the network size.*

Exercise 17.14 *Show how to compute the depth of a tree with the Update algorithm.*

Part Four

Appendices

A

Pseudocode Conventions

Rather than presenting the algorithms in this book as programs written in an existing programming language, a pseudocode is used for the formal description of algorithms. Pseudocode is concise and "user-friendly", where a real program is often obscured by details concerning a rigid syntax.

Pascal-like pseudocode. The pseudocode used in this book very much resembles the language Pascal. An algorithm is usually given as the local algorithm of a process of the system, whose name is used as a subscript to the variables of the program. Process names can be used as array indices, and set variables are used. The variable $Neigh_p$ is the set of processes to which p is connected (the *neighbors* of p).

Assignment ("$a := expression$"), conditional statement ("**if** *condition* **then** *statement*", with an optional "**else** *statement*" part), and loop ("**while** *condition* **do** *statement*") are used with the same meaning as in Pascal. The **forall** statement has the form "**forall** $x \in X$ **do** *statement*", where x is a formal parameter and X a set, and means that *statement* will be executed for each element x of X in turn. The order in which the elements get their turn is not specified, but the statement is only used where the order does not matter. For example, if the number of messages received from each neighbor of p must be initialized to zero, we write

forall $q \in Neigh_p$ **do** $R_p[q] := 0$.

In all cases, instead of a single statement a semicolon-separated list of statements, enclosed between **begin** and **end**, may be used. Line breaking and indentation are formally meaningless, but are supposed to reflect the block structure of programs.

Message passing. The operations "send" and "receive" are used to describe message passing in the pseudocode. A message consists of a *message-type* and zero or more (type-specific) *data fields*. For example, assume that each process must send to its neighbors its identity (process name) and its degree (number of neighbors). To this end a message of type **info** can be used with two data fields, namely the identity and degree of the sender. This message is denoted as $\langle \mathbf{info}, a, b \rangle$.

The send operation must be given a message (its type and the value of its data fields) and a destination (which is a neighbor of the sender). The value of a data field is given as an expression that can be evaluated by the sender. To send its identity and degree to process q, process p may execute

    send $\langle \mathbf{info}, id_p, |Neigh_p| \rangle$ to q.

The shorthand "shout" is used to send a message to all neighbors, i.e., the statement "shout $\langle \mathbf{info}, id_p, |Neigh_p| \rangle$" is to be read as

    forall $q \in Neigh_p$ **do** send $\langle \mathbf{info}, id_p, |Neigh_p| \rangle$ to q.

To receive a message, its type as well as formal parameters for the data fields of the message and its sender must be specified. To receive the information regarding the identity and degree of a neighboring node, process p may execute

    receive $\langle \mathbf{info}, a, b \rangle$ from q.

This operation removes one message of type **info** from the communication system; after this operation the first and second data field and the sender of the message are available as a, b, and q. In this form, the receive operation does not specify from which neighbor a message must be received, but the sender of the received message becomes known after the operation.

A process may need to receive a message from a specific process, say q_0; in this case it uses the operation

    receive $\langle \mathbf{info}, a, b \rangle$ fromthis q_0.

Occasionally we want to express that messages of different type can be received and that afterwards the action depends on the type actually received. This is expressed (e.g., in Algorithms 7.7 and 7.9) by writing:

    receive m from q ;   (* or: fromthis q *)
    if m is $\langle \mathbf{info}, a, b \rangle$ **then** *statement* **else** *statement*

The parameter q used by p to describe a neighbor of p for the purpose of sending or receiving a message is called the *address* of the neighbor. In

var $rec_p[q]$ for each $q \in Neigh_p$: **boolean init** false ;

begin while $\#\{q : rec_p[q] \text{ is false}\} > 1$ **do**
                    begin receive $\langle \mathbf{tok} \rangle$ from q ; $rec_p[q] := true$ **end** ;
     send $\langle \mathbf{tok} \rangle$ to q_0 with $rec_p[q_0]$ is false ;
     receive $\langle \mathbf{tok} \rangle$ from q_0 ; $rec_p[q_0] := true$;
     decide
end

Algorithm A.1 CONTROL-ORIENTED NOTATION (TREE ALGORITHM).

the case of *direct addressing* the address is equal to the identity of process q; this implies that all neighbors of process q use the same address for q. In case of *indirect addressing* the address is a name local to p; the neighbors of process q may use different addresses for q in this case; see Figure 2.5.

The communication between processes can be either *asynchronous* or *synchronous* (see Section 2.1). If communication is asynchronous (which will always be assumed unless stated otherwise) a send operation can always be executed immediately. The message is stored in the communication subsystem until it is removed by the execution of a corresponding receive operation. A receive operation suspends the executing process until a message of the specified type is available to be received. If communication is synchronous, no temporary storage of the message is possible. In this case, both send and receive operations may suspend the executing process, because the execution of the send operation and the corresponding receive operation are synchronized. The sender or the receiver, whoever is the first to start the operation, is suspended until both processes are ready to execute the operation. Then the message exchange takes place and both process continue the execution of their algorithm.

Control-oriented versus event-driven notation. The overall control structure of an algorithm may be expressed in two ways, namely, explicitly in a *control-oriented* description or implicitly in an *event-driven* description of the algorithm. Both alternatives are possible for each algorithm, but in many cases one of the two descriptions is more convenient than the other.

The control-oriented notation of an algorithm consists of a declaration of its variables and a semicolon-separated list of statements enclosed between **begin** and **end**. The execution of the local algorithm consists in this case of a single execution of this statement list. The variables can be initialized

var $rec_p[q]$ for each $q \in Neigh_p$: boolean **init** false ;
   $sent_p, dec_p$: boolean **init** false ;

$\mathbf{R}_p$: { A message $\langle \mathbf{tok} \rangle$ has arrived }
   begin receive $\langle \mathbf{tok} \rangle$ from q ; $rec_p[q] := true$ **end**

$\mathbf{S}_p$: { $\#\{q : rec_p[q]$ is false$\} = 1$ and $sent_p = false$ }
   begin send $\langle \mathbf{tok} \rangle$ to q_0 with $rec_p[q_0]$ is false ;
      $sent_p := true$
   end

$\mathbf{D}_p$: { $\#\{q : rec_p[q]$ is false$\} = 0$ and $dec_p = false$ }
   begin *decide* ; $dec_p := true$ **end**

Algorithm A.2 EVENT-DRIVEN NOTATION (TREE ALGORITHM).

---

at the beginning of the statement list, but we also allow the initial values to be given with the declaration.

As an example, consider Algorithm A.1, which is a control-oriented notation of the tree algorithm (Algorithm 6.3). Because the statement list describes the entire control flow of the local algorithm, non-determinism must be explicit in the program. In Algorithm A.1 there is non-determinism in the receive statement, because no corresponding sender is specified explicitly. It is harder to express a non-deterministic choice between sending and receiving a message, but it can be done if incoming channels can be tested for the availability of a message:

if a message $\langle \mathbf{info}, a, b \rangle$ is available on channel q
   then begin receive $\langle \mathbf{info}, a, b \rangle$; ... **end**
   else begin send ... **end**

Non-determinism is more easily expressed (because it is implicit) in the event-driven notation of an algorithm. This notation consists of a declaration of variables together with the initialization of these variables, followed by a list of *actions*. Each action consists of a boolean expression (the *guard* of the action) and a statement (its *body*). An action is *enabled* (or *applicable*) when its guard evaluates to true. The action bodies can be executed arbitrarily often and in any order, with the restriction that an action is only selected for execution when it is enabled.

As an example, consider Algorithm A.2, which is an event-driven notation of the same tree algorithm. Because each statement can be selected for execution arbitrarily often (provided its guard is true), it must be explicitly programmed that the send operation and the *decide* operation are executed only once. In Algorithm A.2 this is done using the $sent_p$ and dec_p flags.

We do not make fairness assumptions regarding the execution of event-driven programs; that is, it is not required from the execution model that an action that is enabled for an infinitely long time is eventually executed. Thus, it is the responsibility of the programmer to ensure that no essential actions suffer from starvation (are never selected because other actions of the program are always selected).

B

Graphs and Networks

As the topology of a distributed system is usually modeled by a graph, some knowledge of graph theory and its terminology is useful in the study of distributed algorithms. Also, graphs are used sometimes in proofs and mathematical arguments about distributed algorithms (see, e.g., Section 8.2).

In Section B.1 some general definitions and terminology are introduced, and in Section B.2 some specific classes of graph are discussed.

B.1 Definitions and Terminology

A graph can be thought of as a collection of points (called the *nodes* of the graph) some of which are connected by lines (the *edges*); see Figure B.1. In case of directed graphs, the edges have a direction and are drawn as arrows. In case of weighted graphs, a numerical value is assigned to each edge.

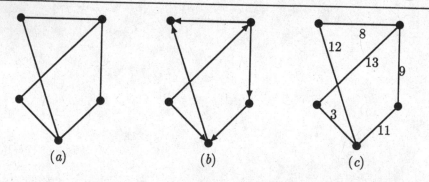

Figure B.1 GRAPHS, (*a*) UNDIRECTED, (*b*) DIRECTED, (*c*) WEIGHTED.

B.1.1 Undirected Graphs

An undirected graph G is a pair (V, E), where V is a set called the *node set* of G and E is a collection of unordered pairs from V. That is, an element of E is a pair $\{u, v\}$ with $u, v \in V$. To shorten the notation, we write $uv \in E$ instead of $\{u, v\} \in E$. Because the pair is unordered, $uv \in E$ is equivalent to $vu \in E$. The edge uv is called an *incident edge* of u (and of v). If $uv \in E$, the nodes u and v are said to be *adjacent*, or *neighbors*. The *degree* of a node is the number of edges incident to it, or, equivalently, its number of neighbors. The graph is called *regular* (of degree δ) if all nodes have the same degree (δ).

A *path* of *length* k between v_0 and v_k is a sequence $P = \langle v_0, \ldots, v_k \rangle$ of nodes such that for each $i < k$, $v_i v_{i+1} \in E$. In this path, v_0 is the begin node and v_k the end node. A *cycle* is a path of which the begin node equals the end node. A path is called *simple* if the nodes v_0 through v_k are all different. A cycle is called *simple* if the nodes v_1 through v_k are all different.

The *distance* between u and v, denoted $d(u, v)$, is the length of a shortest path between u and v. The *diameter* of G is the largest distance between any two nodes. An undirected graph is *connected* if there exists a path between each pair of nodes. An undirected graph is called *acyclic* if it contains no simple cycle of length three or more.

A graph $G' = (V', E')$ is called a *subgraph* of G if $V' \subseteq V$ and $E' \subseteq E$. G' is called a *spanning subgraph* if $V' = V$. G' is called an *induced subgraph* if $E' = \{uv \in E | u \in V' \land v \in V'\}$. A *connected component* of G is a maximal connected induced subgraph G' of G; that is, G' is a connected induced subgraph, but if V' is extended by any node, the subgraph induced by it is no longer connected. The connected components constitute a partition of the graph, consisting of a single component if and only if the graph as a whole is connected.

A graph is called a *planar graph* if it is possible to draw the graph in the plane without crossing edges. A graph is called *outerplanar* if it is possible to draw the graph in the plane without crossing the edges and with all nodes on the border of the picture. The following properties of planar and outerplanar graphs are of interest.

(1) A planar graph with N nodes has at most $3N - 6$ edges.
(2) A planar graph has at least one node of degree five or less.
(3) An outerplanar graph has at least one node of degree two or less.

B.1.2 Directed Graphs

A directed graph G is a pair (V, E), where V is the node set, and E is a collection of ordered pairs from V. That is, an element of E is a pair (u, v) with $u, v \in V$. To shorten the notation, we write $uv \in E$ instead of $(u, v) \in E$. Because the pair is ordered, $uv \in E$ is *not* equivalent to $vu \in E$. Most of the definitions for undirected graphs have a slightly modified counterpart for directed graphs.

The edge uv is called an *outgoing edge* of u and an *incoming edge* of v. If $uv \in E$, v is called an *out-neighbor* of v, and v is called an *in-neighbor* of u. The *in-degree* of a node is the number of its incoming edges, and the *out-degree* is the number of outgoing edges. The degree is the sum of the in-degree and the out-degree.

A path of length k from v_0 to v_k is a sequence $P = \langle v_0, \ldots, v_k \rangle$ of nodes such that for each $i < k$, $v_i v_{i+1} \in E$. In this path, v_0 is the begin node and v_k the end node. A *cycle* is a path of which the begin node equals the end node. As for undirected graphs, a path is called simple if the nodes v_0 through v_k are all different, and a cycle is called simple if the nodes v_1 through v_k are all different.

The distance from u to v, denoted $d(u, v)$, is the length of a shortest path between u and v. The diameter of G is the largest distance from any node to any other node. A directed graph is *strongly connected* if there exists a path from each node to each other node. A directed graph is called *acyclic* if it contains no simple cycle of length two or more.

Subgraphs, spanning subgraphs, and induced subgraphs are defined for directed graphs exactly as for undirected graphs.

B.1.3 Weighted Graphs

A (directed or undirected) graph is *weighted* if for each pair u, v with $uv \in E$, a numerical value ω_{uv} is defined. The weight assignment is called *symmetric* if, for each pair, $\omega_{uv} = \omega_{vu}$. In a weighted graph, the weight of a path is defined as the sum of the edge weights over the edges in the path.

If no weight assignment is assumed for a graph, it is called *unweighted*.

B.2 Frequently Used Graphs

This section defines and discusses some classes of graph that occur frequently in the study of distributed algorithms, namely, rings, trees, forests, grids, tori, cliques, and hypercubes. As can be seen from many results in this book, computations in distributed systems can often be performed more efficiently on networks of restricted topologies than on networks of arbitrary (but connected) topology.

Let, in the sequel, $G = (V, E)$ be a graph, N the number of its nodes, and D the diameter.

B.2.1 Rings

The ring topology is a circular arrangement of nodes, and is often used as a control topology in distributed computations. Some networks (e.g., Token Rings [Tan96, Sec. 4.3]) arrange the nodes in a ring physically, but in other cases the ring is merely used as an embedded control structure. To give each process its turn (to perform some function) in a round-robin fashion, the processes circulate a message among them; v_0 sends it to v_1, v_1 to v_2, etc, until in arrives at v_{N-1}, which sends it to v_0 again.

Definition B.1 *A ring is an undirected, connected, regular graph of degree two.*

The ring can be characterized in several ways.

Theorem B.2 *The following are equivalent for an undirected graph G.*

(1) *G is a ring.*
(2) *There exists a one-to-one mapping from V to $\{0, \ldots, N-1\}$ such that the neighbors of node i are nodes $i-1$ and $i+1$ (modulo N).*

To exploit the advantages of the ring topology in other network topologies, a spanning ring can sometimes be defined in a graph $G = (V, E)$; that is, a set $E' \subseteq E$ is selected such that (V, E') is a ring. Unfortunately, not every graph contains a spanning ring (Hamiltonian cycle) and it is NP-complete [GJ79] to decide whether a given graph has one. It is possible, however, to define a *virtual ring*; in this case, successive nodes in the ring are not necessarily neighbors in the original graph. Bakker and Van Leeuwen [BL93] describe a distributed algorithm for constructing a virtual ring in which the distance between successive nodes of the ring is at most three.

B.2.2 Trees, Forests, and Stars

A tree is a graph that contains a minimal number of edges connecting its nodes (see Theorem B.4), and as a result computations on tree-shaped networks may have a very low communication complexity. For decentralized computations, an additional factor that contributes to the low complexity of computations on trees is that an efficient decentralized wave algorithm for trees exists (Algorithm 6.3).

Definition B.3 *A tree is an undirected, connected, acyclic graph.*

Trees can be characterized in the following ways [CLR90].

Theorem B.4 *The following are equivalent for an undirected graph G.*

(1) *G is a tree.*
(2) *Between any two nodes there exists a unique simple path.*
(3) *G is connected, but becomes disconnected if any edge is removed.*
(4) *G is connected and $|E| = N - 1$.*
(5) *G is acyclic and $|E| = N - 1$.*
(6) *G is acyclic, but becomes cyclic if any edge is added.*

A tree $T = (V, E)$ is *rooted* if there is a unique designated node r called the *root*. If u is a node on the (unique) simple path between v and r, u is called an *ancestor* of v, and v is called a *descendant* of u. If, moreover, u and v are neighbors, v is called a *son* (or *child*) of u, and u is called the *father* (or *parent*) of v. The subgraph induced by the descendants of u is a rooted tree (with root u), called the *subtree* of u. The *depth* of the tree is the maximal length of any simple path from the root to a node.

Every connected graph $G = (V, E)$ contains a spanning tree; that is, a set $E' \subseteq E$ can be chosen, such that (V, E') is a tree. Moreover, if G is not itself a tree, the spanning tree can be chosen in different ways. The edges in E' are called *tree edges* and the edges in $E \setminus E'$ are called *frond edges*.

Several classes of spanning tree are of interest in distributed computing.

(1) *Low-diameter spanning tree.* If the spanning tree must be chosen to minimize the total time necessary for a computation on it, it is desirable that the diameter is as small as possible. The optimal sink tree constructed in the proof of Theorem 4.2 has a diameter that is at most twice the diameter of the entire network. Such a tree can be constructed using the algorithms described in Chapter 4 and Section 12.4.

(2) *Minimal-weight spanning tree.* The number of edges in a spanning tree always equals $N - 1$ (see Theorem B.4 (4)), but in a weighted graph the weight of the tree (sum of the edge weights over the edges of the tree) is usually not the same for every possible spanning tree. If the total communication cost for a computation in a spanning tree must be low, the subtree must be chosen so as to minimize the

weight of the tree. If all edge weights are different, the minimal-weight spanning tree is unique (Proposition 7.18). A distributed algorithm for computing this unique tree was given by Gallager *et al.* [GHS83], and is treated in Section 7.3.2.

(3) *Restricted-degree spanning tree.* If the computation overhead per node must be low, a spanning tree must be selected that has a low degree for each node. The distributed construction of such trees was described by Korach *et al.* [KMZ85].

(4) *Depth-first search tree.* A spanning tree is a depth-first search spanning tree if each frond edge connects a node and a descendant of that node. Depth-first search trees are used in many algorithms that operate on graphs, such as algorithms to test planarity or biconnectivity. They are also used for the construction of interval labeling schemes for compact routing; see Subsection 4.4.2. Distributed algorithms for constructing a depth-first search tree are given in Section 6.4.

Forests are generalizations of trees, and stars are special cases of trees. A graph consisting of a number of isolated trees is called a forest.

Definition B.5 *A forest is an undirected acyclic graph.*

Theorem B.6 *The following are equivalent for an undirected graph G.*

(1) *G is a forest.*
(2) *Between any two nodes there exists at most one simple path.*
(3) *Each connected component of G is a tree.*
(4) *If any edge is removed, the number of connected components of G increases by one.*
(5) *The number of connected components of G equals* $|V| - |E|$.

A forest is rooted if a root node is designated in every tree of the forest. Every graph has a spanning forest, consisting of a spanning tree of each connected component of the graph.

A star is a graph with one special node, the center, and all other nodes are connected only to this center.

Definition B.7 *A star is a rooted tree of depth one. The root of the star is called the center.*

Stars are not usual as a physical connection topology of a distributed systems; rather, stars are the virtual topology used in computations that are controlled by a central process. In such computations, all processes communicate with the center only, thus employing of the entire network only a (spanning) subgraph that is a star; see, for example, Algorithm 6.6.

Theorem B.8 *The following are equivalent for an undirected graph G.*

    (1) *G is a star.*

    (2) *G is connected and contains at most one node of degree larger than one.*

B.2.3 Cliques

In a clique, sometimes also called a *complete graph*, each pair of nodes is directly connected by an edge.

Definition B.9 *A clique is a graph with diameter one.*

As is the case for stars, cliques are rarely used as a physical connection topology. This is so because the high number of edges of the graph would require a large amount of hardware. In most networks not every pair of nodes is directly connected, and communication between non-adjacent nodes requires that all nodes on a path between these nodes cooperate. If, however, this cooperation is invisibly implemented in the "low" layers of the system, the network may be regarded as a clique in its "higher" layers.

Theorem B.10 *The following are equivalent for an undirected graph G.*

    (1) *G is a clique.*

    (2) $E = \{uv : u, v \in V \text{ and } u \neq v\}$.

    (3) $|E| = \frac{1}{2}N(N-1)$.

    (4) *Each node has degree $N - 1$.*

B.2.4 Grids and Tori

In an $n \times n$ grid there are $N = n^2$ nodes, arranged in n rows of n nodes each. Each node is connected to the nodes above it, right and left of it, and under it; see Figure B.2. The $n \times n$ torus is similar, but in addition the leftmost and rightmost node of each row are adjacent, and the uppermost and lowermost node of each column are adjacent; see Figure B.2. Grids and tori are popular topologies for use in the design of multiprocessor computers. Because the degree of each node is at most four, it is possible to realize these topologies physically from Transputer chips. The topologies are very suitable for performing computations on matrices.

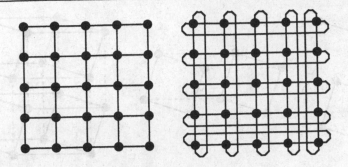

Figure B.2 A GRID AND A TORUS.

For the formal definition of these topologies, recall that $\mathbb{Z}_n$ is the set of integers modulo n.

Definition B.11 *The $n \times n$ grid is a graph on $N = n^2$ nodes for which the nodes can be uniquely labeled with elements from $\{(i, j) : 0 \leq i, j < n\}$ in such a way that nodes (i, j) and (i', j') are adjacent if and only if $(i = i') \wedge (j = j' + 1)$ or $(i = i') \wedge (j = j' - 1)$ or $(i = i' + 1) \wedge (j = j')$ or $(i = i' - 1) \wedge (j = j')$.*
The $n \times n$ torus is a graph on $N = n^2$ nodes for which the nodes can be uniquely labeled with elements from $\{(i, j) : i, j \in \mathbb{Z}_n\}$ in such a way that nodes (i, j) and (i', j') are adjacent if and only if $(i = i') \wedge (j = j' + 1)$ or $(i = i') \wedge (j = j' - 1)$ or $(i = i' + 1) \wedge (j = j')$ or $(i = i' - 1) \wedge (j = j')$ (here arithmetic is modulo n).

The $n \times n$ grid has $2n(n-1)$ edges, contains nodes of degree two, three, and four, and its diameter is $2(n-1)$. The $n \times n$ torus has $2n^2$ edges, is regular of degree four, and its diameter is $2\lfloor \frac{n}{2} \rfloor$.

B.2.5 Hypercubes

Like grids and tori, hypercubes are often used in the design of multiprocessor computers. They combine a reasonably small diameter with a reasonably small degree; both diameter and degree equal $\log N$, where N is the number of nodes. The topological properties of this class of graphs were studied by Saad and Schultz [SS88].

Definition B.12 *The n-dimensional hypercube is a graph on $N = 2^n$ nodes where each node can be assigned a unique element from the set of*

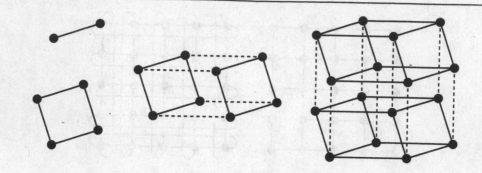

Figure B.3 Hypercubes of dimension 1, 2, 3, and 4.

labels $\{(b_0, \ldots, b_{n-1}) : b_i = 0, 1\}$ *in such a way that*

$$E = \{uv : \text{the labels of } u \text{ and } v \text{ differ in one bit}\}.$$

The hypercube is regular of degree n, and has diameter n. There are different ways to view hypercubes, and some interesting graph-theoretical results are reported in [SS88]. First, the labeling as mentioned in Definition B.12 is far from unique; if G is an n-dimensional hypercube, exactly $2^n n!$ such labelings can be found.

An $(n + 1)$-dimensional hypercube can be constructed by taking two n-dimensional hypercubes and connecting corresponding nodes. In Figure B.3, the edges between the corresponding nodes are drawn as dashed lines.

If we fix one labeling of the nodes of a hypercube, it is not difficult to prove the following statement. If u and v are adjacent, the neighbors of u and the neighbors of v are connected in a one-to-one way. By this we mean that each neighbor of v is adjacent to exactly one neighbor of u, and vice versa. It is more difficult to see that (together with some additional, rather trivial conditions) a one-to-one connection between neighbors of adjacent nodes is sufficient for a graph to be a hypercube.

Theorem B.13 *The following are equivalent for an undirected graph G.*

(1) *G is a hypercube of dimension n.*
(2) *$N = 2^n$, G is regular of degree n, G is connected, and for each pair u, v of adjacent nodes, the neighbors of v and the neighbors of u are connected in a one-to-one way.*

Summary. Table B.4 summarizes the main characteristics of the graph classes discussed in this section.

Graph	degree	$|E|$	D	Remarks
Ring	2	N	$\lfloor \frac{N}{2} \rfloor$	
Tree	varies	$N-1$	$< N$	
Forest	varies	$< N$		
Star	1 or $N-1$	$N-1$	2 or 1	$D=1$ iff $N=2$
Clique	$N-1$	$\frac{1}{2}N(N-1)$	1	
Grid ($n \times n$)	2, 3, 4	$2n(n-1)$	$2(n-1)$	$N = n^2$
Torus ($n \times n$)	4	$2n^2$	$2\lfloor \frac{n}{2} \rfloor$	$N = n^2$
Hyperc. (n dim.)	n	$2^{n-1}n$	n	$N = 2^n$

Table B.4 CLASSES OF GRAPH.

B.3 Sense of Direction

It was observed by Santoro [San84] that the communication complexity of distributed computations is influenced by, apart from the actual topology, the following factors.

(1) *Topological awareness.* In order to exploit the advantages of a specific topology, it is sometimes necessary that the processes "know" that they are connected in a topology of this class.

For example, the election problem (Chapter 7) can be solved in a clique network using only $O(N \log N)$ messages. However, if the optimal algorithm for arbitrary connected networks is used in the clique, $\Omega(N^2)$ messages will be exchanged. Thus, to exploit the advantage of full connection, the processes must know that they are in a clique.

(2) *Sense of direction.* The routing of information through a network can be done more efficiently if the edges incident to each node are labelled with the "direction" to which they lead in the network. Such information allows us to find a short (usually, optimal) path to a node, to which only a long path is known.

As an illustration of the advantages of sense of direction, consider Figure B.5, where a section of a grid network is depicted. Node v has issued a request for some resource, which has been forwarded by several nodes (that do not have the requested resource) and has finally arrived at u, which has the resource. Because u observes that the request message has been forwarded three times to the right, twice down, and three times to the left, u sends the reply upwards. Instead of following the request path backwards (over eight edges) the reply is sent via a path of length two. Clearly, the shorter return path can only be found if the nodes "know" for each of their incident edges in what direction they lead.

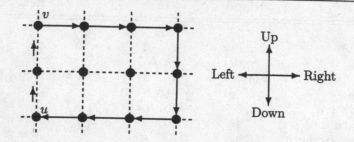

Figure B.5 EXPLOITING SENSE OF DIRECTION.

Of course, what the "directions" in a graph are depends on its topology. In each case we assume that, for each node, the edges of that node are locally labeled with the "meaningful directions" for that class of graphs. If $\mathcal{S}$ denotes the labeling, write $\mathcal{S}_v(u)$ for the label that is assigned to edge uv in node v; the same edge is labeled $\mathcal{S}_u(v)$ in node u. The set of existing labels is the same for each node; the size of that set, $\mathcal{L}$, equals the degree of the network, because within each node, edge labels are unique. To give a sense of direction, an additional global consistency condition must be verified. It will now be explained for four classes of graph what sense of direction means for this particular class.

Rings. As the ring is regular of degree two, there are only two directions in the ring; we call them "*Prev*" (previous) and "*Next*". Of course, if u is the "*Next*" node after v, then v is the "*Prev*" node before u; if this relation is

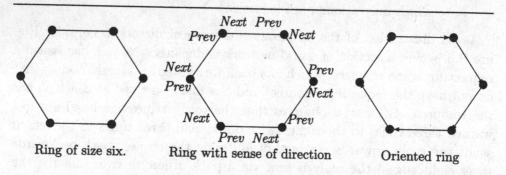

Ring of size six.   Ring with sense of direction   Oriented ring

Figure B.6 SENSE OF DIRECTION IN A RING.

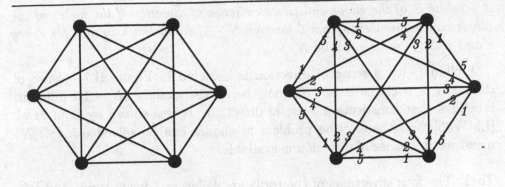

Figure B.7 SENSE OF DIRECTION IN A CLIQUE.

satisfied for each pair of adjacent nodes, the orientation is globally consistent; see Figure B.6.

Definition B.14 *A labeling of the ring is an assignment at every node of different labels from the set {Prev, Next} to the edges incident to that node. A labeling S of the ring constitutes a sense of direction if for all adjacent nodes u and v,*

$$S_u(v) = Prev \iff S_v(u) = Next.$$

Sense of direction in a ring is not unique; there are two edge labelings satisfying these constraints. It will always be assumed that rings have a sense of direction. Clearly, if one node sends a message via its *Next* edge, and each node that receives the message again forwards it via its *Next* edge, all nodes will receive the message before it returns to the first node. Usually, this is the only direction in which the communication channels are used, and it is often assumed that the ring is directed as indicated in Figure B.6.

Cliques. The clique of N nodes has degree $N - 1$; its directions are numbered from 1 through $N-1$, i.e., $\mathcal{L} = \{1, \ldots, N-1\}$. A labeling constitutes a sense of direction if a directed Hamiltonian cycle can be fixed in the clique in such a way that edge uv is labeled (in u) with the distance from u to v along this cycle.

Definition B.15 *A labeling of the clique is an assignment at every node of different labels from the set $\{1, \ldots, N-1\}$ to the edges incident to that node.*

A labeling S of the clique constitutes a sense of direction if the nodes of the clique can be numbered from 0 through $N - 1$, in such a way that for every i and j, $S_i(j) = (j - i) \bmod N$.

A clique with a sense of direction is depicted in Figure B.7. Sense of direction in a clique is not unique; there exist exactly $(N - 1)!$ different labelings that constitute a sense of direction. It was shown by Loui *et al.* [LMW86] that the election problem in cliques can be solved using $O(N)$ messages if a sense of direction is available.

Tori. The four directions of the torus are called up, down, right, and left, abbreviated *U, D, R, L.*

Definition B.16 *A labeling of the torus is an assignment at every node of different labels from the set $\{U, D, R, L\}$ to the edges incident to that node. A labeling S of the torus constitutes a sense of direction if the nodes can be renamed with elements from $\{(i, j) : i, j \in \mathbb{Z}_n\}$ in such a way that*

(1) $S_{(i,j)}((i', j')) = U \Rightarrow (i' = i) \wedge (j' = j + 1)$;
(2) $S_{(i,j)}((i', j')) = D \Rightarrow (i' = i) \wedge (j' = j - 1)$;
(3) $S_{(i,j)}((i', j')) = L \Rightarrow (i' = i - 1) \wedge (j' = j)$;
(4) $S_{(i,j)}((i', j')) = R \Rightarrow (i' = i + 1) \wedge (j' = j)$.

Sense of direction in a torus is not unique; if $n > 4$, there are exactly eight different labelings that give the torus sense of direction. A torus with sense of direction is depicted in Figure B.8.

Hypercubes. The n dimensions of the n-dimensional hypercube are numbered from 0 through $n - 1$. There is a sense of direction if all parallel edges are labeled with the same number.

Definition B.17 *A labeling of the n-dimensional hypercube is an assignment at every node of different labels from the set $\{0, \ldots, n - 1\}$ to the edges incident to that node.*
A labeling S of the hypercube constitutes a sense of direction if the nodes can be renamed with elements from $\{(b_0, \ldots, b_{n-1}) : b_i = 0, 1\}$ such that if the label $S_{(b_0, \ldots, b_{n-1})}((c_0, \ldots, c_{n-1})) = i$, then $(b_0, \ldots, b_{n-1})$ and $(c_0, \ldots, c_{n-1})$ differ in exactly one bit, namely, bit i.

Sense of direction in a hypercube is not unique; for an n-dimensional hypercube there are exactly $n!$ different edge labelings that give the hypercube a sense of direction. The definition implies that for adjacent nodes u and

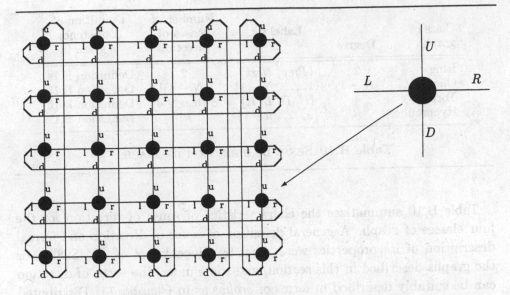

Figure B.8 SENSE OF DIRECTION IN A TORUS.

v, $\mathcal{S}_u(v) = \mathcal{S}_v(u)$; therefore, in Figure B.9 only one label is placed on each edge.

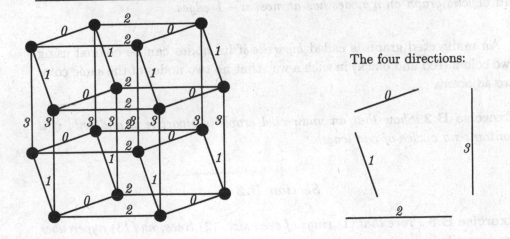

The four directions:

Figure B.9 SENSE OF DIRECTION IN A HYPERCUBE.

Class of graph	Degree	Label set $\mathcal{L}$	Number of senses of direction	Definition of consistency is given in
Ring	2	$\{Prev, Next\}$	2	Definition B.14
Clique	$N-1$	$\{1, \ldots, N-1\}$	$(N-1)!$	Definition B.15
Torus	4	$\{U, D, L, R\}$	8 (if $n > 4$)	Definition B.16
Hypercube	n	$\{0, \ldots, n-1\}$	$n!$	Definition B.17

Table B.10 SENSE OF DIRECTION IN GRAPHS.

Table B.10 summarizes the characteristics of sense of direction for the four classes of graph. A general definition of sense of direction and formal description of its properties were given by Flocchini *et al.* [FMS98]. For the graphs described in this section, and some more, the sense of direction can be suitably described in terms of *groups* as in Chapter 11. Distributed algorithms for computing a sense of direction in hypercubes and tori are given there and in [Tel94].

Exercises to Appendix B
Section B.1

Exercise B.1 *Prove the following for undirected graphs:*
A connected graph on n nodes has at least $n-1$ edges.
An acyclic graph on n nodes has at most $n-1$ edges.

An undirected graph is called *bipartite* if its nodes can be colored using two colors (red and black) in such a way that no two nodes of the same color are adjacent.

Exercise B.2 *Show that an undirected graph is bipartite if and only if it contains no cycles of odd length.*

Section B.2

Exercise B.3 *Prove that* (1) *rings of even size,* (2) *trees, and* (3) *hypercubes are bipartite.*

Exercise B.4 *Prove Theorems B.4 and B.6. (Hint: Use Exercise B.1.)*

Project B.5 *Can any of the four conditions of Theorem B.13 (2), be removed?*

Section B.3

Exercise B.6 *Prove that a clique can be given a sense of direction in exactly $(N - 1)!$ different ways.*
Prove that an n-dimensional hypercube can be given a sense of direction in exactly n! different ways.

Exercise B.7 *Let S be a labeling of a clique. For a path $P = \langle v_0, \ldots, v_k \rangle$, define $Sum(P) = S_{v_0}(v_1) + \cdots + S_{v_{k-1}}(v_k)$. Prove that the following two statements are equivalent.*

(1) *S is a sense of direction.*
(2) *For every path P, P is a cycle if and only if $Sum(P) \equiv 0 \pmod{N}$.*

References

[ABND+90] ATTIYA, H., BAR-NOY, A., DOLEV, D., PELEG, D., AND REIS-CHUK, R. Renaming in an asynchronous environment. *J. ACM* **37** (1990), 524–548.

[ABNLP90] AWERBUCH, B., BAR-NOY, A., LINIAL, N., AND PELEG, D. Improved routing strategies with succinct tables. *J. Algorithms* **11** (1990), 307–341.

[ACT97] AGUILERA, M. K., CHEN, W., AND TOUEG, S. Heartbeat: A timeout-free failure detector for quiescent reliable communication. In proc. *11th Int. Workshop on Distributed Algorithms* (1997), M. Mavronicolas and P. Tsigas (eds.), vol. 1320 of *Lecture Notes in Computer Science*, Springer-Verlag, pp. 126–140.

[AG85] AWERBUCH, B. AND GALLAGER, R. G. Distributed BFS algorithms. In proc. *Foundations of Computation Theory* (1985), pp. 250–256.

[AG91] AFEK, Y. AND GAFNI, E. Time and message bounds for election in synchronous and asynchronous complete networks. *SIAM J. Comput.* **20**, 2 (1991), 376–394.

[AH93] ANAGNOSTOU, E. AND HADZILACOS, V. Tolerating transient and permanent failures. In proc. *Int. Workshop on Distributed Algorithms* (Lausanne, 1993), A. Schiper (ed.), vol. 725 of *Lecture Notes in Computer Science*, Springer-Verlag, pp. 174–188.

[Ahu90] AHUJA, M. Flush primitives for asynchronous distributed systems. *Inf. Proc. Lett.* **34** (1990), 5–12.

[AKY90] AFEK, Y., KUTTEN, S., AND YUNG, M. Memory-efficient self stabilizing protocols for general networks. In proc. *4th Int. Workshop on Distributed Algorithms* (Bari, 1990), J. van Leeuwen and N. Santoro (eds.), vol. 486 of *Lecture Notes in Computer Science*, Springer-Verlag, pp. 15–28.

[ALSY90] AFEK, Y., LANDAU, G. M., SCHIEBER, B., AND YUNG, M. The power of multimedia: Combining point-to-point and multiaccess networks. *Inf. Comput.* **84**, 1 (1990), 97–118.

[ALSZ89] ATTIYA, H., LEEUWEN, J. VAN, SANTORO, N., AND ZAKS, S. Efficient elections in chordal ring networks. *Algorithmica* **4** (1989), 437–466.

[Ang80] ANGLUIN, D. Local and global properties in networks of processors. In proc. *Symp. on Theory of Computing* (1980), pp. 82–93.

[AS85] ALPERN, B. AND SCHNEIDER, F. B. Defining liveness. *Inf. Proc. Lett.* **21** (1985), 181–185.

[Att87] ATTIYA, H. Constructing efficient election algorithms from efficient traversal algorithms. In proc. *2nd Int. Workshop on Distributed Algorithms* (Amsterdam, 1987), J. van Leeuwen (ed.), vol. 312 of *Lecture Notes in Computer Science*, Springer-Verlag, pp. 377–344.

[AW98] ATTIYA, H. AND WELCH, J. *Distributed Computing: Fundamentals, Simulations, and Advanced Topics.* McGraw-Hill, 1998.

[Awe85a] AWERBUCH, B. Complexity of network synchronization. *J. ACM* **32** (1985), 804–823.

[Awe85b] AWERBUCH, B. A new distributed depth first search algorithm. *Inf. Proc. Lett.* **20** (1985), 147–150.

[Awe87] AWERBUCH, B. Optimal distributed algorithms for minimum weight spanning tree, counting, leader election and related problems. In proc. *Symp. on Theory of Computing* (1987), pp. 230–240.

[BA84] BEN-ARI, M. Algorithms for on-the-fly garbage collection. *ACM Trans. Program. Lang. Syst.* **6**, 3 (1984), 333–344.

[Bal90] BAL, H. *Programming Distributed Systems.* Prentice-Hall, 1990.

[Bar96] BARBOSA, V. C. *An Introduction to Distributed Algorithms.* MIT Press, 1996 (365 pp.).

[BB88] BRASSARD, G. AND BRATLEY, P. *Algorithmics: Theory and Practice.* Prentice-Hall, 1988.

[BB89] BEAME, P. W. AND BODLAENDER, H. L. Distributed computing on transitive networks: The torus. In proc. *Symp. on Theoretical Aspects of Computer Science* (1989), B. Monien and R. Cori (eds.), vol. 349 of *Lecture Notes in Computer Science*, Springer-Verlag, pp. 294–303.

[Bel76] BELSNES, D. Single-message communication. *IEEE Trans. Comput.* **COM–24**, 2 (1976), 190–194.

[BGM93] BURNS, J. E., GOUDA, M. G., AND MILLER, R. E. Stabilization and pseudo-stabilization. *Distributed Comput.* **7**, 1 (1993), 35–42.

[BGP92] BERMAN, P., GARAY, J. A., AND PERRY, K. J. Optimal early stopping in distributed consensus. In proc. *6th Int. Workshop on Distributed Algorithms* (Haifa, 1992), A. Segall and S. Zaks (eds.), vol. 647 of *Lecture Notes in Computer Science*, Springer-Verlag, pp. 221–237.

[BGS87] BARATZ, A., GOPAL, I., AND SEGALL, A. Fault tolerant queries in computer networks. In proc. *2nd Int. Workshop on Distributed Algorithms* (Amsterdam, 1987), J. van Leeuwen (ed.), vol. 312 of *Lecture Notes in*

Computer Science, Springer-Verlag, pp. 30–40.

[BHR92] BRZEZINSKI, J., HÉLARY, J.-M., AND RAYNAL, M. Deadlock models
and general algorithm for distributed deadlock detection. Research report,
IRISA, Rennes, 1992. Submitted for publication.

[BIZ89] BAR-ILAN, J. AND ZERNIK, D. Random leaders and random spanning
trees. In proc. *3rd Int. Workshop on Distributed Algorithms* (Nice, 1989),
J.-C. Bermond and M. Raynal (eds.), vol. 392 of *Lecture Notes in Computer Science*, Springer-Verlag, pp. 1–12.

[BL93] BAKKER, E. M. AND LEEUWEN, J. VAN. Uniform *d*–emulations of rings,
with an application to distributed virtual ring construction. *Networks* **23**
(1993), 237–248.

[BLT91] BAKKER, E. M., LEEUWEN, J. VAN, AND TAN, R. B. Linear interval
routing. *Algorithms Review* **2**, 2 (1991), 45–61.

[BLT93] BAKKER, E. M., LEEUWEN, J. VAN, AND TAN, R. B. Prefix routing
schemes in dynamic networks. *Computer Networks and ISDN Systems* **26**
(1993), 403–421.

[BMZ90] BIRAN, O., MORAN, S., AND ZAKS, S. A combinatorial characterization
of the distributed tasks which are solvable in the presence of one faulty
processor. *J. Algorithms* **11** (1990), 420–440.

[Bod86] BODLAENDER, H. L. Distributed computing: Structure and complexity.
Ph.D. thesis, Dept Computer Science, Utrecht University, The Netherlands, 1986 (297 pp.).

[Bod88] BODLAENDER, H. L. A better lower bound for distributed leader finding in bidirectional asynchronous rings of processors. *Inf. Proc. Lett.* **27**
(1988), 287–290.

[Bod91a] BODLAENDER, H. L. New lower bound techniques for distributed leader
finding and other problems on rings of processors. *Theor. Comput. Sci.*
81 (1991), 237–256.

[Bod91b] BODLAENDER, H. L. Some lower bound results for decentralized
extrema-finding in rings of processors. *J. Comput. Syst. Sci.* **42**, 1 (1991),
97–118.

[Bou83] BOURNE, S. R. *The Unix System*. Addison-Wesley, 1983 (351 pp.).

[BP88] BURNS, J. E. AND PACHL, J. Uniform self-stabilizing rings. In proc.
Aegean Workshop on Computing (1988), J. H. Reif (ed.), vol. 319 of *Lecture Notes in Computer Science*, Springer-Verlag, pp. 391–400.

[BT85] BRACHA, G. AND TOUEG, S. Asynchronous consensus and broadcast
protocols. *J. ACM* **32** (1985), 824–840.

[CB89] CHARRON-BOST, B. Mesures de la concurrence et du parallélisme des
calculs répartis. Ph.D. thesis, Université Paris VII, 1989 (129 pp.).

[CBMT96] CHARRON-BOST, B., MATTERN, F., AND TEL, G. Synchronous, asynchronous, and causally ordered communication. *Distributed Comput.* **9** (1996), 173–191.

[CBT97] CHARRON-BOST, B. AND TEL, G. Calculs approchés de la borne inférieure de valeurs réparties. *Inf. Théor. Appl.* **31**, 4 (1997), 305–330.

[CCGZ90] CHOU, C. T., CIDON, I., GOPAL, I. S., AND ZAKS, S. Synchronizing asynchronous bounded delay networks. *IEEE Trans. Commun.* **38**, 2 (1990), 144–147.

[CD88] COULOURIS, G. F. AND DOLLIMORE, J. *Distributed Systems: Concepts and Design.* Addison-Wesley, 1988 (366 pp.).

[CD91] COAN, B. A. AND DWORK, C. Simultaneity is harder than agreement. *Information and Computation* **91**, 2 (1991), 205–231.

[Cha82] CHANG, E. J.-H. Echo algorithms: Depth parallel operations on general graphs. *IEEE Trans. Softw. Eng.* **SE–8** (1982), 391–401.

[Che83] CHEUNG, T.-Y. Graph traversal techniques and the maximum flow problem in distributed computation. *IEEE Trans. Softw. Eng.* **SE–9** (1983), 504–512.

[CHT96] CHANDRA, T. D., HADZILACOS, V., AND TOUEG, S. The weakest failure detector for solving consensus. *J. ACM* **43**, 4 (1996), 685–722.

[Cid88] CIDON, I. Yet another distributed depth-first-search algorithm. *Inf. Proc. Lett.* **26** (1988), 301–305.

[CL85] CHANDY, K. M. AND LAMPORT, L. Distributed snapshots: Determining global states of distributed systems. *ACM Trans. Comput. Syst.* **3**, 1 (1985), 63–75.

[CLR90] CORMEN, T. H., LEISERSON, C. E., AND RIVEST, R. L. *Introduction to Algorithms.* McGraw-Hill/MIT Press, 1990 (1028 pp.).

[CM82] CHANDY, K. M. AND MISRA, J. Distributed computation on graphs: Shortest path algorithms. *Commun. ACM* **25**, 11 (1982), 833–838.

[CM88] CHANDY, K. M. AND MISRA, J. *Parallel Program Design: A Foundation.* Addison-Wesley, 1988 (516 pp.).

[CMH83] CHANDY, K. M., MISRA, J., AND HAAS, L. M. Distributed deadlock detection. *ACM Trans. Comput. Syst.* **1**, 2 (1983), 144–156.

[CR79] CHANG, E. J.-H. AND ROBERTS, R. An improved algorithm for decentralized extrema finding in circular arrangements of processes. *Commun. ACM* **22** (1979), 281–283.

[Cri89] CRISTIAN, F. Probabilistic clock synchronization. *Distributed Computing* **3** (1989), 146–158.

[CT90] CRITCHLOW, C. AND TAYLOR, K. The inhibition spectrum and the achievement of causal consistency. Tech. rep. 90-1101, Dept Computer Science, Cornell Univ., 1990.

[CT96] CHANDRA, T. D. AND TOUEG, S. Unreliable failure detectors for reliable distributed systems. *J. ACM* **43**, 2 (1996), 225–267.

[CV90] CHANDRASEKARAN, S. AND VENKATESAN, S. A message-optimal algorithm for distributed termination detection. *J. Parallel and Distributed Computing* **8**, 3 (1990), 245–252.

[Dav88] DAVIDSON, J. *An Introduction to TCP/IP*. Springer-Verlag, 1988.

[DDS87] DOLEV, D., DWORK, C., AND STOCKMEYER, L. On the minimal synchronism needed for distributed consensus. *J. ACM* **34** (1987), 77–97.

[DFF⁺82] DOLEV, D., FISCHER, M. J., FOWLER, R., LYNCH, N. A., AND STRONG, H. R. An efficient algorithm for Byzantine agreement without authenication. *Information and Control* **52** (1982), 257–274.

[DFG83] DIJKSTRA, E. W., FEIJEN, W. H. J., AND GASTEREN, A. J. M. VAN. Derivation of a termination detection algorithm for distributed computations. *Inf. Proc. Lett.* **16**, 5 (1983), 217–219.

[DHS84] DOLEV, D., HALPERN, J. Y., AND STRONG, H. R. On the possibility and impossibility of achieving clock synchronization. In proc. *Symp. on Theory of Computing* (1984), pp. 504–511.

[Dij68] DIJKSTRA, E. W. Co-operating sequential processes. In *Programming Languages*, F. Genuys (ed.), Academic Press, 1968, pp. 43–112.

[Dij74] DIJKSTRA, E. W. Self-stabilizing systems in spite of distributed control. *Commun. ACM* **17** (1974), 643–644.

[Dij82] DIJKSTRA, E. W. Self-stabilization in spite of distributed control. In *Selected Writing on Computing: A Personal Perspective*, Springer-Verlag, 1982, pp. 41–46.

[Dij87] DIJKSTRA, E. W. Shmuel Safra's version of termination detection. EWD–Note 998, 1987.

[DKR82] DOLEV, D., KLAWE, M., AND RODEH, M. An $O(N \log N)$ unidirectional distributed algorithm for extrema-finding in a circle. *J. Algorithms* **3** (1982), 245–260.

[DLM⁺78] DIJKSTRA, E. W., LAMPORT, L., MARTIN, A. J., SCHOLTEN, C. S., AND STEFFENS, E. F. M. On-the-fly garbage collection: An exercise in cooperation. *Commun. ACM* **21**, 11 (1978), 966–975.

[DLS88] DWORK, C., LYNCH, N. A., AND STOCKMEYER, L. Consensus in the presence of partial synchrony. *J. ACM* **35**, 2 (1988), 288–323.

[Dob99] DOBREV, S. Linear election on unoriented hypercubes and graphs of constant diameter with any sense of direction. Tech. rep., Inst. of Informatics, Comenius Univ., Bratislava, 1999.

[DRS82] DOLEV, D., REISCHUK, R., AND STRONG, H. R. Eventual is earlier than immediate. In proc. *23rd Foundations of Computation Theory* (1982), pp. 196–203.

[DRT98] DOBREV, S., RUŽIČKA, P., AND TEL, G. Time and bit optimal broadcasting on anonymous unoriented hypercubes. In proc. *5th Colloq. on Structural Information and Communication Complexity* (1998), L. Gargano and D. Peleg (eds.), Carleton Scientific Press, pp. 173–187.

[DS80] DIJKSTRA, E. W. AND SCHOLTEN, C. S. Termination detection for diffusing computations. *Inf. Proc. Lett.* **11**, 1 (1980), 1–4.

[DS83] DOLEV, D. AND STRONG, H. R. Authenticated algorithms for Byzantine agreement. *SIAM J. Comput.* **12**, 4 (1983), 656–666.

[ElG85] ELGAMAL, T. A public key cryptosystem and a signature scheme based on discrete logrithms. *IEEE Trans. Inf. Theory* **IT-31**, 4 (1985), 469–472.

[EMZ96] EILAM, T., MORAN, S., AND ZAKS, S. A lower bound for linear interval routing. In proc. *10th Int. Workshop on Distributed Algorithms* (1996), O. Babaoğlu and K. Marzullo (eds.), vol. 1151 of *Lecture Notes in Computer Science*, Springer-Verlag, pp. 191–205.

[FG94] FREIGNIAUD, P. AND GAVOILE, C. Interval routing schemes. Research Report 94-04, LIPS-ENS, Lyon, 1994.

[FGNT98] FLAMMINI, M., GAMBOSI, G., NANNI, U., AND TAN, R. B. Multidimensional interval routing schemes. *Theor. Comput. Sci.* **205** (1998), 115–133.

[FGS93] FLAMMINI, M., GAMBOSI, G., AND SALOMONE, S. Boolean routing. In proc. *Int. Workshop on Distributed Algorithms* (Lausanne, 1993), A. Schiper (ed.), vol. 725 of *Lecture Notes in Computer Science*, Springer-Verlag, pp. 219–233.

[Fin79] FINN, S. G. Resynch procedures and a fail-safe network protocol. *IEEE Trans. Commun.* **COM-27** (1979), 840–845.

[FJ88] FREDERICKSON, G. N. AND JANARDAN, R. Designing networks with compact routing tables. *Algorithmica* **3** (1988), 171–190.

[FL82] FISCHER, M. J. AND LYNCH, N. A. A lower bound for the time to assure interactive consistency. *Inf. Proc. Lett.* **14** (1982), 183–186.

[FL84] FREDERICKSON, G. N. AND LYNCH, N. A. The impact of synchronous communication on the problem of electing a leader in a ring. In proc. *Symp. on Theory of Computing* (Washington DC, 1984), ACM, pp. 493–503.

[FLMS95] FLAMMINI, M., LEEUWEN, J. VAN, AND MARCHETTI-SPACCAMELA, A. The complexity of interval routing on random graphs. Tech. rep. UU-CS-1995-16, Dept Computer Science, Utrecht University, The Netherlands, 1995.

[FLP85] FISCHER, M. J., LYNCH, N. A., AND PATERSON, M. S. Impossibility of distributed consensus with one faulty process. *J. ACM* **32** (1985), 374–382.

[FMS98] FLOCCHINI, P., MANS, B., AND SANTORO, N. Sense of direction: Definitions, properties, and classes. *Networks* **32** (1998), 165–180.

[FR82] FRANCEZ, N. AND RODEH, M. Achieving distributed termination without freezing. *IEEE Trans. Softw. Eng.* **SE–8**, 3 (1982), 287–292.

[Fra80] FRANCEZ, N. Distributed termination. *ACM Trans. Program. Lang. Syst.* **2**, 1 (1980), 42–55.

[Fra82] FRANKLIN, W. R. On an improved algorithm for decentralized extrema finding in circular configurations of processors. *Commun. ACM* **25**, 5 (1982), 336–337.

[Fra86] FRANCEZ, N. *Fairness.* Springer-Verlag, 1986 (295 pp.).

[Fre85] FREDERICKSON, G. N. A single source shortest path algorithm for a planar distributed network. In proc. *Symp. on Theoretical Aspects of Computer Science* (Saarbrücken, 1985), K. Mehlhorn (ed.), vol. 182 of *Lecture Notes in Computer Science*, Springer-Verlag, pp. 143–150.

[FS86] FIAT, A. AND SHAMIR, A. How to prove yourself: Practical solutions to identification and signature problems. In proc. *Advances in Cryptology* (1986), A. M. Odlyzko (ed.), vol. 263 of *Lecture Notes in Computer Science*, Springer-Verlag, pp. 186–194.

[FW78] FLETCHER, J. G. AND WATSON, R. W. Mechanisms for a reliable timer-based protocol. *Computer Networks* **2** (1978), 271–290.

[Gaf87] GAFNI, E. Generalized scheme for topology-update in dynamic networks. In proc. *2nd Int. Workshop on Distributed Algorithms* (Amsterdam, 1987), J. van Leeuwen (ed.), Springer-Verlag, pp. 187–196.

[GHS83] GALLAGER, R. G., HUMBLET, P. A., AND SPIRA, P. M. A distributed algorithm for minimum weight spanning trees. *ACM Trans. Program. Lang. Syst.* **5** (1983), 67–77.

[GJ79] GAREY, M. R. AND JOHNSON, D. S. *Computers and Intractability: A Guide to the Theory of NP-Completeness.* W. H. Freeman, 1979.

[Gos91] GOSCINSKI, A. *Distributed Operating Systems: The Logical Design.* Addison-Wesley, 1991 (913 pp.).

[GP92] GARAY, J. A. AND PERRY, K. J. A continuum of failure models for distributed computing. In proc. *6th Int. Workshop on Distributed Algorithms* (Haifa, 1992), S. Zaks and A. Segall (eds.), vol. 647 of *Lecture Notes in Computer Science*, Springer-Verlag, pp. 153–165.

[GP93] GOPAL, A. S. AND PERRY, K. J. Unifying self-stabilization and fault-tolerance. In proc. *12th Symp. on Principles of Distributed Computing*

(Ithaca, 1993), pp. 195–206.

[GT90] GASTEREN, A. J. M. VAN AND TEL, G. Comments on "On the proof of a distributed algorithm": Always-true is not invariant. *Inf. Proc. Lett.* **35** (1990), 277–279.

[Her91] HERMAN, T. Adaptivity through distributed convergence. Ph.D. thesis, Dept Computer Science, University of Texas at Austin, 1991.

[HH92] HSU, S.-C. AND HUANG, S.-T. A self-stabilizing algorithm for maximal matching. *Inf. Proc. Lett.* **43**, 2 (1992), 77–81.

[HJ90] HARGET, A. J. AND JOHNSON, I. D. Load balancing algorithms in loosely-coupled distributed systems: A survey. In *Distributed Computer Systems*, H. S. M. Zedan (ed.), Butterworths, 1990, pp. 85–108.

[Hoa74] HOARE, C. A. R. Monitors: An operating system structuring concept. *Commun. ACM* **17** (1974), 549–557.

[Hoa78] HOARE, C. A. R. Communicating sequential processes. *Commun. ACM* **21** (1978), 666–677.

[Hoe99] HOEPMAN, J.-H. Self-stabilizing mutual exclusion on a ring, even if $K = N$. Submitted for publication, 1999.

[HP93] HIGHAM, L. AND PRZYTYCKA, T. A simple, efficient algorithm for maximum finding on rings. In proc. *7th Int. Workshop on Distributed Algorithms* (1993), A. Schiper (ed.), vol. 725 of *Lecture Notes in Computer Science*, Springer-Verlag, pp. 249–263.

[HS80] HIRSCHBERG, D. S. AND SINCLAIR, J. B. Decentralized extrema-finding in circular configurations of processes. *Commun. ACM* **23** (1980), 627–628.

[Hua88] HUANG, S.-T. A fully distributed termination detection scheme. *Inf. Proc. Lett.* **29**, 1 (1988), 13–18.

[IJ90] ISRAELI, A. AND JALFON, M. Self-stabilizing ring orientation. In proc. *4th Int. Workshop on Distributed Algorithms* (Bari, 1990), J. van Leeuwen and N. Santoro (eds.), vol. 486 of *Lecture Notes in Computer Science*, Springer-Verlag, pp. 1–14.

[IKWZ90] ITAI, A., KUTTEN, S., WOLFSTAHL, Y., AND ZAKS, S. Optimal distributed t–resilient election in complete networks. *IEEE Trans. Softw. Eng.* **SE–8**, 4 (1990), 415–420.

[IR81] ITAI, A. AND RODEH, M. Symmetry breaking in distributive networks. In proc. *Symp. on Theory of Computing* (1981), pp. 150–158.

[JJN+87] JOHANSEN, K. E., JØRGENSEN, U. L., NIELSEN, S. H., NIELSEN, S. E., AND SKYUM, S. A distributed spanning tree algorithm. In proc. *2nd Int. Workshop on Distributed Algorithms* (Amsterdam, 1987), J. van Leeuwen (ed.), vol. 312 of *Lecture Notes in Computer Science*, Springer-

Verlag, pp. 1–12.

[Kel76]   KELLER, R. M. Formal verification of parallel programs. *Commun. ACM* **19**, 7 (1976), 371–384.

[KK89]   KIROUSIS, L. M. AND KRANAKIS, E. A brief survey of concurrent readers and writers. *CWI Quarterly* **2**, 4 (1989), 307–330.

[KK90]   KRANAKIS, E. AND KRIZANC, D. Computing boolean functions on anonymous hypercube networks. Report CS–R9040, Centre for Mathematics and Computer Science, Amsterdam, 1990.

[KKM90]   KORACH, E., KUTTEN, S., AND MORAN, S. A modular technique for the design of efficient leader finding algorithms. *ACM Trans. Program. Lang. Syst.* **12** (1990), 84–101.

[KMZ84]   KORACH, E., MORAN, S., AND ZAKS, S. Tight upper and lower bounds for some distributed algorithms for a complete network of processors. In proc. *Symp. on Principles of Distributed Computing* (1984), pp. 199–207.

[KMZ85]   KORACH, E., MORAN, S., AND ZAKS, S. The optimality of distributive constructions of minimum weight and degree restricted spanning trees in a complete network of processors. In proc. *4th Symp. on Principles of Distributed Computing* (1985).

[Kna87]   KNAPP, E. Deadlock detection in distributed databases. *Computing Surveys* **19**, 4 (1987), 303–328.

[KP93]   KATZ, S. AND PERRY, K. J. Self-stabilizing extensions for message-passing systems. *Distributed Comput.* **7**, 1 (1993), 17–26.

[LAD+92] LEISERSON, C. E., ABUHAMDEH, Z. S., DOUGLAS, D. C., FEYNMAN, C. R., GANMUKHI, M. N., HILL, J. V., HILLIS, W. D., KUSZMAUL, B. C., ST. PIERRE, M. A., WELLS, D. S., WONG, M. C., YANG, S.-W., AND ZAK, R. The network architecture of the Connection Machine CM-5. In proc. *4th Symp. on Parallel Algorithms and Architectures* (San Diego, 1992), L. Snyder (ed.), pp. 272–285.

[Lam78]   LAMPORT, L. Time, clocks, and the ordering of events in a distributed system. *Commun. ACM* **21** (1978), 558–564.

[Lam82]   LAMPORT, L. An assertional correctness proof of a distributed algorithm. *Sci. Computer Programming* **2** (1982), 175–206.

[LeL77]   LELANN, G. Distributed systems: Towards a formal approach. In proc. *Information Processing '77* (1977), B. Gilchrist (ed.), North-Holland, pp. 155–160.

[LL86]   LISKOV, B. AND LADIN, R. Highly-available distributed services and fault-tolerant distributed garbage collection. In proc. *5th Symp. on Principles of Distributed Computing* (Vancouver, 1986), pp. 29–39.

[LMT87]   LAKSHMANAN, K. B., MEENAKSHI, N., AND THULASIRAMAN, K.

A time-optimal message-efficient distributed algorithm for depth-first-search. *Inf. Proc. Lett.* **25** (1987), 103–109.

[LMW86] LOUI, M. C., MATSUSHITA, T. A., AND WEST, D. B. Election in a complete network with a sense of direction. *Inf. Proc. Lett.* **22** (1986), 185–187. Addendum: *Inf. Proc. Lett.* **28** (1988), 327.

[LSP82] LAMPORT, L., SHOSTAK, R., AND PEASE, M. The Byzantine generals problem. *ACM Trans. Program. Lang. Syst.* **4** (1982), 382–401.

[LSUZ87] LEEUWEN, J. VAN, SANTORO, N., URRUTIA, J., AND ZAKS, S. Guessing games and distributed computations in synchronous networks. In proc. *Int. Colloq. Automata, Languages, and Programming* (Karlsruhe, 1987), vol. 267 of *Lecture Notes in Computer Science*, Springer-Verlag, pp. 347–356.

[LT86] LEEUWEN, J. VAN AND TAN, R. B. Computer networks with compact routing tables. In *The Book of L*, G. Rozenberg and A. Salomaa (eds.), Springer-Verlag, 1986, pp. 259–273.

[LT87] LEEUWEN, J. VAN AND TAN, R. B. Interval routing. *Computer J.* **30** (1987), 298–307.

[LUST89] LENTFERT, P. J. A., UITTENBOGAARD, A. H., SWIERSTRA, S. D., AND TEL, G. Distributed hierarchical routing. Tech. rep. RUU–CS–89–5, Dept Computer Science, Utrecht University, The Netherlands, 1989.

[LY87] LAI, T. H. AND YANG, T. H. On distributed snapshots. *Inf. Proc. Lett.* **25** (1987), 153–158.

[Lyn68] LYNCH, W. C. Reliable full-duplex file transmission over half-duplex telephone lines. *Commun. ACM* **11**, 6 (1968), 407–410.

[Lyn96] LYNCH, N. *Distributed Algorithms*. Morgan Kaufmann Publishers, 1996.

[MA89] MATIAS, Y. AND AFEK, Y. Simple and efficient election algorithms for anonymous networks. In proc. *3rd Int. Workshop on Distributed Algorithms* (Nice, 1989), J.-C. Bermond and M. Raynal (eds.), vol. 392 of *Lecture Notes in Computer Science*, Springer-Verlag, pp. 183–194.

[Mat87] MATTERN, F. Algorithms for distributed termination detection. *Distributed Computing* **2**, 3 (1987), 161–175.

[Mat89a] MATTERN, F. Global quiescence detection based on credit distribution and recovery. *Inf. Proc. Lett.* **30**, 4 (1989), 195–200.

[Mat89b] MATTERN, F. Message complexity of simple ring-based election algorithms: an empirical analysis. In proc. *Proc. 9th Int. Conf. on Distributed Computer Systems* (1989), pp. 94–100.

[Mat89c] MATTERN, F. Virtual time and global states of distributed systems. In proc. *Parallel and Distributed Algorithms* (1989), M. Cosnard et al. (eds.), Elsevier Science Publishers, pp. 215–226.

[McH90] McHUGH, J. A. *Algorithmic Graph Theory*. Prentice-Hall, 1990.

[MM79] MENASCE, D. AND MUNTZ, R. Locking and deadlock detection in distributed databases. *Commun. ACM* **21** (1979).

[MM84] MITCHELL, D. P. AND MERRIT, M. J. A distributed algorithm for deadlock detection and resolution. In proc. *3rd Symp. on Principles of Distributed Computing* (1984), pp. 282–284.

[MNHT89] MASUZAWA, T., NISHIKAWA, N., HAGIHARA, K., AND TOKURA, N. Optimal fault tolerant distributed algorithms for election in complete networks with a global sense of direction. In proc. *3rd Int. Workshop on Distributed Algorithms* (1989), J.-C. Bermond and M. Raynal (eds.), vol. 329 of *Lecture Notes in Computer Science*, Springer-Verlag, pp. 171–182.

[MP88] MANNA, Z. AND PNUELI, A. The anchored version of the temporal framework. In proc. *Symp. on Linear Time, Branching Time, and Partial Order in Logics and Models for Concurrency* (Noordwijkerhout, 1988), J. W. de Bakker, W.-P. de Roever, and G. Rozenberg (eds.), vol. 354 of *Lecture Notes in Computer Science*, Springer-Verlag, pp. 201–284.

[MS79] MERLIN, P. M. AND SEGALL, A. A failsafe distributed routing protocol. *IEEE Trans. Commun.* **COM–27**, 9 (1979), 1280–1287.

[MS80a] MERLIN, P. M. AND SCHWEITZER, P. J. Deadlock avoidance in store-and-forward networks I: Store-and-forward deadlock. *IEEE Trans. Commun.* **COM–28**, 3 (1980), 345–354.

[MS80b] MERLIN, P. P. AND SCHWEITZER, P. J. Deadlock avoidance in store-and-forward networks II: Other deadlock types. *IEEE Trans. Commun.* **COM–28**, 3 (1980), 355–360.

[MS85] MAHANY, S. R. AND SCHNEIDER, F. B. Inexact agreement: Accuracy, precision, and graceful degradation. In proc. *4th Symp. on Principles of Distributed Computing* (1985), pp. 237–249.

[MW87] MORAN, S. AND WOLFSTAHL, Y. Extended impossibility results for asynchronous complete networks. *Inf. Proc. Lett.* **26** (1987), 145–151.

[Nai88] NAIMI, M. Global stability detection in the asynchronous distributed computations. In proc. *Future trends of Distributed Computing Systems in the Nineties* (Hong Kong, 1988), pp. 87–92.

[Nat86] NATARAJAN, N. A distributed scheme for detecting communication deadlocks. *IEEE Trans. Softw. Eng.* **SE–12**, 4 (1986), 531–537.

[Odl84] ODLYZKO, A. M. Discrete logarithms in finite fields and their cryptographic significancce. In proc. *Advances in Cryptology* (Paris, 1984), vol. 209 of *Lecture Notes in Computer Science*, Springer-Verlag, pp. 224–314.

[OG76] OWICKI, S. AND GRIES, D. Verifying properties of parallel programs: An axiomatic approach. *Commun. ACM* **19**, 5 (1976), 279–285.

[Pel90] PELEG, D. Time-optimal leader election in general networks. *J. Parallel and Distributed Computing* **8**, 1 (1990), 96–99.

[Pet82] PETERSON, G. L. An $O(n \log n)$ unidirectional algorithm for the circular extrema problem. *ACM Trans. Program. Lang. Syst.* **4** (1982), 758–762.

[Pet85] PETERSON, G. L. Efficient algorithms for elections in meshes and complete networks. Tech. rep. TR 140, Dept Computer Science, University of Rochester, Rochester NY 14627, 1985.

[PKR84] PACHL, J., KORACH, E., AND ROTEM, D. Lower bounds for distributed maximum finding algorithms. *J. ACM* **31** (1984), 905–918.

[PSL80] PEASE, M., SHOSTAK, R., AND LAMPORT, L. Reaching agreement in the presence of faults. *J. ACM* **27** (1980), 228–234.

[Ran83] RANA, S. P. A distributed solution of the distributed termination problem. *Inf. Proc. Lett.* **17** (1983), 43–46.

[RBS92] RICCARDI, A., BIRMAN, K., AND STEPHENSON, P. The cost of order in asynchronous systems. In proc. *6th Int. Workshop on Distributed Algorithms* (Haifa, 1992), A. Segall and S. Zaks (eds.), vol. 647 of *Lecture Notes in Computer Science*, Springer-Verlag, pp. 329–345.

[RGG96] RUDOLPH, E., GRAUBMANN, P., AND GRABOWSKI, J. Tutorial on message charts. *Comput. Networks ISDN Syst.* **28** (1996), 1629–1641.

[RSA78] RIVEST, R., SHAMIR, A., AND ADLEMAN, L. A method for obtaining digital signatures and public-key cryptosystems. *Commun. ACM* **21** (1978), 120–126.

[Ruž88] RUŽIČKA, P. On efficiency of interval routing algorithms. In proc. *Mathematical Foundations of Computer Science* (1988), M. P. Chytil, L. Janiga, and V. Koubek (eds.), vol. 324 of *Lecture Notes in Computer Science*, pp. 492–500.

[Ruž98] RUŽIČKA, P. Efficient communication schemes. In proc. *SOFSEM98: Theory and Practice of Informatics* (1998), B. Rovan (ed.), vol. 1521 of *Lecture Notes in Computer Science*, Springer-Verlag, pp. 244–263.

[San84] SANTORO, N. Sense of direction, topological awareness, and communication complexity. *ACM SIGACT News* **16** (1984), 50–56.

[Sch91] SCHOONE, A. A. Assertional verification in distributed computing. Ph.D. thesis, Dept Computer Science, Utrecht University, The Netherlands, 1991 (191 pp.).

[Seg83] SEGALL, A. Distributed network protocols. *IEEE Trans. Inf. Theory* **IT–29** (1983), 23–35.

[SES89] SCHIPER, A., EGGLI, J., AND SANDOZ, A. A new algorithm to implement causal ordering. In proc. *3rd Int. Workshop on Distributed Algorithms* (Nice, 1989), J.-C. Bermond and M. Raynal (eds.), vol. 392 of

Lecture Notes in Computer Science, Springer-Verlag, pp. 219–232.

[SF86]   SHAVIT, N. AND FRANCEZ, N. A new approach to the detection of locally indicative stability. In proc. *Int. Colloq. Automata, Languages, and Programming* (1986), L. Kott (ed.), vol. 226 of *Lecture Notes in Computer Science*, Springer-Verlag, pp. 344–358.

[SG84]   SPECTOR, A. AND GIFFORD, D. The Space Shuttle computer system. *Commun. ACM* **27** (1984), 874–900.

[SK85]   SANTORO, N. AND KHATIB, R. Labelling and implicit routing in networks. *Computer J.* **28** (1985), 5–8.

[SK87]   SLOMAN, M. AND KRAMER, J. *Distributed Systems and Computer Networks*. Prentice-Hall International, 1987 (336 pp.).

[SR85]   SANTORO, N. AND ROTEM, D. On the complexity of distributed elections in synchronous graphs. In proc. *Int. Workshop on Graph-Theoretic Concepts in Computer Science* (1985), H. Noltemeier (ed.), Trauner Verlag, pp. 337–346.

[SS88]   SAAD, Y. AND SCHULTZ, M. H. Topological properties of hypercubes. *IEEE Trans. Comput.* **C–37**, 7 (1988), 867–872.

[SS89]   SCHIEBER, B. AND SNIR, M. Calling names on nameless networks. In proc. *8th Symp. on Principles of Distributed Computing* (Edmonton, 1989), pp. 319–329.

[ST89]   SPIRAKIS, P. AND TAMPAKAS, B. Efficient distributed algorithms by using the Archimedean time assumption. *Informatique Théorique et Applications* **23**, 1 (1989), 113–128.

[Ste99]   ŠTEFANKOVIČ, D. Acyclic orientations do not lead to optimal deadlock-free packet routing algorithms. *Inf. Proc. Lett.* (2000).

[T1895]   TARRY, G. Le problème des labyrinthes. *Nouvelles Annales de Mathématique* **14** (1895).

[Taj77]   TAJIBNAPIS, W. D. A correctness proof of a topology information maintenance protocol for a distributed computer network. *Commun. ACM* **20**, 7 (1977), 477–485.

[Tan96]   TANENBAUM, A. S. *Computer Networks*, 3rd edition. Prentice Hall, 1996.

[Tar72]   TARJAN, R. E. Depth-first search and linear graph algorithms. *SIAM J. Comput.* **1** (1972), 146–160.

[Tay89]   TAYLOR, K. The role of inhibition in asynchronous consistent-cut protocols. In proc. *3rd Int. Workshop on Distributed Algorithms* (Nice, 1989), J.-C. Bermond and M. Raynal (eds.), vol. 392 of *Lecture Notes in Computer Science*, Springer-Verlag, pp. 280–291.

[Tel91a] TEL, G. Fouttolerantie in gedistribueerde algoritmen. Lecture Note INF/DOC–91–02, Dept Computer Science, Utrecht University, The

Netherlands, 1991. In Dutch.

[Tel91b] TEL, G. *Topics in Distributed Algorithms*, vol. 1 of *Cambridge Int. Series on Parallel Computation*. Cambridge University Press, 1991 (240 pp.).

[Tel94] TEL, G. Network orientation. *Int. J. Foundations Comput. Sci.* **5**, 1 (1994), 23–57.

[Tel95] TEL, G. Sense of direction in processor networks. In proc. *SOF-SEM'95: Theory and Practice of Informatics* (Milovy (Czech Rep.), 1995), M. Bartošek, J. Staudek, and J. Wiedermann (eds.), vol. 1012 of *Lecture Notes in Computer Science*, Springer-Verlag, pp. 50–82.

[TKZ94] TEL, G., KORACH, E., AND ZAKS, S. Synchronizing ABD networks. *IEEE Trans. Networking* **2**, 1 (1994), 66–69.

[TL86] TAN, R. B. AND LEEUWEN, J. VAN. General symmetric distributed termination detection. Tech. rep. RUU–CS–86–2, Dept Computer Science, Utrecht University, The Netherlands, 1986.

[TM89] TAUBENFELD, G. AND MORAN, S. Possibility and impossibility results in a shared memory environment. In proc. *3rd Int. Workshop on Distributed Algorithms* (Nice, 1989), J.-C. Bermond and M. Raynal (eds.), vol. 392 of *Lecture Notes in Computer Science*, Springer-Verlag, pp. 254–267.

[TM93] TEL, G. AND MATTERN, F. The derivation of termination detection algorithms from garbage collection schemes. *ACM Trans. Program. Lang. Syst.* **15**, 1 (1993), 1–35.

[Top84] TOPOR, R. W. Termination detection for distributed computation. *Inf. Proc. Lett.* **18** (1984), 33–36.

[Tou80a] TOUEG, S. An all-pairs shortest-path distributed algorithm. Tech. rep. RC 8327, IBM T. J. Watson Research Center, Yorktown Heights, NY 10598, 1980.

[Tou80b] TOUEG, S. Deadlock- and livelock-free packet switching networks. In proc. *Symp. on Theory of Computing* (1980), pp. 94–99.

[TU81] TOUEG, S. AND ULLMAN, J. D. Deadlock-free packet switching networks. *SIAM J. Comput.* **10**, 3 (1981), 594–611.

[Vit85] VITÁNYI, P. M. B. Time-driven algorithms for distributed control. Tech. rep. CS–R8510, Centre for Mathematics and Computer Science, Amsterdam, 1985.

[VT95] VERWEIJ, A. M. AND TEL, G. A Monte Carlo algorithm for election. In proc. *2nd Colloq. on Structural Information and Communication Complexity* (Olympia (Greece), 1995), L. M. Kirousis and E. Kranakis (eds.), Carleton University Press, pp. 77–88.

[Wat81] WATSON, R. W. Timer-based mechanisms in reliable transport protocol connection management. *Computer Networks* **5** (1981), 47–56.

References

[WT94]   WEZEL, M. C. VAN AND TEL, G. An assertional proof of Rana's algorithm. *Inf. Proc. Lett.* **49**, 5 (1994), 227–233.

Index

|| (concurrent), 57
~ (equivalent executions), 59
$\mathbf{H}_n$ (harmonic number), 237
$\mathbb{M}(A)$ (multisets), 46
≺, 56, 182
◁ (prefix), 147
→ (transition relation), 45
0/1-decided configuration, 438
0/1-valent configuration, 438

ABD network, 400
accuracy (failure det.), 507
acknowledgement, 77, 86
action, 554
acyclic orientation cover, 163
addressing, 69, 552
adjacent nodes, 557
agreement
    for broadcast algorithm, 471
    for consensus algorithm, 438
    for interactive consistency, 492
algorithm
    Attiya *et al.* (renaming), 447
    Awerbuch, DFS, 212
    Awerbuch–Gallager, 419
    Bracha–Toueg (Byzantine
        broadcast), 463
    Bracha–Toueg (consensus), 453, 458
    Chandy–Lamport, 341
    Chandy–Misra, 121, 153
    Chang, echo, 194
    Chang–Roberts, 234, 323
    Cidon, depth-first search, 214
    credit-recovery, 299
    deterministic, 309
    Dijkstra–Feijen–Van Gasteren, 285

Dijkstra–Scholten, 276
distributed (definition), 46
Dolev–Klawe–Rodeh, 238
fast-convergence, 497
Finn, 199, 232
Fischer *et al.* (knot agreement), 443
Floyd–Warshall, 110
Gallager–Humblet–Spira, 249
global-marking, 351
Itai–Rodeh (election), 323
Itai–Rodeh (ring size), 329
Korach–Kutten–Moran, 260
Lai–Yang, 342
LeLann, 233
local (definition), 46
Merlin–Segall, 120
Netchange, 123, 153, 523, 545
Peleg (election), 232
Peterson, 238, 266
Rana, 302
Safra, 289
Santoro–Khatib, 133, 414
Shavit–Francez, 280
Tarry, traversal, 207
Toueg, 113, 399
Update, 543
vector-counting, 293
alive (of process), 350
alpha synchronizer, 411
alpha-time complexity, 223
alternating-bit protocol, 85
ancestor, 560
AND model (deadlock), 354
anonymous network, 69, 307, 309, 526
applicable action, 554
application layer, 22

587

Printed in the United States
By Bookmasters